History of
INDUSTRIAL EDUCATION
in the United States

Dr. Melvin L. Barlow *is Professor of Education, University of California, Los Angeles, and Director, Division of Vocational Education. He did undergraduate work and earned his master's degree at the University of Southern California, obtained his Doctoral degree from the University of California, Los Angeles. He is a member of numerous policy making committees and serves as technical editor and consultant for publications and projects in vocational education. He has served as writer and staff director for major national advisory councils in vocational education. A licensed professional engineer in California, Dr. Barlow has written for and worked with industrial arts groups across the country.*

*He is the Historian for the American Vocational Association.*

Melvin L. Barlow

# History
## of
# INDUSTRIAL
# EDUCATION
## in the United States

Chas. A. Bennett Co., Inc.
Peoria, Illinois

---

PHOTOS                                                         *Page*

★ ★ ★
*For*
*Alice and Ralph*
★ ★ ★

# *Preface*

For two decades or more it has been difficult for people in the field to study the background of industrial education. Earlier historical periods were treated quite well, and some books have dealt with later legislative matters and social implications of industrial education in a democracy. Still, the story of industrial education since 1917 has not been readily available to the person who desires to develop some background information on its more recent aspects. A few enterprising scholars have made attempts to provide for this lack by preparing special syllabi for their students. But by and large the history has remained buried in thousands of pages of reports, magazine articles, and other unorganized literature.

Summarizing the literature and gleaning from it a story of industrial education presents many problems. In the first place the literature is extensive, and difficult decisions must be made about what to include and what to leave out. Sometimes the record is not too clear about significant trends,

and there are many blanks. Statistical data have frequently provided only a few clues to interpretation. Studies and trends can be followed for only a short period of time, and then the story stops —there is no more information.

The problem of what to do about the contributions of individuals in industrial education was most perplexing. Tracking down their records is a bit difficult and the significance of their contribution was not always clear. So with reluctance the idea of telling the main story in terms of people was largely abandoned. They enter the picture as circumstances project their points of view into the problem at hand. A few personalities shine along the way because they were so intimately involved with the industrial education movement and because they chose to write extensively about their concerns in the development.

Similarly the schools of industrial education are not delineated in such a way as to represent their full story. Some schools are mentioned merely because they were related to a particular facet of the history under review, but other fine, continuously strong contributions of many schools were of necessity not detailed. The story of the schools of industrial education, like that of the people, must await another day for review in history.

Probably the most frustrating problem has been that of terminology. It is "all mixed up" in the historical record —at times so obscure as to defy interpretation. When a writer used the term *manual training* when he should have used industrial arts, I followed the procedure of recording his views in his own terminology. In general, however, when left to my own devices and free from the pressure of an actual situation, I have chosen to use contemporary terminology. That I have done so consistently may be open to question.

Some people regard the confusion of terminology as a serious problem in industrial education. It does add certain stress, but the historical record is as it is, and I have tried to represent men and their times in the terminology they used. It is a fact of the history that this situation has existed. Bennett, for example, largely ignored the term "industrial arts," even when others were finding it appropriate.

In preparing the history of industrial education, material was gathered from a variety of sources. The major part of the research was conducted in Washington, D.C. The libraries of Congress; the Department of Health, Education, and Welfare; the National Education Association; the AFL-CIO; and the Archives of the United States were consulted extensively. The Division of Vocational and Technical Education, U.S. Office of Education, was generous in supplying materials and making files available. The historical documents of the American Vocational Association were researched with a fine-tooth comb. Dr. William E. Warner, Ohio State University, made his historical collection available for study. The entire historical file of the Mississippi Valley Conferences was loaned for review by Dr. Verne C. Fryklund. The personal files of James E. McKinney, American Technical Society, Chicago, were made available for study. The California State Library, the library of the San Francisco Mechanics Institute, and that of the University of California were consulted frequently. The historical files of the Division of Vocational Education, University of California, provided much of the source material.

Among the journals reviewed were *Manual Training Magazine (Industrial Education Magazine)*, 1898-1939; *Vocational Education*, 1912-14; *Industrial Arts and Vocational Education*, since 1914; the *Industrial Arts Teacher* and the *Journal of Industrial Arts Education* of the American Industrial Arts Association; and the proceedings and publications of the National Society for the Promotion of Industrial Education, the National Society for Vocational Education, the Vocational Education Association of the Middle West, and the National Education Association. In addition journals and pamphlets from many states were examined. Other information about industrial education is where you find it, and it may be found in the most out-of-the-way places.

I am indebted to a long list of people who took time to be concerned about the history and who offered their constructive suggestions. Among these are

7

Mrs. Kirsten Vanderberg, Textbook Consultant, California State Department of Education; Dr. John P. Walsh, Assistant Administrator, Manpower Administration, U.S. Department of Labor; Dr. Walter M. Arnold, Assistant Commissioner, Division of Vocational and Technical Education, U.S. Department of Health, Education, and Welfare; Mr. Lane Ash and Mr. Earl Bowler, Division of Vocational and Technical Education, U.S. Office of Education; Dr. Marshall Schmitt, Industrial Arts Consultant, U.S. Office of Education; Dr. Kenneth Dawson, former Executive Secretary, American Industrial Arts Association; Dr. M. D. Mobley, Executive Director Emeritus, Mr. Lowell Burkett, Executive Director, and Miss Gwen Hoelscher, Publications Secretary, American Vocational Association; Mr. Lawrence Rogin, Director, Department of Education, AFL-CIO; and Mr. Svend Grabe, Director, International Vocational Training Information and Research Center, Geneva, Switzerland; Dr. David Allen, Supervisor, Trade and Technical Teacher Education, Division of Vocational Education, University of California, Los Angeles (California State Department of Education); Mr. Lee W. Ralston, Director of Practical Arts, Los Angeles County Schools; Mr. Ernest G. Kramer, Assistant Superintendent for Vocational Education, Washington State Department of Education; Mr. Richard S. Nelson, Chief, Bureau of Industrial Education, and

Dr. Robert L. Woodward, Industrial Arts Consultant, Bureau of Industrial Education, California State Department of Education; and my wife, Alice D. Barlow, Counselor, Palisades High School, Los Angeles, who had the last word in inspecting the manuscript.

Editors are hard to get along with—it's a built-in occupational trait—and the editors of the Chas. A. Bennett Co., were no exception to the rule. But there was a difference. Senior editor Paul Van Winkle had a deep and abiding personal concern that the history of industrial education be made available for study. His wealth of background information and his personal interest were most helpful in smoothing the rough spots encountered during the research and writing. We had many hours of discussion in Peoria, Los Angeles, and the convention cities of professional association meetings, probing special facets of the history. Michael Kenny, Associate Editor, made the final review of the manuscript.

This history was prepared because of a deep personal conviction that industrial educators can plan effectively for the future only to the extent that they have developed a perspective of the past. If the history helps to sharpen that perspective, the effort in producing it has been worthwhile.

MELVIN L. BARLOW

Los Angeles, California
February 23, 1967

# Table of Contents

13

# Chapter 1

# The Heritage

The Greeks · The Romans · The Middle Ages · The Renaissance and the Reformation · The Beginnings of Educational Reform · Apprenticeship in Colonial America · The American Manual Labor Movement · Summary · Recall Questions · Research Questions · Suggestions for Further Reading

The roots of industrial education reach deep into the historical past. The mores of every culture leaving a written record have included unmistakable evidence of this fact. However, most trade education in the ancient nations was conducted in a father-son relationship. It was not until the advent of apprenticeship, which in itself is very old, that we find distinctive patterns of teaching industrial processes. It was only "this morning," in a historical sense, that attention was given to industrial education as a part of the educational program generally provided for youth. It was later yet before any significant gains were made.

## The Greeks

### Slave-degraded Sparta

The structure of "the glory that was Greece" rested upon a self-sufficient system of slave industry and agriculture. Production of Greek sustenance was largely the job of the slave or near-slave population, and therefore was for the most part considered menial. The citizens of militaristic Sparta were forbidden by Lycurgus "to exercise any mechanical trade." The burden of production in Sparta fell upon the Perioeci, a group of the "dwellers about," who were in a sense slaves once removed. They were free men, but they were second class citizens in that they had no political rights. The Perioeci tilled the land outside Sparta, worked the quarries, mined the iron, and made all of the products required by Sparta.

Certain of their families in hereditary succession supplied the cooks for the military messes. . . . The Perioeci of the seacoast towns carried on the commerce of Laconia. Manufacturing, too, . . . was in

15

their hands. Laconian shoes which Aristophanes' Athenians valued, the red uniforms of the Spartan soldiers, their weapons, iron and steel products, houses and household furniture, tableware, clothing, etc.—all were made by the Perioeci.[1]

Whatever craftsmanship was needed to support the Spartan citizens came from the Perioeci. The details of how they managed to develop and transmit their skill and artistry are unknown. The Spartans did not produce a history or leave a literary account of their lives, so we are forced to mere conjecture and a few secondary accounts by later Athenians for evidence of what might have passed for industrial education. It seems evident (1) that craftsmanship was a family affair, producing only those articles desired by Sparta, and (2) that little if any encouragement was given to creative imagination beyond the needs of the army. Spears, swords, and heavy shields were provided the soldiers. Death in battle was a high honor; survival of a defeat—disgrace. " 'Return with your shield or on it,' was the Spartan Mother's farewell to her soldier son."[2]

### Freedom-degraded Athens

The rise of Athens was accompanied by an increase in the practice of trades required by the growing city. A definite occupational classification developed, regulating various workers into a caste system. The industrial workers, although free people, were generally of the second class. Governmental reforms of Solon, c. 600 B.C., created industrial opportunities which grew as trade with other areas increased. The Assembly of Athens, in Socrates' day, included cobblers, carpenters, coppersmiths, and shipmerchants. The free workers organized clubs representative of their occupations: stonemasonry, marble cutting, woodworking, pottery making, and others.[3] Socrates was said to have been a member of the sculptor's club.

These organizations had the earmarks of academic clubs rather than of trade unions. "Socrates belonged to and lived in hearty sympathy with the working classes," but was not a worker.[4] The theorists scorned the trades to a much greater extent than they did agriculture because agriculture seemed to contribute more directly to healthful living. Some of the theorists were mindful of the necessity and dignity of labor, and could recognize honest craftsmanship with some degree of pride. Others, and Plato is a good example, could not think of education as having any connection with manual activities.

Then let us not leave the meaning of education ambiguous or ill-defined. At present, when we speak in terms of praise or blame about the bringing-up of each person, we call one man educated and another uneducated, although the uneducated man may be sometimes very well educated for the calling of a retail trader, or of a captain of a ship, and the like. For we are not speaking of education in this

[1] Ernest Carroll Moore, *The Story of Instruction, The Beginnings*. New York: The Macmillan Company, 1936, p. 15.

[2] Will Durant, *The Life of Greece*. New York: Simon and Schuster, 1939, p. 81.

[3] *Ibid.*, pp. 282-283.

[4] L. F. Anderson, "Some Facts Regarding Vocational Training Among the Ancient Greeks and Romans," *School Review*, XX, No. 3, March 1912, p. 192.

narrower sense, but of that other education in virtue from youth upwards, which makes a man eagerly pursue the ideal perfection of citizenship, and teaches him how rightly to rule and how to obey. This is the only education which, upon our view, deserves the name; *that other sort of training, which aims at* the acquisition of wealth or bodily strength, or *mere cleverness apart from intelligence and justice,* is mean and illiberal, and is not worthy to be called education at all.[5]

Despite this judgment, the work of the artisan is our best evidence of Greek achievement. During the Golden Age of Greece, construction of public buildings reached its peak. Durant reports that during the sixteen years 447-431 B.C., Athens spent the equivalent of $57,600,000 on public buildings and artwork. "The spread of this sum among artisans and artists, executives and slaves, had much to do with the prosperity of Athens under Pericles."[6]

Greece was raised up by manual labor; then new leaders felt superior to manual expression after they had taken over. Although Athens produced a large number of craftsmen, the nature of their training does not seem to have been a matter of public notice or concern. No regulated patterns of instruction have survived: the culture produced its craftsmanship as if by magic. Of course, those involved with formal education did not generally engage in industrial pursuits and hence cannot be expected to have been concerned with the problems of the "low mechanic," whom Aristotle would even have

barred from citizenship. Since such work was not productive of "virtue," it could be ignored, even though the work was essential to Athenian supremacy. All we know is that the "technician, like the scientist, learned his job in a very simple, archaic way, the way of personal relationship between master and pupil, craftsman and apprentice."[7]

## The Romans

### The Great Imitators

"The grandeur that was Rome," like "the glory that was Greece," produced little evidence to indicate that either industry or artisanship was ever held in very high official esteem. And yet the great public works, aqueducts, buildings, and roads, required a high level of craftsmanship for their construction.

Throughout a long history, the craftsmen and artisans of Rome were composed of a mixture of slaves and freemen. They acquired their skill in the only way possible, that is, through family apprenticeship. The father taught the son. "There can be little doubt that youths learned how to make tools, farming implements, boats, weapons, etc., by the apprenticeship method."[8]

Westermann cites in considerable detail an apprentice contract made out in 183 A.D., under the rule of the Roman

---

[5] *Laws,* I, 644. Author's italics.

[6] Durant, *op. cit.,* p. 329.

[7] H. I. Marrou, *A History of Education in Antiquity.* New York: Sheed and Ward, © 1956, p. 191.

[8] James Mulhern, *A History of Education—A* Social Interpretation, Sec. Ed. New York: The Ronald Press Company, © 1959, p. 192.

emperor Commodus.[9] Terms of the contract were specific: there was no confusion concerning the obligation of the master-workman to "teach his trade to Heraclas." Heraclas was to be taught the art of weaving for five years. After two years and seven months, he began to draw pay, starting at 12 drachmas a month (originally a drachma meant enough to buy a "handful") and graduating to 24 drachmas during the fifth year. In addition, a tunic was provided yearly, one of increased quality each year. He was to receive his food, 20 holidays a year, and had to abide by his obligations to the master. If either party violated any of the provisions he paid a fine of 100 drachmas to the party abiding by the contract and an equal amount into a government treasury. Heraclas made the contract and consented to its provisions, but his friend, Thonis, signed for him, since Heraclas was illiterate.

The references to vocational training found in the records of ancient Roman life are of interest chiefly for the examples they afford us of transition from the apprenticeship to the school system. This transition seems to have occurred first in what are known as the professional vocations, those involving intellectual rather than manual labor. By the fourth century A.D. architects and mechanicians seem to have been trained at least in part by school methods.[10]

## The Middle Ages

### A Thin Thread of Light

The so-called Middle Ages account for approximately a thousand years of history between ancient and modern. Beginning in the early 300's and extending into the early 1300's, the period is divided into two nearly equal parts. The turning point between the *early* and *later* Middle Ages is marked at 800, when Charlemagne was crowned Holy Roman Emperor.

Christianity had all but triumphed over the pagan Mediterranean world in 313 when the Edict of Milan removed the last obstacle to the development of the Christian church. The first monasteries, in which the lamp of academic learning was to burn for a millenium, appeared shortly thereafter. In the monks' work, we also find a thin thread of industrial education.

One of the most important events of the early period was the establishment of a scriptorium by Cassiodorus. Scriptoria became a major religious contribution of the monasteries; large numbers of manuscripts were copied and distributed throughout the Christian world.

It is interesting to note that strong elements of apprenticeship were to be found in the formal training plans of the monks who copied the manuscripts. The famous Benedictine rule, in setting a pattern for the numerous functions of the monasteries, established manual labor in an honorable and preferred position. At least seven hours of manual labor were required of the monks each day. Agriculture, and some phases of the trades, composed a large part of the manual labor requirement, and, by the very nature of the work,

---

[9] W. L. Westermann, "Vocational Training in Antiquity," *School Review*, XXII, No. 9, November 1914, pp. 605-606.

[10] Anderson, *op. cit.*, p. 201.

involved an apprenticeship type of learning. Thus apprenticeship and manual labor were built into the foundations of Christianity and the preservation of learning. Unfortunately, education existed primarily for the church; the masses remained illiterate.

Towns with true modern features first arose in the later Middle Ages. They were marked by the development of a merchant class and a class of skilled artisans.

The merchants engaged in retail or wholesale trade, in commerce with other towns and over the seas, and developed many banking and legal practices. In order better to control their economic interests, the merchants organized into guilds. The skilled artisans soon organized into craft guilds. In both merchant and craft guilds an effort was made to control the quantity and quality of production, to keep down competition, and to provide thorough training for those who were accepted as apprentices to the guild. The guilds became very influential in the life of the cities. The first craft guild of which we have record is the Candlemakers' guild in Paris in 1061.[11]

The educational activities of the guilds fell naturally into two categories:

1. Education at the elementary level for the children of guild members. Clergymen were employed to teach children the elements of reading, writing, arithmetic, and religion. The guild paid for this instruction from a "well-filled treasury." "Many of these early guild schools developed, during the Renaissance, into institutions of the humanistic type."[12]

2. The apprenticeship indenture system. Sons of journeymen were indentured to a master who agreed to train the apprentice in the skills of the craft and, in addition, to provide other instruction, including religion. The indenture obligated the master to provide food, clothing, shelter, and usually medical care in addition. In return, the apprentice was bound to his master for a term of years. "The length of apprenticeship varied from two or three to seven to ten years. The apprentice spent his time in the shop running errands and engaging in the simpler processes pertaining to the craft."[13]

## The Renaissance and the Reformation

### Groping for Freedom

The Renaissance, a period of about 250 years, began in the fourteenth century with a great revival of learning—for the few. Rediscovery of the literature of Greece and Rome and the escape from medievalism were for the most part of little importance to the great masses of people. Humanism and the concept of the importance of man were slow to filter down to the ranks of humanity, but a trend was started that would place increased value upon the "here and now" rather than upon the "hereafter." Latin had long been the language of religion and learning, but the man in the street could neither read nor understand that language. The spirit of the Renaissance could not influence the mores of society until the

---

[11] Flaud C. Wooton, *A History of Education*, Parts 1 and 2. Los Angeles: A Mimeographed Edition by the Author, 1956, p. 91.

[12] *Ibid.*, p. 107.

[13] *Ibid.*

language barrier had been penetrated. The use of the vernacular in writing was popularized somewhat by the appearance of Dante Alighieri's *The Divine Comedy* and Giovanni Bocaccio's *Decameron* in the fourteenth century.

An age of geographical and scientific discovery evolved, and printing became a common carrier of knowledge. It was a new age of sculpture and of art which produced the masterpieces of Ghiberti, Donatello, Cellini, da Vinci, and Michelangelo. The medieval roots of humanity thrived in the new soil of individuality and the freedom and dignity of man. Even though the culture of the Renaissance—the revolt from the chains of the medieval world —favored the relatively few who were educated, in time this group, pushing toward the world of the future, would draw their illiterate brothers with them.

During the whole of this wonderful and terrifying period of contrasts and conflicts, we may find the stabilizing influence of industry, trade, and craftsmanship. Society became dependent upon the new burgher class and the arts-and-crafts guilds. The school of industrial education during the Renaissance was the same as it had been from time immemorial—the father-son or master-apprentice system. During the formal period of instruction on the job the apprentice could learn all of the aspects of the trade or craft from his father or master. The length of time— seven years more or less—was sufficient to provide a large variety of learning experiences: by imitation and emula-

tion the apprentice would acquire the skills and understandings required. "In some trades the master was required by his gild [sic] to teach reading and writing to his apprentices, and a master was not to take any more apprentices than he could 'keep, inform, and teach'."[14] The success of the system depended to a great extent upon the master who could set a worthy example and inspire the apprentice to find joy in personal expression.

Whatever may have been its weak points the medieval apprenticeship system is by no means to be despised; it was well adapted to the social and economic conditions of the time. The household, the small shop, and the gild [sic] were the great factors in industrial life. There was . . . no great gulf between employer and employee. The apprentice became a part of his master's household and was given a home and instruction in a trade at but little expense save that of time. If the master did his duty, skill and artistic ability were developed in the lad. At the end of his term of service he passed into the ranks of the master craftsmen and looked forward to a life of comparative economic security and perhaps of some honor as a skilled artisan or merchant, and as a citizen. If there was little opportunity for him to rise out of his class there was great opportunity for him to rise in it.[15]

**Strong Effects in Religion**

In a sense the Reformation was merely an extension—adjusted by time and circumstance—of the Renaissance. However, in Germany the Reformation did have a significant religious base, in which religion acted as a catalyst in speeding up the process of social change. The seeds of revolt in Ger-

---

[14] Charles A. Bennett, *History of Manual and Industrial Education Up to 1870*. Peoria: The Manual Arts Press, 1926, p. 22.
[15] *Ibid.*, p. 28.

many had been planted much earlier. It was a simple accident of chronology that placed Martin Luther, an Augustinian monk and professor of Theology at the University of Wittenberg, in the leader's position. Luther, following the customary normal university process of issuing an invitation to debate theological issues, sought in his famous *Ninety-five Theses* to debate the sale of indulgences. Through no effort on his part, the incident got completely out of control and he was excommunicated. He fought back by scathing attacks upon the evils of the Roman Church. His new doctrines were readily received by the German people, who were looking for a reason to approve religious revolt.

Although Luther's zeal was in the direction of a new religion based upon the Bible as the authority, and not on church doctrine, he and his colleagues profoundly influenced the development of education in Germany and the Scandinavian countries. Luther cannot properly be called enthusiastic for anything resembling industrial education, but the educational tenor of his reforms was highly influential. In his *Letter to the Mayors and Aldermen of All the Cities of Germany in Behalf of Christian Schools*, in 1524, he says:

> My idea is that boys should spend an hour or two a day in school, and the rest of the time work at home, learn some trade and do whatever is desired, so that study and work may go on together, while the children are young and can attend to both.[16]

It would be late in the 1800's before the idea of combining trade and academic education in the schools was tried seriously.

## The Beginnings of Educational Reform

Traditional ideas of educational theory and practice were supplemented generously by the views of educational reformers from the sixteenth to the nineteenth centuries. As literate use of the vernacular spread, the common man became more important in the eyes of leaders, and his education became at least a matter of casual notice. Now and again, a faint tribute to some phase of industrial education would drop from the pen of some writer or wedge into the common educational experience of some school. Drawing was taught at Mulcaster's Merchant Taylor's School after 1561; John Locke thought that trade education might be useful; and Jean Jacques Rousseau desired that Emile learn the carpentry trade, spending one or two whole days each week with a master carpenter. Be it noted that, although Rousseau felt that man needed to work in order to live, he would be sure that Emile would raise himself to the "state" of a carpenter, not merely to the occupation of a carpenter.

Educational theory was one thing, making the theory work another. Rousseau's *Emile*, published in 1762, was read two years later by an eighteen-year-old boy who was so touched by the direct simplicity of the work that he was inspired to organize a school that would embody some of the ideas of Rousseau.

---

[16] Frederick Eby, *Early Protestant Educators*. New York: McGraw-Hill Book Company, Inc., © 1931, p. 71.

## Pestalozzi

Johann Heinrich Pestalozzi, Swiss educator, the "father of modern elementary education," evolved a system of educational theory and practice from which industrial education borrowed heavily during its formative years. The concept that *im*pression resulted from *ex*pression was a fundamental principle of Pestalozzi's, and it became the basis of learning in his school, in which the child was allowed to "learn by doing." "I come to the conviction," says Pestalozzi, "that the fundamental error—the blind use of words in matters of instruction—must be extirpated before it is possible to resuscitate life and truth."[17] Thus Pestalozzi rejected pure word knowledge, which had been not only the *basis* but the *whole* of education, and turned to the pathways of nature and natural environment as the appropriate setting for learning. This was largely a matter of timing with Pestalozzi: Books could, of course, be consulted with profit, since they contained the storehouse of accumulated knowledge of the past and provided a means of following the march of civilization, but books must be subjected to criticism and inquiry and not accepted without question. The only system of instruction appealing to Pestalozzi was one that led the mind to original discovery. Books were to be used "to supplement experience, and to supply those facts that are not readily accessible by direct investigation."[18]

Obtaining knowledge through experience had no substitute. Pestalozzi's "object lessons" led directly to drawing, writing, reading, speaking, geometry, history, geography, and other subjects. Through his method of object teaching, "the idolatrous worship of words was placed under the ban of human intelligence; and when he so eloquently and faithfully demonstrated the necessity of observing and respecting the individuality of every child, arbitrary authority and routine became obsolete."[19]

Pestalozzi came to advocate industrial training because he realized that it was fundamental to the future economic dependence of the poor children in his care. He felt that they could find a means of subsistence through the practice of several different kinds of crafts. He wished to include an adequate training for agriculture, for domestic management, and for industry. He felt that vocational training which failed to provide an equal cultivation of the head and the heart would only degrade the individual and reduce his status to that of "one slavishly trained merely for making a living." Furthermore, it was simply inadequate as a means of education.[20]

Thus, industry became a means to an end but not the "all" of his educational aim. His emphasis upon industry as a means of general education came at a later period in his work. He developed the point of view that cultivat-

[17] Herman Krusi, *Pestalozzi: His Life, Work and Influence.* Cincinnati: Wilson, Hinkle and Co., 1875, p. 152.

[18] *Ibid.,* p. 188.

[19] *Ibid.,* p. 168.

[20] Lewis Flint Anderson, *Pestalozzi.* New York: McGraw-Hill Book Company, Inc., 1931, pp. 101-102.

ing knowledge and neglecting skill produced not only a one-sided education but an individual out of phase with his environment. He could see in industrial training many benefits to the harmonious development of a man. These attitudes find expression at many points in his books *Leonard and Gertrude* and *How Gertrude Teaches Her Children.* The values of industrial education were not limited to the poorer elements of the masses, although it was with this group that Pestalozzi's philanthropic efforts were centered.

*Pestalozzi's influence.* Pestalozzi's influence was felt strongly in the United States, particularly after 1860 through the work of Edward A. Sheldon in Oswego, New York. However, the United States version of Pestalozzianism had little direct effect on the development of industrial education, even though it is implicit in the fundamental goals of industrial education. Some direct evidence of Pestalozzi's influence in the United States may be found in the earlier work of Joseph Neef.

## Neef

Francis Joseph Nicholas Neef taught under Pestalozzi's direction at Bergdorf for approximately three years. In 1803, he married Eloise Buss, a sister of one of Pestalozzi's assistants, and soon thereafter departed for Paris to open a school. His school attracted the attention of Napoleon and Talleyrand, and more importantly from our point of view, the attention of a delegation of men from the United States which included the philanthropist, William Maclure. After considering the schools

he had seen in Europe, Maclure sent for Neef and offered him aid in opening a school in America.

On what terms . . . would you go to my country, and introduce there your method of education? I have seen Pestalozzi, I know his system; my country wants it, and will receive it with enthusiasm. I engage to pay your passage, to secure your livelihood. Go and be your master's apostle in the new world.[21]

Maclure's contract with Neef was signed in Paris on March 19, 1806. Neef spent three years learning the English language and preparing his *Sketch of a Plan and Method of Education.* In 1809, he opened his school in Philadelphia which he continued for three years, at which time he moved to Village Green, in Delaware County, Pennsylvania. One of Neef's young students, David Farragut, was destined to become famous a half century later for his statement, "Damn the torpedoes! Full speed ahead!"

Of his days at the Village Green School, Farragut later said:

I accompanied my friend Captain Porter to Chester where I was put in a school to a queer old individual named Neef. His method of instruction was simple in the extreme; he had no books but taught orally such subjects as he desired us to understand. In the afternoon it was customary for us to take long walks, accompanied by our instructor. On these occasions Mr. Neef would make collections of minerals and plants, and talk to us about mineralogy and botany. The course of study was not very regular but we certainly had an opportunity of gaining a great deal of useful information and worldly knowledge. We were taught to swim and climb, and were drilled like

[21] Joseph Neef, *Sketch of a Plan and Method of Education.* Philadelphia: Printed for the Author, 1808, p. 5.

23

soldiers—branches of instruction to be accounted for, probably, by the fact that the old gentleman had been one of Napoleon's celebrated guards. I do not regret the time passed at this school, for it has been of service to me all my life.[22]

The Village Green School failed, and Neef moved to a farm near Louisville, Kentucky. In 1825, he was called to New Harmony, Indiana, to become a teacher in a school organized by Robert Dale Owen in cooperation with William Maclure. In this school, which was organized along the lines suggested by Pestalozzi, physical labor was combined with moral and intellectual culture. Unfortunately, the New Harmony experiment came to an end in 1828. Of the many reasons cited for its failure, the one that seems most credible is that it merely transplanted the Pestalozzian system without Americanizing it.

### Von Fellenberg

Philip Emanuel von Fellenberg, onetime associate of Pestalozzi, organized and conducted a variety of educational activities at Hofwyl, Switzerland. He paid special attention to the education of the various social classes, including both extremes, in an effort to promote harmony among the classes and improve the general conditions of human life. Agricultural and industrial instruction were combined with some elements of literary instruction in an educational experiment with strong social implications. Manual activities were stressed for all students, but the emphasis was placed upon literary activities for well-to-do students and

upon practical aspects for the poor children. All teaching was inspired by Pestalozzian principles.

Fellenberg's Academy at Hofwyl was intended for the sons of rich families. From time to time it included the sons of Europe's prominent noblemen. (Robert Dale Owen attended Fellenberg's Academy.) Fellenberg's Farm and Trade School provided instruction for the poor children. Under the direction of an imaginative assistant, Joseph Wehrli, the school was a reflection of the best of Pestalozzian theory and practice. The children were properly clothed and fed. Their manual labor activities in agriculture were related to their school studies, providing a source of real interest in school work for them. Trade instruction was provided by skilled craftsmen, representing a dozen or more trade areas, who were employed by the school as a part of their regular work.

This afforded an exceptional opportunity for a young man to select and learn a trade. So it came about that when a boy was old enough to become an apprentice, instead of continuing at farm work, he was allowed to select a trade which he would follow during his working hours for the remainder of his life at Hofwyl.[23]

Fellenberg's Hofwyl school attracted much attention in Europe and in America. William C. Woodbridge, editor of the *American Annals of Education,* featured in many issues "Sketches of Hofwyl," which brought to American educators a wealth of information concerning this noble experiment in education. These ideas influenced developments in the United States.

---

[22] Loyall Farragut, *Life of David Glasgow Farragut.* New York: D. Appleton Co., 1879, p. 50.
[23] Bennett, *op. cit.,* pp. 137-138.

## Froebel

Friedrich Wilhelm Augustus Froebel studied with Pestalozzi at Yverdon. He was particularly impressed by the use of drawing and practical work in the school. A predecessor of Froebel, Heinrich Gottlieb Heusinger, had developed basic ideas concerning child activity; but Froebel, although acquainted with and influenced by Heusinger's work, became the leader in utilizing handwork in the general education of children.

Froebel's later work in developing the kindergarten was directed by pioneering ideas about self-activity, sense perception, nature, God, the universe, and the mystical power of "unity." His book, the *Education of Man*, published in 1826, explained the basic elements of his theory: the *gifts* and *occupations* which became so important in the kindergarten. It was Froebel's recognition of the central importance of manual and industrial education which led to the major position that manual training later occupied in the kindergarten and the elementary school.

## Others

Many other nineteenth century educational reformers contributed to the growth of the concepts of industrial education. Among them were Uno Cygnaeus, Otto Salomon, Johann Friedrich Herbart, and Tuiskan Ziller. Their contributions and views of activity, handwork, and industry all added emphasis to the necessity of industrial education.

Industrial education provided a natural avenue for educational reform. It was practical, close to the common daily experience of man, and therefore easily understood.

## Apprenticeship in Colonial America

Apprenticeship was practiced throughout colonial America. Although the English system prevailed, appropriate modifications were made by the colonists to suit their particular needs. Laws and conditions of apprenticeship were provided among other instruments of town government: appropriate authorities were delegated responsibility to determine that apprenticeship agreements were honored.

There were two kinds of apprenticeship: (1) The voluntary form followed European customs and traditions, but was not subject, in general, to particular provisions of law, although such agreements were entered in the town records. The apprentice "bound himself" by his own free will in order to learn a trade; (2) Involuntary apprenticeship provided a means of taking care of poor children and orphans. A master, instead of the town, became responsible for their personal and occupational needs.

In general, apprenticeship agreements provided for food, clothing, and shelter; religious training; general education as needed in the trade; knowledge, understanding, and experience in the trade skills; and, finally, for the "mysteries" of the trade, or the techniques which had some elementary scientific basis. These were the traditional elements. Both boys and girls were apprenticed for periods of time varying from five to ten years. Girls usually served until they were eighteen or were married. Apprenticeship started in many instances at the age of eight or nine. ". . . useless occupations, such as minding cattle, were [not] to be tolerated; apprenticeship was not a scheme of exploitation, but was essentially an educational institution." [24] The intent of colonial apprenticeship was clearly to provide some learning in the 3 R's in addition to other requirements.

Seybolt calls attention to the frequency with which parents provided in their wills that their children should be "put out to the trades." [25] In some instances, the trade was specified, but most generally the decision was left to the executor or to the boy. The age of fourteen was most common for entering a trade when provisions to do so had been made in a will. Paying for an education was always a problem in colonial America: the boy who came from a less fortunate family could find opportunities in apprenticeship. A large segment of public elementary education was accounted for in this manner.

## The American Manual Labor Movement

### Extending Educational Opportunities

An education-conscious labor force developed rapidly in the early years of our nation. A labor movement which strongly favored public education promoted the concept of equal educational opportunity at public expense.

Private charity schools and societies of mechanics came into existence during the early part of the nineteenth century in an attempt to supply the educational advantages of apprenticeship for factory workers. Many of these institutions were founded for charitable purposes, but in time also provided regular schools and classes. The Boston Asylum and Farm School, founded in 1814, was devoted to the education of orphaned boys. Each boy selected practical work and study in one of several trades, in addition to a basic academic course. The General Society of Mechanics and Tradesmen, which was founded on November 17, 1785, had by 1821 embarked upon a full-scale educational program. When public education became generally available, this society relaxed its direct participation in educational work. That it did not lose interest is indicated by the fact that as late as the mid-twentieth century it maintained scholarships for craftsmen at New York University and the New York Trade School.

The lyceums and mechanics institutes, which developed during the early years of the nineteenth century, provided additional education for mechanics. The Gardiner Lyceum, founded in 1823, and the American Lyceum of Science and the Arts, proposed by Josiah Holbrook in 1826, were typical. The educational goals of the lyceum were broad enough to include the cultural needs of the artist, the farmer, and the mechanic.

The mechanics institutes directed their attention primarily to the vocational needs of their members. Prominent among them were the Franklin Institute, Philadelphia, 1824; the Maryland Institute for the Promotion of the Mechanic Arts, Baltimore, 1826; the Ohio Mechanics Institute, Cincinnati, 1828; and the San Francisco Mechanics Institute, 1854. There were many

---

[24] Robert F. Seybolt, *Apprenticeship and Apprenticeship Education in Colonial New England and New York.* New York: Teachers College, Columbia University, 1917, p. 38.

[25] *Ibid.*, pp. 99-103.

others. It was not uncommon to find reading rooms, libraries, public lectures, cabinets of models and apparatus, and day and night schools as a part of the institutes' programs. Practice and science were combined to the benefit of the mechanic and industry.

Another phase of the manual labor movement developed with the formation of manual labor academies. In addition to studies in the academy, each student worked in a shop or factory owned by a local businessman, who paid the institution for the student's services. The expense of education was reduced materially. Distinctions between rich and poor tended to break down. It was contended that the combination of studies and labor contributed to the development of better citizens.

The Society for Promoting Manual Labor in Literary Institutions, which was organized in July, 1831, contributed much to the understanding of the values of labor as a part of the literary curriculum. The difference between manual labor institutions and others rested chiefly in the use of the hours of relaxation. In the manual labor school, the student worked at some useful project, while students of other schools occupied their time as they chose. It appears that the Society had no particular quarrel with the curriculum of the manual labor schools: As far as it was concerned, the manual labor did not detract from study.

The Rensselaer Institute was a notable school of the type advocated during this period. Founded by Stephen Van Rensselaer in Troy, New York, in 1824, it opened on Monday, January 3, 1825. Van Rensselaer proposed to instruct persons in the "application of science to the common purposes of life." The institute was a realization of the growing idea of combining science and practical work for a better understanding of the inter-relationships between chemistry, natural philosophy, and mathematics on the one hand, and agriculture and mechanics on the other.

The demands of our national period, combined with the stirrings of the industrial revolution, were strange forces for the American people to control. The factory system directed deadly blows toward apprenticeship; by trial and error, new institutions developed to provide the greatly needed industrial education. Technical institutes in tune with the new social system were founded. After the Civil War, a system of agricultural and mechanical colleges appeared in each of the states in response to the national interest in industrial education. Following closely behind were the private trade schools, corporation schools, and the "new education" which reflected the desire of the masses for things practical. At the same time, American public education struggled to provide educational opportunity for all the people.

*Summary*

The origin of industrial education is lost in antiquity, but ancient nations obviously depended upon forms of industry and upon craftsmanship for economic and civil survival. The products of the forge, the field, and the quarry brought wealth to these nations through commerce, and provided materials for war. That craftsmanship was highly developed can be inferred from the treasures that remain to identify these early cultures. For thousands of

27

years, the process of teaching and learning related to this industrial craftsmanship was a family affair, conducted largely through the father-son and master-apprentice relationships. That such was the case seems clear from the records of the Greeks, the Romans, and the Middle Ages.

During the Renaissance and Reformation, something like formal industrial education came into being. The guilds had added a definite mark of respectability to craftsmanship, and craftsmanship itself had grown concurrently with geographical, economic, and scientific advancement. Luther's educational plans made provision for trade education, and the general tenor of humanism, in recognizing the worth of the common man, further strengthened the position of industrial education.

Educational reforms of the sixteenth and seventeenth centuries provided for industrial education in theory and in some instances actually included industrial-related instruction in programs of formal education. Rousseau's Emile was destined to become a carpenter—not just an ordinary carpenter, but a craftsman of high distinction who was well educated in other areas. Mul-

caster's famous school placed emphasis upon drawing as an element of instruction.

In the nineteenth century, positive gains of lasting significance were made in the utilization of the elements of industry in education. Pestalozzi, with his homespun philosophy and practical ideas about education, became a center of attraction for educators in Europe and America, and his ideas bore fruit in the United States. Fellenberg, Froebel, and Herbart, aided by money and scientific evidence, created educational environments that advanced the early Pestalozzian gains in the United States. These influences supplemented the existing apprenticeship systems, the lyceums and mechanics institutes, and the numerous societies of craftsmen, and lent sustenance to the development of special schools in which industrial education was given new emphasis.

Thus a "new education" emerged in America in the late nineteenth century. Into the crucible went traditional educational ideas, social and economic needs, patterns of educational reform, and newer ideas from Russia and Scandinavian countries to form the beginnings of manual and trade education.

---

## Recall Questions

1. The burden of production for Sparta fell upon what group of people? How was this group related to the citizen class?

2. Why do we know so little about the nature of industrial education in Sparta?

3. How did Plato regard manual activities as an element of education?

4. What were some of the elements of an apprenticeship agreement in ancient Roman times?

5. What two educational activities were characteristic of the guilds?

6. What threads of industrial education do we find in the Renaissance and Reformation?

7. Name the educational reformers whose work had a bearing upon the development of industrial education.

8. Describe apprenticeship in colonial America.

9. What society of mechanics was established immediately following the Revolutionary War and is still in existence?

## Research Questions

1. It has been said that the educational consciousness of America began about 1820. Find evidence to support or oppose the view that interest and positive action in industrial education began about the same time. Identify significant achievements in industrial education from 1820 to 1880.

2. Elementary education and industrial education have much in common from the standpoint of principles. What evidence can you find from the work of Pestalozzi, Fellenberg, and Froebel to support this statement?

## Suggestions for Further Reading

Anderson, Lewis Flint, *History of Manual and Industrial School Education.* New York: D. Appleton-Century Company, 1926.

Bennett, Charles Alpheus, *History of Manual and Industrial Education up to 1870.* Peoria: The Manual Arts Press, 1926.

———, *History of Manual and Industrial Education 1870-1917.* Peoria: The Manual Arts Press, 1937.

Blake, James Vila, *Manual Training in Education.* Chicago: Charles H. Kerr and Company, 1886.

Scott, Jonathan Frence, *Historical Essays on Apprenticeship and Vocational Education.* Ann Arbor: Ann Arbor Press, 1914.

Seybolt, Robert Francis, *Apprenticeship and Apprenticeship Education in Colonial New England and New York.* New York: Teachers College, Columbia University, 1917.

Smith, H. Ross, *Development of Manual Training in the United States.* Lancaster, Pa.: The Intelligencer Print, 1914.

Eighth Annual Report of the Commissioner of Labor, 1892. *Industrial Education.* Washington: Government Printing Office, 1893.

# Chapter 2

# The Crucible of Manual and Trade Education 1870-1906

The Issues · The Leaders · The Results · Summary · Recall Questions · Research Questions · Suggestions for Further Reading

The awakening of educational consciousness in the United States occurred about 1820. General enthusiasm for public schools was slow to develop, but over the next fifty years the idea of the common school, public and free, became woven unmistakably into the fabric of the American culture.

By 1870 the American people had accepted the concept of universal public elementary education, and progress in that direction tended generally to be satisfactory. Beginning with Massachusetts in 1851, state after state had enacted school laws requiring the attendance of youth at least through the eighth grade. This was the spirit of democracy at work. Its indomitable forces were behind a true free public education system within the reach of all.

Simple compulsory education might have satisfied another society, but within the American democracy the drive was very strong and compelling.

High schools had existed in the United States since 1821. Although their growth had been slow, city after city took up the problem of providing education beyond the elementary school. But opposition developed to the idea of such additional schooling paid for out of the public treasury. Private academies existed in abundance throughout the country, although they charged tuition. Sentiment was strong to hold the line, to use caution in setting "dangerous" precedents for further public education.

The legal question of whether a people hold the right to tax themselves for whatever kind of educational system they desired was largely settled by the famous Kalamazoo Case in 1872. With that affirmative decision the way was reasonably clear for the high school to become the dominant educational institution in America. It was sometimes referred to as the "people's college," which indicated that courses

30

must suit individual needs of students. This involved a vastly expanded curriculum and introduced many new practical subjects. Within the new environment of public secondary education, industrial education found its beginnings.

## The Issues

Education needed by all men became the goal, and slowly but steadily more and more children were brought under the influence of the common school. A large percentage of the children were the sons and daughters of workingmen and laborers, and the common school would largely represent all of their formal educational experience. If the studies and methods of the common school were to be adapted to the needs of any class of people, then it ought to be the working class.

### Criticism of the Common School

Upon the basis of the special needs of the working class the curriculum of the common school became the target for general criticism. The critics felt that the curriculum was not appropriate for the special needs of the working class. School work was bookish. Words were taught instead of ideas. Too many things were taught, and these were taught because of fashion rather than fitness. The school was intent upon cultivation of the "knowing powers," to the exclusion of "activity." In order to correct the inadequacies of the common school program, various reforms were generously recommended. The

school should concentrate on fewer subjects, should distinguish between knowledge and skill, and should recognize that skill cannot be obtained except by practice. The student should be tested by calling upon him to demonstrate by practice what he had learned, not merely by having him tell about it. Only the useful and necessary parts of arithmetic should be taught, and the curious or disciplinary elements should be avoided. Skills in composition should replace much of the excessive emphasis upon grammar. Plain and rapid penmanship should prevail in instruction, with "fancy flourishes" considered as an extra. Reading should be taught as a means of obtaining knowledge. Drawing should cultivate perception and develop the power of exact comprehensive observation. Such reforms would provide time that could be devoted to natural sciences and "other things which every intelligent working man needs to know."

The constructive critics of the common school tended to live dangerously, as they dared to cross or move upstream relative to the prevailing educational current, in their efforts to secure favorable attitudes toward introduction of new ideas into the curriculum. S. R. Thompson remarked that, "Culture and discipline are not so much dependent upon *what* is taught, as upon *how* it is taught."[1] In 1877 J. R. Buchanan raised an issue that was already old, yet one which would long continue to be a jumping off point for both the critic and the defender of the curriculum, when he said, "Education

---

[1] S. R. Thompson, "Relations of the Common School to Industrial Education," NEA *Proceedings*, 1877, p. 220.

should be a preparation for life and should be like the life to which it prepares." [2]

### Drawing Gains a Foothold

Drawing had always been popular in classes conducted by the Mechanics' Institutes throughout the country. The influence of its success weighed heavily in the new curriculum. Drawing as a part of the education for all boys found many supporters because of its everyday uses on the farm, at home, and in the world of industry. In a book published in 1868, John Hart emphasized drawing, saying, "A workman who is ready and expert with his pencil, who has learned to put his own ideas, or those of another, readily on paper, is worth fifty percent more than his fellows who have not this skill." [3]

Schools in various parts of the country were moving in the direction of introducing drawing as a regular part of the school program. Educators sensitive to community pressures were thinking of the expanded curriculum of the future and the additional responsibilities of the public schools. "Every system of technical and industrial education must begin with the public school." [4] The manual training movement had not yet begun, but the coming events were casting their shadows on the educational world.

### Influence of the Morrill Act

No small part of this influence had come from the Morrill Act of Congress in 1862, which provided for the establishment of agricultural and mechanical colleges.

Although the Morrill Act represented a victory for the proponents of agricultural and mechanical education, there is very little evidence to indicate that the writers of the law had even a hazy conception of what kinds of schools might result. The law provided that "the leading object shall be, without excluding other scientific and classical studies . . . to teach such branches of learning as are related to agriculture and the mechanic arts . . . in order to promote the liberal and practical education of the industrial classes in the several pursuits and professions in life." [5] The college programs which did result were generally satisfactory, but in some instances they were contrary to expectations, largely because the colleges did not seem to make it their "leading object" to bring agriculture or mechanics into prominence.

The intense desire of the public for practical education is illustrated by the following quotation:

For all this munificence [the Morrill Act], it [the Congress] naturally expects a return in the increase of public intelligence, and in the improvement of the country. It contemplates great progress in the industrial pursuits of the nation. It looks to see the farms, the workshops and the various mechanical and mining operations, brought under the control of science, and conducted by an educated people. It anticipates a period when every man

---

[2] *Ibid.*, p. 223.
[3] John S. Hart, *In the School-Room*. Philadelphia: Eldredge and Brother, 1868, p. 263.
[4] California, *Sixth Biennial Report of the Superintendent of Public Instruction, 1874 and 1875*. Sacramento: G. A. Springer, State Printer, 1875, p. 96.
[5] *United States Statutes At Large*, XII, Chapt. 130, p. 504.

in the nation shall by the results of educated labor, be placed above want, and become a contributor to the general welfare.[6]

Although such discussions were directed toward problems in college-level programs, many of the opinions expressed would have future value to other levels and kinds of industrial education.

## Educated Labor—the Goal

Differences between skilled labor and educated labor were deemed to be largely differences of the degree and kind of education. The skills taught in the programs of the new colleges were supposed to have the character of genuine work, and students were not to be involved in play-work, if the best ends of instruction were to be served.[7] The need for competent instructors who were skilled in the various aspects of industry did not go unnoticed. It was pointed out that in addition to the important handicraft aspects of instruction the well known principles of science should be applied to the products of the machine work and to the processes involved in their production. Much was said about the equal cultivation of the head, the heart, and the hand as representing a totality and completeness of instruction. Supplanting liberal education did not become a goal of industrial education. Instead, it was clearly the intent to provide a combination of liberal and practical education so that both areas would be

enlarged and benefited, and that the so-called "industrial classes" would have an education equivalent to that of the literary and professional classes.

The idea of "educated labor" generally meant that the laborer, along with developing skill in his industrial pursuit, should also have instruction in liberal arts and in philosophy. As the following quotation points out, laborers were often at a disadvantage in society, and would remain so until they acquired tools that transcended mere skills. "The manual-laboring classes sometimes justly complain that they are oppressed by unjust legislation, that their rights are not properly regarded by our law-makers, and that those who are more intelligent than they are take advantage of their ignorance."[8] The answer was obviously in the direction of an education which could be incorporated in the public schools so that general culture and hand culture could be carried on harmoniously.

There was agreement concerning the reasonableness of the demand for industrial training, for it was recognized that the decay of the apprenticeship system made industrial education a national necessity. One of the early educational developments in response to this need was the Manual Training Movement. The St. Louis Manual Training School is one of the more famous examples of what this movement accomplished. Its design was copied in other cities.

---

[6] G. W. Pinney, *The New Education, Objections to the System as Taught in the University of California Together With the Memorial of the California State Grange and Mechanics Deliberative Society.* Oakland: Butler and Stillwell, Steam Book and Job Printers, 1874, p. 40.

[7] NEA *Proceedings*, 1877, p. 237.

[8] NEA *Proceedings*, 1879, p. 203.

## The Leaders

Into the crucible of manual and trade education came the theories, beliefs, and practices of the educational leaders of the time. Emergence of practical education as a consideration in the curriculum of the public school was much in the news, and the movement had its ardent proponents and its severe critics. The pages of educational literature between 1875 and 1900 record both sides of the argument in full.

The two principal personalities—judging from the quantity of their written views—were Calvin M. Woodward and William T. Harris. To a lesser extent E. E. White and John D. Runkle were involved in the discussions. The story of the educational battle of the century can be cast in a brief form by reference to these four persons, although occasional reference to others will serve to clarify some basic issues.

### Calvin M. Woodward

Early Activities. Events leading up to the establishment of the St. Louis Manual Training School began in 1855, when the trustees of Washington University established the O'Fallon Polytechnic Institute. For many years the Institute performed services similar to those of the mechanics' institutes, conducting evening schools for apprentices and journeymen, which included classes in mathematics and drawing. In an address on April 23, 1857, John How, President of the Institute, indicated that it was the desire of many St. Louis citizens to organize an institution having all the advantages of the mechanics' institutes in other parts of the

country and in Europe. The O'Fallon Polytechnic Institute was successful from the very beginning, even though financial difficulties and the Civil War were hard problems to overcome.

In 1865 Calvin M. Woodward began his teaching career at Washington University. In 1866 he became principal of the O'Fallon Polytechnic Institute, and two years later, when the Institute was organized as a part of the engineering department of Washington University, he was made dean of that department.

Manual Training Idea Takes Root. Sometime between 1868 and 1871 Woodward decided that the engineering students should construct models made of wood to illustrate certain mechanical principles. When he learned that the students had little aptitude in using hand tools he asked the university carpenter, Noah Dean, to demonstrate their use. By 1871 a new workshop, modestly equipped, was placed at Dean's disposal. The work was carried out under Woodward's supervision.

In an address given at Washington University on October 24, 1873, Woodward made reference to his method of combining theory and practice, indicating that the things studied and taught had immediate and intrinsic values, and that a student could not understand a process or an experiment until he had performed it. He made a plea for a systematic extension of manual education, saying that, "It is the best aid towards securing a wholesome intellectual culture, and it is the only means for making that culture of practical use." [9]

---

[9] C. M. Woodward, *The Manual Training School*. Boston: D. C. Heath and Company, Publishers, 1887, p. 256.

A description of the shopwork prepared by Woodward for the Washington University catalog of 1875 shows the manual training ideas at work.

During the past year the students of each class [students in the polytechnic classes were required to attend, while the classical students were at liberty to attend] have worked systematically in the shop under the direction of the professors, assisted by a skillful carpenter and a pattern-maker. The general method of conducting this work is as follows: A sketch of the piece or task to be constructed is given a class with all needed dimensions. Each student then makes a careful drawing of it to some convenient scale, with details and exact measurements. The class then goes to the shop, is furnished with the requisite materials and tools, and each member is shown by an expert how to execute the work. Every piece must be reasonably perfect or it is rejected and a new one is required. Although the students work in the shop no more than four hours per week, the experience is valuable. It is not supposed of course that skilled work can be produced by this method, but it is certain that such training will make better judges of workmanship.[10]

By 1877 the single shop was no longer satisfactory, and larger quarters were found in an old house nearby.

On May 16, 1878, Woodward, who was much in demand as a speaker, read a paper on the subject of manual education before the St. Louis Social Science Association. He discussed the strengths and weaknesses of education in general and then built up to the idea that manual education should be a general part of the educational system. He advanced the idea that all of the manual arts, the mechanical processes, and the tools used in common in the trades and occupations should be arranged in a systematic course of instruction and incorporated into the general system of education. Woodward reasoned that by thus teaching the essential principles involved in all trades it would be unnecessary to teach any one trade as such.

The Manual Training School is Born. Through Woodward's initial efforts, a group of prominent businessmen, industrialists, and educators began a series of meetings in the interests of founding a school for the manual arts. The industrialists were looking for a better class of trained workers, and it was on this assumption that their support had been so readily obtained. Enthusiasm was high, and financial assistance was offered. After a series of meetings a plan was finally presented to the Trustees of Washington University and adopted by that group on June 6, 1879. The St. Louis Manual Training School of Washington University was planned for boys of intermediate grades, starting at the age of fourteen. This was to be a school of general education on a new plan.

Woodward had used the name "Manual Training" in published articles and in discussions about the proposed school. When the name of the school was under discussion, Woodward suggested "Manual Training School." At first Chancellor W. G. Eliot rejected the name because it had an army flavor about it, and he felt it was not indicative of the intellectual nature of the work.[11] Also the chances were

---

[10] *Ibid.*, p. 9.
[11] Charles P. Coates, *History of the Manual Training School of Washington University,* Bulletin 1923, No. 3, Department of the Interior, Bureau of Education. Washington: Government Printing Office, 1923, p. 60.

great that it would be confused with the "Manual Labor Schools" which had appeared in abundance throughout the country in the previous half century.

At a later period Chancellor Eliot accepted the name, but not without a thorough search of dictionaries and etymologies, which seemed not to suggest to him an appropriate name. He felt that the name Manual Training School was misleading and belittling, and that it might create a prejudice against the school.

The prospectus for the new school, which Woodward prepared in October 1879, was probably the earliest practical formulation of the ideas of manual training for the secondary school; it is the basis for calling the St. Louis school the "Pioneer Manual-Training School." On September 6, 1880, the first class of fifty boys, selected by examinations, began their studies in the first manual training school in the United States. Inscribed over the entrance to the new building were these words of Woodward, which expressed his hopes for the new educational venture:

Hail to the skillful cunning hand!
Hail to the cultured mind!
Contending for the world's command,
Here let them be combined.

Woodward was interested in manual training for industrial purposes, but he was perhaps even more interested in the value of manual training in the general education of students. His slogan, "Put the whole boy in school," indicated his belief that manual training would increase the holding power of the high schools. He felt that the excessive drop-out rate of the high

school was directly related to the traditional classical curriculum. The first students in 1880 were enrolled in a program which consisted of two hours of woodshop and one hour each of mathematics, science, Latin or English, and drawing.

At the end of the school year, on June 16, 1881, a display of student work and actual demonstration of the teaching methods was scheduled for public presentation. The *Missouri Republican,* June 17, 1881, reported the affair in considerable detail and with credit to the school and to Woodward. The reporter noted that several prominent Chicago men were present and that one of them said to Professor Woodward, "We shall not be ashamed to follow in your lead if only we can."[12]

Manual was the most popular secondary school in St. Louis for many years, and grammar school graduates eagerly sought admission. Its popularity was high among business and industrial groups, and during times of financial stress or when equipment was needed, these groups willingly supplied money. Woodward expressed the opinion many times that Manual was "fortunate in its friends."

Student enrollment never exceeded 316 students (1892-93 and 1903-4) and during the period 1882-1910 was never lower than 200. During its 35 year history a total of 7,864 students enrolled, and of this number 1,346 were graduated. Manual's graduates turned out to be remarkably successful in their life's work, but they were a select group to begin with. Because the school had the reputation of being "tough" the faint of heart seldom sought admission.

---

[12] Coates, *op. cit.,* p. 26.

36

On the other hand there was some competition among the more capable students to gain admission.

On February 8, 1910, Woodward submitted his resignation from his various posts at Washington University. He was 72 years of age and had spent nearly 45 years at the university. From time to time after his retirement he attended meetings of the managing board. On January 12, 1914, he passed away at his home in St. Louis.

For several years enrollment and general interest in Manual had steadily declined. Enrollment in 1914-15 was 141 students, the lowest in 33 years. Manual instruction needed by the university's preparatory students was being supplied adequately by the programs in the city high school. So on February 5, 1915, Manual was united with another department of the university and at the close of the school term, Woodward's Manual Training School ceased to exist. New pathways had been found leading to the cultured mind and the skillful hand.

### E. E. White

In the fall of 1880, President E. E. White of Purdue University entered the discussion of what the public schools should teach. He recognized that while the state had the right to teach any subject which might "promote the general welfare," it was not obligated to do so. He distinguished between *general* and *special* in education, pointing out that, "The elements of technical knowledge which are of general application and utility may clearly be taught in the public schools." [13]

White was emphatic in his view that trades should not be taught in the public schools because this would direct public education away from its primary purpose. Although he was in accord with the principle that the head and the hand should be trained together, he felt that the "statement that the public school should teach every pupil to work with his hand while it trains him to think with his head [is] impractical and misleading." [14] The guardians of liberal education considered technical education as a "deceptive farce," impractical, a potential threat to the intellect, and completely unacceptable in the public schools.

White told an NEA audience in 1880 that it was impossible to teach trades in the public schools because of the number of trades. It would, he said, be "manifest injustice" to attempt to do so,[15] and would crowd the trades with workmen and reduce the compensation of skilled labor. White did advocate a program of technical education that provided for half of each school day to be devoted to labor and the remainder spent in the regular school program. While he did want to cultivate respect for honest labor and a taste for industrial pursuits, he was firmly set against a "weak attempt to make artisans."

### John D. Runkle

John Daniel Runkle, a graduate of the Lawrence Scientific School of Harvard University, was one of the first

---

[13] E. E. White, "Technical Training in American Schools," *Education*, November 1880, p. 116.
[14] *Ibid.*, p. 119.
[15] *Ibid.*, pp. 222-228.

ten faculty members of the Massachusetts Institute of Technology. In 1868 he left his post as professor of mathematics to become the acting president of MIT. In 1870 he was made president.

**Runkle and Students Visit Exposition.** The Centennial Exposition, held in Philadelphia from May to November 1876, attracted more than eight million visitors. Tucked away under a stairway in Machinery Hall were the cabinets of models sent by the Imperial Technical School of Moscow.*

In June, 1876, Runkle and a large party of students and faculty members from MIT spent two weeks at the Centennial Exposition, clearly bent on searching for things of value to their school. Runkle discovered the Russian exhibit, which fired his imagination and provided an answer to one of his pressing problems, that of finding a method of giving practical training to engineering students. The major part of the problem was the actual method which was needed. Runkle reported his ideas as follows: (1) separate instruction shops from construction shops; (2) provide only one kind of work in each shop; (3) provide as many work stations and tools for each station as a teacher can reasonably handle in one instruction period; (4) graduate the instruction in each shop according to the difficulty of the operation.

In this manner a reasonable degree of skill would be acquired, with maximum economy of time. Runkle felt that such shop instruction was not unlike the instruction given in the chemistry and physics laboratories, and that it should bear the same relationship to the parent course. Credit for developing these ideas of shop instruction is usually given to the Russian school and to its director, Victor Della-Vos. Concerning the general influence of the Russian exhibit Coates says:

It is certain that the influence of the Russian school on American education did not extend beyond the giving of the original impulse. There never was any American drawing on Russian education in Russia; moveover, there is no evidence that anything written in Russian or by Russians, except Della-Vos's description of the Philadelphia exhibit, was ever consulted by American educators.[16]

There was no question but that Runkle was inspired by what he saw of the Russian exhibit, and his quick mind immediately formulated plans for utilizing the ideas. He reported to the Corporation of the Massachusetts Institute of Technology and made recommendations concerning instruction shops for engineering students. Long before the Centennial Exposition was over the Corporation had granted approval of Runkle's plan. The program required for engineering students could be elected by others. In addition to providing work for the students at MIT, a new school of secondary grade (School of Mechanic Arts) was opened to grammar-school students who could pass the required examinations.

---

* Hidden thus from prominent view, the Russian exhibit would easily have been overlooked. This seems to have been the case with Woodward, for he never mentioned in his writings that he saw the exhibit. Woodward consistently leads one to believe that the true nature and importance of the Russian system of manual training came to him through the eyes and imagination of Runkle.

[16] Coates, *op. cit.*, p. 57.

It was Woodward's opinion that Runkle had looked deeper into the problem than had Della-Vos, and that he not only saw shop instruction as an essential element in the education of a mechanical engineer, but also perceived its value in general education. Runkle's discovery excited many education-conscious groups. It was these groups which in turn discussed this idea and spread interest in this new direction in education.

Runkle discussed the Russian system at the NEA meeting in 1877, indicating that prior to discovering the Russian system and seeing its advantages at Massachusetts Institute of Technology, American schools had been sending engineers into the field with their hands tied. Until then, engineers had had a good technical education, but they had little knowledge, and absolutely no skill, in connection with the practical aspects of construction. It was not possible to send graduate engineers into an apprenticeship in order to learn certain fundamentals which they lacked. Runkle believed that practice in technical work should be a part of every week's work, it should be carried out in a businesslike atmosphere of reality, and the student should not receive any pecuniary return for his labor.[17] In Runkle's view the distinguishing feature of the Russian system was that art was fundamental to it. In the years that followed, attempts were made to establish a satisfactory working relationship between art and manual training.

## William T. Harris

Another prominent American educator who spoke with a loud voice and whose ideas were heard by the masters of educational direction was William T. Harris. He was well informed concerning European educational ideas, and while serving as Superintendent of Schools in St. Louis, he introduced kindergarten work and became one of the proponents and leaders of elementary work in science. From 1889 to 1906 he served as the U.S. Commissioner of Education.

Harris was ever the friendly enemy of manual training. He could support manual training, but only on his terms. "I have no patience with those who advocate industrial education at the expense of the general education now given in the common schools," he wrote in June, 1886.[18] He could not abide the thought of training for skill in certain "knacks" as an answer or substitute for the general disciplines. His order of education was such that the first consideration was related to citizenship; the second, "to the intellectual mastery of the scientific view of the world," and the third, to education that pertains to the business of making a living. Harris was not to be taken in by the wild claims of manual training or of industrial education. He wrote, "No parent would prefer to have his children know how to work skillfully in preference to knowing how to behave morally, and how to act according to the accepted code of manners."[19]

---

[17] NEA *Proceedings*, 1877, p. 241.
[18] William T. Harris, "Industrial Education in the Common Schools," *Education*, June 1886, p. 607.
[19] *Ibid.*, p. 608.

The devotees of manual training believed that in their classes children could learn both moral and mannerly behavior.

Strong arguments in favor of industrial education and manual training could not shake Harris from his view that it was the function of education to cultivate the humanities as a first step, and then, perhaps, the industrial faculties. He could not accept the idea that manual training activities were entitled even in a remote way to infringe upon the curriculum which had served society well for so long a period of time. Manual training in its proper place was a good idea, but even good ideas could be recommended for the wrong reasons. Manual training "was first defended on the preposterous ground that it is educative in the same sense that arithmetic, geography, grammar and natural science are educative." [20]

**Other Voices**

"Our present school exists on the presumption that it is the product of our present civil society," wrote Robert Seidel, a Swiss educator.[21] He indicated also that this had been true of all previous societies. There had been a close relationship between educational theories and social revolutions, and during social revolutions great leaders in education had always appeared. "Each form of society begets its form of education, and each stage of the economic development of mankind implies a definite system of education and instruction." [22]

Seidel knew well the educational program of his native Switzerland. He knew of the influence of the practical Pestalozzi and of the changes in education in Germany, France, and America. The change was inevitable—it was the manifest destiny of education—and so strongly did Seidel feel this change that he predicted:

So surely as with civil society the ideas of the culture of mankind, natural development, and observation made their way into the pedagogy of the time, so surely with the new order of society will its principle, labor, achieve its citizenship in the system of education. Struggling against it is in vain. The future in the state, as well as in pedagogy, belongs to labor.[23]

"I have regarded good training in manual arts as more than equal to literary instruction for intellectual progress, [and] it is the very backbone of moral education," wrote J. R. Buchanan, who also claimed that the industrial system was the *true liberal education.*[24] Gradually the new education included among its proponents well known educational leaders. Men such as John Dewey aided the cause. G. Stanley Hall, who once criticized manual training programs as "these thin curricula" which hover aimlessly between liberality and utility, later wrote, "Next to moral education, . . . industrial training

---

[20] William T. Harris, "Vocation Versus Culture, Or the Two Aspects of Education," *Education,* December 1891, p. 201.

[21] Robert Seidel, *Industrial Instruction: A Pedagogic and Social Necessity,* Translated by Margaret K. Smith. Boston: D. C. Heath and Company, 1887, p. 4.

[22] *Ibid.,* p. 9.

[23] *Ibid.,* pp. 10-11.

[24] J. R. Buchanan, "The Moral Influence of Manual Training, NEA *Proceedings,* 1883, p. 45.

is by general consent the greatest and most urgent problem confronting the American people." [25] Slowly the attitudes of educators seemed to be changing. Where once there was opposition and indifference in professional groups, the pattern had changed to one of encouragement and cooperation. Bennett said of the meeting of the NEA Department of Superintendence in 1901 ". . . there was not enough criticism or opposition of any sort [related to industrial education] to stimulate a healthy discussion." [26] Leaders in the manual training movement were concerned with "wholeness" in the program and did not restrict their vision to limited values.

## The Results

### Attitudes in Favor of Manual Training

The rationale against manual training was harsh; but, undaunted, the proponents of manual training and industrial education struggled to maintain their position. They asserted that the lack of practical education in the public schools represented a deficiency in the school system. They could point to the fact that graduates from high schools were not well prepared to earn a living and that the school should be more concerned with this problem. The aims of education proposed by the advocates of manual training amounted to a criticism of the established system of education, and it was natural to resent such criticism and to discourage efforts at reform of the curriculum.

For more than two decades after 1870 the integration of manual training with the school curriculum was fought out in the pages of the educational journals and in the conventions of professional educators. Few educational questions have excited so many schoolmen. Points of view ranged from blind faith in manual training to bitterly obstinate opposition to its introduction in any form or at any place in the curriculum. Nor did one have to choose one extreme or the other, for there was a continuum of viewpoints, with many positions between the extremes.

The manual training movement provided many new, fresh, and realistic viewpoints for the late-nineteenth-century educator in search of change. He could see potential educational goals become reality through the process of manual training. Such training represented a relief from the drudgery and boredom so often found in the schools of the period. Some of the new proposals were obviously visionary, but this was regarded as a minor problem by the converts to the manual training idea. Discovery of various potential values in manual training created a chain reaction in which each new value discovery provided the tap roots for others.

Critics who claimed that manual training interfered with intellectual culture were given the answer that industry was the natural assistant and invigorator of intellectual education. Pupils would obtain general mental improvement faster when hand and mental labor were united. Manual training tended to provide understanding in addition to knowledge.

---

[25] G. Stanley Hall, *Educational Problems*, 2 vols. New York: D. Appleton Century Company, 1911, I, p. 540.
[26] *Manual Training Magazine*, Vol. II, No. 3, April 1901, p. 187.

## Emergence of Trade Education

Mechanics had customarily solved their own educational problems by establishing mechanics' institutes, mechanics' libraries, and professional associations. In the early years of the nineteenth century the workingman had battled to obtain equality of education for his children. Even his wildest dreams did not include the teaching trades in the free public schools.

The idea of "educated labor" as opposed to merely "skilled labor," was gaining acceptance, but this differentiation was not followed by appropriate changes in the public school curriculum. However, lack of immediate action did not discourage the proponents of trade education. The necessity of providing a vast number of workers could not be overlooked by educators. They were particularly appalled by the failure of apprenticeship to meet the needs of labor, and the old ideas of manual labor schools were frequently revived. Thomas Hampson informed an NEA audience in 1885 that manufacturing cities should have one or more manual labor schools to be attended by volunteer classes from the public schools for two or three hours each day.[27] In increasing numbers, educators thought of the industrial need, and attempted to determine the relationship of the public schools to the problem. One of the main issues to be overcome was the matter of attitude in approach to the problem. "Instead of saying, we will not teach trades, we should aim to provide a

large and constantly increasing series of trade schools, until all boys, and girls too, in all trades, shall have the benefits of well-devised and thorough instruction therein."[28]

**Hampton Institute.** One of the first private trade schools was the Hampton Institute, organized by General Samuel Chapman Armstrong in 1868. Armstrong was convinced that if a free Negro race was to find adjustment in society, education would become a vital factor in that adjustment. He succeeded in interesting the American Missionary Society in the school, and the Society purchased a large estate on the Hampton River. Providing skilled Negro labor was a necessary step in the reconstruction period following the War between the States. Furthermore, trade training was combined with the elements of a liberal education in order that the Negro might improve his character and social status. The Hampton Institute led the way in the education of Negroes. Booker T. Washington was one of its students.

**New York Trade School.** The first school to offer specific trade training with supplementary studies directly related to each trade was the New York Trade School, founded by Colonel Richard Tylden Auchtmuty in 1881. As a result of his study of labor problems, Auchtmuty developed a pattern of trade training designed to give pre-employment instruction as well as supplementary instruction for employed workers. Any male over seventeen years of age might enroll in the school

[27] Thomas Hampson, "The Apprenticeship Question and Industrial Schools," NEA *Proceedings*, July 1885, pp. 151-159.
[28] Selim H. Peabody, "The Value of Tool-Instruction as Related to the Active Pursuits in Which Pupils May Subsequently Engage," NEA *Proceedings*, July 1889, p. 103.

if he could profit from the instruction. Although tuition was charged, much of Auchtmuty's personal fortune was used to support the school. Among the many benefactors of the school was J. Pierpont Morgan, who provided a generous endowment in 1892.

**Hebrew Technical Institute.** In contrast to the plan of instruction of the New York Trade School, the Hebrew Technical Institute, founded in New York City in November 1883, offered a greater range of subjects of a general nature. It may be classed more properly as a technical school rather than a trade school. The need for a school of this nature arose because of the number of Jewish immigrants coming to this country in the late years of the nineteenth century. Many were in poor economic circumstances and became a burden upon the Jewish charitable organizations.

The school required that an applicant be a resident of New York City, strong and healthy, of Jewish faith, and at least twelve and a half years of age. Each applicant was required also to supply letters of recommendation testifying to his scholarship and character.

**Williamson Free School of Mechanical Trades.** Still another departure in trade training developed with the establishment of the Williamson Free School of Mechanical Trades in Philadelphia in 1891. The school was endowed by Isaiah V. Williamson, merchant and philanthropist of Philadelphia, and was designed to take the place of the old apprenticeship training. Boys from 16 to 18 years of age were bound as indentured apprentices to the school trustees for three years. After preliminary courses were completed, a student was assigned to a trade by the school trustees. Due regard was given to the inclination and adaptability of the boys for the trade to which they were assigned. Williamson was convinced that the abandonment of apprenticeship resulted in idleness, vice, and crime, and constituted a threat to society. The school was entirely free—no charge was made for clothing, food, or instruction. Only the most worthy of all applicants were accepted by the board of trustees.

The Williamson School was founded at a time when the manual training movement was growing in popularity. The school subscribed to the nature of the movement and actually added work, preliminary to trade instruction, along the lines of manual training. It was felt that such instruction was necessary and, since manual training had not been widely established at that date, many of the pupils from the public schools would not have had such training.

**Comparison of Types.** The New York Trade School, the Hebrew Technical Institute, and the Williamson Free School of Mechanical Trades each represents a type of school which developed during the initial period of the trade school movement. The New York Trade School offered specific trade training with directly related scientific instruction. The Hebrew Technical Institute offered a limited amount of specific trade training, was organized in the manner of a technical institute, and combined trade training with the subject matter of general education. The Williamson school started with a program of manual training for all students, added some general education, and finally offered specific, intensive trade training. As mentioned, students

43

at the Williamson school were apprenticed to the board of trustees and lived at the school. Other schools which developed during the early years of the trade school movement usually adopted one of these plans. The exceptions are found in the corporation schools, which attempted to revive the old type of apprenticeship to meet their particular needs.

## Corporation Schools

As industrialization continued, many employers supported some form of industrial education. Those who could do so usually prefered to conduct their own systems of education. The others usually supported the plan of industrial training in the public schools.

R. Hoe and Company. In 1872 the firm of R. Hoe and Company, New York manufacturers of printing presses, was confronted with a demand for improved machinery. This required a more intelligent class of workmen, and to obtain them the company established a school which met two evenings a week. The school was free and was open to employees of the firm, both men and boys. Suppers were provided by the company immediately upon the close of the day's work, and instruction began in the early evening. Among the subjects studied were English, mechanical drawing, arithmetic, geometry, and algebra. The studies were directly related to the work of the firm.

Attendance was not compulsory, but advancement within the firm was measured in part by special preparation for it. The graduates were preferred over other workers because it was felt they were better equipped to do the work entrusted to them. The school proved to be satisfactory, and after thirty years of operation the company was convinced that a superior class of workmen was their reward.

General Electric Co. In 1900 the General Electric Company of Lynn, Massachusetts, established an apprenticeship system which combined the activities of shop and classroom. Selected for study were academic courses which would develop for the apprentice a better understanding of machines and machine parts. Included in the studies were courses in interpretation of mechanical drawings, sketching, and design of auxiliary tools required for modern manufacture. The plan of combining apprenticeship with industrial science was evidently successful, since the company was satisfied with the results and the system was widely copied.

Baldwin Locomotive Works. In 1901 the Baldwin Locomotive Works of Philadelphia established school programs for three classes of their personnel. The first class was organized for those who had completed elementary school but who had not reached 16 years of age. They attended school three evenings a week for three years and studied arithmetic, geometry, mechanical drawing, and shop practice. The second class included those employees over 18 who had completed a more advanced educational program. This group attended school two evenings a week for two years and studied such subjects as chemistry, advanced mathematics, and mechanical drawing. The third group was composed of graduates of colleges and other advanced institutions. They were not required to attend classes but were required to read technical journals and turn in synopses of the various articles. The attitude of the Baldwin Locomotive Works

44

toward education in general was that better elementary schools would provide more efficiently for the apprenticeship system and that evening schools were necessary in order that working boys might supplement their daily shop experience.

**The Ludlow Manufacturing Company.** Organization of schools by industrial concerns followed similar patterns. In almost every case the company noted in the employee deficiencies which interfered with efficient production. The purpose of the school programs was to remedy the deficiencies. The Ludlow Manufacturing Company of Ludlow, Massachusetts, found that in their forty years of operation not one of the overseers or first line supervisors in the textile mill had been educated in the village schools. It was evident to the company that they must either depend upon men trained abroad or encourage the local schools to provide an education which would fit boys in the village for responsible positions in the mills.

**The Role of the Public School**

It was common knowledge that there was a need for trained mechanics in the United States and that the apprenticeship system was not able to cope with the situation. The idea that American youth had a right to expect some preparation for occupation as a part of his public school work was finding support among some educators. The fact that manual training groups had some responsibility or obligation in this regard was attracting the attention of many leaders of the manual training movement. It was possible to satisfy

this need in part by an evening program using the manual training facilities, supplemented by special equipment if necessary, in order to teach elements of the trades. Trade instruction could be taught in the manual training schools, provided that it was preceded by a thorough course in manual training.

**Promotion by NEA**

Charles H. Keyes, president of the NEA Department of Manual Training, announced at the Charleston convention in 1900 that he had received demands from various parts of the country for a consideration of the relation of manual training to trade training. The letters indicated interests in either one of two items: The first concerned the establishment of public trade schools; the second insisted that the public schools should include more work for business, vocation, or trade, "without sacrificing their general culture aims." Keyes pointed out that manual training groups had been steadfast in their point of view that manual training was entirely educational and did not have economic or utilitarian aims. "They even prayed to be delivered from their friends who were fond of announcing the discovery that one of the consequences of good manual training was the development of technical skill readily turned to use in the trades," he reported.[29]

Keyes urged the Department to remember that a significant number of the manual training school pupils would go into the trades, and that a year or two of manual training would increase the power and general intel-

---

[29] *Manual Training Magazine*, Vol. II, No. 1, October 1900, p. 46.

ligence of students bent in that direction. Furthermore, it was the mission of the school to help the student discover himself, and this purpose could not be achieved better than in the area of manual training.

**Pioneer Work in Massachusetts**

Charles F. Warner, principal of the Mechanic Arts High School of Springfield, Massachusetts, recognized the growing need for manual training to make some positive effort to contribute to the solution of this problem, which was then of national significance. Warner indicated that it was not possible for manual training to remain aloof. He took this stand knowing full well that, "One who advocates such a connection will probably be stigmatized as a deserter from the ranks of true educational manual training." [30] Warner's suggested program provided adequate attention to English, mathematics, science, and history, and provided in addition a sufficient amount of time in mechanic arts practice. He was of the opinion that the time devoted to mechanical work could be increased in order to give thoroughness to the teaching for the required trades, without infringing upon the academic work.

**Pioneer Work in California**

The four-year plan adopted by George A. Merrill, director of the California School of Mechanical Arts in San Francisco, began with two years of manual training during which the student had an opportunity to explore and discover which of the trades he wished to learn. During the last two years the student deepened his knowledge and skills in his chosen trade, and at the same time took an adequate amount of academic studies.

**NEA Proposal**

Because of the interest concerning the relationship of manual training to trade education, the NEA proposed a resolution as follows:

WHEREAS, Great interest has been manifested in the relation of manual training to trade instruction; and WHEREAS, it is suggested that trades should be taught at public expense; be it therefore *Resolved*, that a committee of five be appointed by the president to investigate the subject during the coming year, and report at the meeting of the department next year. [31]

The committee appointed consisted of Charles H. Keyes, supervisor of schools, Hartford, Connecticut, Chairman; J. H. Van Sickle, superintendent of schools, Baltimore, Maryland; Dr. H. H. Belfield, principal, Mechanic Arts High School, Springfield, Massachusetts; and George A. Merrill, principal, California School of Mechanical Arts, San Francisco.

Although the discussions continued in other meetings, a formal written report of the committee may not have been prepared. Subsequent discussions and the writings of industrial educators suggest that the topic continued to be under investigation.

**Arthur D. Dean's Proposal**

Many boys left school before they had an opportunity to attend the manual training high schools and thus con-

---

[30] *Ibid.*, p. 47.
[31] *Ibid.*, p. 50.

tributed to much of the poor work and unpleasant labor conditions of the time. Because these boys were about fourteen, at an age when their minds were receptive to the essentials of education, Arthur D. Dean proposed a course in trade education. Dean, who later became Chief of the Division of Vocational Schools in Albany, New York, urged a program consisting of arithmetic, English, bookkeeping, elementary science, and manual instruction. About half of the school day was to be given over to academic work and the other half to shop. This was almost identical to the plan which Merrill had found so successful in San Francisco. The essential features of Dean's plan were as follows: First, "The shop work ought to begin with a course in sloyd a little more extensive than the present grammar-school course, and its educational value ought to be emphasized;" and second, "gradually the trade element ought to be introduced, and finally the pupil, choosing his trade, would enter upon the course of instruction prepared for that trade."[32] Dean felt that such a course would tempt many grammar-school boys to remain in school longer.

Dean's proposal for the day-school program was based upon experience gained in evening classes for trades, which had been in operation since 1898 at the Mechanic Arts High School in Springfield, Massachusetts. The evening school attracted students who were employed in narrow specialties with no opportunity for advance-ment. They had a desire to learn but lacked the opportunity to do so. Students usually attended school two nights each week for two and a half hours each night. Although the school provided specific training related to trade areas, it was noted than an even broader training was desired by the students. This was provided in part by making mathematics, drawing, and electricity a part of the general background for all students. Many of the graduates had been able to increase their wages as a result of attendance at the evening school, and a few who were unemployed at the time of their admission to the school had been able to secure employment.

## Relationship of Manual Training to Trade Education

The growing interest among the proponents of manual training to do something specific about meeting the need for trade training did not include a desire to convert the manual training high school into a trade school. The existing program of manual training was intended to be left without change, but it was recognized that the environment of the manual training school did offer "a fairly wide field for a choice which may be made later."[33] Furthermore, the group to be served was large.

The most complicating factor of all was that no one knew what kind of industrial training was really needed. If this could be determined, then finding the appropriate place for trade

[32] Arthur D. Dean, "An Experiment in Teaching Trades at Public Expense," *Manual Training Magazine*, Vol. II, No. 3, April 1901, p. 149.

[33] George H. Bryant, "Recognition of the Trade Idea in Manual-Training Courses of High-School Grade," *Manual Training Magazine*, Vol. II, No. 4, July 1901, p. 201.

education in the public schools would be an easier task. Some educators held prejudices concerning the development of a utilitarian element in education, while others were of the opinion that utilitarian aims were the foundation blocks of education.

Bennett felt that trade instruction opposed the tradition of the American free-school system; a high degree of specialization at an early period in life was not desirable; trade schools could produce a surplus of workers in some areas; the idea favored one class in the community at the expense of the other; and that the cost of trade education made it impossible for public schools to assume the burden. Although Bennett did recognize the need for trade instruction, he expressed his belief "in the ability of the manual training work to do all in this direction that should be expected of the public schools. Manual training schools are doing much more to relieve the demand for trade schools than many persons are willing to admit." [34]

### Douglas Commission

Despite the conflict of opinion concerning trade education, necessity forced the issue, demanding attention and action. One of the most significant developments in gathering the forces of industrial education for the trades was the Douglas Commission in 1906. The Commission, which had been appointed in 1905 by Governor William

L. Douglas of Massachusetts, reported on the need for public industrial education of a trade nature. [35] This report caused influential industrial educators to think of manual training as only one aspect of a larger problem of industrial education.

James P. Haney devoted his editorial in the July issue of the *Manual Training Magazine* to the work of the Douglas Commission. Haney was concerned that the language of the report was not more forceful. It frequently used the word "may," which he felt was a weakness.

Some of our Munich friends have ordered things a bit better. They have tucked a "must" in their law, so that in the latter city even chimney-sweeps go to a part-time industrial school which teaches the art of chimney sweeping. Very clever people the Germans, albeit some of their words are so long they sag at the hyphens. [36]

### Summary

Social need for industrial education developed in relationship to the economy of the nation. As industrial development proceeded to become the dominant factor in the economic life of America, its educational implications commanded attention. For a half-century a variety of forces—manual labor schools, lyceums, mechanics institutes, and associations of craftsmen—placed an emphasis upon the need for industrial education. These forces tended to operate outside the mainstream of pub-

---

[34] "Reports From Associations," *Manual Training Magazine*, Vol. V, No. 1, October 1903, p. 37.

[35] Massachusetts, *Report of the Commission of Industrial and Technical Education*, Senate Document No. 349. Boston: Wright and Potter Printing Co., April 1906, pp. 3-7.

[36] *Manual Training Magazine*, Vol. III, No. 4, July 1906, p. 225.

lic education. They were more a convenience to society than an integral part of general social development. About 1870 the situation had reached critical proportions in that the needs were great but the solutions were not adequate. From 1870 to 1906, concerted attention and action was focused upon the general problem of industrial education. Out of the crucible of discussion came the foundation for a new era in education.

The issues were clear. The common school was criticized because it failed to reflect the life for which it was supposed to prepare youth. On the other hand there were arguments that the moral background of the school program was in reality the best preparation for life. And so the heated debate continued without clear evidence that either side was correct, but with a strong suspicion that both extremes were essential.

Though certain aspects of industrial education were regarded as anti-intellectual, drawing was not. Its educational values appeared to be sound, and its addition to the curriculum of the common school spread rapidly across the nation. Thus, one of the practical arts was established in high esteem as a vehicle of the total education of the individual.

Establishment of Agricultural and Mechanical Colleges [Morrill Act of 1862] did much to clarify the image of industrial education in the public mind. Throughout the nation the values of such instruction were proclaimed as an element of social progress.

These colleges were a step toward the goal of educated labor, but a step which required much more attention to the development of industrial education in the public schools. The Morrill Act would greatly benefit those who were able to attend the colleges, but the vast majority of the public, who could profit from similar instruction, would be ignored unless some reflection of the purposes of the colleges could develop also in the common schools.

Many prominent people participated in the discussion about industrial education in the late years of the nineteenth century. The proponents were enthusiastic about new educational values to be gained. The antagonists were fearful that existing values would be sacrificed for the sake of unproven theoretical considerations. But the viewpoint of society was changing and a new social spirit aided the development of attitudes in favor of the early manifestations [manual training] of industrial education.

From the standpoint of industrial education in the public schools, the two principal products of the crucible were: (1) Development of a strong and expanded manual training program, and (2) the emergence of trade education.

Private trade schools set the pace in contributing to the development of an educated labor force. Corporation schools formed industrial education programs appropriate for their corporate objectives and found their efforts amply rewarded.

Pioneer work in establishing industrial education was developed on many fronts. Some states took action as states, individual initiative was apparent in other states, the NEA moved toward adopting industrial educators' points of view, and individuals cited their observations concerning the general development of industrial education. Finally the greatest boost of all came from the report of the Douglas Commission in Massachusetts, 1906, whose thorough investigation of the nature of, and need for, industrial education served as a catalyst to increase enthusiasm for such education. The report was the opening wedge of the vocational drive to follow.

## Recall Questions

1. Identify the specific issues suggested as the principal ingredients in the crucible.
2. Summarize the arguments for and against the development of industrial education.
3. Name some of the schools that developed following the emergence of trade education.
4. What were some of the related proposals, suggestions, and pioneer developments characteristic of the period, 1870-1906?
5. Review the problems related to selecting the name of the St. Louis Manual Training School.

## Research Questions

1. Review the historical development of industrial education in your state for the period 1870-1906. What issues were involved? To what extent were the leaders in your state influenced by national leaders such as Woodward, Harris, and others? What were the results in your state in terms of the development of manual training and trade education?
2. Consult the following references and prepare a list of principles of industrial education that are valid today.

## Suggestions for Further Reading

Coates. Charles P., *History of the Manual Training School of Washington University.* U.S. Department of the Interior, Bureau of Education, Bulletin 1923, No. 3, Washington: Government Printing Office, 1923.

*Education*, 1880-1906.

*Manual Training Magazine*, 1900-1906.

Massachusetts, *Report of the Commission of Industrial and Technical Education*, Senate Document No. 349. Boston: Wright and Potter Printing Co., April 1906.

NEA, *Proceedings*, 1870-1906.

Woodward, Calvin M., *The Manual Training School*. Boston: D. C. Heath & Company, Publishers, 1887.

# Chapter 3

# The Vocational Drive

National Society for the Promotion of Industrial Education · Federal Bills for Vocational Education · Commission on National Aid to Vocational Education · The Smith-Hughes Act in the Making · Summary · Recall Questions · Research Questions · Suggestions for Further Reading

American industry needed mechanics. If manual training was not producing them, then some educational agency would have to do so. The movement which began to take shape in 1906 was dedicated in part to this goal. No criticism of the objectives of manual training was intended, but an emphasis was desired upon the educational aspects of manual training that would lead directly to employment. It was not expected that a short period of time in the secondary school would produce a skilled mechanic for industry, but it was hoped that a modicum of intensive training, for boys who had selected a particular occupation for their life's work, would facilitate entry into an occupation and speed their progress in and adjustment to the occupation. Nevertheless, in the years to follow, the problem of whether the school could or could not produce a

skilled mechanic would be debated endlessly and inconclusively.

General understanding of the vocational significance of manual training grew in proportion to the growth of manual training in general. During the years immediately after 1900 the vocational values of manual training were so obvious that they could no longer be ignored. Indeed, the Commission on the Reorganization of Secondary Education in 1913 recognized "vocational efficiency" of the pupil as the major purpose of instruction in the manual arts.

No small part of the movement to develop vocational training out of parts of manual education came about through the creative imagination of some staunch supporters of manual training itself. This produced a new program of vital social significance— beyond the natural vocational significance that was inherently a part of manual training.

Private trade schools had been in existence for nearly a quarter of a century. Corporations organized their own schools to satisfy their educational needs. The Douglas Commission had found that not only was there a demand for such a program, but the need was so critical that an adequate program would have to be supported in part or in whole by public funds. The formation of an association to promote the professional interest and understanding of industrial educators and to acquaint the public with the need for industrial education was timely and of great interest.

### National Society for the Promotion of Industrial Education

During the spring of 1906 two men sought to turn the interest in industrial education into a program of united action. The result was a powerful group, worth full attention here. The prime movers were Dr. James P. Haney, Director of Manual Training for the New York Public Schools, and Professor Charles R. Richards, Teachers College, Columbia University. The first formal meeting to discuss formation of an organization was held on June 9, 1906, at the Engineers Club in New York City. The 13 men attending this meeting were of the opinion "that a deep and widespread interest prevailed throughout the country in industrial education."[1] A subcommittee of five was appointed to continue discussions during the summer and early fall. Finally, on Friday, November 16, 1906, an organization meeting was held at Cooper Union in New York City, presided over by Dr. Haney and attended by approximately 250 businessmen and educators. A constitution was approved; officers and a board of managers were elected.

The purposes of the new organization were identified in the constitution as follows:

The objects of this Society shall be to bring to public attention the importance of industrial education as a factor in the industrial development of the United States; to provide opportunities for the study and discussion of the various phases of the problem; to make available the results of experience in the field of industrial education both in this country and abroad, and to promote the establishment of institutions for industrial training.[2]

At eight o'clock on the same evening the first meeting of the newly organized Society was held in the assembly hall of Cooper Union. Nicholas Murray Butler, President of Columbia University, presided. The tenor of the addresses which followed is exemplified in part by the remarks of Milton P. Higgins, President of the Norton Company, Worcester, Massachusetts.

Has not the time come when industrial education . . . will touch the man who works with tools, the artisan in general engaged in all the productive industries, the man who controls the ponderous machine, who guides the instrument of precision, the workman upon whom the engineer must ever depend to realize his ideals? Skill is the counterpart of knowledge. Is it too much to expect that through

---

[1] National Society for the Promotion of Industrial Education, [hereinafter cited as NSPIE], *Proceedings of the Organizational Meetings,* Bulletin No. 1, January 1907, pp. 15-16.
[2] *Ibid.,* p. 10.

skill given to the workman, there may result a better life, a better citizenship, and also a higher culture?[3]

Other addresses included those of President Butler; Frank A. Vanderlip, Vice-President, National City Bank, New York; Frederick P. Fish, President, American Telephone and Telegraph Company, Boston; and Miss Jane Addams, Head of Hull House, Chicago. There seemed to be no question in the minds of the speakers concerning the importance, value, or necessity of rapidly expanding the means of industrial education throughout the country.

### Early Bulletins

During 1907 the Society issued three bulletins. In July a *Selected Bibliography on Industrial Education,* prepared by Charles R. Richards, was issued in response to numerous requests. In September *A Symposium on Industrial Education,* collated by James P. Haney, was issued. It consisted of replies, from leaders in labor, management, and education, to a request from the Society for "some succinct statements concerning the relative desirability of industrial instruction." One of the 33 persons who responded was President Theodore Roosevelt:

This question is vital to our future progress, and public attention should be focused upon it. Surely it is eminently in accord with the principles of our democratic life that we should furnish the highest average industrial training for the ordinary skilled workman. But it is a curious thing that in industrial training we have tended to devote our energies to producing high grade men at the top rather than in the ranks.[4]

In October the Society issued a bulletin on *Industrial Training for Women.* The bulletin was prepared by Florence M. Marshall, Director of the Boston Trade School for Girls, and a member of the Society's subcommittee on industrial education for women.

### Early Meetings

From the very beginning the Society had been confronted with the problem of finding a common base for agreement among labor, management, and education about principles and requirements of education. Bringing industrial education prominently before the general public and promoting its development required that the major forces concerned work together with a minimum of strife. The first annual convention, in Chicago, January 23-25, 1908, provided the opportunity for each of these forces to assert its hopes and fears for industrial education.

Charles W. Eliot, President of Harvard University, spoke on "Industrial Education as an Essential Factor in Our National Prosperity." He was concerned with the confusion of definition; more important, he endorsed manual training as *a very useful element in the curriculum,* and thought that public trade schools were necessary in order to meet the requirements of a rapidly changing industrial economy.

James W. Van Cleve, President of the National Association of Manufacturers, spoke on the topic "Industrial Education from the Standpoint of the Manufacturer." He showed statistics to

[3] *Ibid.,* p. 15.
[4] NSPIE, *A Symposium on Industrial Education,* Bulletin No. 3, September 1907, pp. 6-7.

indicate that the need for industrial education greatly exceeded the number of schools thus far created; he urged extending and rounding out the educational system; he endorsed the activities of the Society in securing cooperation between education and industrial groups; he proposed that the office of Commissioner of Industrial Education be established in an appropriate governmental bureau; and finally, he pointed out:

The only way in which we can get this skill, in grade and volume at all adequate to our demands, is to give industrial education to all our American boys, beginning it in the lowest grades of our public primary schools, and making it free as the air and sunlight.

. . . .

The door of industrial opportunity must be thrown wide open to every American boy by means of free trade schools so that his superior originality, initiative and versatility may have an open field for their exercise. Then will the world's choicest prizes in industrial, social and intellectual supremacy be ours.[5]

The Society's President, Henry S. Pritchett, who was also president of the Carnegie Foundation for the Advancement of Teaching, discussed "The Aims of the National Society for the Promotion of Industrial Education." Pritchett pointed out that the Society intended to bring together four groups of persons: (1) those involved directly with industrial callings, (2) the great manufacturers who depend upon trade skills, (3) the teachers involved in teaching the skills, and (4) the American public. The Society intended to work out the problems of industrial

education by cooperation in a spirit of industrial peace, and to open the door of opportunity so that men and women might surely become effective in the industrial life of the country. Pritchett made it clear that the work of propaganda would require the services of a person who could give full time to the basic interests of the Society. He stressed that the Society was dedicated to broad aims rather than purely parochial ones:

This great problem of industrial education is after all only one part of the larger problem of education which has to do with national fitness, with national respect for law and order, national discipline, and national efficiency in government. It is all a part of the problem which today is set before democracy, and democracy is yet on trial.[6]

Carroll D. Wright, President of Clark College, Worcester, Massachusetts, speaking on "The Apprenticeship System as a Means of Promoting Industrial Efficiency," expressed the fear that the propagandizing for industrial education would obscure the advantages of the apprenticeship system. He nevertheless believed that separate industrial schools should be organized for trade instruction, especially since the ordinary schools had been devoted primarily to purely academic subjects. He stated emphatically that the industrial school could not turn out full-fledged skilled mechanics. However, he could see the benefits of combining the two systems—academic and industrial—to produce the most efficient and skilled workmen.

---

[5] NSPIE, *Proceedings of First Annual Meeting,* Chicago, Part I, Bulletin No. 5, April 1908, p. 21.
[6] *Ibid.,* p. 27.

The first annual meeting reached into the heart of industrial education; the present condition was assessed, imperative needs were described, and the group looked to the future. Labor presented its case, management cited its industrial aims, and education speculated upon a vastly improved and expanded program for industrial education in the public schools.

The Society had set for itself the task of convincing the public of the need for public education to provide preparation for industrial occupations. At the national level the group had already been quite successful. Although some suspicion existed concerning the "real" intent of the Society, all parties seemed to be seeking common ground upon which to build a public system of industrial education. However, conviction at the national level was not sufficient. The real battle had to be fought at the state and local levels. For this reason the Society commenced immediately to organize state branches. State committees were formed by extending invitations to prominent representatives of employer and employee groups, to educators, and to the general public. Some state committees formed immediately, and quickly initiated the work of molding public opinion with gratifying results.

It was the plan of the national Society to recommend the conversion of state committees into self-acting and self-supporting state branches. On March 14, 1908, the executive committee adopted by-laws to govern the organization of these branches. The committee also prepared a suggested constitution for state branch use. By November, 1908, state branches had been organized in Alabama, Georgia, Massachusetts, Montana, Ohio, Pennsylvania, Rhode Island, and Virginia. Twenty-nine states had organized state committees, while only eight states—Arkansas, Delaware, Florida, Maryland, Mississippi, North Dakota, Nevada, and Wyoming—had no organized body.

Membership in the national Society by the end of 1908 had reached nearly 900. The second meeting, in Atlanta, November 19-21, 1908, followed a pattern of organization similar to the January, 1908, meeting. There were addresses by well known and influential persons representing industry, labor, and education. Inherent in the purposes of the national society was the ultimate aim of obtaining federal support for industrial education. The Society moved in this direction not on the basis of slipshod methods but by deliberate and painstaking means, insisting that the great problems be considered from every angle.

**An Abortive Aid Bill**

In 1907 Representative Charles R. Davis of Minnesota had introduced a bill in Congress calling for a plan of federal education to be supported by funds from the Congress. Davis discussed his plan at the Atlanta meeting, then asked that the Society be "an active agent in support of this measure."[7] However, the bill was not supported by either the Society or the Commissioner of Education. This, plus lack of support from other groups interested in

---

[7] NSPIE, *Proceedings, Second Annual Meeting, Atlanta, Georgia,* Bulletin No. 9, June 1909, p. 102.

federal aid to vocational education, caused the bill to fail. In withholding support, leaders of the Society insisted first that a thorough investigation of the status and the future needs of the entire field of industrial and vocational education was necessary before an adequate bill could be prepared.

Later the Society acquired the necessary data and formulated a federal bill which was championed by Senator Hoke Smith of Georgia. In 1908, however, Smith was Governor of Georgia. He had been invited to serve as toastmaster at the opening banquet of the Atlanta meeting. There was never any question concerning where Smith stood in relation to the purposes of the Society:

It is a great problem you have undertaken. I do not know that there is a greater problem, or so great a problem in our country. It reaches our position in national commerce. It will solve the question as to whether our manufactories and our industrial growth are to maintain that place in the world's commerce to which our best resources entitle us.

. . . .

No system of education or manufacture is logical which undertakes to carry a youth as far as he has to go through school and college and drops him without having done anything to teach him how to do that which will most probably aid him to make his daily livelihood.[8]

Elmer Ellsworth Brown, United States Commissioner of Education, voiced a similar sentiment:

We are idealists and we are going to continue to be idealists. I believe in our university education. I believe in the liberal culture of our lower schools; but I believe just as strongly in that doctrine which has been enunciated in the clearest terms tonight by the Governor of this Commonwealth that no part of our education should be considered complete until it has given the pupil power to grapple with the real work of the working world into which he has to go.[9]

Making the most of the national trend in education, the Society geared its activities to the "vocational drive" that was enunciated so clearly in the annual meetings. Members were determined to study and interpret the vocational trend before embarking upon any action program to make the desire a reality. In keeping with this determination, a committee had been appointed at the first national meeting to prepare a report on the "Relation of Industrial Training to the General System of Education in the United States." The committee submitted its final report at the third annual meeting in Milwaukee in 1909.

The report took up the problem of nomenclature, outlined the general problem faced in attempting to provide industrial education for the youth of the United States, and indicated in a general way the possible groups to be served and the kinds of schools which seemed to be necessary. The Society recognized that, although it had gathered a certain amount of information, far more would have to be collected before a reasonable plan of action could be formulated. The gathering of such data was beyond the resources of the Society; it would have to be done by some comprehensive agency.

The Society therefore sent a resolution to President William Howard Taft, recommending that he urge the Congress to provide an appropriation

---

[8] *Ibid.*, pp. 16-17.
[9] *Ibid.*, pp. 36-37.

in the budget of the Commissioner of Education so that the "national study" which seemed imperative could be carried out. The resolution did not directly produce the action requested, but it did bring formally to the atten- of governmental bodies the imperative needs of industrial education on a national scale. The report may have indirectly influenced the appointment of the Commission on National Aid to Vocational Education four years later.

## Federal Bills for Vocational Education

### The Dolliver-Davis Bill

As we will see in another chapter, the American Federation of Labor contributed immeasurably to the promotion of federal aid for vocational education. It had long been friendly to the aims of the field, and at its meeting in Denver in November, 1908, it adopted a resolution providing for a study of industrial education. The president of the AFL appointed a committee "to investigate the methods and means of industrial education in this country and abroad, and to report its findings, conclusions, and recommendations to the next annual meeting of the American Federation of Labor." [10]

The American Federation of Labor's committee met twice, in New York the following August, and in Washington in October. Its report was made at the Toronto Convention in November, 1909. The interest expressed by business organizations, boards of trade, labor organizations, and educators

satisfied the committee that the demand for industrial education was based on real need. Misfits found throughout industry were offered as additional proof that action was necessary. The committee reported, "If we are to secure industrial supremacy, or even maintain our present standards in the industrial world, we must in some way in our educational system acquire an equivalent to our old apprenticeship system."[11]

The committee investigated the apprenticeship system thoroughly and invited comments from leaders in the field. It had investigated the cooperative industrial education plan. It studied past legislation for education and received comprehensive reports on the educational programs of private companies and private trade schools. A statement was prepared giving organized labor's position in favor of unification of effort of all groups in order to arrive at the optimum solution of the problem.

Finally the committee drafted a bill for Congressional enactment based upon its findings and conclusions. Ar· thur E. Holder, Chairman of the Legis· lative Committee of the American Federation of Labor, was instructed to secure its introduction in Congress. Senator Jonathan P. Dolliver of Iowa, Chairman of the Senate Committee on Education and Labor, agreed to introduce the bill and to champion its provisions. The bill was introduced in the Senate in January, 1910, and referred to the Committee on Agriculture and Forestry. The hearings were conducted

---

[10] American Federation of Labor, *Industrial Education*. Washington: American Federation of Labor, 1910, p. 5.

[11] *Ibid.*, p. 9.

on April 12 and 13, 1910. The bill provided for the preparation of teachers of vocational subjects and for the appropriation of money and the regulation of its expenditure.[12]

### The Page-Wilson and Smith-Lever Bills

The original bill failed, and a revised bill was introduced in the Senate on April 6, 1911, by Senator Carroll S. Page of Vermont. The Committee on Agriculture and Forestry, after a brief consideration, recommended that the administrative features of the bill should be further revised in order to articulate better with the laws of the several states. Furthermore, the Committee passed a resolution providing:

. . . that Senator Page, as a subcommittee of one, be instructed to correspond with leading educators and others interested in the purposes of the proposed measure, and to report to the full committee the result of his investigations, and to submit a bill amended to conform to the suggestions he may receive from such correspondence or any he might have to make. And that the committee approves the general purposes of the bill.[13]

Senator Page wrote to the superintendents of public instruction in every state inviting their comments, criticisms, and suggestions. He asked particularly that the superintendents point out changes that would be necessary to conform to the laws of their states. Letters were written to governors and men of prominence in all fields of labor and industrial life. In most instances the response was enthusiastic and

extremely helpful in pointing out specific revisions. When all of the supplementary information had been received, a subcommittee studied the bill word for word and prepared a revision according to the suggested changes. In presenting the bill to the Senate on June 5, 1912, Senator Page said, "The present bill is a consensus of opinion far more unanimous than is the case with most portions of our constructive legislation."[14] In his introductory remarks the Senator pointed out that the bill dealt with the welfare of boys and girls, of mature workers, and of homemakers to a greater extent than any measure before Congress in the preceding fifty years.

Although the bill made considerable progress during the session, a congested legislative calendar prevented its final consideration. Then, early in the next session of Congress, 1914, the agricultural extension provisions of the bill were removed and enacted into law as the Smith-Lever Act. The remaining provisions of the bill were set aside for additional study by a national commission—a measure designed to relieve a deadlock that had come about between two factions in Congress.

## Commission on National Aid to Vocational Education

On January 20, 1914, the Congress approved a joint resolution authorizing the President to appoint a commission to study national aid to vocational

---

[12] United States Senate, *Hearings Before the Committee on Agriculture and Forestry*, April 12, 13, 1910. Washington: Government Printing Office, 1911, p. 1.

[13] Carroll S. Page, *Vocational Education*, Senate Document No. 845. Washington: Government Printing Office, 1912, p. 4.

[14] *Ibid.*, p. 5.

education.[15] The resolution provided that the nine members of the Commission report to the Congress not later than June 1, 1914. The Commission was organized on April 2, 1914, with Senator Hoke Smith of Georgia as chairman. Other members were Senator Carroll S. Page of Vermont; Representative D. M. Hughes of Georgia; Representative S. D. Fess of Ohio; John A. Lapp, Director, Indiana Bureau of Legislative Information; Florence M. Marshall, Director, Manhattan Trade School, New York City; Agnes Nester, President, International Glove Workers' Union, Chicago; Charles A. Prosser, Secretary, National Society for the Promotion of Industrial Education, New York City; and Charles H. Winslow, Special Agent, Bureau of Labor Statistics, Washington, D.C.

The Commission prepared a questionnaire which was sent to representatives of various departments of the federal government, representatives of national organizations, and private individuals, who submitted replies both in person and by letter. In six months of investigation the Commission compiled two volumes of testimony. Each person to appear before the Commission was given ample opportunity to present his point of view or that of the organization he represented. He was asked to submit written answers to the questions the Commission had previously asked, and to present any other information which he wanted the Commission to consider. Presentations before the Commission bore all the earmarks of an interrogation. Both positive and negative statements were pursued relentlessly. [Captain Douglas MacArthur, later a renowned general of World War II, was among those who appeared in support of vocational education.]

The National Education Association presented a lengthy and strong endorsement of the bills for vocational education then before Congress. The point of view of organized labor had often been presented to the public in such a way that confusion existed concerning just where labor stood in connection with problems of public instruction. There was no doubt, however, in the testimony presented by Mr. Hamilton when he met with the Commission on the evening of April 23, 1914.

Mr. Chairman and members of the commission, the American Federation of Labor, which I represent here, is in favor of industrial education, with a very strong reservation, and that is that industrial education shall be conducted by the State and not by any private interests; in other words, we believe that the United States should cooperate with the States in establishing a system of industrial education, and which practically comprises trade training. We necessarily and naturally are more interested in the boy or the girl who wants to learn a trade, and we would like to have them educated along particular lines, not given a theoretical education without any practical [aspects]. As a matter of fact, the labor movement itself, as expressed by the American Federation of Labor, is thoroughly in harmony with education along every channel, where it is feasible. We are in favor of the agricultural colleges, and their extension work. We are in favor of universities, and, in fact, every system of education that gives to the various sections of our society an opportunity to become educated either along general or special lines, but more

---

[15] *Report of the Commission on National Aid to Vocational Education,* 2 vols. Washington: Government Printing Office, 1914, I, p. 9.

particularly we are interested in the rising generation to be given an opportunity; that is, that part who are expected or compelled to earn a livelihood by their own hands. But we desire that they shall be educated in a practical way.[16]

Mr. Cheney, who represented the NSPIE, presented an interesting and well prepared statement to the Commission. In a sense this was one of the "big days" for the Society because the Commission was dealing with the fundamental purpose for which it existed. Cheney was well equipped with the facts and figures essential to preparing legislation for vocational education. One portion of his lengthy statement, often overlooked, is most significant:

The society has existed from its start with consecutive earnestness for the promotion of a public support and for the creation of public interest in the training for useful occupations. It stands for a definite purpose, and what I want to say is not in any way in criticism or in hostility to the aims of a cultural, academic, and common-school system. I only have come, and I think the national society has come, to feel distinctly that the aim of training for useful occupation must from start to finish be absolutely differentiated for the present from that of a general and cultural training.[17]

The idea of separation was a key point in the development of industrial education, even though it drew much criticism. However, the Society wanted industrial education, during its early growth, to be unhampered by educational prejudice. Industrial education was viewed as "the missing link connecting training with life." Cheney and the Society believed that some phases of industrial training could in time be merged with other areas of education. The separation in the beginning did not "by any means mean that it must always be so."

Charles R. Richards, Director of Cooper Union, brought to the attention of the Presidential Commission one of the imperative elements in the Society's program—the need for facts and for thorough investigation of the problem. As previously pointed out, the Society did not support the Davis bills in 1907 simply because these bills had not been prepared with sufficient evidence of a real need and—what was even more important—data to support a plan of action based on that need.

There is a great and pressing need for an analysis of our industries as the first step in forwarding an intelligent program for the training of the workers. We need an intensive study of the work and of the requirements of the work of the wage earners in the specific occupations of each industry. Not until this has been done will it be possible for us to know, in any accurate or comprehensive way, either the kind of training which any group of workers should have or how it can best be given. As a Nation we are singularly lacking in this kind of information. In European countries much advantage has been gained in establishing schemes of industrial education, because our neighbors across the waters are already in possession of this knowledge. They have been studying their industries and gathering such data for over half a century, and furthermore, have been collecting it as a great national asset and service.[18]

It has been estimated that the direct and indirect testimony presented before the Presidental Commission represented the points of view of more than

---

[16] *Ibid.*, Vol. II, p. 181.
[17] *Ibid.*, Vol. II, p. 246.
[18] *Ibid.*, Vol. II, p. 259.

12,000,000 persons. The overwhelmingly favorable regard for vocational education must have pleased the leaders of the Society, for it reflected in part the effectiveness of their program of propaganda.

The final report of the Commission contained discussion on seven major issues: (1) the need for vocational education; (2) the need for national grants to the states for vocational education; (3) the kinds of vocational education for which national grants should be given; (4) aid to vocational education through federal agencies; (5) the extent to which the national government should aid vocational education; (6) the conditions under which grants for vocational education should be given; and (7) proposed legislation. The Commission found that public sentiment showed the need for vocational education; that an urgent social and educational need existed; and that national grants were necessary because the problem was too large to be worked out on a local basis; the states varied widely in their ability to carry the cost of vocational education. The Commission justified national grants on the basis of the interstate and national character of the problem. The solution of the problem was related to the general welfare of the nation.

The Commission recommended that grants be given for stimulating vocational education and for the training of teachers; for partial payment of the salaries of teachers, supervisors, and directors; and for the support of a federal board for making studies and investigations useful in vocational schools. The schools thus aided should be publicly supported and controlled

and should be of less than college grade. In consideration of the total findings and recommendations, a proposal for legislation, including a draft of a bill for vocational education, was made a part of the final report.

On June 1, 1914, the report of the Commission on National Aid to Vocational Education was referred to the Committee on Education of the House of Representatives and ordered to be printed. Thus a significant step had been taken. The aims of the Society seemed to be near realization, now that its reports and bill had reached the Congress. The Society's members felt that their propaganda had been effective in presenting an honest appraisal of vocational education, an appraisal which could become the backbone of legislative action.

The report of the Presidential Commission became a source book for future reference; it may well be considered a classic in the literature of vocational education.

### The Smith-Hughes Act in the Making

It was nearly a year and a half after the Commission on National Aid to Vocational Education reported to Congress, before some positive action resulted. Then, on December 7, 1915, Senator Hoke Smith of Georgia introduced Senate Bill 703, entitled:

*An Act to provide for the promotion of vocational education; to provide for cooperation with the States in the promotion of such education in agriculture and the trades and industries; to provide for cooperation with the States in the preparation of*

61

*teachers of vocational subjects; and to appropriate money and regulate its expenditure.*

The bill was read, referred to the Committee on Education and Labor, and printed in the *Congressional Record*. Thus began the odyssey of the Smith-Hughes bill.

On February 10, 1916, Representative Dudley M. Hughes of Georgia introduced House Bill 11250, which was read and referred to the House Committee on Education. Two days later the Hughes bill was reported back to the House without amendment, accompanied by House Report No. 181. In describing vocational education, the report reads as follows:

It is especially designed to prepare workers for the more common occupations in which the great mass of our people find useful employment. As here used it means that form of education whose controlling purpose is to give training of a secondary grade to persons over 14 years of age for increased efficiency in useful employment in the trades and industries, in agriculture, in commerce and commercial pursuits, and in callings based upon a knowledge of home economcs.[19]

The report compared vocational education in the United States and Germany as follows:

The American people have hardly begun the work of providing for the practical education of these millions of our wage workers. In this whole country there are fewer trade schools than are to be found in the little German kingdom of Bavaria, with a population not much greater than that of New York City. There are more workers being trained at public expense in the city of Munich alone than in all the larger cities of the United States, representing a population of more than 12,000,000. It is substantially true that practically every German citizen who could profit by it may receive vocational training for his life work in the schools and classes supported out of the public treasury.[20]

The report indicated that the three sources of manpower waste—the involuntarily idle, the imperfectly employed, and the improperly employed—must be eliminated before increased production could begin. The authors of the House report felt that the aspirations of most young people were denied in an educational world that prepared only the few for college. The drop-out rate in the early years of schooling was deplored. Not only did students leave without an adequate general education, but they also had no special training to fit them for work. It was stated that vocational courses would attract and hold students because they would be able to obtain suitable preparation for useful employment. The cultural values of vocational education were recognized and deemed to be a valuable addition to the total general education of students. Observations were made concerning previous national grants and the contributions of these grants to the development of the nation. Proposed allotments to the states were described, and an outline of a future bill was suggested.

Senate Bill 703 was reported out of committee accompanied by Senate Report No. 97, a little more than a page in length.

---

[19] U.S. House of Representatives, *Vocational Education*, House Report No. 181. Washington: Government Printing Office, 1916, p. 1.

[20] *Ibid.*, p. 2.

We commend to the consideration of the Senate the report of the Commission on National Aid to Vocational Education, which explains in detail the bill now reported, and gives reasons for its adoption. This report is so full that your committee deem it unnecessary again to go into details upon this subject.[21]

On April 20, 1916, Senator Smith called the attention of the members of the Senate to the bill and asked that they give it careful consideration. On July 19, 1916, two amendments to the vocational bill were authorized upon the request of Senator Smith. On July 22, 1916, Senator Smith asked the Senate to go into a "Committee of the Whole on the State of the Union," to consider the vocational bill. Senator Page addressed the Senate at length on the provisions of the bill and the virtues of vocational education.

In the House of Representatives on July 29, 1916, Representative Hughes discussed the provisions of the Act for vocational education and then, in a fashion similar to that of Senator Page, presented at great length the arguments in support of the bill. On the last day of July the Senate considered minor amendments to the vocational bill. Discussion was brief, a few objections were made and withdrawn, and in the end the Senate passed the bill. At this point Senator Smith made a comment that provides a view into the general attitudes of Congressmen concerning the bill.

The truth is, on this side [Democratic] my colleagues seem largely to have looked to me to work upon the bill, as I have been working on it for several years, and I know the Senators on the other side of the Chamber realize the splendid work that has been done with reference to this measure by the Senator from Vermont [Carroll S. Page]. . . . The responsibility for the measure would have continued with him rather than to have fallen to me but for the change that took place in the organization of the Senate three years ago. With the Republican majority he was leading in the work and I was helping him. Since that time, as I am Chairman of the Committee on Education and Labor, the situation is reversed just a little, but I am always glad to stop at any time the opportunity is presented to give to the Senator from Vermont every possible credit for his splendid work upon this subject, and almost to regret that we have a Democratic majority and that he has not charge of the bill instead of myself.[22]

During the months that remained in the session of Congress, the House calendar was congested with problems largely connected with the war in Europe, so that final consideration of the vocational education bill was not possible.

In his message to Congress on December 5, 1916, President Woodrow Wilson called attention to the vocational education bill and urged action, saying:

At the last session of the Congress a bill was passed by the Senate which provides for the promotion of vocational and industrial education which is of vital importance to the whole country, for the critical years of economic development immediately ahead of us in very large measure depend upon it. May I not urge its early and favorable consideration by the House of Representatives and its early enactment into law? It contains plans which affect all interests and all parts of the country and I am sure there is no

---

[21] U. S. Senate, *Vocational Education*, Senate Report No. 97. Washington: Government Printing Office, 1916, p. 2.

[22] *Congressional Record*, 64th Congress, 1st Session, Vol. LIII, p. 11874.

legislation now pending before the Congress whose passage the country awaits with more thoughtful approval or greater impatience to see a great and admirable thing set in the way of being done.[23]

Immediately thereafter the House took the bill under consideration again. In the days that followed there were long and frequent presentations by members of the House concerning the vocational education bill. Upon the conclusion of these presentations the Senate bill was read to the House. Mr. Hughes then moved that the House strike out the Senate bill and substitute the House bill. The motion was agreed to, and it was announced that this bill would be taken up on the second day of January.

On January 2, 1917, Representative Austin of Tennessee commented as follows:

Now, I want to commend the gentleman of Georgia [Mr. Hughes] in charge of this bill. This measure, I am sure, is not all he would like to have it. He has had to contend with the Senate committee, and we have all been here long enough to know that in proposed legislation, where there is conflict of opinion, we must concede and compromise; but I want to commend him for his hard, efficient, and zealous work, and at the same time I want to say that the State of Georgia never committed a greater mistake than in not returning him to Congress. Had his reelection been submitted to a vote of this House, in my opinion there would not have been a dissenting voice. He would have been the choice of every Democratic and every Republican Member. [APPLAUSE] While I have served in this House eight years, I would rather go out of it with my name as the author of a vocational education bill than anything else to my credit.[24]

On the final day of discussion in the House fellow members took advantage of the concluding minutes of the debates to pay tribute to Mr. Hughes.

While he will leave here on the 4th of March, he will never be forgotten by the boys and girls of this great country, for he will by this bill erect to himself a monument more imperishable and enduring than any monument of brass or of marble. By being instrumental in securing the passage of this bill and putting it upon the statute book as a law of the land, he will have a monument in the minds and in the hearts of the present generation and generations yet to come.[25]

The *Congressional Record* notes that these remarks were followed by GREAT APPLAUSE.[26] Mr. Hughes acknowledged the tributes of the members of the House and then moved that the bill be reported to the House, with the recommendation that the amendments be agreed to and the bill passed. After a third reading the bill was passed.

Arthur E. Holder, as legislative chairman for the American Federation of Labor, followed the bill's progress and commented on the final discussions:

During the debate in the House, members complimented and praised Mr. Hughes. On the final passage of the bill in the House, the members were so elated

---

[23] *Congressional Record*, 64th Congress, 2nd Session, Vol. LIV, pp. 32-33.

[24] *Ibid.*, p. 761.

[25] *Ibid.*, p. 1081.

[26] Nevertheless the State of Georgia did honor Dudley M. Hughes with a monument, in the form of the Dudley M. Hughes Vocational School, in Bibb County, dedicated on October 5, 1955. It would have been difficult to find anyone more in tune with the "vocational drive" of the early years of the twentieth century than Hughes was. He has been referred to as "a man with a vision" in vocational education.

that they arose en masse and vigorously applauded. Never at any time was any allusion made to political party credits in debate. We are proud of the fact that this great educational humanitarian measure passed Congress by almost unanimous vote without any partisan claims or antagonism.[27]

The differences that remained between the Senate and House bills were resolved, final legislative action was completed on February 17, and the bill was sent to the President. On February 23, 1917, President Wilson sent a message to the Senate announcing that he had on that day signed Senate Bill 703, the vocational education bill.

The National Society for the Promotion of Industrial Education was conducting its tenth annual convention at Indianapolis, February 21-24, 1917. News of the signing was sent to the convention by wire from Washington. The dramatic announcement of the event was received with equal drama. Charles W. Sylvester, longtime treasurer of the American Vocational Association, was able to recall that "pandemonium broke loose." The Society had achieved its first major goal.

## Summary

The National Society for the Promotion of Industrial Education became the focal point of all interests for the promotion and development of the vocational phase of industrial education. Labor, management, industry, government, business, education, and the public at large joined in support of the purposes of the Society. Committees of the Society probed many

areas of the total problem and were intent upon obtaining the facts and opinions of all concerned in relation to the drive for a nationwide program of industrial education. Though the Society wanted a federal bill that would provide funds for industrial education, it did not support the Davis Bill in 1907. This bill was introduced in good faith and in support of the Society's purposes, but the Society could not urge its passage because a thorough study of all related elements had not been made. A fear existed that haste would cause some important considerations to be overlooked.

The first bill to have serious consideration was the Dolliver-Davis Bill in 1910. Although it failed of enactment during that session of Congress, a revision was introduced by Senator Page in 1911. The bill made little progress, but Senator Page was authorized, as a subcommittee of one, to secure supplementary information. After a thorough investigation, revised versions of the bill were presented to Congress. Finally a compromise was reached, and in 1914 the agricultural extension provisions of the bill were enacted into law as the Smith-Lever Act. Simultaneously a national commission was appointed to study the need for other legislation.

It was the report of the Commission on National Aid to Vocational Education, 1914, that marked the beginning of the final steps toward passage of the bill. The evidence was overwhelmingly positive and the critical issues had received thorough review. But there were endless delays, and it was late in

[27] Arthur E. Holder, "Brief History and Progress of the Vocational Education Act," Reprinted from *The Machinists' Monthly Journal*, August 1919, p. 7.

1915 when Senator Smith introduced a bill. Early in 1916 Representative Hughes introduced a similar bill in the House. Agreement was reached upon the small differences, but a congested legislative calendar and the war in Europe pushed the bill into the background.

On December 5, 1916, President Woodrow Wilson urged action on the bill. The matter was taken up early in 1917 by both Houses of the Congress, and the Vocational Education Act of 1917 (the Smith-Hughes Act) was signed into law on February 23, 1917.

From every point of view Congress was pleased with its action. As evidence of unanimity Senator Smith, a Democrat, went out of his way to point out that Senator Page, a Republican, was the real force and authority behind the bill. Similarly in the House of Representatives, Hughes was praised by his colleagues for his efforts in securing the passage of the bill.

With the legislation a reality, the National Society for the Promotion of Industrial Education turned their attention toward building the professional structure required to sustain and enhance the new program of industrial education.

## Recall Questions

1. What was the central purpose of the National Society for the Promotion of Industrial Education?

2. What were some of the key arguments advanced in support of industrial education in the early meetings and publications of the national Society?

3. What bills were introduced in support of industrial education between 1907-1914?

4. Describe the odyssey of the Smith-Hughes bill from 1915-1917.

5. What was the basis for the feeling of Congress that something good had been achieved with the passage of the Smith-Hughes Act?

## Research Questions

1. Study the report of the Commission on National Aid to Vocational Education, and identify the issues that contributed to an attitude about vocational education. Summarize these issues in your own words in a paper, "The Case for Vocational Education."

2. Read the *Congressional Record* for the period December 7, 1915 to February 23, 1917. Analyze each major statement about vocational education, and identify the issues, pro and con.

## Suggestions for Further Reading

*Congressional Record*, 1907-1917.

National Society for the Promotion of Industrial Education, *Proceedings*, 1907-1917.

*Report of the Commission on National Aid to Vocational Education*, 2 vols. Washington: Government Printing Office, 1914.

# Chapter 4

# *Professional Associations*

Eastern Arts Association · Western Arts Association · The National Society for Vocational Education · Vocational Education Association of the Middle West · American Vocational Association · National Education Association · American Industrial Arts Association · Iota Lambda Sigma · Epsilon Pi Tau · The Ship · Local and State Organization Relationships · Summary · Recall Questions · Research Questions · Suggestions for Further Reading

The basic elements of the industrial education movement in America are reflected conspicuously in the activities of professional associations. Persons directly involved with industrial education needed strong professional association in order to reassure and question themselves continuously about the nature, motives, direction, and values of of their work.

Industrial educators, as individuals, always were dedicated to their educational task and seldom entertained any doubt concerning its importance in the general scheme of education. But an individual was limited in his ability to develop a system of values upon which industrial education could grow. Professional associations provided the environment in which the considered judgment of a group could be sharpened, thus helping to define for each person the larger values involved in his efforts. In this way, the process of professional association tended to create motivation among members: It satisfied a need. This explains, at least in part, why the associations were largely successful in their activities.

Certain clearly defined attitudes of the public about education in general aided the cause of the industrial education movement. The nation in the twentieth century felt its educational obligation deeply. By 1919, all of the states had provided for compulsory education. The industrial economic base of the nation was growing rapidly. The social need of industrial intelligence had been recognized, and education leading directly to employment was considered a justifiable goal.

These fundamental ideas encouraged the organization of professional associations in industrial education; in fact, local, district, regional, and state groups of teachers organized throughout the nation. The spheres of interest and influence of several of these groups came to encompass the entire nation. The earlier history of these groups is cited by Bennett.[1] By 1918, six professional associations in industrial education had become of national significance. These were: (1) Eastern Arts Association; (2) Western Arts Association; (3) National Society for Vocational Education; (4) Vocational Education Association of the Middle West; (5) the Manual Arts Conference; and (6) the Department of Vocational Training and Practical Arts of the National Education Association. Five of these organizations will be discussed in this chapter. Because of the special conditions surrounding the Manual Arts Conference, its achievements and contributions will be treated in a separate chapter.

These six associations were joined in 1926 by the American Vocational Association. In addition, other groups developed whose work as professional associations cannot be overlooked—namely, the American Industrial Arts Association, Epsilon Pi Tau, and Iota Lambda Sigma.

These professional associations, subject to the forces of expanding educational vitality in America, each in his own way, became interpreters of the social force and functioned as centers of action in the growth of industrial education.

## Eastern Arts Association

It is not difficult to find evidence of this organization's industrial interests. The eighth annual convention was in session on April 6, 1917, when Congress passed the declaration of war. Ordinary activities during the Philadelphia convention were obscured somewhat by a number of "war speeches" considering what the association could do in the national crisis. Nevertheless, the association was concerned primarily with professional topics: discipline and the use of industry as an interest vehicle for art, language, mathematics, and dramatics. Consideration was also given to the necessity for art appreciation and to the status of the United States in developing its own industrial point of view.

The spring meeting of the Association in New Haven in 1918 also had about it an air of war emergency, but delegates were urged to focus their attention upon "retaining the continuity of instruction" despite the war. The convention program was representative of the usual extremes and varieties of the interests of the delegates. They considered the aims of teaching art, the conservation of the individual in art, the pupil's capacity for artistic expression, and a number of rather specific elements of the manual training program. A strong spirit of Americanism was much in evidence at the convention, and hope was voiced that this spirit might at some time be expressed in art.

---

[1] Charles A. Bennett, *History of Manual and Industrial Education 1870-1917*. Peoria, Illinois: The Manual Arts Press, 1937, pp. 492-505.

Mrs. Honore Willsie, editor of the magazine *Delineator,* pointed out that, "The artist who first pictures on canvas the story of American freedom will make a valuable contribution to the American cause at this time."[2]

During the earlier years of the Eastern Arts Association the members' interests had been, in the main, common; there was little necessity for subdivisions or sections of the Association. But by 1922 the organization had become much larger, and its annual conference included separate meetings for such sections as art, industrial arts, elementary industrial arts, household arts, part-time education, and vocational education. At this stage of development Bennett observed that "the Association is made up of groups that are not much acquainted with each other, and seem to have very little in common except the spirit of educational progress and loyalty to the organization."[3] The diversity of interests was a product of expansion in the size of the organization, and the officers were aware that steps needed to be taken to break strong lines of separation and to recapture solidarity and mutual acquaintance. One of the elements of common interest appeared to be the program of the junior high school, in which a majority of the members found identifiable responsibilities.

The records of the meetings of the Eastern Arts Association indicate that members were interested in making a sustained effort to vitalize education.

Ways of improving the quality of instruction and of improving the efficiency of their work, in all areas of interest, were persistent themes of convention programs. School exhibits of art in industry and visits to schools in the convention city were usual features of the convention program. "A member's exhibit, consisting of individual paintings and designs, attracted considerable attention and proved that many of our teachers can *do* as well as teach."[4] Later conventions grew to be many-sided in character. Strengthening the work in drawing, color, design, and composition was a constant goal. A small sampling of other topics for consideration and discussion included art anatomy, threshold pottery, vocational education, vocational guidance, part-time schools, and manual arts. The importance of standards in craftsmanship was everywhere apparent; members of the Association seemed almost to be carrying a banner saying, "There Must Be Pride in Craftsmanship."

The Association was frequently concerned with the "deplorable situation" of indifference to the arts and to the belief that anyone who works with his hands belongs to an inferior class. At the Philadelphia convention in 1927, the famous sculptor, Lorado Taft, included in his message to the group:

One of our leading educators tells us . . . that the tacit implication in most schools is: "Now, Johnny, study hard so that you will not have to work when you

[2] George M. Morris, "The New Haven Convention of the Eastern Arts Association," *Manual Training Magazine,* Vol. XIX, No. 10, June 1918, p. 362.
[3] Charles A. Bennett, "The Eastern Arts Convention," *Manual Training Magazine,* Vol. XXIII, No. 11, May 1922, p. 386.
[4] "The Eastern Arts Association Convention," *Industrial Education Magazine,* Vol. XXVI, No. 12, June 1925, p. X.

grow up." This attitude is unfortunate in more ways than one. It tends to separate us into classes. When the ambition of half of our people is to avoid work with the hands—when they despise those who have to work—it is indeed a dangerous time for democracy.[5]

The blue collar-white collar concept of the social structure of work was ever-present in professional discussions. It seems a matter of fact that our past ideals have tended to favor class distinction. It is even more a matter of fact that unskilled labor had been tried in America and had failed. The new opportunity for America was to produce skilled workers. At the Hartford convention in 1928, Ernest W. Butterfield, State Commissioner of Education in New Hampshire, discussed "Three Vocational Objectives": (1) skilled production, (2) courteous commerce, (3) gracious living. He laid part of the blame for the failure to attain these objectives on teachers in general and their attitudes concerning work, saying: "Academic teachers still believe in predestination, not for heaven, but for Harvard." [6]

The theme for the 1929 convention in New York City centered around the title "Improvement in Teaching the Arts." One of the highlights of the convention was a speech by William H. Kilpatrick of Teachers College, Columbia University, entitled "Some Basic Considerations Affecting Success in Teaching." Kilpatrick clearly did not believe that a child's ability would necessarily find a way to assert itself. He felt that a child with special ability needed encouragement and stimulation in order to become effective. "Talent," he said, "manifests itself in the line of greatest cultivation." And, concerning the degree of talent, he said, "There is much more in any child than we can get out." [7]

With respect to its professional goals, industrial education was always somewhat out of place as a part of the Eastern Arts Association. Industrial education leaders were consistent in efforts to emphasize the art value of industry, and the actual program in the public schools did bear evidence of this emphasis, but professional attachment to the Eastern Arts Association was in many ways artificial.

## Western Arts Association

The group which later became the Western Arts Association was formed in 1893 as the Western Drawing Teachers Association. In 1904 the name Western Drawing and Manual Training Association was adopted. The purpose of the Association as shown in its constitution was as follows: "Its object shall be the promotion of Art Education and Manual Training in schools and particularly in the public schools." [8] At the Chicago convention in 1919, the name was changed to the Western Arts

[5] "The Eastern Arts Association Convention," *Industrial Education Magazine*, Vol. XXVIII, No. 12, June 1927, p. 16A.

[6] Charles A. Bennett, "The Eastern Arts Convention at Hartford," *Industrial Education Magazine*, Vol. XXIX, No. 12, June 1928, p. 4A.

[7] "Eastern Arts Convention," *Industrial Education Magazine*, Vol. XXX, No. 11, May 1929, p. 36A.

[8] Western Drawing and Manual Training Association, *Twelfth Annual Meeting Report*, April 25-28, 1905, p. 3.

Association. At the same time the Association altered its purpose somewhat with the following statement: "Its object shall be the advancement of the teaching of art, manual training, household arts, and allied subjects in schools and particularly in the public schools."[9] The new name was a compromise which was intended to include a wide variety of arts. The art that went into the making of a chair or a piece of textile was thought to be as "fine" as the art included under the general term of "fine arts." The need for art in education and in industry was thought to be great. Discussions of the need of art in the day-to-day lives of the American people absorbed the attention of the Association in many of its programs. The close attachment of the Association to the Chicago Art Institute influenced its convention programs in many ways, but not to the exclusion of basic problems of manual training.

The 1920 convention in Detroit was the first under the Association's new name. The name, with its emphasis on art, was suggestive of the changing times. President Harry A. Wood suggested that the Association might well concentrate its efforts on making a more artistic America, with particular reference to the common things of everyday life. Discussion topics such as "color and design as applied to manual training," "industrial design," and "a more artistic America," established the keynote for themes in future years.

It was noted at the 1921 convention in Peoria that the attendance of manual training and industrial teachers was small compared with earlier conventions; other conventions during 1921 seemed to attract more industrial education teachers. Therefore making art education practical was a key feature of the 1922 convention. Practical emphasis upon art and design was thought to be a public necessity brought on by quantity production. The nation still imported many of its designers from Europe. The ratio of schools of industrial art in Germany to those in the entire United States was approximately three to one.

Enthusiasm of the 1922 convention for increased emphasis upon art resurrected the discussion of relative subject matter values. Frank Leavitt, Associate Superintendent of Schools, Pittsburgh, held the opinion that, "Whether a course is vocational or cultural depends wholly upon the use the students will make of the things they learn."[10] During the final meeting of the 1922 convention the following resolution was adopted unanimously:

WHEREAS, the development of art in its relation to industry is a matter of National importance,

*Be it resolved* that this Association expresses its commendation of the attitude of the United States Bureau of Education toward the movement for the promotion of art in industry and for its publication of the pamphlet *Industrial Art as a National Asset*, and that this Association fervently hopes that the Bureau may be provided with funds which will enable it to occupy its proper position of leadership in this movement for art education which is essential to the best future development of American industry.[11]

---

[9] Western Arts Association, *Annual Report 1919*, p. 237.
[10] Emanuel E. Ericson, "The Western Arts Association," *Manual Training Magazine*, Vol. XXIII, No. 12, June 1922, p. 424.
[11] *Ibid.*, p. 425.

One of the main features of Western Arts Association conventions was the round table discussion. A member of the Association was assigned the responsibility of organizing and conducting the discussion. Members of the round table could freely share their views in these off-the-record exchanges, and frequently the consensus in certain areas of interest would result in plans for positive action. As an example, in the Dayton convention in 1924, the round table adopted a resolution calling for the establishment of a national Commission on Art Education.

It was apparent that a clearer differentiation was needed among kinds of instruction to be given in the various schools. Also the problems of credit granted for entrance in high schools and colleges needed study, as did the larger problem of preparing art teachers. It was proposed that the national commission comprise three representatives of each of the following organizations: Western Arts Association, Eastern Arts Association, American Federation of Arts, College Art Association, and the American Institute of Architects.

Efforts to establish a successful union of art and manual training through the Western and Eastern Arts Associations, and efforts to capture the professional interests of both art and manual training educators, diminished materially with the beginning of the 1930's. Nevertheless, art left its mark upon the industrial education movement.

In 1947 the Western Arts Association and the Eastern Arts Association joined two other regional groups to form the National Art Education Association, a department of the National Education Association. This development severed completely the professional relationship of art and manual arts. But by 1947 the concept of manual art was a dead issue and had long since been replaced by industrial art.

It is important to point out again that although attempts at professional association of art and industrial arts failed, still the art motif in industrial arts surged forward with continuous vigor.

## The National Society for Vocational Education

The Smith-Hughes Act had been passed by both houses of Congress by the time the National Society for the Promotion of Industrial Education held its annual convention in Indianapolis, February 21-24, 1917. The meeting was an anniversary celebration, marking a decade of work.

The banquet on Thursday evening, February 23, was the occasion of two special treats. First, a long letter from Senator Carroll S. Page was read to the members. The Page Bill had not passed the Congress, but it had created a legislative climate favorable to passage of the Smith-Hughes Act. The failure of his bill did not dim the Senator's enthusiasm for vocational education. He said in his letter:

Accept my heartiest congratulations on the passage of the great measure for which your organization has struggled so long and faithfully—the measure providing for federal aid for vocational education. . . . I am sure, that, measured by its immense importance to the boys and girls of this country, it is incomparably the most important piece of constructive legislation passed by Congress in this generation. . . . Permit me, in so far as I properly may, to wish your organization God speed, and to express to its membership the country's deep appreciation of the most valuable aid which has extended through the trying period during which we have worked together to bring about the passage of this most important legislation.[12]

The devotion of Senator Page to the cause of vocational education was almost without parallel. Throughout the long years he worked toward the passage of a vocational education bill, his open mind and enthusiasm, combined with almost unlimited effort, made a deep impression upon the educators working with him.

The second treat was the reading of the telegram announcing that President Wilson had on that day signed the Smith-Hughes Bill. The goal toward which the Society had directed its efforts had been realized, and the major problem in the "promotion" of industrial education was solved. During the next year preparation was made to change the name of the Society to the National Society for Vocational Education, a change approved during the Philadelphia convention in February, 1918. David Snedden, of Columbia University, was elected the first president of the National Society.

Senator Page had pointed out that the Society had a responsibility to aid in directing the realization of the great potential created by the legislation. "Your work, however, is not completed," he said, and in truth it had just begun.

Much of the convention activity in the years that followed was directed toward problems of program organization, teacher training, administration, and similar problems confronting vocational education under the new Smith-Hughes Act. The industrial education section of the Philadelphia convention in 1918 was devoted almost entirely to teacher training. Industrial education from the point of view of the manufacturer, the worker, and the educator, with emphasis upon such specific points as "vestibule" training or "foreman" training, was among the numerous topics of discussion which occupied the attention of the industrial educator.

However, these educators were not totally absorbed with the mechanical phases of their organization or with perfecting its operational details. They were much in touch with economic, labor, and social problems. Charles A. Prosser, addressing the convention in Detroit in 1922, summarized the situation as follows:

In every stage of social development, society has set up a more or less definite concept of what constituted a desirable citizen. Sometimes this idea of citizenship has been that of the entire social organization and sometimes different groups within the organization have held distinct notions as to what would be desirable in the membership of the group. In some way, good, bad, or indifferent, the youth as a social recruit was more or less equipped to take his place in the social body. As the types of social organizations changed, social standards changed with them and brought corresponding changes in the ideals of different ages regarding the elements or factors in good citizenship —in other words changes in the specifications or requirements of the social job.[13]

[12] "The Indianapolis Convention," *Manual Training Magazine*, Vol. XVIII, No. 8, April 1917, p. 348.

[13] Charles A. Prosser, "Apprenticeship for Life—An Old Idea," *National Society for Vocational Education, Bulletin No. 34*, November 1, 1923, p. 1.

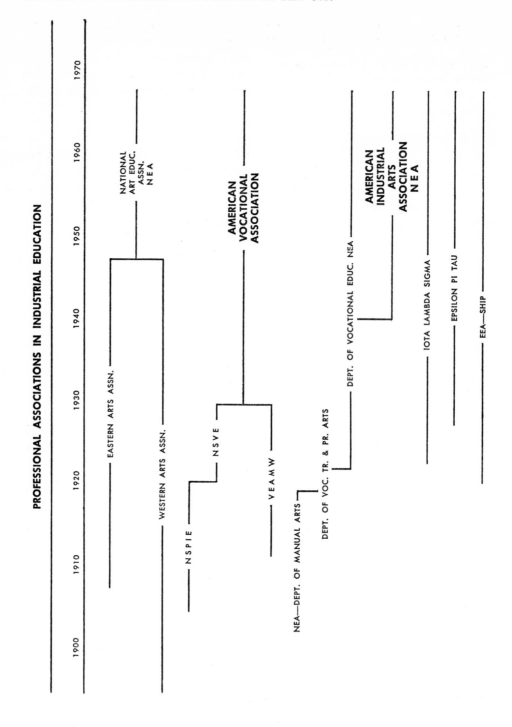

PROFESSIONAL ASSOCIATIONS IN INDUSTRIAL EDUCATION

Industrial education was reaching toward broader and more inclusive goals. "To earn a living as well as to live—to become an economic unit of society" was one of the three objectives commonly quoted at the annual conventions. The other two objectives characteristic of industrial education were: "To be good citizens; to become effective units of society," and "to approach the fine things of life—to become in a measure, a more cultured unit of society." [14]

In September, 1922, the first issue of the *Vocational Education Magazine* was published by the Society. A professional journal, as a means of intercommunication among all those interested in vocational education, had been considered "an urgent necessity." David Snedden, editor-in-chief of the magazine, made it clear that the new publication was not intended to compete with the "excellent journals . . . now devoted to manual and industrial arts" but was created because the exigencies of public support of vocational education demanded an appropriate magazine. The magazine was discontinued with the January, 1925, issue because of financial problems; its function is performed today by the *American Vocational Journal*.

## Vocational Education Association of the Middle West

Until 1914 the center of activity of professional associations in industrial education was on the Atlantic seaboard. However, industrial education problems unique to the Mississippi Valley created a desire for meetings of vocational educators who were interested in resolving these issues. Informal meetings began late in 1913, and the association was formalized on January 16, 1914, at the Chicago City Club, with the organization of the Vocational Education Association of the Middle West. William J. Bogan, Principal of Lane Technical High School, was elected first president. The depth and breadth of the Association's interests can readily be seen from its stated purpose:

[The objects of the Association] shall be to study problems relating to Vocational Education and to bring the results of this study to public attention for the purpose of fostering types of education that will meet the vocational needs of youth and the reasonable demands of industry for efficient workers, while preserving those elements of general education essential to efficient citizenship in democracy.[15]

The Association's first annual meeting, in Chicago, February 5-6, 1915, was attended by one thousand persons. The two days were highlighted by spirited discussions of the control of vocational education. In the years that followed, the Association became a center of influence in the Mississippi Valley. Its annual meetings acted as a sounding board for controversial issues which were vital to vocational education in general and especially to the progress of industrial education. Using a mailing list supplied by the *Manual Training Magazine*, letters were written to a large number of persons known

---

[14] Robert O. Small, "What Is the Job or the Function of the Part-Time Schools?" *National Society for Vocational Education, Bulletin No. 34*, November 1, 1923, pp. 8-9.

[15] "A New Association," *Industrial Arts Magazine*, Vol. I, March 1914, p. 113.

to have interests in vocational education, to challenge them to local action and to participation in the activities of the Association. It was pointed out that as educational leaders they needed to know all of the arguments for and against "our own theory of vocational education." This association, like the others, was deeply motivated to produce an educational system directly in tune with the social and economic needs of the people.

The following quotations, gleaned from the January, 1917, meeting, indicate the Association members' perceptiveness.[16]

We do not speak of "blind alley jobs" any more; we call them juvenile occupations, paid for as such.—David Snedden

Organized labor believes that the activities of the public school room should be enlarged to the maximum.—Matthew Woll

The business of the school is to stand between the union and the employer for the best in the child and the work.—C. A. Prosser

At five a child is wrenched from God's education and placed in a dusty red school house as dry as hay.—Herbert Quick

Prior to the passage of the Smith-Hughes Act, the Association was concerned with ways of increasing state aid for vocational education. Views from various states were freely exchanged. Vocational guidance in one form or another was included in all of the early meetings of the Association. As World War I approached, members discussed the necessity of providing effort on a war basis. Opinions were sought from men of national prominence. John Dewey talked on the subject of "Vocational Education in the Light of the World War" at the convention in February, 1918. After the war, a series of topic related to the war and vocational education were included on convention programs. For example, David Snedden discussed the "Lessons of the War for Vocational Education" at the meeting in March, 1919.

After the passage of the Smith-Hughes Act, the Association directed attention to such problems as class operation and teacher training, with a view toward working in accord with the new law. The convention programs of the Association allowed members to share one another's practices and to learn how the various states were handling particular aspects of vocational education. Field trips during the conventions permitted visting educators to see other schools in action. The relationship of vocational education to general education was prominent in the list of convention topics. Striving for greater efficiency in instruction was seldom omitted from a program. Convention highlights were nearly always centered around the annual banquet, which attracted outstanding speakers.

The convention in Detroit in November, 1922, was held in cooperation with three other national associations: the National Society for Vocational Education, the National Vocational Guidance Association, and the American Home Economics Association. The program seems to have included a great array of talent from every part of the United States. Convention programs encouraged dynamic professional ac-

---

[16] "Gleaned from the Chicago Meeting," *Manual Training Magazine,* Vol. XVIII, No. 7, March 1917, p. 297.

tivity among the members, and new horizons of professional interest appeared to develop concurrently.

## American Vocational Association

By 1920 the major professional associations were in competition with each other to capture the interest and enthusiasm of industrial educators. Three of the groups were basically regional in their interests, one was actually national, and another, the National Society for Vocational Education, while pursuing stated national objectives, was in reality strongly regional. From time to time casual interest had been expressed concerning the appropriateness of organizing one strong and truly national society. One of the first significant moves in this direction was a joint meeting of the National Society for Vocational Education and the Vocational Education Association of the Middle West.

The joint convention was held in Chicago, February 19-21, 1920. It was described as the largest and most representative convention ever held in America in the interests of vocational education.[17] Delegations were sent from every state in the nation. A year of planning for the joint meeting produced a balanced program to satisfy the interests of every delegate. The spirit of hearty cooperation between the two associations was apparent throughout the convention, although at its close each group held its own business meeting and elected its own officers for the coming year.

The joint meeting in Chicago made a deep impression upon both groups. The value of the combined talents of a larger group to the cause of vocational education was self-evident. Independent meetings of both associations had produced an element of serious competition, and unless remedied, could continue to do so. This was quite noticeable in the 1922 conventions, which were scheduled only a week apart. The competition was not intended, but it was nevertheless real; interested observers called attention to the problem by directly suggesting that the National Society be strengthened and its regional activities expanded.[18] The most urgent and immediate problem, of course, was to determine a plan for a national organization. In January, 1923, Bennett reported what appeared to him to be the consensus.[19] In brief, the desired organization would be a union, or federation, of the National Society for Vocational Education, the Vocational Education Association of the Middle West, the American Home Economics Association, and the National Vocational Guidance Association. The federation in turn would then become a department of the National Education Association, but would retain a separate management and identity.

NEA President William B. Owen supported this proposal enthusiastically and appealed to vocational teachers

[17] "The Chicago Convention," *Manual Training Magazine,* Vol. XXI, No. 8, April 1920, p. 278.

[18] "A National Scheme of Organization for Vocational Teachers and Supervisors," *Manual Training Magazine,* Vol. XXIII, No. 10, April 1922, pp. 356-357.

[19] Charles A. Bennett, "Shall We Have an Adequate National Organization of Vocational Teachers," *Industrial Education Magazine,* Vol. XXIV, No. 7, January 1923, pp. 191-192.

with the practicality of the arrangement. Finally, he admonished them: "You can't live perpetually alone; you can't solve the vocational education problem alone. Our cards are on the table. We need your help and we offer you ours." [20]

In the February and March, 1923, issues of the *Industrial Education Magazine,* Bennett outlined a plan of organization which seemed to meet and solve all difficulties. An adequate organization would need to (1) be national in scope, (2) provide for a large group of teachers with similar interests [Bennett identified the total group as teachers of industrial arts, agriculture, home economics, art, commerce, and vocational guidance], (3) provide a means of solving the differences in policy and finding common ground for action.

Edwin A. Lee, former president of the Vocational Education Association of the Middle West, proposed an organization which included a national council and supporting regional groups.[21] According to Lee's plan the national council would (1) formulate national policies relative to vocational education in its national significance, (2) establish working relationships with other organizations national in character, (3) edit and manage the publication of a national magazine, (4) coordinate activities of the regional organizations, and (5) maintain a research staff for making studies and gathering information of importance to vocational education.

In Lee's plan the function of the national council was to be primarily administrative; the regional organizations were to be inspirational. The regional organizations would (1) organize and hold at least one meeting each year, (2) cooperate with the national council in carrying out policies, (3) cooperate with local organizations and subdivisions of other national organizations, and (4) carry on research studies of local significance.

Representatives of the American Home Economics Association, the National Society for Vocational Education, the National Vocational Guidance Association, and the Vocational Education Association of the Middle West met in Chicago on February 26, 1924, to discuss amalgamation proposals. The vested interests of the groups appeared to be nearly irreconcilable. However, before adjournment a Council for Vocational Education was formed and given five purposes (1) to furnish a means whereby the various societies engaged in vocational education and allied activities might cooperate with each other, (2) to provide a clearing house for exchange of ideas and the development of the activities of these organizations, (3) to furnish an opportunity to present a united front in furtherance of aims, (4) to furnish a means of closer association with NEA, and (5) to study the possibility of a still closer affiliation among these associations.

The Council met for the first time in December, 1924. Some progress was made in the direction of its purposes but no definite decisions were reached

---

20 *Ibid.,* p. 191.
21 Edwin A. Lee, "The Future of Vocational Education Associations in the United States," *Industrial Education Magazine,* Vol. XXIV, No. 10, April 1923, pp. 301-302.

at this meeting or at the second meeting in February, 1925. Interests were too varied to find a common ground. However, it was quite apparent that the Middle West Association and the National Society for Vocational Education did not differ significantly in their aims. Therefore discussion and planning between these two groups continued.

For almost a year the possibility of a strong national organization had occupied the attention of leaders in industrial education. Bennett and his editorial staff brought prominently to the attention of the readers of the *Industrial Education Magazine* the progress and issues involved in the proposed organization. In the spring of 1925 the Vocational Education Association of the Middle West passed the following resolution:

*Whereas:* The Vocational Education Association of the Middle West, during the past few years, has sought to reach an agreement with the National Society for Vocational Education in order to prevent the undesirable duplication of annual conventions in the territory of the Mid-West association, and

*Whereas,* the National Society for Vocational Education has recently provided for a reorganization of that Society, dividing its territory into four regional groups of states corresponding to the grouping adopted by the Federal Board for Vocational Education and providing for a regional association in each, and

*Whereas,* it has been proposed that the Vocational Education Association of the Middle West become the regional association for the National Society for Vocational Education for the Central divisions of states, therefore be it

*Resolved* that the Vocational Education Association of the Middle West hereby instruct its Executive Committee to continue their negotiations with the National Society for Vocational Education.[22]

The National Society for Vocational Education was anxious to continue its name without important change because it had a long history of work and influence on a national basis. On the other hand the Vocational Education Association of the Middle West had developed a strong organization which had supplied a real need, and it was believed that the same type of organization could be developed in the other territories of the United States. There was strong sentiment in favor of a large national organization, within which regional organizations could both meet in common and still be free to attend to their own problems as they saw fit.

Representatives of the two Associations continued their discussions, which were to lead to a new kind of professional organization, retaining the strengths and eliminating weaknesses of the earlier groups. Finally, the joint committee of the two Associations, after several protracted meetings, produced a new constitution and suggested a list of officers, which was approved by the executive committee of each organization.

The National Society for Vocational Education met in Cleveland, December 3-5, 1925, for its nineteenth annual convention. The name of the Society was changed to the American Vocational Association, the new constitution was

---

[22] "The Greater National Society," *Industrial Education Magazine,* Vol. XXVI, No. 10, April 1925, p. 283.

adopted, and the proposed amalgamation with the Vocational Education Association of the Middle West was endorsed. As president of the newly formed American Vocational Association, the Cleveland convention elected Edwin A. Lee, Director of the Division of Vocational Education, University of California, whose plan had stimulated the new union. Lee's vigorous acceptance of the responsibility "inspired confidence among those who did not know him before. They know now that they have a vital force at the head of the new organization; and those who have known him longer can vouch for the fact that he is an efficient administrative officer." [23]

The spirit and morale of the convention delegates seemed suddenly to be lifted by their act of amalgamation. L. H. Dennis—who was to become executive secretary—wrote, "We find ourselves in a situation where the leaders in vocational education have a finer faith in each other and a greater belief in the great work in which we are all endeavoring to do our part." [24] Lewis Gustafson was also impressed by the visible evidence of enthusiasm, cordiality, unanimity, and general harmony among the large number of persons in attendance.

The final step in the amalgamation awaited only the action of the Vocational Association of the Middle West. This action was taken unanimously at the Des Moines Convention, March 17-20, 1926. No regret was expressed concerning the demise of the old organization; only the hope and promise of the future occupied the attention and thoughts of the delegates. Charles A. Prosser addressed the convention on the topic "The Magic Chance of Vocational Education."

If you want the magic chance get in on the new movement. That's the chance in manual training; that's the chance in vocational education; that's the chance in art. Manual training, vocational education and art education have made more progress than any other departments of education. [25]

Leaders of industrial education in the United States hailed the new American Vocational Association as a mark of progress, and saw its inception as the start of a new era in vocational education. AVA had inherited from the parent associations a rich background of experience upon which to build for the future and with which to meet the imperative problems of the field. Lee initiated a vigorous campaign of publicity and charged AVA members with obligations to form strong state associations and to secure representation in large numbers at the annual convention. The first convention of the American Vocational Association was held in Louisville, December 2-4, 1926. [26]

Since its formation in 1926 the American Vocational Association has planned and conducted its activities with

[23] "The A.V.A.," *Industrial Education Magazine,* Vol. XXVII, No. 7, January 1926, p. 208.

[24] L. H. Dennis, "The Cleveland Convention," *News Bulletin—American Vocational Association,* Vol. I, No. 1, February 1926, p. 4.

[25] Charles A. Bennett, "The Merger Wins Unanimously at Des Moines," *Industrial Education Magazine,* Vol. XXVII, No. 11, May 1926, p. 353.

[26] For a comprehensive study of the AVA see Carl R. Bartel, *Origin, Development and Work of the American Vocational Association.* (Unpublished Doctoral Dissertation, Graduate School of the University of Missouri, 1959), 517 numbered pages.

the view of providing maximum service to vocational and practical arts education. In addition to its official publication, the *American Vocational Journal*, the AVA maintains cooperative relationships with other educational organizations, thus on the one hand extending its influence and program and on the other hand providing members an opportunity to keep informed on educational matters of a wide variety. Perhaps its major contribution is its active interest in legislative matters which in one way or another have a bearing upon vocational education. Bartel and others have held the opinion that the AVA has been the organizing and driving force behind most of the vocational education measures that have come before Congress. There is strong evidence that Congressional leaders have had confidence in and respect for the AVA throughout its history.

The American Vocational Association holds an annual convention, usually in December. The convention city is selected on a rotating basis so that the meeting is held in various parts of the nation. The membership of the AVA exceeds 36,000 (1965); convention attendance of two to four thousand people places some limitations upon selection of convention cities.

The AVA maintains an office in Washington, D.C. Its work is conducted by an executive director, an assistant executive director, and a staff of professional and clerical assistants. Operating policies are derived from a board of directors (elected officers of the Association) and from resolutions of the House of Delegates. Each state is entitled to send official delegates to the annual convention from its state association. The number sent is based upon the state's percentage of national membership. Official business of the delegates is consummated in the meeting of the House of Delegates at the annual convention.

The fiftieth annual convention—counting from the first meeting of the NSPIE—was held in St. Louis, December 3-7, 1956. The occasion was marked by the publication of a special issue of the *American Vocational Journal*, "Fifty Years of Progress in Vocational and Practical Arts Education." This issue is a rich source of information about the historical background in these fields of education.

## National Education Association

The National Education Association organized a Department of Industrial Education in 1875. For a few years the Department was largely concerned with industrial education as it was related to the engineering schools. Then, with the founding of the St. Louis Manual Training School in 1880 and the subsequent growth of manual training throughout the United States, meetings of the Department began to deal with various facets of manual training. So strong was this interest in manual training that in 1890 the name of the Department was changed to the Department of Industrial and Manual Training.

The subject of manual training and technical schools was the fourth most popular topic at NEA meetings during the period 1858-1890 [according to an analysis made by William T. Harris in 1891]. Forty-five papers had been presented on the topic.

The great frequency of manual training as a topic is explained by its appeal to those who advocated a practical education and the subject enlisted some ardent proponents, even though Harris, Marble, and other critics denied its disciplinary value.[27]

The impact of manual training became so strong during the closing years of the nineteenth century that in 1899 the name of the NEA Department was changed again, to the Department of Manual Training. It is interesting to note how general sentiment influenced the NEA Department: its name was changed in 1899 to reflect manual training only, because the large majority of persons who attended the annual meetings of the Department were leaders in manual training.

It has been shown in Chapter Two that attention to vocational education, trade schools, and the push for Congressional aid for vocational education was of rising interest during the early years of the twentieth century; naturally these changes were reflected in the organization of the NEA Department. In 1914 the name was changed to the Department of Vocational Training and Practical Arts. Then in 1919, when federal aid had heightened interest in vocational education, the name was duly changed to the Department of Vocational Education.

Many educators have felt that the national professional association for vocational education should be a department of the NEA. This point of view was held by Bennett and others when discussions were taking place to organize the American Vocational Association.

The Milwaukee convention of NEA in 1919 devoted a great deal of time to resolutions designed to secure appropriate changes in education. Among these resolutions was one with the title, "A National Policy of Vocational Education." The policy reads as follows:

A high standard of intelligence, general vocational efficiency, physical and moral fitness and civic devotion are not only dependent upon an efficient system of public education of all our youth, but also upon the reaction upon human values of the occupations in which the people of the nation engage. If we are to be a homogeneous people generally, happy and prosperous, generally living full, rich, contributive lives, the work which we must do must continue through our lives, the development begun in the earlier years, devoted to specific and formal schooling. To this end industry in this country must be reorganized. All industry must become educational to those who engage in it. The workers must find in their work an opportunity for self-expression and self-development. Human—not commercial—value must be placed first in our great industrial establishments. The rank and file of those who produce the wealth must, through their organization, share in the control of the policy of the institutions for whom they work. They must find an educative realization of their life's purposes in the output of their daily toil and in the sharing in the direction of the policy guiding its production.

Vocational education must have as its purpose educational industry. Inasmuch as the general policy of Vocational Education in this country is directed by those responsible for the administration of the Smith-Hughes Law, we urge those thus responsible to adopt such a policy in interpreting and administering this law that the above named ends may be furthered by the system of vocational education now developing under this law; namely [that

---

[27] Edgar B. Wesley, *NEA, The First Hundred Years.* New York: Harper & Brothers, 1957, p. 49.

students] in the schools and departments organized under the Smith-Hughes Law shall be made competent as far as humanly possible for sharing in the control of the policy of the institutions in which they may afterward be employed and that they shall be inspired, so far as is humanly possible, with an impulse to continue their education through the instrumentality of the occupation for which they may be trained, and in which they may be afterward engaged.[28]

The NEA committee sponsoring the resolution did not contain anyone of prominence in the field of vocational education, and, furthermore, the committee was known to have been somewhat lukewarm to the field. At any rate the policy resolutions were drafted without the knowledge of the NEA Department of Vocational Education, which was also engaged, at the same time, in drafting resolutions on vocational education.

The NEA "policy" touched off a vitriolic blast from vocational educators, who maintained that the resolution was ill-advised, incorrect, inconsistent, and most certainly astonishing.[29] Other vocational education sympathizers could see a glimmer of truth in the policy resolution, and they advanced a more tempered, philosophical view of the situation. Clarence E. Howell, Supervisor of Industrial Arts, Lincoln, Nebraska, thought it strange that no vocational educator was included on the committee, but he reacted to the policy as follows:

We so-called vocational men need to get our heads above the sphere of our own little world now and then. We are Cock of the Walk just now, but it may not always be so,—there are others in the educational planet who are still worth listening to on the big problems ahead. Let's put ourselves in the other fellow's place once in a while, and thereby gain a perspective, and a sympathetic understanding of educational problems, rather than just our own problems. Hats off to the N.E.A. policy! [30]

Since 1926 the NEA Department of Vocational Education has been relatively inactive, decreasingly so with each year. Wesley's discussion of "Who Talked About What" shows that during the ten year period, 1930-1939, vocational education ranked eighth in the order of frequency of topics among 71 papers presented.[31] In recent years papers on vocational education have been presented at the annual NEA convention, but the Department has ceased to be a significant force in the general area of vocational education.

## American Industrial Arts Association

The American Industrial Arts Association was organized during the annual conference of the American Association of School Administrators in Cleveland in 1939. In 1942 AIAA became a department of the National Education Association. The decision to form a department of industrial arts in

---

[28] "Vocational Education at the N.E.A." *Industrial Arts Magazine*, Vol. VIII, No. 9, September 1919, p. 369.

[29] Arthur F. Payne, "The NEA Adopts a So-Called National Policy of Vocational Education," *Industrial Arts Magazine*, Vol. VIII, No. 9, September 1919, pp. 364-365.

[30] Clarence E. Howell, "Commending the N.E.A. Resolution on Vocational Education," *Industrial Arts Magazine*, Vol. VIII, No. 10, October 1919, p. 425.

[31] Wesley, *op. cit.*, p. 53.

NEA was prompted by the Association's recognition of a need for closer affiliation with leadership in the general field of education.

The organizational meeting in 1939 developed in connection with a national conference on industrial arts teacher education held on February 27-28. Invitations were issued by William E. Warner, and the conference was sponsored by Epsilon Pi Tau as a part of that fraternity's tenth anniversary celebration. Warner pointed out that progress in industrial arts was a direct responsibility of teacher educators, and that the time was ripe to appraise their policies and programs. The Depression of the thirties had caused a broad expansion of industrial arts education beyond what were generally thought to be its normal limits. Warner cited evidence of confusion, disproportionate emphasis due to expediency, shoddy selection techniques, inappropriately equipped laboratories, incompetent personnel, and absence of reasonable accrediting regulation as examples to show the need for professional study of the teacher education program. Approximately twenty leaders of industrial arts teacher education responded to the invitation. During the second day of the meeting the guidelines for forming the American Industrial Arts Association were developed. William E. Warner was elected as the first president.

The first annual convention of the AIAA was held in Minneapolis on July 2, 1940, in connection with the annual meeting of the NEA. The conventions of 1941 and 1942 were held during the annual meetings of the American Association of School Administrators, in Atlantic City and San Francisco, respectively. Wartime restrictions prevented conventions for the next four years, although meetings of the executive committee were held each year and the purposes of the Association were kept in motion. Conventions were resumed in 1947 and are held in the spring of the year in various cities throughout the nation.[32]

In purpose the AIAA strives to improve, advance, and raise the status of industrial arts in education and among educators. The Association is concerned with standards of teaching and with representation of industrial arts on the national level. The purpose is stated in terms of improving the industrial arts program in the public schools alone.

Two related groups sponsored by the Association are: the American Council for Industrial Arts Teacher Education, formed in 1950; and the American Council of Industrial Arts Supervisors, organized in 1951. These two groups have met annually, usually on the day previous to the opening of the AIAA convention.

In membership the Association has grown from approximately 4,000 in 1954 to 10,000 in 1965.

A full-time executive secretary, Kenneth E. Dawson, was appointed January 2, 1961, and an office is maintained in the NEA Building in Washington, D.C. In the fall of 1941 the executive committee of AIAA decided to publish a professional magazine. The first issue

---

[32] Comprehensive documentation concerning the Association may be found in the unpublished manuscript of DeWitt Hunt, *History of the American Industrial Arts Association*. Washington: American Industrial Arts Association. [Not dated but containing documentation to 1960.]

of the *Industrial Arts Teacher* was dated April, 1942. In 1964 the magazine was redesigned and issued under the title *The Journal of Industrial Arts Education.*

## Iota Lambda Sigma

Iota Lambda Sigma is a national professional fraternity of industrial educators. Its membership consists of teachers, supervisors, and administrators of industrial arts and trade and industrial education. The professional purpose of the fraternity is to promote the cause of industrial education by recognition of scholarship and professional training and to create and maintain a closer bond of fraternity among persons in higher education who pursue professional work in industrial education.

The Alpha Chapter of Iota Lambda Sigma was founded at the Pennsylvania State College on July 21, 1925. First officers of the Alpha Chapter were: E. C. Youngbluch, president; R. L. Punnett, vice-president; and Charles P. Scott, secretary-treasurer. The charter group consisted of thirty members. Arthur D. Dean, author of the fraternity ritual, was the first person to receive an honorary membership. The first person to act as a faculty advisor to the fraternity was William Penn Loomis, who was head of the college's department of industrial education.

F. Theodore Struck, as a later faculty advisor to the Alpha Chapter, saw in the professional fraternity of Iota Lambda Sigma a potential for creating and sustaining leadership among the rapidly growing groups of industrial educators. Through his efforts chapters were established in other colleges and universities. A charter was issued by the Common Pleas Court of the State of Pennsylvania, County of Centre, officially incorporating the Alpha Chapter and the Grand Chapter.

The tentative constitution of the Grand Chapter was distributed to the other chapters, which were asked to take similar action. In addition, the chapters were asked to elect an official representative, with the power to act, to attend a meeting for the purpose of organizing a Grand Chapter. The meeting was held in Milwaukee, Wisconsin, on December 11, 1930. The group that met as official representatives of the various chapters, reviewed, discussed, and finally adopted a constitution for the Grand Chapter. The Grand Chapter officers elected at that meeting were president, F. Theodore Struck, Alpha; vice-president, Clyde H. Wilson, Beta; and secretary-treasurer, George H. Resides, Alpha. The next morning, on December 12, 1930, a breakfast meeting of 28 members of Iota Lambda Sigma constituted the first annual meeting of the Grand Chapter. The Grand Chapter holds a meeting each year in the same city and at the same time as the annual meeting of the American Vocational Association. By February, 1960, 25 local chapters had been established.

## Epsilon Pi Tau

Seminar discussions with graduate students at the Ohio State University in the late 1920's confirmed in the mind of Professor William E. Warner the necessity for a professional fraternity for industrial education. Both industrial arts and vocational industrial education needed strong leadership. A portion of that leadership could come from, and be stimulated by, a professional fraternity.

Greek lettered fraternities had a magic about them, and such an organization, cast among the traditions and *mores* of university life, was calculated to produce a stimulating effect of deep professionalism among the members. Warner consulted with colleagues, and with their assistance developed an appropriate ritual. [Charles A. Bennett contributed generously to the writing of the ritual and was made an honorary member in December, 1930.] Among the ideals which the fraternity sought to emphasize through its members were the skill of real craftsmanship, social relationships, and research. These ideals were historically fundamental to the total movement of industrial education, and the fraternity sought a better understanding of the ideals in their broadest sense.

Warner formally conducted the first initiation and installed the Alpha Chapter on Saturday, March 13, 1929. In the years that followed, the fraternity grew rapidly. Twenty-three chapters were installed by 1942. In the years following World War II, the fraternity grew so rapidly that by May, 1961, Warner could report that there were 68 chapters in 27 states and also in Canada, the Philippines, Puerto Rico, and Thailand. Furthermore, fraternity members were known to be at work in 40 nations. Immediately following the annual meeting of the American Industrial Arts Association in Pittsburgh, April 16-19, 1962, Warner embarked on a world tour for the purpose of

studying "The Progress of Our Profession in Europe, the Middle East and Southeast Asia, to Install Some Chapters, Present Certain Honors, and Confer With Interested Leaders Over the Fraternity's Proposal of a Program of International Research and Development."

Epsilon Pi Tau has made contributions to industrial education through its extensive programs, through its numerous projects, and through its various publications. Meetings of Epsilon Pi Tau are held during the annual conventions of the American Industrial Arts Association and the American Vocational Association.

## The Ship

The Ship is an organization of representatives of commercial firms who are engaged in selling in the school field. Since its formation in 1922, this group has had a significant influence upon the development of industrial education.

The Ship reportedly had its origin as a kind of by-product of the Western Arts Association convention in St. Louis in 1922.[33] One evening several of the commercial representatives at the convention were sitting in the Chase Hotel lobby, talking informally. During the discussion, Fred Bishop of the Frederick Post Company suggested the idea of forming an organization of commercial men in the school field.

Frank K. Phillips of the American Type Founders Company was so intrigued with the idea and the opportunity it presented that he proceeded to work out a basic plan. Ideals of

---

[33] "The Ship," Included as a supplement to the *American Vocational Association News Bulletin,* Vol. IV, No. 3, August 1929, n.p.

service and attainment, friendship, and fair dealing were foremost in his mind when it occurred to him that The Ship would be an ideal name, for it seemed to him to signify faithfulness, stability, and honesty. His proposal the next morning was immediately adopted.

The name, The Ship, suggested that the officers should have nautical titles. Phillips was designated as the first Captain. The only educator ever to have a billet on the Ship was Arthur D. Dean, who for several years was Chief Broadcasting Officer and later Chief Radio Operator. The Ship was actually launched at the Western Arts Association convention at Dayton, Ohio, in 1924.

Early in its history The Ship initiated the practice of recognizing outstanding service in the field of industrial education by conferring the title "First-Class Passenger" upon deserving educators. Carl T. Cotter was the first person so honored. In 1939 "The Ship's Citation" became a permanent part of the exhibitor's program at the AVA convention, and Charles A. Bennett was the first person to be honored in this manner. In later years an award known as "The Ship's Man of the Year" became a part of the annual convention of the American Industrial Arts Association. On the bow of the mythical ship is its motto—*Ich Dien* (I serve), the motto of the Prince of Wales.

One of the great values of The Ship has been in the planning and operating of commercial exhibits at industrial education conventions. A *deck officer* is appointed to sit in on the planning meetings of the convention committees. The deck officer's experience as an exhibitor at many conventions is invaluable to convention committees. Gen-

erally he represents all the exhibitors in such things as the selection of appropriate exhibit areas, shipping problems, storage facilities, and prizes, and he also handles the special problems of individual exhibitors.

Although The Ship is a "social organization," its contributions are significant in the development of industrial education. The Ship promotes an atmosphere of mutual trust, understanding, and cooperation among exhibitors and members of industrial education professional associations, a relationship which transcends mere seller and consumer relationships.

Many of the commercial representatives are former industrial education teachers. New equipment, supplies, processes, and services have developed from these relationships, which in turn have aided the improvement of instruction in industrial education. This close relationship between the actual industrial education needed and the requirement to supply the need has brought industrial education much closer to representatives of industry and technology than would otherwise have been possible. Constant cooperation and consultation between commercial firms and industrial educators often shortens the time lag between the development of industrial processes and the start of teaching about them.

At the American Vocational Association convention in Los Angeles in December, 1960, the official name of The Ship was changed to the Educational Exhibitors Association—Ship. The EEA—Ship organization has pledged itself to work with educators in the promotion of industrial, vocational, technological, and practical arts education. Furthermore, the organization is dedicated to improving service through better educational exhibits, improved trade practices, and cooperation with educators in worthy projects. This relationship is unique to industrial education; no counterpart exists for other professional associations.

## Local and State Organization Relationships

With the beginning of industrial education as an area of emphasis in the public schools, numerous small local groups of persons with professional interests were organized. No particular pattern appeared to dominate in these organizations, since they represented geographical areas most convenient to the purposes and sizes of the groups. The following names represent the general trend: Essex County Arts Association, Philadelphia Mechanic Arts Teachers' Association, North Texas Vocational Teachers Association, Vocational Education Society of Boston, Industrial Arts Club of Central California. It was characteristic of these groups to change their names as they changed in size to encompass larger areas, or as they included in their membership persons of related interests.

The existence of many purely local groups led to combinations into larger units, such as state associations. However, the small local groups not only continued to function, but did so with improved status (and perhaps greater purpose) as chapters of the state group. It is important to note that the national professional associations, if they are to be effective in their purposes, must be backed up by these smaller units. The total complex organizational structure must have clear and uninterrupted channels of communication directly to individual members. This process appears to work two ways. The existence of many small organizations eventually produces a large national group; or, if a national group is created, it must organize smaller units if it is to be more than an honorary society.

Small local units of industrial educators provide vital social and professional relationships. Development of these relationships is highly important because progress in industrial education must begin at the point of student-teacher activity. Otherwise, the efforts of state and national organizations may be of little consequence.

The historical record of industrial education includes many reports of the activities of local groups, significant because they represent action at the very heart of industrial education. The number of these organizations is far too large for their individual achievements to be exhaustively documented; however, the nature of these groups can be illustrated by a few examples.

### Oklahoma City

A Department of Manual Training was organized at the convention of the State Teachers Association of Oklahoma, December 20-21, 1909. The name of the organization was the Oklahoma Manual Training and Drawing Association.[34] The Association held meetings each year during the convention of the State Teachers Association, but apparently did not engage

---

[34] Marion E. Franklin, *A History of Industrial Education in Oklahoma Up to 1950.* Tahlequah, Oklahoma: Northeastern State College Printing Department, 1954, p. 34.

in any professional development programs between conventions. Franklin estimates that at most not more than a dozen schools in the state were offering manual training when the Association was organized.[35]

### Detroit

A 1917 report of the Detroit Manual Training Club shows that the Club had established the practice of sending its president on a trip each year to visit schools, to talk with teachers and students, and to report back to the Club "all the new ideas" he could find. When L. G. Burgess visited Chicago, Milwaukee, and Minneapolis, his report to the Club indicated that all of the instructors he visited had agreed that if youth could be taught "judgment" or "mechanical sense" or the ability to think about what he was doing, it was not necessary to worry about the facts he was expected to learn.

### Boston

At the May, 1919, meeting of the Boston Manual Training Club, Charles W. Parmenter talked on the topic, "Present Tendencies in Technical Education." He felt that the trend was toward a balance of two extremes: (1) formal exercise, logically and progressively arranged, but lacking in industrial significance; and (2) production without regard to fundamental principles. The Club members discussed Parmenter's address. The sentiment of the Club was strongly for the educational values of manual training as obtained by "true craftsmanship."

### Pittsburgh

On Saturday, May 22, 1930, the Manual Training Teachers of Pittsburgh played their annual baseball game. The historical record tells us that the affair "took the form of a big get-together for the men representing industrial education in the Pittsburgh schools."

### San Francisco and Los Angeles

David Allen in his study of professional associations in industrial education in California described the early organizations as follows:

The fifteen-year period, from 1896 to 1911 saw the beginning and growth of professional industrial education organizations in both the San Francisco and Los Angeles areas. In the north industrial education teacher organizations were always a part of the California Teachers' Association. The predominant organization was the Manual Training and Drawing Teachers' Association.

In the south an organization was attached to the Southern California Teachers' Association, and an independent organization existed well, the Pacific Manual Training Teachers' Association. The organizations had many of the same members and officers. There were many joint meetings held throughout this period.[36]

Allen goes on to say that in-service training and opportunity for socialization were the chief contributions of the associations to the teachers' well-being; both led toward the improvement of instruction.

### Significance of Local Activity

The significant point of these and hundreds of other reports of local

---

[35] Author's personal note. The chairman of the executive committee of the Oklahoma Manual Training and Drawing Association was R. R. Barlow, manual training teacher, Mounds, Oklahoma, my father.

[36] David Allen, *The History of Professional Industrial Education Organizations in California.* (Unpublished doctoral dissertation, University of California, Los Angeles), 1962, p. 112.

activity is that industrial education personnel were joined in professional association and were working toward improvement in their understanding of both the field and each other.

## Summary

Professional associations have played an important role in the growth and development of industrial education. In fact, professional associations appear to be an essential aspect of any educational movement. The quality and quantity of educational contributions find their origin in the activities of professional associations.

The first professional organization to have concerns in the area of industrial education was the National Education Association which organized a Department of Industrial Education in 1875. When the manual training movement had become well established, the Department changed its name to the Department of Industrial and Manual Training in recognition of the contemporary emphasis in the general area.

In later years the Eastern Arts Association and the Western Arts Association placed an emphasis upon manual training and then in turn upon manual arts. Industrial education seemed only to "exist" in these Associations. There is scarcely any evidence of significant contributions to industrial education. Probably it was the broad interests of the associations that created the major problem. Asserting that art and manual art were both "fine" arts did not make them so.

With the attainment of federal aid the National Society for the Promotion of Industrial Education changed its name to the National Society for Vocational Education, but its influence tended to be largely regional. The Vocational Association of the Middle West, organized in 1914, grew rapidly under the stimulation of vocational education by the Smith-Hughes Act. Leaders in' both Associations recognized the fallacy to two competing associations and by mutual consent joined forces to become the American Vocational Association in 1925. The pressure was strong for further identification of AVA with the National Education Association, but the new national organization decided to remain independent of NEA, with the result that the Department of Vocational Education of NEA functioned with decreasing influence and importance.

In the meantime the industrial arts movement had grown significantly; even though AVA provided an emphasis upon industrial arts, motivation was strong to form a separate association. Part of this motivation may have developed because of animosity among certain leaders of the industrial education movement.

However, in 1939, the American Industrial Arts Association was formed as the national professional association for industrial arts. It was not until after World War II that significant achievements were noted. The Association grew rapidly during the two decades following World War II. The Association reached full professional status with the appointment of a full-time executive secretary in 1961.

Two professional fraternities, Iota Lambda Sigma and Epsilon Pi Tau, provide further motivation for the professional development of industrial education. The fraternities work in cooperation with the national professional associations. Finally the Educational Exhibitors Association—Ship, a social organization of firms engaged in selling in the school field, contributes much to the *esprit de corps* of industrial education. This group supports many projects in the interests of the growth and development of industrial education, and encourages professional development of industrial educators.

State and local organizations interested in industrial education have long existed throughout the nation. The specific purposes and programs of these organizations vary widely, but all are concerned in general with improvement of industrial education.

With one exception the significant professional organizations in industrial education have been discussed in this chapter. The exception is the group known as the Mississippi Valley Conference, whose activity, beginning in 1913, has provided leadership, enthusiasm, and motivation in professionalizing industrial education. Although strictly regional in nature, the Mississippi Valley Conference occupies a unique position in the historical scene. Therefore the next chapter will deal exclusively with that group.

## Recall Questions

1. Identify the five professional organizations discussed in this chapter.
2. For what reasons did each organization exist?
3. Describe Iota Lambda Sigma, Epsilon Pi Tau, and EEA—Ship. What contributions do these organizations make to the improvement of industrial education?
4. Summarize the general purposes and contributions of the professional organizations in industrial education.

## Research Questions

1. From the general historical background of your state, develop a chronology of the activities of professional associations in industrial education and discuss their relationships with other educational associations.
2. What contributions to the improvement of industrial education in your school can you trace to local, regional, or state associations in industrial education? Document your answer with specific reference to published materials.

## Suggestions for Further Reading

Professional periodicals of:
American Industrial Arts Association
    *Journal of Industrial Arts Education*
American Vocational Association
    *American Vocational Journal*
National Education Association
    *Proceedings of Annual Meetings*

Chapter 5

# Mississippi Valley Conference[1]

First Meeting, 1909 · The 1913 Conference · Chicago, 1914 · Conferences 1915-1929 · Depression Years, 1930-1934 · Conferences 1935-1940 · Bawden Retires as Chairman · Conferences 1946-1950 · Conferences 1951-1960 · Fryklund Retires as General Chairman · Postscript · Summary · Recall Questions · Research Questions · Suggestions for Further Reading

**W**hile en route to Europe in the early spring of 1908, Charles A. Bennett stopped briefly in New York to visit with Robert W. Selvidge, at that time a student at Teachers College, Columbia University. A portion of their discussion was concerned with the general condition of manual arts in the Middle West. The Middle West had developed a number of teacher training programs during the early 1900's, and the necessity of sharing viewpoints was evident to both Selvidge and Bennett. By mutual agreement (although the idea appears to have been suggested by Selvidge) they decided to call a conference of men responsible for the preparation of teachers of manual arts, in order to discuss common problems.

## First Meeting, 1909

Nearly a year and a half later, in October, 1909, Bennett wrote to Selvidge (who in the meantime had returned to the University of Missouri) that he had not forgotten the proposed conference. Bennett suggested the names of persons to be invited and further suggested that the meeting be held at Bradley Institute, in Peoria, on November 11-13, 1909. Selvidge agreed, and accordingly Bennett sent letters outlining the plan of the con-

---

[1] Resource materials for this chapter consisted largely of the historical file of the proceedings of the Mississippi Valley Conferences. These materials were made available by Dr. Verne C. Fryklund, conference chairman. Some of the footnotes for this chapter will refer to "Historical File" as the source of material from the official records of the Mississippi Valley Conference. Much of this material has not been bound or paged, hence the rather loose documentation.

ference to those who were to be invited. In his letter he said, "There is great need of an opportunity for the teachers and organizers of manual training to get together in close conference where they could express all their heresies without being reported in the educational papers and exchange views on questions of vital importance."[2]

The program of the conference was as follows:

*Thursday, November 11, 1909*

Welcome by Dr. T. C. Burgess

"Our Unscientific Attitude." Robert W. Selvidge, chairman.

"Controlling Ideas in the Selection of Problems in the Manual Arts; (a) for the Grades, (b) for the High Schools." Oscar L. McMurry, chairman.

Dinner given by Mr. and Mrs. Bennett at their home.

*Friday, November 12, 1909*

"Possibilities and Limitations of Industrial Work in the Grades." Fred D. Crawshaw, chairman.

"Value of Different Factors in the Preparation of Teachers of Manual Arts." William T. Bawden, chairman.

Dinner given by the Manual Arts Press at the Creve Coeur Club.

*Saturday, November 13, 1909*

"Is There Room in the Course of Study for the Art Crafts?" George F. Buxton, chairman.

"Summary of Topics Discussed." Charles A. Bennett, chairman.

Five states were represented at the conference. Twelve men who were responsible for, or concerned with,

teacher training in the manual arts attended the conference. They were: L. A. Bacon, Indianapolis, Indiana; C. H. Bailey, Cedar Falls, Iowa; W. T. Bawden, Normal, Illinois; C. A. Bennett, Peoria, Illinois; L. H. Bruch, Macomb, Illinois; G. F. Buxton, Menomonie, Wisconsin; F. D. Crawshaw, Urbana, Illinois; M. L. Laubach, Terre Haute, Indiana; O. L. McMurry, Chicago, Illinois; W. Sargent, Chicago, Illinois; R. W. Selvidge, Columbia, Missouri; and L. W. Walstron, Chicago, Illinois.[3]

A number of these people met informally in May, 1910, at the Western Drawing and Manual Arts Association Convention at Minneapolis; some met again in May, 1912, at that association's convention in Cincinnati. They planned to meet formally in December, 1912, but did not actually meet until the following year.

## The 1913 Conference

The 1913 conference is of particular significance because it represents the determined effort of ten men to provide leadership and to stimulate activity leading to the solution of immediate problems in manual arts. At that time no general arrangement existed to coordinate teacher training activities or to stimulate research. Development left entirely to individual initiative did not appear satisfactory.

On the first day of the conference, Ira S. Griffith presented a mimeographed proposal for a four-year training course of college grade for teachers

---

[2] *Historical File.* [Also reported in William T. Bawden, *Twenty Years of Progress in the Manual Arts.* Peoria, Illinois: The Manual Arts Press, March 1, 1930, p. 10.]

[3] *Historical File.*

of manual arts. This proposal represented the recommendations of the Manual Arts Department of the University of Missouri. The conferees discussed the idea in great detail and then raised a number of questions for general discussion. The questions were as follows: [4]

1. Shall we recommend that a four-year course be offered to prospective teachers of the Manual Arts?

2. Are we in favor of the ratio of three hours of shopwork to one hour of credit, or two hours to one of credit?

3. Shall manual arts courses be given on a cultural basis to students not specializing in manual arts?

4. What academic subjects shall be required in a four-year course?

5. Shall we allow students to go through the four-year course without any foreign language requirement?

6. Will this language requirement be dependent on whether the students took foreign language in the high school?

7. Should we include in the Freshman and Sophomore years all of the traditional manual arts courses of the manual training high school?

8. Shall general or preliminary psychology be included in the Junior year work?

9. Shall any psychology be required?

10. Is it important that normal schools offering four-year courses should adopt the university division of work into two years of cultural before two years of professional work?

11. What subjects should enter into the manual arts requirements for graduation?

12. Should sociology be required or elective?

13. Should an informational course be given on tools and materials either in connection with or separate from classes in shopwork?

14. Is there need of a special course in care and use of machines and the installation of the same?

15. Should engineering drawing and architectural drawing be included in the course?

16. Ought not this Conference try to outline courses in the manual arts for high schools?

Although these points were discussed in detail, the conferees did not attempt to formulate an entire four-year course for the training of manual arts teachers. However, they did adopt unanimously the following resolutions: [5]

1. We strongly endorse the practice of offering a four-year course of college grade for the preparation of teachers of manual arts.

2. In estimating credits we favor the commonly accepted academic method: namely, three hours of the student's time to one hour of credit. This may be interpreted, for example, as three hours of shopwork to one of credit; or it may be two hours of shopwork and one hour of preparation for one hour of credit; or it may be one hour of recitation and two hours of preparation for one hour of credit.

3. We are in favor of offering courses in the manual arts as cultural subjects in any year of the college course.

4. In foreign language instruction for students preparing to teach the manual arts, we believe that the combined requirement of both the high school and the college should not exceed three years.

5. We favor a minimum of one-fourth of the entire four years' work and a maximum of one-half to be devoted to the manual arts.

---

[4] *Historical File.*
[5] *Historical File.*

94

The group also devoted time to the subject of the training of teachers for vocational schools. No action was taken concerning the various problems raised, nor did the group formulate any particular conclusions on the topic. Bennett, who acted as secretary, did suggest five points which he felt represented a reasonable conclusion.[6]

1. The schools cannot get efficient men from the trades because these men, if they know their trades thoroughly, can get more pay in the industries than the schools can offer.

2. Owing to the division of labor in the industries very few man are learning their trades thoroughly enough to become teachers in vocational schools.

3. There is a difference between general schooling and general education; men who are to teach must have the latter even if they have very little of the former.

4. In order to get the best kind of preparation for teaching, the man from the shops must supplement his practical experience with instruction in the training school for teachers, and the man from the technical school must get practical shop experience besides his pedagogic training.

5. Training schools for teachers can give all the preparation except the trade experience and they can go a long ways in that direction.

Included among the topics discussed was the evaluation of credits between institutions. Facilitating the transfer of credits was important in itself, but the group also felt that the creation of uniform standards would be a means of dignifying the manual and industrial arts and aid in securing proper recognition from the academicians. In later years the group devoted much time and attention to the problem of evaluation. Such study tended to strengthen the curriculum simply through the exchange of ideas about the values to be found in the field.

At the business meeting it was agreed that the conference should consist of the persons who were present, those who had attended the previous meetings, and such other persons as the group might desire to invite. It was also agreed that only one person should be selected from an institution; that no matters concerning the policies of the conference be published without the consent of the members; and that in public statements concerning the conference it would be called "A group of men from institutions in the Mississippi Valley engaged in training teachers of manual arts."

### Chicago, 1914

The Conference met at the University of Chicago, November 19-21, 1914. After the usual greetings and an address by Charles H. Judd, of the University of Chicago, the conferees settled down to the business of committee reports. These reports included "Salaries of Manual Training Teachers," "Evaluation of Units of Credit," and "Preparation of Vocational Teachers." During the year the committees had been at work attempting to find the best possible solutions to their assigned problems. William T. Bawden, who had made the arrangements for the meeting [room, bath, and meals at the Hotel Del Prado, $3.00], was not present at the 1913 conference; he was

---

[6] *Historical File.*

attending Teachers College, Columbia University, completing work for a doctor's degree—the second granted in industrial education.

Following the custom set in eariler meetings, the Conference agreed upon a number of resolutions which summarized their work and which indicated direction for the immediate future. Also the resolutions had the effect of setting standards for teachers in industrial education, which were much needed.

The resolutions for the 1914 conference were: [7]

1. *Resolved,* that this Conference favors the principle of State certification for admission as workers into the skilled trades and certain classified industries.

2. *Resolved,* that this Conference favors the policy of having the State retain control of the education of the youth until he is established as a thoroughly competent worker in his vocation, and to this end, it is believed that the State should cooperate in providing, so far as may be necessary, actual instruction within the industries.

3. *Resolved,* that the members of this Conference believe that promising material for the vocational shop teacher is to be found in the professionally prepared manual training shop teacher who supplements his equipment by not less than one year's experience in the trade; and also in the skilled mechanic who supplements his trade equipment by not less than one year's special professional preparation.

4. *Resolved,* that this Conference favors the policy of giving professional preparation for teaching to selected journeyman workers in industry, including such plans as the following: (1) special institutes; (2) night school continuation classes; and (3) full time residence courses; with the provision that, so far as possible, such professional training should extend over a period equivalent to not less than one school year.

5. *Resolved,* that this Conference favors the intensive analysis of many typical industrial occupations as a basis for the organization of courses of study for preparation for such occupations.

6. *Resolved,* that the members of this Conference believe that it is essential that provision shall be made of opportunities for vocational education for individuals who are employed in the occupations for which they desire further special preparation, but also that opportunities should be provided that will encourage the progress of individuals into more desirable occupations.

7. *Resolved,* that the Conference expresses its appreciation of the interests in its problems and deliberations manifested by the U.S. Bureau of Education in sending a representative to Chicago.

8. *Resolved,* that the Conference expresses its appreciation of courtesies received during its meetings at the University of Chicago, with special thanks to Messrs. Leavitt, Parker, Filbey and Bobbitt.

The first resolution, favoring state certification of workers, grew out of a presentation by Robert W. Selvidge at the 1913 meeting. Selvidge believed that there should be certification for entrance to the industries, just as there was certification to practice law or medicine. He further believed that such certification should be under the control of the educational authorities. The logic of Selvidge's presentations at both the 1913 and 1914 conferences caused the members to request that he continue studying the possibility of

_____

[7] *Historical File.*

96

such practice and keep the members of the conference advised of his progress.

It was also voted at the 1914 conference that United States Commissioner of Education, P. P. Claxton, be requested to call the conference for the next year.

## Conferences 1915-1929

Commissioner Claxton complied with the request, then assigned William T. Bawden to represent him. Upon completing his studies at Columbia University, Bawden had entered government service as a Specialist in Industrial Education with the Bureau of Education. He issued invitations to all "institutions in the Mississippi Valley States engaged in training teachers of the manual arts and industrial education." These institutions were to designate official representatives to the next conference. Invitations were also issued to state departments of education in the same area. Membership increased to the extent that 31 persons attended the conference held at Chicago Normal College, December 9-11, 1915.

The topics discussed at this and succeeding conferences indicate the wide variety of interests among the members as well as their desire to get at the roots of some of the really puzzling problems with which they had to cope as teachers and teacher educators. Practice teaching, evaluation of credits for transfer, and testing the results of teaching appeared frequently on the programs. Conference committees working from year to year considered standards for manual arts work, prin-

ciples of industrial education, terminology, and teaching combinations that defined what subjects a manual arts teacher should teach in addition to his major area, and, even more important, how far a combination of subjects should be allowed to progress.

In December, 1916, the Conference met at the Peabody College for Teachers, Nashville, Tennessee, at the invitation of President Bruce R. Payne. Payne was not present for the opening session but was represented by Professor Charles A. McMurray. Although McMurray was considered an "outsider" by the Conference—he was not directly involved in manual training— he did provide encouragement and enthusiasm. In his rough notes of the discussion by McMurray, Bawden summarized the presentation in four major sections.

1. There have been a number of rather well defined stages of manual arts in the schools. In the first stage the emphasis was upon the practical values of manual arts (made the boy handy). This represented in part a protest against the wholly scholastic work of the school. In the second stage the emphasis was upon accurate joints and rather definitely outlined set of models to be constructed. The third stage ushered in the idea of the useful model which represented the application of definite principles or processes. The fourth stage indicated the influence of the arts and crafts movement and gave recognition to the importance of the aesthetic element. This element became one of the dominant elements in manual arts. In the fifth stage, manual arts which had entered the curriculum with little recognition, achieved a place of recognition as one of the important parts of the school work along with the traditional (or cultural) subjects.

2. The introduction of manual arts provided a relief from the mental work required of other studies. Manual arts was considered to have real subject matter knowledge such as knowledge of tools, materials, processes, and construction. Design became of prime importance and thought dominated this activity.

3. Manual arts furnishes good examples of organized subject matter through its units of instruction. The whole is considered before the details are taken into account. Such values are largely lacking in other subjects.

4. The whole development of the industrial arts (manual arts) is basic to the solution of the large industrial education problem. Such experiences should be provided early in the child's career and the pre-vocational experiences should be allowed to function. The proper carrying out of this idea is the most important problem in the whole field of education.[8]

The Commissioner of Education continued to call the annual conferences during the time that Bawden was located in Washington. Reports of the conferences were printed by the Bureau of Education as Industrial Education Circulars. This gave wider circulation to the work of the Conference than would otherwise have been possible. The agenda for each meeting was constructed by surveying the members to determine what subjects or topics they wished to take up at the coming meeting. In addition, members often felt it necessary to pursue some topics for a prolonged time, and standing committees were appointed with this responsibility. In general, the mainstream of discussion in the conferences was related to the problem of teacher preparation in manual arts and industrial subjects.

Admission to membership in the conference had been limited to only a small number of persons. This was not done in order to be exclusive, but rather as an expedient to permit a free exchange of thought, utilizing the advantages of small groups and informal discussion. The programs were not "loaded" to such an extent that time for discussion was restricted. Each topic was assigned to a member of the Conference who was an authority on it, and each received thorough consideration. During the first twenty years the conference devoted:

25 sessions to problems of teaching, testing, and standards.
21 sessions to administrative studies.
19 sessions to curricula for the preparation of manual arts teachers.
13 sessions to underlying philosophy.
10 sessions to shop organization, arrangement, and equipment.
8 sessions to junior high school programs.
8 sessions to Smith-Hughes vocational topics.
4 sessions to senior high school programs.
4 sessions to topics related to World War I.

Analysis of the conference topics provides additional insight into the motivations behind the Mississippi Valley Conferences. Attention had been focused upon problems of teaching. If progress couldn't be shown at this point—the teacher-student contact—all other progress would become less meaningful. Help the teacher solve in-

---

[8] *Historical File.* In this particular case I have chosen to use Bawden's rough notes of McMurray's presentation rather than refer to a printed account in order to capture Bawden's impression. The notes have been condensed, but the central idea is preserved.

structional problems, help him measure student progress, help him devise standards of instruction, and then move to other areas of need. This was the essence of attention to the problems of the teacher.

Because the Mississippi Valley Conferences had been organized by persons with teacher preparation, it was only natural that they would devote much time to the program, progress, and trends in teacher education. They were concerned with fundamental principles of program content both in teacher education and in the school program of manual arts. So philosophical doctrines would have great interest to the members of the conference.

It is quite apparent that two decades of professional study of the problems of manual arts were devoted to issues central to building the program.

The twentieth anniversary conference was held in Peoria, Illinois, December 12-14, 1929. Part of the meeting was given over to taking stock of the progress of twenty years and to recognizing outstanding achievement. The most honored person at the conference was Charles A. Bennett, "the Dean of the Manual-Arts Movement in America." On behalf of the members of the Conference, William E. Roberts presented him a bouquet of twenty roses and a desk set as evidence of appreciation for his untiring efforts. When called upon to review some of the historical background of the Conference, Bennett said that it was difficult for him to realize that he had begun teaching manual training 42 years earlier. Based upon this long ex-

perience, his opinion was that the Conference had been a maker of history.

This Conference during the past 20 years has made a notable, unpretentious contribution to the progress of public education. By wholly democratic methods it has influenced the thought and practice of leaders in teacher-training institutions within its territory, and through them the instruction given to thousands of young people.[9]

Robert W. Selvidge prized the fine spirit of comradeship developed during the twenty years and felt that the accomplishments of the Conference each year were worth more than any other professional activity during the twelve months. William E. Roberts indicated that "the development of our work in Cleveland, so far as I have had any influence upon it, during the 15 years that I have been a member, has been due directly to my reactions to the things I have gotten from this conference."[10]

The membership list of the Manual Arts Conference, corrected to January 1, 1930, indicated that there were 73 members from 19 states. Fifty-eight were representatives of colleges, universities, normal schools, and teachers colleges.

## Depression Years, 1930-1934

The general theme of the conference held at Ohio State University, December 18-20, 1930, was postgraduate courses for teachers of manual arts and industrial subjects. Graduate programs leading to the master's degree varied

[9] William T. Bawden, *Twenty Years of Progress in the Manual Arts.* Peoria, Illinois: The Manual Arts Press, March 1, 1930, p. 4.

[10] *Ibid.,* p. 19.

widely throughout the nation in their subject matter content. Few, if any, courses in industrial education could be counted as credit toward a doctoral degree. The need for advanced professional work was evident to the conference members, but graduate curricula in industrial education were still in a process of slow evolution. The idea appeared to be somewhat of an enigma to deans of graduate schools, according to the information provided for the Conference by A. C. Newell. The members were disturbed that a large percentage of graduate work was confined to the administrative and professional phases of education. The subject matter of the field had been largely excluded.

Throughout the years one characteristic of the conferences which has been strikingly evident, even to the casual observer, has been the determined effort of the members to probe deeply into all sides of a question or discussion topic. There is also much evidence to indicate that the members were somewhat impatient with the slow pace of progress. Bennett, who frequently assumed the role of providing a general summary of the conference, said of the 1931 meeting:

This conference has proved that we reflect the fears as well as the enthusiasms of the social and educational environment in which we live. In a period of depression we have held a depression conference. We are depressed because we cannot live up to our ideals.

We are worried because we do not know what to do with students in the senior high school. We are fretted because we have become the football in the game between credit for shop experience and academic ideals. We fear we will lose caste (which we never really had) if we do not find our work listed more often in the records of research. When we get a top view of our own teacher-training curriculum, we are amazed that it is an unorganized mass, or mess, and we wonder who will deliver us from our friendly enemies in the college faculties. We are afraid the legislators will repeal the Smith-Hughes Act. And worst of all, we are shocked that we have no high-sounding objectives to have emblazoned on our banner when approached by the makers of meaningless phrases or the unfriendly evaluators of courses of instruction.

But this is only one side of the picture. This conference has given us encouragement because we have seen the seamy side of our problems as well as the attractive pattern side.[11]

The 1931 conference was not entirely depressing; the members found their work interesting and rewarding despite the general economic depression of the times.

Although the topics were chosen by consensus of the members and therefore usually were varied, each conference seemed to have a general theme. In the 1932 conference the theme was Research Problems in Manual Arts. Elements of research in industrial education were thoroughly discussed, and a list of 159 theses from 11 institutions was presented to indicate the nature and scope of recent research. Both the limitations and the values of graduate research in industrial education were evident to the members of the conference. They could see special value in finding a means of publishing research and studies for general distribution but were at a loss to determine an appropriate way to accomplish this task.

---

[11] *Historical File.* Report of the twenty-second Manual Arts Conference, p. 20.

The twenty-fifth anniversary meeting was held in Peoria, Illinois, December 13-15, 1934. Fifty persons attended, representing 15 states. Six of the group had attended the first meeting in 1909: C. H. Bailey, W. T. Bawden, C. A. Bennett, F. D. Crawshaw, M. L. Laubach, and R. W. Selvidge. The program consisted of the following topics: [12]

1. New Teaching Techniques in Shopwork and Drafting.

2. Selection, Organization, and Shop Use of Related Informational Material.

3. What Should Be the Content of the Various Shop and Drafting Courses in the Teacher-Training Curriculum?

4. Objectives of a Department of Industrial Arts in the Teacher-Training Institution.

5. Why Should We Not Seek Progress Through General Agreement on an Industrial-Arts Program for the Junior High School Period, Consisting of Six Fundamental Shop Courses, Recommending One Course for Each Semester During the 7th, 8th, and 9th Years?

6. What Next in Industrial Education? The Changing Social Order, and Its Effects on Industrial Education.

Bawden was the general chairman of the conference (a responsibility he had held since 1914), Selvidge was the toastmaster for the anniversary dinner, and Bennett filled his traditional role by summarizing the conference.

The proceedings of the banquet give a good picture of the major considerations. Selvidge opened the dinner meeting with the following remarks: [13]

For 25 years we have been getting along without speeches but this evening we are engaged in a departure from this procedure as a part of our celebration. During this time, without speeches, we have been engaged in professional writing. Our writing has involved 72 authors who have produced 295 titles which represent quite a contribution. I doubt if any group in the country in any special field has made a greater contribution.

We are frequently asked, What questions has this conference settled? This represents a mistaken notion as to our objectives. One of our traditions has been not to pass resolutions and attempt to settle problems. But I will venture to assert that the discussions during the 25 years have done more to settle problems than all the resolutions passed by all the associations concerned with industrial education. Confidence born of these discussions has been a real factor in determining and setting up policies.

Our influence has been not wholly in the writing and addresses but has been found in a broader and more subtle influence. As Carlyle said, "No idlest word thou speakest but is a seed cast into eternity." The influence of our discussions has gone out and permeated the whole field of industrial education.

Selvidge then introduced "one of the most distinguished friends of industrial education," William J. Bogan, Superintendent of City Schools, Chicago, who talked on the topic "The Teacher and Educational Progress."

---

[12] *Historical File.* Mimeographed outlines of the 25th Anniversary Meeting, pp. 6-7.

[13] *Historical File.* Mimeographed outlines of the 25th anniversary meeting, p. 35. The remarks by Selvidge were reconstructed from Bawden's rough notes. Although Bawden did not compile the material for the historical record concerning the 25th meeting until some years later—dated July 18, 1956, at Santa Barbara, California—comparison of his handwriting would indicate that these notes were made at a much earlier date than 1956, and since the notes are titled "Banquet Thurs. 6:30" it is presumed that they were made in 1934. I have taken the liberty of filling in the words which Bawden's shorthand did not contain, but about the intent of Selvidge in his remarks there can be no doubt.

Bawden was the second speaker at the dinner meeting.[14]

He spoke briefly of his temptation to develop a theme on what had happened in the past few years. He found this to be "well-nigh irresistible" but chose instead the topic of "The Second Twenty-Five Years." He admitted that he used the topic merely to gain the audience's attention and said that he would have some difficulty in looking even five years into the future. But it was the future, and the immediate future at that, which was his greatest concern. His address consisted of three parts: (1) the general problems of industrial arts, considered as a movement, or as a phase, or as an essential, integral part of education; (2) the problems of the institution, or department, charged with the responsibility of preparing teachers of industrial arts subjects; and (3) the problems of the manual arts conference as an organization.

During the first part of his address he encouraged the members by indicating that they had in their power the opportunity to determine whether or not a person was educated. He spoke of "the fallacy of the fundamentals of education." He was not against the three R's but did oppose the misleading attitudes about them that worked to the detriment of the industrial arts. It was his view that education really begins when students start to use the tools and fundamentals of construction. Bawden called attention to "indifference and inconsistency in high places," on the part of institutions of higher learning, to the industrial arts movement. The educational policies of such institutions provided a place for industrial education, but their practice, relative to their policy, did not. A more aggressive attitude was urged in order to promote the advantages of industrial arts.

Bawden's second consideration regarding the problems of the teacher training institutions was based on a list of topics discussed at previous conferences. He selected the five most persistent, the five topics that continued to be urgent. "More careful selection of prospective teachers" had been discussed frequently, and the problem of raising standards of admission was never more pressing if industrial arts was to keep up with the trends of the times. "Development of versatility in shop teachers" continued to demand attention: Bawden estimated that eighty percent of the high schools offering the program were limited to the services of only one industrial arts teacher. This alone should indicate that placing in a school a teacher who can do only one thing (for example, teach woodwork) is an error. From previous discussions Bawden deduced that "more general agreement on a program of industrial arts" was one of the most significant topics to come before the conference, and he urged its thorough discussion. "Development of ability to speak effectively" had become a necessity in teacher education because the teacher "is expected to make a creditable appearance" in his relationships with the students, the faculty, and the community. Bawden believed that the public's partly unfavorable impression of industrial arts could be traced to this one phase of teacher education. Finally, Bawden's look into the immediate future suggested that "more

---

[14] *Historical File.*

effective use of text materials" was a prerequisite to progress for the new generation of industrial arts teachers.

The third part of Bawden's address considered the Conference as an organization. The Conference had been an informal association of persons who met together for the purpose of seeking and offering help on certain problems of common interest. He pointed out that the group had kept its own counsel and was indifferent to publicity. Bawden felt that the membership policy should be reviewed. Fewer than half of the active membership had generally attended the conferences with any degree of regularity. The fringe of inactive members was missing the benefits of the assembly. It was time to state a policy of conference attendance as prerequisite to active membership.

Bawden then turned his attention to the publication of an annual report. There were no reports during the early years of the Conference. Mimeographed summaries of the meetings had been prepared for the years 1914 through 1917. From 1918 to 1923 the reports had been printed by the Bureau of Education. No report was prepared for the 1924 meeting. From 1925 through 1933 the conference members, at their own expense, had printed and distributed records of the conferences. Bawden asked for some policy with respect to reports.

Bawden commented at some length on the leadership in industrial educational research which had been provided by the conference members. "Scarcely a year has passed without the assignment of at least one session to reports of research problems or to the discussion of plans for research." The Conference had listened to reports and participated in discussions of methods, organization, and machinery of research; and a committee of the Conference members had prepared an annotated list of 800 graduate theses and dissertations.[15] This committee had been active over a period of time under the chairmanship of Professor W. L. Hunter of Iowa State College. Bawden commented upon the "deep obligation" of the Conference for the furtherance of this monumental task.

It was clear that the Conference could render a unique and valuable service to institutions of higher learning by making available its members' judgments concerning the most profitable lines of research. This idea Bawden placed before the Conference as an imperative responsibility. Collective effort and constructive teamwork, Bawden pointed out, had been characteristic of the group. He cited the book published by Charles A. Bennett, *Industrial Arts in Modern Education,* as an example of a team effort.

Bawden's address could not have been other than a stimulating experience for the members. He had assessed the power of the Conference, and had shown that in the future more organized effort would be required.

---

[15] *Annotated List of 800 Graduate Theses and Dissertations in Industrial Arts Education and Vocational-Industrial Education Accepted by Institutions of Higher Learning in the U.S. 1892-1933.* Apparently this was distributed to the members of the Conference at the meeting in Chicago in December, 1933. This is a valuable research tool; any institution fortunate enough to have a copy on file should provide for the careful custody of the document. It apparently has not been reissued and no similar document for the same period is known to exist. Fortunately a copy is available in the Library of Congress.

## Conferences 1935-1940

The record is exceedingly sketchy in regard to the significant content of the conferences from 1935 through 1940, all of which were held in Chicago. The referendum plan for determining topics was continued during this time, however, and the list of topics indicates a wide range of interests. It may be presumed, therefore, that each meeting continued to provide the members an opportunity "to set their educational watch"—to borrow an expression from G. Stanley Hall. During the 1935 conference the discussion topics included the industrial arts program in the junior high school; the relation of industrial arts to other areas of education; the changing social order and its effects upon industrial education. In addition there were the perennial topics of certification, teacher training, and graduate study.

On March 10, 1936, Bawden sent a memorandum to all of the active members in which he proposed establishment of a number of committees. At the same time he requested that each committee make a report to the 1936 conference. At the time there were committees on biographical bulletins about conference members, on the six fundamental shop courses, on the relation of industrial arts to the experimental organization of the school, on the minimum essentials of a curriculum for the professional preparation of teachers, and on graduate study.

Also in March, 1936, Bawden reproduced some of the previous conference suggestions which had been made "for the good of the order" and added his own suggestions. A section of the memorandum is reproduced in full because it provides an insight into the inner workings of the Conference and leads one to a more substantial view of the determination to strive for excellence.

This is too largely a *closed corporation.* We should modify our procedure in some way, to bring about wider dissemination of the valuable ideas and material produced in our meetings.

The *outlines* submitted by speakers are too *condensed;* they are almost meaningless to anyone who did not hear the discussion; they are of relatively little value to us after 30 days. We should encourage the presentation of scholarly papers.

The Conference seems to be drifting away from its unique purpose and function, that of a forum for intensive roundtable discussion of vital problems; and with the reading of papers, it is rapidly approaching the status of *one more convention* to divide our time and money. I hope this drift can be checked.

Our programs are coming more and more to deal with *theories* rather than with the *practical* problems that need to be solved and presented to a group of hungry teachers out in the field. Papers can be had in abundance; but the type of open, frank, constructive, conclusive *discussion,* such as has characterized our Conferences, can be had nowhere else.

Since leaving Chicago, several members have written, protesting against the growing tendency to read papers; also, against the tendency for the assigned speakers to appropriate too much time for the presentation of material, thus leaving too little time for discussion.

Also, objection has been urged against the present plan of building the program from the topics receiving the largest number of "votes" in the referendum; the point being that someone should exercise some discretion is selecting the topics that are most vital and significant to the cause as a whole, rather than those that happen to receive the votes.

The duties of the General Chairman have never been defined; consequently I feel free to announce that the instructions to leaders of discussion for the program of the 1936 Conference will include the following:

1. No speaker will be permitted to read a paper, although any member who cares to do so may submit mimeographed or printed copies of a paper, to be distributed to members.

2. The time allotted to the speakers (or Committee) for opening the discussion will be limited to 45 minutes, the remainder of the time to be available for *discussion* from the floor.

3. Each speaker assigned to a part in opening the discussion will be requested to formulate from three to five *theses,* conclusions, statements, or recommendations, which are to be the basis for his part of the discussion. I believe that a return to this practice, which has proved so satisfactory in the past, will tend to meet the objection that "the outlines are too brief and sketchy;" and will at the same time tend to meet the demand for "papers," by offering an acceptable substitute.

4. Each speaker will submit 100 mimeographed copies of a sheet containing the "theses," together with the same number of copies of any other supporting or amplifying material, as he may elect. This will provide one copy for each Active Member, whether in attendance, or not, also one copy for each Guest, and a few extra copies for good measure.

5. In preparing mimeographed material for distribution, speakers will be requested to follow a uniform style of spacing, paragraphing, and enumerating, in accordance with a Memorandum of Instructions furnished by the Chairman.

*Comment*—If any one of the foregoing provisions is not acceptable to a majority of Active Members, it can and will be changed. It will require just 32 postcards or letters, expressing objection, to eliminate or modify any item. By this simple device, the affairs of the Manual Arts Conference will continue to be adminis-

tered in the most direct and democratic manner possible, and in accordance with the wishes of the Active Members.[16]

Although no evidence is available to show precisely what effect the memorandum had on the members of the Conference, one can deduce that Bawden held a winning hand. Some of his suggestions may not have been accepted at the 1936 meeting, but there can be no question that he stirred up the group to a new level of activity; in that sense, he won.

After the Committee on the Six Fundamental Shop Courses reported on their study, the 32 members present voted as follows for eight subjects to be recommended for the 7th, 8th, and 9th grades.

| | |
|---|---|
| Electricity | 22 |
| Drawing | 22 |
| Graphic Arts | 18 |
| Woodworking | 17 |
| Metalworking | 15 |
| Ceramics and Plastics | 8 |
| Power | 4 |
| Automotives | 4 |

## Bawden Retires as Conference Chairman

Previously, on September 25, 1941, Bawden had sent the following memorandum to each of the active members of the conference:

With great reluctance I have decided that the time has come when I must relinquish the assignment of General Chairman of the Manual Arts Conference. That this step must be taken at some time is inevitable; it seems best to take it now. It is nevertheless a difficult thing to do, for this has been one of the most highly prized honors of my career.[17]

---

[16] *Historical File.* Proceedings, 1934-1941.
[17] *Historical File.*

Bawden appointed a nominating committee consisting of H. J. Smith, Dean C. A. Bowman, and Dean A. F. Siepert to determine his successor as chairman of the Conference. Formal action concerning his request to be relieved as chairman was taken at the Minneapolis conference in the form of the following resolution:

*Whereas,* Dr. William T. Bawden, who has served us as General Chairman for more than a quarter-century, now expresses earnest desire to be relieved of this responsibility, and

*Whereas,* his request seems justifiable in view of all surrounding facts and circumstances,

*Be it Resolved,* Therefore, that Dr. Bawden's desire be honored, that we thank him sincerely for long, arduous, and efficient assistance to us in the work of our great interest, that we take special note of the professional spirit, fairness, and informality that have been engendered and strengthened in us, that this action be made a matter of record in our minutes, and that it be transcribed, for Dr. Bawden, in a form constantly and conveniently to remind him of our pride in his accomplishments and of our gratefulness for his aid.[18]

In addition to the resolution, Bennett was called upon to speak for the Conference in appreciation of Bawden's work. Bennett recalled many of the specific facts of Bawden's career and spoke glowingly of their close association over the years. He pointed to many of the characteristics of Bawden's chairmanship, "his willingness to sacrifice himself" in order that he might render the best possible service, and his dedication to the real values to be obtained from the Conference.

Selecting Bawden's successor was

serious business. The success of the Conference depended largely upon the general chairman and upon his dedication to the task. The nominating committee suggested the following rigorous criteria as appropriate to govern the selection of a new chairman:

The person selected for this position should be—

Good enough in appearance so that he may face us three days a year without incurring our discomfort.

Old enough to have good sense and judgment.

Old enough in the Conference to know its aims and precedents.

Old enough in the group to have absorbed some of Bawden's techniques of managing and presiding.

Young enough to serve us for many years.

Busy enough to understand how an additional load of work may be assumed.

One who will meet us cordially, pep us up, hold us in line with the topic of each session, compose our differences, and send us home eager to meet again.

This is what we have had in our respected long-time leader.

This is what we want for the years just ahead.

The nominating committee submitted its report recommending that Verne C. Fryklund, then associate professor of industrial education, University of Minnesota, be elected as general chairman. The Conference accepted the recommendation unanimously.

## Conferences 1946-1950

No conferences were held during the years of World War II because of restrictions on travel and related complications. The thirty-third conference,

---

[18] *Historical File.*

held in Chicago, November 14-16, 1946, was the first under the chairmanship of Verne C. Fryklund. The meeting was concerned with two main problem areas. The first was a new look at the Conference as an organization. The second involved a number of smaller problems which had developed as a result of the war.

The war had created serious shortages of professionally trained teachers in all areas, but in the area of industrial education the shortage was critical. Emergency methods of teacher recruitment—particularly with regard for the minimum essentials—was one topic of discussion. It was known that many young people were not electing industrial arts as a teaching field, and many former teachers did not return to teaching after the war. The Conference was also concerned with some elements of the surplus war materials which were available in abundance to the schools.

A committee assigned to report upon selected research studies in industrial education compiled a list of 204 such studies. Problems of graduate study in industrial arts and various concepts of graduate work were highlights of the conferences that followed.

Beginning with the 35th conference, in 1948, the identification of "Manual Arts Conference" was dropped and the term "Industrial Arts Conference" was used instead. No official mention is is made of this change of title, but its timeliness is unquestionable since manual arts and manual training belonged to a past age.

Concentrated attention was given to industrial arts as a factor in the general education of youth during the 1948 conference. In a similar manner industrial arts and life adjustment education

found a satisfactory relationship in the discussions. Attention to an almost forgotten area—industrial arts in elementary schools—captured a degree of attention, as did the problem of selecting students for trade preparatory classes.

Problem-solving in industrial arts graduate programs, air-age education, and problems related to the technical, professional, and academic preparation of industrial arts teachers occupied much time during the 1949 and 1950 conferences.

## Conferences 1951-1960

Paraphrasing an earlier description of the annual meetings, it might be said that they represented a "conference of men from institutions in the Mississippi Valley states engaged in teacher education in industrial arts and industrial education." The conditions of membership had been adjusted from time to time so that the teacher education group was augmented by representatives of state departments of education, city schools, and educational journals. But in the main the representation consisted of persons from colleges and universities, who were engaged in teacher education in industrial arts and industrial education. The membership had been fixed at a maximum of 65 which included representatives from 19 states.

A rough classification of the discussion topics of this period indicates that approximately 36 percent were related to teacher education problems, 14 percent to research, 12 percent to graduate programs, and 10 percent to a broader outlook for industrial arts, beyond the limitations of teacher education.

## Teacher Education and Related Topics

Teacher education topics were generally directed toward improvement, upgrading, and change rather than toward a hold-the-line or status-quo point of view. How can we improve our techniques for selecting industrial arts teachers? How can we do a better job of meeting the general education requirements for teachers? How can we best meet the student's individual needs? How can we improve our evaluation of instruction? These were questions commonly raised for discussion.

Examination of the course content and teacher education program in general was pursued with questions or topics such as: How should we determine the content of industrial arts courses? What subject matter areas are essential in the preparation of industrial arts teachers? What changes in content must be made to meet the needs of the technological age? What mathematics and science requirements should we have? How do we bridge the gap between theory and practice? Many of these questions had been frequently discussed in the conferences of past decades. However, since the Conference members were sensitive to the effects of social change, growing industrialism, and increased school enrollment, they felt the need to reexamine certain problems which had been temporarily solved or put aside.

## Research

It had been the practice of the conference to keep reasonably well informed on the progress of research in industrial education. Accordingly the programs provided for reports of recent research, particularly that which was of significance to industrial teacher education. Critical areas of industrial arts in which research was needed were studied by committees. The Conference did not limit its interest to what had been done, or what should be done in its own field, but desired to learn the implications for industrial arts of research in teacher education in general.

## Graduate Programs

The Conference was greatly concerned with the growth, content, and direction of graduate programs in industrial education. Many reports and surveys were made for the benefit of the group, reporting such things as the degree to which the needs of industrial arts teachers were being met by graduate programs, the upgrading of in-service teachers by graduate programs, and comparisons and generalizations concerning programs for the master's and doctor's degrees. On at least two occasions the Conference investigated the problem of using shopwork for graduate credit. Specifically their concern was with the problem of dignifying shopwork so that it could become acceptable in graduate schools.

## The Broad Outlook

Industrial arts programs in colleges and universities had been largely dedicated to the preparation of teachers of industrial arts, but there was evidence to indicate that industrial arts teacher education institutions possibly had a much broader responsibility. With this possibility in mind the Conference members took up such topics as: (1) To what extent are industrial arts and industrial education departments offering degrees and courses that do not qualify graduates to teach but prepare them for industry? (2) Many graduates of industrial arts programs enter industry; therefore, should training for industrial education teachers be broadened to include preparation for industrial employment? (3) What additional characteristics of a technological society should be reflected in a program of industrial arts? (4) What contributions can industrial arts make in a program of accelerated scientific education? (5) To what extent should industrial arts serve engineering, technician training, or other special industrial needs? [19]

### Other Conference Concerns

*Professional organizations and professional relationships* were included frequently in the 1951-1960 discussions. The Conference considered the functions of the professional associations in industrial education and reviewed the need for a separate national professional organization for industrial arts teachers, which, of course, was in existence. Implied in these discussions was fear that the growing number of professional organizations and splinter groups would actually weaken the cause of industrial education. At one conference the question was raised: How important is it whether we call industrial arts general education or vocational education? The feeling seemed to be that the most important questions were: How useful is industrial arts, and exactly how is it taught?

*The promotion and development of industrial arts in elementary education*

were discussed. Recommendations were made concerning rooms and equipment considered essential for such classes in the elementary school.

*Communications and public relations* were also frequent discussion topics. A portion of such discussion was related to the nature of public relations and to the necessity for the industrial arts teacher to become aware of his responsibilities in this area. In addition there were discussions of two persistent problems which had escaped solution: What does the school administrator need to know about industrial education so that he may better supervise his teachers in the field? How can industrial educators do an effective job of informing administrators, guidance personnel, and academic teachers of the learning advantages to be gained through industrial arts?

*State supervision* of industrial arts was discussed. Attention was paid to those states which had an industrial arts educator to supervise this type of education as well as to those where the supervision was done by the state supervisor of trade and industrial education.

### Fryklund Retires as General Chairman

Verne C. Fryklund retired as president of Stout State College on September 1, 1961, and moved first to Santa Monica, California, and later to San Clemente, California. He had been the general chairman of the Industrial Arts

---

[19] History does seem to have a way of repeating itself. Around the turn of the century manual training leaders had noticed that a large number of the high school graduates were going directly to work. Their action created, in part, the area of trade and industrial education to support vocational needs, and manual training dropped primary responsibility for vocations. Again, in the 1950's it became apparent that many persons trained for industrial arts actually enter industry.

Conference for twenty years. Fryklund presided for the last time at the 48th conference in Chicago, November 9-11, 1961. To succeed him, the Conference selected Hoyt H. London, Head of the Department of Industrial Education, University of Missouri.

The Industrial Arts Conference membership list, corrected to November 20, 1959, identified 188 persons who had participated in Conference activities; active members, 63; associated members, 51; former active members, 25; former active members deceased, 49.

## Postscript

### Death of Robert Washington Selvidge

The death of Robert W. Selvidge on November 16, 1941, at age sixty-nine, represented a loss of one of the main strengths and sources of inspiration of the Conference. The Conference had existed because of Selvidge's vision that the intensive, informal discussion of a small group of key persons in the area of manual arts would provide ways of solving problems. Eight members of the Conference attended the funeral in Columbia, Missouri, on November 18. In addition, many leaders of industrial education were in attendance. Selvidge was one of the twelve charter members of the Conference and the first of three prime movers (with Bennett and Bawden) to pass away.

Selvidge apparently had a real understanding of the responsibility compelling persons in the area of industrial education toward improving the quality of that education. Evidently he longed to find people with the ability to make realistic appraisals of the industrial education program and the courage to do something constructive about its needs. In his very first discussion at the conference in 1909 he had talked about "Our Unscientific Attitude" and dared to challenge the group with such statements as: "The greatest trouble right now is not that the people are unconvinced or unwilling, but that *we* don't know what we are talking about," and "Only on account of reverence for the dead do we have a crowded curriculum, and *no time* to do what needs to be done," and, "We should be careful to have reasons rather than excuses for what we are doing." His ability to get at the heart of a problem and to work with important aspects undoubtedly went a long way in creating that vast army of friends who paid him the final tribute in November, 1941.

During the conference only a month before, in Minneapolis, the chairman had been authorized to send a telegram to Selvidge as follows:

Members of Manual Arts Conference assembled University Minnesota regret illness prevents you from being here and send this greeting to express hope you may be cheered by memories of years of outstanding service and best wishes of devoted friends.

Later in the day (October 24) the following telegram was received from Selvidge:

I greatly appreciate your message from the Conference. I want to assure you that in all these years no one has received greater pleasure from it than I have. I am hoping that it will continue to give the same degree of happiness and pleasure that it has in the past.[20]

---

[20] *Historical File.*

And thus in his final days a great leader continued to urge the pursuit of things good for industrial education.

## Death of Charles Alpheus Bennett[21]

On Wednesday, June 17, 1942, the second of the Conference's "prime movers" passed away. Charles A. Bennett, who was seventy-eight at the time of his death, had been instrumental in organizing the first conference in 1909 and had attended twenty-nine of the thirty-two meetings held proir to his death. Ill health prevented his attendance in 1938, 1939, and 1940; however, upon learning that Bawden had planned to resign as chairman, Bennett resolved to attend the 1941 conference, and did so.

Bennett had been a participant at each of the conferences, performing his leadership role in various capacities. Most significantly, it was Bennett who, in the final summary session, outlined for the Conference what had taken place. The thirty-two conferences had been an inseparable part of his life. He was indeed the "Dean of Manual Arts" through this phase of his professional career.

## Death of William Thomas Bawden[22]

The last of the triumvirate, William T. Bawden, passed away at his home in Santa Barbara, California, on Wednesday, April 27, 1960, at the age of eighty-four. The story of his professional life, like those of his conference colleagues, is itself a history of industrial education. He had served as a teacher, teacher educator, school administrator, writer, and editor. His experience and his personality influenced the Manual Arts Conference for nearly a half-century.

His death was the occasion for many tributes from industrial educators throughout the nation who vied with each other to tell of Bawden's achievements and influence. Selvidge, Bennett, and Bawden had faith in the power of people in industrial education, and the conferences had been a sounding board for critical analysis and a briefing room for ventures into the future largely because of this doctrine.

### Summary

Professional associations provided an opportunity for industrial educators to share ideas in general, but seemed not to provide an opportunity for close review of specific issues: details of teacher education, for example. It was this problem that Bennett and Selvidge had in mind when the first meeting of teacher educators for manual training was called in 1909.

The first significant conference was held in 1913. The questions raised, the resolutions adopted, and the general conclusions reached represented a consensus that could have immediate impact upon the development of teacher education. The conference in 1914 was no less significant and represented a

---

[21] For a comprehensive study of the life and professional contributions of Charles A. Bennett, see: Gerald K. Hammer, "Charles Alpheus Bennett, Dean of Manual Arts," (Unpublished doctoral dissertation, University of California, Los Angeles), June 1962.

[22] I cannot resist a personal note. Bawden was associate superintendent of schools in Tulsa, Oklahoma, during the years I was a student at the Tulsa Central High School. Bawden was known to all of the students in industrial education. It was possible at that time, probably due to his leadership, to take an industrial arts course each semester and still go on to college— all this and heaven too!

more determined effort to capitalize upon group experiences in reaching patterns for improvement in teacher education.

During the next decade and a half, the group continued to meet annually. The group was small, long speeches were not permitted, and free exchange of thought became the strength of the conferences. Beginning in 1915, and upon request of the group, the conferences were called by the U.S. Commissioner of Education. Reports from the conferences were printed by the Commissioner of Education for general distribution.

On the occasion of the twentieth anniversary, members of the Conference took stock of their progress. Over the years their discussions had the central theme of improving teacher education, but many related issues had been introduced. A review of this work was prepared by Bawden and issued by the Manual Arts Press under the title of *Twenty Years of Progress in the Manual Arts.*

The conferences after 1930 continued in the same spirit as previously; attention to contemporary problems, and reaching a consensus about courses of action. It might be said that a new ingredient—looking into the future—was characteristic of the meetings after 1930; however, it should not be inferred that the group ever had its attention fixed solely on the past. Early in the record of the Mississippi Valley Conference the group had respected the value of research and had devoted time to a study of previous research. In 1933 an annotated list of 800 graduate theses and dissertations (1892-1933) was compiled and made available to the members of the Conference.

The significance of the Conference can be easily overlooked by students of industrial education because there have been few analyses made of its activities; relationship of the Conference to progress of industrial education is therefore not well known. One obstacle to the professional advancement of manual and industrial arts had been the lack of a "home base" in a professional sense. Several professional associations had made contributions to the progress of industrial arts, but a central organization wholly dedicated to industrial arts did not exist. In one sense the Mississippi Valley Conference served as a central coordinating agency after 1909. [The assumption that the American Industrial Arts Association, after 1939, became the recognized central agency for Industrial Arts seems obvious.]

Focus of attention upon Selvidge, Bennett, and Bawden is justified because they nurtured professional advancement in industrial arts. They were the ring-leaders in the Mississippi Valley Conference during the early years. Where one was making a concerted effort on some phase of industrial arts, the tracks of the other two could usually be found.

The professional equivalent of the Mississippi Valley Conference for the vocational phase of industrial education during the period 1917-1933 was vested in the Federal Board for Vocational Education. The coming of age of trade and technical education, stimulated by the central agency represented by the Federal Board for Vocational Education, is the next step in the general analysis of the history of industrial education in the United States.

## Recall Questions

1. What was the rationale that led to the organization of the Mississippi Valley Conference?

2. What key items were considered in the 1913 and 1914 conferences? How are these related to contemporary problems?

3. In what ways did the conferences contribute to the professionalization of industrial arts, 1909-1960?

## Research Questions

1. Review the Industrial Education Circulars published by the U.S. Office of Education, 1915-1930, and make a list of the major contributions to industrial arts originating in the discussions of the Mississippi Valley Conference.

2. Read Bawden's *Twenty Years of Progress in the Manual Arts* and determine which, if any, of the major values of industrial arts, as identified in 1930, have been disproven by contemporary attitudes and practices.

## Suggestions for Further Reading

Bawden, William T., *Twenty Years of Progress in the Manual Arts.* Peoria, Illinois: The Manual Arts Press, 1930.

U.S. Department of the Interior, Bureau of Education, *Industrial Education Circulars.*

# Chapter 6

# Federal Board for Vocational Education

First Organizational Activities of the Federal Board · Conferences with the States · First Policies of the Federal Board, 1917 · The Board as an Example of Federal-State Relations · The Federal Board, 1921–1925 · The Federal Board, 1926–1932 · Demise of the Federal Board · Postscript · Summary · Recall Questions · Research Questions · Suggestions for Further Reading

The long campaign to gain federal aid for vocational education was intensified early in 1916. Committees of Congress had moved slowly with certain aspects of the proposed Smith-Hughes bill, particularly with the provision for a Federal Board for Vocational Education. Several amendments had been proposed in an effort to clarify the purpose, function, and organization of the Federal Board. The National Society for the Promotion of Industrial Education, the American Home Economics Association, the National Association of Manufacturers, and the American Federation of Labor all endorsed the idea of a representative board, and in 1914 the Commission on National Aid to Vocational Education had recommended the establishment of such a board.

At this point in the campaign the United States Chamber of Commerce delivered a master stroke. First, its education committee submitted a favorable report on federal aid for vocational education, and second, in April, 1916, the Chamber sponsored a nationwide referendum on the subject. The Chamber's resolutions concerning a federal board were endorsed with enthusiasm. Only 12 states cast negative votes, and in these instances the maximum opposition was 42 percent. In effect this endorsement became a mandate that Congress could not overlook. By July both the Senate and the House had reached an agreement concerning the nature of the proposed board.

One of the stumbling blocks was the unusual provision that it be almost entirely independent, responsible only to

Congress. This became so controversial that it developed into a prime target for criticism. However, the attitude of the Commissioner of Education, Philander P. Claxton, contributed toward establishing an independent board by eliminating a possible alternative. Claxton took the position that the staff of the U.S. Office of Education was not properly constituted to administer the provisions of the Act.

Therefore, the Smith-Hughes Act provided for the appointment of a Federal Board for Vocational Education to administer the provisions of the Act. The seven-member Board consisted of four ex-officio members (the Secretaries of Labor, Commerce, and Agriculture, and the Commissioner of Education) and three additional members to be appointed by the President. On June 29, 1917, Arthur E. Holder, representing labor; Charles H. Greathouse, representing agriculture; and James P. Munroe, representing manufacturing and commerce, were appointed by President Woodrow Wilson. These appointments were later confirmed by the Senate. The ex-officio members of the Board were David F. Houston, chairman, Secretary of Agriculture; William C. Radfield, Secretary of Commerce; William B. Wilson, Secretary of Labor; and Philander P. Claxton, Commissioner of Education. On July 21, 1917, the Board met for the first time in Washington, D.C.

The American people, through their representatives in the Congress, had accepted as a public responsibility the vocational preparation of a large group of workers and youths preparing to become workers. Funds to promote and develop vocational education and consultative services from state boards of vocational education, were the inducements offered to public schools which facilitated their acceptance of the challenge.

The first task confronting the Board was the preparation of a plan of organization to encompass appropriate working relationships with the states. Although the Smith-Hughes Act was quite specific with regard to the intent of Congress, many operational details were reserved for the Board to develop. The Board's second major task was the development of general policy for the operation of the vocational programs.

## First Organizational Activities of the Federal Board

The Board's unanimous choice for chief executive officer was Charles A. Prosser, director of the William Hood Dunwoody Institute in Minneapolis. Prosser met with the Board on July 30 and subsequently made arrangements for a leave of absence from his position. The Board also appointed directors for the fields of agricultural education, industrial education, home economics education, and research. Lewis H. Carris, of Trenton, New Jersey, was appointed assistant director for industrial education.

In order to provide the service required by the Smith-Hughes Act, the Board divided the country into five regions: North Atlantic, Southern, North Central, West Central, and Pacific. An agent was assigned to each region, and made his headquarters in a centrally located city. The regional agents appointed to represent industrial education were: Harry B. Smith, New York City; Roy Dimmitt, Atlanta; Robert J. Leonard, Indianapolis; J. C.

Wright, Kansas City; and Benjamin W. Johnson, San Francisco. All appointees had occupied positions of trust in their respective states and brought to the Federal Board a valuable background of experience in teaching and administration.

The basic activity of the Board was of course supervising the expenditure of federal funds according to the principles of the Act.[1] Supervision was accomplished through reviews of reports from the states and from the regional agents. Supervision was limited to determining whether the states had complied with the provisions of the Act. Although the Federal Board had no dictatorial powers, it did have the right to disapprove.

In addition to the responsibility for supervision, the Board also made studies and investigations, and prepared reports which would be useful to the states in promoting and developing their programs. By October 1, 1917, the staff numbered 47. With a staff of this size, the Board could turn its attention, in part, to preparing studies and investigating the progress of and need for vocational education in particular geographical areas and for specific occupational groups. The results were published and distributed to the states. During its first four years the Board produced 68 bulletins, including 29 on trade and industrial subjects.

## Conferences with the States

The Smith-Hughes Act represented a scheme of cooperation between the federal government and the individual states. The Act had made provisions for this cooperative arrangement to extend to the fields of agriculture, home economics, and the trades and industries. The cooperative arrangement was based upon four fundamental ideas:

First, that vocational education being essential to the national welfare, it is a function of the National Government to stimulate the States to undertake this new and needed form of service; second, that Federal funds are necessary in order to equalize the burden of carrying on the work among the States; third, that since the Federal Government is vitally interested in the success of vocational education, it should, so to speak, purchase a degree of participation in this work; and, fourth, that only by creating such a relationship between the central and the local Governments can proper standards of educational efficiency be set up.[2]

A conference with representatives of the states was held by the Federal Board during the period August 17-28, 1917. The purposes and general principles of the law were discussed with each representative. It was imperative that the states understand clearly the fundamentals involved. A stenographic record of each discussion was given to the representative so that both the Board and the state would know precisely the agreements which had been reached. The nature of these discussions can be seen by referring to records of the conference with the California representative.

Will C. Wood, Commissioner of Secondary Schools for the State of California, met with the Federal Board

---

[1] The Federal Board for Vocational Education was also responsible for the vocational rehabilitation of disabled persons. This phase of activity is not treated here because it does not pertain to this study.

[2] Federal Board for Vocational Education, *Statement of Policies, Bulletin No. 1*. Washington: Government Printing Office, 1917, p. 6.

on the afternoon of August 23, 1917. Prosser outlined in specific detail the provisions which must be included in the contractual agreement between the state and the federal government in order that the state might receive federal funds in support of the vocational program proposed in its plan. During the discussion of teacher training, Prosser said:

The whole success of this matter depends upon two things—proper supervision and proper teachers, properly trained teachers; and we are urging States to put their energies as far as possible into those two things.[3]

Prosser probed deeply into the small operating details of the California plan, with emphasis upon the teacher and his qualifications. For example:

Prosser: Suppose I wanted to be a teacher of machine shop practice in California and I went to your office; what would you say I would have to be now?

Wood: For machine shop practice you would have to show first of all a common school education or the equivalent. We would have to be satisfied that your use of English was satisfactory.

Prosser: Suppose I said "ain't" once in a while?

Wood: Well, I am inclined to think you would be turned down, unless you could show that you were an exceptional teacher of a mechanical art. We are not so strict on that line that we cannot overlook things of that kind, but we do desire that our employees shall use language that is ordinarily satisfactory, anyway. In addition to that we would require that you show, I should say, six years of work as a journeyman in addition to an apprenticeship.[4]

It was obvious that Prosser wanted to be of real assistance to the states as

plans were prepared, but at the same time the Board made no attempt to control the nature of the plan. It was the Board's opinion that each plan should reflect the unique problems and practices of the state concerned and should not become difficult to administer because of a burden imposed by the federal group.

## First Policies of the Federal Board, 1917

In November, 1917, the Federal Board for Vocational Education issued its first policy bulletin. The Board interpreted its role as that of assisting the states to "extend and democratize" their programs of secondary education by adding to the curriculum a program of broad practical training. The bulletin was intended to guide the states in conducting their programs. It was necessary that the state plans meet the minimum requirements of the Act, or as the Board indicated, that they be "in conformity with the spirit and purpose" of the Act. Standards, therefore, could be determined partly through the Act, partly through the activities of the Board, and partly through the state plans. Agreement between the Board and the state representatives was essential for vocational education to function effectively.

Policy Bulletin No. 1 provided an overview of the administrative structure of the Federal Board. It restated certain key sections of the Smith-Hughes Act, followed by the Board's interpretation of the meaning of the

---

[3] "California," *Federal Board for Vocational Education Conference With State Boards for States Accepting the Act of February 23, 1917.* Washington, D.C.: U.S. Office of Education, August 23, 1917, p. 12.

[4] *Ibid.*, p. 20.

section. One section, which was certainly fundamental, yet apt to be misunderstood, concerned the group of persons for whom vocational education was intended.

The Federal board desires to emphasize the fact that vocational schools and classes are not fostered under the Smith-Hughes Act for the purpose of giving instruction to the backward, deficient, incorrigible, or otherwise subnormal individuals; but that such schools and classes are to be established and maintained for the clearly avowed purpose of giving thorough vocational instruction to healthy, normal individuals to the end that they may be prepared for profitable and efficient employment. Such education should command the best efforts of normal boys and girls.[5]

Ten items relating to the program of industrial education were included in the policy bulletin in the form of questions and answers. These policies and interpretations are paraphrased as follows:

- The minimum age for entrance in the all-day program was 14 years; this presumed that the persons were capable, both physically and mentally, to do the work.
- Students enrolled in classes in cooperation with industry were considered to be enrolled in an all-day school, provided that the shop work and the class work were coordinated and were under the general supervision of a school instructor.
- The all-day school was intended to follow the general nine-month school year.
- An "hour" was interpreted to be a clock hour of sixty minutes rather than the variable school "period."
- The work of the school shop was assumed to meet the requirements of "useful or productive basis" when the

work compared favorably in economic value with products completed in a shop or factory. In other words the school shop should resemble a regular shop in as many aspects as possible.

- "Industrial subjects" were interpreted broadly as the work inherent in the occupation that enlarges the trade knowledge of the worker. For example, in a printing class, related subjects such as English for printers, art in printing, estimating costs, science related to printing, and hygiene of the trade would be representative of industrial subjects appropriate for reimbursement. It was the policy of the Board that such classes should be taught by a teacher who had satisfactory experience in the trade.
- The Board emphasized that evening industrial programs must not enroll persons under the age of 16.
- The instruction in "evening industrial schools" must be confined to that which supplemented the daily employment of the individual.
- Money from the Smith-Hughes Act was provided to pay in part the salaries of instructors of part-time schools or classes providing instruction for working boys and girls. Such instruction was intended to increase the knowledge of the worker in his occupation.
- The funds also supported courses which gave eligibility for promotion and which improved the worker's knowledge of subjects that he did not complete in school, particularly subjects that tended to increase civic or vocational intelligence.

## The Board as an Example of Federal - State Relations

Administration of the Smith-Hughes Act by the Federal Board for Vocational Education created a new kind of relationship between the federal government and the states. The Morrill

---

[5] Bulletin No. 1, *op. cit.*, p. 17.

Acts, which had allocated federal money for vocational education at college level, had provided that the federal government deal directly with one or two institutions in any particular state. But the Smith-Hughes Act provided money for the promotion and development of vocational education in the secondary schools, and because of the complexity of educational organization throughout the country, it was necessary that the federal government deal only with one Board of Control within each state, not with individual schools directly. The Federal Board thus intended to direct all its official activities with any one state to the Board for Vocational Education of that state. Far from enslaving vocational education to federal control, this form of administration has promoted the free working of the democratic process, a condition in which vocational education has thrived.

Within the minimum limits of the Act and of the plan that each state prepared, the states had a number of responsibilities. For example, the state had to select the institutions to provide teacher training, and determine whether the courses in local schools met the requirements of the Act and the plan. Controversies within a state were matters to be settled by the State Board. Although both the state and the federal governments were responsible for seeing that money was used as efficiently as possible, the Federal Board was concerned "only with the question of whether or not the State Board is subletting the contract of vocational education and training voca-

tional teachers as the work done according to the plan which it proposed and which the Federal Board approved." [6] So in 1918 the Federal Board for Vocational Education restated its position in the administrative scheme and emphasized the states' responsibility and control.

As stated, agents of the Federal Board had been assigned to each of the five regions to facilitate the orderly promotion and development of vocational education through a closer relationship with the state boards. Among the agents' responsibilities was that of gathering data and statistics concerning the growth of the program. For the year ending June 30, 1918, reports indicated that 121,812 students were enrolled in the trade and industrial program. They were taught by 3,276 teachers. In addition, 45 teacher training centers had been established with a total staff of 95 teacher trainers.

When the National Society for Vocational Education held its annual convention in Philadelphia, February 21-23, 1918, the Smith-Hughes Act was one year old. Naturally, a major portion of the program was devoted to the experiences of the first year with the national program of federal aid to vocational education. Three members of the Federal Board addressed the convention. One of them was Lewis H. Carris, assistant director for industrial education. Carris devoted his entire speech to the subject of training teachers for trade and industrial instruction. While providing little, if any, new information, Carris did review thoroughly the principles he considered

[6] Federal Board for Vocational Education, *Second Annual Report, 1918.* Washington: Government Printing Office, 1918, p. 15.

relevant. In particular he emphasized the relationship of teacher training to certification:

In order to make the teacher-training scheme effective, it will be necessary to have the very closest coordination of this work with any scheme of certification which legalizes the employment of teachers in Federal aided vocational schools.[7]

This point of view was representative of the relationships that had developed in many of the states.

The 1919 report of the Federal Board presented evidence that progress had been made in every phase of the vocational program. But with progress a number of new problems developed, the solution of which required closer relationships with the states. Prior to the passage of the Smith-Hughes Act only a few state boards had any experience, on a statewide basis, with vocational education in the secondary schools. While the Federal Board recognized its responsibility to assist state boards, the 1919 report declared emphatically that, "Promotion of vocational education within a State is primarily the task of the State Board for vocational education of that state." Regional agents provided assistance to state boards and would, upon request from a state official, participate in state or local meetings in order to provide these groups with the benefit of their experience. As the program of vocational education grew, the states depended more and more upon assistance from the Federal Board.

Prosser addressed the National Society for Vocational Education in 1919 and brought to the attention of the Society some of the salient points con-cerning policies and problems of administering the Smith-Hughes Act. Apparently the roles of the state and federal governments in matters of vocational education were easily misunderstood. Prosser emphasized the democratic nature of the relationship: The Board was not a "one man" power, bending all to its will. Such an autocratic point of view would be foredoomed to failure. Such power, he said, "wouldn't last any longer than a cake of ice on a New York pavement on a July day."

Two state superintendents responded to Prosser's statement. R. O. Small of Massachusetts indicated that he felt no special obligation to the Board, that Massachusetts had conducted and would continue to conduct an exemplary program of vocational education. However, his experience was that the Federal Board had not interfered in the program, had given "considerable help," so that the Commonwealth of Massachusetts was altogether pleased with the relationship. Superintendent C. P. Cary of Wisconsin, on the other hand, was not quite so pleased: The regularly constituted educational machinery of the state had been by-passed in the matter of selecting a state board for vocational education.

Certain inexperienced men were suddenly chosen to be wiseacres in the matter of vocational education—men who had never given any consecutive thought to education were brought together to constitute a State Board. Now, these were very good gentlemen in their way, but their way is not the way of education. They do not know any more about education than any other group of intelligent people that you might chance to meet; but

---

[7] National Society for Vocational Education, *Problems of Administering the Federal Act for Vocational Education*, Bulletin No. 26, May 1918, p. 26.

suddenly they are invested with this power to carry on educational work in Wisconsin. They did not know whether they were afoot or a-horseback.[8]

Cary wanted the Smith-Hughes Law changed so that the states would be forced to recognize for this purpose the educational authorities already existing within these boundaries.

In order to provide more attention to the states' problems and to clarify its relationships with the states, the Federal Board held a national conference in St. Louis in February, 1919, the day previous to the annual meeting of the National Society for Vocational Education. In the months that followed, similar meetings were held in each of the regions. Experience during the formative period of vocational education demonstrated to the Board the necessity for frequent group and individual conferences. At first the Board regarded these meetings as a means of receiving guidance from the states. However, when the Act and its provisions became more generally understood by all states, the meetings became largely a means of sharing experiences among state representatives. The benefit to the national program from the cooperative work of the states and the Federal Board in conference was readily apparent. This cooperative arrangement in working out problems and planning for the future has continued to be one of the real strengths of the vocational education movement in the United States.

By the end of the fiscal year 1919, advances had been noted in state supervision of trade and industrial education. Twenty states were employing full-time supervisors. The quality and quantity of classes meeting industrial needs had grown, with the largest increase in enrollment in the part-time and evening schools. Teacher training programs had increased over the nation, as had the general understanding of the meaning of vocational education. Summation of the advances also brought clearly into focus the vast underdeveloped areas of trade and industrial education. These areas employed large numbers of persons in need of the educational benefits provided by the state under the provisions of the Federal Act. The 11,000,000 wage-earning women in the labor force in 1919 constituted an educational problem of immediate concern.

The economic loss both to the worker and employer which results from permitting great numbers of girls and women to enter the industrial world without skill, training, or other preparation—there to shift for themselves as best they may—is focusing the attention of the public on the need for trade and industrial training for girls and women.[9]

In 1919, an expanding industry viewed the woman worker as "destined to become an increasingly important factor" in the growth of the national economy. Her industrial training needs became concerns of the national program of vocational education. [See Chapter 12.]

In its 1920 report, the Board provided data concerning the gains, both in breadth and depth, of the program

[8] National Society for Vocational Education, *Lessons of the War, the States and the Smith-Hughes Act*, Bulletin No. 28, June 1919, p. 54.

[9] Federal Board for Vocational Education, *Third Annual Report, 1919*, Vol. I, Vocational Education. Washington: Government Printing Office, 1919, p. 66.

of trade and industrial education throughout the nation. Special attention was given to the services that the federal group had been able to provide for state boards. These services were summarized in four different categories.

First were the services related to the training of trade and industrial teachers. The Board considered these services "an extremely important part" of its work. Although skilled craftsmen were selected as teachers for the trade and industrial subjects, the mere possession of occupational skill did not help the craftsman to understand the principles and practices of "the teaching trade." The Board held conferences and distributed materials to be used in training craftsmen to teach. Graduates of teacher training courses were known to be generally superior as teachers to craftsmen who did not have the benefit of such instruction.

The second service was concerned with the preparation of educational trade analyses. Much of this service, available through regional conferences, consisted in providing the states with methods of preparing analyses which would accurately identify various aspects of the teachable content of a trade. In addition the Board made analyses of a number of trade areas and distributed this information to the states. The reception given to these bulletins by the states was most gratifying.

The third service was concerned with foreman training. The Board provided a format for the content and methods of conducting foreman training conferences. The purposes of such conferences were obvious, since improvement of the foreman in relation to his job was of great concern to industry. Employees of State Boards for Vocational Education conducted hundreds of foreman conferences in industry. Problems studied, reviewed, and solved in such conferences were directly related to improving the efficiency of industrial production. Development of this activity throughout the nation firmly established a desirable rapport between industry and public education.

The fourth service of the Federal Board was in connection with developing simple and inexpensive methods of conducting local surveys in order to secure information about industrial employment and training needs. This enabled schools to correlate more effectively with the industrial community.

Charles A. Prosser served as director of the Federal Board for Vocational Education from August 15, 1917, to November 1, 1919, at which time he returned to his position at Dunwoody Institute. The Board did not appoint a new director until July 1, 1920. L. S. Hawkins, as Assistant Director for the Vocational Division, reported directly to the Board, as did Uel W. Lamkin for the Rehabilitation Division. Mr. Lamkin was appointed director on July 1, 1920, and served until August 10, 1921.

## The Federal Board, 1921-1925

The Federal Board was constantly alert to its proper role in relationship to state governments. The principle of federal grants-in-aid for practical education had become a matter of permanent national policy. It therefore became a proper function of the federal government to cooperate with the states in the effort "to make popular public-school education purposeful and useful, to enrich its content and practical value, to make it democratic and universal, and by so doing to make it effective for the promotion of public welfare and good citizenship." [10]

Consequently, during the early 1920's the Federal Board was unusually attentive to its responsibility of service to the states, in order that promotion and development of industrial education could be maximized. State supervision improved and increased; regional conferences were held with increased attendance and with evidence of greater perception of the vocational problem in the various areas; foreman and instructor training grew rapidly in each region; and industrial education for girls and women extended beyond the traditional trades for women and moved into the mechanical and manufacturing industries.

By 1922 the Federal Board could report with justification that the program promoted in the interests of industrial workers was indeed meeting the needs of workers in many ways. [11] An opportunity had been provided wherein the worker could improve his "intellectual attainment." More general participation in "citizenship problems of democracy" was noted in many areas of the nation. The economic value of industrial education, both to the individual and to society, in itself proved the worth of the program. Labor and education had found a practical com-bination—a direct contradiction to the "mudsill" theory, which assumed that labor and education were incompatible.

In June, 1922, the *Newsletter* of the National Society for Vocational Education reported on the accomplishments of the Federal Board during its first five years. [12] The *Newsletter* indicated that the publications of the Board had been "extremely helpful," being used by thousands of people. The Board was complimented for its many conferences with state officials and teachers and for its recognition of the needs in special fields of vocational education. The *Newsletter* concluded as follows:

The Federal Board for Vocational Education, coming into service after some ten years active campaigning by social economists, business men, organized labor, and educators, for more extended vocational education under public support, fell heir to a host of partially formulated aspirations and proposals. It gave them shape and organized them to meet administrative conditions. The Board was in a favorable situation to effect a large amount of educational experimentation and testing. Its accomplishments constitute one of the outstanding facts in the history of American Education. [13]

The functions of the Federal Board had been determined to fall within three classifications: (1) efficient administration of the Federal funds; (2) research and studies to promote and improve vocational education; and (3) assistance to the states in their promotion and development activities.

---

[10] Federal Board for Vocational Education, *Fifth Annual Report, 1921.* Washington: Government Printing Office, 1921, p. 20.

[11] Federal Board for Vocational Education, *Sixth Annual Report, 1922.* Washington: Government Printing Office, 1922, p. 57.

[12] This was a report of a special committee of the Society, probably issued as a defense of the Federal Board. The Board had been under attack by a number of individuals over its activities in vocational rehabilitation.

[13] National Society for Vocational Education, *Newsletter,* June 1922, p. 12.

The 1924 report of the Board gave specific attention to these three functions.[14] The first and third functions had been previously reviewed by the Board as a regular reporting feature. But the function of research had to wait until the administrative and working relationships had become stabilized. The purpose of the Board's research program was simply one of securing information and experience which would be of assistance to the states. It was a matter of policy with the Board that such research was intended to be largely experimental so that it could result in proven methods. In many instances the Board's experimental research program was worked out in cooperation with one or more states. By the end of 1924, the Board had issued 23 bulletins in trade and industrial education reporting research and investigation projects. Demand from the states for this information was so large that it was necessary to reprint a number of the bulletins.

The Board's report in 1925 emphasized the improvement previously noted in the teacher training program for trade and industrial education. Earlier plans had not been effective, but a general readjustment of teacher training had contributed materially to the total growth. Even in 1925, with particular attention to teacher training, the Board reported that the most effective plans had not been achieved, and the whole matter of teacher training required considerable experimentation and research.

As has been said, the Board provided service to the states by direct assistance through training conferences and "intensive schools of instruction" and by indirect relationships with state boards and teacher training institutions.

It had been the practice of the Federal Board to hold two- or three-day conferences prior to the annual conventions of the national societies. The rationale behind this practice was perfectly reasonable, but the number of conferences the federal body was called upon to organize had grown to proportions that were not reasonable; thus it became necessary to make some reductions. So in the fall of 1924, the Board announced a series of just three regional conferences for July and August, 1925. The significant part of the arrangement was the length of the conferences. Instead of two or three days, the conferences were planned for two weeks' duration. The Federal Board was moving deliberately toward using the conferences as schools of instruction. They were specially designed for state supervisors, teacher trainers, and city directors. Based on seminar and conference plans, they were organized so the members were involved in "not less than 70 hours of intensive work." This was a bold but imperative move, by which the Board demonstrated both leadership and democratic orientation.

The Board also reported numerous special developments secured in trade and industrial education during the year.[15] Special training conferences, development of apprenticeship, extension

---

[14] Federal Board for Vocational Education, *Eighth Annual Report, 1924.* Washington: Government Printing Office, 1924, pp. 6-31.

[15] Federal Board for Vocational Education, *Ninth Annual Report, 1925.* Washington: Government Printing Office, 1925, pp. 88-89.

of foreman training conferences to newer industries, new trade schools, new short-unit courses, and other ventures testified to real accomplishment. The Board's directory of organized training indicated that federal aid had been provided in support of training for 146 different lines of work.

On August 11, 1921, the directorship of the Federal Board passed from U. W. Lamkin to J. C. Wright, who began a 24-year tenure. His four years of experience prior to becoming director were in trade and industrial education.

### The Federal Board, 1926-1932

The report to Congress in 1926 emphasized the results of nine years' performance. Little change in administrative relationships with the states had taken place during the fiscal year of 1926. The operating relationships had become reasonably stabilized so that routine procedures freed the personnel of the Board for attention to other aspects of national concern in vocational education. The Board detected among the states a broader conception of the service they were responsible for. This was thought to be evidence of a healthy condition for program growth. Labor had participated to a greater degree in contributing knowledge and service toward effective program growth. Some states, evidently without prodding from the Federal Board, had devised schemes of itinerant teacher training to assist the isolated instructor.

In 1927, the Board included in its report a rather short discussion of what

actually became one of its chief contributions—that of standards. The Board contrasted early program development stages with later development stages. In the first stage the orientation was one of "accomplishing the result somehow," but during the second stage the emphasis was upon "securing of results with some degree of efficiency." The Board's desire to apply principles of "efficiency engineering" found eager acceptance in the states. However, there were practices that alarmed the Board. For example, it was a fundamental principle with the federal group that the instructor must be a competent craftsman. In general education this fundamental was measured by the possession of academic degrees. A distinct tendency to carry the latter point of view into vocational education seemed a danger signal that program standards would suffer.

The Board believes that should the time ever come when vocational programs will be conducted by individuals who have been selected on the basis of their academic degrees rather than on the basis of mastery of their occupations, vocational education of the type contemplated under the national vocational education act will become inefficient and will fail to render the social service which Congress and the framers of the act intended should be rendered.[16]

The real problem was—as it still is— the selection of persons qualified on both counts, that is, by experience and education.

Noted also in 1927 was the increasing tendency to develop apprenticeship programs as a cooperative effort of employers, labor, and schools. The Board

---

[16] Federal Board for Vocational Education, *Eleventh Annual Report, 1927.* Washington: Government Printing Office, 1927, p. 26.

regarded this as one of "the most promising methods of properly training recruits for the skilled trades."[17] A trend toward more adequate provision of vocational education for employed workers was heartily approved in the Board's report.

In the 1928 report the Board redefined its conception of vocational education as "that form of education and training in any field of human activity which assists people, young and old, to get a job, to keep a job, to improve on the job, to get a better job, and to believe in their job."[18]

By 1929 the Board reported to Congress that the passage of the George-Reed Act would enable the Board to provide additional service to the states in the development of their programs; particularly desirable was service which could be supported by research work conducted by the Board. The report also pointed to decided improvement in state plans, better standards of organization and operation, and improved teacher education. These were conditions which tended to safeguard federal funds, and the Board seldom lost sight of an opportunity to keep this thought before Congress.

The Board also indicated that there was an increased demand for published materials, a demand it was attempting to meet. During the fiscal year 1929, it had published 38 bulletins, monographs, and other reports.

The Board was keenly aware of the necessity of appropriate relationships with state boards, so the reports to Congress clearly delineated both special and routine relationships. In the 1930 report, for example, the Federal Board shared with the Congress some of the problems then being considered through these cooperative relationships. The problems included teacher eligibility requirements, out-of-school youth, student selection, teacher training, qualifications of administrators, and retraining displaced workers. John McCarthy pointed out that the accomplishments of the Board were worthy of prominence in the history of total American education. But, McCarthy continued, "Unfortunately those who write educational histories are too far removed from the developments of vocational education to give due credit to these great accomplishments."[19]

The Board was notably attentive to all the problems and issues facing the nation, that had implications for vocational education. A good example is the economic collapse which precipitated the depression of the 1930's. In the 1931 report, the Board called attention to the problem of unemployment and its relationship to vocational training. Almost immediately upon recognizing the need, the Board began working in cooperation with the states to develop "a constructive policy" in connection with training for unemployed workers. Although the Board could not deal with the general causes of unemployment, it could, and did, consider the plight of the unemployed worker and means of aiding him.

[17] Ibid.

[18] Federal Board for Vocational Education, Twelfth Annual Report, 1928. Washington: Government Printing Office, 1928, p. 1.

[19] John A. McCarthy, Vocational Education: America's Greatest Resource. Chicago: American Technical Society, 1951, p. 58.

No one in 1917 could have foreseen the great industrial depression; there were no specific provisions in the Smith-Hughes Act for coping with such a crisis. However, the Board held that it was in keeping with the spirit of the Act for it to contribute toward solving educational problems of unemployment. Many adult workers lost their jobs through causes beyond their control. The possibility of finding another job was often directly related to the availability of suitable training. A general preparatory training program for unemployed adults was "manifestly impractical" because of the length of time it would have required and because adults were not enrolled in schools.

The board is suggesting to the States, therefore, that existing trade preparatory schools or courses shall admit unemployed adults for thorough training in some specialized unit, in preparation for available jobs, to the extent to which their facilities permit and the need has been indorsed by a local representative advisory committee.[20]

A similar arrangement was recommended for part-time schools and courses. To the "pound of cure," the Board added "an ounce of prevention" by pointing out the advantages of extension training for employed adults.

To the extent to which adult workers take advantage of the opportunities provided in the evening school to upgrade themselves and become more resourceful and better qualified in their occupations, they are protecting themselves against the loss of their jobs due to technological advances in their occupations. It is one of the primary functions of the evening school to render this sort of service.[21]

In the 1932 report to Congress the Federal Board included an organization chart showing all of the positions and persons involved in their professional contributions. Included were data to bring the Congress up to date on the growth and development of vocational education. Also, a comprehensive review of research and service activities of the Board was included, to show conclusively how its influences had helped develop new programs in the states.

### Demise of the Federal Board

Vocational education was the victim of congressional economy measures in the early 1930's. On February 24, 1932, an Economy Committee was organized by the House of Representatives for the purpose of curtailing federal expenses. On April 25, this Committee submitted a report proposing some drastic steps in connection with vocational education and the Federal Board for Vocational Education. It was recommended that the permanent annual appropriations under the Smith-Hughes Act be reduced in the sum of ten percent for the fiscal year 1934, and progressively by ten percent more for each year thereafter, so that by the end of the fiscal year 1942 the appropriations would have been abolished. The permanent annual appropriation to the Federal Board for administration was also abolished; the report recommended the substitution of a year-to-

[20] Federal Board for Vocational Education, *Fifteenth Annual Report, 1931*. Washington: Government Printing Office, 1931, p. 10.
[21] *Ibid.*, p. 11.

year appropriation of the same amount, $200,000. This too was to be eliminated at the end of the fiscal year 1942.[22]

Although there was much sentiment in favor of these moves, there was also a storm of protest. Concurrently with the report of the Economy Committee, various senators and representatives were reading into the *Congressional Record* resolutions, memorials, and petitions against curtailment of funds for vocational education. As an example, on April 26, Representative William H. Sutphin of New Jersey introduced into the *Congressional Record* views of some of his constituents, who practically demanded retention of federal aid for vocational education. Sutphin cited many values of the program, then challenged the Committee concerning its alternative proposals, characterizing them as "simply an attempt to slowly and surely abolish vocational education rather than destroy it by immediate action."[23] Finally Representative Sutphin urged his colleagues to action, saying:

It is my earnest and sincere hope that every member of the House of Representatives will vote against this attempt to abolish the appropriations for vocational education entirely or to suspend or curtail it in any measure.[24]

On Friday, April 29, 1932, House discussion reached deeply into the fundamental purposes of federal participation in vocational education. One member of the House found it difficult to believe that the Economy Committee had given the subject "more than cursory attention," because otherwise it would have found evidence that the need for federal aid existed. The move was regarded as a false economy because, "It will not save a dollar." On the other hand, some members of Congress argued that it would return the problem of vocational training to the states, where it belonged. In rebuttal it was recalled that the Congress had previously appropriated money "for the erection of monuments in honor of Indian chiefs," millions had been provided to "dredge and widen streams barely navigable by punts," and huge sums of money had been allocated "to irrigate waste land when a vast number of fertile acres were growing up to bushes."

And now when it is proposed to continue an appropriation for vocational education—an appropriation that dollar for dollar has in results accomplished as much as any like amount ever before appropriated by the Federal Government—an attempt is made to strangle it.[25]

In the end, the logic of the opinion in favor of retaining the permanent appropriations for vocational education prevailed. The Federal Board for Vocational Education, however, fared badly. Parallel with the general economy measures and with the review of permanent funds was the desire to consolidate governmental agenices in order to reduce expenses. The President was authorized to issue executive orders to this effect, although a Senate amendment mentioned specifically that the Federal Board for Vocational Edu-

---

[22] 72nd Congress, 1st Session, *House of Representatives Report No. 1126,* April 25, 1932, pp. 6-8.

[23] *Congressional Record,* 75:9300.

[24] *Congressional Record,* 75:9301.

[25] Reprint from *Congressional Record,* 75, April 29, 1932, p. 6.

cation "shall not be abolished." On December 9, 1932, President Herbert Hoover, by executive order, attempted to transfer to the Office of Education the duties, powers, and functions of the Federal Board for Vocational Education, and instructed the Board itself to serve in merely an advisory capacity to the Secretary of the Interior. This action encountered opposition in Congress (principally on the basis that the incoming President should have the opportunity to reorganize the Executive Department.) Hence a resolution was passed in January, 1933, which postponed the reorganization.

Congressional opposition was supported by the American Vocational Association, whose legislative committee was quick to muster sentiment in opposition to the proposed change of status for the Federal Board. Vocational educators, too, were strongly against any change in the Board, and said as much in thousands of letters to the Congress. Furthermore, in April, 1932, in connection with general discussion of the economy measure, the House had reviewed reasons for establishment of an independent board. They had held that the opposition to it was "largely the result of misinformation and misunderstandings" concerning the work of the Federal Board. The reasons advanced for continuing the program of vocational education under an independent board were essentially the same as they had been in 1917. It was imperative that a practical program intended by the federal acts be under the direction of persons who understood the nature and values of practical work. Generous reference was made to the testimony and rationale of 1916-1917, which Congress had used in

establishing the necessity of the Board. No evidence had been advanced in the discussions of 1932 to show that the interested parties had protested against "anything with which the Board has been concerned." Evidence revealed that national organizations such as the American Federation of Labor, United States Chamber of Commerce, national manufacturers' associations, and others, had voluntarily adopted resolutions commending the work of the Board.

Tampering with the Federal Board for Vocational Education was looked upon by industrial educators as only slightly short of a major crisis. The American Vocational Association kept key vocational educators of the nation well informed about the day-to-day developments. The *Industrial Education Magazine*, however, which was usually dependable in keeping its readers informed of such developments, largely ignored the whole matter. In March, 1933, Bawden summarized the annual report of the Federal Board for 1932, but he did not mention any of the proposed changes in the operation of the Board. In his review of industrial education for 1933, Bawden ventured the opinion that the change was "undoubtedly the most important and far-reaching event of 1933 in industrial education." Yet the details, the arguments, and the divergent views concerning the Federal Board were not presented, nor did the magazine take a position either in defense of the Board or in sympathy with the change.

It is understandable why William N. Doak, Chairman of the Federal Board for Vocational Education, did not urge positive action. His position as Secretary of Labor placed limitations upon his vigorous opposition to measures initiated by the administration. Nevertheless, his subtle recognition of the controversy is to be noted in his article in the May, 1932, issue of the *American Vocational Association News Bulletin*. The title of the article was "Changing Economic Conditions and Vocational Education." He reviewed the social and economic conditions which led up to the passage of the Smith-Hughes Act, pointed to the achievements of the past 15 years, and complimented vocational educators in general for their wholehearted cooperation. His identification of vocational education's achievements and the Federal Board's relationship to those achievements was an open invitation to vocational educators to advise their congressional leaders on the matter of the Federal Board. This the vocational educators did, through the well organized channels of the American Vocational Association. Their efforts, however, did not prevent the change of status.

Early in March, 1933, the Act was amended, authorizing the President to make certain reorganizations in the Executive Department. On June 10, 1933, President Roosevelt transferred the functions of the Federal Board to the Department of the Interior and ordered that the Board serve in an advisory capacity without compensation. On October 10, 1933, the administrative functions of vocational education were transferred to the U.S. Office of Education. After 1933 the Board ceased to be an important force in vocational education, and it met infrequently in its advisory capacity. Finally on May 16, 1946, President Truman, by executive order, abolished the Federal Board; its valuable contributions, however, had been terminated 13 years earlier.

*Postscript*

Control of the vocational program was obviously regarded as one of the key issues throughout the life of the Federal Board. During the formative period of national legislation the American Federation of Labor, the National Education Association, and other groups sought to clarify this element of control. It is understandable why the Federal Board would be so keenly aware of, and sensitive to, appropriate relationships with the states.

Precedent existed prior to 1917 for the federal government's interest in legislation of an educational, social, and moral nature. This interest was manifested in many ways, such as in the government's concern for "dependent peoples," and in the general desire to eradicate illiteracy. The establishment of the Bureau of Education in 1867, the Morrill Act, and other acts gave evidence of the government's attempt to seek a more vigorous role. The problem of control was present in every act of the Congress, but at no time previous to the Smith-Hughes Act had it been so prominent, nor had it created so much discussion. All bills in connection with vocational education prior to the passage of the Smith-Hughes Act had provided for cooperative relationships between the states and the federal government. As first proposed, the 1917 legislation would have set up programs to be administered by a federal unit. However, certain educators felt that this would lead to a dual system of education, and so they spoke out in defense of a unified system.

By terms of the Smith-Hughes Act, the Federal Board had six basic responsibilities: administrative, advisory, service, research, quasi-judicial, and regulatory. An independent board had been established by Congress for the following reasons:

1. To provide serviceable education and training which would assist people to "get a job, hold a job, or get a better job."

2. To prevent the work from becoming so academic in character that it would fail in its fundamental purpose.

3. To insure that the funds would be used as intended and not diverted to general education.

4. To recognize that vocational education was a means of bringing economic benefits both to employers and to employees.

Because of its independent nature the Board could equitably represent labor, employers, and other interested parties; it had been entirely free of partisan politics, a situation about which Congress had boasted in 1917 and again in 1932.

Persons who believed that the independent status of the Board tended to separate vocational education from the other areas of education went to the extreme of retarding the program. The problem of control was, and still is, a touchy subject. Yet, "Every effort was made by the Board in its relations with the States to avoid a dictatorial attitude, and these relations were throughout the period of its administrative activity entirely on a basis of service and cooperation."[26]

For nearly 16 years the Federal Board held a leading role in the development of vocational education. Dele-

gating its powers and changing its function to an advisory one were, in the opinion of educators and labor leaders, "steps backward in industrial education progress." The American Federation of Labor regarded the action as a "serious mistake" and urged the President to restore the Board, but opposition groups eventually won out.

Nevertheless, evidence indicates that the Federal Board, as an experiment in relationships and control, was highly successful.

## Summary

One of the fundamental issues for discussion during the final phases of planning for the Smith-Hughes Act was the nature of the administrative structure necessary to establish appropriate working relationships with the states. Various national associations, including labor, supported the recommendation of the Commission on National Aid to Vocational Education that a Federal Board be authorized. Establishing the Board as an independent agency, responsible only to Congress, was a highly controversial matter. However, the Commissioner of Education supported this move because the U.S. Office of Education was not properly constituted to administer the provisions of the Act.

The Board consisted of the Secretaries of Labor, Commerce, and Agriculture, and the Commissioner of Education as ex-officio members, and three other members appointed by the President to represent labor, agriculture,

---

[26] Lloyd E. Blauch, *Federal Cooperation in Agricultural Extension Work, Vocational Education and Vocational Rehabilitation,* Office of Education, Bulletin 1933, No. 15. Washington: Government Printing Office, 1935, p. 215.

and manufacturing and commerce. The Board met for the first time on July 21, 1917. Charles A. Prosser was appointed director. Subsequently a staff was appointed to carry out the responsibilities of the Board.

In less than a month after the first meeting of the Board, arrangements were made for conferences with representatives of each of the states concerning their plans for utilizing the funds available for the promotion and development of vocational education. The Board assisted the states in making their plans but made no attempt to control the nature of these plans. The only requirement was that the plans include provisions to meet the minimum requirements of the Smith-Hughes Act.

The Board also assisted the states by providing general policy in relation to the Act and by interpreting the various sections of the Act. The early bulletins of the Federal Board became guides for the states to use as they developed their own procedures in relation to the general policy. The federal-state relationships that developed in the implementation of the Smith-Hughes Act helped to clarify the role of the Federal Board as one of providing service to the states in many ways. Service was first and always of major concern. In general, however, the functions of the Federal Board for Vocational Education were: (1) efficient administration of the federal funds, (2) research and studies to promote and improve vocational education, and (3) assistance to the states in their promotion and development activities. The Board reported to Congress each year.

Through regional and national conferences and a variety of publications the Board developed standards of performance that represented a consensus among industrial educators. This provided a convenient base from which the pursuit of quality could be launched and which suggested areas where intensive research was required.

The Federal Board for Vocational Education was a victim of the great depression of the 1930's. Economy measures in government forced the Board to relinquish its independent status and to become an advisory board, with the administrative functions transferred to the Department of the Interior. But Congress did not reduce funds of the Smith-Hughes Act.

The Federal Board for Vocational Education was a test of federal-state relationships in a partnership of education; and the Board passed the test with flying colors. The evidence indicates that the relationship was successful, that it worked for the improvement of quality and quantity of vocational education, and that it was sensitive to social and economic needs of the nation.

Despite strong opposition the administrative functions of the Board were transferred to the U.S. Office of Education on October 10, 1933. For 16 years, 2 months, and 19 days, the Board had a direct influence upon building a national framework for vocational education. During the next twelve and a half years the Board served in an advisory capacity, but its impact on vocational education was negligible.

The staff of the Board had remained intact during the transfer to the U.S. Office of Education; thus its influence survived in the background of experience of the staff. This was a favorable situation in which to continue the work in the Office of Education.

132

## Recall Questions

1. What were the provisions of the Smith-Hughes Act regarding membership of the Federal Board?

2. Identify by name and position the first members of the Federal Board for Vocational Education.

3. What were the three functions of the Federal Board?

4. For what purposes did the Federal Board hold conferences with the states in August, 1917?

5. What were the ten items of policy and interpretation for vocational education in the first issue of Policy Bulletin No. 1?

6. How did the Federal Board view its role in relationship with the states? Explain.

7. Upon what basis was the administration of the Federal Board transferred to the U.S. Office of Education?

## Research Questions

1. Study the Smith-Hughes Act and the publications of the Federal Board for Vocational Education, and write a paper giving an analysis of the control of vocational education by the Federal Board.

2. Review the publications of the Federal Board for Vocational Education and prepare a summary of the influences of the Board upon the various facets of vocational education. Cite specific references.

## Suggestions for Further Reading

Blauch, Lloyd E., *Federal Cooperation in Agricultural Extension Work, Vocational Education and Vocational Rehabilitation,* U.S. Department of the Interior, Bulletin 1933, No. 15, Washington: Government Printing Office, 1935.

Hawkins, Layton S., Prosser, Charles A., and Wright, John C., *Development of Vocational Education.* Chicago: American Technical Society, 1951.

Lee, Edwin A., *Objectives and Problems of Vocational Education, Second Edition.* New York: McGraw-Hill Book Co., Inc., 1938.

Roberts, Roy W., *Vocational and Practical Arts Education, Second Edition.* New York: Harper and Row, 1965.

# Chapter 7

# U.S. Office of Education[1]

**The Specialists in Industrial Education · Trade and Industrial Education Branch · National Conferences · National Teacher Training Conferences · Regional Conferences · National Leadership Development Conferences · Research in Trade and Industrial Education · Area Vocational Education Branch · Reorganization of the Division of Vocational and Technical Education · Summary · Recall Questions · Research Questions · Suggestions for Further Reading**

From the beginning the commissioners of the U.S. Bureau of Education were deeply interested in the impact of industrial education upon the school systems of the nation. They varied considerably, however, in their attitudes about it and in their influences upon its development. Most outspoken of the commissioners against industrial education was William T. Harris. We know that prior to his appointment, Harris had been a frequent antagonist. In professional associations he could be depended upon to harass the proponents of industrial education. Whereupon, of course, the great champion of manual

training, Calvin M. Woodward, would come to the rescue, and the ensuing verbal battle would be fought to a standstill.

The tenure of William T. Harris as Commissioner of Education began on September 12, 1889, and ended on June 30, 1906—the very years in which industrial education came into visible maturity. Harris had no choice but to recognize the national movement. From time to time his reports made objective reference to these developments, even though his personal point of view apparently did not change. Unknowingly Harris may have been a benefactor of

---

[1] The U.S. Office of Education was first established as an independent government agency (1867), but was transferred in 1869 to the Department of the Interior where it had the title of the Bureau of Education. In 1939, the Bureau was transferred to the Federal Security Agency and was renamed the Office of Education.

industrial education; for when he attacked manual training as a "deceptive farce" and chided those who would substitute certain "knacks in education" for the disciplines, he unquestionably forced industrial education leaders to define and stand upon their fundamental principles.

Harris was followed in office by Elmer Ellsworth Brown whose tenure extended to June 30, 1911. Brown, a Californian, did not hold the negative views of his predecessor. He supported federal aid for industrial education, and he said so in 1908 as a speaker at the second annual meeting of the National Society for the Promotion of Industrial Education, held in Atlanta, Georgia. Brown was introduced by the toastmaster of the evening, the Honorable Hoke Smith, Governor of Georgia, who implied in his introduction that it was time that the U.S. Bureau of Education expand its services to industrial education.

Commissioner Brown held the opinion that industrial education was an essential factor in our national prosperity. He urged that this development "be kept in the closest sympathetic relation with the schools that make for our culture." His attitude is shown clearly in the conclusion of his address:

. . . You need to keep a constant influence at work, directing the minds of men in this country to the things that are best in our industrial education. I hope that you will have the leaders to do those things, and I hope that you will do them, that you will do a great upward work there, but I hope that that upward work will lead our national government and our state government at no distant day to assume that work

as a part of their work, as one of the ways in which education, state and national, is to serve the national good. . . .[2]

Brown was succeeded by Philander Priestley Claxton, who served from July 8, 1911 to June 1, 1921. Claxton continued with his support and, like Brown, was a frequent contributor to the professional work of the National Society for the Promotion of Industrial Education. Claxton engaged the services of leaders to supply him with information about the developments of the industrial education movement for inclusion in his annual reports. For several years these contributions were prepared by William T. Bawden. Finally, through Claxton's efforts, a position was created in the U.S. Bureau of Education for a Specialist in Industrial Education. To this position Claxton invited William T. Bawden, who assumed the duties of the office on November 6, 1914.

## The Specialists in Industrial Education

### William T. Bawden, November 6, 1914-October 16, 1923

Bawden was a national figure in the field of manual training. Yet his appointment was greeted as a significant step in the general promotion of industrial education. After all, manual training was representative of almost all industrial education, if one considers influence of programs in the public schools. But Bawden's participation cannot be considered one-sided, for he was frequently involved in the national

[2] E. E. Brown, "Unifying Influence of Industrial Art," National Society for the Promotion of Industrial Education, Bulletin No. 9, Proceedings, Second Annual Meeting, June 1909, p. 40.

program of trade and industrial education. He was a prolific writer and, as the only representative of industrial education in the U.S. Bureau of Education, was deeply involved in many aspects of vocational and practical arts. At the beginning of Bawden's tenure there were approximately 46,000 students enrolled in manual training in the public schools of the nation. Instruction was provided by 861 instructors (564 men and 297 women).[3]

A large part of Bawden's work was promotional, involving efforts to provide a climate in which progress could be made. He conducted industrial education conferences called by the commissioner of education, participated in surveys, prepared reports for the commissioner, and in his spare time wrote articles for a variety of journals. In addition he was called upon for an extensive amount of editorial work on publications in general. During the nine years of his work with the Bureau of Education, Bawden attended 31 national conferences and participated in public school surveys in Butte, Montana; Memphis, Tennessee; Wilmington, Delaware; Elyria, Ohio; Alexandria, Virginia; Washington, D.C.; and at Bradley Polytechnic Institute, Peoria, Illinois. He conducted industrial education surveys in Bridgeport, Connecticut; Richmond, Virginia; and Wilmington, Delaware. He was director of state surveys in North Dakota, Arkansas, and Oklahoma; and conducted city surveys in San Francisco, California; Wheeling, West Virginia; and Elizabeth City, North Carolina. Ben-

nett estimated that Bawden traveled approximately 1,800 miles a month. Because his work and contacts were broad in scope, he made hundreds of friends across the nation.

His personal relations were so cordial (and so becoming an "officer of the Government," as Bennett described him) that when he attempted to retire from his position as chairman of the Manual Arts Conference, the members would not accept his resignation. This same degree of cordiality extended to his relationships with Commissioner Claxton.

It was not surprising, therefore, that in the fall of 1923, Bawden accepted an invitation from Claxton (who had become superintendent of schools in Tulsa, Oklahoma) to become assistant superintendent in charge of that city's vocational and practical arts education.

In the Bureau of Education the same cordial relationships existed between Claxton's successor, John James Tigert, and Bawden. Tigert viewed Bawden's service as conspicuously meritorious. But value had not been recognized in terms of salary; on the other hand, the financial arrangement at Tulsa was inviting. Thus Bawden moved back into school administration. He was Claxton's choice "from the entire field."

### Maris M. Proffitt, January 1, 1925–January 24, 1946

It was not until January 1, 1925, that the position of Specialist in Industrial Education was again filled, in the person of Maris M. Proffitt. Proffitt had

[3] Department of the Interior, U.S. Bureau of Education, *Statistics of Certain Manual Training, Agricultural, and Industrial Schools, 1913-1914*, Bulletin 1915, No. 19. Washington: Government Printing Office, 1915, pp. 28-29.

extensive teaching experience both in industrial arts and trade and industrial education. He had been a superintendent of schools for five years, and during the six years immediately preceding his appointment he had been a professor of trades and industries at the University of Maryland; he had also been the state supervisor of industrial education for Maryland. The appointment may have been made in part because of the strong desire of teachers for information on "how to do it" and for help in general organization of courses and methods of teaching.[4] Proffitt certainly had the required experience to provide leadership.

During the first six months in office, Proffitt worked in eleven states in connection with industrial education conferences and meetings of professional associations. Part of the work was in cooperation with the regional agents of the Federal Board for Vocational Education, and part with representatives of state departments of education where attention was focused upon objectives and problems of industrial arts.

In the three years that followed, these services were continued; in addition Proffitt gave attention to needs of his field in school building construction, to development of industrial education courses for students in small communities, to teacher education and related problems, to exploratory courses, and to plans for out-of-school youth and adults. A distinct trend was reported by the commissioner of education in 1928 toward general accept-

ance of the aims of industrial arts and toward its recognition as a "part of the general education program and not a phase of a special type of education."[5]

Progress in industrial education in terms of its many areas of growth was given special attention in the 1929 report of the commissioner. With such progress came a host of other considerations which commanded attention. These included teacher education, teacher certification, and research directed toward improvement of instruction.

However, a reorganization of the Office of Education occurred in 1930. In effect the change placed the Specialist in Industrial Education one step lower in the administrative organization. A new department (Research and Investigation) was created and Proffitt became one of two consultants directly responsible to an assistant commissioner. Proffitt's work was to plan, conduct, and report upon research and special investigations in the field of industrial education.

In 1930, the new department began compiling a bibliography of industrial education reading materials and undertook research into part-time programs in industrial education; into courses of study in industrial education divisions of teacher training institutions; and (with the American Vocational Association) into performance abilities of industrial arts students in junior high schools.

In 1931, the department continued its emphasis upon conducting studies

[4] *Industrial Education Magazine*, Vol. XXVI, No. 8, February 1925, p. 221.

[5] U.S. Department of the Interior, *Report of the Commissioner of Education, 1928*. Washington: Government Printing Office, 1928, p. 18.

in industrial education rather than upon extensive surveys or attendance at meetings in the field. The strong influence of vocational guidance upon industrial education was noted also in the reports of the commissioner.

### Changes After 1932

During Proffitt's service in the Office of Education, the title of his position was changed from Specialist in Industrial Education to Specialist in Industrial Arts. Two situations contributed to this change. First, the functions of the Federal Board for Vocational Education were transferred to the Department of the Interior in 1933 and were assigned to the Office of Education. Second, the recognition of industrial arts as an area of importance in the public school curriculum enabled the Office of Education to emphasize instruction in industrial arts by changing the title of the specialist.

### John R. Ludington, June 14, 1948-December 1, 1954

On June 14, 1948, after a two-year vacancy in the position, John R. Ludington succeeded Proffitt as Specialist in Industrial Arts. His background and experience included public school teaching, teacher education, editorial experience (including three years as special editor for industrial arts for the *American Vocational Journal*), and extensive activity in the work of professional organizations. At the time of his appointment Ludington was a professor of industrial arts education at North Carolina State College. In addition he served as the state supervisor of industrial arts for North Carolina.

Ludington carried on many of the traditional responsibilities of the pre-

vious specialists; he attended conferences and meetings of professional associations, and provided consultative services. But a significant variation of professional responsibility appears to have developed during the six and a half years of his service. The variation may be roughly described as "team-type" work, in which studies and publications of the Office of Education became the product of two or more persons working as a team. The advantage was that the influence and understanding of industrial arts were projected into a larger, and at times foreign, environment. Accordingly, studies concerning life adjustment education, drop-outs, holding power, secondary education, pupil analysis, the slow learner, the junior high school, and other topics tended to make the contributions and values of industrial arts better known.

The period immediately after World War II was marked by rapid expansion of industrial arts throughout the nation, and the Specialist in Industrial Arts held a key position from the standpoint of the general evolvement of his field in the expanding public school curriculum.

On December 1, 1954, Ludington was assigned to direct a program of civil defense education, so he relinquished his assignment in industrial arts.

### DeWitt T. Hunt, January 24, 1955-June 30, 1956

On January 24, 1955, DeWitt T. Hunt joined the staff of the U.S. Office of Education, on temporary assignment, as the Specialist in Industrial Arts. He was on leave of absence from his position as head of the school of industrial arts education and engineering shop-work at Oklahoma Agricultural and Mechanical College. To his new position Hunt brought much experience in industrial education, as a teacher in Texas, as a teacher educator, and as a member of numerous committees and commissions relating both to education in general and industrial education in particular. He had been president of the American Industrial Arts Association, and at the time of his appointment was serving as editor of *The Industrial Arts Teacher*.

After a year and a half of service, in which he carried on the work generally required, Hunt returned to his position in Oklahoma.

### Marshall L. Schmitt, January 28, 1957-

Marshall L. Schmitt was appointed Specialist in Industrial Arts, January 28, 1957. Schmitt's background of teaching in industrial arts and his experience as a teacher educator at Oswego State Teachers College and the University of North Carolina, as well as his work with professional associations, was appropriate for promoting the work of industrial arts in the Office of Education.

One of the immediate problems that Schmitt undertook was to bring up to date national data about industrial arts. These data were important for developing an adequate overview of the national program. Such basic knowledge was needed for continued promotion and development. Schmitt's curriculum analysis study, 1961, provided a review of the instructional topics listed in 39 state curriculum guides and covered the general instructional areas of industrial arts. A national survey of industrial arts in the public schools (in process 1963-64) was the first of its kind ever made for the field. Response from 2,400 schools indicated that there was active interest in the study; 95 percent of the principals and 90 percent of the teachers responded.

Beginning with Schmitt's tenure as Specialist in Industrial Arts, the Office of Education has expanded the services of the Specialist by providing additional clerical assistance and by adding a full-time research assistant. Although these are signs of progress, the number of persons representing industrial arts in the Office of Education is entirely too small in relation to the number of teachers and students in the total field.

### The Function of the Specialist in the Contemporary Scene

The function of the Specialist in Industrial Arts is in a general way the same as the function of the Office of Education. Responsibilities which fall upon the Office of Education are also responsibilities of the Specialist. However, the change in specific function from Bawden's day to the present has in some respects been great. Bawden was one of the comparatively few employees of the Bureau of Education. Although he gave attention to industrial education on a broad basis, in addition he was called upon to serve the Bureau at times as a professional educator in situations far afield. During his last few years, much of Bawden's time was spent in administrative work as an assistant to the Commissioner of Education. During the four decades since Bawden's resignation, the number of persons employed in the Office of Education has grown to more than 1,700. Industrial arts is only one among many areas having the benefit of specialized attention.

In general the Specialist in Industrial Arts is responsible for the following:

- To perform professional work involved in initiation and formulation of programs in industrial arts.
- To identify and evaluate problems.
- To plan and conduct research, surveys, and studies.
- To disseminate information to improve education in the United States by providing accurate and up-to-date information on public industrial arts programs.
- To exercise leadership and provide advisory services.
- To review and make appraisals of practices in industrial arts.
- To make final recommendations concerning the recognition, evaluation, and solution of problems in industrial arts for which criteria have not been established.
- To maintain liaison with other areas and professional organizations.
- To write for publication.
- To attend conferences.
- To exercise leadership in promotion of cooperative relationships with educational groups.

## Trade and Industrial Education Branch

Fifteen million people were out of work on March 4, 1933, when Franklin D. Roosevelt was inaugurated as President. His administration—the New Deal—promised relief, recovery, and reform. Pledges of drastic reduction in the expenses of government included a proposal to reorganize the Federal Board for Vocational Education. This proposal roused the legislative committee of the American Vocational Association to action, and after a number of conferences with government officials in May, 1933, agreement was reached to study the general situation of the Federal Board.

By Executive Order, on June 10, 1933, the functions of the Board were transferred to the Department of the Interior, and on October 10 were assigned to the Commissioner of Education. In a public statement on November 28, 1933, Harold L. Ickes, Secretary of the Department of the Interior said:

This transfer of the functions of the Federal Board for Vocational Education is not to be interpreted as any curtailment of the activities of the Federal Government in the field of vocational education. Both Commissioner Zook and I have long been deeply interested in vocational education, and we both propose to promote the development of this highly important part of the field of education vigorously.[6]

The title of John C. Wright, Director of the Federal Board for Vocational Education, was changed to Assistant Commissioner for Vocational Education, with "no change in duties."

Despite much anxiety in connection with the changes, President Roosevelt's appointments to the Federal Board (then acting in an advisory capacity) drew hearty approval from the *AVA Journal and News Bulletin*. The appointments included Lincoln Filene, a businessman from Boston; Henry Ohl, Jr., President of the Wisconsin State Federation of Labor; and Clarence Poe,

---

[6] William T. Bawden, "Review of Industrial Education in 1933," *Industrial Education Magazine*, Vol. XXXVI, No. 1, January 1934, p. 6.

editor of *The Progressive Farmer,* Raleigh, North Carolina.

The appointments of Messrs. Filene, Ohl, and Poe to membership on the Federal Board for Vocational Education gives us hope that again the working people of America, both employed and unemployed, will be assured of a permanent program. . . . All those interested in the vocational school movement in America have good reason to feel gratified for the President's recent appointments to the Federal Board for Vocational Education.[7]

There was a distinct feeling among vocational educators that the appointments indicated an intention on the part of the administration to give the "Federal Board an opportunity to again become an active and participating factor in the vocational school movement in America."[8] For some time there had been spokesmen in business, labor, and education who advocated the view that the only practical and effective way to develop vocational education was to have it guided "by men who are close to the actual problems of agriculture, industry and labor."[9] The appointments were regarded as a sign that this view had also been accepted by the government administration.

The new deal for vocational education resulted in a vastly different administrative structure. All of the vocational services functioned as a part of the U.S. Office of Education, but maintained their identity through the office of an Assistant Commissioner for Vocational Education. Under these conditions and in this environment the trade and industrial education program continued.

## Administration of Trade and Industrial Education

Under the original Federal Board, and later the Office of Education, the actual title of the group responsible for the general administration of trade and industrial education changed from time to time; during the early years it was called Trade and Industrial Education Service; most recently the title has been Trade and Industrial Education Branch. Similarly the title of the chief administrative officer changed. By the early 1960's he was known as the Director.

The work of the trade and industrial education branch also changed. During the early years, immediately after the passage of the Smith-Hughes Act, much attention was given to the preparation of manuals of instruction. (Use and Preparation of Food, 1919; Foreman Training Courses, 1919; Theory and Practice of the Machinist's Trade, 1919; and on throughout the years—more than 100 such publications.) Little instructional material existed, so members of the Trade and Industrial Education Service set out to fill the void. Attention was also given to inspection of trade and industrial education programs to be sure that the states were complying with the federal law. By the 1960's attention was definitely upon development of leadership among the states, and the program reviews tended largely to emphasize leadership rather than mere "inspection and compliance." This change evolved as a natural process, the states becoming more

---

[7] *AVA Journal and News Bulletin,* Vol. X, No. 3, September 1935, p. 59.
[8] *AVA Journal and News Bulletin,* Vol. X, No. 4, November 1935, p. 135.
[9] *Ibid.,* p. 135.

sophisticated in the organization and administration of their programs with the passage of time. The American Vocational Association had provided much attention to standards of performance and to evaluative criteria. Therefore it was not so essential that the Office of Education continue its initial practices with the same degree of emphasis.

Much of the change of emphasis in the work of the Trade and Industrial Education Branch was reflected in the personalities of its directors and the working relationships they maintained with the states. State leaders had learned to depend in a large measure upon the guidance they received from the Trade and Industrial Education Branch, and both new and routine ideas of procedure were presented to the Branch for suggestions and comment. These professional reviews, backed up with knowledge of the program on a nationwide basis, were valuable contributions to the development of trade and industrial education in the various states.

### Administrative Officers, 1922-1964

The chief administrative officer for trade and industrial education at the time of the transfer of the functions to the Office of Education was Frank Cushman. He had been a regional agent of the Federal Board during the period 1918-1922 and was appointed chief of trade and industrial education on July 1, 1922. He served in this capacity until June 30, 1939.

Layton S. Hawkins was appointed chief of trade and industrial education in 1939 and served until May 31, 1947. Hawkins had an earlier period of service with the Federal Board

which extended from 1917 to 1921. During the period 1940-1945, he was also the Director of Vocational Training for War Production Workers.

From July 13, 1947 to February 1, 1953, the position of chief was held by Walter H. Cooper.

Laurence Borosage was appointed to the position on February 2, 1953. Borosage was a graduate of the Milwaukee Vocational School. He had extensive experience in industry, including work as a machinist. He was the first chief to hold an earned doctorate. At the time of his appointment he was serving as a teacher educator at the Michigan State College. On July 1, 1954, Borosage resigned and returned to his university position.

On June 6, 1955, John P. Walsh was appointed as Director of the Trade and Industrial Education Branch and served in this capacity until June, 1962, when he was appointed Deputy Director, Office of Manpower, Automation and Training in the U.S. Department of Labor.

Earl M. Bowler, Assistant Director of the Branch, was appointed Acting Director and served until February 19, 1964, when he was assigned as chief of the Professional Services Section of Manpower Development and Training Program. Merle E. Strong then served as Acting Director until September 25, 1964, when the reorganization plan of the Division of Vocational and Technical Education became effective.

### National Conferences

Much of the information in trade and industrial education to be transmitted to the states was issued in the form of bulletins, circular letters, and other informal statements. Prior to 1933, of course, these memoranda came from the Federal Board for Vocational Education, and after 1933 from the U.S. Office of Education. In the early formative years of the trade and industrial education program, the flow of information was largely one way, from the national office to the states. As the degree of sophistication in program organization, administration, and development improved in the states, the Office of Education called national conferences in order that state leaders might have an opportunity to share ideas and thus reach conclusions through group processes. These conferences served as a communication device among the states and with the Office of Education. In a sense each conference was a sounding board for problems in trade and industrial education; out of them came a consensus which became the guide or ideal for progress.

### Minneapolis Conference, Summer 1921 [10]

The first national conference conducted by the Trade and Industrial Education Service of the Federal Board was held in Minneapolis, with 63 persons from various parts of the nation attending. The conference served as a means of crystallizing ideas concerning organized teacher training for part-time, evening, and all-day teachers. Also it devoted substantial attention to the "newer problem of training men to teach foremanship classes." Foremanship training was regarded as one of the best means of promoting the entire program of trade and industrial education in the states.

Immediately following this conference 14 supplementary conferences were held, each in a different state. These conferences involved key personnel from education, industry, management, and labor.

### Minneapolis Conference, Summer 1922 [11]

The second national conference was held for four weeks during the summer of 1922. In general the conference, attended by 42 people from 24 states, duplicated the 1921 conference. However, members largely represented states that had not participated before.

### Blue Ridge, North Carolina, Conference, August 4-16, 1924 [12]

The third conference, called as a regional meeting, is considered national in scope because it followed the general pattern of the first two, set up problem study organization for later conferences, and sharpened the need for occasional national conferences. Fifty-nine persons from 12 southern states (60 percent of the group came from Texas, Oklahoma, and North Carolina) and a conference staff of six representing the Federal Board for Vocational Education comprised the total group. During the two-week period, members were divided into

---

[10] *Sixth Annual Report to Congress of the Federal Board for Vocational Education, 1922.* Washington: Government Printing Office, 1922, p. 50.

[11] *Ibid.*

[12] Federal Board for Vocational Education, *Report of Trade and Industrial Education Conference Held at Blue Ridge, North Carolina, August 4-16, 1924,* Misc. 617.

groups to consider four problems: (1) training of trade teachers, (2) training of part-time general continuation teachers, (3) city supervision of industrial education, and (4) plant training and foremanship courses. The conference was conducted by an experienced leader from the Federal Board.

Although the conclusions of each conference group seemed but to reinforce principles, issues, or points of view already known, the plan did serve to permit the members of a large group to review standards with all of the benefits of small-group discussion, and enhanced the opportunity for a comparison of ideas and experiences.

### Blue Ridge, North Carolina, Conference, 1926 [13]

The fourth national conference, conducted during the summer of 1926, is presumed to have followed the pattern of the 1924 conference. No detailed report of this conference is known to exist.

### Minneapolis Conference, August 17-28, 1936 [14]

The fifth national conference in trade and industrial education was called in 1936. Ninety-three persons from 34 states attended. The conference was planned and conducted by members of the Trade and Industrial Education staff. Upon completion of each section conference, conclusions were drawn. These conclusions were later amended and approved by the total conference group. Although the

conference staff provided direction and assistance, it did not exert pressure toward any particular decision. In content the conference covered a wide range of subject matter including advisory committees, teacher training, apprenticeship, distributive occupations, guidance, and a study of wages paid to part-time students. In addition some time was spent in review of past accomplishments of vocational education and in looking toward future developments. The 232-page report constituted an up-to-date, practical handbook for trade and industrial educators which could be used to evaluate, promote, and develop their state and local programs.

### Supervisory Personnel Development Conference, Washington, D.C., May 7-11, 1956

Development of programs for supervisory personnel had been a consistent activity of the national office of trade and industrial education from its beginning in 1917. Supervisory training programs had been much in demand during World War II, and in the years following the war this demand became wider. Consequently a number of states employed professional staff specialists in the area of supervisory training. The unprecedented activity in supervisory training brought an expressed need for a degree of uniformity, continuity, and coordination of effort among the states. Committees of the American Vocational Association brought the problem into focus and requested that the Trade and Indus-

---

[13] Frank Cushman, Chief of the Trade and Industrial Education Service, Office of Education, refers to this conference in the opening ceremonies of the 1936 conference in Minneapolis.
[14] U.S. Department of the Interior, Office of Education, *Report of National Conference on Trade and Industrial Education*, Misc. 1853. Minneapolis, Minnesota, August 17-28, 1936.

trial Education Branch, Office of Education, call a conference of specialists to consider the elements of supervisory training.

Eleven specialists, all from different states that had well developed programs, were invited to a conference at Washington, D.C., in May, 1956. Assisted by representatives of the Office of Education and other governmental units, the conferees embarked upon a study which had the following objectives:

- To explore the nature of successful programs of key States in the four regions in the field of supervisory development.

- To ascertain what elements in successful programs might be valuable for use by vocational educators in other States.

- To determine what might be done to assist States in establishing, improving, or accelerating supervisory development programs.

- To structure a plan, including a bulletin, helpful to the States interested in gearing supervisory development to the needs of industrial establishments.[15]

The conference group studied and discussed problems and trends, training needs—including instructional material—the need for qualified personnel to teach supervisory training, uniform terminology, definition of scope of program, and criteria for evaluation of statewide programs. Finally the group came to general conclusions concerning principles that should apply to the development of supervisory curricula.

## Instructional Materials Development Conference, Washington, D.C., January 19-23, 1959

Preparation of instructional materials for trade and industrial education had grown in terms of need to the point that it commanded national interest and concern. Many states had provided special attention to this need, had organized instructional materials laboratories, and in general were making contributions to the improvement of instruction. It was quite evident, however, that solving the real problem of the preparation of instructional material required cooperative action among the states. Therefore, the Office of Education in January, 1959, called a conference of 25 specialists from 22 states.[16] The conference was coordinated by the Trade and Industrial Education Branch.

Conference members considered the types of curriculum materials needed, the responsibilities for preparing them, state organizational patterns for curriculum development, and their evaluation, validation, articulation, development, exchange, distribution, and promotion. In addition the groups identified and suggested assignment of certain responsibilities in connection with implementation of the findings of the conference.

As an outgrowth of these recommendations, a National Professional Curriculum Materials Committee was appointed. Two representatives from each of the four regions (see page

---

[15] U.S. Department of Health, Education, and Welfare, Office of Education, *Report of Supervisory Personnel Development Conference, May 7-11, 1956*, p. 1.

[16] U.S. Department of Health, Education, and Welfare, Office of Education, *Cooperative Action for Instructional Materials Development in Trade and Industrial Education*, OE-84000. Washington: Government Printing Office, 1959.

151) and a representative of the Office of Education comprised the nine-member national committee. The committee's purposes were to provide co-ordination, to seek uniformity in terminology and format, and to provide a clearinghouse, all in order to stimulate the development of appropriate materials. Meetings of the committee were held in October, 1959, February-March, 1960, and January, 1961. Among its accomplishments was the establishing of curriculum laboratories in several states.

**Trade and Industrial Education for the 1960's** [17]

It had been some time since the last conference for the purpose of reviewing and planning the entire program of trade and industrial education. The conference in Kansas City, April 27-May 1, 1959, was the largest national meeting ever held for a specific end of this kind: 207 representatives from 47 states, the District of Columbia, Puerto Rico, the Virgin Islands, and the Philippines attended. Representatives of state, national, and local programs participated in small committees to solve specific problems. The conference also assembled as a total group to hear panel discussions and individual presentations concerning developments in teacher training, supervision, challenges, "portraits" of trade and industrial education, untapped resources, investment, and images of the future.

Specific attention was directed toward the topics "Some Major Challenges in Trade and Industrial Educa-

tion," and "Some Vehicles for Meeting Major Challenges." After discussions, the group summarized its recommendations, taking into consideration the viewpoints of state directors and supervisors, teacher trainers, practical nurse supervisors, and local directors. All who attended had an opportunity to take an active part in the conference. The value of the meeting was so strongly imprinted upon the minds of the group that trade and industrial conferences were planned for the next five years. Included were proposals for intra- and inter-regional meetings for 1960 through 1963, and a national meeting for 1964. The meetings were held as planned.

**Significance of the Conferences**

The national conferences to consider the problems confronting state and local trade and industrial supervisors have been effective. Many states had common problems because the major issues tended to be national in concern. Still, the problems required state and local solutions. The conferees had an opportunity to identify significant aspects of national problems and to reach a consensus about desirable and effective state and local principles and practices.

The conferences served also to identify items that needed special study. One of these was teacher training.

*National Teacher Training Conferences*

Teacher training was inherently a part of every conference involving

---

[17] U.S. Department of Health, Education, and Welfare, Office of Education, *Trade and Industrial Education for the 1960's*, OE-84001. Washington: Government Printing Office, 1959.

trade and industrial educators. Their discussions and conclusions invariably had direct or related implications for the preparation of instructors. Deficiencies could often be traced to teacher education; progress and success could be likewise diagnosed.

Teacher education has been inseparable from the total trade and industrial education program; however, regional and national conferences devoted entirely to teacher education have been few in number.

### New York City Conference, April, 1946

Educators had frequently discussed the problem of expanding and improving the use of audio-visual instructional aids in trade and industrial education. Many of those most directly concerned had experience with such materials of instruction during military service in World War II. More generous use appeared to have value. Accordingly, at the Buffalo convention of the American Vocational Association in February, 1946, a few individuals, in conference with L. S. Hawkins, Chief of Trade and Industrial Education, Office of Education, reached an agreement to conduct an audio-visual education workshop for a selected, small group of trade and industrial teacher educators. Gilbert G. Weaver, teacher educator in New York City, offered the use of his laboratory space, equipment, and instructional staff for the proposed conference, and in addition agreed to plan and conduct the workshop.

Key states were invited to send representatives to the New York workshop for a three-week period in April and May, 1946. When the workshop group convened it consisted of 12 persons from widely scattered geographical locations and from the U.S. Office of Education. The members of the workshop received instruction and actual experience in preparing charts, slides, posters, and blackboard drawings, and in the use of tape recordings, motion pictures, and film strips in trade and industrial teacher education.

The workshop was immediately successful and two significant outgrowths were observed: (1) States that had not previously had audio-visual instruction in their teacher education program began to include such instruction, and (2) supplementary regional workshops were held at the University of Texas and the University of California, Los Angeles, in cooperation with state representatives of trade and industrial education. Subsequently, informal meetings of the workshop group were held in connection with the conventions of the American Vocational Association. The workshop also heightened the desire of the participants to probe more deeply into related elements of teacher education, seeking improvement.

### Washington, D.C., Conference, April 12-23, 1948

The conference in New York had provided an opportunity for the conference members to concentrate upon audio-visual instruction and to adopt points of view concerning the adaptation of these devices in teacher education programs. At the AVA meetings in St. Louis, 1946, and in Los Angeles, 1947, follow-up reports from teacher trainers indicated that much interest had been created since the New York meeting.

147

Out of these meetings on progress came a request for [another] workshop type of conference for the purpose of studying what has been developed for various teacher training programs, and to work out suggestions on unification of course titles; content within the courses; and, needed expansion and improvement.[18]

When the request for the conference was approved by the Office of Education, 14 teacher educators representing 13 states met with representatives of the Trade and Industrial Education Service in Washington, D.C.

Members of the workshop had sent to the Office of Education, in advance of the meeting, copies of the teacher training materials developed in their states. These materials were discussed, and experiences were shared. Then a report was prepared which summarized the findings of the group. The findings consisted of seven parts:

*Part one:* A report of teacher training courses, with a suggested order of presentation, based on an analysis of course content. The purpose of each course was indicated, and a listing of the major headings or topics which the course covered was included.

*Part two:* Teacher training proposals for full-time teachers, coordinators, supervisors, and directors. All agreed that a preservice teacher training course was imperative, and that the course would in fact precede other courses in teacher training.

*Part three:* An analysis of the training program for part-time trade and industrial teachers. Again members were of the opinion that preservice teacher training was imperative, but

since the group could not agree upon one plan, two alternative plans were suggested.

*Part four:* Suggestions to be followed for emergency teacher training programs. "When large numbers of teachers must be trained to meet training requirements, caused by any type of a national or local emergency, a thoroughly tested program of teacher training should be available for immediate use."[19] Emergency programs required superior teachers; hence the quality of the teacher training program available was most important.

*Part five:* A report entitled "Instructional Material for Apprentices" merely called attention to the necessity for joint participation, on a nationwide basis. It was recommended that assignments for the production and distribution of instructional material be made to certain states, and that the U.S. Office of Education take the lead in following up on the matter.

*Part six:* A discussion and recommendation of methods for conducting teacher training.

*Part seven:* Suggested ways of utilization and follow-up on the report of the Washington meeting.

It is noteworthy that representatives of 13 states could agree upon small details in teacher training. This suggested that the supposed regional or geographical differences were in reality not significant. Furthermore the conference group represented both large and small programs of trade and industrial education and teacher training.

---

[18] Federal Security Agency, United States Office of Education, *Report of Second Inter-Regional Conference in the Field of Teacher Training, Trade and Industrial Education,* 1948, p. 1.
[19] *Ibid.,* p. 25.

## Kansas City Conference, May 12-16, 1958

Programs for the training of teachers of trade and industrial subjects require critical evaluation and revision to keep pace with developing professional standards, advancing certification requirements, and a rapidly changing technology. Such critical evaluation of an activity can result in the discovery of needs.[20]

On this premise, a national conference on trade and industrial teacher training was called at Kansas City, Missouri, May 12-16, 1958, by the U.S. Office of Education. Ninety trade and industrial teacher educators from 41 universities and colleges and from 37 states and territories met for critical examination (2,430 man-hours of deliberation) of certification requirements, teacher competencies, curriculum development, preservice and inservice teacher training, training of women teachers, and the preparation of administrators and supervisors.

It is significant that in 1958 the states desired to assume more responsibility for the improvement of their teacher training programs than they had in previous years. The assigned state roles are also significant:

Each state will study its present teacher training program, first, for improvements in its present framework and structure, and second, for changes in structure if it is placing limitations on the program. This should be a joint enterprise of teacher educators, State supervisors, and administrators.

When new State plans are prepared, provisions for teacher training will probably be a little different than at present.

Certification requirements will have a thorough evaluation; there will be more flexibility in the major provisions in State plans.[21]

From 1906 to 1917 leadership in formulating ideals and practices in trade and industrial teacher education tended to come from the National Society for the Promotion of Industrial Education. From 1917 to 1933, leadership generally seemed to originate with the trade and industrial education service of the Federal Board for Vocational Education. In both instances it was largely a one-way process, in that published bulletins provided a pattern for states to follow and suggested what the state should do, with recommendations concerning the details of the problem. From a professional point of view these recommendations were sound, and they did suggest reasonable patterns for teacher preparation. However, except in isolated instances, they did not allow the states to participate in the discovery of the goals and purposes of teacher education. In a large sense this condition also prevailed during the period from 1933 to the end of World War II. This does not imply that the states were "muzzled" with no opportunity to assert their own creative ideas—far from it. But the influence from Washington was strong and compelling. No one actually objected. The Washington influence was probably the main reason why many of the teacher education programs were successful.

As noted, the three national teacher training conferences after World War

[20] U.S. Department of Health, Education, and Welfare, Office of Education, *New Dimensions in Trade and Industrial Teacher Training,* Circular No. 548, 1958, p. iii.
[21] *Ibid.,* p. 66.

II were entirely different. The approach to the problem of improvements in teacher education moved more along the lines of the states sharing their experiences in professional meetings and then reaching new conclusions about teacher training. The role of the Trade and Industrial Education Branch, Office of Education, was largely that of a catalyst; the Branch provided the environment in which goals for improvement could be reached. In the case of the Kansas City meeting, the states looked to the Branch for leadership, and the Branch obliged by providing the environment and encouragement for the state leaders to discuss their programs in detail. In addition the Branch provided the results of carefully prepared analyses of survey data as "grist for the mill," and other statistics which the conference members used during their discussions. The states were specifically asked to inform the Office of Education, Trade and Industrial Education Branch, concerning the role that they desired the Office of Education to take. These recommendations, as summarized by the Office of Education, indicated that plans should be made for action as follows:

1. Promote the development of sound research programs to continually explore new frontiers in teacher education.
2. Assist the several States in the development of experimental programs to test and validate the research findings.
3. Assess the developments through the gathering and critical analysis of statistics pertinent to trade and industrial teacher education in order to provide bases for further development and to establish trend information.

4. Provide ways and means for the coordination of the development of instructional materials for all phases of the trade and industrial education program, including teacher training materials.
5. Establish an advisory committee on teacher education and curriculum development for the purpose of coordinating such development.
6. Coordinate work conferences for the purpose of developing the tools and techniques to assist in the orderly expansion of the teacher education program, including promotional materials, evaluating devices, screening and testing instruments, etc.

The leadership role of the Office of Education is spelled out in action words:

L   *Locate* the best practices and make them known to the profession.
E   *Examine* critically the pertinent research findings.
A   *Adapt* and/or *adopt* recommendations for program improvement.
D   *Distribute* the information to the point of application.
E   *Experiment* to determine the most effective and efficient methods.
R   *Remove* obstacles that would prevent the development of new procedures.
S   *Search* for the real truths and share them.
H   *Hasten* the reporting of important findings.
I    *Initiate* a continuing series of workshops and conferences.
P   *Participate* professionally.[22]

The evidence shows that leadership by the Trade and Industrial Education Branch had been effective in providing encouragement and incentive for the states to make improvements in teacher education, and that the states definitely wanted the Branch to continue in this leadership role.

---

[22] *Ibid.*, pp. 66-67.

## Regional Conferences

For the purpose of providing assistance to the states, the nation is divided into four regions: North Atlantic, Central, Southern, and Pacific. A program specialist is assigned to each and is the direct representative of the director of the Trade and Industrial Education Branch. The function of the regional program specialist is important. To most of the trade and industrial education people in the region, he *is* the Office of Education. The extent to which the Office assists in a particular region depends largely upon the person assigned to regional responsibilities and upon the ways and means he uses to accomplish his work.

A regional program specialist is given broad responsibilities in order to permit wide development. He is expected to be well enough acquainted with the entire region to make an overall appraisal of its program and needs, to detect special problems, and to be in a position to determine which problems should command the attention of the Office of Education; further, he must recommend a program of action to the Office for additional or special service to a particular region. His dual role of representing the Office of Education to the region, and of representing the region to the Office, makes him equally responsible to keep local, state, and regional groups aware of the Office's problems, and to become better acquainted with the work and direction of the Office and with other national education agencies.

In order that the program specialist may render the most effective service to a region, he is expected to consult frequently with local, state, and national groups to build up his understanding of the educational, economic, labor, and social trends that affect his region. He performs some research and does professional writing, but to a larger extent he is concerned with the development of others' research and professional writing in his region and with the appropriate exchange of information thus advanced.

In order to facilitate this exchange, to encourage professional growth of personnel, and to promote program development in the region, the specialist from time to time arranges regional conferences. This is usually done with committees which assist in the development of an agenda adapted to the needs and urgent problems of the region. Through the years each region has had such conferences. The nature, duration, and direction of the conferences change with the times and with the needs as regional groups determine them. It is not possible to provide a complete listing of all regional conferences and their achievements. In fact only a very few formal reports of these conferences have been made. But the arrangements concerning two regional conferences—perhaps in some sense typical—will help to indicate the function of all conferences.

### Central Regional Conference, Des Moines, March 22-24, 1960

Sixty-nine representatives from 13 states, assisted by five representatives of the Trade and Industrial Education Branch of the Office of Education, met in a three day conference. The conference for 1960 was formulated by a planning committee after careful study and evaluation of the regional meeting of 1958. The conference theme was

151

"Strengthening Trade and Industrial Education for the 1960's." Included in the conference topics were discussions of recent developments in the program of trade and industrial education, research, and instructional materials. The group was concerned also with concepts of "self-development" as indicated by the following conference topics: Quest for Quality, Developing Local Leadership, and Developing Technical Competencies. The real value, always difficult to measure and judge, probably arises from the sharing of the viewpoints of Office of Education personnel with those of regional, state, and local leaders who are actually involved in programs of trade and industrial education.

### North Atlantic Regional Conference, New York City, April 4-6, 1960

Sixty-nine representatives from 12 states and the District of Columbia, assisted by five representatives of the Office of Education, met in conference discussions having the theme "Tooling Up for 1965." A regional committee assisted in the preparation of the program, which was directed toward meeting the needs and interests of the North Atlantic Region. Class organization, teacher training, technician training, curriculum development, research, and safety were among the topics presented and discussed.

### Planning in Other Regions

In a similar fashion, conferences were conducted in the Southern and Pacific regions. These conferences offered the only opportunity for many persons to meet representatives of the Office of Education. Insight into the nature of the national program, the discussion of national trends, and the review of the direction of trade and industrial education as seen from Washington added perspective to regional matters.

The opportunity to talk with the persons in other states about professional problems was another valuable outcome of the regional conferences. Such discussions not only led to the exchange of ideas but frequently resulted in new regional projects of common interest.

### National Leadership Development Conferences

For years, especially from 1950, the growth of the program in trade and industrial education had far exceeded the development of leadership, which had become an imperative problem. The problem was national in scope and needed the attention of a national group. First discussions concerning leadership training were program items of the Policy and Planning Committee for Trade and Industrial Education of the American Vocational Association. A subcommittee was organized in 1954, under the chairmanship of James R. D. Eddy, to explore the possibility of plans for training "newly appointed supervisory personnel." [23] The subcommittee's plan was approved by the Policy and Planning Committee at the San Francisco convention of AVA in December, 1954. Due to the nature of the pro-

---

[23] U.S. Department of Health, Education, and Welfare, Office of Education, *National Leadership Development Conference in Trade and Industrial Education*, Circular No. 477, 1956, p. 1.

posed conference, the plan was referred to James H. Pearson, Assistant Commissioner for Vocational Education, U.S. Office of Education, with the request that the Office sponsor and underwrite the costs of the conference. Pearson approved the idea and proceeded to make preliminary arrangements.

A special committee was appointed and a meeting was held in San Francisco, February 26 and 27, 1955. [This meeting was an extended part of the Pacific Regional Conference on Trade and Industrial Education.] The committee explored the idea of leadership conferences in considerable detail, suggested some procedures, and agreed:

... that the purpose of a leadership development conference would be to provide potential leaders with an opportunity to identify and evaluate the basic concepts of trade and industrial education through the study and discussion of problems in administration, supervision, and organization of vocational programs to the end that the skills of leadership would be strengthened throughout the United States.[24]

The plan from the San Francisco meeting was discussed subsequently in regional conferences and approved.

On April 30, 1955, Pearson called a meeting in Washington, D.C., to consider detailed arrangements for a national leadership conference. It was concluded that the first conference should be held August 1-12, 1955, at the Colorado State University, Fort Collins, Colorado. A second preliminary meeting was called by Pearson in Washington, D.C., for June 10-12, 1955, at which time the final plans

were made for the Fort Collins conference, including selection of leaders and resource personnel, and the preparation of the agenda.

### The Fort Collins Conference, August 1-12, 1955, Colorado State University

Fifty-nine persons, representing 33 states, several territories, and the District of Columbia, attended the conference. The staff of five was aided by seven resource people who made special presentations. The basic conference plan consisted of a general presentation by a resource assistant or a member of the staff, followed by group discussion—there were four groups—on topics or problems related to the presentation. The main topics were:

1. Industrial, Economic, and Social Conditions that Require Proficiency and Full Utilization of Industrial Workers of the Nation.
2. Principles and Practices of Trade and Industrial Education.
3. The Place, Functions, and Importance of Trade Extension Training.
4. The Place, Functions, and Importance of Preparatory Training.
5. Important Program Requirements.
6. Federal, State, and Local Administrative Relationships in Vocational Education.
7. Organization and Utilization of Advisory Committees.
8. Requirements for Trade and Industrial Teachers.
9. Selection, Placement, and Follow-up of Trainees.
10. The Trade and Industrial Supervisor's Responsibilities.
11. Public Relations.[25]

Three evaluations of the conference were made—one by the conferees, a

[24] *Ibid.*
[25] *Ibid.*, pp. 110-113.

second by a special committee [not directly connected with the conference operation], and a third by the conference staff. Details of these evaluations were included in the report of the conference and used in preparation for the second conference.

The first conference produced an enthusiastic response to the role played by the Office of Education, Trade and Industrial Education Branch, in promoting the development of leadership. The final report of the independent evaluation committee read as follows:

The Independent Committee feels that this type of activity is a definite and important function of the Vocational Education Division of the U.S. Office of Education; that only as such activities are sponsored by the U.S. Office of Education will they be nationwide in character and composition of membership. Further, it will require the backing and leadership of the Federal Office so States will regard the training experience with the real importance it deserves.[26]

### The Lafayette Conference, July 30-August 10, 1956, Purdue University

Fifty-nine persons representing 39 states and territories attended the second conference, which was conducted by a staff of six, assisted by 15 resource persons who made special presentations. The second conference followed a pattern similar to that of the first. Although some adjustments, additions, and deletions were made—based upon the reports of the evaluation committees—at its close the Office of Education merely reported:

It would seem that a background of experience in conducting a program suitable for the development of national leaders in trade and industrial education is being accumulated. There appears to be emerging a pattern that should provide a maximum opportunity for the various States and the Office of Education, Trade and Industrial Education Branch, to work together to develop strong leadership in the field of vocational education.[27]

### The Ithaca Conference, August 12-23, 1957, Cornell University

The third leadership conference, held on the campus of Cornell University, was attended by 52 participants from 31 states and two territories. The conference was conducted by a staff of nine, supported at one time or another by 31 resource persons.

The Ithaca conference advanced beyond those of 1955 and 1956 in its scope and methods. The conference tended to cover broader areas, with the intent of providing leadership, and involved the use of many new techniques of group discussion and participation. It was intended that the actual presentations and the arrangements be models for the participants. The conference moved from a pedestrian treatment of issues in trade and industrial education toward a more dynamic approach to stimulate intellectual creativity.

The keynote of the conference was quite personal in delegating responsibility: "To recognize the need for each of us to become better developers of leadership at all levels of supervision and administration." [28]

---

[26] U.S. Department of Health, Education, and Welfare, Office of Education, *National Leadership Development Conference in Trade and Industrial Education*, Circular No. 492, Washington: Government Printing Office, 1956, p. 1.

[27] *Ibid.*, p. 2.

[28] U.S. Department of Health, Education, and Welfare, Office of Education, *National Leadership Development Conference, Trade and Industrial Education*, Circular No. 519, 1957, p. 4.

## The Columbus Conference, July 28-August 8, 1958, The Ohio State University

The fourth conference, held on the campus of The Ohio State University, was attended by 56 conferees from 36 states and territories and the District of Columbia. The conference was conducted by a staff of six, assisted by 22 resource persons. Although objectives remained stable, the Columbus conference was marked by even more striking methodological departures. There were listening teams, evaluation groups, leadership groups, women's groups, and task forces, all designed to make more meaningful the actual participation of the conferees in their small-and-large group leadership experiences. All of the activities focused upon the idea of being alert to change: "Changing occupational patterns and production processes present a continuing challenge to trade and industrial educators—a challenge that places a premium on existing leadership and calls for the discovery and development of new leaders." [29]

Evaluation of the conference provided reasonable evidence that the system was in fact achieving its goals.

## The San Luis Obispo Conference, August 17-28, 1959, California State Polytechnic College

A conference staff of two, assisted by eight resource persons, met a conference group of 25 representing 12 states and territories, at the California conference. A restatement of goals was made: "The objectives of these conferences have been modified to meet the educational, social, economic, and industrial needs of the period. The underlying objective has been that of developing skilled leaders with vigor and astuteness in trade and industrial education." [30] Although previous methods and techniques prevailed at the San Luis Obispo conference, the outstanding feature was the pursuit of the task force concept, which provided a single problem requiring both large and small group action.

## The Menomonie Conference, August 8-19, 1960, Stout State College

The 43 persons who attended this conference represented twenty states and two territories. The staff of eight was aided in its work by 13 resource persons who participated individually in the activities at appropriate stages. In purpose the conference in Menomonie, Wisconsin, held the line of its predecessors, but again in methodology it differed considerably. The differences were largely in the degree to which conference members were involved in various action situations such as "buzz" groups, listening teams, case study analyses, and other techniques calculated to enhance participation. Presentations by resource persons were thoroughly analyzed by the group.

Emphasis was placed upon philosophy of trade and industrial education, teacher competencies, teacher education, manpower developments, curriculum materials, the role of management

[29] U.S. Department of Health, Education, and Welfare, Office of Education, *Leadership Development in Trade and Industrial Education, 1958,* OE-84010, Circular No. 626, 1960, p. v.

[30] U.S. Department of Health, Education, and Welfare, Office of Education, *National Leadership Development Conference, 1959,* OE-84013, 1960, p. 3.

and labor in training of manpower, improving coordination and supervision, public relations, measuring student achievement, and other problems that were deemed critical in the development of excellence in trade and industrial education. The rapidly changing and growing program placed an even greater premium upon competent teachers and upon adequate curriculum materials; therefore the conference was focused upon these elements.[31]

### The Washington, D.C., Conference, July 30-August 10, 1962, Sheraton-Park Hotel

The National Leadership Development Conference held in Washington, D.C., 1962, expanded its field notably and adopted a new emphasis. It was not limited to trade and industrial education. All of the vocational services participated in the conference, which had a "Manpower Development and Training" theme. After the Manpower Development and Training Act was signed by President John F. Kennedy on March 15, there were serious questions to be discussed concerning the legislation, which focused upon unemployment due to automation, shifting labor market demands, and other economic changes. Despite the emphasis upon the Act, however, the conference included topics with a leadership orientation in many related areas.

Forty-seven persons from 25 states and the District of Columbia attended. Discussion and conference leaders were selected from the staff of the Division of Vocational and Technical Education.

In addition to the other activities the conference group worked on a task force assignment related to the study of vocational education in a five county area of the hypothetical State of Euphoria. The task force technique, which had worked successfully in other conferences, was particularly appropriate in the Washington, D.C., conference because it led to group decisions about a total program of vocational education which the previous conferences had not considered. On the other hand, the complexities involved and the limited time available made depth of penetration difficult to achieve. The fact that a conference was held at this time did set the stage for situations to be confronted in the future, when the Vocational Education Act of 1963 became a reality.

### The University Park Conference, August 5-16, 1963, The Pennsylvania State University

In 1963 the leadership conference was again limited to the area of trade and industrial education. Fifty-one persons from 28 states and two territories attended. The organization pattern was not unlike that of the conferences before 1962. Although the group of conferees was homogeneous in its representation of a particular area of vocational education, its activities were broad in scope. The content covered a wide range of practical problems that the leader had to cope with in the growing complexity of new program development.

The conference roll call and the resource staff were the largest in the

---

[31] U.S. Department of Health, Education, and Welfare, Office of Education, *National Leadership Development Conference in Trade and Industrial Education*, OE-84013, 1960, p. iii.

group's history. Thirty-one persons appeared at different times before the group, to set the theme for discussion of a particular topic. This was a distinct advantage, in that each resource aide was well known for his leadership in the problem area under discussion.

## The Fort Collins Conference, July 27-August 7, 1964, Colorado State University

The 1964 conference was held at Colorado State University in the same location where the conferences had started a decade earlier. There had been nine conferences during the ten-year period. (A conference was not held during 1961.) Two members of the staff of the first conference, Walter M. Arnold and Earl M. Bowler, participated as staff members for this anniversary conference.

The conference group of 56 included five women, 11 state supervisors of trade and industrial education, and a variety of other local, area, and state coordinators and supervisors. The staff and resource persons were 23 in number.

Conference methodology was a sample of the many successful techniques used in past conferences. In addition, an emphasis was placed on leadership skills, and the conference environment was conducive to developing a sound knowledge, understanding, and appreciation of the emphasis needed in the future of trade and industrial education.

## Significance of the Leadership Conferences

That each conference was successful in meeting its objectives was demonstrated by the evaluative instruments used.

Groups of trade and industrial educators from different states were removed from their normal working environment and set to work in study and discussion of common problems. At once it was realized that there were many ways to solve the same problem. Furthermore the combined experiences of the group frequently produced new ideas and procedures of value to all. Individual members could measure the progress of their state in relation to other states and could detect whether they were ahead or behind in any particular development.

During the decade of the first nine conferences more than 400 trade and industrial educators participated. In terms of location and attendance, the conferences served all sections of the nation. Programs were chosen to be representative of the critical issues in trade and industrial education, and each of the conferences tended to be provocative.

Perhaps one of the most significant developments to result from the conferences has been the *esprit de corps* which has developed among the conferees. Personal friendships have been added to professional understanding, and a better communication network has spread across the nation in the area of trade and industrial education.

These gains would not have been possible without the farsightedness of James R. D. Eddy and James H. Pearson. Nor would the program have been carried into action without the leadership of the Trade and Industrial Education Branch of the Division of Vocational and Technical Education.

157

## Research in Trade and Industrial Education

Prior to the early 1950's, emphasis upon research in trade and industrial education by the states can scarcely be discerned. Certainly there were many community surveys, trade analyses, standards of various kinds, and evaluative criteria prepared in relation to the "going" program. That is the point: Such research was largely a secondary part of other programs, not their primary objective. Obviously one could argue that these studies did provide information about the progress and direction of the program, that changes were made on the basis of such data, and that therefore the process was in accord with the essential idea of research. It seems rather pointless, however, to debate the issue when it is clear the goal of trade and industrial educators was not research as such.

Research as a regular function of the "going" program of trade and industrial education received much emphasis after World War II. The National Association of Industrial Teacher Educators, American Vocational Association, had compiled lists of theses and dissertations in industrial education which were published periodically by the U.S. Office of Education. These lists indicate the general direction of research, but they also show that few of the projects were directed toward the most urgent matters confronting trade and industrial education. Therefore, state directors and supervisors were urged to provide funds for research and to stimulate research activities by exerting leadership in that direction.

The first significant review of the need for research in trade and industrial education after World War II was reported by Allen T. Hamilton in 1954. Major purposes of the review were:

1. Emphasize the need for a greater stress on research.

2. Stimulate research activities.

3. Stress the fact that research in trade and industrial education cannot be justified unless the findings contribute to the development and improvement of the program and are used to achieve that end.

4. Call attention to the need for enriching teacher training through a study of the professional problems that confront the teacher, supervisor, coordinator, and administrator in the operating program.

5. Encourage teachers, coordinators, supervisors, and administrators in the operating program to utilize research methods in solving their professional problems.

6. Emphasize the need for directing greater effort toward giving an understanding of research methods in professional courses offered in teacher-training institutions.

7. Show the indispensability of research in effective state supervision and teacher training.

8. Indicate that members of state boards for vocational education and the State Director as their official representative have a continuing need for factual data relating to many problems in trade and industrial vocational education which can be obtained through organized study and investigation.

9. Emphasize the fact that the State Supervisor of trade and industrial vocational education is responsible for promoting research in the state unless special provisions are made for someone else to assume that duty.[32]

---

[32] Allen T. Hamilton, *Research in Trade and Industrial Vocational Education.* Chicago: American Technical Society, 1954, pp. 38-39.

Hamilton's report was widely circulated and created a need for a national conference to review the entire problem and to make plans for developing a nationwide research program in trade and industrial education.

## Washington Research Conference, June 13-17, 1955

The Division of Vocational Education, U.S. Office of Education, called a conference for the purposes of (1) listing a series of problems in trade and industrial education about which more factual data were needed, (2) suggesting a procedure which the Office of Education should follow in cooperating with the states in conducting a program of research, and (3) outlining forms that could be used to secure the necessary data concerning research from the field. The 19 persons who attended this conference, in Washington, D.C., represented 15 states.

The conference discussions and subsequent survey of the states, regarding specific research needs and activities, indicated that 21 states were conducting research studies. The research problems in trade and industrial education that needed emphasis were listed as follows: [33]

1. The impact of industrial trends on trade and industrial education.
2. Procedures and standards for selecting students for training in day trade and industrial courses.
3. The philosophical, economic, psychological, and social bases for trade and industrial education.
4. Determining the attitudes of certain groups of people toward trade and industrial education.

5. Determining ways and means to provide more adequate related instructional materials.
6. Establishing occupational areas and program standards for vocational technical education.
7. Learning activities that have most value for youths preparing for trade and industrial occupations.
8. Methods of extending and improving training services for adult workers.
9. The establishment and acceptance of the responsibility for placement and follow-up of trade preparatory students at the local level.
10. Comparing the general type of trade and industrial program, cutting across craft lines, which includes two or more families of occupations with the specific types of program organized within craft or trade fields.
11. The field service activities engaged in by teacher trainers in trade and industrial education.
12. The training and activities of all personnel rendering guidance service to secondary school students.
13. The relative advantages and disadvantages of the comprehensive high school versus the separate vocational school.
14. The relationship of consecutive hours of organized instruction and supervised practice to efficient training for trade and industrial occupations.
15. The extent and nature of training needed for trade extension teachers.

Washington was the site of a further discussion of research in industrial education, held on February 13, 1958, in connection with the national meeting of State Directors and Executive Officers of Vocational Education. This second discussion was partly a reaction to

---

[33] U.S. Department of Health, Education, and Welfare, Office of Education, Division of Vocational Education, *Research and Studies in Trade and Industrial Education,* Misc. 3495, December 1955, pp. 25-35.

the conference just described. The research section of this second Washington meeting was conducted by Lynn A. Emerson, professor emeritus, Cornell University. He observed that much research was of an "applied" nature, local in character, but that little attention had been paid to research in the basic sciences and disciplines that underlie industrial education.[34] Although some results had been very good and did supply needed information, there were indications of considerable superficiality and lack of depth. Emerson noted that this situation could be expected, since most vocational educators were practical minded and tended to shy away from research jobs. Besides time, research required "energy and concentrated reflective thinking," in Emerson's words. Few people in industrial education were really qualified for such work.

Emerson saw the basic problem: Research has not been closely related to the day-to-day program; thus its significance was not generally understood.

Research by university personnel in industrial education had suffered because of heavy teaching loads, lack of orientation among some of the university staff, and lack of funds to support research. Emerson hit upon another key point when he said: "Possibly research by industrial educators has been neglected because their superior officers do not recognize its value, and do not give sufficient recognition to the research efforts of the subordinates."[35]

## Research Activities of the American Vocational Association

Assignment of research responsibilities to committees has been a continuous part of the work of AVA since 1926. A special research committee was established in 1940, leading to development of the Committee on Research and Publications, organized in 1943. The publications of this committee have provided information which was previously not available. A cooperative relationship has existed between the Division of Vocational and Technical Education, U.S. Office of Education, and the AVA in the matter of special publications, which prevented unnecessary duplication of effort.

In 1959 the title of the Research and Publications Committee was changed to Publications Committee, and it was again reorganized. Representatives of each of the AVA divisions served. Also, subsequently the Division of Trade and Industrial Education, AVA, developed a divisional committee on research in order to stimulate research activity within the particular area.

The organizational structure for research was then complete within the AVA, and a pattern for cooperative relationships between the U.S. Office of Education was established.[36]

## AVA-USOE Research Relationships

The Research Committee of the Division of Vocational and Technical Education, U.S. Office of Education,

---

[34] U.S. Department of Health, Education, and Welfare, Office of Education, *Research in Vocational Education*, February 13, 1958. (Mimeographed.)

[35] *Ibid.*, p. 6.

[36] For a more comprehensive treatment see, Carl L. Bartel, "Origin, Development and Work of the American Vocational Association," (unpublished doctoral dissertation, University of Missouri, 1959), p. 515 ff.

and the Research Committee of the American Vocational Association have worked cooperatively since 1960 in the promotion of research.

Annual joint meetings of the groups are held and the two committees have jointly sponsored national research seminars. In 1963, such a seminar was held at Purdue University, and in 1964, seminars were held at Purdue University, The Ohio State University, and the Pennsylvania State University.

### Area Vocational Education Branch

Active national interest in technical education and urgent demands for technicians led the Trade and Industrial Education Branch to request that a meeting of a selected group of educators be called in connection with the annual convention of the American Vocational Association in St. Louis, December, 1956. Twenty-one persons responded to the invitation from James H. Pearson, Assistant Commissioner for Vocational Education. John P. Walsh, Director, Trade and Industrial Education Branch, was chairman and conference leader of the meeting, held on December 5.

The meeting was essentially a "freewheeling" session for exchanging ideas and determining the extent of interest in solving problems of technical education. Pearson pointed out that the real question was not one of getting into technical education; vocational educators were already involved. The real problem was to identify what the

Office of Education should do to improve technical education. After considerable discussion the consensus was that the Office of Education should take leadership in the problem of technical education to the extent of employing personnel in appropriate categories, and of conducting national and regional conferences on the problem.

The first national conference on vocational technical education was held in Washington, D.C., May 13-17, 1957. Twenty educators responded to the invitation. The conference was conducted under the chairmanship and direction of Lee W. Ralston, Director of the Division of Practical Arts, Los Angeles County Schools, Los Angeles, California. Office of Education personnel participated in the meeting, as did a number of resource specialists. Commissioner of Education Lawrence Derthick challenged the participants with the thought that it was their responsibility to keep ahead of the times—not just up to date. Pearson emphasized the challenge by saying, "If there is one group of educators in this country that must be sensitive at all times to our technological advances and our economic and social changes, it is those in vocational education." [37]

During the week, the conference members reached conclusions concerning some of the difficult problems, but they were plagued with uncertainties in defining the work of the technician and his role in the industrial life of the future. The Washington meeting was considered a preliminary event, in which agreements were to be reached

---

[37] U.S. Department of Health, Education, and Welfare, Office of Education, *Vocational Technical Education, A Report of a National Conference,* Washington, D.C., May 13-17, 1957, p. 1.

that could be discussed in regional meetings with a larger group of vocational educators.

Before the close of the Washington conference, regional conferences were planned for the following places and dates: San Francisco, October 15-17; Milwaukee, October 28-30; Ogden, Utah, November 5-7; Memphis, also November 5-7; and Asbury Park, New Jersey, November 12-14, 1957. The five conferences were held within one month, with 42 states, three territories, and 196 persons participating. The conferences established the fact that a real need existed for technical education throughout the United States, that the various states were ready, willing, and able to move into a more expanded program of technical education, and that they looked to the Trade and Industrial Education Branch, Office of Education for leadership. Additional conferences were held in some states to determine more specifically self-interest and needs.

The next step in developing programs of vocational technical education was the preparation of a special bulletin to clarify understanding of vocational technical occupations and to provide related information.[38] Lynn A. Emerson was employed as a special consultant to the Division of Vocational Education, U.S. Office of Education, for this purpose.

## National Defense Education Act of 1958

By passing the National Defense Education Act of 1958, Congress acted to strengthen the national defense and to expand and improve certain educational programs which were thought to be representative of critical national needs. Title VIII of the act concerns Area Vocational Education programs. In connection with the statement of findings and purposes, the Act reads as follows:

The Congress hereby finds that the excellent programs of vocational education, which States have established and are carrying on with the assistance provided by the Federal Government under the Smith-Hughes Vocational Education Act and the Vocational Education Act of 1946 (the George-Barden Act), need expansion to provide vocational education to residents of areas inadequately served and also to meet national defense requirements for personnel equipped to render skilled assistance in fields particularly affected by scientific and technological developments. It is therefore the purpose of this title to provide assistance to the States so that they may improve their vocational education programs through area vocational education programs approved by State Boards for vocational education as providing vocational and related technical training and retraining for youths, adults, and older persons, including related instruction for apprentices, designed to fit them for useful employment as technicians or skilled workers in scientific or technical fields.[39]

During discussion of the bill in the Senate, and upon the advice of The Governors' Committee on Federal-State Relations, an amendment was added to Title VIII to limit the use of the funds to programs necessary to the national defense. The amendment in Section 303(a)(3), reads as follows:

---

[38] U.S. Department of Health, Education, and Welfare, Office of Education, *Vocational-Technical Education for American Industry*, Circular No. 530, 1958.

[39] Public Law 85-864, 85th Congress, 2nd Session, Section 301, September 2, 1958.

That *funds* appropriated under Section 301 of this title *be used exclusively* for the *training of individuals* designed to fit them for useful employment *as highly skilled technicians* in recognized occupations requiring scientific knowledge as determined by the State board for such State in fields necessary for the national defense.[40]

It was further provided that Title VIII of the National Defense Education Act would amend the George-Barden Act and become Title III of that Act. All of the provisions concerning Federal-State relationships would then apply to the Area Vocational Education programs.

### Establishment of the Branch

It was commonly assumed that the program provided by Title III of the George-Barden Act would become an additional responsibility of the Trade and Industrial Education Branch, Division of Vocational Education, Office of Education. Instead, however, the Area Vocational Education Branch was created for this purpose. This new branch, separate and distinct from the others, was established because other branches had been created in response to other titles of the National Defense Education Act, and Assistant Commissioner Pearson felt it imperative to make similar arrangements for the new title. Also, under a branch arrangement, the problems of budget, personnel, and other operational issues would receive additional attention.

State departments of education, in response to the Area Vocational Educational program, generally followed the procedure of adding a new area

of interest directly to the Trade and Industrial Education organization of the state. In only a few states was an area organization made separate from the trade and industrial organization. The Area Vocational Education Branch became an official part of the Vocational Division of the Office of Education on July 1, 1959. Soon thereafter the name of the Division was changed to the Division of Vocational and Technical Education.[41]

### Reorganization of the Division of Vocational and Technical Education

The Panel of Consultants on Vocational Education (see Chapter 15) made a number of recommendations concerning the future direction of vocational education. The Panel did not presume to cast a precise working model of the entire national structure of vocational education, but it did make three points relative to the Office of Education.

First, the division having major responsibility for vocational education in the Office of Education should be headed by a "well-trained, experienced, and capable vocational educator who should report directly to the Commissioner of Education." The Panel considered that the position of the chief administrative officer for vocational education was entirely too low in the administrative structure of the Office of Education. This situation, if continued, would be a deterrent to progress, the Panel believed. Second, the

---

[40] *Ibid.* [Author's italics.]

[41] A discussion related to the work of the Area Vocational Education Branch is to be found in Chapter 15.

163

Panel placed a premium upon "professional competence" as the "prevailing policy for leadership personnel in this Federal agency," and urged salary, authority, and responsibility to attract and hold the most capable people. Third,

It is recommended that the State be considered the regional agency for the operation and administration of vocational and technical education, and that the services of the Federal agency be concentrated at the Washington office of the Office of Education.[42]

The Panel felt that if the highly specialized services were dispersed into regional offices, they would not be equally available to the states.

It was expected that some reorganization would take place in the Vocational and Technical Division. However, when Commissioner Francis Keppel announced the reorganization on August 17, 1964, the administrative position of the Assistant Commissioner for Vocational Education remained the same, a part of the Bureau of Educational Assistance Programs, headed by an associate commissioner.

Reorganization within the Division of Vocational and Technical Education proceeded under the direction of Walter M. Arnold, Assistant Commissioner for Vocational Education. Arnold was guided by the fundamental ideas expressed in the Vocational Education Act of 1963. These were:

1. The programs of vocational education are to be geared to labor market needs, both immediate and future, on local, State, regional, and national bases.

2. The programs to be offered under the terms of the 1963 Act will prepare students for employment in a great variety and range of jobs. Training will include the entire occupational spectrum, excluding only those jobs which the Commissioner of Education determines to be generally considered professional or which require a baccalaureate degree.

3. The Vocational Education Act of 1963 embodies the philosophy that all our citizens must have access to education and training that is of high quality and realistic in terms of opportunities for gainful employment. This service should be available to all, from the least able and the disadvantaged to those of high level of technical ability.

4. The new Act provides for vocational education programs to be conducted in any type of school or educational institution.

5. The Act places special emphasis on periodic evaluation of goals and progress. The States are required to evaluate their programs and vocational services continuously in the light of labor market needs and the needs of all groups in all communities in the State.

6. Research and development, long tools of successful businesses and industries, are assigned an important place in the future of vocational education.[43]

Arnold's staff was involved in the design of a new operating structure for the Division, that would embody the fundamental provisions of the act of 1963. Its final reorganization structure is shown in the chart on the opposite page.

The major change in the reorganization, as shown by the chart, is the provision for the activities of the Division to be divided among three associate directors: (1) for professional resources, (2) for field administration,

---

[42] U.S. Department of Health, Education, and Welfare, Office of Education, *Education for a Changing World of Work*, OE-80021. Washington: Government Printing Office, 1963, p. 254.
[43] Walter M. Arnold, "New Directions in Vocational Education," *American Vocational Journal*, Vol. 39, No. 7, October 1964, pp. 10-11.

# DIVISION OF VOCATIONAL AND TECHNICAL EDUCATION

and (3) for research and development. The Associate Director for Professional Resources administers three branches. The following quotation discusses those branches and also describes the other two associate directors:

*Student Instruction Branch*—with specialists in secondary, postsecondary and adult instruction programs for groups such as the socioeconomically disadvantaged.

*Occupations Branch*—with specialists in the occupational categories. [An emphasis upon trade and industrial education will be located here.]

*Auxiliary Service Branch*—with specialists in curriculum development, teacher education, facilities, vocational guidance, and work-study programs.

*The Associate Director for Field Administration.* The Field Administration staff will function as the operating arm of the Division, providing administrative direction and coordination to a field service staff in each of the nine regional offices of the Department of Health, Education, and Welfare. . . . It will serve as the channel through which professional consultation and assistance is made available to the regional offices and to the states.

*The Associate Director for Research and Development.* The third major function is unique in the history of the Division. This function is authorized under

Sec. 4(c) of the Vocational Education Act of 1963.

. . . .

The new Research and Development staff will be committed to these objectives.

- The establishment of standards for federally sponsored research and development projects.
- The utilization of research and development resources of related disciplines. This will involve enlisting the services of economists, sociologists, psychologists, and other professional workers to assist in evaluation and planning.
- Coordination and assistance in the expansion of State and regional research and development capabilities.
- The promotion and implementation of innovative programs with built-in provisions for evaluation.
- The implementation of research and development projects concerned with preparing and motivating individuals for life-long productive careers.
- The communication and dissemination of relevant information derived from federally sponsored and State supported projects.

To accomplish these objectives the Research and Development staff will be concerned with:

165

Employment Opportunities—including the identification of labor market trends and emerging job opportunities and their relationship to training needs; the common skills associated with clusters of jobs; development of vocational counseling and guidance data reflecting emerging employment opportunities, and the development of model local, State and regional job surveys.

Human Resources Development—focusing on the individual needs of vocational students; improved ways of teaching culturally deprived youngsters; development of basic learning skills; motivation of career guidance techniques at various age levels.

Educational Resources Development and Training—improving vocational education curricula, facilities, teacher training and recruitment, guidance and counseling techniques and instructional materials; encouraging and evaluating pilot and demonstration programs at State and local levels; devising new and imaginative ways of meeting the problems of continuing education.[44]

The major purpose of the reorganization was increased efficiency. Arnold placed value upon the plan because it not only provided a sounding board for ideas from the field, but it gave assistance, advice, and support which streamlined the communication from the Division to the states.

In the states the reorganization met with reaction that ranged from complete endorsement to violent opposition. Only a minimum of information had been available to the states, which created concern among some vocational educators. They viewed the future as an adjustment to an unknown quantity, probably because their method of operation with the branches of the Office of Education was being disrupted.

## Reorganization Continues

The new organization was scarcely six months old when change was again in the making. Several federal acts had assigned responsibilities to the Office of Education; consequently the Commissioner sought to review the organizational structure in order to improve the efficiency of operation. These activities came to an abrupt halt when the President announced, on April 15, 1965, that a task force had been established to "study the organization and staffing of the Office of Education."

The task force recommendations were announced on June 18, and the organizational structure provided for four Bureaus: Bureau of Elementary and Secondary Education; Bureau of Adult and Vocational Education; Bureau of Higher Education; and Bureau of Research.

Within the Bureau of Research, a Division of Adult and Vocational Education Research was created to administer the research program authorized by Section 4(c) of the Vocational Education Act of 1963.[45]

Thus the responsibility for research in vocational education was removed from the direct administration of the Division of Vocational and Technical Education. Such research was now the function of a Division-level unit within the new Bureau.

The Division of Vocational and Technical Education again came up for review, and various branches, sections, and units were regrouped. On August 16, 1965, the Commissioner approved an organization built around five basic

---

[44] Walter M. Arnold, op. cit., pp. 13-14.
[45] "Organizational Structure of USOE Vocational-Technical Division," American Vocational Journal, Vol. 40, No. 7, October 1965, pp. 31-33.

elements which accomplishes the following:

1. Translates major delegated authorities and responsibilities into clearly identified staff functions.
2. Establishes appropriate administrative levels with effective channels of operation to carry out these administrative and program responsibilities.
3. Establishes four Branches with appropriate sections and units to provide national leadership and expertise in vocational-technical education and manpower development.
4. Provides channels of communication between all levels of state, national, regional and local agencies and institutions which provide substantive programs of vocational and technical education.
5. Gives visible identity to major occupational fields in the line of administration and establishes the position of "chief" of these services with supportive staff.[46]

The result of the administrative adjustment produced the following organization chart. (Page 168).

These changes in the organizational structure of the Division of Vocational and Technical Education may have been well considered from the standpoint of organizational structure, but state and local leaders in vocational education were far from pleased. Reaction set in immediately, first at the Minneapolis convention of AVA in 1964, and again at the Miami Beach convention in 1965.

### Reaction at AVA—Minneapolis Convention, 1964

The National Association of State Directors of Vocational Education is a professional group of major importance in the normal affairs of vocational education. The state directors are continually alert to change, and when the

relocation of the Division of Vocational and Technical Education in the administrative structure of the Office of Education failed to materialize, they expressed their points of view concerning the staffing pattern as follows:

WHEREAS, the functions and staffing pattern of vocational education in the U.S. Office of Education continues to be assigned under the Bureau of Educational Assistance Programs, and

WHEREAS, the Federal Vocational Education Acts have imposed added and broadened administrative responsibilities upon the Vocational and Technical Division of the U.S. Office of Education, and

WHEREAS, the fulfillment and discharge of these responsibilities must be effected in cooperation with other governmental agencies and their counterparts in the 50 States and the several territories, and

WHEREAS, in the interest of National economy and the public welfare, and to facilitate maximum program effectiveness, it is essential that the Vocational and Technical Division in the U.S. Office of Education have Bureau status,

THEREFORE, BE IT RESOLVED, that the State Directors of Vocational Education in their 46th Annual Convention reaffirm their position, taken at the 45th Convention, and continue their strong recommendation for the establishment within the organizational structure of the U.S. Office of Education a Bureau of Vocational and Technical Education under an Associate Commissioner.

Similarly, when the internal reorganization of the Division of Vocational and Technical Education occurred, the State Directors went on record as follows:

WHEREAS, the Vocational and Technical Division of the U.S. Office of Education has been restructured for administrative purposes, and

WHEREAS, it is recognized the basic and primary function of the Division is to

---

[46] *Ibid.*, p. 33.

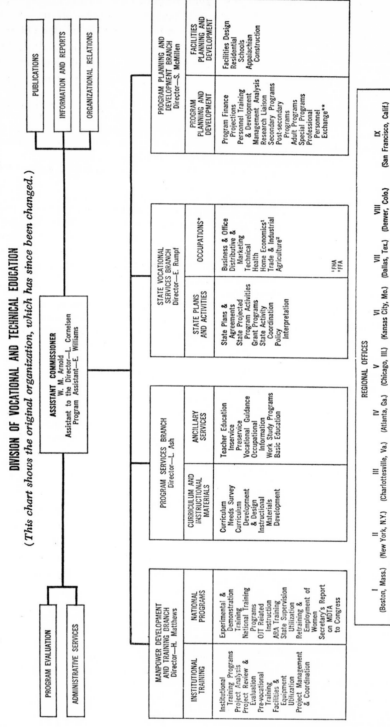

DIVISION OF VOCATIONAL AND TECHNICAL EDUCATION

*(This chart shows the original organization, which has since been changed.)*

render service to the States in their administration and conduct of effective programs of vocational and technical education, and

WHEREAS, the organizational structure through which this service is rendered has direct and significant implications for the States and their programs,

THEREFORE, BE IT RESOLVED, that the State Directors endorse the principles involved in the reorganization, pledge to the U.S. Office of Education the support of their association in the implementation of the services to be provided, and at the end of one year informally assess and appraise the effectiveness of the services.

The AVA House of Delegates also proposed a resolution at its Minneapolis meeting in December, 1964, concerning the organizational pattern for vocational education. The resolution touched on such points as: the years of effective federal-state relationships, the significance of the available consultative services, and a sense of alarm that the reorganization "dissipates" the gains. Then it concluded as follows:

THEREFORE, BE IT RESOLVED, that the officers of the American Vocational Association be directed to take whatever steps are appropriate and necessary, including soliciting support of members of the National Congress and the President of the United States to get the organizational structure for the administration of vocational education in the United States Office of Education changed so that more clearly defined administrative channels will be effected, which will result in more effective working relationships between state and federal officials and thus encourage the further development of needed leadership in the several program fields of vocational education and the strengthening of all phases of vocational and technical education, and,

BE IT FURTHER RESOLVED, that the

American Vocational Association strongly recommends that there be established within the organizational structure of the United States Office of Education, a Bureau of Vocational-Technical Education under an Associate Commissioner, well qualified with training and experience in the field of vocational education, with divisions within the Bureau for each vocational area.[47]

The resolution was passed by a substantial vote even though some of the delegates disagreed upon what they had voted for; the actual course of action to be taken is somewhat clouded in the resolution. However, two points stand out in clear view. First, the vocational educators wanted a strong leadership role for the Division in its relationships with the states, and second, they wanted the Division moved up in the administrative structure of the Office of Education to the status of a Bureau.

### Reaction at AVA—Miami Beach Convention, 1965

The nation's vocational educators were not pleased with the events of 1965 concerning the administrative position of the Division of Vocational and Technical Education. When they met at the Miami Beach convention in December, 1965, they discussed this matter and presented to the delegates a resolution concerning the status of federal administration of vocational education. The resolution, which was passed unanimously by the House of Delegates on December 10, is presented in full because it identifies the issues succinctly.

WHEREAS, the American Vocational Association approved resolutions urging

[47] Resolutions, House of Delegates, American Vocational Association, *Minneapolis Convention*, December 10, 1964. (Mimeographed.)

Bureau status for vocational and technical education in the U.S. Office of Education, as set forth in Resolution 14 in 1964, and

WHEREAS, the Panel of Consultants for Vocational Education, appointed at the request of the late President John F. Kennedy, recommended: "That a single agency in the Federal Government perform the following functions in vocational and technical education.

1. Be responsible for the administration and supervision of the Federal vocational education acts and/or portions of Federal acts related to vocational and technical education in the schools of the Nation.

    a. The division within the U.S. Office of Education to perform these functions should be headed by a well-trained, experienced, and capable vocational educator who should report directly to the Commissioner of Education.

    b. Professional competence should be the prevailing policy for leadership personnel in the Federal agency, with salaries, authority, and responsibility sufficient to justify employment and retention of the most capable personnel.

2. Be responsible for liaison and coordination with Federal agencies and other organizations and their activities as they are related to the vocational and technical education program," and

WHEREAS, vocational leaders are greatly displeased with the present administrative posture and level of vocational education in the U.S. Office of Education, and

WHEREAS, the extent and importance of vocational education warrants the administration of the program at a higher level in order that more effective communication may be obtained in connection with policy-making and decisions vital to the vocational education program as an integral part of the total education program, and

WHEREAS, it is essential for the administration of vocational education at the Federal level to have status comparable to that of other Federal agencies to insure that the interests of vocational education

are appropriately represented at the National level, and

WHEREAS, research programs funded under section 4-C of the Vocational Education Act of 1963 are now being administered by a separate Bureau of the Office of Education which is not in keeping with the intent of the recommendations of the Panel of Consultants, and in principle should be more directly related to the administration of vocational education, and

WHEREAS, educational leaders suggest the possibilities of establishing the administration of vocational education as a Bureau or a separate office answerable to the Secretary of HEW.

THEREFORE, BE IT RESOLVED, that the AVA Board of Directors work diligently at an early date to secure a higher status for the administration of vocational education at the Federal level, and

BE IT ALSO RESOLVED, that the AVA Board of Directors (a) provide for an appropriate study to determine the services and/or functions that should be carried out by the Federal agency administering vocational education, (b) that from such a study the place of vocational education in the structure of the Federal government be identified, and (c) that such a study include positive and definite proposals to be made to appropriate Federal officials, and

BE IT FURTHER RESOLVED, that members of AVA be urged to let their members of Congress know that they are displeased with the fact that the Federal administration of vocational and technical education is at a low structural level, that it has been placed at a lower administrative level than it was formerly, even though Federal funds for the program have been greatly increased, and that the program is suffering because of lack of an adequate number of personnel in high level leadership positions knowledgeable about vocational and technical education at the Federal level, and thus the program is not being given the leadership in policy and decision-making authority it needs and warrants.[48]

---

[48] Resolutions, House of Delegates, American Vocational Association, *Miami Beach Convention*, December 10, 1965. (Mimeographed.)

It is clear that vocational educators regarded their responsibility for trade and technical education to be of increasing importance in the social and economic development of the nation. It is equally clear that they regarded a strong national office as essential in providing guidance and leadership needed for the states to cope with the problems of technology and the proper preparation of workers.

## Summary

The U.S. Office of Education has figured prominently in the leadership role related to the development of industrial education since 1914. For nearly two decades after 1914, industrial education was represented by only one person in the Office of Education. In the beginning the concern was largely concentrated in the area of manual training and manual arts; but later, when the vocational education movement was beginning to take form, this area was added to the primary responsibilities of the Specialist in Industrial Education.

The efforts of William T. Bawden are particularly noteworthy because of his catalytic role in bringing together the forces of industrial education. The professionalization of industrial education required a focal point, and this was largely found in the office of the Specialist in Industrial Education.

The big change came in 1933 when the activities of the Federal Board for Vocational Education were transferred to the Office of Education. This move brought under the aegis of the Office a number of people whose titles and responsibilities were identified by "trade and industrial education." The title of Specialist in Industrial Education was changed to Specialist in Industrial Arts. This move tended to reduce the possibility of conflict of interests, but even more important it focused attention upon industrial arts as an area of industrial education.

For 26 years (1933-1959) the vocational emphasis of industrial education was vested in the Trade and Industrial Education Branch of the Division of Vocational Education. The Branch stimulated growth and development by means of national program conferences (some with emphasis upon supervision, instructional materials, and teacher training), regional conferences, national leadership development conferences, and activities related to research.

In 1959 the Area Vocational Education Branch was established. This Branch had vocational interests in industrial education beamed largely toward the preparation of highly skilled technicians. Its formation removed the area of technician training from the Trade and Industrial Education Branch as a major phase of concern.

With the passage of the Vocational Education Act of 1963, the door was open for major change in vocational education, and part of this change was exemplified in 1964 in the complete reorganization of the Division of Vocational and Technical Education. The Trade and Industrial Education Branch ceased to exist as such, and its functions were carried out with a greatly reduced staff as a part of the new Occupations Branch.

171

## Recall Questions

1. What were the significant responsibilities of the Specialist in Industrial Arts, and how have these responsibilities changed during the fifty year period, 1914-1964?

2. Name the Specialists in Industrial Arts, 1914-1964.

3. What are some distinguishing characteristics of the various types of conferences sponsored by the Trade and Industrial Education Branch?

4. Why was the Area Vocational Education Branch created, and what were some of its principal duties?

5. Describe briefly the reorganization of the Division of Vocational and Technical Education.

## Research Questions

1. Review the publications issued by William T. Bawden during his tenure of office as Specialist in Industrial Education, and draw conclusions about the major purposes he was seeking to achieve. What changes can you detect through the years?

2. Review the reports of national and regional conferences of trade and industrial education, and draw conclusions about the major purposes these conferences were attempting to achieve. How did these purposes change with time?

3. Compare your answers to the two preceding questions. What were the similarities and differences of purpose between the specialists and the conferences? What implications can you draw from this comparison?

## Suggestions for Further Reading

Source materials related to the industrial-education activities of the Office of Education are to be gleaned from the printed reports of the Office. Bibliographies of all publications of the U.S. Office are available, beginning with those of 1867. Mimeographed reports and staff studies are harder to find. However, the Archives of the United States is a valuable source of information. No general comprehensive treatment of the topic is known to exist. The best library source of these materials is that of the Department of Health, Education, and Welfare, Washington, D.C.

The following journals provide supplementary reading material:

*American Vocational Journal*
*Industrial Arts and Vocational Education*
*Industrial Education Magazine*
*School Shop*
*The Industrial Arts Teacher*
*The Journal of Industrial Arts Education*

# Chapter 8

# Industrial Arts Teacher Education

The Status of Teacher Education in 1918 · After World War I and the Early 20's · AVA Bulletins—Improving Instruction in Industrial Arts · Five Teacher Education Studies · Other Reports from the Professional Literature · Yearbooks of the American Council on Industrial Arts Teacher Education · Summary · Recall Questions · Research Questions · Suggestions for Further Reading

Thin threads of evidence in the historical background of industrial arts suggest that definitive teacher education may have started as early as 1873 at the Massachusetts Normal Art School. Also prior to 1890 other schools gave special attention to the selection of manual training teachers. Even at that time there was little question about the need for good instructors; however, it was not until 1891 that the first recognized course for training such teachers was conducted at the New York College for the Training of Teachers (later Teachers College, Columbia University) by Charles A. Bennett.

Bennett's work here extended from 1891 to 1897. During this period the enrollment grew rapidly, new methods of teacher training were introduced, and in 1893-94 the first two-year program for the training of manual arts teachers in the United States was introduced. Other achievements associated with Bennett and his work included the first summer school in manual training, the first program to grant degrees, and the first graduate course in manual training.[1] Practices commonly accepted in teacher education in general were adapted to the specific conditions surrounding manual training. There were no other models to follow. Bennett and those associated with him

---

[1] For a detailed analysis of Bennett's work at Teachers College see, Gerald K. Hammer, "Charles Alpheus Bennett, Dean of Manual Arts," (unpublished doctoral dissertation, University of California, Los Angeles, 1962).

173

simply projected a program of teacher education into a new area of instruction.[2]

In the years that followed, other institutions organized programs for the training of special teachers of manual arts. Still there were no standards. The programs of teacher preparation were different in each institution because there were no commonly accepted objectives or goals. It was precisely this situation that occupied the attention of Bennett and Selvidge that day in 1908 when they discussed the need for professional meetings concerning teacher preparation. Neither man wanted all teacher preparation to be alike. They did hold the opinion, however, that if persons having responsibility for such training could discuss the various aspects of their programs, they could reach a consensus on general purposes. Furthermore such a discussion would act as a means of evaluation and thus would stimulate improvement.

## The Status of Teacher Education in 1918

In 1918, at least 184 institutions were offering curricula of varying lengths designed to prepare teachers of manual arts. Programs were found in 43 states in state universities and agricultural colleges, normal schools and teachers colleges, and in private and municipal institutions.

Albert F. Siepert reported that, "An almost infinite variety of courses are being offered in these schools," and that they varied in length from part-time to four-year courses which were "becoming comparatively common."[3]

Only 14 land-grant colleges were offering four-year curricula for the training of manual arts teachers in 1917, but the demand for manual arts teachers with four years of training was not large. A larger number of programs requiring a much shorter period provided stiff competition to the four-year programs. Prerequisites were so varied that classification was nearly impossible. Some schools required high school graduation, some required only four years of trade experience, and others required a combination of both high school and trade experience.

A student at the Williamson Free School of Mechanical Trades (Philadelphia) who desired to teach manual arts, spent three years as an indentured apprentice (to the Board of Trustees), worked two years in a trade, and then returned for 11 months of teacher training. At Bradley Institute a teacher of "automobile work" completed one year of technical study and then spent at

---

[2] An interesting sidelight is related to the development of teacher education in trade and industrial education. Teacher education for the vocational side of industrial education was developed in theory and put into practice by persons with experience in manual training. Many of these persons were instrumental in contributing to the development of trade and industrial teacher education as a separate entity. For example, Bennett's first assistant at Teachers College was Frank H. Ball. Later Ball served with John Dewey in Chicago, held a number of positions in manual training in other areas, and became President of the State Teachers College in Santa Barbara, California. When the Smith-Hughes Act was passed in 1917, California was faced with developing a new area of teacher education. Ball was appointed by the State Board for Vocational Education as the first supervisor of trade and industrial teacher training, located at the University of California, Los Angeles.

[3] Albert F. Siepert, *Courses of Study for the Preparation of Teachers of Manual Arts*, U.S. Department of the Interior, Bureau of Education, Bulletin 1918, No. 37. Washington: Government Printing Office, 1919, p. 10.

least three months in a commercial garage. At this point, if his work had been satisfactory, he returned to Bradley for a second year of instruction in pedagogy, general and technical courses, plus practice in teaching.

Siepert compared teacher preparation programs with reference to course content, length, and description. For a selected group of 13 institutions he summarized the requirements for academic, professional, and technical subjects. One of the thirteen institutions made no academic requirements, while another required six subjects. Eleven of the institutions required work in English composition but varied in time from 48 clock hours to 120 clock hours. Three institutions made provision for the student to select academic subjects as electives.

All 13 of the institutions required instruction in professional subjects, but with extreme variations in the time devoted to each. The table below, summarized from Siepert's study, shows these variations:

The range of technical subject matter may be seen from the course titles: *Woodwork*—elementary, cabinetmaking, turning, patternmaking, carpentry, finishing, upholstery; *Metalwork*— bench metal, art metal, sheet metal, forge, machine shop, foundry; *Craftwork*—bookbinding, clay and pottery, leather; *Drawing*—mechanical, machine, architectural, freehand, design, blackboard, woodwork design; *Printing*; *Paper and Cardboard*; *Construction Material*; and *Forestry*. Few electives were recognized except by one institution that provided for 180 clock hours of electives! The minimum requirement for any total course was 45 hours; the maximum was 450.

Considerable variation existed in buildings, shops, and equipment. Of course the manual arts courses required a substantial outlay of funds in this regard. Siepert indicated that buildings and equipment should be representative of "good practice" rather than "elaborate practice"; otherwise the student would find it difficult to adjust to

| Course | Number of Institutions Requiring Course | Range of Requirement— in Clock Hours |
|---|---|---|
| Psychology | | |
| Elementary general | 9 | 54-120 |
| Educational | 4 | 67-120 |
| Child study | 2 | 48-60 |
| History of education | 6 | 50-72 |
| General methods | 7 | 54-60 |
| History of manual arts | 11 | 18-100 |
| Organization of manual arts | 8 | 18-120 |
| Administration of manual arts | 3 | 36-100 |
| Special methods | 6 | 36-180 |
| Observation | 1 | 60 |
| Practice teaching | 10 | 36-270 |
| School administration | 2 | 54-96 |
| Principles of education | 1 | 54 |
| Education electives | 1 | 180 |

"mediocre conditions outside." Except for woodwork, no normal school was very well equipped. Siepert's general evaluation was that equipment ranged "from elaborate to meagre."

Data concerning 108 instructors show that 45 percent held a baccalaureate degree, five percent a master's degree, and 18 percent held a "diploma" (which Siepert did not identify, but it was presumably for high school graduation). It was implied that 32 percent were not high school graduates. Thirty-six instructors from four institutions had an average of nine years of teaching experience and approximately three years' trade experience.

Siepert's summary of "the general problem" is of particular interest because it provides a first hand view of the status and trends of manual arts teacher education in 1918. The following paraphrased points were gleaned at random from his study:

1. There was a growing tendency toward a common standard.

2. Two-year courses had many common elements of subject matter and methods of procedure.

3. Practice teaching varied as to character, length of time required, and conditions under which the teaching was done.

4. Two-year normal school graduates found employment in grammar schools and in some high schools.

5. High school positions were generally held by men with bachelor's degrees.

6. The trend was toward four-year programs in general colleges and universities.

7. Universities tended to place much emphasis upon education courses and to give little consideration to actual shop practice. Prime consideration was not given to the man being trained, "with reference to his having, or acquiring, the skill required as the basis for effective teaching."

8. The supply of teachers was small compared to the demand; the number needed was increasing, and the means of preparation was limited.

9. "An analysis of the problems must make evident the need of one with *ability to teach the things he himself can actually do.*"

10. It was common practice to "pick up" a mechanic from the trades. "Having found this man, we still have the problem of training him to be an effective teacher with the spirit, the point of view, and the attitude toward education, toward industry, and life in general which we need in leaders of boys and men." (This appeared to be influenced by the Smith-Hughes Act.)

11. Teacher training was not entirely successful, and new directions had to be found; the four-year programs seemed to be moving in the right direction.

12. Teacher training courses for technical subjects should be made up of elements selected "because of their contribution to the end or ideal in mind."

13. There was no reason why foreign language should be made a requirement—according to Siepert.

14. "Teacher-training institutions need to make a more thorough analysis of the work industrial teachers must do and to arrange curricula which directly and specifically fit individuals for their work."

In short, manual arts teacher education in 1918 existed in a number of institutions dispersed throughout the United States, but its program was only slightly short of chaotic. There was neither a central clearinghouse of information, except for the Mississippi Valley Conference, nor a national association devoted to improvement and professionalization. It simply grew, unrestrained by commonly accepted professional goals, and its nature was subject only to individual interpretation. The decade of the roaring twenties would provide the first significant attempts to "take up the slack" and to suggest evaluative processes.

### After World War I and the Early 20's

Many things had been learned from industrial education activities in World War I. It was evident that peacetime provisions for industrial education had lagged far behind the recognized demand. It also seemed inevitable that the reconstruction era would create a larger demand for young workers with practical mechanical ability. Viewing the situation just after the war, Bawden urged the schools to consider the problem carefully and take appropriate action. Specific recommendations for action were suggested for the Bureau of Education, state departments of public instruction, members of the Mississippi Valley Conference, and educational institutions.[4] In general, because more liberal financial support for industrial education was needed, public interest was being solicited. From the

standpoint of general program improvement in industrial education, the war had pointed to the importance of three definite aims: (1) the necessity of adjusting instruction to the needs and capacities of students; (2) the importance of expanding instructional programs to reach a larger group of students; and (3) the necessity of testing the qualifications of teachers.

The trade and industrial teacher-training program, stimulated by the Federal Board for Vocational Education, limited its attention to the training of trade teachers. The Mississippi Valley Conference, however, had a wider range of interests. Although its concern was predominantly for teachers of manual training, the conference viewed its role as one which included aiding the progress of teachers of trade and industrial education. Thus many of the conferences developed broad discussions.

The 1919 Mississippi Valley Conference, held at the University of Cincinnati, reviewed the progress of a number of institutions in teacher training and considered at length the problems of itinerant-teacher training with respect to the needs of teachers of special subjects in rural and village schools. While the intent was clearly one of expansion, improvement, and to some extent uniformity of program, there were dangers to be avoided in promoting the latter. "Dr. E. K. Strong, Jr., urged the teacher of manual arts and industrial subjects, as well as teachers of other subjects, not to lose sight of the deficiencies and the entire inade-

---

[4] William T. Bawden, *Lessons from the War and Their Application in the Training of Teachers*, U.S. Department of the Interior, Bureau of Education, Industrial Education Circular No. 1, January 1919, pp. 10-12.

quacy of the uniform curriculum." [5] Practice teaching (or laboratory teaching, as some preferred to call it) had many times been the subject of discussion, and it was regarded as a particularly important phase of teacher training. In this connection, the pros and cons of good lesson planning were investigated at length.

The opportunity to observe examples of good teaching was considered imperative since it provided a background for improvement. "Dr. Strong maintained that it is self-evident that anyone who is to teach should be taught how to teach." [6] In general, only a small number of persons had an opportunity to receive suitable preparation for the difficult job of teaching in a special field which required a considerable amount of investigative study, review, and creative planning.

A one-day conference of specialists in industrial education was called by the Commissioner of Education in February, 1920. Twenty-nine states sent 104 representatives to Chicago to consider the topic, "Examples of Good Teaching in Industrial Education." Charles H. Judd, Director, School of Education, University of Chicago, summarized the day's discussion. He pointed out that the United States lagged behind European countries in the preparation of industrial teachers, and that we were "inexcusably negligent" in this matter. It had been as-

serted at the conference that one could go into an industry and find craftsmen who would make better teachers than some of the graduates of the teacher-training schools. "Such a confession surely discredits somebody," he said. [7] Judd indicated that the fact that such a statement could be made seriously should be a matter of deep concern.

In continuing his summary, Judd called attention to the necessity of improvement in the machinery of teacher training and the general lack of standards of professional training for teachers. It was not possible to be satisfied with teacher training as it stood.

In this country today the teachers of more than 1,000,000 children have less than eighth-grade schooling themselves. There is a technic of teaching—make no mistake about that. And we must convince the public that teachers *must be* trained for their work—must be given this technic. [8]

As indicated previously, much of the progress in industrial teacher training came from persons associated with the Mississippi Valley Conferences. The 1920 Conference, held at the Indiana State University, was concerned with the general topic of higher standards for industrial teachers. Reports from working committees were presented. The nature of the reports is indicated in a review of the program for that year. [9] Topics discussed were: Occupational Analysis as a Basis for Determining the Content of Trade Courses;

---

[5] William T. Bawden, *Progress in the Preparation of Industrial Teachers,* U.S. Department of the Interior, Bureau of Education, Industrial Education Circular No. 5, July 1920, p. 17.
[6] William T. Bawden, *Examples of Good Teaching in Industrial Education,* U.S. Department of the Interior, Bureau of Education, Industrial Education Circular No. 6, July 1920, p. 2.
[7] *Ibid.,* p. 10.
[8] *Ibid.,* p. 11.
[9] William T. Bawden, *Higher Standards for Teachers of Industrial Subjects,* U.S. Department of the Interior, Bureau of Education, Industrial Education Circular No. 7, January 1922, pp. 1-2.

Itinerant Teachers of Manual Arts in Rural and Village Schools; Progress in the Development of Plans for Preparing Teachers of Industrial Subjects; The Need of More Vital Contacts Between School and Industry; The Program of the Junior Employment Service; Problems of Manual Arts Teaching in the Intermediate School or Junior High School; The Special Problems of the Teacher in Part-Time Classes; and Occupational Training Work in the United States Army.

The task of improving instruction, raising standards, and securing a much better result from the instruction was, in part, the problem of supervision. Forty-two supervisors of instruction in shopwork and drafting, meeting in Baltimore, March 23, 1921, considered their work from the point of view of improving instruction. However, deficiencies in the preliminary training of the teacher seemed to stand in the way of any easy solution. In summarizing the discussion, Frank M. Leavitt, associate superintendent of public schools, Pittsburgh, said:

Much of the teacher-training service outlined in this discussion ought to be given by someone else before these teachers come to us. Supervisors ought not to have to struggle with "brand new" teachers, wholly uninstructed in the technic of teaching.

Teachers should realize that the chief duty of a specialist is to make an analysis of his own job, which will be a measure of his own efficiency. We should place on the teacher the responsibility for appealing to the supervisor for help on the points in which he is deficient.[10]

In December, 1921, members of the Mississippi Valley Conference contin-ued their quest for improvement of instruction and for new insights into the process of training teachers. They reached the following conclusions concerning the junior high school program:

(a) Enriched courses for pupils of this period are now possible because more time and better equipment are becoming available.

(b) The prevocational motive should not be the only one; courses should not aim wholly, or even chiefly, at teaching the methods of large factory production. Individual craftsman methods are still as important as ever. Both should be employed.

(c) More kinds of industrial work should be given, metal work as well as woodwork, and a larger variety of industrial processes and materials should be included, but without sacrifice of thoroughness and high ideals of workmanship.

(d) The methods of instruction must be such as to keep alive the creative impulse in handwork. There must be emotional satisfaction in the work as well as intellectual. The element of design and beauty must be present, and this is not inconsistent with teaching the methods used in productive work.

(e) More broadly trained teachers must be secured for this instruction. The training colleges must produce results from such material as they can get, but should make an effort to get the best.

(f) The smaller cities and towns need the most help from the training colleges. The large cities are in a better position to take care of themselves.

(g) Teachers of manual arts in junior high schools must know productive processes.

Finally, as recommended by Dean Whitney, (a) manual arts and vocational educators should not expect to accomplish their purposes immediately. They should be content to go slowly, and (b) they should not isolate themselves; they should

---

[10] William T. Bawden, *Helping the Shop Teacher Through Supervision*, U.S. Department of the Interior, Bureau of Education, Industrial Education Circular No. 10, February 1922, p. 9.

mix more with the so-called academic teachers; for, after all, education is and must continue to be a unit.[11]

The conference members were probing deeply for the ways and means of achieving quality both in course content of manual arts and in the training of teachers. No one entertained doubts about the importance of the teacher in the process, and quality in teaching was pursued with determination.

In the spring of 1923, Bawden conducted a conference in Providence, Rhode Island, for ninety shop teachers and supervisors from nine states for the purpose of discussing teacher improvement. The outstanding features of the various addresses were summarized under five headings as follows:

1. The necessity for professional improvement. It has been very clearly shown that good schools require good teaching. Teachers of vocational subjects have in many instances taken up this profession well prepared so far as actual trade knowledge is concerned, but lacking in presenting their subjects, organization, vision, etc. It therefore becomes imperative that they seek additional training while in service.

2. Means of improvement. The ambitious teacher can find many opportunities for making himself more efficient by means of vacation study, extension courses, correspondence courses, systematic private reading, and by obtaining leave of absence for advanced study.

3. The responsibility rests largely with the State. The professional instinct of some teachers is of such a nature that they require little direction and certainly no compulsion in connection with the seeking of professional improvement.

Others, however, for various reasons need some direction and guidance, and in many cases efficiency is not apt to be at its highest level unless definite requirements are set up by either local authorities or the State. In the last analysis it would seem that the responsibility for the training of teachers while in service must rest largely with the State.

4. Importance of the cooperation of industry and the schools. Industry travels so fast and changes so rapidly that our schools will perhaps always be somewhat in the rear. The significant fact, however, emphasized by one of the speakers regarding the contrast between the dozen or so subjects taught in our school shops and the thousands of occupations as shown in an analysis of the industries of even one State is something educators will need to give much thought to in the future.

5. The sane point of view with respect to vocational guidance. During the past few years much nonsense has been both said and written in connection with vocational guidance, as a result of which this very significant movement has been more or less retarded. Vocational counseling is a scientific problem and must be handled as such. Its correct application in our school work will eventually be of vast benefit to both pupils and industry.[12]

Bawden's conferences were getting at the heart of the problem. The five summary points were keys to stability which developed as the result of self-appraisal. The goals implied were realistic and represented a consensus. Clearly manual arts personnel needed to meet these issues squarely, but the central point of responsibility was teacher education.

After World War I and during the 1920's, the reconstruction of education

---

[11] William T. Bawden, *Preparation of Teachers of Manual Arts and Industrial Subjects*, U.S. Department of the Interior, Bureau of Education, Industrial Education Circular No. 7, January 1922, pp. 1-2.

[12] William T. Bawden, *Means of Improvement for Teachers in Service*, U.S. Department of the Interior, Bureau of Education, Industrial Education Circular No. 19, October 1923, pp. 16-17.

continued vigorously. High school enrollments grew significantly larger each year, bringing school administrators face to face with students having special interests, desires, and objectives. An expanding curriculum was inevitable; one facet of the expansion was the subject area of industrial arts—emerging slowly from its manual arts cocoon. Industrial arts found a host of problems which needed resolution for comfortable coexistence in the growing educational system. It was obvious that teacher education would play an important role in the future. No wonder that Siepert sought to find an answer to the question, "Where are we now?" in order to look forward to the future; no wonder that the Mississippi Valley Conferences pushed relentlessly for quality in teacher education; no wonder that Bawden, capitalizing upon his position in the Bureau of Education, helped to create an environment conducive to progress in teacher education. Industrial arts teacher education needed inspired leadership and forces were at work to provide it.

## AVA Bulletins—Improving Instruction in Industrial Arts

Few groups of educators have pursued quality in instruction as relentlessly as have those in industrial arts. At almost any point in time, from the beginning of manual training, it is possible to document their professional activities related to the improvement of the instructional process. However, critics had suggested that industrial arts educators were not in agreement concerning either acceptable objectives or content of their program. In addition, it was asserted that they lacked a clear-cut view of the standards to be expected of students.

Industrial arts educators who attended the American Vocational Association convention in Los Angeles in December, 1927, considered some of their imperative problems. Subsequently, the group requested the AVA Executive Committee to appoint a committee to study these problems. Early in 1928, W. E. Roberts, C. F. Bauder, W. T. Bawden, C. A. Bowman, E. E. Ericson, M. M. Proffitt, and R. W. Selvidge were appointed. Although the group was known as a committee on "Standards of Attainment in Industrial Arts Teaching," its assignment was not definite. It decided to limit preliminary work to "a study of those things which the boy should know and be able to do" at the end of the junior high school period.

### Standards of Attainment in Industrial Arts Teaching

The committee made its *first report* on December 7, 1929. One thousand copies of the report were printed and offered for sale at ten cents each. This edition lasted less than one month.

During the next few years, with a number of internal changes in the committee, progress was made in studying objectives, procedures, curriculum problems, learning or teaching units, practical applications of methods and materials, and other related items. The *final report* was presented at the American Vocational Association convention in Pittsburgh on December 7, 1934. Between 1934 and 1941, six printings of the report were made, which provided 11,000 copies for distribution. The committee's summary of objectives, as stated in 1934, was as follows:

181

1. To develop in each pupil an active interest in industrial life and in the methods of production and distribution.

2. To develop in each pupil the ability to select wisely, care for, and use properly the things he buys or uses.

3. To develop in each pupil an appreciation of good workmanship and good design.

4. To develop in each pupil an attitude of pride or interest in his ability to do useful things.

5. To develop in each pupil a feeling of self-reliance and confidence in his ability to deal with people and to care for himself in an unusual or unfamiliar situation.

6. To develop in each pupil the habit of an orderly method of procedure in the performance of any task.

7. To develop in each pupil the habit of self-discipline which requires one to do a thing when it should be done, whether it is a pleasant task or not.

8. To develop in each pupil the habit of careful, thoughtful work without loitering or wasting time (industry).

9. To develop in each pupil an attitude of readiness to assist others when they need help and to join in group undertakings (cooperation).

10. To develop in each pupil a thoughtful attitude in the matter of making things easy and pleasant for others.

11. To develop in each pupil a knowledge and understanding of mechanical drawing, the interpretation of the conventions in drawings and working diagrams, and the ability to express his ideas by means of a drawing.

12. To develop in each pupil elementary skills in the use of the more common tools and machines in modifying and handling materials, and an understanding of some of the more common construction problems.[13]

## Improving Instruction in Industrial Arts

Great influence of the *Standards of Attainment in Industrial Arts Teaching* was claimed in the following statement: "It is probable that no other publication in the field of industrial arts has been used by so many teachers and administrators. Certainly none has exerted equal significance upon the progress of industrial arts in public education in this country."[14]

In December, 1939, the stock of *Standards* had been nearly exhausted. The committee recommended an extensive revision, which was promptly approved by the AVA Executive Committee. One member of the original committee, C. F. Bauder, found it necessary to resign. The following men were added to the committee: J. F. Friese, V. C. Fryklund, A. B. Mays, G. F. Weber, and Homer J. Smith, who was designated as chairman.

Some of the material in the 1934 report did not appear to be applicable to the major problems of 1939. Numerous suggestions had been made for revision of the bulletin; new material had become available. The committee recommended that the revised report be titled *Improving Instruction in Industrial Arts*. Then, before the work could be completed, World War II had begun and the revision became temporarily a war casualty. Eventually the work of the committee of twelve was completed by a subcommittee consisting of Bawden, Mays, and Smith and, in February, 1946, the revised bulletin

---

[13] American Vocational Association, Industrial Arts Section, *Standards of Attainment in Industrial Arts Teaching,* December 7, 1934, p. 12.

[14] American Vocational Association, Industrial Arts Division, *Improving Instruction in Industrial Arts,* June 1946, p. 7.

182

was submitted to the AVA convention at Buffalo.

The revised list of objectives was summarized as follows:

These purposes or assumed outcomes of industrial-arts work are stated in terms of teacher attempts rather than in the usual terms of departmental or field aims. They should be considered as cumulative and unified rather than as nine distinct ends or effects.

1. Interest in Industry.—To develop *in each pupil* an active interest in industrial life and in the methods and problems of production and exchange.

2. Appreciation and Use.—To develop *in each pupil* the appreciation of good design and workmanship, and the ability to select, care for, and use industrial products wisely.

3. Self-discipline and Initiative.—To develop *in each pupil* the habits of self-reliance, self-discipline, and resourcefulness in meeting practical situations.

4. Cooperative Attitudes.—To develop *in each pupil* a readiness to assist others and to join happily in group undertakings.

5. Health and Safety.—To develop *in each pupil* desirable attitudes and practices with respect to health and safety.

6. Interest in Achievement.—To develop *in each pupil* a feeling of pride in his ability to do useful things and to develop worthy leisure-time interests.

7. Orderly Performance.—To develop *in each pupil* the habit of an orderly, complete, and efficient performance of any task.

8. Drawing and Design.—To develop *in each pupil* an understanding of drawings, and the ability to express ideas by means of drawing.

9. Shop Skills and Knowledge.—To develop *in each pupil* a measure of skill in the use of common tools and machines, and an understanding of the problems involved in common types of construction and repair.[15]

Ten thousand copies of the revised bulletin were printed in June, 1946, and an additional ten thousand copies in September, 1948.

It was evident that industrial arts educators were eager to receive the bulletins concerning objectives. This was something tangible, a foundation for industrail arts' future development. Furthermore, program development based upon a common set of objectives could produce standards of performance and become the basis for extensive evaluation.

## A Guide to Improving Instruction in Industrial Arts

In 1951, when the supply of the bulletins was again depleted, a new committee, with Chris H. Groneman as chairman, was appointed to prepare a more detailed edition. Through the use of workshops, subcommittees, and a final editorial committee, the bulletin was expanded and published in July, 1953. Nearly 100 people had contributed in one way or another. The new edition had been prepared for one major purpose: "To assist the teacher of industrial arts in improving the quality of industrial arts instruction."[16]

The nine objectives for industrial arts as suggested in the 1946 revision were retained in the 1953 edition of the bulletin, but with a new treatment which gave the reader a fuller understanding concerning the objectives. Following the statement of each objective was a paragraph which further defined its meaning. The committee

---

[15] *Ibid.,* p. 51.

[16] American Vocational Association, *A Guide to Improving Instruction in Industrial Arts,* July 1953, p. 3.

then listed a number of student be-
haviors which characterized achievement of the objective and, in addition,
suggested activities which the teacher
might use in order to obtain desired
behavior.

### Industrial Arts in Education

In 1958, the Industrial Arts Policy
and Planning Committee, Industrial
Arts Division, American Vocational
Association, issued a small brochure
containing succinct statements defining
and describing industrial arts education. Industrial arts was defined as:

. . . the study of industrial tools, materials, processes, products, and occupations pursued for general education purposes in shops, laboratories, and drafting
rooms.

The unique contributions of Industrial
Arts are:

1. To help learners develop a degree
of skill as they solve problems with tools,
materials, and processes of industry.

2. To provide exploratory experiences
in a variety of industrial activities.

3. To develop the skill and knowledge
necessary to produce and use working
drawings.[17]

The purpose of industrial arts as
indicated by the Policy and Planning
Committee was to

. . . foster the development of a strong
foundation in technical skills, consumer
knowledges, and attitudes regarding matters needed for happy and effective living. Public secondary education should
provide every boy and girl the opportunity
to work with the tools and materials of
industry, thereby acquiring an understanding of our technological developments.[18]

This brochure was distributed
widely and served as a quick reference
to the purposes of industrial arts.
Nothing had been added which would
show any significant departure from
past objectives.

### Evaluative Criteria for Industrial Arts Education

In 1961, the Industrial Arts Policy
and Planning Committee published
evaluative criteria for industrial arts
education. The committee felt that the
greatest value of the publication would
be to promote discussion between
teachers, supervisors, and others. It was
suggested that an individual teacher
might use the guide as an instrument
of self-evaluation. The *Criteria* included sections on physical facilities,
the teacher, and the instructional program—activities and materials, methods of evaluation, student records, and
instructor records.

The AVA bulletins relative to the
improvement of instruction did not
represent all of the industrial arts effort
in teacher education, but this long-
term project was one of the significant
contributions.

The influence of the AVA bulletins
upon the general standardization of
teacher education was particularly significant. Through the publication of the
bulletins the committees sought to establish areas of common agreement
which all teacher education programs
could use as a guide. The bulletins
tended to draw together the various related elements of industrial arts teacher
education, and a closer rapport among
teacher educators developed.

---

[17] American Vocational Association, Industrial Arts Policy and Planning Committee, *Industrial Arts in Education*, 1958, p. 1.

[18] *Ibid.*, p. 2.

## Five Teacher Education Studies

Information was needed continuously concerning the status and trends of teacher education in the nation. Procedures had not been developed to keep this information current, and the only approach to providing the desired information was vested in occasional studies. Five of these studies seem to represent well the status and trends at various periods since 1941.

The National Association of Industrial Teacher Trainers, an affiliate of AVA, recommended at its meeting in St. Louis, December, 1938, that a study be conducted of the educational preparation of industrial arts teachers. Following the practice of the research committee, Verne C. Fryklund, one of its members, was assigned to head the study.[19]

### The Fryklund Statistics

The ninety publicly supported teacher education institutions consisted largely of universities, state colleges, and teachers colleges. One of the institutions had had an industrial arts program for 48 years; three others for more than forty years; six for over 35 years; 62 departments had been functioning 16 to 35 years; 12, from six to 15 years; and six had been organized within the five years preceding the study. Seventy of the ninety institutions identified the industrial arts teacher education departments as either *industrial arts* or *industrial education.*

Eighty-six of the institutions granted baccalaureate degrees with 14 different titles to industrial arts teacher graduates. One institution granted no such degree, and three others failed to supply information for the study. Variation in semester credits for the first degree ranged from fewer than 105 to more than 146.

The 329 instructors of industrial arts teacher education held the following degrees:

| | |
|---|---|
| Doctorate | 8.5% |
| Master's | 60.7% |
| Bachelor's | 22.5% |
| No degree | 4.6% |
| Not specified | 3.7% |

There seemed to be little question but that the preferred degree for industrial arts teacher educators was moving rapidly toward the doctorate.

Seventy-five percent of the instructors reported previous industrial work experience (ranging from 1 to 32 years) with an average of 3.7 years.

Wide variations were found in the industrial arts teacher candidate's course requirements in education, English, social studies, mathematics, sciences, psychology, music, fine arts, and languages, and in the subject matter of industrial arts.

The study included a detailed analysis of directed teaching practices in the various institutions. This aspect was personalized by including the actual comments, pro and con, of the respondents, about directed teaching.

### The F. Theodore Struck Study

At the 1939 convention of the National Association of Industrial Teacher

[19] Verne C. Fryklund, *Industrial Arts Teacher Education in the United States,* Bulletin No. 2, National Association of Industrial Teacher Trainers. Bloomington, Illinois: McKnight and McKnight, 1941.

Trainers at Grand Rapids, Michigan, the research committee was assigned a study of industrial teacher education at the graduate level. F. Theodore Struck, chairman of the research committee, was asked to assume the major responsibility.

Information was obtained from 32 institutions in 22 states. Struck summarized the findings as follows:

1. Twenty-four of the thirty-two institutions studied offer graduate instruction in both vocational-industrial education and industrial arts; four offer instruction in vocational-industrial education only.

2. Sixteen institutions offer undergraduate instruction in both vocational-industrial and industrial arts education. Four offer such instruction in vocational-industrial education only, five in industrial arts only, and four in neither.

3. The majority of institutions administer their graduate offerings in industrial education in the College (or School) of Education.

4. There is a very wide variation in prerequisite undergraduate requirements in the major field.

5. Fourteen of the thirty-two institutions have no specific course requirements. Most of the others specify one, two, or three courses. Of twenty-five such required graduate courses nineteen were mentioned only once. The course most commonly required is Administration and Supervision of Industrial Education, which was mentioned seven times.

6. Thirty-one of the thirty-two institutions make possible the meeting of all requirements in summer sessions only.

7. The range of offerings of professional courses is very large and there is a small degree of uniformity of practice.

8. Of ninety staff members teaching graduate courses, eight held the bachelor's degree only, fifty-six held master's degrees, twenty-four held the Ph.D. degree, one the Ed.D., and one the honorary LL.D.

9. Only four institutions reported provision for "stipend scholarships" in industrial education, and only five have graduate fellowships available for students in industrial education.

10. For the period August 31, 1938 to September 1, 1939 there were enrolled in graduate courses in "Vocational-Industrial Education," 1,303 students; in "Industrial Education," 505 students; and in "Industrial Arts," 1,031 students. Forty-three per cent of the total number were not candidates for graduate degrees.

11. During 1938-1939, 222 master's degrees and nine doctor's degrees were granted in industrial education.[20]

The most striking feature of the study seemed to be the variety in the graduate program. Although the need for complete agreement on every detail was not suggested by Struck, or by the research committee, some aspects of the situation were "most disturbing," such as the wide variation in entrance standards, which Struck felt was most in need of attention.

Arthur B. Mays viewed the study as one of significance in industrial teacher education and urged industrial educators to read and study the report. The study revealed significant progress, but many tasks were indicated which had to await the end of World War II. Mays wrote:

The leadership in this area of education faces some difficult problems in the years just ahead concerning graduate study. This is a good time to get all the facts available and prepare to move forward when the present unsettled conditions are ended. Dr. Struck's study will help those who are trying to prepare for a new day.[21]

---

[20] F. Theodore Struck, *A Study of Industrial Teacher Education at the Graduate Level*, American Vocational Association, Research Bulletin No. 2, December 1941, p. 31.

[21] Arthur B. Mays, "A Significant Study of Industrial Teacher Education," *AVA Journal and News Bulletin*, Vol. XVII, No. 2, May 1942, p. 111.

## The Siepert Study, 1942

A. F. Siepert, who in 1918 led the van of inquiry into professional preparation of teachers, made a study of "Trends in the Preparation of Industrial Arts Teachers" in 1942. He secured data from 55 teacher training institutions located in 32 states.

He found a growing importance of state colleges as a source for industrial arts teachers, and indicated that many of the colleges appeared to be moving toward offering a master's degree. He also found that the old two-year programs had almost disappeared and that minimum credit for an industrial arts major was rising to a point between thirty and forty semester hours. He cited certain points of interest, as follows:

1. The State A. & M. Colleges tend to stress the engineering type of approach with mathematics and science predominant.
2. The Teachers Colleges give greater emphasis to courses in education with social studies also prominent.
3. The "general shop" idea tends to cause diversity in training to give teachers at least limited competence in several fields.
4. The high school teachers are being expected to bring greater technical skill and knowledge in a more narrow field of specialization.
5. New topics or subjects are still being added to the industrial field, e.g., aeronautics, textiles, power, ceramics, etc.
6. Preparation of vocational teachers for trades and industry is finding increasing recognition.[22]

Siepert noticed also a definite trend toward promoting the position of industrial arts in the public schools. Published reports (he cited Fryklund's report, the bulletin *Standards of Attainment in Industrial Arts Teaching*, and others) were helping shape the practices of industrial arts teacher education institutions, and such publications had also reached a large group of educators outside the immediate field.

The war influence upon technical training had produced an abundance of material concerning teaching problems. Siepert felt that there was a danger in focusing attention upon immediate needs; in this connection he raised several questions which would occupy the attention of professional educators for many years after World War II.

1. How can we meet all of the demands and keep our sense of balance?
2. How can we prepare teachers for the smaller school systems, many of which have a general shop or call for varied teaching fields, and at the same time prepare the candidate for the larger school systems?
3. What shall be our attitude and practice toward women teachers and girls taking industrial arts courses?
4. What is the solution for the teacher shortage? What about "refresher" courses for teachers now in service? What can be done with surplus teachers—English, social studies, art, music—as prospective industrial arts teachers?
5. How can we meet the challenge of the opportunities presented by short-time training with pay and better salaries in the schools operated by the armed forces?
6. How can we attract the best high school graduates to enter the profession of industrial arts teaching?[23]

[22] Albert F. Siepert, "Trends in the Preparation of Industrial Arts Teachers," *AVA Journal and News Bulletin*, Vol. XVIII, No. 1, February 1943, p. 22.
[23] *Ibid.*, pp. 22, 31.

### The Williams and Meyer Study

The American Council on Industrial Arts Teacher Education made a nationwide study of teacher education programs in industrial arts as a preliminary measure in preparing the council's first yearbook. The data for a ten-year period 1941-1951 provided the following information: [24]

1. The number of schools offering industrial arts teacher education programs increased from 166 in 1941 to 200 in 1951, a gain of twenty percent.

2. The number of professional educators engaged in industrial arts teacher education increased from 604 in 1941 to 1,018 in 1951, a gain of 69 percent.

The data revealed other significant changes. One of the most interesting items in the yearbook is a composite profile of 500 teacher educators. This profile reads as follows:

He was born in New York state in 1909 and is forty-two years of age. He is married, has two children, and is the holder of a Master of Arts degree. He has taught over seven years in the public schools and approximately ten years in institutions of higher learning. He has contributed very little along the lines of published materials. He is twice as likely to be a member of the American Industrial Arts Association and/or the National Education Association as he is to hold membership in the American Vocational Association and/or the National Association of Industrial Teacher Trainers. The chances are about even that he has travelled abroad and that he is a member of Epsilon Pi Tau. His chief avocational interest is that of out-door sports.[25]

Despite extreme differences among the institutions offering industrial arts teacher education, their personnel and curricula, the yearbook includes an interesting profile of a "typical" program of industrial arts teacher education.

The "typical" program has been established for 28 years, hence the date of establishment is 1923. It is designated as an Industrial Arts Department, but while it is more likely to be in a School or College of Education than in any other single institutional subdivision it is less likely to be classified under Education than under some alternate grouping.

The department has five faculty members, with a head who ranks as professor, one associate professor, one assistant professor, and two instructors. These men deal with about one hundred industrial arts majors, some full-time, and some part-time students, reasonably equally divided. It is not likely that there is a graduate program, for only one in three institutions has such a program. If one exists it is handled by the regular staff, and has ten graduate students pursuing work.

The staff members' professional preparation is most likely to include the attainment of a master's degree. Less than one-half the departments have a staff member possessing a doctor's degree. Instructors may have a master's degree—many do not.

This typical program offers a total of 105 semester hours of work and includes 19 hours of woods, 14 hours each of drawing and metals, 11 hours each of graphic arts and professional courses, 8 hours of electricity, and 5 hours each of crafts and general shop. Other courses, in which transportation experiences predominate, total 18 semester hours. This program leads to a bachelor of science degree, usually designated as a bachelor of science in education. If a master's de-

[24] Walter R. Williams and Harvey K. Meyer, *Inventory-Analysis of Industrial Arts Teacher Education Facilities, Personnel and Programs.* Washington: American Council on Industrial Arts Teacher Education, 1952, p. 2.

[25] *Ibid.*, p. 4.

gree is offered, it is probably a master of arts in education or a master of education degree.[26]

Although the yearbook indicated that industrial arts had traveled a long hard path from the manual training of the 1880's, and therefore had every reason to be proud of its achievement, the council regarded this achievement merely as a marker in the path of history and urged "a new sense of mission," "new goals," and "renewed devotion to the ideal of industrial arts opportunities for all American youth."

### The Schmitt-Hunt Study, 1956-1958

During Dewitt Hunt's short tenure of office as Specialist for Industrial Arts, U.S. Office of Education, he initiated a survey of industrial arts teacher education programs. Hunt left the Office of Education before the returns could be analyzed. Eventual tabulation by Marshall Schmitt revealed that about 58 percent of the questionnaires were returned. The data were over a year old by the time that Schmitt became Specialist in Industrial Arts.

Although the data were thought to be largely inconclusive, certain conclusions did seem justifiable. These were:

1. Most of the institutions training industrial arts teachers used the term "industrial arts" in their department titles.
2. Three titles—head, chairman, and director—designated the administrator of the department. "Head" of department was preferred, and most of these men achieved the academic rank of professor.
3. More industrial arts teacher educators achieved the academic rank of assistant professor than any other rank.

4. Very few teacher educators did not possess a college degree.
5. A considerable proportion of the staff did not devote full time to teaching and/or administering industrial arts courses.
6. There was little unanimity in the title of the first and second level professional degrees awarded graduates by the industrial arts teacher education institutions.
7. Some teacher education institutions offer a wide variety of two-year associate degrees and/or certificates not pertaining to industrial arts teaching.
8. Many curricula leading to degrees, other than industrial arts teaching, are administered by some departments training industrial arts teachers.
9. There was an increase in the number of graduates at all degree levels during the 1953-54, 1954-55 school years.
10. A little more than four-fifths of the first degree graduates either taught industrial arts or entered military service.[27]

### Significance of the Five Studies

Not until the formation of the American Council on Industrial Arts Teacher Education, in 1950, had any professional group devoted itself solely to the problems of such education. Prior to 1950, therefore, studies tended largely to represent occasional interests of other professional organizations and of individuals. Studies of teacher education had of course been made by graduate students, but because of the exigencies of thesis and dissertation writing these were seldom definitive to the point of showing national trends.

Adjustments in teacher education seemed easier to make when facts were available to show an existing situation and when it was possible to identify

---

[26] *Ibid.*, pp. 4-7.
[27] Marshall L. Schmitt, and Dewitt Hunt, *Survey of Industrial Arts Teacher Education Programs*, U.S. Department of Health, Education, and Welfare, Office of Education, 1958, p. 24.

significant trends. Fryklund's study provided a factual analysis of the undergraduate program. Having solved this problem it was only natural to review the graduate program, which was the purpose of Struck's study.

Identification of trends, as in Siepert's 1942 study, opened the door to an inventory-analysis of teacher education by Walter R. Williams and Harvey K. Meyer in 1952.

Each of these studies provides some means of evaluation. The more comparative data available, the greater will be the tendency to adjust teacher education programs to generally acceptable higher standards. The Specialist for Industrial Arts, U.S. Office of Education, has continuing responsibilities in regard to the quality of teacher education and for keeping the profession aware of status and trends. However, it would appear that the principal responsibility for keeping track of the facts, showing the trends, and suggesting the standards, falls largely to the American Council on Industrial Arts Teacher Education.

## Other Reports from the Professional Literature

In many respects the professional literature has been merely a "safety valve" in teacher education. It has provided an opportunity for teacher educators to share advanced ideas, make recommendations, and inform the professional group of the status of a particular venture at a particular time. The story of industrial arts teacher education as found in professional literature is disconnected. Following the historical background from this point of reference is much like reading a book five pages a day, but starting at a different place each day and with no plan of progression for reading. Nevertheless the articles in the professional journals are an important part of the historical background, for they do reinforce many ideas of the period in which they were written.

### Larsson—The Voice of Experience

Early in 1919 Gustaf Larsson, principal of the Sloyd Training School in Boston, set forth some fundamental ideas on teacher training, ideas that still have merit more than a half century later. He did not believe that the training of teachers of the manual and industrial fields should necessarily be different from the training required of other teachers. Only the subject matter would vary.

In view of these facts, it seems that the essential qualification in any teacher is first, a proper understanding of and sympathy with the pupils; second, a professional training in the art and methods of teaching; and third, a mastery of the subject-matter.

We take these qualifications in order of importance, for in the case of teachers of industrial subjects the selection is often made on a reverse plan, a person being sometimes selected merely for his superior technical attainments. The result of such selection is detrimental to education. The lack of professional training in these teachers is often overlooked, as they are known as "special teachers." There should be no "special teachers," but always teachers of special subjects and having professional preparation.[28]

---

[28] Gustaf Larsson, "Manual Training, Its Teacher and Its Methods," *Manual Training Magazine*, Vol. XX, No. 5, January 1919, p. 176.

Larsson's enthusiastic support for and participation in teacher education were elements that provided some stability in the growing concern for appropriate advances in industrial education.[29]

### Proffitt Report, 1924-1926

M. M. Proffitt called attention briefly to the implications of the development of the general shop for teacher education. The general shop plan of organizing instruction required a much better prepared teacher of industrial arts than was usually available. The normal schools and the colleges had not provided an adequate supply of such teachers. Experience was required with a variety of crafts; teachers needed to apply and adapt their skills to projects for pupils with varying abilities and interests.

Proffitt cited an arrangement with the Indianapolis public schools and Purdue University in which a plan had been evolved for in-service teachers. The work was organized for a period of two semesters on an extension basis, with 17 lessons each semester. It included instruction in the manipulation of tools and equipment, applied to projects for seventh and eighth grade students. Reading and research problems related to the projects were provided. The teachers were involved in the preparation of three types of instruction sheets: information, operation, and job. The same subject was usually assigned to two persons who worked independently to prepare the material. In conference a composite was made which was mimeographed and distributed to all members of the class. By the end of the first semester 55 information sheets, 46 operation sheets, and 28 job sheets had been prepared for items directly related to subjects and projects suitable for use in the general shop.

During the second semester the in-service teacher education consisted of special units on sheet metal, foundry, and concrete work. Lesson sheets were prepared for these projects.

Proffitt's summary of industrial education during the biennium 1924-26 included only one reference to teacher education, in which he said that there were

. . . occasional efforts toward the reorganization of teacher training work in teacher training institutions to meet special needs of manual arts instructors, especially for such new types of work as represented by the general shop teacher.[30]

### Proffitt Report, 1926-1928

Much discussion of teacher qualifications occurred during the biennium. This resulted in changes in the curricula of teacher training institutions. State boards of education tended to increase certification requirements, and local schools tended to move toward higher qualifications for industrial arts teachers. The trend of cooperation between a local school system and a

---

[29] Larsson's Americanized Sloyd was not only popular in elementary education; his influence was felt throughout the entire manual training field. It has been said that he never lost his enthusiasm for the work, which must have accounted in part for its success. On the occasion of Larsson's death, July 23, 1919, Bennett referred to him as one of the "makers of manual training" in America.

[30] M. M. Proffitt, *Industrial Education in 1924-1926*, U.S. Department of the Interior, Bureau of Education, Bulletin 1927, No. 29, 1927, p. 29.

teacher training college for the purpose of upgrading industrial arts teachers had been continued.

A conference was called by the State Department of Education in California, December, 1926, for the purpose of considering problems involved. It was agreed at this conference:

. . . that 40 semester hours of shop work be prescribed as a basic course, with 10 electives in shop work, making a total of 50 semester hours of shop work for a degree. The 40 hours of prescribed shop work include woodwork, machine shop, auto mechanics, wood finishing, electricity, sheet metal, plumbing, leather work, forging and welding, mechanical and architectural drawing, and cement and concrete construction.[31]

The State Department of Education in Pennsylvania reached a decision that after 1931 all teachers of industrial arts must have three years of college work when applying for a certificate to teach industrial arts, and that after 1932 such persons would be required to hold a degree. The highlight of the period, insofar as Proffitt could determine it, was the tendency to increase requirements for industrial arts teachers in academic, professional, and shop work.

### Shane's Study of Educational Requirements

In March, 1930, Adolph Shane reported on the special educational requirements for teachers of manual arts or industrial arts as distinct from vocational educators. Based on data from 47 states, the study provided information on the minimum educational attainment beyond high school required by each of the states. These data are shown in the accompanying chart, which was included in Shane's study.

Shane concluded his report optimistically by saying:

With only four or five States now requiring less than one year of education and professional training beyond high school for industrial-arts teachers, and with other States increasing their present requirements, the trend is definitely upward, and it will probably not be long before a college degree will be the common minimum requirement of industrial-art teachers every where.[32]

### Evaluation of Professional Preparation

In 1933, John F. Friese reported on a study of 154 teachers who had been asked for their judgment of various subjects included in the teacher training program. Friese prepared a composite of all replies and reported an order of value in three categories as follows:

**Shop**
 Mechanical and machine drawing
 Woodwork
 Sheet-metal work
 Design
 Machine shop
 Electricity
 Pattern making
 Wood turning
 Printing

**Professional**
 Psychology (general)
 Practice teaching
 Organization of industrial arts
 Methods (general)
 Teaching of industrial arts
 Shop administration—management
 History of industrial arts
 Equipment

---

[31] M. M. Proffitt, *Industrial Education 1926-1928*, U.S. Department of the Interior, Bureau of Education, Bulletin 1929, No. 21, 1929, pp. 21-22.

[32] Adolph Shane, "Educational Requirements of Industrial-Arts Teachers," *Industrial Education Magazine*, Vol. XXXI, No. 9, March 1930, p. 341.

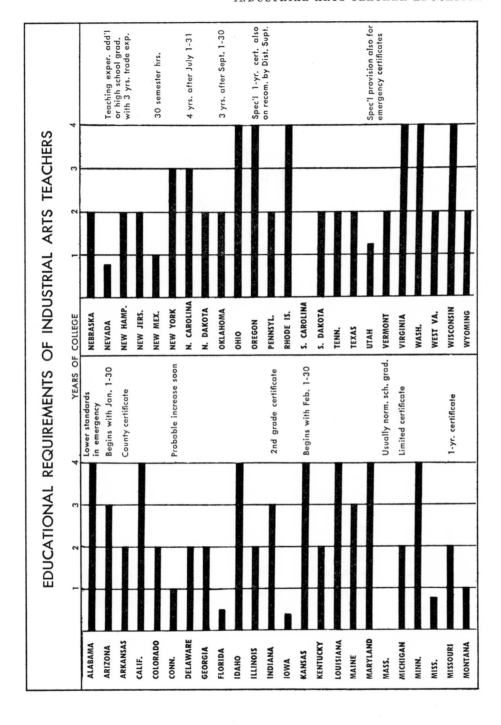

Curriculum construction
Safety and health
Lesson plans
Project method
History of vocational education

**Academic**

Mathematics
English
Physics and chemistry
History
Sociology

Friese further reported that 5.16 semesters of preparation was considered a minimum for initial successful teaching. Although a low requirement, it did indicate that improvement had taken place.

Industrial-arts teachers believe that to meet present conditions one-half of their training should be devoted to shopwork and drawing, one-fourth to professional subjects, and one-fourth to academic subjects.[33]

**Abilities of Industrial Teachers**

In an address before the American Vocational Association, December, 1933, Verne C. Fryklund emphasized the necessity of adequate selection procedures. "There can be no defense for a policy of encouraging young people to prepare for occupations for which they lack the obvious and necessary personal qualifications," he said. Fryklund's study was based upon extensive objective evidence. He suggested the following points for consideration as a means of general improvement in teacher selection.

1. Some refinement of the methods of selecting the personnel who choose to enter industrial teaching is possible. Testing procedure provides splendid supporting information if not, as yet, a completely worthy substitution for older methods of selection. It must be kept in mind, however, that there is demanded a shortening of the period of time required to make decisions upon entry. This period must, for economic reasons, come before or very soon after one enters training, rather than when one is nearly through with his preparation.

2. A testing procedure is suggested for selecting those who possess the highest measurable traits of the kinds desired. Further experimentation is needed, and high correlations should eventually be sought between test results and success on the job. Reasonable assurance can be placed at the outset upon elimination of those who fall in the lower 25 per cent according to population.

3. The facts here presented show the high level at which certain desirable traits can be expected in the excellent shop teacher. Teacher trainers should not overlook these desirable qualities; they should not lessen the usefulness of the industrial teacher to his community by neglecting and overlooking the importance of supporting academic preparation. This preparation must be held to a high standard. There is little excuse for tolerating academic incompetence on the part of the potential shop teacher, inasmuch as his responsibility of molding youth is fully as great as that of other teachers. Upholding the academic as well as the shop standard, in the preparation of industrial teachers, also provides that test of stamina that indicates a possession of those qualities needed in the excellent teacher who can be creative and dynamic in pursuit of his chosen profession.[34]

Fryklund was hitting hard at the soft spot in education—teacher competence. It was clear, from his point of view, that teacher educators were in control of the matter. Upon their

[33] John F. Friese, "Shop Teachers' Evaluation of Courses in Professional Preparation," *Industrial Education Magazine,* Vol. XXXIV, No. 7, January 1933, p. 126.
[34] Verne C. Fryklund, "The Abilities of Industrial Teachers," *Industrial Education Magazine,* Vol. XXXVI, No. 2, March 1934, p. 63.

judgment rested the future of industrial arts.

## Undergraduate Training of Industrial Arts Teachers

Benjamin W. Leib, reporting on undergraduate training of industrial arts teachers in 1936, advanced the view that the major contributing factor in the lack of teacher preparation was related to minimum requirements in the amount of specialized courses. Leib, a professor of industrial arts at State Teachers College, Kirksville, Missouri, based his analysis upon four major issues.

1. Beginning teachers of industrial arts generally are not sufficiently well prepared to meet the challenge of the modern industrial-arts department in a good high school.
2. Manipulative skills ordinarily can not be learned with the same relative rapidity as ideational subject-matter.
3. The beginning industrial-arts teacher can not expect to acquire the necessary manipulative skills and technical information while he is on the teaching job.
4. Graduate schools generally do not recognize manipulative work as of graduate level. This applies in the field of industrial-arts education.[35]

In his do-or-die conclusion Leib pointed out that:

Since industrial-arts teachers generally do not receive adequate special preparation in the undergraduate teachers college; since development of manipulative skills requires a relatively large amount of time; and since industrial-arts teachers have little or no opportunity for improving their manipulative skills and increasing their fund of technical information

either in service or in graduate school; it would appear that the undergraduate teachers colleges which prepare teachers for industrial arts should increase the relative amount of time given to the special training of these students, or else should retire from this special field of service.[36]

Leib left very little room for doubt as to his point of view, and no doubt at all as to the sincerity of his feelings on the issue.

## The Master's Degree

By 1937 about forty institutions were offering the master's degree in industrial arts education. Most of the institutions offered a full-time program, although some provided for graduate study only in summer programs. Emphasis in graduate study was centered upon research and teaching.

According to Otto A. Hankammer, the key to progressive graduate study was the staff of the institution offering advanced work. Hankammer had determined that 37 percent of the staff in graduate programs held the doctorate, 53 percent the master's, and ten percent the bachelor's degree.[37] Proper academic rank, adequately trained staff, and laboratories of research (rather than skill development) were essential items in the further development of graduate study, according to Hankammer. He made it crystal clear that *professional development* characteristics should be expected in graduate work rather than *skill development* characteristics, which he believed were the province of the undergraduate program.

---

[35] Benjamin W. Leib, "Undergraduate Training of Industrial-Arts Teachers," *Industrial Education Magazine*, Vol. 38, No. 4, September 1936, pp. 202-203.

[36] *Ibid.*, p. 203.

[37] Otto A. Hankammer, "The Master's Degree in Industrial Arts Education," *Industrial Education Magazine*, Vol. 39, No. 4, September 1937, pp. 178-180.

Immaturity of the graduate program created many problems which in time would be solved. However, Hankammer was quite specific on the point that "experimentation and change" should be essential characteristics of the evolving program.

## Trends in Industrial Arts Teacher Education, 1940

The trends identified by Proffitt in 1940 included one reference to teacher education. He cited the general increase of requirements in almost every aspect. A college degree was uniformly required, and in some locations even a fifth year was demanded. Educators generally agreed that these higher standards were appropriate, and also that the work done in earning the degree must become increasingly relevant to industrial arts education. Proffitt was not particularly impressed by the tendency to have industrial arts teachers "merely take more of the academic subjects."

A great disadvantage may be had, however, from giving industrial arts teachers a baptism of professional education, including attention to present movements in the whole field of education, to administrative practices governing the organization and operation of public-school systems, to the psychology of child life and development, and to the study of changing social patterns in life and the part that industrial life plays in such changes.[38]

Despite these negative feelings Proffitt said that there was evidence to indicate that industrial arts teachers found the study of such topics interesting and valuable as a background for professional development.

## A Laboratory for Teachers

Lethargy is a universal problem; in industrial arts, elements of lethargy could be detected in the attitude of instructors and in the sameness of student activity. In-service activities in Indianapolis, under the direction of Harry E. Wood, uncovered the fact that teachers were not interested in things they knew little about or which required a great amount of energy. The pattern of routine offered many attractions to the teacher.

Wood attempted to improve opportunities, at least, by providing an experimental laboratory which was available to teachers in small groups, or as individuals, at times when teachers could be expected to be free for such work. Here the teacher could see excellent projects in their finished stage, together with directions and examples of their development. The demonstrations and displays were said to be new, attractive, and inspiring.

No longer may the teacher lay claim to the fact that he has no opportunity to place before his class certain of the newer innovations in the manual arts. He cannot lay claim to being too busy for there is developed for him and with him as a part of his regular teacher-training program the projects that he will need.[39]

Among the general outcomes of the experiment was a "contest idea" which stimulated teachers to create interesting innovations.

---

[38] M. M. Proffitt, *Trends in Industrial Arts,* Federal Security Agency, Office of Education, Pamphlet No. 93, 1940, pp. 14-15.

[39] Ammon Swope, "The Training of Industrial Arts Teachers," *American Vocational Association News Bulletin,* Vol. V, No. II, May 1930, p. 36.

## Basic Preparation for Teachers, 1948

The preparation of industrial arts teachers was a threefold problem, according to Gordon O. Wilber. It involved (1) preparing to teach—method and related elements, (2) becoming contributing citizens in society, and (3) training to perform as technicians and craftsmen.

Wilber reasoned as follows: "Administrators are demanding and communities are expecting that the industrial arts teacher be a cultured person who can meet other teachers and members of the community on an equal basis socially as well as professionally." [40] He noted that industrial arts teachers were required to have from 21 to 60 semester hours in the liberal-cultural area. In technical training, rather than competencies in only one or two fields, the teacher was expected to know a wide variety of basic industrial processes. The necessity for exploration and guidance, the acceptance of the general-shop idea, and the enrichment and broadening of unit shops were all steps which made it particularly difficult for industrially trained craftsmen to adjust to teaching requirements. Wilber reported that the practice of having school shop courses taught by engineering instructors was an obstacle to effective training in industrial arts. The students would tend to follow special examples and practices of the instructor which differed from what they had been told to do; it was imperative that this part of preparation be directed by industrial arts men.

In professional preparation Wilber found a great diversity of opinion and practice. He cited particularly the variety of practices in cadet teaching experience.

## In-Service Preparation of Industrial Arts Teachers

The necessity of in-service education had become well established. It was a teacher's recognized obligation to avail himself of such training. Chris Groneman cited four in-service programs as typical: (1) city supervision; (2) teacher training college follow-up; (3) national, state, and regional supervision; and (4) self-improvement. [41]

City supervisors could develop rapport through visits and consultations with individual teachers, by providing teaching demonstrations and directed observations, teacher committee work, course revision, and a variety of other means. Teamwork in developing tests, preparing evaluative criteria, and judging effectiveness of teaching were cooperative enterprises which produced results.

Teacher training colleges had found that follow-up and field work with teachers were valuable in-service development programs. Groneman cited an instance of a critic teacher from one teacher training institution who spent his full time with the master teachers in schools cooperating in assignment of student teachers. In 1948 approximately 14 states had appointed state supervisors of industrial arts, and

[40] Gordon O. Wilber, "The Basic Preparation for Industrial Arts Teachers," *American Vocational Journal*, Vol. 23, No. 5, May 1948, p. 13.
[41] Chris H. Groneman, "In-Service Preparation of Industrial Arts Teachers," *American Vocational Journal*, Vol. 23, No. 7, September 1948, p. 21.

their work—devoted to upgrading programs through advice and assistance to superintendents, stimulating statewide activities of a professional nature, and meeting with local and regional groups of teachers—was thought to be an important step toward in-service training. Self-improvement as a means of inservice development consisted of a variety of activities. Short courses, professional magazines, general industrial literature, workshops, clinics, and membership in professional organizations could all be counted upon to exert some influence upon the teacher. This was the aspect of teacher improvement that an instructor engaged in simply because he felt it professionally important for him to do so.

### Values from the Professional Literature

The chief value to be gained from the professional literature lies in the opportunity for industrial arts educators to share their viewpoints with one another. The literature contains many expressions of procedure and philosophy which have been generated from purely local or regional experiences. It also contains examples of "action research" dealing with problems of concern to teacher educators. Such reporting is unregulated in the sense that it comes into existence only when an individual is motivated to prepare his material for publication. Also, such studies tend to be planned without sufficient attention to other research; thus major areas of the industrial arts curriculum are left unexplored. Nevertheless, an article published about a new idea, procedure, or device stimulates experimentation by others who have similar or related interests or problems.

One thing is certain, however. Over the years, efforts to achieve quality in industrial arts teacher education have captured the attention of a substantial group of educators. Furthermore, these educators have viewed the program in a broad sense and cannot be criticized for preoccupation with minor elements of teacher education.

## Yearbooks of the American Council on Industrial Arts Teacher Education

### The First Yearbook, 1952

The American Council on Industrial Arts Teacher Education was established in 1950. This group, which is associated with the American Industrial Arts Association, is the only professional group in the nation whose total effort is directed toward improving industrial arts teacher education. The Council's first yearbook, published in 1952, consisted of an inventory-analysis of industrial arts teacher education.

### The Second Yearbook, 1953
### "Who's Who" in Industrial Arts Teacher Education

The second yearbook, 1953, was devoted to an analysis of industrial arts teacher education in terms of its human composition. It was noted that 73 percent of the teacher educators claimed one of 15 states as their place of birth—Illinois, Indiana, Iowa, Kansas, Michigan, Minnesota, Nebraska, New York, Ohio, Missouri, Oklahoma, Pennsylvania, Tennessee, Texas, and Wisconsin. Less than two percent were foreign born, and these persons came chiefly from Canada, France, England, and Sweden. The average family had

198

1.94 children. The teacher educators' average age was 41.9 years. Publications: 12 percent had written one or more books and 27 percent had contributed at least one article to a professional magazine. Professional preparation: 12 percent held the doctorate, 75 percent the master's, and 12 percent the bachelor's degree. Only one percent did not have a college degree.

The yearbook contains the following conclusion:

It is evident . . . that industrial arts teacher education is a full-fledged profession, worthy of a permanent place in the circle of higher education. The profession is young, yet well equipped for its task both in terms of fomal education and professional experience.

It is somewhat surprising, however, to find that about one of every five industrial arts teacher educators has had no experience in public school teaching. The study also seems to indicate a need for an increase in the production of professional books.[42]

## The Third Yearbook, 1954
## Techniques of Selection and Guidance of Graduate Students

George F. Henry undertook this study. Information was obtained by questionnaires, supplemented by a study of college catalogs.

Problems of selection, appraisal, retention, and guidance of graduate students depended upon the particular institution. Generally, however, smaller schools tended to have fewer requirements. The controlling elements of selection and admission were most frequently based upon an analysis of the

student's scholastic records. Little difference was discovered in the caliber of students who followed different degree options. There was no evidence to indicate that the age of the student should become a controlling factor of selection. The evidence did indicate that more attention should be given to the needs of graduate students with teaching experience who had the desire to improve their teaching. Henry recommended that:

. . . more emphasis be placed on individualized selection. The personal qualities of the student, his maturity and experience, his ability to reason, his perseverance and ardent pursuit of an objective are often more significant for purposes of retention than is his failure to have attained, or his attainment of, a high scholastic average in the undergraduate college.

Special attention should be given to the problems of selection of students who are peculiar to the program of industrial arts education.

A clear definition of "admission to candidacy" should be made and inserted in college and university catalogs so that a common interpretation may be made by all who read it.

There is a decided lack of information on prognosis of success in graduate study in industrial arts education. It is recommended that administrators be encouraged to publish their ideas and findings for the benefit of the graduate programs in the United States.[43]

## Fourth Yearbook, 1955
## Superior Practices in Industrial Arts Teacher Education

The fourth yearbook, 1955, was intended to provide a profile of the fron-

---

[42] Walter R. Williams and Roy F. Bergengren, *Who's Who in Industrial Arts Teacher Education*. Washington: American Council on Industrial Arts Teacher Education, 1953, p. 4.

[43] Roy F. Bergengren, Jr., George F. Henry, Talmage B. Young, *Leadership • Graduate Selection • Textbook Analysis, Yearbook 3.* Washington: American Council on Industrial Arts Teacher Education, 1954, p. 117.

tier of industrial arts teacher education. An inventory of superior practices in the field was sent to 202 schools in 45 states. Members of the departments surveyed were asked to rate the items on the inventory as "practiced or achieved in a superior manner," "practiced or achieved to a limited extent," or "absent as a practice or of minor significance." The study was based on data from 147 schools in 40 states.

In addition to responding to the inventory, the institutions were asked to describe some of their superior practices. A major portion of the yearbook was devoted to these responses. The actual situations indicated how the institutions interpreted their role in the improvement of practices in teacher education. In summary the yearbook indicated:

Many of the items in the Inventory are searching in their nature and were designed to ferret out practices that are essentially a departure from the traditional program. Such items were incorporated in the instrument to determine the awareness of the profession to the demands of a highly technical democracy. Similarly other items were intended to obtain an indication of the concepts of learning and of the educational philosophies which undergird our teacher-education programs.

The study has revealed points of strength and weakness among present practices. Each of the chapters has an obvious absence of pertinent responses to one or more items. These items, it will be conceded, are new departures in many respects but their performance or pursuit is decidedly in keeping with advocated practices and Industrial Arts teacher needs.

Finally, the Yearbook should serve as a resource publication for teacher educators. Through this volume the educator can locate institutions and programs that have met with success in various aspects of teacher preparation. In this respect the book becomes an annotated cross reference of superior practices.[44]

An outstanding contribution of the yearbook is that it reports actual superior practices rather than theoretical models.

### The Fifth Yearbook, 1956
### Problems and Issues in Industrial Arts Teacher Education

The 1956 Yearbook was prepared so that each chapter presented a complete problem, including its analysis, suggested solutions, and related information. Teacher educators were urged to use the yearbook in a variety of ways: as a basis for discussion in professional meetings, by selecting an issue and developing it fully for publication in a professional journal, by making the yearbook available to persons outside the council, and by sponsoring an experiment or conducting research based upon one or more of the issues and problems raised.

In connection with the chapter concerning "The Human Element," it was reported in summary that:

The learning takes place through differentiation of perceptual fields which are, in some respects, known only to the individual. Gaining insight into human behavior is facilitated by engaging in a direct study of the pupils. In this way we begin to see some elements in their perceptual fields and we begin to recognize their ends and concerns in life. These needs and concerns of pupils are the

---

[44] R. Lee Hornbake and Donald Maley, *Superior Practices in Industrial Arts Teacher Education, Yearbook 4, 1955.* Washington: American Council on Industrial Arts Teacher Education, 1955, pp. 156-157.

foundation on which industrial arts curriculum content and teaching method may well be based.[45]

Other problems and issues consisted of those related to the demands of a contemporary culture, the derivation of goals and purposes of instruction, concepts of curriculum and method, evaluation, general education, technical education, and professional education. The general problem of agreement on principle but wide diversity of performance was cited as one of the major challenges of the profession. The common weaknesses of teacher education programs were identified as:

. . . insufficient emphasis upon professional education in programs of preparation for secondary school teaching; lack of integration of understandings, attitudes, and appreciations; inappropriate learning activities and teaching techniques; misdirected methods courses; and neglect of in-service professional education.[46]

## The Sixth Yearbook, 1957
## A Sourcebook of Readings in Education

The 1957 Yearbook brought attention to some of the significant, up-to-date writings, points of view, and generally accepted concepts of education, and the relationships of these concepts to industrial arts. The approach to the general problem was made with seven major topics: philosophical viewpoints, psychological theories, curricular approaches, instructional methods, guidance procedures, community and professional relations, and educational evaluation. In part the yearbook noted criticism that little attention had been given to industrial arts in relation to other areas of education. The editors reported:

The technique is one of surveying some of the most significant writings in these seven areas and attempting to synthesize them, producing useful, well-considered ideas about education. Only then are the applications made and implications drawn for industrial arts. This process . . . should help to rectify the situation. If the criticism was unfair to begin with, this volume will help to prove our case.[47]

The 1957 Yearbook is indeed an excellent sourcebook for persons who wish to match their general orientation in the field of industrial arts with their educational surroundings. Even so, the value of the book is not limited to industrial arts teachers; its content should have appeal for a larger group.

## The Seventh Yearbook, 1958
## The Accreditation of Industrial Arts Teacher Education

Although teacher educators had discussed accreditation for a number of years, little effort had been devoted to systematic study, review, and planning of accreditation in the field of industrial arts. The decision to approach the problem in a thoroughly professional manner resulted in the appointment of a committee to take appropriate action. The seventh yearbook, 1958, represents a condensed version of a major, seven-year study of the

---

[45] C. Robert Hutchcroft, Editor, *Problems and Issues in Industrial Arts Teacher Education, Yearbook 5, 1956.* Washington: American Council on Industrial Arts Teacher Education, 1956, p. 51.

[46] *Ibid.,* p. 215.

[47] Carl Gerbracht and Gordon O. Wilber, Editors, *A Sourcebook of Readings in Education, Sixth Yearbook, 1957.* Washington: American Council on Industrial Arts Teacher Education, 1957, p. xi.

process of accreditation, a report of a national survey, the evaluative instrument, and other related data. In connection with the role of industrial arts education in self-improvement, the Council took the position that:

Industrial arts teacher educators recognize the need for improvement through program evaluation, and they are doing something about it. With this evaluation instrument and the supplement provided the National Council for Accreditation of Teacher Education, it is hoped that industrial arts educators will take a renewed interest in improving their programs and will share proved effective techniques with others in the profession. . . . National leadership has been provided . . . and . . . the task now remaining must be performed at the departmental level.

In addition to evaluating going programs, departmental personnel may also want to cooperate in formulating more effective methods for improving industrial arts teacher education. . . . This instrument has not been offered as final. . . . It is an initial step in developing an ongoing improvement program for industrial arts teacher educators in the United States.[48]

### The Eighth Yearbook, 1959
### Planning Industrial Arts Facilities

One step in unifying industrial arts education—a step which had been too long neglected—was professional attention to the total problem of industrial arts facilities. The literature was abundant with reviews of local and state efforts in the planning of facilities, and many teachers and supervisors had shared their rather subjective views with others in the profession.

However, national recognition, coordination, and identification of successful, recommended efforts in the planning of facilities had not evolved.

The decision of the council to rectify this error by devoting the 1959 Yearbook to the problem was most appropriate and timely.[49]

The yearbook provides a wealth of material concerning equipment selection, architectural and engineering practices, planning and evaluation of facilities, shop and laboratory plans, photographs of actual installations representing the best ideas, and a variety of other information. Marshall Schmitt showed trends over a half century by contrasting the haphazardness of the past with careful planning for modern requirements. Robert L. Woodward provided recommendations for the number and types of industrial arts laboratories for junior and senior high schools as a function of enrollment.

Here at last was a sourcebook for industrial arts planning. The yearbook contains the best of principles, practices, and theory, gleaned from the total experience of the nation's professional staff of industrial arts educators, and from recognized consultants.

### The Ninth Yearbook, 1960
### Research in Industrial Arts Education

The post World War II era in education has been identified by a marked increase in attention to research. In fact the intensity of research activity could almost be subject to a major criticism, for in such preoccupation al-

---

[48] Verne C. Fryklund and H. L. Helton, *The Accreditation of Industrial Arts Teacher Education, Seventh Yearbook, 1958.* Washington: American Council on Industrial Arts Teacher Education, 1958, p. 64.

[49] Ralph K. Nair, Editor, *Planning Industrial Arts Facilities, Eighth Yearbook, 1959.* Washington: American Council on Industrial Arts Teacher Education, 1959.

ways lurks the danger of forgetting other fundamentals. Nevertheless, the research background was as imperative in industrial arts as in any other area of education. Research produces the facts upon which evaluation and improvement can be made. The Council's 1960 Yearbook cites significant research in industrial arts teacher education, highlights other research completed by industrial arts educators, suggests procedures and theoretical orientation for research in industrial arts, and finally gives consideration to the research needed. In summary it points out that:

The problems concerning the lack of coordinated research in the field of industrial arts and industrial arts teacher training should be evident to the reader. . . . Through research, we must evaluate our entire system of education if we hope to provide our youth with the necessary knowledges and skills to preserve the leadership this nation needs to bring it through the critical years ahead—economically, socially, and from the standpoint of national defense.[50]

## The Tenth Yearbook, 1961
## Graduate Study in Industrial Arts

Analyzing what is known about industrial arts education and the nature of the social forces which influence the field is one of the consistent, imperative tasks of industrial arts educators. Another such task is the development of graduate programs which effectively provide a realistic environment, comprehensive frame of reference, and proper attitude for the student.

The tenth yearbook, 1961, provided attention to both of these matters. It dealt with the general evolution of industrial arts in public education with reference to its scope, its claim as a discipline, and the elementary, secondary, and collegiate programs. It also examined industrial arts graduate programs *in action*: The evolution of and trends in graduate study, as well as the relationship between graduate and undergraduate programs, were reviewed in depth by means of examples of programs on the graduate level.

One result of graduate study which can be measured rather easily is the number of advanced degrees which have been issued. For the 25-year period 1930-1955 studies show that 3,420 master's degrees were granted and 371 doctor's degrees. It appeared that the master's degree would become a "minimum requirement in teaching." As to the future of the doctorate, the yearbook reports:

Probably the greatest problem facing the profession in relation to the doctorate is the limited number of programs in existence. Many industrial arts teachers have been forced to enter programs that provide little or no professional training in industrial arts or industrial education. Under these circumstances, they select majors such as art education, teacher education, administration and supervision, and secondary education. While these programs provide the professional education aspects, they often fail to provide the opportunity to gain further insights into the problems and needs of industrial arts. That is, their education courses are not related to their major interest (industrial arts) and they have no contact with an advisor versed in industrial arts.[51]

[50] Raymond Van Tassel, Editor, *Research in Industrial Arts Education, Ninth Yearbook, 1960.* Washington: American Council on Industrial Arts Teacher Education, 1960, p. 119.

[51] Ralph P. Norman and Ralph C. Bohn, Editors, *Graduate Study in Industrial Arts, Tenth Yearbook, 1961.* Washington: American Council on Industrial Arts Teacher Education, 1961, p. 156.

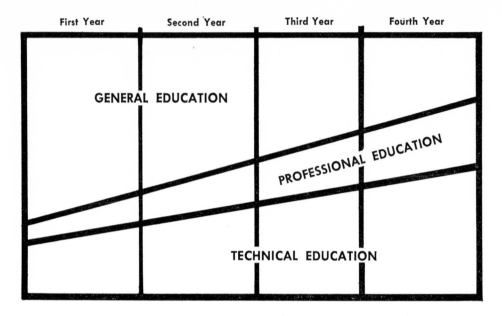

## The Eleventh Yearbook, 1962
### Essentials of Preservice Preparation

The eleventh yearbook offered a general rationale for a program of pre-service education for industrial arts teachers. The writers had in mind the following objectives:

1. To identify and state some basic assumptions and arguments underlying the essentials of the general, professional, and technical preparation of industrial arts teachers.
2. To recommend minimum standards of preservice education for industrial arts teachers as to (a) nature, (b) quantity, and (c) sequence in a program which is consistent with the developed rationale.
3. To identify ways in which we can select better individuals who aspire to industrial arts teaching.[52]

These objectives were reached in the chapters which developed the background and purpose of preservice preparation, the general professional and technical education phases, and the elements of student selection; and by the implications of significant elements and trends for the total program of preservice teacher education. It was determined in the summary that the program generally allotted 62 semester hours to general education, 20-21 semester hours to professional education, and 41-42 semester hours to the technical phases of industrial arts. This resulted in a total number of units required for graduation which ranged between 123 and 125 semester hours. The program was represented graphically on the chart above.[53]

The chart shows how a typical industrial arts teacher candidate would divide his time among the three main divisions of preservice education during his undergraduate years.

---

[52] Donald G. Lux, Editor, *Essentials of Preservice Preparation, Eleventh Yearbook, 1962.* Washington: American Council on Industrial Arts Teacher Education, 1962, p. 3.
[53] *Ibid.,* p. 173.

## Yearbooks, 1963-66

A yearbook planning committee of the American Council on Industrial Arts Teacher Education has the primary responsibility for looking ahead to major issues for consideration in each of the yearbooks. Members of the committee serve staggered terms so that not more than two persons retire from the committee each year, and two new persons are added. This provides the continuity essential for adequate attention to the major forces influencing the teaching process in industrial arts.

Yearbook twelve, 1963, *Action and Thought in Industrial Arts Education,* was addressed "to all who would listen or read things which cause our subject matter to advance." In addition it provided ideas calculated to facilitate action among industrial arts educators.

The thirteenth yearbook, 1964, considered the general area of *Classroom Research in Industrial Arts.* Because of the wide gap that generally exists between the producers of research (college personnel) and the consumers of research (classroom teachers), the yearbook committee directed its attention toward making the consumers of research contributors to the production of research. This was visualized under the general heading of research that classroom teachers can do. The yearbook was essentially an abbreviated research handbook for industrial arts teachers.

In 1965 the yearbook (fourteenth) was devoted to *Approaches and Procedures in Industrial Arts.* Broadly the yearbook treated: (1) the curriculum area of industrial arts and its place in the educational structure, (2) effective teaching procedures, and (3) efficient organizational practices. The body of knowledge of industrial arts was cast in a modern progressive setting.

The yearbook for 1966 (fifteenth), *Status of Research in Industrial Arts,* was in effect a report to the profession identifying in a single volume significant research completed in industrial arts related to: (1) objectives, (2) evaluation, (3) teaching methods, (4) teacher education, and (5) staff studies and nondegree research. In addition the general problem of securing funds for research in industrial arts teacher education was reviewed.

### Significance of the Yearbooks

The yearbooks of the American Council on Industrial Arts Teacher Education have been effective in the improvement of teacher education. Not only do the books embrace the entire professional area of teacher education, but the cooperative nature of their preparation reaches into the remote areas of the industrial arts program and builds standards, goals, and objectives, by common consent and with general acceptance.

## Summary

Teacher education in industrial arts began prior to the turn of the century when the program was in its manual training stage. First efforts varied greatly—some good, others poor. Nevertheless the attempts had sufficient vitality to sustain the movement toward improvement of instruction. That any effort was made at all during the early years can be attributed to individual initiative. Here and there manual training teachers would come to the realization that it was possible to have better programs which in turn would be keys to progress. So these individuals found ways to make progress through their own efforts.

Three of these early leaders were Bennett, Bawden, and Selvidge. Each had developed his own ideas, and wanted to share them. In addition each was anxious to learn from others who had experience with the general problems of teacher education. The Mississippi Valley Conferences are representative of the first constructive efforts to coordinate and promote sound principles of industrial arts teacher education. In 1918 Siepert made his study of the status of teacher preparation in manual arts; already for more than two decades attention had been paid to the problem of such teacher training, and some progress was evident.

Immediately following the first World War, Bawden set out with determination to bring into open view many related facets of teacher education. Through conferences and publications of the Bureau of Education, interest was heightened. Also, Mississippi Valley Conference members had the foresight to encourage publication of documents related to teacher education. It is easy for one to reach the conclusion that Bawden stood head and shoulders above the entire field in contributions to the promotion and development of teacher education. However, such a conclusion needs to be tempered by other observations. Bawden was a prominent leader in the field. He also had access to a most effective printing plant (the Government Printing Office); coupled with

his willingness to serve, this led him into the limelight more frequently than many of his colleagues. However, it is quite safe to assume that Bawden was not moving against the prevailing current of opinion; he was a part of that current, and the elements of progress attributed to him in print were in reality a consensus of many persons.

By 1927, forces represented by the interests of teacher education in industrial arts caused the formation of a committee of the American Vocational Association for the purpose of studying the entire problem of industrial arts teacher education and the improvement of instruction. AVA bulletins and reports about industrial arts teacher education issued in 1929, 1934, 1946, and 1951 were printed in large quantities and widely distributed. It was observed that no other bulletins concerning industrial arts had been used by so many persons or had such stimulating effect upon the progress of industrial arts. In 1959 and 1961, the Industrial Arts Policy and Planning Committee of AVA issued additional bulletins designed to inform and to create an environment for progress.

Teacher education studies promoted by the National Association of Industrial Teacher Educators, in the early 1940's, also had a stimulating effect upon the improvement of industrial arts teacher education. In addition, individual studies, reports of observations, points of view, and research reviewed in the professional journals made contributions toward improvement.

All lacked at least one essential ingredient—continuity. There were few sustained or prolonged efforts of any magnitude until 1950, when the American Council on Industrial Arts Teacher Education was formed. The Council provided, between 1952 and 1962, eleven yearbooks directly concerned with the professional treatment of the total program. In many respects it could be argued that the professional study of industrial arts teacher education *began* in 1950. Most certainly the yearbooks contributed more toward standardization and development of a unified viewpoint than any other publication during the period.

There is little similarity between the teacher education of Bennett's first program in 1891 and the comprehensive program reported in the Council's twelfth yearbook in 1962. Only in one element—the desire to have better teachers—has there been no change.

## Recall Questions

1. What are some of the "firsts" in teacher education attributed to Bennett?

2. What were the significant conclusions reached by Siepert in his 1918 study?

3. Identify some of the elements of the historical development in industrial arts teacher education between 1917 and 1927.

4. What significant changes in the objectives of industrial arts can you find in the reports of the AVA committees on industrial arts?

5. Of the "Five Teacher Education Studies" which one do you feel had the greatest impact on teacher education? Why?

6. What is the most important function of professional literature?

7. Outline the major issues treated in the first twelve yearbooks of the American Council on Industrial Arts Teacher Education. In your opinion has the Council's attention to teacher education been narrow or broad? Why?

## Research Questions

1. Prepare a *time line* for teacher education in industrial arts and show the persons and events in historical perspective. Include important books, by date of publication. List locations where major events took place.

2. Study the chapter in detail and prepare a short analysis of professional development of teacher education staffs in regard to degrees held. Arrange this information in chronological order and reach conclusions about the trends in professional development.

## Suggestions for Further Reading

American Council on Industrial Arts Teacher Education, Yearbooks, 1952 to present. Other publications as suggested by footnote references.

# Chapter 9

# Trade and Industrial Teacher Education

The Society's Bulletins on Teacher Training · Teacher Training Requirements of the Smith-Hughes Act · Teacher Training, 1917-1933 · Teacher Training from 1934 Through World War II · The Post-War Years · Looking Forward from Historical Perspective · Summary · Recall Questions · Research Questions · Suggestions for Further Reading

**I**n its early years the National Society for the Promotion of Industrial Education recognized the need for a sound program of trade and industrial teacher education. Establishment of such a vocational program was proposed by persons who envisioned teacher education as one of the foundation blocks of the entire movement. In a sense teacher education was intended to be a "built-in" quality control in trade and industrial education; the program could be no better than its teachers.

This attitude was a product of the environment in which the National Society was created. Charles R. Richards, founder of NSPIE, had been influenced strongly by the professionalism and progressivism of the rapidly growing Teachers College at Columbia University, where he was a member of the faculty.[1] James Earl Russell, Dean of Teachers College, had previously brought to that institution an array of talented men whose work had created new dimensions of interest in teacher education throughout the nation.

Members of the Society were well acquainted with the growth and development of the teacher training activities which had been initiated by Charles A. Bennett at Columbia University in 1891. Indeed some of the Society's members had participated.

It is not surprising, therefore, that the Society devoted a session of its sixth annual meeting to problems related to the training of teachers. This

---

[1] For additional study of the environmental background, see Lawrence A. Cremin's chapter on "Pedagogical Pioneers," in *The Transformation of the School*. New York: Alfred A. Knopf, 1961, pp. 127-176.

*National Society for the Promotion of Industrial Education. Atlanta, Georgia meeting, November 19-21, 1908. (See discussion beginning on page 52.)*

Charles A. Bennett, a leading industrial educator of the early twentieth century. (Among numerous references see passages beginning on pages 92 and 111.)

Dr. Charles A. Prosser, first director of the Federal Board for Vocational Education. (See references on pages 115 and 122, among others.)

*President John F. Kennedy and members of the Panel of Consultants on Vocational Education. This photograph was taken on the White House lawn, November 27, 1962, when the Panel presented its final report. In the foreground with the President are (at left) Benjamin C. Willis, Panel chairman, and (at right) Melvin L. Barlow, author of this book. (See discussion beginning on page 427.) Photograph by Abbie Rowe, White House Photographer.*

208C

*President Lyndon B. Johnson at the signing of the Vocational Education Act of 1963. Standing (left to right) are Dr. William B. Logan, Ohio State University; Dr. M. D. Mobley, American Vocational Association; and Dr. William G. Carr, National Education Association. (Signing of the Act is discussed on page 452.)*

session took place on December 5, 1912. Mrs. Mary Schenck Woolman, President, Women's Educational and Industrial Union, Boston, and Miss Florence Marshall, Principal, Manhattan Trade School for Girls, New York, suggested a number of principles and policies which should prevail in training teachers of girls who would be students in industrial classes.[2] Teachers especially trained for working with women were deemed essential. The ordinary normal school did not offer satisfactory arrangements for the training of trade teachers. These schools had not placed value upon occupational experience as a background requirement; this was essentially a new concept in teacher education. Mrs. Woolman and Miss Marshall recognized that trade experience in itself did not insure good teaching, largely because the teacher might hold a narrow point of view educationally and was likely to give greater emphasis to the product than to the pupil. They did propose, however, that both the best teachers and the most skilled trade workers were needed and, while the combination was difficult to find, it should be an essential goal.

Principles and policies were also formulated by David Snedden, Massachusetts Commissioner of Education, and Charles R. Allen, Agent for the Massachusetts State Board of Education, for the selection and training of teachers for classes of boys. These principles and policies did not differ significantly from those suggested for teachers of girls.[3] Snedden and Allen did, however, call attention to certain problems that teachers would face in dealing with adolescents: It was evident that teachers who transferred from the secondary schools to instruct trade classes would not be acceptable; a school environment could not replace actual experience. Instruction for both boys and girls required (1) that the teacher be selected from the industry or trade area concerned and (2) that he should have special preparation in instructional methods and aims.

At the annual meeting in 1913, the Society voted to continue the study of selecting and training teachers as follows:

To have needed experiments for the training of teachers carried on under favorable conditions; to publish the results of these experiments for the benefit of the country; to issue special reports and bulletins on the problem; and to induce state officials to adopt effective schemes for certifying and preparing instructors.[4]

## The Society's Bulletins on Teacher Training

Throughout the year 1913 committees of the Society, appointed by the executive committee, studied the problems of certification and training of teachers. Authority was granted by the Society, at its annual meeting in October, 1913, to publish the results. In February, 1914, the Society issued its Bulletin No. 19 concerning selection and training of teachers for state-aided industrial schools for boys and men.

[2] National Society for the Promotion of Industrial Education, *Proceedings Sixth Annual Meeting*, Philadelphia, December 5-7, 1912, Bulletin No. 16, pp. 41-43.

[3] *Ibid.*, pp. 67-69.

[4] National Society for the Promotion of Industrial Education, *Proceedings Seventh Annual Meeting*, Grand Rapids, Michigan, October 23-25, 1913, Bulletin No. 18, p. 252.

It was contended that a new plan of certification was needed and that the state should be the sole certifying authority, with certification to be based upon proper examinations. The Society developed at great length the rationale for both certification and teacher training. Examples and plans for each were given in a comprehensive report which set the stage for future standards in teacher training and certification. It was the first significant publication on the topic, and its principles were destined to influence teacher education during the next half century.

Much attention was devoted to the problem of, "Who is going to teach the teachers?" The Society's point of view concerning qualities of the teacher educator is so fundamental and has had such a lasting influence that it is reproduced in summary form as follows:

*The leader for the teacher's training class* should be a man who brings to the work more than a knowledge of general psychology and the established teaching methods of traditional schools. He should have a first hand and thoroughgoing knowledge of the social, economic, industrial and educational problems of the industrial and trade school; he should be thoroughly familiar with its methods of organization and administration and with its teaching practice. A fair measure of the special equipment which such a leader must have in order to conduct successfully such a training course for prospective teachers would be his ability to serve as an acceptable leader in the practical discussion of their problems before a training class for industrial or trade school teachers who are already in service. A glance at the suggested contents of the course of training which is later recommended as indicative of the kind of preparation for

teaching which the student qualifying for service in industrial and trade schools must have, will show at once that the requirements for the leader of the training class as outlined above are certainly none too great and probably entirely too meagre.

No one can successfully induct others into experience he has never had himself. It is obvious that only those who have themselves served as teachers or directors of such schools would be able to measure up to the standard. The few rare leaders of this kind who are available for training purposes are not sufficient to meet the present need and the demand rapidly coming upon us. This will make it necessary to employ, to a considerable extent at least, as such leaders, those who have added to all other necessary qualifications for the task, an intimate familiarity, through close contact with the practice and the problems of the schools for which they undertake to prepare teachers.[5]

The Society's executive committee desired the highest possible standards for persons who were to serve in the capacity of teacher educator. They recommended that such a person prepare for the responsibility by taking leave from any current teaching position "even at financial sacrifice," to add to his academic background; that he visit industrial and trade schools; that he serve as a student teacher in some of these schools and take part in faculty meetings; and in general that he broaden his background and bring into his view an enlarged understanding of the task he was to undertake. The committee was just as adamant concerning the necessity of the leader's keeping himself constantly prepared for his total responsibility in teacher education.

The members expressed suspicion to-

---

[5] National Society for the Promotion of Industrial Education, *The Selection and Training of Teachers for State-Aided Industrial Schools for Boys and Men*, Bulletin No. 19, February 1914, pp. 23-24.

ward the value of certain kinds of educational travel when they recommended that the prospective teacher educator "stay away from Germany and its schools until at least he has learned intimately to know those of his own country." [6] The influence of Europe was strong in the early development of the trade and industrial movement, but some methods needed drastic reorganization to become acceptable in the United States.

A revised edition of Bulletin No. 19 was issued in February, 1917, concurrent with the passage of the Smith-Hughes Act. This again emphasized methods of selection, certification, and training of teachers, both men and women; it became the guide used by the states preparing to embark upon a program of trade and industrial education in the public schools.

In this connection we have noted elsewhere that organized labor, as early as 1912, took a strong position concerning the kind of person who should be selected as a teacher, agreeing—as might be expected—that training in theory alone could not provide effective teachers of trades. What was needed was a combination of theory and practical experience. The Committee on Industrial Education, American Federation of Labor, also held the opinion that the head of a school employing teachers with practical and methodical backgrounds must himself have more than a "textbook acquaintance with the great industrial world." [7]

## Teacher-Training Requirements of the Smith-Hughes Act

The Smith-Hughes Act provided that $1,000,000 of the total sum appropriated be reserved for the purpose of preparing teachers for instruction in vocational education classes. [8] The money was divided among agriculture, home economics, and trade and industrial education, in such a way that not more than 60 percent, nor less than 20 percent, could be expended for any one of the services. This arrangement not only made it possible, but actually made it a requirement, for each of these areas to have at least a minimum program of teacher education. The emphasis upon teacher training is shown in section 12 of the Act, which reads as follows:

That in order for any State to receive the benefits of the appropriation in this Act for the training of teachers . . . of trade [and] industrial . . . subjects, the State Board of such State shall provide in its plan for such training that the same shall be carried out under the supervision of the State board; that such training shall be given in schools or classes under public supervision or control; that such training shall be given only to persons who have had adequate vocational experience or contact in the line of work for which they are preparing themselves as teachers, supervisors, or directors, or who are acquiring such experience or contact as a part of their training; and that the state board, with the approval of the Federal Board, shall establish minimum requirements for such experience or contact for teachers

---

[6] *Ibid.*, p. 106.

[7] 62d Congress, 2d Session, Senate Document No. 936, *Industrial Education,* August 17, 1912, p. 20.

[8] For the fiscal year ending June 30, 1918, only $500,000 was appropriated. This amount was increased each year until the full $1,000,000 was authorized for the year ending June 30, 1921.

. . . of trade [and] industrial . . . subjects.[9]

The influence of the National Society for the Promotion of Industrial Education is indicated clearly in the provisions of the Act.

In March, 1917, the Society issued Bulletin No. 25, which was concerned with an interpretation of the Smith-Hughes Act and which included a discussion of the requirements which the states had to meet in order to take advantage of the Act. The information was consistent with the Society's earlier interpretations of the kind of teacher training and certification which seemed desirable. For the benefit of the state, the bulletin was keyed to certain sections of the Act which indicated the relationships and responsibilities of the Federal Board for Vocational Education and the state boards.

In the late summer of 1917, the Federal Board held a series of conferences with representatives of state boards of education concerning state plans which were to be submitted to the Board for approval. In each of the conferences the Board inquired, in considerable detail, about the exact intentions of the state toward teacher training programs. (See Chapter 6, pp. 116-117.) Although all state plans were different, they subscribed to the principles advocated by the Society and met minimum requirements of the Smith-Hughes Act.

## Teacher Training, 1917-1933

The teacher training requirements of the Smith-Hughes Act did thrust upon the states a new problem for which they were not prepared. Only a very few states had programs of trade and industrial education, and fewer still had given any attention to the special problem of training trade and industrial teachers. In short, a background of experience in trade and industrial teacher training did not exist. The normal schools in many sections of the country had programs for manual training teachers, but such preparation did not meet the exacting requirements of the Smith-Hughes Act.

The demand for trade and industrial teachers is a comparatively recent one, and educators have been somewhat doubtful regarding the nature of the training that trade teachers should have. The lack of a definite plan for teacher training has retarded the progress of vocational education. The supply of properly trained teachers is still the controlling factor in the development of this popular and promising type of education.[10]

The problem of teacher training was complicated further by the large number of trade areas represented and by the different kinds of classes to be offered. Teachers were required for all-day schools, part-time schools, evening schools, and continuation schools. Furthermore it was imperative that teacher training be given in special classes limited to persons preparing to teach in trade and industrial fields.

During the summer of 1917, the discussions between the Federal Board and representatives of the states were related in part to the ways and means for solving state teacher training problems. Despite many shortcomings and

---

[9] 64th Congress, S. 703, February 23, 1917.

[10] Chester D. Jarvis, *Vocational Teachers for Secondary Schools*, Department of the Interior, Bureau of Education, Bulletin 1917, No. 38, Washington: Government Printing Office, 1917, p. 25.

uncertainties, programs of teacher training were organized. By June 30, 1918, courses were being given in 45 institutions by professionals totaling 95. Training was provided for 1,091 prospective teachers during the first year.

The Federal Board had insisted at every opportunity that certification of trade and industrial teachers should require special consideration by the states. It was recognized that a man qualified by practical experience would not necessarily be able to meet the general requirements for teachers in any particular state. However, it was not considered necessary for a man to abandon his trade in order to enter training as a trade teacher. The specific view of the Federal Board in the fall of 1918 is shown by the following analysis:

It is, of course, essential always that the teacher shall be able to teach, but it does not follow that he shall always qualify as a professional teacher. It is much more important that the instructor in carpentering, for example, at least as regards shopwork instruction, shall be a competent carpenter than that he shall have attended a normal school. Provided he can teach carpentering to beginners, he fulfills the chief professional requirement for a vocational teacher of carpentering. This is the prime requisite and all other qualifications are secondary. He must be of good moral character, and unobjectionable in every respect, but provided always, that he can teach carpentering, he should be judged and certified in other respects as a man, rather than as a professional pedagogue.[11]

The Federal Board urged that states having little or no flexibility in their certification system present the prob-lem to the appropriate state board and request that an adequate system be devised. Also the Federal Board continued to drive home the ideas that a trade teacher *must know his trade* and *how to teach* and that the states should not consider the teacher training responsibility lightly.

In connection with the Federal Board's desire to have teacher training established and in good working order, it frequently called attention to programs in operation. Charles L. Jacobs, Director of Teacher Training, trade and industrial education, University of California, reported two classes in 1919 with a total of 49 students, two-thirds of whom were teaching regularly. Jacobs said that the content of the teacher training program consisted of craft analysis, methods of teaching, class management, theory and history of vocational education, and supplemental subjects.[12] These subjects, together with directed observation, assistant teaching, and teaching under supervision, made a total of 288 clock hours of teacher education. It almost goes without saying that students with this training were in demand as teachers.

The Federal Board's role in promoting teacher education was shown also in its announcement of a special course in administration of industrial education which was planned for Teachers College, Columbia University, during the summer of 1919. The course was designed for persons who held responsible positions in industrial education but who wished to advance themselves.

[11] Federal Board for Vocational Education, *The Vocational Summary*, Vol. 1, No. 4, August 1918, p. 15.
[12] Charles L. Jacobs, "Teacher Training for Trades and Industries," *The Vocational Summary*, Vol. 1, No. 10, February 1919, pp. 10-11.

213

It is interesting to note that the course, which lasted six weeks, was intended to be a full time undertaking for those who enrolled. The announced plans suggested that the student would be occupied with activities which would give him a broad insight into elements of industrial education.

### Reaction in the States

In 1919 the University of Illinois formed a center in Chicago for trade and industrial teacher training. A 240-hour program was offered over a period of two years. As described by James McKinney, an assistant professor at the University of Illinois, the program reflected the following attitudes: The trade teacher should have a point of view which was conducive to serving the community, to developing skilled workers, and to providing down-to-earth counseling. He should be a recognized craftsman in the ranks of labor, have the ability to see his trade from the point of view of a teacher, and develop the ability to teach and to manage a class. McKinney, who later was an editor for the American Technical Society and president of the American School, concluded his review of the Chicago center with the following plea:

We are just on the threshold of this vast domain of vocational education, and it behooves those who have been intrusted with the task of training shop teachers to recognize that the larger part of the problem will be to take a man who in his life experience has developed in some marked degree that scarce attribute of judgment (that undefinable quality of meeting a new situation and handling it with common sense) and develop and direct this quality for the new job of teaching.[13]

In May, 1920, New Jersey announced its system of selecting candidates for trade and industrial teacher training programs.[14] The first candidates, recruited by newspaper advertisements, were required to be within the age range of 23-40, have at least six years of trade experience, and have completed the eighth grade. The prospective teachers were then rated by several examiners who first studied their experience background and then conducted an oral examination. All examinations were restricted to subjects in which the candidate claimed experience. The independent ratings were thought to be adequate in selecting the best of craftsmen for teaching.

New York established 25 scholarships, of $2,000 each, for persons who had at least five years' trade experience, in order that they might attend the vocational department of a state normal school for systematic training as teachers.[15] This action by the Regents of the University of the State of New York was indicative of strong desire to attract the best possible persons into the field of trade and industrial teaching.

Early in the development of trade and industrial teacher training some states organized auxiliary services. As an example, a research and service center was established by the Division of

---

[13] James McKinney, "The Chicago Center for the Training of Trade Teachers," *The Vocational Summary*, Vol. I, No. 12, April 1919, p. 13.

[14] J. G. Spofford, "New Jersey System of Selecting Candidates for Trade and Industrial Teacher Training," *The Vocational Summary*, Vol. III, No. 1, May 1920, pp. 11-13.

[15] "Fifty Thousand Dollars for Industrial Teachers' Scholarships," *The Vocational Summary*, Vol. III, No. 2, June 1920, p. 24.

Vocational Education, University of California, on July 1, 1920, with Miss Emily G. Palmer in charge.[16] The first task of the center was to produce analyses of occupations which attracted a large number of workers. There was little or no instructional material available for many occupations, so the analyses were intended primarily as guides for teachers.

In a similar manner other states were making progress in adapting principles of teacher education to their own particular conditions.

## Idea of Occupational Tests Introduced

In April, 1919, at St. Louis, the U.S. Commissioner of Education, Philander P. Claxton, called a conference of industrial education specialists to consider the implications of the Army trade tests which had been used so successfully during World War I. Included among the participants were Lieutenant Colonel E. K. Strong Jr., professor and head of the department of industrial education, Carnegie Institute of Technology, and Lieutenant Colonel W. V. Bingham, head of the department of psychology, Carnegie Institute of Technology.

Military personnel had been classified from a number of points of view including occupation, trade skill, and previous occupational experience. The total trade examination consisted of an oral test, a picture test, and a performance test. The Army had data on 250,000 soldiers. The big question

raised by the 94 members of the conference (from 24 states) was: Would these tests be of value to the state boards of vocational education, in helping to select teachers for trade schools?[17] In general the answer was affirmative, but it was emphasized that the trade test should be used in connection with other selective devices and not as the final measure. Although the tests were still in the stage of "crude tools," it did appear that they could be one of the measures used to determine a candidate's eligibility for a teaching position. The Army leaders stressed that the tests must be considered supplementary only, and not used in place of "searching personal interviews and inquiry into a man's record and experience."

In later years some states capitalized upon the trade test concept as a means of establishing the quality of the teacher's occupational background. In a few states occupational tests were developed extensively; the program of occupational testing in California is a good example of such development.

## Progress in Teacher Education

During the summer of 1922, vocational courses were offered in 31 states and in 60 educational institutions.[18] A majority of the courses were suitable for the training of trade and industrial teachers, and many had been planned specifically toward this end.

Very little accurate information had been made available concerning the actual progress of trade and industrial

[16] "Research and Service Center at University of California," *The Vocational Summary,* Vol. III, No. 7, November 1920, p. 109.

[17] William T. Bawden, *The Army Trade Tests,* Department of the Interior, Bureau of Education, Industrial Education Circular No. 4, April 1919, p. 26.

[18] National Society for Vocational Education, *Newsletter,* June 1922, pp. 25-29.

teacher training during the five years following the Smith-Hughes Act. Indeed the Federal Board had not previously asked for much specific information. However, in January, 1923, the Federal Board sent questionnaires to all of the states in order to secure a more realistic view of the status of teacher training. Although only 37 states replied, it was felt that the information was sufficiently definitive that a follow-up on the other 11 states was unnecessary. The replies showed that 305 trade and industrial teacher trainers (211 employed by institutions, sixty by state boards, and thirty-four by local boards) had provided training for 7,370 teachers during the year 1922.

Even less was known about the actual qualifications of the teacher trainers, since the Federal Board had not required this information. Later, however, in response to a specific request, statements on the individual qualifications of 262 teacher trainers were furnished by the states. The summary of qualifications was as follows:

- Sixty percent had completed college; half of this group had one year or more of trade experience.
- Twenty-four percent had completed one or more years of graduate work.
- Fifty-one percent had completed one or more years of teaching industrial subjects.
- Sixty percent had one or more years of trade experience.
- Forty-eight percent had one or more years of administrative experience.

Therefore the minimum qualifications of teacher trainers in a majority of states appeared to be as follows:

1. Graduation from a four year college or university or equivalent.
2. At least one year's experience in teaching shop or related subjects.
3. At least one year's experience in an administrative capacity.
4. At least one year of industrial experience.[19]

This was not a discouraging report. Nevertheless, the Federal Board pressed continually for improvement in the quality of training and for greater breadth of viewpoint about the nature, purpose, and relationships of the teacher training program with other facets of trade and industrial education.

Training was still regarded as a continuous process which could not be completed wholly in a teacher training institution.[20]

According to the terms of the Smith-Hughes Act, at least one-third of the money allotted for trade and industrial education was required to be spent for the part-time instruction of youth who were wage earners and who had left the environment of the full-time school. This group represented such a large segment of the younger wage earners that from the standpoint of the Federal Board it required "a competent corps of specially-trained teachers" in order for the success of the part-time school to be assured.[21]

The Board desired "superteachers"

---

[19] Federal Board for Vocational Education, *Yearbook 1923*. Washington: Government Printing Office, January 1924, p. 262.

[20] Federal Board for Vocational Education, *Training Supervisors of Trade and Industrial Education*, Bulletin No. 139, December 1929, p. 3.

[21] Federal Board for Vocational Education, *Program for Training Part-Time School Teachers*, Bulletin No. 85, June 1923, p. v.

and indicated the following characteristics which were thought to be appropriate.

1. They should have a strong abiding sympathy for boys and girls and a desire to help them meet their problems. The type of person who makes a successful boy scout or camp-fire girl leader or social-service worker would meet this requirement.

2. They should possess resourcefulness and tact in meeting new or difficult situations and should embody a happy combination of dignity, reserve, and sense of humor.

3. They should be likable and optimistic and should radiate enthusiasm. Their vitality, imagination, and initiative should inspire confidence.

4. Their observations should be wide and accurate, their experience broad and inclusive.

5. Their habits and standards should be acceptable to the people and worthy of emulation.

In addition to the personal characteristics mentioned the general training and practical experience which will be of large value to the prospective part-time teacher may well include:

1. Mastery of the subject matter or content of instruction, whether academic or technical, and of manipulative skill.

2. Experience as a wage earner comprehensive enough to give an understanding and appreciation of the problems which confront working children.

3. Understanding of the fundamental social and economic principles underlying the institutions of our complex society.

4. Adequate experience in the practical work of the occupational field in which the individual is to teach. This is most essential.[22]

The Board also set forth a comprehensive list of the minimum professional requirements for the teacher of the part-time student, and then outlined a program of training for such teachers. It was assumed that, in addition to other requirements, courses in economics, sociology, and general and educational psychology were appropriate.

The Board then suggested that the teacher training program be organized into seven units

Unit I—Aims, purposes, and problems of part-time education. Introductory course, 12 to 22 hours. This will probably work out to be a 16-hour unit offering 1 semester hour of credit.

Unit II—Social, economic, and educational background producing the present social, industrial, and school status of the junior worker. Illustrative advanced course, 32 hours or 2 semester hours of credit.

Unit III—Determination of aims and objectives of the part-time school. Sixteen to 32 hours or 1 to 2 semester hours of credit.

Unit IV—Analysis and organization of instructional material suited to selected aims and training objectives in the part-time school. Sixteen to 32 hours or 1 to 2 semester hours of credit.

Unit V—Methods of teaching and instructional management, with special adaptation to part-time school problems. Thirty-two to 64 hours or 2 to 4 semester hours of credit.

Unit VI—Follow-up, visitation, and coordination of activities. Sixteen to 32 hours or 1 to 2 semester hours of credit.

Unit VII—Vocational, social, moral, and educational guidance and occupational placement in the part-time school. Thirty-two hours or 2 semester hours of credit.[23]

In summary, the Federal Board proposed a minimum program of training for the part-time teacher which ranged from 156 to 246 clock hours, or from

---

[22] *Ibid.*, p. 6.
[23] *Ibid.*, pp. 7-8.

10 to 15 semester credit hours. The proposal was presented in workable detail in that the purpose of the unit was explained, an outline of the unit was presented, and suggestions were made concerning the methods of instruction to be used.

**Trends**

In 1926 the Federal Board reported a number of trends and developments in trade and industrial teacher training. At the beginning of the program nearly all of the states had developed residence courses which required from two to four years of preparation before teachers were available. This procedure did not seem to meet the need, so the states soon began to favor some type of extension program in which teacher training courses were offered in several locations to small groups, scheduled at times most convenient for the prospective teachers.

In 1917 there was need for a short simple training course for teaching mechanics, who were desirous of becoming supervisors in vocational schools, how to teach what they knew.

Advantage was taken of experience gained in Massachusetts and during the war to develop such a special course. In connection with this work one bulletin has been published and nine separate training conferences have been held with State representatives. This training program is now accepted and in general use in the States.[24]

In addition many of the states were beginning to adopt summer session programs in cooperation with colleges and universities. This arrangement seemed to have so many factors in its favor that the Board predicted the summer session approach to teacher training would grow.

There were other arrangements which involved the principle of *itinerant teacher training*. Under this principle, teacher trainers or representatives of the state board, or some combination of the two, provided teacher training in many locations throughout a state, for short periods of time, and in addition provided direct assistance to the individual, with concentrated attention to his problems. Teacher trainers assigned to institutions had limited their activities to on-campus courses in the early days. However, the itinerant plan provided a new emphasis, to the apparent benefit of the program of trade and industrial education.

By 1926 a definite trend was established in professional development. Promotion to positions of supervision and administration was dependent upon professional growth. Pressure from local school officials heightened the desire of teachers to hold college degrees.

This demand for credit toward a degree has also resulted in the organization of special summer-school courses for trade teachers, where they may take courses in industrial education and academic courses for general improvement leading toward college degrees.[25]

As the program of trade and industrial education grew, the need for teacher education increased proportionally. Even so, irregularities were noted in the teacher education program, with an explanation as follows:

In view of the fact that the problem of training trade and industrial teachers is

[24] Federal Board for Vocational Education, *Ninth Annual Report to Congress*, 1925, p. 17.
[25] Federal Board for Vocational Education, *Tenth Annual Report to Congress*, 1926, p. 113.

not one of enrolling students in four-year courses in residence at a college or university, but is largely one of securing skilled trades people and carrying on professional improvement work with them in the cities or localities where they are employed, it is altogether probable that the curves for training teachers of trade and industrial education will continue to show such irregularities as are manifested at the present time, as the program is still largely in an experimental stage.[26]

Growth was particularly noticeable in the area of providing programs for apprenticeship, plant training programs, foremanship, and special services to specific industries. Trade schools throughout the nation were expanding their programs, enlarging their buildings, and extending their course offerings. Under construction were such schools as the Frank Wiggins Trade School, Los Angeles, a project of the public school system.

Melvin Lewis conducted a status study of trade and industrial teacher training in the United States for the year 1926.[27] From the study he was able to recommend: (1) that the training of trade teachers be delegated to an educational institution, (2) that both resident and extension courses be provided, (3) that the content of the courses be aimed at imparting teaching techniques, (4) that the course be approximately 180 hours in length, (5) that age not be considered as a factor, (6) that applicants have completed elementary school as a minimum, and (7) that both apprenticeship and journeyman experience be required in addition to good qualities of character and health.

Lewis further suggested that the actual teacher training curriculum (180 hours) consist of organization and administration of vocational education, special methods of teaching, occupational analysis, demonstration and practice teaching, shop organization, management, making reports, and keeping records. Although Lewis believed that educational institutions should be delegated the responsibility for initial training, he felt that the in-service program should be a joint responsibility with the state board.

At first the policy in teacher training had been largely one of accepting all who applied. By 1927 the Federal Board had detected a change in this policy. The tendency at that time seemed to involve more selectivity. This change apparently came about because teacher trainers had become more attentive to the actual need for teachers. The Federal Board regarded this trend as encouraging.

Enrollment in trade and industrial teacher training courses tended to fluctuate from year to year, showing both sharp increases and decreases in the number of persons involved as students. This trend was influenced by the practice in some states of uniting the teacher training classes for manual training and industrial arts with those for vocational-teacher training. High enrollment figures under such conditions represented a false index to the number of vocational teachers trained. The Federal Board urged an end to this practice.

Enrollment figures were distorted by

---

[26] *Ibid.*, pp. 95-96.
[27] Melvin S. Lewis, "The Status of Trade and Industrial Teacher-Training in the U.S. in the Year 1926," *American Vocational Association News Bulletin*, Vol. III, No. 1, February 1928, pp. 22-23.

219

the fact that some states abandoned their courses in residence in favor of holding classes only during the summer session. Also many local supervisors had instituted in-service programs, in which teachers furthered their own education while remaining on the job; frequently these figures were not included. Because the Federal Board had asked for enrollment in teacher training classes only, individual help to teachers in an informal program did not appear in reports. It was was also apparent in 1928 that some degree of stability had evolved and that there was relatively little turnover among full-time trade teachers who had completed the training required.

**Revised Standards**

In March, 1929, the Federal Board issued a revised edition of a bulletin concerning standards of organization, administration, and operation of trade and industrial education. This restatement of standards was based upon a dozen years of experience and growth of industrial education. The Board's point of view concerning the qualifications of teacher trainers was in agreement with the position of the earlier statements of the National Society for the Promotion of Industrial Education. The Board suggested that teacher trainers should have three years of practical work experience in a trade or industrial occupation; two years of teaching in state approved classes; three years of experience in administration or supervision in the field of

trade and industrial education; and the equivalent of 540 clock hours of special professional preparation which would bear upon philosophy of vocational education, supervision and administration, trade analysis and other curricular studies, and methods of training trade teachers.[28] Concerning the general educational background of teachers, the Board indicated only that, "Teacher trainers who have demonstrated their success in training trade and industrial teachers in the several States possess a very wide diversity of academic attainment and general education." [29]

The Board insisted that teacher training programs be adapted to state needs, that they be comprehensive, and that they function efficiently. The Federal Board's concentrated attention on teacher training created a similar response at the state and local levels. The "one very definite practice" which the Board could detect by 1931 was the trend toward offering much of the teacher training as either in-service, or on-the-job. The pre-employment type, or the long term program involving residence courses at a college or university, had been largely abandoned.

In 1930 the Board published a comprehensive bulletin concerning the training of trade and industrial teachers. A chapter was devoted to background and general development, including a discussion of the Board's rulings, and assignment of responsibilities. Another chapter dealt with the

---

[28] Federal Board for Vocational Education, *Trade and Industrial Education,* Second revised edition, Bulletin 17, March 1929, pp. 122-123.

[29] *Ibid.,* p. 123. Although many states revised their programs of teacher training and adopted the standards suggested by the Board in 1929, they have been slow in making further changes. The 1965 pattern, in some states, bears a striking relationship to the 1929 standards.

fields to be served and the needs to be met—in general a treatment of the scope of the total program. Attention was given in another chapter to the types of teacher training courses offered in 1930. A discussion of the various types of organizations for teacher training and the general recommendations of the Board were also included.

The Board urged teacher training institutions to provide a three- to six-week summer program. Some states evidently followed the practice of hiring teacher trainers for nine or ten months, assigning them to an institution, and then leaving them free during the summer, according to the college or university custom. This procedure had certain drawbacks. "The summer school session at an institution offers a real opportunity in the way of giving courses to bona fide vocational teachers who are regularly employed during the school year in the various cities of the State." [30] Of special note is the fact that the summer session program provided opportunities for nurturing a professional spirit among trade teachers.

The Board pointed out that many state supervisors of trade and industrial education were not thoroughly aware of their responsibilities in relation to teacher training and consequently used inadequate methods of evaluation. "The final test of any teacher-training program is whether or not the quality of teaching being carried on in the classroom is gradually improved." [31]

Although teacher training was a part of the program of trade and industrial education, many of its problems were distinct from the problems of supervision and program development. Teacher trainers employed by a designated institution were primarily responsible for the training of teachers and not for supervising or promoting programs. The question of how far the teacher trainer should be involved in organizational and promotional work depended upon circumstances and had to be decided in consultation with the state supervisor.

In summary, it is apparent that during the period 1917-1933, the Federal Board for Vocational Education exerted a significant influence upon the content, growth, development, and general improvement of trade and industrial teacher education. Meanwhile the states were building up experience backgrounds of their own which would eventually merge, under the leadership of the U.S. Office of Education, into a national system of standards, procedures, and content for teacher education.

## Teacher Training from 1934 Through World War II

One of the better results of the depression was the men of superior quality were attracted to teacher training classes. Of course, they would have been eligible for admission to the program at any time, but when jobs were plentiful they sought the higher pay of industrial employment. When jobs were scarce, they sought any avenue

---

[30] Federal Board for Vocational Education, *The Training of Teachers for Trade and Industrial Education*, Bulletin No. 150, June 1930, p. 156.
[31] *Ibid.*, p. 156.

of employment, and many highly skilled craftsmen with excellent experience found their way into teaching. This trend was evident to the U.S. Office of Education in 1933.

The influx of superior persons tended to raise the standards of teacher training and stimulated development of in-service training among teachers already employed.

### Four Significant Reports

In 1934 the Office of Education arranged for the publication of four reports on trade and industrial teacher training which had been made at the American Vocational Association meeting in Detroit the previous December. U.S. Commissioner of Education, George F. Zook, in the foreword to the publication wrote that, "These four papers contain data of permanent value to administrators and teacher trainers in the field of vocational education." [32]

The first report, by G. D. Whitney, Director of Vocational Teacher Training, University of Pittsburgh, was concerned with the upgrading of vocational teachers in service. He reached the following conclusions:

1. There is no best way to up-grade teachers in service. Size of community or State, location of institution, and general organization of the work must be taken into account.
2. The principle of more and more contact on or near the job is of great importance.
3. Classes at a convenient point geographically are useful in both preemployment and postemployment teacher train-

ing, but are perhaps more valuable in the former than in the latter.
4. The kind and amount of postemployment training will vary with the selection of the teacher and the amount of his preemployment training.
5. No teacher is so well prepared that he does not need further training on the job.
6. The local supervisor, where one exists, is the most important individual in the continued growth of the local teaching staff.
7. The State supervisor or teacher trainer is able to further the growth of teachers in service in certain definite ways, but can neither take the place nor accept the responsibility of the local supervisor in this respect.
8. The growth of teachers in service involves a return to industry periodically in order to keep up to date.
9. Recognition, such as involved in a degree, is becoming more and more important, although it should not be allowed to interfere with basic skill on the teaching job. Rather it should be thought of as raising the status of a good, well-prepared teacher to a higher power.
10. Finally, as the vocational school becomes a more and more important part of the public-school program, there will be a demand for objective measures of success; also the teacher who merely teaches the skill and technic of a trade will be challenged to improve his practice to include training for citizenship and other broad educational objectives which are now coming to *loom so large* in the public eye. [33]

The second report, by J. B. Spofford, Assistant for the Training of Teachers of Trades and Industries, Trenton, New Jersey, described the methods used in selecting persons to be trained as vocational instructors. Spofford reviewed the educational qualifications of trade instructors, the trade qualifica-

[32] U.S. Department of the Interior, Office of Education, *Vocational Teacher Training in the Industrial Field,* Vocational Education Bulletin, No. 172, 1934, p. iii.
[33] *Ibid.,* p. 8.

tions, the trade-technical qualifications, and personality, and came to the following conclusion:

It would appear from these reports of the States that educational background, industrial experience, and personality are vital factors which must be determined as far as possible in selecting personnel for teacher-training classes. Fundamentally, the trade teacher must be adequately equipped with an educational and industrial background together with the trade skills necessary to give assurance of his having something to teach after he is trained as a teacher. Furthermore, it must be ascertained that the trade-technical teacher has an appreciation of the application of his subjects to the manipulative processes and skills of the industry, so that he may tie up the trade-technical subjects with trade experiences. Finally, every effort must be made to determine the personality characteristics of the prospective teacher by securing as much information as possible concerning his habits, his social life, his temperament, and his probable ability to adjust himself to a teaching position.[34]

The third report, by George E. Meyers, Professor of Vocational Education and Guidance, University of Michigan, delved into the procedures to be followed in giving attention to the needs of individual students in teacher training courses. Meyers was aware that situational factors affected all considerations. Nevertheless, he could see at least four steps of general importance: (1) The teacher educator must know the needs of each student. (2) The student should become conscious of his own needs. (3) The course content should make provisions for meeting individual student needs. (4) The teaching methods must be flexible enough to meet these needs. Meyers

stated that some people would feel this to be an impossible task, but he was firm in his point of view. The teacher trainer with an adequate conception of education:

. . . will be on the alert to inform himself as to the special needs of each student in his class; to help each student become aware of his own needs; to bring together a wealth of illustrations, projects, and other material pertaining to his course; to draw from this material with reference to the needs of individual students; and to make use of lesson sheets, class discussions, reports by individual students, and other methods of teaching in order to promote this process of development in each member of his class. At any rate this conception will give meaning and purpose to all of these procedures that are essential, if he is to give adequate attention to the needs of individual students who take his course.[35]

The fourth report, prepared by Benjamin W. Johnson, Assistant Director, Division of Vocational Education, University of California, Los Angeles, consisted of a comparative study of the methods of certification of trade and industrial teachers. Johnson considered all types of teachers and surveyed all of the states, seeking information concerning certification. He reached the following conclusions:

1. It is gratifying to find that some 40 States specify teacher training for their vocational teachers of evening adult classes. To what extent is the training given, and how?

2. The general education specified for shop teachers is surprisingly low. Over half the States are satisfied with only elementary education and nine States make no specification whatever. With the rise in standards of employment in most industries calling for technical skill, and

[34] *Ibid.*, p. 12.
[35] *Ibid.*, p. 17.

the great increase in the number of high-school graduates, it is a very serious deficiency to permit such a low standard. Every shop teacher should acquire a high-school training, or its equivalent, within a reasonable time if the standard of admission is less than high-school graduation. [This is quite interesting as a milestone compared with today's standards.]

3. The . . . teacher training specified does not seem to be consistent. Idaho designates 20 clock hours, Oregon 40, and New York 480. Why is this wide variation? It there justification for the very low requirement *in over half* the States, when the standards for teachers of other subjects are higher?

4. Should there not be more provision made for upgrading of trade and industrial teachers with opportunity for promotion by grades and classes? Certification and college credit should be granted for each advance dependent upon attainment in professional training and broadening experience, both in successful teaching and in the trade. Michigan has such a plan, Colorado likewise, and California to some degree.

5. In view of rapid economic and industrial changes, trade and industrial teachers should be able to acquire new adaptations of their trade or even new trade abilities within their field by pursuing trade training courses and thereby gain added certification based upon achievement to be checked by trade tests.

6. The recognition of trade and technical training as partial equivalent for trade experience above, say, 2 years' minimum, as is done by several States, should be encouraged and in accord with the present industrial trends and with the basic philosophy of trade education.

7. To what extent are the provisions, prescriptions, or requirements for teaching standards based upon known and tested outcomes? In raising the standards will they be based upon definite abilities desired or just a device to limit the supply of teachers to an intellectual group?

8. Loose, indefinite, or even lax statements of requirements seem to be covered in some States by a plea for flexibility in their programs.

9. With industry seeking better standards of work, and employment further stimulated by the N.R.A. is it not high time that a better standard than just "three years of journeyman experience" be set up by every State for determining trade proficiency? Only three States reported the use of trade tests in determining present trade ability.[36]

The four reports are important not because of new information contained, but because they provide evidence that earlier principles had sustained the test of time. After nearly twenty years these principles continued to be sound. The decision to print and distribute the reports brought the information directly to all teacher educators in the nation.

### A Selection of Views

A national conference on trade and industrial education was conducted by the U.S. Office of Education in Minneapolis, August 17-28, 1936. A substantial part of the conference was devoted to teacher training. Charles A. Prosser directed the discussion concerning the problems of teacher selection and training of instructors.

Prosser indicated that the experience gained during the twenty years of operation needed to be analyzed and interpreted, and that particular attention should be paid to what might be called mistakes in teacher selection and training. He presented his material to the group by identifying a number of discussion items which he thought represented mistakes. He then indicated why the item was a mistake and finally considered what could be

---

[36] *Ibid.,* pp. 30-31.

done about it.[37] As an illustration of the treatment of these items, in the "Prosser fashion," the following example is typical.

*Academic requirements are given preference over mechanical skill and knowledge in selecting the shop instructor.*

This was a mistake from Prosser's point of view because so few men have a high degree of both. Teachers in the trade and industrial fields need mechanical skill and knowledge, not the ability to quote Shakespeare, as Prosser put it. "As academic requirements are raised, trade competency in the successful applicants will be lowered," he stated. Prosser's answer to the question, "Can anything be done about it?" was, "Yes, by preferring mechanical skill and knowledge to unreasonable academic requirements." In a similar fashion Prosser considered a total of 47 different items which in his estimation were stumbling blocks in the program of selection and training of teachers.

The *Digest of Annual Reports,* which was issued each year by the Office of Education, and which summarized the work of the year, contained practically no information about the progress of trade and industrial teacher education during the period 1934-1942. In part this may be accounted for by general economy measures of the Government, directed toward reducing the volume of information which was printed. However, other reports from the professional journals indicate a degree of experimentation and critical thinking in relation to adjustments in teacher education.

**Cooperative Plan.** A plan of conducting teacher education on a cooperative basis was one of the new developments in 1937. The regular program in New York City, under the direction of Gilbert G. Weaver, consisted of 12 or 13 different courses, requiring 480 clock hours of instruction. It was conducted over a period of about four years and provided for 32 credit hours. Although fairly satisfactory, the program had one fundamental defect: inadequate provision had been made to afford opportunity for practice teaching.

Weaver's experimental plan, which had the approval of the New York City Board of Education and the New York State Board of Education, was intended to overcome the lack of practice teaching. Under the new "Cooperative Plan" 30 teachers-in-training were chosen by examination from a list of 306. This group of 16 men and 14 women represented 12 trade areas. Their training was given in the daytime rather than in the customary night classes. Each week they spent 15 hours in schools as helpers to regularly assigned instructors, and 16 additional hours attending classes. Appropriate compensation was arranged for these teachers-in-training. The experimental program not only speeded up the process of completing the teacher training requirements but in addition it provided a direct relationship between the theory and practice. This is noted in Weaver's conclusions about the project:

---

[37] U.S. Department of the Interior, Office of Education, *Report of National Conference on Trade and Industrial Education,* Misc. 1853, December 1936, pp. 7-25.

The plan has been in operation a relatively short time, but there is every indication that it will be a marked success. The local school administrators and school principals have extended their unqualified cooperation and express their enthusiasm concerning the practicability of the scheme and its ultimate results. The members of the teacher-training staff have noted considerable contrast between the point of view of the day group and the evening groups under their instruction. The day group has a greater appreciation for the teacher-training courses as they are motivated by the contacts and needs of their daily work as an assistant teacher. It is the hope of those concerned that an extension of this plan may be possible in succeeding years.[38]

The success of the program was undoubtedly due in part to the extensive planning which preceded it.

**Professional Organization.** The year 1937 also marked the beginning of an important professional organization which was devoted entirely to industrial teacher training. At the San Antonio convention of the American Vocational Association, the industrial arts and the trade and industrial teacher educators proposed the organization of a group which would exercise a strong influence on industrial education and serve the interests peculiar to teacher training. The resulting organization was the National Association of Industrial Teacher Trainers (later changed to Teacher Educators). First officers were: George E. Meyers, University of Michigan, President; R. W. Selvidge, University of Missouri, Vice President; Homer J. Smith, University of Minnesota, Secretary-Treasurer. Three additional persons, later to be known as trustees—

Russell J. Greenly, Purdue University; V. P. McKinley, University of Alabama; and Lynn E. Stockwell, University of California—were selected, and the total group constituted the executive committee.

Over the years the National Association of Industrial Teacher Educators has been a strong force in stimulating improvements in teacher education, in developing sound attitudes toward research, and in issuing publications of value. Among the most popular of its publications are the summaries of theses and dissertations in industrial education.

**Experience and Training.** In the fall of 1937, Arthur F. Dodge presented an informative review of the experience and educational considerations of importance in training trade and industrial teachers. His conclusions were as follows:

The most important factor in the success of a vocational shop teacher is efficiency in his trade. To insure this, two years of work in the trade beyond apprenticeship should be required and further proof of mastery of his trade should be demanded by references from employers or by trade tests or both.

The next most important factor is the ability to teach. This cannot be guaranteed by completion of any particular course, but it is probable that the requirement of a pre-service course, however short, dealing specifically with the problems of a vocational shop teacher would help to improve latent teaching ability and would also provide information of value as a basis for selection.

Present requirements with respect to amount of formal education are much too low, but in actual practice this has no ill effect as superintendents consistently give

---

[38] Gilbert G. Weaver, "Training Vocational Teachers on a Cooperative Basis," *AVA Journal and News Bulletin,* Vol. XII, No. 2, May 1937, p. 90.

preference to the teachers with the most academic credits, sometimes at the expense of trade proficiency.

Certain requirements should also be established to insure professional growth after employment. First, trade proficiency should be maintained by requiring teachers to work in their trade for a full summer, at least every third year.

Second, teaching ability should be improved by requiring completion within a reasonable time of approximately eight semester hours in courses dealing directly with the problems of the vocational shop teacher and the philosophy of vocational education. Attendance at meetings of State Vocational Associations, sectional round table conferences, and the completion of other courses in the field of education should be encouraged. The most effective means of improving teaching ability, however, is through the supervision of the local supervisor and principal.

Third, the attainment of a broad, liberal education should be encouraged. Perhaps attendance at summer school every third summer, or its equivalent, would not be to much to require until the completion of four years of college work.[39]

*Trade-Extension Teachers.* In 1939, David F. Jackey emphasized the responsibility of teacher educators for the quality of instruction in trade extension.[40] He pointed out that extension classes must truly represent a program for the extension of knowledges and skills, and that confusion concerning objectives should not exist. In addition to the usual qualities desired in extension teachers, the knowledge of teaching essentials was imperative. Furthermore, Jackey held the opinion that the wise teacher would discover the occupational weaknesses of each member of his class and then, through the most effective, sophisticated techniques (a responsibility of teacher educators), lead the members of the class to achievements consistent with their abilities.

*Challenge and Change.* A variety of social, technological, and economic changes, with implications for teacher training, called for immediate attention. Lynn A. Emerson reviewed some of the trends and pointed specifically to the problems and challenges for teacher trainers.[41] New teacher training programs were needed, as well as revision of current programs, to meet the need for better technical education and for the training of semi-skilled workers. Allotments of time to various phases of teacher training needed adjustment, with more emphasis on the upgrading of teachers. This is turn called for greater incentives to promote such professional and technical upgrading, thus keeping pace with social and technological change.

In Emerson's view the methods of selecting teacher trainees and eventually inducting them as new teachers had to change, because the scope of trade and industrial education had vastly increased. Emerson's address to the State Supervisors and State Teacher Trainers at the Grand Rapids convention of the American Vocational Association reached sympathetic ears; action based on his proposals could strengthen vocational education.

[39] Arthur F. Dodge, "What Should Be the Education and Training of a Trade and Industrial Education Teacher?" *AVA Journal and News Bulletin,* Vol. XII, No. 3, September 1937, p. 176.

[40] David F. Jackey, "Foreman Training Conferences and Extension Classes," *AVA Journal and News Bulletin,* Vol. XIV, No. 1, February 1939, pp. 34-35, 38-39.

[41] Lynn A. Emerson, "Socio-Economic Trends and Industrial Teacher Training," *AVA Journal and News Bulletin,* Vol. XV, No. 1, February 1940, pp. 50-54.

**Teacher Trainers.** A study of teacher preparation by the Office of Education, released in 1941, showed that teacher trainers often held their position in combination with other assignments. For example: [42]

Teacher trainer, full-time position, 23 cases; combined with supervisor, 20 cases.

Assistant teacher trainer, full-time position, 29 cases; combined with state director and supervisor, 4 cases; combined with assistant supervisor, 2 cases; combined with executive officer, director and supervisor, 1 case.

Local supervisors and local directors, full-time position, 104 cases; combined with teacher trainer for distributive education, 2 cases.

The study also indicated that more than half of the teacher training was conducted by persons who had local rather than statewide responsibility.

Most states required teacher trainers to have from one to eight years of experience in a trade or industrial occupation. Most states required trade and industrial teaching experience of from two to five years; in addition, the same number of states required supervisory experience. Required courses in trade and industrial education ranged from 180 to 640 clock hours; but only 26 states specified four years of college or its equivalent.

It was reported that of the persons holding the title of "head teacher trainer," 34 percent (24) held the doctoral, another 52 percent (37) held at least the master's, and the remaining 14 percent (10) held at least the bachelor's degree. There were no reports of persons with the title "head teacher trainer" who did not hold a college degree. [43]

Similarly it was reported that of persons with the title "assistant teacher trainer," 25 percent (29) held the doctoral, another 51 percent (61) held at least the master's, and the remaining 24 percent (28) held at least the bachelor's degree. There were no reports of such persons who did not hold a college degree.

During the war years from 1942 through 1945, teacher training activity varied considerably but was usually masked by the importance of and concentrated attention to war-related work. During the early war years, states reported increased activity in conducting methods classes, in revising outlines of instruction, in preparation of instructional material, and in teacher training for war production. Many states reported that they had lost teacher trainers to military service and to government activities related to the war, and that these persons could not be readily replaced.

By 1944 the Office of Education could identify trends toward decentralizing teacher training activities, such as designation of institutions on a localized basis and the development of itinerant teacher training. It appeared that the standards were maintained despite the war. A trend was noted also toward including technical content, such as mathematics and science, in teacher training courses.

---

[42] Federal Security Agency, Office of Education, *The State and the Preservice Preparation of Teachers of Vocational Education,* Bulletin No. 219, 1941, p. 39.
[43] *Ibid.,* p. 50.

By the end of the fiscal year 1945, a pronounced movement toward general revision and improvement of formal teacher training courses was reported. An emphasis was given to short, intensive, preservice teacher training courses. State and local supervisors assisted in the redevelopment of plans.

The adjustment of teacher training to the harsh conditions of the depression and later to the easier economic standards associated with war production provided valuable guides for the future. The adjustment also contributed to the desire of trade and industrial teacher educators to review their programs and to set new goals of achievement.

The need for quality in teacher education had been a consistent challenge for three decades. In the post-war years, necessity of excellence in teacher education was heightened to match the technological advances.

## The Post-War Years

In 1946 the teacher training load reported by the states indicated that the numbers of persons trained tended to increase; in some states the load was exceptionally heavy. Teacher educators continued to point out the necessity of enriched course content (science and mathematics) in the program. They also indicated criticism of teacher training courses which tended to become formal and lacked depth. (Such criticism probably grew out of experience in military training programs.) Finally, a definite movement toward flexibility in teacher education was apparent.

World War II did strange things to teacher educators and to trainees alike. The "quickie" methods of learning to teach were applicable in only a narrow sense. Thousands of cards and certificates were issued to certify a person who had completed "10 easy lessons" in teaching techniques. The situation caused Walter B. Jones, Director of Vocational and Technical Teacher Education, University of Pennsylvania, to recall a famous line from Pope's *Essay on Criticism*, "A little learning is a dang'rous thing." Jones used it as a theme in discussing how much more there was to teaching than could be learned in ten lessons.

Four rigidly stated steps of instruction were known to all trade and industrial teacher educators and were very popular during World War II. Yet, Charles R. Allen had adapted them to industrial education as far back as World War I, when he served as a member of the training staff of the United States Shipping Board. The steps had originated in the Herbartian educational philosophy. They were based on excellent principles, but Jones pointed out that teacher training limited to the narrow formalistic method is likely to be ineffective.

It is especially unfortunate for future trainees in vocational education classes if such teachers believe that their present level of professional competence, based on such meagre training and experience, is acceptable in public vocational schools as the finished product.[44]

"The first course," wrote Jones, "is only professional foot wetting and not an over-all plunge."

By 1948 some states were planning

---

[44] Walter B. Jones, "A Little Learning Is a Dang'rous Thing in Teacher Training," *American Vocational Journal*, Vol. 22, No. 10, December 1947, p. 41.

teacher training laboratories which could do much toward developing a functional approach to teacher education. Trade testing, which Bawden had brought to the attention of industrial educators in 1919, began to attract the attention of trade and industrial educators again. Some states had well organized programs of trade testing, supervised by competent psychologists. The National Association of Industrial Teacher Educators had promoted experimentation in the field.

Paul Lofgren, Supervisor of Occupational Testing, Division of Vocational Education, University of California, reviewed the California trade testing program, which consisted of a written test and a performance test. Other tests, as in English, civics, and social adjustment, were included as a part of teacher selection. The *written tests* were prepared from questions submitted by persons of recognized competency in the trade area and were edited to eliminate a variety of psychological errors. The *performance tests* were supervised by a committee of judges who were representative of labor, management, and education and who were also competent craftsmen in the trade area concerned. Apparently every phase of a trade was "completely and adequately" sampled. The number of written questions and the length of the performance test were functional to the complexity or simplicity of the trade. Lofgren indicated that:

1. The questions in a given written test have a difficulty gradation such that an individual with the slightest experience in the field can answer some of them, but no tradesman can answer all of them correctly. Hence each candidate is held within measurable bounds.

2. The reliability of the ratings is acceptably high with few exceptions.

3. An improvement of rating reliability seems to have resulted from the introduction of a special personality rating scale, the primary purpose of which is to syphon off the "halo" effect from the skill ratings.[45]

Lofgren indicated that there were no satisfactory substitutes for ratings of *known dependability* and that achievement of dependable ratings would require the combined experience of teachers, teacher educators, supervisors, and a trained test constructor and statistician.

One of the most significant events in teacher education during the early post-war years was a conference in Washington, D.C., in the spring of 1948. The inter-regional conference provided an opportunity for teacher educators to share their experiences in teacher education and to weigh carefully the influences of the war upon the general progress of teacher education.[46]

Emphasis upon instruction in use of visual aids continued to be reported in many states. In some, the instruction in audio-visual education included laboratory experiences under the direction of persons experienced in the area.

Teacher educators also reported experiments in integration of formal teacher training courses. An example of this development was practice teaching, which was supervised and evalu-

---

[45] Paul V. W. Lofgren, "The Use of Tests in the Selection of Trade and Industrial Teachers," *American Vocational Journal*, Vol. 23, No. 6, June 1948, p. 29.

[46] The report of this conference is discussed in Chapter 7.

ated by classes in administration and supervision.

Trade and industrial teacher education was unique in the variety of application brought about by special conditions and circumstances in the states. Uniformity in teacher training would be most difficult to develop, even if it were desirable. The *Digest of Annual Reports* for 1950 summarized the trends as follows:

1. Methods of testing prospective trade teachers for occupational competency are being studied in several States with the objective of improving the tests and increasing the number of occupations covered.

2. Two States report a study to determine the soundness and effectiveness of the trade and industrial education teacher training program through a research program and statistical analysis.

3. Several States report the use of a so-called "apprenticeship plan" (or cadet teaching) for the induction of new teachers. In this program, the prospective teacher actually teaches under the close supervision of a selected experienced teacher while he is learning. This on-the-job training may be on a part-time or full-time basis, and the apprentice teacher is paid for his work. While he is in training the apprentice is also engaged in the study of professional subjects such as methods of teaching and class management.

4. A large number of States have adopted patterns to be used in the preparation of instructional materials. These States either have conducted or are planning to conduct workshops or laboratories for the purpose of preparing study guides and other instructional materials for use in the training program. The impetus for these trends is provided largely by the operation of the diversified occupations courses in secondary schools.

5. The construction and effective use of visual instructional aids for industrial training continued to receive increased attention in the teacher training programs. Conferences and workshops were conducted in a number of States during the year. Some States maintain central lending libraries of motion pictures, filmstrips, and posters for service to trade and industrial education teachers.

6. Several States are providing professional courses for teachers in privately operated trade schools.

7. The training of conference leaders for supervisory training in industry received increased attention during this year.

8. Some States are giving special attention to the development and operation of courses that are conducted under various names but quite generally cover the purposes, programs, and methods of vocational trade and industrial education and a brief history of the development of the program.

9. In the training of trade and industrial teachers of part-time and evening classes, a number of States are offering short intensive courses. The persons employed to teach these classes are occupationally competent, but many of them have had little or no training for or experience in teaching. They are usually employed full-time in a trade or industrial occupation and are interested in teaching only as a side line. Training programs are conducted on a pre-service basis, or on an in-service basis through group or individual conferences. In a few States, special training pamphlets have been prepared as a basis for instruction. In at least one State, this training service is provided for teachers in isolated places through correspondence instruction.

10. A large number of States report increased emphasis on the improvement of instruction through supervision of teachers while at work. This responsibility is shared by local and State supervisors and by teacher trainers.[47]

---

[47] Federal Security Agency, Office of Education, *Digest of Annual Reports of State Boards for Vocational Education*, June 30, 1950, pp. 61-62.

Throughout most of the 1950's very few significant gains were reported in the area of teacher education. Patterns and experiments previously initiated were repeated or concluded. Instructional materials were improved, and in some instances attempts were made to speed up the time involved in completing teacher training programs. The 1952 *Digest of Annual Reports* indicated that a balanced and complete program for trade and industrial teacher education should include administrative arrangements for six functions that would:

1. Provide facilities for the recruitment, counseling, selection and pre-employment training of trade and industrial teachers.
2. Develop instructional aids for teachers in service.
3. Provide continuing educational opportunities for teachers in service.
4. Follow-up resident teacher training through field contacts for the purpose of checking the effectiveness of all units of instruction, thus leading to the improvement of the teacher-training program.
5. Improve college teaching (professional and technical) based upon the objectives for trade and industrial education in the State and upon the abilities needed by teachers of trade and industrial education courses.
6. Conduct research and studies making direct contributions to the development of the program of trade and industrial education in the State.[48]

From 1953 through 1957 teacher training reports revealed the use of familiar devices such as special courses, institutes, conferences, workshops, and other large and small group meetings. Some specialization was noted in the workshops, such as those devoted to the technology of metals. Research in teacher education, which had been largely dormant, began to show up now and then in reports. Efforts were directed toward relating the training needs to the "changing industrial and social conditions."

## Planning for the Decade of the 60's

It had been a long time since a national conference had been held in the interests of trade and industrial teacher education. State teacher educators had urged the Trade and Industrial Education Branch of the Office of Education to bring leaders together in conference to discuss old and emerging problems. During the week of May 12-16, 1958, ninety representatives of industrial education from 41 colleges, universities, and state agencies, representing 37 states and territories, met in Kansas City.

The conference was dedicated to a critical examination of current thought and practice. From this examination it was hoped that solutions would develop for the pressing problems of teacher education. The stated objectives, as proposed by John P. Walsh, Director, Trade and Industrial Education Branch, Office of Education, were as follows:

1. To examine present certification standards, evaluate their effectiveness, and explore procedures to be used in developing professionally sound standards.
2. To review critically teacher training programs in order to assess their effectiveness in preparing competent teachers.
3. To consider ways and means to meet the challenge of changing requirements brought about by increasing pro-

---

[48] U.S. Department of Health, Education, and Welfare, Office of Education, *Digest of Annual Reports of State Boards for Vocational Education,* June 30, 1952, p. 31.

fessional standards and technological developments.

4. To develop recommendations that will assist the States in establishing the kind of sound programs that are needed to insure the development of competent trade and industrial teachers.[49]

The highlights of the historical background of teacher training were developed, previous teacher training conferences were reviewed, the fundamental responsibilities of the teacher educator were brought into view, and at frequent intervals the entire conference was assembled into smaller units to consider specific questions and to reach a consensus.

Resource material for the conference had been provided by the Trade and Industrial Education Branch, Office of Education. The material reported on a nationwide study of competencies desired in teachers of trade and industrial education. It represented the opinions of 870 persons (503 teachers, 135 state supervisors, 120 teacher educators, and 112 local directors) concerning a list of 107 competencies. Forty percent of the participants in the study indicated that they were basically satisfied with the teacher-education program, 45 percent indicated dissatisfaction, and 15 percent were undecided. This was the most comprehensive study in the field of trade and industrial teacher training ever conducted.

Some time was spent in the conference re-identifying the scope of teacher training and re-analyzing the nature of the program. Diversity in implementation of principles was most apparent.

Although some time also was devoted to identifying weaknesses of teacher education, the most important contribution was the summary of group discussions on "Strengthening Teacher Preparation." Conference members were asked the following questions:

1. How do we go about determining the need for improving the preparation of the day trade teacher?
2. What are we doing *NOW* that could be done better?
3. What should we be doing to prepare day trade teachers?
4. What are the ways of determining the need for improving preparation of evening trade extension teachers?
5. What should we be doing to prepare evening extension teachers that we are *NOT* doing?
6. How can we do better what we are doing now for evening extension teachers?[50]

The discussion was exciting to the members of the conference because they had the opportunity to gain first-hand insight into the actual methods of operating programs for the training of trade and industrial education teachers. Many of the persons in the group were new in the program of teacher education. They could have had no finer review of teacher training.

Broadening and expanding teacher training to include pre-service, in-service, and upgrading programs seemed to be a definite trend in the reviews of 1959. In many states teacher certification studies had been made, generally leading toward increased requirements for teachers, and continuance of college work toward advanced degrees.

---

[49] U.S. Department of Health, Education, and Welfare, Office of Education, *New Dimensions in Trade and Industrial Teacher Training*, Circular No. 548, May 1958, p. vi. (See also Chapter 7 for additional information concerning this conference.)
[50] *Ibid.*, pp. 42-47.

Lack of qualified teacher educators is a story as old as the entire program. In 1959-1960 the problem emerged once again. Teacher education programs had expanded in many states, older teacher educators had retired, and the net effect was a shortage of qualified persons to fill the positions created and vacated. However, teacher educators appointed in 1959-1960 and later were generally better qualified than were the persons they replaced. Many such appointees had completed the doctorate in education or in one of the other disciplines.

Two recurring complaints of teacher educators are: (1) the tendency to overload them with responsibilities not directly related to teacher education, and thus prevent them from assuming their fundamental responsibilities; and (2) the tendency to emphasize the teacher education program for full-time teachers. Two-thirds of all trade and industrial teachers have been employed on a part-time basis, but in teacher education, greater emphasis has been placed on training for the full-time teacher. Obviously this has caused problems, but there are reasons why this situation exists. About half of the teacher educators are resident in institutions of higher education where they see the power structure, or the decision-making role, related to teacher education in a different light from that of other teacher educators. Those who reside in state offices and local districts see the decision-making role in trade and industrial education in terms of labor, management, and industry. Nevertheless, the total teacher education program in all of its aspects has shown remarkable growth and development, and the critical views are focused on somewhat minor phases. The criticism has been largely directed toward improvement of the program.

The national study of teacher education which had been initiated by the Office of Education prior to the conference in Kansas City in 1958 had been completed by 1960. The study was concerned with teacher competencies in trade and industrial education. The level of competence was a direct reflection of the quality of the program. The study attempted to determine the nature of the most important competence categories. Relative values were assigned to each item by successful teachers, teacher educators, and administrators. The 1960 report highlighted the imperative elements of teacher education content and provided a better basis of value judgment than had previously been available. Following is a selection from the summary of findings:

Teachers of trade and industrial subjects need many distinctive skills and abilities in addition to those required by regular classroom teachers. Teachers, teacher educators, and supervisors emphasized the importance of the teacher's ability to develop student attitudes toward safe practices and safety-consciousness in job performance, to develop appreciation of good workmanship, to demonstrate the skills of his trade, to stimulate and maintain interest, and to motivate students to acquire skill and knowledge.

Competencies in the category of teaching methods and techniques were most often rated high in importance while competencies in the category of shop and classroom organization and management rated low in the scale.

Teachers considered "most important" and "very important" those competencies which expressed ability to do something rather than those indicating knowledge or understanding.

The respondents were emphatic in selecting *trade analysis and course construction, methods of teaching industrial subjects, and development of instructional materials* as the three courses contributing most to their teaching success.

Successful teachers and teacher educators ranked high the importance of direct professional experiences in the teacher-preparation program. They rated especially high such experiences as supervised practice teaching, planned observation of teaching, and planned visits to industrial plants.

Local administrators, State and local supervisors, and teacher educators expressed dissatisfaction with the level of preparation of teachers in such areas as preparation of instructional materials, testing and evaluation, and orientation concerning the types, locations, and services of the community organizations concerned with industrial education.

The respondents expressed considerable satisfaction with the level of preparation of teachers in such areas as mastery of the skills of the trade to be taught, understanding of the objectives of trade and industrial education, ability to demonstrate skills, ability to develop safe work habits and tendency to teach at an appropriate level.

Teacher educators and State and local supervisors expressed dissatisfaction with the general level of preparation of trade and industrial teachers. Only 40 percent of this group indicated that they were satisfied with the level of preparation.[51]

The study provided criteria for evaluation of every facet of the teacher education program, and it strongly indicated the need for changes.

### Looking Forward from Historical Perspective

Trade and industrial teacher education was considered essential from the beginning of the vocational movement. The idea scarcely had time to grow—it began in full bloom. No one ever seriously questioned its importance. The fundamental decision in favor of such training was made in an environment of enthusiasm for teacher education in general and at a time when the "pedagogical pioneers" were pressing the educational world with new ideas on teaching, learning, and method. Early leaders in trade and industrial education produced a wealth of ideas, points of view, attitudes, and principles. The Smith-Hughes Act furthered this development by making trade and industrial teacher education a legal requirement.

Although dedication to principles of teacher education had been achieved, its practice was quite another thing. Development of models for actual programs occupied the attention of the National Society for the Promotion of Industrial Education and was a first order of business of the Special Agents of the Federal Board for Vocational Education. Some states were quick to develop satisfactory programs and some fumbled for long periods before defining a pattern. There were false starts: Some programs were patterned too closely after general teacher preparation and others were narrowly conceived and lacking in creative imagination.

During the 16 years of its existence the Federal Board conducted conferences, prepared bulletins, and stimulated the states in a variety of ways to build workable programs of teacher

[51] John P. Walsh, *Teacher Competencies in Trade and Industrial Education*, U.S. Department of Health, Education, and Welfare, Office of Education, OE-84006. Washington: Government Printing Office, 1960, pp. 43-44.

education. The programs which evolved were presumed to meet the requirements in each of the states. No two states developed programs exactly alike, and there were no nationally required standards.

The Trade and Industrial Education Branch of the Office of Education continued, after 1933, to urge states to improve, revise, and adapt their teacher education programs to the ever changing industrial conditions. Additional bulletins were prepared, and conferences were held. A degree of sophistication developed slowly but surely throughout the nation. Teacher educators shared ideas and debated principles in meetings of professional associations. A few research studies provided background information, but there is little evidence to indicate that much of the general research in teaching and learning filtered into trade and industrial teacher education.

Studies and conferences during the post-World War II years have disclosed a wide range of satisfaction with the content and methods of teacher education. The tendency toward uniformity in many aspects is quite apparent. At the same time there is evidence of unrest; change is in the air, but the direction, nature, and amount of change are clouded in uncertainties. In part the unrest is caused by the lack of fundamental research.

At the time this is written, some states are still basing their teacher education plans largely upon their past experience and upon cautious predictions of the future. On the whole, however, the picture is one of change. Many forces are at work which demand change in practice (but not in

fundamental principles). Higher educational achievement for beginning trade and industrial teachers is rapidly becoming the nationwide rule. Early isolationism is slowly dissolving as communications improve. Future teachers in the trade and industrial field will have more in common with other teachers than has been true in the past. However, this field will continue to be distinct from all others because its many specialized areas create unique teacher education problems which arise from the needs of the technological age. Renewed demands for quality in teacher selection, for excellence in teacher education, and for greater sophistication in industrial instruction naturally result as vocational education comes of age.

## Summary

The first plans for trade and industrial teacher training were made long before the passage of the Smith-Hughes Act. The National Society for the Promotion of Industrial Education considered that teacher training was basic to success of the whole program and therefore concentrated its efforts in this direction. As early as 1913, the Society had published a bulletin setting forth a framework for teacher training.

Recommendations of the Society were carried into the fundamental provisions of the Smith-Hughes Act. Money appropriated by the Act was available to the states only on the condition that they provide appropriate training for the teacher of trade and industrial subjects.

One of the most difficult problems

in teacher education has been the relationship between trade experience and academic training. There are many evidences of narrow interpretation and throughout the years the relationship has been beset with conflict. Contemporary rationale places a premium upon both trade experience and academic training as essential aspects in the background of a good teacher.

The period 1917-1933 was marked by a growth in teacher training. The basic concepts had to be put into practice, and there were no models to follow; but the persons assigned responsibility for teacher training were equal to the task, and innovations appeared in many states. The Federal Board for Vocational Education supplied developmental motivation by continual emphasis upon the program's importance.

The idea of using occupational tests was introduced in April, 1919. In some states such tests were integrated into the pattern of teacher education and teacher selection, but uniform acceptance of the idea did not produce uniform action among the states.

The Federal Board continued to "drive home" various principles of teacher training. Teacher educators shared their experiences in professional meetings and in the pages of professional journals. Analysis of reports indicated trends in the mechanics of conducting teacher training, in the content of the program, and in the general professionalization of teacher education.

Early attempts to develop teacher training as part of a four-year college program were largely unsuccessful,

and states were urged to use other procedures. The major difficulty was the length of time required before the teacher was actually available for service. Only with accumulated experience was it possible to revise standards for teacher education; then the goals became increasingly realistic.

After 1933, when the functions of the Federal Board had been transferred to the U.S. Office of Education, the practice of stimulating training was continued. By publishing four reports about teacher training, the Office made available to the states views on upgrading of teachers, teacher qualifications and selection, individualizing instruction by emphasis upon guidance for trade teachers, and methods of certification. The national conference in 1936 devoted a substantial part of its program to teacher training with an emphasis upon "mistakes in teacher selection and teacher training." These "mistakes" were analyzed in conference sessions under the direction of Charles A. Prosser.

In 1937 the National Association of Industrial Teacher Trainers was organized. The group consisted of industrial arts and trade industrial educators who had specific responsibility for teacher training. (In contemporary usage the word "trainers" has been replaced by the word "educators." This change was made official by the Association.) The work of the Association has been significant in many ways, with its emphasis upon the specific problems in teacher education. The summaries of theses and dissertations have been extremely important in the development of research, although this phase has lagged.

237

During the post-World War II years the problem of teacher education received concentrated attention. Expansion of the program and the experience gained during the war were contributing factors. Three significant national conferences were held in the interests of trade and industrial teacher training: in New York City, 1946; in Washington, D.C., 1948; and in Kansas City, 1958. The report of the 1958 conference, *New Dimensions in Trade and Industrial Teacher Training,* consists of a valuable summation of new ideas and elements of encouragement in the new aspects of teacher education.

A national study of trade and industrial teacher education, *Teacher Competencies,* issued in 1960 and conducted by John P. Walsh, was one of the most significant projects ever undertaken because it recorded conditions on a full-scale, realistic basis.

The major problem in trade and industrial teacher education in 1965 was the same as it was in 1917—the need for better teachers. But the degree of sophistication which had developed to meet this perennial problem made a vast difference.

---

## Recall Questions

1. Describe the activities of the NSPIE in teacher training prior to the Smith-Hughes Act.

2. What are the specific provisions of the Smith-Hughes Act concerning trade and industrial teacher training?

3. What were the principal developments in teacher training during the period 1917-1933? After 1933?

4. Identify some of the views of trade and industrial teacher educators during the period, 1936-1946.

5. What changes developed in theory and practice in trade and industrial teacher training after World War II?

## Research Questions

1. Using the 1936 report on trade and industrial education (see footnote 37), prepare a questionnaire on the basis of the "mistakes" identified by Prosser, and administer the questionnaire in your state, on a limited basis. (This should be correlated with other campuses or districts and with the state vocational education office to avoid creating a nuisance.) Then develop a plan of action for improvement.

2. Using the 1960 study by John P. Walsh (see footnote 51), develop a short form of the questionnaire and administer it selectively in your state, so as to avoid nuisance. What convictions can you reach on the basis of your study and how do these convictions compare with the Walsh study? Identify trends indicating change.

## Suggestions for Further Reading

Reports of the Federal Board for Vocational Education, 1917-1933.
*Digest of Annual Reports,* U.S. Office of Education since 1934.
U.S. Department of Health, Education, and Welfare, Office of Education, *New Dimensions in Trade and Industrial Teacher Training,* Circular No. 548, May 1958.
Walsh, John P., *Teacher Competencies in Trade and Industrial Education,* OE-84006. Washington: Government Printing Office, 1960.

# Chapter 10

# Influences on Industrial Arts Since 1917

Influences of World War I Through the Prosperous 20's · The Bird House Era · The Depression and World War II—1929-1949 · Into the Space Age · Summary · Recall Questions · Research Questions · Suggestions for Further Reading

A study of the growth, development, and trends of industrial arts in the schools of the nation provides a fascinating insight into the changes in American education through nearly a half-century. Industrial arts grew in every facet of the program. In numbers of students, for example, the growth was from 50,000 more-or-less in 1917 to roughly 4,000,000 in 1964. However, the drama of the growth and development of industrial arts is not to be found in mere statistical data, but is contained in the discussions, controversies, and educational claims and counterclaims throughout the years. Some influential educators regarded industrial arts as an "upstart" trying to gain a foothold in the educational structure where it was neither wanted or needed; others viewed the development of industrial arts as the vehicle through which the most precious values of education could be realized. There have been few if any years during the last half-century without some incendiary elements of controversial thought rising to the surface and bursting forth in full flame.

This chapter is concerned with the evolution of industrial arts as found in the writings of some of its most ardent proponents. Their points of view provide an index to their moods, fears, and enthusiasms as they attempted to improve the climate for growth. They generally were quick to be critical of their own achievements and continually set higher standards for themselves. But support from the general program of education was difficult to obtain; at times, seemingly modest achievements were in reality major victories. The internal problem of unity combined with change in the program was as difficult to solve as the external problem of finding acceptance in the general curriculum. During most of the history of industrial arts, there has not been one strong organization devoted exclusively to the program; consequently its progress has depended upon the motivation of strong personalities and their groups working in and out of other, better supported movements.

One of the major problems in relating the historical background of industrial arts is that of terminology. In the past "industrial arts," "manual arts," and "manual training" have been used almost interchangeably to mean either the same or different areas of education. Some persons will chafe at any use of the term "manual training," claiming that industrial arts would be more appropriate. However, this chapter does not propose to solve the problem of terminology, and the story as it unfolds here will employ the terms of the historical record.

There were no hard and fast lines representing the end of one primary era of terminology and the beginning of another. However, it is well to recall that the term "manual training" was generally used after about 1876; "manual arts" put in an appearance and drew support beginning about 1894; and "industrial arts" began finding acceptance after about 1910. Each term was supposed to have a meaning all its own. As was pointed out previously (Chapter 3), manual arts gave an improved design concept to manual training, and industrial arts represented a further refinement of purpose and direction. Some of the transitional leaders of the movement never gave in entirely to changes of terminology. For example, Bennett, who championed the use of the term "manual arts,"

never seemed to feel comfortable with the term "industrial arts."

The actual evolution from manual training to industrial arts has been a long slow process. Carved in stone on hundreds of buildings throughout the country are the words "Manual Training" or "Manual Arts," silent reminders of ages now past.

## Influences of World War I Through the Prosperous 20's

The following evokes the feeling of this massive transition period.

### A Trumpet Call

A trumpet sings, and other songs are still;
The close-locked ranks fast gather and are gone,
Leaving a myriad stars in casements hung,
As symbols of the spirit which doth thrill
A mighty nation, as it bends its will
To aid that Cause, which Freedom must see won.
A trumpet sings; it bids the valiant—Come!
Your Country calls; the laggard serves her ill.
But what of those who march not in the van.
How shall they serve who yet must bide at home?
Quick to the thousand tasks which must be done;
Each to his post—Let each now play the man.
And what for song fit for the trumpet's tone?
Why—raise the battle cry of "Carry on"!
                    —James Parton Haney

By 1914 Europe had virtually become an armed camp of two forces, Germany and Austria-Hungary on one side and England, France, and Russia on the other, awaiting only a crisis— which came on June 28—to plunge the adversaries into conflict. Despite pledges of neutrality, and peace efforts by the President, America was gradually drawn into the combat. On April 2, 1917, President Wilson asked Congress for a declaration of war and on April 6, he gained his objective.

Immediately the nation's energy was mobilized: manpower, industry, transportation, agriculture, natural resources, and finance. Mobilization reached into every community, institution, and family. The two major areas of public school industrial education consisted of the long established programs of manual arts and the newly created vocational education program which was to become effective on July 1, 1917. Industrial education, in all of its aspects, sought ways and means of contributing to the war effort.

## The War Program of Industrial Arts

Concurrently with the declaration of war, the Bureau of Education focused attention upon the role of the schools during wartime. The demand for mechanical skill and for technical and scientific knowledge was much out of proportion to the supply available. The meagerness of the educational provision for industrial and scientific knowledge was apparent, although understandable, for never before had such stark need faced the schools. Yet the educational system could contribute to the winning of the war, and to the reconstruction which would follow. In order to formulate the essentials of a war program, the Commissioner of Education called groups of

advisors to Washington to prepare appropriate statements and to suggest procedures for the schools to follow.

The advisors on industrial arts who met in Washington during the week of May 20, 1918, included William T. Bawden, Alfred P. Fletcher, William J. Bogan, Charles H. Lake, George F. Buxton, Charles A. Bennett, Robert W. Selvidge, James A. Pratt, Arthur B. Mays, and William E. Roberts. The needs of both the Army and Navy for trained mechanics, as well as the demand for technical workers in the supporting industries, made it imperative that the high schools provide special training for the young men who were approaching military age.

The demand for large numbers of young people having some practical mechanical ability is so great that no school should hesitate to do what it can in any line of technical and mechanical instruction for which it has, or can secure, the necessary equipment and teachers.[1]

From the War Department and other sources it was determined that the trades and occupations most in need of attention were the automotive, machining, metal fabrication, forging, electrical, building, and drafting. The advisory group determined the foundation work and the trade specialization appropriate for each of the industrial areas. It analyzed instructional units and suggested courses of study that provided detailed information concerning the foundation work and the elements of the specialized trade courses that would follow. Minimum standards for admission, time, equipment, and qualifications of teachers were also

---

[1] U.S. Department of the Interior, Bureau of Education, *Industrial Arts in Secondary Schools in the War Emergency*, Secondary School Circular No. 4, September 1918, p. 3.

suggested. The general recommendations of the advisory group are summarized as follows: [2]

1. The high schools should undertake occupational preparatory training following curricular patterns that paralleled the requirements of the Smith-Hughes Act.

2. The length of time devoted to such instruction should be increased by deleting much of the school work not directly related to war needs.

3. "Practical shopwork in wood and metal" was urged in increasing amounts in the seventh and eighth grades, and rural schools were requested to find the ways and means of adapting "handwork" in their programs.

4. Selection of "practical" teachers was thought to be imperative to meet the demands of shopwork. Skilled craftsmen were cited as necessary for part-time work.

5. Teachers in "technical and industrial fields" were urged to stay on the job and to recognize that their efforts represented a "maximum measure of patriotic service."

The schools of the nation reacted to the challenge and increased their participation in war work.

The advisors sought to increase greatly the number of boys who would receive instruction in technical and industrial work; they sought also to improve the practical effectiveness of the instruction by relating it closely to the practical problems of the war crisis.

The authors of the war emergency program in industrial arts were all well known for their dedication to the field;

therefore it is not surprising that the program they set up reflected the generally accepted philosophy of industrial arts. (1) They tied to the war emergency the necessity to expand programs of industrial education and urged cities which had not started industrial education to do so immediately. (2) They urged careful attention to high standards in the program and pointed to the benefits of industrial arts in terms of general school objectives. (3) They also called attention to certain problems of accepted instruction methods. For example, they discussed the "exercise" method of instruction and the "factory" method, indicating that one was wasteful of material and the other made it hard to keep the student interested. The middle ground, however, offered hope if the two forms were brought closer together.

### Industrial Arts and the Red Cross

One of the most popular activities of industrial arts students during World War I was the program sponsored by the Junior Red Cross. President Wilson announced the formation of the junior membership program and commended the program to the school children of the United States by a proclamation. He urged every school child to participate and told them how their contributions would aid the cause of freedom.

The industrial arts shops were ready-made for service in constructing practical articles so necessary at the front and in hospitals or at military bases at home and overseas. The construction of such articles was integrated into the regular instructional

---

[2] *Ibid.*, pp. 4-5.

program so that uniqueness of design and group participation were maintained as objectives. The knowledge that their productions would be used was a source of enthusiasm. One class in Aberdeen, South Dakota, learned that checker boards were needed in Y.M.C.A. recreation camps and undertook the construction of 100 boards and 2400 checker men.[3]

Art students at the Oswego State Normal School painted names and appropriate insignia on trunk tops for officers. The high schools in Boston and vicinity made 200 game tables to be used in naval cantonments and recreation centers. (In this activity the Manual Training Club of Boston figured prominently.) In Duluth toys were made from waste materials such as cigar boxes and packing cases, a war economy practice. The toys were sold and "a neat sum" was realized for the Red Cross. In Pueblo, Colorado, an industrial arts class, under the direction of instructor H. A. Tiemann, made a war tank float to be used in the third Liberty Loan campaign. During the parade that followed, the float "was one of the biggest features of the demonstration, bringing many applauses from the crowd."[4] Bird houses prepared on a factory basis by students at Saginaw, Michigan, were sold throughout the community. In Los Angeles the school shops "looked, sounded, and smelt like a toy factory," and receipts went to the Red Cross. Thirty thousand chairs and ten thousand tables were sent to homes in devastated areas of France.

Thus throughout the nation countless articles were the war contributions of thousands of students. The nation's shop programs did not demobilize immediately upon the end of the fighting, but carried on their Red Cross work as long as they could make significant contributions to people in the devastated countries. The act of service seemed to have a motivating effect upon the boys in industrial arts classes. Reports indicated that students often chose to make projects for the Red Cross rather than for themselves.

The projects, from knitting needles to tables, were instructional units of the finest order. Students could practice conservation and demonstrate with pride their ability to find better ways of doing the jobs. One industrial arts class joined forces with a French class. They prepared disassembled tables and chairs, wrote assembly instructions in French, and in addition wrote a letter of greeting to the French people. The printed instructions and letters were placed in an envelope and tacked to a piece of the furniture. A postcard addressed to the school was included so that the class could learn where the table found a home in the war-torn land. Viewing the total contribution of a year and a half gave industrial arts instructors a feeling of achievement because the men in their ranks had made a "magnificent showing."

U.S. Commissioner of Education P. P. Claxton urged that the schools remain open during the summer of 1917 and that students take advantage

---

[3] H. P. Gerber, "The Making of One Hundred Checker Boards and 2400 Checker Men," *Industrial Arts Magazine*, Vol. VII, No. 5, May 1918, pp. 186-188.

[4] "A Few Kinks in School War Service," *Industrial Arts Magazine*, Vol. VII, No. 10, October 1918, p. 277.

of it. He saw that the work of the school shops had immediate value to national defense and that, perhaps even more importantly, it might lead to higher interest in industrial skill that would be needed in the post-war era.

Arthur D. Dean could see in the challenge of the war work a golden opportunity for the manual training teacher "to abandon his set of models" and achieve new value from shop teaching. Incidentally, he used the terms manual arts and industrial arts synonymously with manual training. His point of view was expressed as follows:

Dealing with boys under fifteen, as the average manual-training teacher will, it is possible for him to develop a type of manual arts which will serve to create or arouse a set of industrial interests helpful to the boy in determining his life career. With every temptation to a pupil to leave school, the manual-training teacher will now have an unusual opportunity to make his work so attractive and economically so helpful that the boy may see the advantage of paying no attention to industrial-service inducements.

There is time for increasing the field of usefulness of the industrial arts in connection with the problems involved in the junior high school. This type of school is certain to meet with increased favor during and after the war, and the reasons are both educational and administrative.[5]

### Growth and Development of Industrial Arts

George Henry Jensen advocated industrializing manual arts in his presentation to a National Education Associa-tion audience in 1917. His point of view was in brief that, "A newer conception must vitalize the work and give the boys along with their manual arts the elements of practical training for industrial pursuits."[6] He apparently had no intention of making factories out of the schools, but he did feel that one of the weaknesses of manual training was the lack of attention to the technical side of the subject. Students knew little about the manufacture of the tools used in the shop and even less about their material value. To the frequent assertion that manual training contributed little to vocational preparation, Jensen pointed out that the surveys used to prove the point were made at low grade industrial job levels where most of the employees had left school without completing the sixth or seventh grade. Naturally manual training had not contributed to their efficiency—they had not the training. A general study had indicated previously that the dominant aim of manual training was prevocational; that the systematic graded exercise was the most frequent method used; and that the time allotted to manual training in the seventh and eighth grade was approximately 90 minutes per week.[7]

Charles A. Bennett was ever watchful for signs of progress, and he saw such a sign in the more liberal credit allowance for manual arts at the University of Wisconsin. Students who had a considerable amount of credits could

[5] Arthur D. Dean, *Our Schools in War Time—and After*. Boston: Ginn and Company, 1918, pp. 318-319.

[6] George Henry Jensen, "Industrializing the Manual Arts," *NEA Proceedings*, 1917, p. 454.

[7] Joseph C. Park and Charles L. Harlan, *Some Facts Concerning Manual Arts and Homemaking Subjects in One Hundred Fifty-Six Cities*, U.S. Department of the Interior, Bureau of Education, Bulletin 1916, No. 32. Washington: Government Printing Office, 1916, p. 23.

244

pursue graduate studies without penalty. Manual arts counted in their undergraduate background. Bennett was so happy about the situation that he said he "felt like taking a holiday to celebrate." But he also observed that while this was an encouraging step, "An armed guard is still stationed at the door to scrutinize each [manual] course as it enters. It still enters on suspicion."[8] Three years later, in 1923, the University of Wisconsin recognized all of the vocational fields at the graduate level, removing all previous barriers, which made it possible for work toward the master's degree and the doctorate.

### Educational Gains for Shopwork

By 1922, shopwork had made such significant gains in the curriculum that it was justified on the basis of its educational value. Maintaining the program so that it did in fact continue to contribute valuable educational experiences depended in a large measure upon records of student progress. A conference of supervisors of instruction in shopwork and drafting, held in Rochester late in 1922, concluded that accurate records, based on specific objectives, were essential to effective instruction.[9] Much of the concern about the measurement of progress based upon stated objectives came about through the increasingly important place of the junior high school in general educational development. Hence industrial arts educators had likewise to give considerable attention to the

development of clear-cut aims and purposes of industrial arts in the junior high school. Some industrial arts educators declared that manual arts had discovered the "individual pupil" many years earlier and had recognized the necessity of differentiation of ability, motive, and objective. "Our whole program must be conceived on the basis of recognizing the necessity of doing different things for different children."[10]

At many times in the history of industrial education, it is not clear whether a topic under discussion belongs to industrial arts or to trade and industrial education. Part of the confusion arises from the fact that many of the national leaders in one field were also leaders in the other. Furthermore, in many instances such leaders did not stop to distinguish which field was concerned; they were intent upon problem solving on a wide basis. Bawden's conference in Detroit in November, 1922, is an example.

One hundred eighty-two persons from 18 states attended the conference, which dealt with studies about occupations in the public schools. The conference members accepted as their responsibility the devising of means to stimulate the study of occupations and of actually assisting in leadership roles to accomplish the task. A particular goal was to provide assistance to principals, who would appreciate practical suggestions about the solution of the problem. The summary of the confer-

---

[8] Charles A. Bennett, "Editorial Review of the Month," *Manual Training Magazine,* Vol. XXI, No. 10, June 1920, p. 345.

[9] William T. Bawden, *Measuring the Student's Progress in Shopwork,* U.S. Department of the Interior, Bureau of Education, Industrial Education Circular No. 14, October 1922, pp. 1-2.

[10] William T. Bawden, *Manual Arts in the Junior High School,* U.S. Department of the Interior, Bureau of Education, Industrial Education Circular No. 15, November 1922, p. 24.

ence indicates clearly that industrial arts educators had many functions to perform in relation to the vocational guidance of youth in their classes.[11]

Bawden continued his efforts toward probing the critical areas of shopwork. In the spring of 1923 he called a conference of 56 persons to consider standards of eighth-grade attainment in shopwork. The shop teacher had fallen into the habit of using euphemisms to justify his existence and his work, such as pre-vocational, industrial intelligence, "finding-courses," neatness concepts, pursuit of ideals, and others. These had been emptied of meaning by careless use. Some accurate positive statements were needed, statements of what the teacher expected the boy to know and to be able to do when he had completed a particular course. The tendency of teachers, as was largely the custom of the period, to relate all activities directly to a trade or an industry did not appear adequate. During the summary of the discussion Selvidge indicated that, "It makes little difference whether these activities are unclassified with respect to the trade."[12]

The proposed list of activities that a boy should be able to do and the things he should know was to be flexible, allowing the teacher to adjust from time to time, with consideration of the boy and the community he represented. It was hoped that this scheme of activities classification would go a long way toward developing the point that the teacher was actually trying to *teach* something and that the boy was attemping to *learn* something. Selvidge continued his summary of the conference by expanding his interesting point of view related to the general problem of vocational guidance.

> The suggestions . . . have not been directed toward any particular vocation. I believe they should not be. I am firmly convinced at this age and at this degree of progress the future vocation of the boy is too uncertain for us to undertake training in a special field. I believe that the very best training that any boy can have at this age is thorough training in those fundamental social conventions of reading, writing, arithmetic, drawing, speech, good manners, essentials of health, and the things which all men should know and be able to do without respect to their vocations. This is true even of the boy who must enter industry, for jobs that are open to boys of this age do not require vocational preparation.[13]

Arthur D. Dean was a dependable observer of conditions that had a bearing upon the growth and development of industrial arts. Not only had his travels across the nation brought him into many industrial education environments, but his experience and natural abilities made him a competent critic. In his *Industrial Arts Magazine* column for December, 1924, his topic was "Thinking about What?" He wanted to know how industrial arts educators were facing up to the issues at hand, what they believed, and what they did about their beliefs. About the

---

[11] William T. Bawden, *Studies About Occupations in Public Schools*, U.S. Department of the Interior, Bureau of Education, Industrial Education Circular No. 16, 1923.

[12] William T. Bawden, *Standards of Eighth-Grade Attainment in Shopwork*, U.S. Department of the Interior, Bureau of Education, Industrial Education Circular No. 18, October 1923, p. 13.

[13] *Ibid.*, p. 14.

*general shop* he wondered if teachers had a firm understanding of the purposes of the general shop and if they were doing anything to prepare themselves specially to perform their teaching functions. His penetrating questions were concerned with the activities, with what the boy was expected to learn, how leadership was handled, and how the shop was equipped.

Dean challenged teachers to defend their practice in connection with the *short-unit course,* and suggested the possibility that some teachers were treating new ideas on the basis of what they were willing to do rather than upon what should be done. In the area of *mechanical and architectural drawing* he raised the point of the relation between theory and actual practice. Could it be possible that drawing was a subject in itself or was it really a "maid-servant" to bench work? What real place did drawing have anyway in the educational scheme? Could a boy read about drawings and get all of the information necessary without making a drawing? In the area of *household mechanics* he compared some inconsistencies of thinking among teachers: why the teacher who thought he could teach household mechanics was opposed to the general shop. The function of *production* in the shop was treated in so many different ways that Arthur Dean could not feel that teachers had come to grips with real problem solving. Behind the production issue were basic issues of hand and machine skills, coupled with understanding of social and economic problems in the machine age. Could the

need for shop work in *small communities* be solved by a traveling instructor? Dean raised other questions about *instruction in general* with some reference to the actual instructional practice.

Dean's main attack was directed toward lethargy. Evidently he found a number of industrial arts teachers who were content with things as they were, and this he could not accept. There were so many educational issues to be studied that he urged industrial arts teachers to become a part of the educational history of the times, not to be passive bystanders.

## Differentiation of Purpose

Prior to 1900, as we know, utilitarian aims and over-emphasis of economic purpose in shopwork led to the justification of manual training largely on the basis of technical skill. Thereafter, due to the belated influences of Pestalozzi, Froebel, and others—including Colonel Francis W. Parker who protested against the "deadly sequence" of manual training—a new conception of such activities was championed by John Dewey, who could see manual activities as a basis for educational work in general. "The recognition of interests in a useful finished project was but a natural step to a recognition of the pupil's right, within reasonable limitations, to determine what that product should be and how it should be designed." [14] This project concept disturbed both teachers and supervisors. The task of the teacher must become dynamic and in tune with the interests of the student, and the supervisor

---

[14] William E. Roberts, "Changes in the Problems of the Manual Arts Supervisor," *Industrial Education Magazine,* Vol. XXIV, No. 6, December 1924, p. 167.

would be forced to become an educational leader rather than merely an efficient administrator of equipment and supplies. New dimensions in teacher qualifications and teacher education would be required, as would clearer statements of objective. It stirred William E. Roberts to reconsider the high school program.

The problem of manual arts in the high school has been too long "settled." It needs an active "raising" infusion and stimulant. It is a problem worthy of careful investigation and report, based upon an extensive study of existing conditions and needs, and a discovery, if possible, of what the objectives of the high school really are.[15]

Bennett entered the discussion concerning industrial arts in the senior high school by reading a paper on the subject before the Industrial Education Department of the Vocational Education Association of the Middle-West at the St. Louis meeting in 1924. A mild critical review of the paper resulted, which satisfied Bennett's desire for communication. Bennett developed the rationale for his points of view by references to the European beginnings of industrial education and to an analysis of the purpose of the high school. From his point of view, industrial arts courses in the senior high school should be distinct from those of the junior high school.

They should be adapted to the age, capacity, and viewpoint of senior high school students. This means that they should never be "snap courses." They should be just as rich in content and re-

quire just as much effort to complete as courses in English or mathematics or history or any other subject in the same school. The time for mere exploratory or try-out courses has passed. An industrial arts course in the senior high school should be taken only by students who have a fixed purpose to accomplish something worth while in the course, and no teacher should be allowed to give weak courses in the industrial arts for senior high school credit; no courses should be given that are unworthy of credit.[16]

Whenever the objectives of industrial arts were discussed, Bennett believed one should keep in mind that the purpose of the high school was "a preparation for life and for life work" as well as for college. The fact that the high school had been divided into parts, one junior and the other senior, emphasized the necessity for differentiation between the two programs. In a way he was trying to implement the recommendations of Selvidge, Roberts, and others.

The aim of the industrial arts, then, in the senior high school should be, first, vocational, either immediately or remotely; second, cultural; and each course should be planned and taught with reference to the capacity and general background of schooling of the students and with a practical or vocational end in view.[17]

Note Bennett's use of the phrase "immediately or remotely."

Lewis Gustafson, Superintendent of the David Ranken Jr., School of Mechanical Trades, was concerned also with the general orientation of industrial arts. Like others, he found it necessary to review in considerable detail the early development of industrial

---

[15] *Ibid.*, p. 169.

[16] Charles A. Bennett, "Industrial Arts in Senior High Schools," *Industrial Education Magazine,* Vol. XXVI, No. 8, February 1925, p. 226.

[17] *Ibid.*, p. 227.

education in order to show the logic of his viewpoints. Prior to 1900 there had been a distinct tendency to make manual training vocational. Later, the emphasis on the cultural value of manual training led to the virtual abandonment of vocational aims, with some persons strongly disclaiming any intention to teach a trade, and even going to the extreme of renouncing any economically useful goals. In urging the need for a return to useful concepts, Gustafson cited the toast given at a mathematician's banquet, "Here's to mathematics. May they never be of any earthly use!" Of course, this was before the space age!

### The Thin Line

Manual training did change its direction. It may have been pressured by organized labor or public opinion concerning the stigma of hand work. "Whatever the reason, manual training became a part of general education, became definitely and avowedly cultural, and as such it served a useful purpose with honor and distinction."[18]

Times were indeed changing in the mid-1920's. It was necessary for manual training to recognize that it must adjust or suffer grave setbacks. By sponsoring vocational education the Smith-Hughes Law offered an indirect threat to manual training, and finding a new role was imperative in order that it perform a vital and important function in education.

The fact was that the line between what was purely vocational and purely cultural was very thin. The principal difficulty lay in attempts to separate things which were inseparable: manual training and vocational guidance, manual training and pre-vocational training, for example. In fact it was Gustafson's view that manual arts held the key to the question, "Shall we remain drudging mechanics, or shall we become inventive artisans?"[19] Manual arts had many purposes, and influential writers emphasized the evils of "single purpose" in order that those actively engaged in the manual arts would not again fall into the trap of failing to change with the times.[20] Said Bennett:

Today in progressive schools there is an effort to give the pupils real experiences thru making things that may be marketable or that may serve some social use, and to make them by methods which give correct ideas of hand craftsmanship or industrial production or both. Moreover, along with these exepriences in doing real things more attention is being given to making sure that the student gets the "related information" which is essential to an adequate understanding of what he is doing. The effort is constantly to help the student to make the connection between what he does and learns and the real life of adults outside the school.[21]

Purposeful activity in a school was a part of life, and not merely a preparation for it; its values would carry beyond the school—as vocational, as cultural, as the basis of appreciation. The

---

[18] Lewis Gustafson, "What is the Future of the Regular Manual Training Teacher," *Industrial Education Magazine*, Vol. XXVI, No. 9, March 1925, p. 258.

[19] *Ibid.*, p. 260.

[20] James Parton Haney, "Character Values in Training in the Manual Arts," *Industrial Education Magazine*, Vol. XXVI, No. 10, April 1925, pp. 298-299.

[21] Charles A. Bennett, "Changes in Manual Arts Instruction in Relation to Changes in the Philosophy of Education," *Industrial Education Magazine*, Vol. XXVI, No. 12, June 1925, p. 363.

value of manual training for leisure time use was strongly advanced by persons in and out of the field of manual training.[22]

Leaders in manual arts and in the vocational education programs continued to identify appropriate relationships and to investigate how each could best complement the other. Yet confusion of thinking sifted through the school more generally than clarity of definition, with the result that the programs were frequently regarded as rivals or competitors. Despite this image, in some respects the two maintained clear differences. Vocational industrial education tended to train for gainful employment; this purpose was clearly not a purpose of the manual arts program. But in practice such a clear-cut differentiation did not separate the two areas, partly because it was obvious that vital relationships between the two areas existed. W. H. Lancelot reached three conclusions in regard to the contributions that manual arts could make to the vocational-industrial education program:

1. In their relations to the vocational objective, the manual arts and the vocational industrial education programs seem to be in a sense complements of each other, since one provides vocational guidance and the other vocational training. The manual arts courses, then, should operate as a selective agency, finding and sending on the boys who should receive vocational industrial training.

2. In the realization of teaching objectives, the two seem again to stand in a complementary relation to each other.

The manual arts are actually accomplishing certain of the vocational objectives in greater measure than are the training courses in many cases. The contribution to the vocational industrial education program is so considerable that it should not be overlooked.

3. Not the least part of the ultimate contribution of the manual arts to the vocational industrial program will probably be an improvement in teaching methods. The time is apparently not far away when more attention can be given to this in vocational work. At that time, the methods used in the manual arts will be largely drawn upon to the great benefit of all concerned.[23]

On the other hand, manual arts educators were not preoccupied with vocational-industrial relationships. Study of the relationships to other areas of education helped identify the unique contributions of manual arts in the total educational scheme. In this connection Bennett held the following view:

Without fear of contradiction one may say that in no department of education is there better opportunity for experiences that carry rich meanings over into modern life than in the department of the manual arts. The value of the manual arts, then, in general education, from the standpoint of present educational philosophy is that they provide a wide range of experiences that equip the pupil with meanings that make for better preparation for life under present-day conditions.[24]

**Manual Arts in the Junior High School.** In the mid-twenties industrial arts found its greatest hope in the junior high school. Here growth was rapid and much activity was indicated

---

[22] Frederick A. Adams, "Manual Training and Education for the Use of Leisure," *Industrial Education Magazine,* Vol. XXVII, No. 2, August 1925, p. 50.

[23] W. H. Lancelot, "The Contribution That Manual Arts Can Make to the Vocational Industrial Education Program," *Industrial Education Magazine,* Vol. XXVII, No. 11, May 1926, p. 360.

[24] Charles A. Bennett, "The Value of the Manual Arts in General Education," *Industrial Education Magazine,* Vol. XXVIII, No. 2, August 1926, p. 34.

in writings about junior high school manual arts. However, opinions differed widely concerning certain aspects of the program.

William E. Roberts sought to establish order by suggesting definite answers to the following question: "What are the aims of manual arts in the junior high school, and how are they attained in terms of teaching, methods, subject matter and organization?"[25]

In answering the question Roberts conducted a survey of junior high schools in thirteen cities of the Midwest. He described outstanding features of each school and then examined each program in terms of the following general items: (1) The function of manual arts in the junior high school, (2) the objectives of manual arts teaching, (3) methods in manual arts (individual craftsman vs. quantity production), (4) basis for determining subject matter, (5) measuring attainment in manual arts, (6) courses of study, (7) course outlines, (8) the teacher, and (9) equipment and facilities. He then reported on correlated findings that set up a form or standard. Roberts succeeded in getting an answer to his question concerning the nature of the junior high school program, as studied, and in this sense pointed toward elimination of confusion. Although his sample was quite limited, the report which he made was one of the first comprehensive treatments of the subject.

Maris M. Proffitt, in his summary of the biennium, 1924-26, could identify an increase in the number of shops in high schools, a tendency toward compulsory enrollment in seventh and eighth grade industrial arts, an increase in the amount of time devoted to industrial arts, an increase in both interest in and use of visual aids for instruction, and a marked increase of general shops as an orgnization form. It was apparent also that the instructional emphasis was changing more and more from one of skill through developmental experience to one of industrial intelligence.[26]

"Manual arts instruction forms an essential part of any successful junior high school course of study. It will make better citizens, happier workers, and result in a bigger democracy through the intelligent cooperation upon the part of all of our boys who have had this training."[27] In this manner, Howard L. Briggs answered the question, Why do we teach manual arts?

**Principles and Rationalizations.** It was not uncommon for such general questions to be asked of various phases of education, and it was just as common for the educators concerned to relate the purposes of their work to whichever educational philosophy prevailed at the time. Thus Briggs identified three basic phases of living as related to *producing, consuming,* and *securing contentment and satisfaction from relationships with the general environment and with fellow men.* (1) Manual arts activity met the test of

[25] William E. Roberts, *Manual Arts in the Junior High School,* U.S. Department of the Interior, Bureau of Education, Bulletin 1924, No. 11, p. 1.

[26] Maris M. Proffitt, *Industrial Education in 1924-1926,* U.S. Department of the Interior, Bureau of Education, Bulletin 1927, No. 29, 1927, p. 29.

[27] Howard L. Briggs, "Why Do We Teach Manual Arts?" *Industrial Education Magazine,* Vol. XXIX, No. 2, August 1927, p. 61.

producing a marketable commodity through numerous related activities. (2) Most certainly, aspects of experience in consumer education were integrated in manual arts courses. Many shop projects were for home or personal use, which provided a natural avenue for building consumer concepts. (3) As for the third point, the achievement of taking a piece of raw material and fashioning it into a final product brought the boy into many valuable relationships in and out of school. In addition, the boy's pride in the work that he had completed and his dependence upon his fellow class members were further justifications of manual arts in the scheme of education for general purposes.

Thomas R. Foulkes went further in the enumeration of particular values of manual training, in an analysis of the process of teaching pupils to think, as part of their shop experience. In this matter educational administrators and philosophers had left the educational practitioner in the dark. The concept was certainly acceptable; it was the implementation that was difficult. The manual arts teacher needed some vehicle or "gimmick" in order to invite student resourcefulness; some means by which the student could find out if his thinking was straight. Job sheets, instructor demonstrations and verbal instructions, acquaintance with the basic tools and equipment were all preliminary to the process. Once the project had been selected, the student was led to "think the job through" by a series of questions, which resulted in a daily plan slip, prepared in advance,

for the student's work the next day or days. Even the slip itself was a part of the instruction in lettering, and class time was used in order to make the plan slip a definite part of the instructional process.

The pupil, according to Foulkes, became more dependent upon himself for some ideas, although the instructor was available to assist. In this case he became a guide instead of a dictator.

But most important of all is the possibility which this plan offers, as no academic work can possibly do, of training in habits of success. Instead of half success, or failure, every boy can have a real thrill every day in manual training. He sets his objective, plans thru successfully accomplishing every day the thing he sets out to do. This means at least one thrill of victory every day to every boy in manual training, and that, to the boy, makes the game worth while! [28]

### Dignity of Work

Among the other expressed objectives was to develop understanding of the dignity of work. In the fall of 1927 Harold Feuerstein wrote that practical arts instructors were in an excellent position to make progress on this phase of education. They could demonstrate analogies more easily than would be possible in the academic classroom. Feuerstein believed that the dignity of a position was measured by quality of work and the sincerity of the worker, not by financial rewards or academic considerations. People failed to see the dignity in various lines of work because of a tendency to measure the prestige of an occupation by the length and breadth of its educational

---

[28] Thomas R. Foulkes, "Teaching Pupils to Think in Manual Training," *Industrial Education Magazine,* Vol. XXIX, No. 3, September 1927, p. 96.

requirements. Feuerstein described a practical demonstration of a more objective viewpoint. First the instructor prepared for the demonstration by obtaining a large fish bowl, filling it nearly full with water, and mounting it on a pedestal so that the whole class could see it. Then a number of small blocks were prepared. Some of the blocks were soiled, some were clean but "loaded" with lead, some were rough, and some were smooth. Each block represented typical students and the bowl represented the world. The instructor's accompanying monologue was as follows:

Each of you are sooner or later going to leave school. Some of you will appear very rough and unfinished when you leave school. You will look something like this. (Hold up a rough block.) Some of you will go to college and become polished like this. (Hold up a smooth block.) Some of you, though you may look rather worthless like this block (hold up a dirty unleaded block), will work hard and finally reach the top; you will win success. Now I am going to take these blocks and tell them to go to work. I will place them in the bowl and stir them so they will travel around the world for a time, then we will see which ones will reach the top, or in other words which will be successful. (Stir the water, place all the blocks in the water and as the water is stirred continue to explain as follows.)

Do you see that polished block at the bottom? That worker must be lazy. He does not seem to want to reach the top. Now do you see the block that was so dirty? It is getting polished by moving around in the water. And look at that rough block. No matter how many times it is pushed about it reaches the top. That is the way all workers should do. Try to reach the top. (Now let the water rest

and continue to explain.) Though some of the workers in the bowl appeared to be neat and finished workers they did not reach the top because inside of them there was something wrong. They were not what they appeared to be. Now as I look at you I see some boys who appear to be good workers, I see some who appear to be rough and crude. It is up to you to swim about and look for a place on top; it is up to you to respect everyone no matter how rough they may be; it is up to you to sink to the bottom or swim to the top.[29]

The important part of Feuerstein's demonstration is not its appropriateness. Rather, such a demonstration represents evidence that industrial arts educators were in fact thinking beyond the shop project and viewing their students as individuals who had contributions to make for the good of society. He cautioned practical arts teachers about some of the hazards of the demonstration, such as giving the idea that all students can become supervisors and administrators by just working hard. To Feuerstein the shop was alive with opportunities for the teacher to stress the dignity of work.

Myron J. Files, in discussing the ways in which manual training gave concreteness to ideas, said:

It is one thing to teach a student formulae for standard operations and quite another to teach him to think and feel in terms of harmony, pattern, and the varying values of different materials. It is of no tremendous advantage for a boy to learn how to build a chair or a chicken coop, but it is an increase in personal power to learn to "think" shapeless oak or pine into objects of beauty and utility embodying ideals of beauty drawing in

[29] Harold Feuerstein, "Teaching Practical Arts Pupils the Dignity of Work," *Industrial Education Magazine*, Vol. XXIX, No. 4, October 1927, p. 123.

the mind. Whoever teaches manual training ought to be more of a teacher than a woodturner.[30]

**Growth Trends**

At the end of the 1926-28 biennium there was notable growth in industrial arts. The need for special qualifications for supervisors of the curriculum was much discussed, and club activities for students were highly recommended. Reflecting interest in motion, model boat and airplane construction became very popular in the junior high school. Also, girls had enrolled in home mechanics courses, and industrial arts projects seemed to have definite relationships to home and leisure time activities for girls.

Maris M. Proffitt, as a specialist in the field of industrial education in the U.S. Office of Education, provided data for the biennial surveys of education that related to the growth and development of industrial arts education. The report for the biennium 1928-30 points up some significant trends and provides an excellent summary. The place and function of industrial arts in the curriculum had been the subject of almost continuous discussion. By 1930 its place in the general school program was generally accepted, and the tendency was more and more to make industrial arts a requirement in junior high schools. Proffitt observed the following trends:

1. To make shop work in the industrial arts a required course somewhere in the junior high school grades.

2. To make the exploratory objective, including the development of general industrial intelligence, the principal aim of the industrial arts work at least through the first and second years of the junior high school grades.

3. To consider industrial arts as a general education subject, governed by the same principles as govern the purpose and organization of courses for general education training.

4. To establish the user's or consumer's values as the aim for any course offered beyond those provided in the junior high school in accordance with the exploratory and industrial-intelligence objectives. Some advance has been made in theory and a little in practice relative to establishing a clear distinction between industrial courses in the senior high school offered as industrial arts courses in general and vocational-industrial courses offered for employment purposes.

5. To organize instruction for the exploratory objective on the basis of the general shop type of course.

6. To increase the number of shop activities included in a course for realizing the exploratory aim. The tendency to break away from woodwork as the most exclusive type of shop activity was especially noticeable in some States.

7. To standardize in a general way the activities, projects, and quality of work for the industrial arts in the junior high school grades.

8. To raise the qualifications for industrial arts teachers.

9. To provide a 4-year curriculum in industrial arts in teacher training colleges.

10. To organize industrial arts clubs for project work on the interest and ability levels of junior high school pupils as an integral part of the industrial arts program.[31]

There was also evidence that industrial arts educators felt secure from the

---

[30] Myron J. Files, "Manual Training Gives Concreteness to Words," *Industrial Education Magazine,* Vol. XXIX, No. 7, January 1928, p. 233.

[31] Maris M. Proffitt, Biennial Survey of Education in the United States, *Chapter IV, Industrial Education,* U.S. Department of the Interior, Office of Education, Bulletin 1931, No. 20, 1931, p. 18.

claim that a positive declaration of the employment aims of vocational-industrial education would weaken the place of industrial arts in general education. Conversely, they felt secure in writing off direct preparation for employment as an aim of industrial arts. Courses with mixed objectives were thought to be inefficient, representing "neither good industrial arts nor good vocational-industrial work." This thinking, more than anything else, established the principle of differentiation, although there was a possibility that confusion might still exist in practice.

### AVA Vice President for Industrial Arts

The first convention of the American Vocational Association, in 1926 at Louisville, Kentucky, did not feature any major phase of industrial arts education. There was certainly a reason for programing industrial arts, because some AVA members were national leaders in the field. But if industrial arts was discussed in any way, it does not show in the printed record of the convention.

Nevertheless, before the second convention of AVA, in Los Angeles, December, 1927, a committee on industrial arts had been appointed. This committee, the first under the banner of AVA, consisted of some familiar names: William E. Roberts, Supervisor of Manual Arts, Cleveland, Ohio (Chairman); Clyde Bowman, Stout Institute, Menomonie, Wisconsin; A. F. Siepert, University of Chicago, Chicago, Illinois; William H. Stone, The Ohio State University, Columbus, Ohio; and Frank M. Treat, State Di-

rector of Vocational Education, Cheyenne, Wyoming.[32]

A section meeting on industrial arts, organized by the AVA committee, was held for the first time at the Los Angeles convention. Roberts, Ericson, Proffitt, and Selvidge participated in the program.

In February, 1928, the committee on industrial arts was reconstituted. Siepert, Stone, and Treat retired. William T. Bawden, then Associate Superintendent of Schools, Tulsa, Oklahoma; William R. Ward, Supervisor of Manual Training, Trenton, New Jersey; and E. E. Ericson, Head of the Department of Industrial Education, State Teachers College, Santa Barbara, California, were the new members.

One of the speakers at the Industrial Arts Education section at the Los Angeles convention was H. B. Wilson, Superintendent of Schools, Berkeley, California, whose topic was "The Place of Industrial Arts in the Public School Program." Wilson made the following points:

1. In offering a fair and adequate democratic educational program the industrial arts are necessary. They help to enrich the courses of study, . . . [meeting] the needs that normally arise in the life of the child from the first grade through the high school. Change is the outstanding need of these times and in education a varied course of study helps to provide profitable opportunities for the child's living during these succeeding changes.

2. The industrial arts subjects increase the opportunities for success on the part of all the children.

3. The industrial arts subjects increase the child's opportunity to discover himself vocationally.

[32] *American Vocational Association News Bulletin,* Vol. II, No. 4, November 1927, p. 6.

4. The industrial arts subjects make for democratic, cooperative understanding and neighborliness.

5. The industrial arts subjects make for richness of each individual's personal life.[33]

A second speaker at the industrial arts section was William John Cooper, Superintendent of Public Instruction in California (to become the United States Commissioner of Education, February 11, 1929), who spoke on the topic "The Destiny of Industrial Arts in the Senior High School." Superintendent Cooper described the difficulties involved in predicting the place of industrial arts in the senior high school and indicated that the experiments with manual arts high schools had not fulfilled hopes and expectations.

During the next few years the membership of the industrial arts committee changed a number of times, but the committee continued to plan and conduct discussions at the AVA convention on industrial arts themes. At the New York convention in 1931, the program was for some reason relegated to a rather minor place, which caused some concern among the industrial arts teachers. R. W. Selvidge was appointed a committee of one to take up the matter with the AVA executive committee. In May, 1932, Selvidge reported his progress.

Years of experience and careful study of our educational problems have brought a clearer understanding of the functions and fields of vocational education and the industrial arts. It has become clear that there is no real conflict between these two phases of education, but that each supplements the other. It seems desirable, therefore, that people interested in these fields should work together in harmony and without jealousy.[34]

Selvidge requested the executive committee to recognize industrial arts as a major group of AVA and to provide a vice-president to represent this group on the executive committee. The members assured him that the matter would be given their attention. However, an organizational change would necessitate an amendment to the constitution; that could only be accomplished at the next annual meeting in Kansas City.

At the Kansas City convention in December, 1932, the constitution was so amended by approval of the House of Delegates. Industrial arts was given representation on the executive committee. R. W. Selvidge became the first vice-president for industrial arts education.

### Effect of the Twenties on Industrial Arts

The period from the end of World War I to the depression was one of significant growth of industrial arts in all aspects. The subject matter reached more junior high school students and the trend was definitely toward required courses for boys.

Confusion inherent in the aims, objectives, and purposes of industrial arts occupied much of the attention of professional groups. It could scarcely be said that the matter was settled for all time, but consideration did bring forth new understanding of inherent values. The practical realistic approach of in-

---

[33] *American Vocational Association News Bulletin*, Vol. III, No. 1, February 1928, p. 12.

[34] R. W. Selvidge, "Recognition of the Industrial Arts," *American Vocational Association News Bulletin*, Vol. III, No. 2, May 1932, p. 16.

dustrial arts was in accord with the general development and expansion of education during the period.

Despite general development, the period did not produce a uniform movement. It did produce many influential individuals, as well as the tendency to develop special group interests within the field of industrial arts, revolving around these individuals.

### The Bird House Era

*When activity is at its best, either physical or mental, it has back of it all the individual's powers and resources. The whole being urgently calls out for and demands this activity. The self wills it fully and completely, interest and desire prompt it, the entire organism affirms it and gives itself gladly to it, no part of the self is latent or withheld.*

*—Anonymous* [35]

The "project" is one of the readily identifiable characteristics of industrial arts. In the main the project, as we know it, is of twentieth century origin, and the project method of instruction represented somewhat of a revolt against older methods of instruction and older subject matter classifications. As previously indicated the project grew out of the experimental work of John Dewey around the turn of the century and seemed to possess values of motor expression and social participation. It represented also a release from the formal, highly structured nature of academic learning. The learning-by-doing concept had been urged by Rousseau and practiced successfully by Pestalozzi, Fellenberg, and others. The project in industrial education developed as a natural evolution from both practical and theoretical considerations. Dewey was intrigued by the possibilities of industrial education and was continuously its strong supporter, for it provided an ideal social and intellectual motivation for learning.[36]

In industrial arts the child could realize social goals and at the same time engage in activities that would require him to think and to solve problems. Selection of projects was important. Not just any project would do. It must meet the tests of social significance, intellectual activity, and a variety of other values.

When industrial education as a whole moved out of the realm of the "exercise" and into a world of "projects," take-home construction bloomed in industrial arts classes. One of the favorite projects was the bird house. In a way it represented the entire project concept of the twentieth century till World War II.

The bird house project was stimulated by a growing national interest in birds, which had been promoted largely by the National Association of Audubon Societies. It caught on as a strong reflection of American topical obsession.[37]

---

[35] Quoted in William H. Kilpatrick, *Source Book in the Philosophy of Education.* New York: The Macmillan Company, 1924, p. 203.

[36] John Dewey, "The Need of an Industrial Education in an Industrial Democracy," *Manual Training and Vocational Education,* Vol. XVII, No. 6, February 1916, p. 414.

[37] John James Audubon (1785-1851) attracted remarkable attention in the United States and in England with his beautiful ornithologies. Although he was not a scientist or trained specialist, his keen observations and attractive paintings were based upon a life-long, absorbing interest in birds. His paintings of American birds have been reproduced in many volumes. In 1886 George Bird Grinnell coined the term "Audubon Society" which became the name of

Just when man first constructed a home for his small feathered friends is lost in obscurity, as is the first manual arts project on the bird house. We do know that a wave of enthusiasm for bird house construction swept the nation. The bird house era provided an opportunity for cooperative activity of the home, the school, and the community. The projects were seldom in the realm of "just doing something," but were calculated to include educational value. Frequently bird house construction was motivated by a contest, with numerous prizes, in which the school and the community could show appreciation for the interest students were taking in their surroundings. News of bird house construction contests were advertised generously.

Students were asked to think through the style of the house. "Does it suit your bird?" they would be asked. The student had much more to think about than just lumber, paint, and nails. Decisions concerning whether the house should be stationary or swinging, the nature of ventilation, and provisions for cleaning the house at the end of the season had to be made. All bird houses had to meet the practical requirements of the species they were meant to attract. Artistic aspects were always present, and students were impressed with the fact

that the bird house should be pleasing to "the human kind who have to look at it."

In 1916, Albert F. Siepert, then Professor of Education at Bradley Polytechnic Institute, issued a small book with the engaging title, *Bird Houses Boys Can Build*. The book was reissued in 1926, and revised and reissued again in 1936.[38] Here were many helpful suggestions for both the instructor and the boy about the major industrial arts project of the time. The book included a short review of the habits and nature of nine different birds; construction hints, instructions for placing the completed houses; notes and construction hints on feeding shelves and shelters; bird baths, including an idea for a concrete structure, and a short discussion of bird enemies. The boy could scarcely miss Siepert's point that bird enemies were definitely *persona non grata,* for he suggested a number of diabolical schemes for their harassment and eradication. Siepert's very brief discussion of bird "mysteries" could only have stimulated further investigation. The reader was also introduced to other sources of information: the U.S. Department of Agriculture, magazines, Audubon Society publications, and thirteen books on the subject of birds, including one by Frank J. Ball, *A Year With Birds.*

an organization concerned with the appreciation and protection of bird life. In time Audubon Societies were organized in many states. Interest in their activities increased to the point that in 1905 a National Association of Audubon Societies was formed in Washington, D.C. By 1914 the association started its work in applied ornithology. Its purpose was to encourage people generally to attract birds to their homes and to become interested in their protection and study. Systematic instruction in bird lore reached many school children (as Junior Audubon members); literature and lectures had a decided influence upon adults in promoting popular sentiment toward the work of the Audubon groups. Millions of bird-protection mailing pieces reached American homes each year.

[38] Albert F. Siepert, *Bird Houses Boys Can Build*. Peoria, Illinois: The Manual Arts Press, 1916.

It was clearly a sign of the times that E. E. Ericson wrote about some of the important yet oftentimes forgotten points in designing bird houses. Ericson used the analogy of an architect who designs a dwelling for a particular family. The architect consults with the family, determines particular tastes and standards of living, and seeks members' particular desires concerning the home he is to design and build for them. Some dwellings, Ericson observed, showed evidence of having been built without loving care and adequate planning, and they were therefore not likely to be pleasing to the occupants. Ericson indicated that many boys had built bird houses, then found to their dismay that the birds did not select the house for nesting. He recognized this as a failure to design the house to fit the needs of the species. "It was fit for neither bluebird, nor wren, nor martin, nor flicker, nor any other bird which has self-respect enough to require the American standards of living." [39]

The related information which was necessary for constructing a bird house was enormous. For example, if a boy wanted to prepare a house for a wren, the opening could not be large enough for a blue jay or sparrow hawk; in fact it had to be precisely ⅞" in diameter in order to exclude the English sparrow. Ericson urged teachers to follow an educational plan which would lead to sound construction. First, the instructor should talk to the boys about the various peculiarities of birds, especially local representatives. It was the instructor's job to get the boys interested enough to do some investigations of their own. Second, the location of the bird houses should be studied. What kinds of birds would it be possible to attract in this location? Instructors were urged to help the students understand the habits of birds in relation to a particular environment. Third, when the first two requirements had been satisfied, the student could begin studying the specifications for a particular dwelling. It was recommended that the student make a sketch of the proposed house and that he use reference materials which would provide assistance on critical dimensions. The finish of the bird house was highly important and should fit in with the surrounding construction. If it were to be used near a stucco dwelling, for instance, the exterior of the bird house could be finished in stucco, also. But, "On the other hand, some birds—the chickadee for instance—want to be inconspicuous, and this requires that a house be painted in grey or green and put in some secluded spot." [40]

## Some Typical Reports

In the spring of 1922, a bird house construction project was introduced in the seventh grade at Rumford, Maine. Eighty new houses for birds of the community were constructed. Although design was emphasized in relation to the requirements of certain birds, the project involved a considerable general study of birds as a prerequisite activity. Prizes were offered for the best design and workmanship.

[39] Emanuel E. Ericson, "Designing Bird Houses for Particular Occupants," *Manual Training Magazine*, Vol. XXIII, No. 10, April 1922, p. 343.

[40] *Ibid.*, p. 345.

Frank W. Neil wrote about a contest in the public schools of Helena, Montana, in the spring of 1924. Bird house construction involved the cooperation of other school departments, which not only advertised the contest but provided information concerning bird protection and care. Bird house projects were a regular part of the manual training program in the sixth, seventh, and eighth grades. "It is a project [in] which the boys supplement their shopwork not only with art posters, but study the subject matter pertaining to bird study in regard to the habits and economic value in destroying injurious insects, their eggs, and weed seed."[41] The stores cooperated in displaying the bird houses to the best advantage, with special window decorations. Local merchants offered prizes for the best houses, as selected by a committee of the community.

The manual training department of the Buffalo public schools, in cooperation with the Boy Scouts of America, constructed 314 bird houses in a city-wide community project in which 32 prizes were offered by local merchants. Many people of the community visited the exhibit, which was displayed in the windows of one of the business establishments. "The purpose of the contest, primarily, was to stimulate the interests of the boys of Buffalo in bird life and out-of-door activities."[42] Although the rules of the contest were general, it was imperative that the boy

acquire some understanding about the life and habits of the bird for which the house was constructed. "The manual training men say that since a few boys have made houses and erected them in their neighborhood and have secured song birds as 'renters' or 'tenants' a keener interest is manifested and a greater love for birds and their protection has evidenced itself."[43] The bird house contest "gave added incentives to other subjects since so many teachers of other subjects took up bird house building as oral work in English, for writing letters, for ordering materials, for geography lessons, in civics, and even lessons of thrift."[44]

C. Anthony Van Kammen described the activities of the Grand Rapids, Michigan schools in 1925. The bird house exhibit was accompanied by a bird-recognizing contest sponsored by the local Audubon Society. Mounted specimens of the local birds were obtained from a museum, identified by numbers, and placed in a local store window. School children could enter the contest by obtaining an entry blank containing the numbers. Prizes were offered and the local papers provided publicity. Later the seventh and eighth grade drawing classes made sketches of the birds, and one energetic fourth grade teacher stimulated some of her pupils to participate in the contest and in the drawings.

The value of birds to the community is common knowledge and most everyone

---

[41] Frank W. Neil, "Bird House Contest, Helena, Montana," *Industrial Education Magazine*, Vol. XXV, No. 11, May 1924, p. 8.

[42] Hiram E. Greiner, "Hundreds of Houses for Buffalo Birds," *Industrial Education Magazine*, Vol. XXV, No. 7, January 1924, p. 188.

[43] *Ibid.*, p. 189.

[44] *Ibid.*

## WILL-YUM                    By Dave Girard

enjoys the early morning song of the wren and bluebird and . . . the untiring flight of the martins as they race after mosquitos or sit in long lines on the telephone wires or about their houses twittering to each other. Those who do not appreciate the feathered friends about them and who cannot recognize their common bird neighbors by both song and sight lose much joy in living.[45]

---

[45] C. Anthony Van Kammen, "Bird House Exhibit and Bird Recognizing Contest," *Industrial Education Magazine,* Vol. XXVI, No. 9, March 1925, p. 277.

As regularly as the arrival of spring, the bird house project became a familiar item in manual arts programs throughout the nation. Each spring, enthusiasm was built anew. In the spring of 1926, M. E. Dodge of the Stanley McCormick School, Burnsville, North Carolina, provided readers of *Industrial Education Magazine* with a review of three interesting bird houses. Dodge was particularly concerned with providing sixth and seventh grade students with an opportunity to show originality in design. Houses built from his "hollow log" suggestions were attractive to many students. "This problem is especially suitable for boys who are expected to pay for the material they use, as the cost is practically nothing. The woods and every wood pile are sources of supply." [46]

Sanger Crumpacker of McPherson, Kansas, reporting on manual arts activities during the school year 1926-27 indicated that the community exhibit was sponsored by the Y.M.C.A. during their annual Pet and Hobby show. Again, store windows were made available for displays. Only seventh and eighth grade classes participated in the contest. The houses were judged by the businessmen of the community. Originality, fitness to purpose, and skill in workmanship were the bases of judging. All entries were supposed to be built to meet the needs of the birds in the area. The boys evidently took the task of originality in stride because the display indicated a range of entries from simple box construction to an elaborate house with some of the characteristics of a medieval castle.

E. F. Stokes reported in February, 1928, that the bird house program for school No. 37 in Indianapolis, Indiana, proved to be a successful and spirited one, with 150 boys involved. The four points which were characteristic of the program were: (1) a study of birds, (2) individuality in plans, (3) workmanship, (4) utility, with each boy striving to make his bird house appropriate for the potential occupant. Stokes mentioned with special emphasis the cooperation among departments of the school in connection with the contest, particularly the English department which assigned students to read and write stories about birds.

With the return of spring in 1929, William L. Hunter took the trouble to review the bird house situation in the interests of stimulating what appeared to him to be lagging enthusiasm in manual arts programs. Hunter gave credit to shop teachers for knowing about bird houses "from A to Z" but cautioned them as follows: "Sometimes . . . the shop teacher forgets that there is a new crop of boys in his shop every spring, just as there is a new crop of birds out among the trees." [47] Hunter felt that the bird house project should have as strong an appeal for these boys as always. He assumed an early origin of the bird house, indicated by the fact that Noah gave shelter to birds, but the project as it was known in 1929 originated after Dewey's appeal to provide interest in teaching.

---

[46] M. E. Dodge, "Three Interesting Bird Houses," *Industrial Education Magazine*, Vol. XXVII, No. 9, March 1926, p. 301.

[47] William L. Hunter, "Boy Interests and the Bird-House Problem," *Industrial Education Magazine*, Vol. XXX, No. 9, March 1929, p. 340.

He reasoned that the thousands of bird houses built each year were proof that the philosopher's words had been heard in the school shop.

Hunter illustrated his paper on the bird house situation by supplying photographs of five attractive projects bearing the following titles: (1) The Log House, "Rustic Inn"; (2) The Stucco House, "Birdies' Paradise"; (3) The Birch-Bark House, "Jennie Wren's Delight"; (4) The One-Log House, "Rest-A-Bit"; and (5) The Camouflaged House, "Tumble-Inn." Hunter cited again the values which the casual observer does not see in the completed project: challenge to the boy's ability, opportunity to express individuality, parental interest and appreciation, community enthusiasm as expressed by the local service clubs and merchants who made attractive displays when the project was accompanied by a sponsored contest in the community. Hunter's final comment probed deeper into the heart of the industrial arts program. "A teacher may keep shop, or he may be a leader of boys. It all depends on whether or not he keeps alive to the interests of youth, and inspires the boys to be the kind of citizens today that he would like them to be tomorrow." [48]

Utilization of the bird house project seemed to have no bounds. The Tulsa, Oklahoma, Rotary Club sponsored a Boys' Home and sent a number of the boys each year to a Y.M.C.A. Boys' Camp, the expenses being paid by the club members. In 1929, in order to accommodate a growing number of boys who wanted to go to the camp, the Rotary Club tried to work out a plan by which the boys could earn money to pay their own expenses; the club consulted the public schools for ideas.

Conferences with school officials resulted in the approval of the Board of Education to use the school shops. Industrial arts teachers agreed to organize and conduct the work. The Rotary Club purchased the materials and managed the sale of the product. The project selected was the bird house. Thirty-two boys met at the school shops for two hours on 15 Saturday mornings and produced 455 houses suitable for wrens, bluebirds, flickers, and martins. All of the houses were sold (the City Park Board purchased 245) and the net profit from the project was $233.75.

On the whole, the attitude of the boys was exceptionally fine, and the interest displayed was very heartening. Most of the boys seemed to appreciate the Big Brother attitude of the Rotarians, and did their level best. . . . Letters written from the camp by the boys to the sponsor members of the Rotary Club showed their deep appreciation of the efforts made in their behalf. The whole undertaking proved decidedly worthwhile, and was a most interesting experience for the boys and for the instructors as well.[49]

### The Bird House Era in Retrospect

Interest in the bird house project waned during the bitter depression. By the end of World War II it was almost nonexistent. New interests captured the attention of the boy and his instructor. For example, aluminum "birds" flying at nearly the speed of

---

[48] *Ibid.*, p. 341.
[49] Roy V. Ludlow and Raymond G. Johnson, "Giving the Under-Privileged Boy a Chance," *Industrial Education Magazine*, Vol. XXXI, No. 3, September 1929, p. 90.

# BIG GEORGE!  By Virgil Partch

## "They just dont build houses like they used to."

sound offered new dimensions. The bird house was a casualty of the efforts of industrial arts educators to extend the range and scope of industrial arts activity, and of the general march of technology.

Few people mourned the passing of the bird house, but in its wake was left a golden legacy of successful educational experiences. Few modern projects compare in richness of experience. It is evident that countless boys took genuine interest in the bird houses they built. The project was also

264

cast in an environment that brought the school, the parent, and the community into new relationships. The boy learned a great deal about the natural world around him, and the nature of the project was such that it provided a basis for many cooperative in-school activities with other subject matter areas.

There is another side to the story that is not so well known or documented; but to leave the impression that all manual arts educators were thoroughly satisfied with the bird house as a project would be false. Some teachers held that the bird house represented little if any progress away from the days of the mortise-and-tenon joints. The intense interest of Audubon Societies, women's clubs, and civic groups was regarded as an advertising scheme; the educational value of the project was considered secondary. A bird house was fine from a nature study point of view but it was poor manual training.[50] Education stood still each spring while the entire school became absorbed in bird house construction. The voice of criticism, however, was no match for the wave of enthusiasm that gave precedence for three decades to the bird house project in manual arts.

## The Depression and World War II—1929-1949

The prosperity of the twenties broke its back in October, 1929, with the stock-market crash. By 1932 the national income had dropped to 27 billion dollars, from a high of 85 billion.

The volume of business had dropped 50 percent, agriculture 57 percent. Foreign trade decreased by two-thirds of its 1929 value. There were staggering unemployment and relief rolls.

Like all other aspects of American life industrial arts "tightened its belt" during the depression. However, there are few evidences that the depression created any degree of real panic among industrial arts educators. School enrollment was increasing, and the tenor of discussion in industrial arts during the early thirties was one of optimism. Chief topics included the future, change, attitudes, and philosophy. Perhaps the discussions were too optimistic, since they seem not to have dealt realistically with problems that involved economic needs.

### The Elements of Change

In 1933 leaders in industrial arts education were looking toward the mid-century and the challenges that the future offered. The future appeared reasonably bright, since the impending war and the problems attendant upon swift technological progress could not be anticipated. Even so, the necessity for industrial arts to adjust with changing conditions was virtually unquestioned. Industrial arts, as one of the practical subjects, had both a place in the educational program and a responsibility to contribute valuably to that program.

Improvement was a general goal, but it could not be achieved in a general way. Much of the anticipated improvement had to come from individual efforts. Meeting the challenge of

---

[50] Milton Clauser, "The Standardization of Manual Training," *Industrial Arts Education*, Vol. VI, No. 8, August 1917, pp. 315-316.

the future required teachers of "more than common ingenuity," instructions that "reflect new modes of teacher preparation," and general educators "who sell our stock in a better market." Homer J. Smith held that progress needed a broad front, backed up by concepts of "goodness" that were known and understood by all industrial arts educators—to the last man.

The challenges of the future had to be seen in terms of certain things to be accomplished, certain attitudes to be held in common, and certain needs to be recognized by the profession. New ways must be developed to acquaint principals and superintendents with the program of industrial arts and its purposes. Industrial arts was not obligated to duplicate industrial processes as found in the factory and other places, but it was obligated to sample and explain such processes.[51]

The values of industrial arts had been "sampled" by relatively few school youths, and a better cross-section of the school population was desired: actually 100 percent of the male enrollment!

If industrial arts is really a function of full development and if our results are as good as we insist that they are, we stand rebuked until every American boy has these advantages regardless of his school connections. Our slogan may well be—industrial arts for every American boy and trade training for carefully selected boys in the number that can be placed.[52]

Did progress in the 1930's improve over the past? Were new objectives and standards created? Let us see.

The status, progress, and public im-

age of industrial arts rested upon the teacher's environment, which was directly related to his efficiency. The call was issued for better selection of teachers and improvement in their quality through higher educational standards. As desiderata these were safe assumptions, but the fundamental intellectual curiosity of individual teachers was personal with each; only the environment of his preparatory years could make lasting impressions upon him. Many times through these years industrial arts educators called attention to the way in which a beginning teacher tended to follow his instructor in methodology—teaching as he was taught. Professional associations appeared to offer the best opportunity of in-service training, to set standards, to develop testing procedures, and to prepare instructional material. But few local organizations had sound objectives for in-service teacher training.

The time spent in any one industrial arts subject varied widely from school to school, state to state, and grade to grade. There were variations in depth of learning. George K. Wells reported a visit with a teacher who had inquired of students what they did and what they had learned the previous year. The boys could not tell him; no definite impressions were left.

The boys had the attitude that the industrial arts shop was a place to do as they pleased. The training institutions must therefore impress the student with the importance of systematic procedure if we are to have standards used.

If we can agree upon objectives and set

[51] Homer J. Smith, "The Challenge of the Future," *American Vocational Association News Bulletin,* Vol. VIII, No. 1, February 1933, p. 28.
[52] *Ibid.,* pp. 28-29.

266

up courses in terms simple enough for the average teacher to comprehend, if the training institutions can train their students in these aims and objectives, if we can develop teacher organizations to promote and study the field, we can set industrial arts on the high plane that it deserves.[53]

Nearly every facet of industrial arts was pictured in a process of change, and shop activity received its share of critical review. The trend was directed toward a greater variety of activity in the shop from day to day and from week to week.

I can't think of anything more boring than going to a class every day and knowing beforehand just exactly what is going to happen. A good industrial teacher, like any other good teacher, should have a dozen arrows in his quiver.[54]

The need for change was a characteristic of the depression years. Actual achievement of the desired changes proceeded slowly and depended almost entirely upon individual desires to respond to the "invitation."

### Attack on Terminology Confusion

As pointed out at the start of this chapter, one consistent trend from the beginning of the industrial education movement has been its struggle with terms and concepts, causing confusion in oral and written communication. Minor skirmishes with this annoyance have occurred from time to time. That it should become an issue at the Cleveland convention of the Western Arts Association in 1929 is not a surprise.

However, some positive action was taken, which was considerably beyond the usual course of events. A section of the Western Arts Association had been known as the "Manual Training Section," and a question was raised concerning the appropriateness of the terminology. A committee was appointed, with William E. Warner as chairman, to look into the matter.

The committee compiled a master word list in which terms were categorized into groups that had some common element, such as terms pertaining to research (assumption, thesis), terms describing a method of teaching (integrated activity), and others. Similarly, criteria were developed to exclude from the list certain terms, such as the names of individuals (Bonser), and terms which were obvious (boy), among others. The process of the research was itself confusing, but in the end the committee managed to come to general agreement concerning definitions, which included descriptive words which were thought to contribute less to the confusion. The definition of industrial arts is chosen as an example.

Industrial arts is one of the *Practical Arts,* a form of general or non-vocational education, which provides learners with experiences, understandings, and appreciations of materials, tools, processes, products and of the vocational conditions and requirements incident generally to the manufacturing and mechanical industries.

These results are achieved through design and construction of useful products in laboratories or shops, appropriately staffed and equipped, supplemented by

---

[53] George K. Wells, "Status, Trends and Outlook of Industrial Arts in the United States," *American Vocational Association News Bulletin,* Vol. VIII, No. 2, May 1933, p. 28.

[54] Homer J. Smith, "Beliefs About Industrial Arts," *Industrial Arts and Vocational Education,* Vol. XXIII, No. 1, January 1934, p. 5.

readings, investigations, discussions, films, visits, reports, and similar activities characteristic of youthful interests and aptitudes in things industrial.

The subject of *Industrial Arts* belongs peculiarly within junior and senior high school areas for such purposes as exploration, guidance, the development of avocational and vocational interests and aptitudes, specific manual abilities, desirable personal-social traits growing out of industrial experiences, ability to choose and use industrial products wisely, all coupled with the aesthetic relationships involved. In general its purposes are *educationally social* rather than *vocationally economic,* although in the senior high school it may increasingly emphasize vocational objectives in a non-legal sense, for certain students.

*Industrial Arts* includes such industrial representations as drawing and design, metal work, wood work, textiles, printing, ceramics, automotives, foods, electricity, and similar units, either as separate offerings or in various combinations common to the "General Shop" or LABORATORY OF INDUSTRIES. [Warner's term.]

The term *laboratory* is more appropriate when the offering is provided upon an experimental or developmental basis, as is commonly done in the junior high school; and the term *shop* may be more appropriate where the work is carried on rather upon the production or economic basis, as may be done in the senior high school.

The term Industrial Arts is generally displacing the historical but narrow term *Manual Training*; and in common usage it has substantially the same significance as the term *Manual Arts*; although *Industrial Arts* emphasizes in addition the all-around arts of industry rather than just manipulative or "manual" aspects of artistic construction implied in the term Manual Arts.[55]

In the definition above, 76 professional terms were used for distinctions either made or implied. The committee suggested that this was further evidence of the need for using words and terms accurately. The committee indicated that members had received the greatest possible benefit from the investigation and felt that every person in the profession should be constantly involved in personal study of terms and terminology in order for general progress to be made.

Another attempt to reduce confusion was the preparation of a chart (on opposite page) showing the conceptual framework in which industrial arts educators viewed the nature of their program. The chart contains more than 60 items and may seem a bit bewildering. Note, however, that it is child-centered in concept.

F. C. Whitcomb explained the chart in part as follows:

"The boy" is made the center of the picture. It is he rather than subject matter that represents the purpose of the school and of teaching. His needs and interests provide the approach to what shall be taught and how it shall be taught. The chart is an interpretation of Practical Arts as general education. It is recognized that Practical Arts represents a large and significant aspect of vocational education, but the chart only sets forth the place of general education in vocational guidance and an intelligent understanding of vocations.[56]

In other words, the chart attempted to place the boy in focus for the teacher, to show that the teacher's whole purpose was related to changes in the boy and not in the material things in the shop.

[55] William E. Warner, Elroy Bollinger, Herbert H. Hutchinson, *The Terminological Investigation,* Western Arts Association, Vol. XVII, No. 2, March 20, 1933, p. 27.

[56] F. C. Whitcomb, "A Broader Outlook," *American Vocational Association Journal and News Bulletin,* Vol. XII, No. 1, February 1937, p. 28.

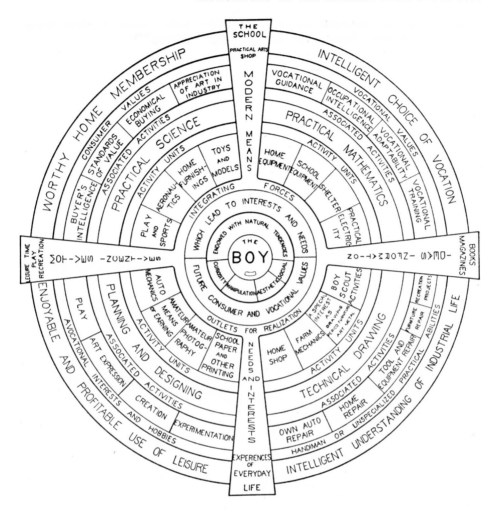

## Examination of Values

The depression did close some schools and it did have an effect upon industrial arts. As mentioned earlier, from one point of view it would appear that educators ignored the depression, because they said so little about it. The most frequent citations were general, and reference was usually made to "the present conditions" or to "present day needs." Presumably this meant the depression and its general effect upon education.

The fact that industrial arts educators devoted much discussion to values, philosophy, and similar topics was not a direct reaction to the depression. There has been a continuous record of such discussions; hence the depressed economic condition seems not to have produced anything unique in this regard. That is to say, an examination of values did occur during the depression, but most likely not because of it. What the depression did do was to influence the emphasis given to certain values. For example, the value of

269

industrial arts as a solution to the problem of excess leisure time was well known prior to the depression. However, "present conditions" were such that this value now seemed especially relevant. Schools were urged to broaden their activity, with the view that leisure, normal or forced, provided opportunities for industrial arts to make additional contributions to the general welfare.[57]

The age of too much leisure time is not around the corner—it is here. The age of sociological and technological change is not an academic fancy of the future—it exists. Leaders in education are doing their best to meet the changed civilization. If the industrial-arts program is as sound and purposeful as its adherents claim, it will meet gladly the challenge of today.[58]

Similarly, search for a working philosophy of industrial arts education has been a familiar theme. The fact of its appearance in papers and discussions during the depression was not as significant as the frequency with which it appeared. It was a part of the continuous effort to keep teachers out of the doldrums and to encourage and motivate them to additional achievement. William L. Hunter, in a heart-to-heart talk on what should be accomplished in and by the school shop, urged teachers to consider fundamental ideas and to move from this base to new achievements. "It takes a much bigger teacher to direct natural inter-

ests than to maintain army discipline." [59]

The shop environment provided desirable conditions for enhancing the growth and development of children, but some teachers were permitting routine to prevent an experimental approach. "It is just as easy to discover an experimental attitude in an industrial-arts laboratory as it is for a prospective visitor to a home to discover a smallpox sign. The one invites you in quite as forcibly as the other tells you to stay out." [60] The challenge of social change brought forth many opportunities for industrial arts to achieve purposes that had been frequently ignored. Whatever the accomplishments, there was considerable talk about themes that go back to Dewey's firm position.

In identifying the values of industrial arts, one writer after another would highlight the fact that the area had primary responsibility for "changes in boys" rather than changes in wood or metal. Certain of the important values were easy to neglect, as Arthur B. Mays noted:

First, there is inherent in the industrial arts experiences the possibility of developing the important intellectual habit of analyzing and planning every undertaking before beginning work, and the supplementary habits of concentration and persistence when once a project is undertaken.
• • •

---

[57] Emerson William Manzer, "Industrial Arts and Leisure," *Industrial Arts and Vocational Education,* Vol. XXII, No. 12, December 1933, pp. 374-377.

[58] Frederick J. Moffitt, "Industrial Arts Meets the Challenge," *Industrial Arts and Vocational Education,* Vol. XXV, No. 3, March 1936, p. 85.

[59] William L. Hunter, "A Philosophy of Industrial-Arts Education," *Industrial Arts and Vocational Education,* Vol. XXVI, No. 10, October 1937, p. 315.

[60] William L. Hunter, "A Philosophy of Industrial-Arts Education," *Industrial Arts and Vocational Education,* Vol. XXVI, No. 11, November 1937, p. 356.

The second value, too often neglected, is that of a genuine appreciation of beauty in design and construction.

• • •

The third of the greatly neglected values in industrial arts education is moral education.[61]

Mays reminded industrial arts teachers that the youth of 1937 needed much assistance in the changing world. The three values—good mental habits, appreciation of beauty in structure and design, and high moral standards and behavior—were required in modern living and could easily be a part of the daily experiences in industrial arts, provided that the teacher would consciously bring them to the fore.

Educators in the field looked with favor upon progressive tendencies in industrial arts, but not to the extent of abandoning the subject matter—an extreme measure which some enthusiasts of progressive education had actually suggested. Nevertheless, the progressive education movement did affect industrial arts. Some of the significant practices or trends were reported as follows. Some were not new, notably the second and third points. However, the list represents a strong bid for a richer program, and makes specific suggestions. Terminology and phrasing reflect both the Dewey philosophy and more sophisticated methods of expression. Note how the expressions compare with reports of the Prosser era.

1. More emphasis upon pupil development and emergent outcomes as evidenced in the objectives which stress attitudes, appreciations, and habits, and less emphasis upon manual skills.

2. A change of emphasis from vocational and prevocational education to general education as the aim of the industrial arts.

3. An increased emphasis upon practical projects in place of abstract exercises and formal models.

4. A greater emphasis upon flexibility, variety, and enrichment of content as evidenced by the growth of the general shop, the use of suggestive plans rather than rigid courses of study, and the increasing number of shop subjects or activities.

5. Less teacher dictation and more pupil initiative and freedom in the selection of projects, and in the choice of materials and methods of carrying the learning units to completion.

6. An increased number of instructional devices to care for individual differences, and to broaden the experiences of the pupils. Such devices include the excursion, movies, instruction sheets, shop manuals, and shop reference books.

7. An increased tendency to correlate shop courses with other courses in order to integrate the pupil's experiences.

8. The use of improved tests and scales for diagnosing, building, and evaluating in the learning process.[62]

Maris M. Proffitt, in a general treatment of the interpretation of industrial arts in American schools, provided a comprehensive image for the mid-1930's.[63] He stressed the contribution of industrial arts to educational values of a general nature and indicated that

---

[61] Arthur B. Mays, "Neglected Values in Industrial Arts," *American Vocational Association Journal and News Bulletin*, Vol. XII, No. 1, February 1937, pp. 60-61.

[62] C. H. Christopherson, "Significant Progressive Education Tendencies in the Industrial Arts," *American Vocational Association Journal and News Bulletin*, Vol. XV, No. 2, May 1940, p. 109.

[63] Maris M. Proffitt, *Industrial Arts—Its Interpretation in American Schools*, U.S. Department of the Interior, Office of Education, Bulletin 1927, No. 34. Washington: Government Printing Office, 1938.

subject matter and experiences were derived from and in tune with contemporary society.

Proffitt and his committee related the program of industrial arts to every facet of public education in which the need for the objectives and typical experiences of industrial arts would find a place in the curriculum: elementary, junior and senior high schools, and adult and higher education. Never before had a treatise been prepared on industrial arts and the school curriculum that was so realistic and practical, and showed such a clear understanding of goal relationships.

### Concepts and Images in the Early 1940's

Again and again industrial arts educators have expressed the wish for a more tenable philosophy on which to base the principles of their field, or for an improved understanding of current philosophy.

Excursions in Principles and Philosophy. Confusion of *principles* (or *policy*) and *philosophy* has always been found in industrial education, as well as in art education, home economics, and other skill fields. More often than not the two terms have been used synonymously. However, it is clear that principles develop from a philosophy. Over the years, as we know, many industrial arts educators have tried their hand at setting forth a philosophy and a set of principles. In 1940 John F. Friese propounded the following list:

1. Learning and developmental experiences in industrial arts, through types of experiences not otherwise available, are essential in the complete social education of every boy in a dominantly industrial democracy.

2. The industrial arts constitute a group of school experiences which embrace the most fundamental procedure in Education: namely, learning through a combination of seeing, hearing, thinking and doing.

3. Industrial arts is a convenient and natural agency for educational correlation.

4. The vehicle of learning, the problem, job, or educational project, is the physical expression of a pupil's educative experiences and growth.

5. Industrial arts provides a ready avenue of self-expression for large numbers of persons who find many other avenues for such experiences closed.

6. Industrial arts is fundamentally and naturally child centered in its concepts and in its practice of methods, subject matter, and control.

7. In industrial arts, as in other school activities, what little carry-over value or transfer of training occurs takes place more as a result of the methods of teaching employed than through the particular significance of subject matter.

8. Industrial arts and vocational industrial education are complementary parts of a complete industrial education—and education based upon important factors of current industrial life and development.

9. The objectives of a particular industrial-arts course or activity must be in harmony with those of the industrial-arts department of which it is a part; the aims of the department in turn with the aims of the junior high school, senior high school or secondary education as a whole; and finally the aims of secondary schools must culminate in recognized contributions to all organized or formal education.

10. The teacher's plan of organization and his control of personnel, equipment, supplies, products, and safety, contribute many of the desirable outcomes of the industrial arts.

11. Industrial arts abounds in natural situations conducive of creative or problem solving.

12. Industrial arts provides a ready and natural agency for a degree of foundational training in industrial versatility.

13. In the teaching of industrial arts,

the teacher is more important than space, equipment and supplies.[64]

Here is a summation for the industrial arts teacher to live by that is reasonably acceptable and reasonably reflective of a total philosophy. Compare with the pupil-centered principles, on page 271.

**Where does industrial arts fit in the system of public education?** Every subject matter area is called on to define and defend its right to a place in the curriculum. The logic of the 1940's continued to hold that industrial arts belonged in the curriculum. Rationales were developed in abundance to support this conclusion. C. S. Van Deusen said of industrial arts that, "It can, and does, develop better understandings of the industrial age and prepares the individual for a place in an industrial society." [65] In general the theme was that industrial arts functioned effectively as a social subject and was part and parcel of the general education of every student "who expects to live with, and use, the products of industry."

One of the "lifelines" in the evolution of industrial arts is that its program has adjusted with changes in the educational format. As new goals, purposes, and values were stressed, industrial arts found identity with the prevailing educational thought. Major historical changes were characterized in 1941 as belonging to five distinct periods.

1. The *exercise period* in which abstract exercises were made for their disciplinary values.

2. The *sloyd period* in which useful articles were made that appealed to the pupil's interests without much regard for their design and beauty.

3. The *arts and crafts period* in which design and artistic expression were stressed rather than tool manipulation.

4. The *industrial period* in which an attempt was made to provide occupational training in the general educational program.

5. The *industrial-arts period* in which a sharp line of demarcation has been drawn between manual activities for general purposes and those for specific occupational training.

The latter has given rise to the development of the "General Shop" and more to the "Laboratory of Industries," which has been introduced by Dr. William E. Warner, of Ohio State University.[66]

It might be reiterated that industrial arts fit into the school program because of the industrial nature of the social order. Methods, activities, and media have changed significantly from early beginnings. One of the more significant changes was that of teacher education in which industrial arts had continually raised requirements.

**Contributions to Functional and General Education.** Literally, it took a long time for industrial arts to get out of the basement; it took even longer before it began to get out of the basement in the minds of academic educators! The problem was in part created and perpetuated by industrial arts teachers themselves, through what might be called "ghetto psychology";

[64] John F. Friese, "Philosophy of Industrial Arts for American Education," *Industrial Arts and Vocational Education*, Vol. XXIX, No. 1, January 1940, pp. 2-4.

[65] C. S. Van Deusen, "Place Program, and Function of Industrial Arts," *Industrial Arts and Vocational Education*, Vol. XXIX, No. 7, September 1940, p. 257.

[66] Heber A. Sotzin, "Industrial Arts in a System of Public Education," *Industrial Arts and Vocational Education*, Vol. XXX, No. 9, November 1941, p. 366.

that is, a tendency to support their subject by reference to whatever imperatives were in vogue, yet keeping the same old program. For example, in the manual training era, when "faculty psychology" was much in the news, manual training was justified as a device to train all of the faculties. Some educators did not think so; nevertheless the claim persisted even though little attempt was made to revise methods and attract a higher type of student.

Changing the minds of the general educators had been in part the purpose of the monograph, *Industrial Arts—Its Interpretation in American Schools,* published by the U.S. Office of Education in 1937. In the 1940's the effort continued. Here is an example of a moderate approach.

Now, if we create the impression which we do not care to do—that industrial arts is a sort of panacea or cure—for all the ills of the secondary school program, we are only going to bring ourselves into disrepute. But, if we can get the secondary school administrator to go along with us on the proposition that industrial arts contributes a great deal to the education of this mass of youngsters, if the industrial arts program will assist 20 or 30 per cent of these youngsters, we are doing our part; we are making a contribution.[67]

The educational goals of the 1940's were expressed frequently in terms of individual development to maximums of ability, success in living, and social adjustment. Leading industrial arts educators viewed their program as a crucible in which the metals of manhood are fired and tempered as a part of all education.

The industrial arts are a vital curriculum area in the general education program and should be treated as such. They are prepared to stand shoulder to shoulder with the other departments of our schools in the attack on and the solution of those problems which challenge public education and should make a unique contribution to the solution of many problems which develop from our complex industrial civilization.[68]

To convince others that industrial arts did valuably contribute to functional and general education, it was necessary to do more than merely insist that such contributions were being made. The literature of the period provides ample evidence that educators were not concerned only with concepts and images, but were motivated to seek positive action.

State Supervision of Industrial Arts. For more than two decades the value of State Supervision, or special consultative services, had been recognized. In 1940, two states, New Jersey and New York, employed full-time state supervisors of industrial arts. In other states a variable amount of assistance was provided in part-time service.[69] However, the movement of the 1940's was definitely toward securing a supervisor of industrial arts in every state. There was little, if any, objection to this move; it was supported wholeheartedly by city supervisors.

In March and April, 1942, William J. Micheels reported a number of

---

[67] Earl L. Bedell, "Contribution of Industrial Arts to a Functional Education," *Industrial Arts and Vocational Education,* Vol. XXX, No. 4, April 1941, p. 142.

[68] James E. Hopkins, "Contribution of Industrial Arts to General Education," *Industrial Arts and Vocational Education,* Vol. XXXII, No. 9, November 1943, p. 375.

[69] Roy G. Fales, "State Supervision of Industrial Arts," *Education,* Vol. CX, No. 9, May 1940, pp. 579-586.

recommendations, based upon comprehensive research of the problem, concerning state supervision. These recommendations are in part as follows:

1. A state supervisor of industrial arts should be appointed in each of the states for the purpose of coordinating the aims and efforts of this particular field of education.

2. It is strongly recommended that national and state-wide groups give of their material and editorial resources for further study, discussion, and clarification of the programs and problems of state supervision of industrial arts.

3. Local, state, and national groups should cooperate in clarifying the type of supervisory relationships which *ought* to exist between the state supervisors of trade and industrial education and industrial-arts teachers.

4. Industrial-arts teachers should be more adequately and more definitely informed by their state departments of education as to the type of supervisory help they can expect from such agencies.

5. It is recommended that state department of education officials make concentrated efforts to promote, establish and visit clubs of industrial-arts teachers in different sections of their states.

6. Each state, now not doing so, should establish a news letter or similar publication for the benefit of industrial arts teachers.

7. It is recommended that further study be made of the semantic propensity of the term state supervisor. [Other terms such as evaluator or co-ordinator had been suggested.]

8. It is recommended that more detailed research be made concerning state supervision of industrial arts.

9. Definite need exists for a careful study of the personal qualities which characterize successful and competent state supervisors who visit industrial arts teachers.

10. The United States Office of Education has shown special interest in industrial-arts education and may well be encouraged to increase its services to this field. It might act as a clearing agency, looking to the establishment of more state supervisory positions and clarifying the functions and relationships of such positions. It might, logically, exert its influence in sponsoring federal aid to this field in view of the fading line of demarcation between the general and vocational aspects of industrial education.[70]

The "fat was in the fire," so to speak, on the issue of state supervision. These moves were practically demanded of every state; attention was called to the imperative elements of state supervision.

## War-Related Activities

A shortage of skilled civilian manpower, so necessary for national defense, developed early in World War II. Solving this problem was obviously more in the realm of vocational education than that of industrial arts. Still, leaders in industrial arts did virtually the same as leaders in every other area of education; that is, they focused their attention upon definite contributions their field could make to the defense of the nation.[71] It is significant that when "the chips are down," when the choice is between national survival and the full preservation of the way of life, it is cold, hard reality that always prevails. High idealism—education for more abundant life, education for leisure, and the like—is all but forgotten.

---

[70] William J. Micheels, "State Supervision of Industrial-Arts Education," *Industrial Arts and Vocational Education*, Vol. XXXI, No. 4, April 1942, p. 157. [See also March issue, pp. 135-138.]

[71] Fred C. Finsterbach, "Industrial Arts in the Defense Program," *Industrial Arts and Vocational Education*, Vol. XXX, No. 3, March 1941, pp. 107-108.

Industrial arts activity centers turned attention to many tasks related directly to defense and the war related interests. Also, teachers left the classrooms and shops by the thousands to serve in the armed and civilian forces directly contributing to war production. The shortage of industrial arts teachers created an emergency situation, a situation that was solved in a variety of ways, but with some emphasis upon "conversion training" and upon recalling retired craftsmen into service.[72]

Did industrial arts change radically because of the entrance of the United States into combat? No, although some teachers did tend to emphasize certain values of industrial arts out of proportion to others, and perhaps did stress projects with a war orientation. But these were emergency conditions; any tendency to emphasize a particular phase of industrial arts was meant only to provide the student with an opportunity to become more aware of the emergency environment, and should not be considered a distortion of essential principles and purposes. Fundamental goals of industrial arts remained constant and prominent throughout the war effort, even though it was important for industrial arts educators to develop the practical relationship of their area to the war.

The total war effort, I believe, will be enhanced by industrial-arts teachers doing what they are equipped by tradition and present circumstances to do, and not by attempting to break into a field that they are not under present circumstances equipped to do. War industries are not asking or expecting our secondary schools to change a program which has been an industrial asset in times of peace. Obviously, if the function of industrial-arts teaching was a vital educational necessity before the present crisis, it is no less so now. It is just as important for *basic* training now as ever. Teachers of industrial arts must keep their perspective, believe in their cause, and stay on the job. It is far easier to make ammunition than it is to make men.[73]

Nevertheless, in response to the natural desire of instructors and students to make a tangible contribution, industrial arts pupils made thousands of articles for the Red Cross, the U.S.O., and the armed services.[74] Many of the achievements were spectacular, as in World War I. For example, model airplanes were needed by the armed services for recognition training. A large percentage of the schools of the nation took up the challenge and were given appropriate recognition for their service in the model airplane program. "One boy, Joe Bashore of Wyandotte, Michigan has made one each of the fifty types of model planes requested by the Navy, and has been given the rank of Admiral Aircraftsman."[75]

The model aircraft project continued with about 6,500 schools participating. Thousands of planes were shipped to receiving centers for inspection. Yet,

---

[72] G. H. Silvius, "Intensive Training to Provide Industrial-Arts Teachers During the War," *Industrial Arts and Vocational Education*, Vol. XXXI, No. 8, October 1942, pp. 321-322.

[73] Steward Scrimshaw, "Responsibilities of Industrial Arts in the Present Crisis," *Industrial Arts and Vocational Education*, Vol. XXXII, No. 2, February 1943, pp. 51-52.

[74] Louis V. Newkirk, "Industrial-Arts Education in the War Effort," *Industrial Arts and Vocational Education*, Vol. XXXII, No. 3, March 1943, pp. 89, 91-92.

[75] J. C. Wright, "Model Aircraft Project to Continue," *AVA Journal and News Bulletin*, Vol. XVII, No. 3, September 1942, p. 134.

although model building was adaptable to almost any part of the industrial arts program, instruction limited to the making and flying of model airplanes was not in keeping with the principles of the field. Students learned, in addition, to understand principles of flight, to know what was meant by terms such as lift, drag, and thrust, and how these forces influenced the performance of the model. In this manner a project in keeping with the war effort became a valuable educational experience.[76]

Follow-up studies disclosed that the training was sufficiently thorough that young men who went into the civilian forces were not only able to hold a responsible position but to advance rapidly—a tribute to their industrial arts instruction.[77] The studies also vindicated to some extent the broadened program of industrial arts, because the reason for advancement was not limited to skill development: Work habits, attitude, use of instructional materials, team work, and a variety of other values were concerned.

Ericson reported an interesting, informal study of industrial arts during the war which indicated that industrial arts projects were generally representative of the opportunities and demands of the all-out war effort.[78] He also noted a significant increase in technical and specialized work that in some cases paralleled what was offered in vocational education, but he believed this was temporary and due largely to the war.

The problem of finding enough teachers was even more critical; it constituted a definite threat to the program. Many industrial arts leaders were giving attention to post-war plans and to the possible changes in objectives or direction that industrial arts might take after the war. Some of the leaders consulted by Ericson were apprehensive that the emphasis upon engineering and industrial accomplishments would make the problem of recruiting of industrial teachers difficult after the war.

One of the noticeable changes in industrial arts due to the war activity was the decided increase in the enrollment of girls. In Chicago the number increased from 15 in 1939 to 25,000 in 1943! Another change was apparent in the field of guidance. The necessity of emphasizing certain occupational areas made it possible for the students to sample occupational life in a variety of situations and thus to establish their likes and dislikes prior to seeking employment.[79] To the industrial arts curriculum were added new courses which were evidence of the war-related change. Not only related aeronautics, but electronics and power were given direct impetus.

[76] Gordon O. Wilber, "Industrial Arts Can Help Keep 'Em Flying," *AVA Journal and News Bulletin*, Vol. XVII, No. 3, September 1942, pp. 139-140.

[77] R. H. Roberts, "Relation of Industrial Arts to War Industries," *Industrial Arts and Vocational Education*, Vol. XXXII, No. 3, March 1943, pp. 101-104.

[78] E. E. Ericson, "Wartime Developments in Industrial Arts Education," *AVA Journal and News Bulletin*, Vol. XVIII, No. 3, September 1943, pp. 13-14.

[79] R. H. Roberts, "Wartime Emphasis on Industrial Production and Its Effect on the Industrial Arts Program," *Industrial Arts and Vocational Education*, Vol. XXXIII, No. 4, April 1944, pp. 139-142.

277

## A New Day in Post-War Reconstruction

It was inevitable that war-related experiences would vastly influence post-war programs of industrial arts education, evoking higher standards from elementary school through senior high school and sometimes even suggesting entirely new programs.[80] Uncertain though the future was, the changes suggested for industrial arts were sufficiently varied to provide a means of adjustment to whatever conditions came to prevail.[81] How was one to improve industrial arts? As in the past, recommendations started with improving the teachers! A prescription for potential industrial arts teachers, from a supervisor's point of view, suggested that they should have:

1. The same general education required of other teachers, so that all of them will have a common meeting place in their thinking and discussions.

2. At least a minor in mathematics and science, so that industrial arts and these allied subjects may be closely coordinated.

3. Training in art and design applied to industrial arts.

4. A wide general shop experience with much experimenting and designing with new materials and machines.

5. Training that will develop the desire and ability to experiment, to try new materials and techniques. (This is not to be confused with tinkering.)

6. Training in sociology to make them sensitive to the industrial and social trends and needs of their community.

7. Work experience in industry; if possible, in their major fields; but in any event, work experience. This work experi-ence should be a part of their college requirements, with placement and supervision by college coordinators.

8. A sound basic training in vocational guidance.

9. A thorough course in general and industrial safety practices.[82]

Compare these recommendations with those in the early manual training movement. Note similarities which suggest the never-ending struggle to "say things better."

In December, 1943, the American Vocational Association appointed an official planning committee in industrial arts—with nationwide interests in mind—to operate under the direction of the AVA Vice President for Industrial Arts, who at that time was Arthur B. Mays. The chairman of the planning committee was E. E. Ericson.

The Industrial Arts Planning Committee made its firts report at the AVA convention in Philadelphia in December, 1944. Recommendations were as follows:

1. The issuing of a pamphlet presenting a brief statement of the values and the logical position of industrial arts offerings in the general education program for the various age levels in public education.

2. A study of curriculum revision for teacher-education programs in industrial arts and a plan for recruiting promising candidates for prospective teachers in the field of industrial arts.

3. A study of problems pertaining to the need of state supervision in industrial arts and suggested procedures for state supervision.

4. A study of aircraft education in in-

---

[80] Arthur B. Mays, "A New Industrial Arts for a New Day," *Industrial Arts and Vocational Education*, Vol. XXXII, No. 10, December 1943, pp. 402-404.

[81] Dean M. Schweickhard, "Industrial Education a Reconstructive Force," *Industrial Arts and Vocational Education*, Vol. XXXIII, No. 1, January 1944, pp. 1-4.

[82] Verne L. Pickens, "Industrial Arts in the Post-War Era," *American Vocational Journal and News Bulletin*, Vol. XVIII, No. 1, February 1943, p. 15.

dustrial arts with some proposal concerning teacher preparation for teaching industrial arts aircraft work.[83]

Subcommittees were assigned to investigate the four problems and to prepare recommendations for publication.

Aviation education had frequently been discussed by industrial arts leaders because they sensed that the air age had arrived and that industrial arts needed to determine the extent to which the new age should be represented to the instructional program. In Los Angeles, Claude E. Nihart, Director of Vocational and Practical Arts in the Los Angeles City Schools, reported the development of aviation mechanics shops in industrial arts programs in a number of high schools. The aims of these programs were:

1. To develop an active interest in and understanding of the broad field of aviation, with its vocational opportunities.
2. To provide for a practical type of experience in aviation mechanics for all students who are interested in aviation.
3. To give training in the use of tools, materials, and processes peculiar to aviation mechanics.
4. To offer preliminary training for those students who later intend to enroll for approved vocational training courses in aircraft mechanics and aircraft engines.
5. To provide a working knowledge of aviation mechanics for students who expect to fly military, commercial, or private aircraft.
6. To provide experience in aviation mechanics for those students who intend to study aeronautical engineering in technical schools and universities.[84]

The program had won wide accept-

ance in California and had the cooperation of the California State Department of Education and the Aviation Education Service of the Civil Aeronautics Administration.

The growth and development of industrial arts during the post-war years included many interesting features such as "Industrial Arts on Wheels." In Kern County, California, an itinerant shop on wheels made visits to ten different schools, providing a half-day of industrial arts instruction for students who would otherwise be denied such opportunities. The shop was fitted out on a trailer, hauled by a station wagon, and included a jig saw, jointer, wood lathe, drill press, and a chest of small tools and materials. (Illustration on following page.)

Sturdy bench tops along the sides of the trailer afford work space for small classes in rural schools. Vises fitted to the bench tops grip the work, electric motors power the machinery.

At mid-morning the dozen younger boys reluctantly surrender their tools and bench places to a group of older pupils. All morning the air is filled with the rasp of saws and the hum of motors.

At noon the tools go back to their appointed places. Until next week, the industrial arts instructor rolls away to meet an afternoon class at another rural school miles away.

This Kern County Rural Schools experiment in a traveling shop program has evolved from a program to encourage industrial arts in small schools. . . .[85]

Some schools became enthusiastic about the program, purchased tools of

---

[83] "Planning Committee Reports," *American Vocational Journal*, Vol. XX, No. 1, January 1945, p. 31.

[84] Claude E. Nihart, "For Air Age Fledglings," *American Vocational Journal*, Vol. XX, No. 3, March 1945, pp. 36-37.

[85] D. Dale Easter, "Industrial Arts on Wheels," *American Vocational Journal*, Vol. XX, No. 8, October 1945, p. 17.

their own, and investigated the possibility of employing a full-time industrial arts teacher.

In general, the post-war period was characterized by increased attention to the expansion of the industrial arts program, by a rededication to the objectives of industrial arts, and a realignment of industrial arts to the general education program.[86] The words *modern* and *comprehensive* were frequently used in oral and written presentations of the immediate post-war era, indicating an attempt to bring subject matter and teachers up to date and to disclaim any previous attachment to narrowness in either fact or theory.

### Into the Space Age

Industrial arts was no different from other areas of education in its new attempts to evaluate and define its purpose, determine its direction, and adjust its course in the most effective manner possible. But industrial arts checked upon itself continuously with a persistence and determination that may have been unusual. A concerted front in the educational world was obviously important: Certain standards needed to be reached and certain understandings shared by all industrial arts educators. It was a case of adjustment by adding the new concepts without losing the proven values of the old; and it was a case of interpretation and reinterpretation of principles, purposes, objectives, and goals. In a sense it was a problem of professional in-service training concerning fundamental elements.

It was probable that a majority of industrial arts educators held the objectives of industrial arts to be essen-

[86] Arthur B. Mays, "Needed Emphasis in Industrial Arts," *Industrial Arts and Vocational Education*, Vol. XXV, No. 7, September 1946, pp. 270-281.

tially the same as the objectives of general education. They identified their work in terms of broader educational aspects. The school shop or laboratory was an educational center where students could learn with greater understanding the meanings of their industrial environment, including both social and material aspects. But in order to achieve more, instructors needed clearer understanding of their teaching aims.

In the fall of 1946, Louis V. Newkirk undertook to identify the teaching objectives of industrial arts. In his view the eight primary aims were to:

- Develop the ability to plan and build projects using a variety of tools and construction materials in a workmanlike manner.
- Give experiences that will increase understanding of modern industry and that will lay the foundation for and help determine vocational interests.
- Develop the ability to read and make working drawings, charts and graphs.
- Develop the ability to recognize quality and design in the products of industry.
- Develop the ability to maintain and service in a safe and efficient manner the common products of industry.
- Provide an objective medium for expression in mathematics, science, language, arts, and social science.
- Develop an interest in crafts as a valuable medium for creative expression in leisure time.
- Give experiences that will develop social understanding and the ability to work effectively with others as a leader or as a member of a group.[87]

The nature of the emphasis upon these general teaching aims would vary from place to place, from one grade level to another, and ultimately would be dependent upon the students themselves.

Industrial arts educators felt that the industrial arts gave emphasis and importance to other school subjects. This required not only an extraordinary insight into planning, experimenting, investigating, organizing, and evaluating, but also appropriate arrangements for fundamental activities.

These fundamental activities should include:

Teaching and improving upon basic skills common to each area; democratically establishing the regulations to which all are expected to conform and which are to govern routine affairs of working in the laboratory; making certain pupils are learning about raw materials; providing opportunities each semester for individual projects, for small-group projects, and for class projects employing quantity production techniques; and by acquainting pupils with trade and industrial practices and products through the use of various media of communication.[88]

The changes in other areas of education could provide sources for new effort. For example, Arthur B. Mays could see in the expansion of the vocational-industrial program—at the upper levels of the high school and into the post-high school area—a corresponding opportunity for expansion of industrial arts in the junior high school program. Also new materials and techniques which were introduced in abundance after World War II demanded closer relationships with chemistry and physics. "Indeed, there are

[87] Louis V. Newkirk, "Teaching Aims of Industrial Arts," *American Vocational Journal*, Vol. XXI, No. 10, December 1946, pp. 12-13.
[88] J. Osborne Johnson, "A Formula for Industrial Arts," *American Vocational Journal*, Vol. XXI, No. 8, October 1946, p. 21.

now present areas in the curriculum where it is difficult to determine where physics leaves off and industrial arts begin," Mays observed.[89] These changes called for better industrial arts teachers in the future—better from every point of view. It was a challenge for teacher educators to grasp the full situation and integrate newer ideas into their programs.

This all means that greater demands will be made upon the intelligence, originality, knowledge, and skill of industrial arts teachers than ever in the history of this field of study. The brightest and best boys in high school shop courses should be encouraged to prepare to become industrial arts teachers. The future is bright indeed for this subject but the price of success grows ever greater and the demands on ability constantly more exacting.[90]

**State Supervision**

As mentioned previously, the growth of industrial arts in the schools needed state leadership. Therefore, leaders had directed strong emphasis toward state supervision to "unify the purposes, interests and practices of the teachers of industrial arts, most of whom normally have little contact with their fellow teachers of the same subject."[91] Such state leadership could develop common objectives and clearer definitions of subject matter. Roy G. Fales held that industrial arts could not exercise its fundamental general education responsibilities, and at the same time provide a foundation for vo-

cational education, without leadership in the form of a supervisor attached to the state department of education.

There was no doubt whatsoever of the value of state supervision: experience had shown that the quality of programs—and the quantity—always increased with good supervision. In the original draft of the vocational bill S. 619, later passed by the seventy-ninth Congress as the George-Barden Act, 1946, a provision had been included to authorize the appropriation of funds for state supervision of industrial arts. However, prior to the final passage of the Act, an item for supervision of industrial arts and a number of other items were deleted, and the burden of financing state supervision was left to the individual states.

Development of supervision increased at a rapid pace after World War II, with special supervisors appearing on the educational scene for subject matter areas that had not previously been included. Token supervision had been given industrial arts at the state level in various forms, usually associated with another area of education. This pattern was not successful, and many industrial educators shared the belief of Chris Groneman: "The industrial arts teacher is entitled to a clear-cut program of supervision by a specialist in his own field."[92] Noting that the selection of a statewide supervisor of industrial arts required careful consideration, Grone-

---

[89] Arthur B. Mays, "New Demands Upon Industrial Arts," *American Vocational Journal*, Vol. XXI, No. 10, December 1946, p. 32.

[90] *Ibid.*, p. 32.

[91] Roy G. Fales, "State Supervision for Industrial Arts," *American Vocational Journal*, Vol. XX, No. 3, March 1945, p. 48.

[92] Chris Groneman, "State Supervision for Industrial Arts," *American Vocational Journal*, Vol. XXI, No. 10, December 1946, p. 15.

man suggested some of the general attributes of a good supervisor:

The State supervisor of industrial arts must:

- Know the objectives and the purposes of the statewide educational system and the industrial arts field.
- Be constantly aware of changing policies which may affect the field.
- Be practical and tactful in that he needs to know and coordinate the desires of his supervisors and his constituency.
- Keep in touch with other supervisors or members of the state staff and know the programs they are planning.
- Have a knowledge of equipment and tools—kinds, sizes, and appropriateness for specific programs.
- Have general information on materials, uses, and applications for particular localities.
- Be acquainted with supervisors in other states, recognize their problems, and be willing to exchange ideas.
- Be able to recommend tests and measurements, give advice on how tests should be given, know the most satisfactory types, and assist teachers in formulating worth-while results from tests.
- Be recognized as a professional leader within the state and be in a position to give advice and counsel for statewide and district conventions.
- Be capable of lecturing at important meetings for industrial arts, vocational education, general education, and leaders in industry.
- Participate in national policy forming meetings, programs, association and convention sessions.
- Maintain a record system of all teachers and be able to make recommendations when vacancies exist.[93]

There were other qualifications that might receive consideration, but any state with a supervisor who met the above qualifications would indeed be fortunate.

## Criticism

Undeniably, some remarkably good things were happening in industrial arts. Courses were more widely taught than ever, and teachers were increasingly better qualified. The casual observer might have felt that the progress made was the only true measure. Virgil Volla, Supervisor of Industrial Arts, in Los Angeles, was not a casual observer; he wanted to look at the entire program, not just the part that looked pretty. "Industrial arts should be the richest subject in the curriculum," he said, "but by and large, from top to bottom, prestige, recognition, consideration, and support are lacking."[94] Volla was well aware of the good points of the program, but he knew that the inadequacies of industrial arts would not go away by simply ignoring them; failure to do something about them would be disastrous. (What he actually said was that it would relegate industrial arts to the fate of the wooden Indian!)

Volla recalled that some educational groups had already identified the "4 F's" of industrial arts: (1) failure to define objectives, (2) failure to provide real leadership, (3) failure to do a real training and in-service training job, and (4) failure to establish standards of facilities and teaching. Despite the evidence of progress, many other indictments could be made against industrial arts: negligible or

---

[93] *Ibid.*, p. 16.

[94] Virgil Volla, "Will Industrial Arts Survive?" *American Vocational Journal,* Vol. XXI, No. 10, December 1946, p. 23.

wholly inadequate offerings; industrial arts taught on a vocational basis; concentration of efforts in some schools entirely upon low-level-of-ability students; misunderstanding of terminology; lack of prestige and recognition; and a host of others. Volla was not discouraged, but he did feel that the profession needed to adopt a more wholesome attitude and needed, more pertinently, active performance to rid itself of those things which prevented the program from shining with full brilliance in the school world.

A strong reply from William E. Caswell singled out some of the gains in industrial arts as more characteristic. The progress from an extra-curricular activity to the accepted status of an essential subject was alone sufficient evidence of remarkable achievement. As for its failures, Caswell offered a perennial argument: school administrators did not understand industrial arts as they should. "It seems there would be a better appreciation of the objectives and problems of the practical phases of education," he said, "if academic teacher education included a minimum requirement in industrial education." [95]

The polarity in the thinking of large numbers of industrial arts educators is represented in this example of charge and rebuttal. On the one hand, Volla directed his attention to areas in which gains were small or non-existent, and placed the burden of responsibility for improving the situation upon the shoulders of industrial arts educators themselves. Caswell, on the other hand,

looking to the brighter side, urged further progress based upon accomplished gains, and singled out as the most urgent of conditions to be remedied the failure of school administrators to understand the program. One may assume, however, that Caswell would have agreed with Volla that the initiative rested with industrial arts educators, as it is unlikely for other groups suddenly to become converted to a field on their own initiative.

### Improving Instruction

If the development of industrial arts education can be said to have a single concept or theme running throughout its history, a strong case could be made for the theme "Improving Instruction." This aspect of industrial arts was viewed from every angle. Most of the reviewers had practical suggestions drawn from their experience as teachers and supervisors. From a large field of knowledge it was necessary for the teacher to select important elements that matched the child's experience and ability to use these elements in instruction. The possibilities of capitalizing upon the exploratory and guidance features of industrial arts were enormous. Yet no straight line of objectives had been set.

Teachers must determine in their own mind what they are exploring: Is it the boy? Is it industrial possibilities? What is this exploration for? It should be definitely for the purpose of giving boys and girls a background for their proper educational choice. [96]

One of the prime assets of good in-

---

[95] William E. Caswell, "Promoting Industrial Arts," *American Vocational Journal*, Vol. XXII, No. 2, February 1947, p. 10.

[96] Frank C. Moore, "Improving Instruction in Industrial Arts," *American Vocational Journal*, Vol. XXII, No. 5, May 1947, p. 7.

struction was keeping good records and using these records in terms of the potential possibilities of the students. Correct usage of tools was imperative. Some instruction about the material used, the history, manufacture, limitations, and substitutes were all legitimate aspects of good industrial arts. Care of the machines in the shop could not be neglected. The home of the student was an important factor in building relationships with the school program of industrial arts; hobbies in the home were potentially useful in strengthening this relationship. There were numerous possibilities of developing general educational goals; but the teacher had to work hard in seeking and helping to establish the appropriate environment for such learning to take place. Much of the improvement of instruction depended upon method. Only in a well-organized class—one, for example, in which the instructor had developed methods of determining the actual results of instruction—would the fundamental purposes of industrial arts be achieved.

The guidance function of industrial arts, particularly vocational guidance, has always been somewhat of a controversial issue. Traditionally, the teacher has been seen as occupying the most desirable position to function in some aspects of guidance, but little evidence appears in the historical record to indicate that this function has been fulfilled. Because the environment of industrial arts lends itself ideally to opportunities for guidance, one might expect that teachers would look forward with anticipation to locating and utilizing guidance opportunities. Possibly the reason for not doing so is that generally teachers do not recognize among traditional activities in industrial arts those most conducive to promoting the goals of guidance. Stanley J. Pawelek, in 1948, suggested that the instructor:

- Emphasize the dignity of industrial occupations in group discussions, lectures, and reports of students.
- Make field trips to industrial plants and business concerns.
- Show movies and slides of industrial and business occupations.
- Assign individual student reports about professions, trades and other callings. Include items such as income, hours, hazards, retirement, tenure, legal regulations, promotional routes, etc.
- Study legislation affecting management and labor, young workers, unions, etc.
- Discuss the demand for certain types of workers in your community and other communities. Include professions.
- Arrange lectures by local professional men, laborers, merchants, etc.
- Show how important a part a high school education plays in going on to remunerative employment.
- Discuss the value in later life of the courses the students are now studying.
- Discuss the value of such items as dress, appearance, personality and character traits, in living a satisfying life.
- Discuss the advantages and disadvantages of teaching industrial arts and teaching in general.
- Utilize various industrial exhibits in stimulating interest in those industries.
- Use bulletin board for displaying interesting guidance materials.
- Secure and study copies of the many available charts and booklets describing the various occupational pursuits.
- Have individual students report on the work their fathers do.
- Keep constantly alert for evidence of special aptitudes and abilities that certain students possess—or do not possess. Take occasional opportunity to discuss their ambitions with them personally and privately.

• Study each pupil thoroughly and become well informed of his background, interest, and abilities so you can counsel him wisely if occasion demands.[97]

Industrial arts teachers were already including many of these suggestions in their programs—it would have been difficult to ignore them. But Pawelek stressed their vocational guidance value and suggested that, in following through with them, the teacher should be more conscious of their significance. Pawelek did not include better use of the project in his list. This, too, has much guidance value.

### The Many Faces of Industrial Arts

The fact that industrial arts is not a single-goal activity allows it to fit the many needs of individuals and groups; and the many faces of industrial arts show vividly in the historical record. One of the frequently discussed functions is related to recreation.

An article that appeared in 1948 suggested that there are five functions of industrial arts in a well-planned recreation program.[98] (1) The industrial arts department acts as a "Central Agency" for recreation by fostering projects; for example, suggesting a model shop that could be duplicated in the home. Industrial arts would in general become a center of activity related to recreation in the home. (2) The second function was related to the "out of school hours of children." The crafts would be well adapted to this function. (3) The third function was related to activities of "children during the summer months." This function could have all of the aspects of a summer school but would be highly motivating and of specialized interest to individuals. (4) The fourth function was related to coordinating with "social agencies" in their programs for youth and leisure time activities. Industrial arts teachers could not only provide leadership, but some of the teachers in training could participate in real situations as a part of their class preparation. (5) The fifth function of industrial arts was related to the "adult recreational activities." This was adaptable either to formal classes or to a club arrangement.

Another face of industrial arts was related to aiding the handicapped. The record of industrial arts brings to light many instances of the significant role industrial arts can play in the readjustment of students to normal activities. Handicaps, such as the loss of an arm, are hardships difficult to overcome, yet perseverance and a strong desire on the part of the handicapped student can lead to successful accomplishments. Tools and equipment take on special significance: the vise becomes another arm, for example.

An interview with an arm amputee disclosed the following attitudes and suggestions:

1. The creation and building of projects in the shop proves that, with a little extra time and patience, the handicapped can do as well in shop as the other students.

2. The skills developed in the shop

---

[97] Stanley J. Pawelek, "The Guidance Function of Industrial Arts," *American Vocational Journal*, Vol. XXIII, No. 1, January 1948, p. 15.

[98] Lynne C. Monroe, "Recreation—An Industrial Arts Function," *American Vocational Journal*, Vol. XXIII, No. 3, March 1948, pp. 18-19.

program help the handicapped students to gain confidence to face and defeat obstacles that may come up in the future.

3. The shop program teaches him many complicated processes and gives him experiences that he can use in his everyday life.

4. It aids him in obtaining a feeling of self-sufficiency and proves to him that he does not always have to rely on others.

5. Above all, industrial arts gave this handicapped youth a desire to become a well-rounded, well-adjusted student.[99]

Teaching for better use of leisure in adulthood and old age is one of the perennial values of industrial arts. Retired persons frequently fall back upon previous industrial arts experiences as a means of gaining the satisfaction of achievement. The arts and crafts have therapeutic value for thousands who have become victims of that accident of chronology—retirement.

One only has to experience the great satisfaction which comes from *carving* in leather, or *using the potter's wheel,* or perhaps *in making a copper bowl,* or as Dr. George Cutten, formerly president of Colgate University, *pounding silver bars into silverware,* to know that the completion of the project, not its monetary value, is the thing that is pertinent, [and to learn of] the deep satisfactions that come from the *doing,* the *creating.*[100]

### Professionalization of Industrial Arts

In one form or another the professionalization of industrial arts teaching has formed a significant part of the growth and development in the field.

In the space age, industrial arts needed new leaders and needed them in greater quantity; it needed new books and other publications that would be the product of experience tempered with considered judgment. Research was needed in all forms and on almost all topics related to industrial arts. DeWitt Hunt felt that an organization of the faculty members of teacher education institutions of industrial arts was imperative. He suggested the name "The American Council on Industrial Arts Teacher Education" as appropriate for the organization, and urged that one of its objectives be the publication of a yearbook.[101]

Hunt also suggested that a wholesale movement toward advanced degrees, at least through the Master's, was imperative. Increased quality and quantity of state and local supervision was also necessary. Included in his suggestions was the development of "membership mindedness": attendance at national, state, and local conventions was evidence of professionalization.

The American Industrial Arts Association, founded in 1939, moved forward with renewed drive after World War II to increase its membership and to be concerned generally with the professionalization of the field. A new constitution was proposed and adopted in 1949-1950 that did much to regularize an orderly movement toward professionalization.[102]

[99] Harry A. Sturges, "Industrial Arts for the Handicapped," *Industrial Arts and Vocational Education,* Vol. XLI, No. 8, October 1952, p. 256.

[100] Golden Romney, "Teaching for Leisure in Adulthood and Old Age," *Industrial Arts and Vocational Education,* Vol. XLII, No. 2, February 1953, p. 32.

[101] DeWitt Hunt, "Professionalization of Industrial Arts Teaching," *American Vocational Journal,* Vol. XXIII, No. 8, October 1948, pp. 9-10. (Note: Both of these ideas were developed. The ACIATE was founded in 1950 and the first yearbook was issued in 1952.)

[102] "Revision of Constitution," *The Industrial Arts Teacher,* Vol. X, No. 1, October 1950, pp. 7-10.

## Industrial Arts and the Dynamism of Space

The social, the economic, the scientific, the artistic, the citizenship, and the exploratory aspects of industrial arts are being taught today in many places much better than was ever envisaged by the industrial-arts philosopher of a decade ago and they are being taught by, of all persons, those who are qualified to teach them.[103]

The history of industrial arts has been a history of adjustment to socio-economic conditions in an educational environment. The tendency has been to assess continuously the present, to find its implications for teaching industrial arts, and to dip "into the future as far as the eye could see." On the one hand this tendency has produced an industrial arts which is dynamic and which seeks to attach itself to the highly honored element of value currently in vogue. On the other hand it has produced a reasonably "satisfied" group of educators who move with caution into the unknown of the future. The tug of war between the "ultra" progressive and the "moderately" progressive has kept industrial arts in motion, producing along the way only a minimum of hysteria.

In one sense the space age challenged the right of industrial arts to exist. At the same time industrial arts educators could see many opportunities to enhance the purposes and motivations of the space age through their program. It was the one area of secondary education that, without much revision, could immediately assume a space age orientation. First, the field was closer to industry than was any other part of the general curriculum:

Industrial arts is a study of the dominant factor of our modern civilization—industry; as such, industrial arts is an integral part of modern general education. The industrial-arts student is concerned with tools, materials, and processes; the accumulation and application of information about things technical and mechanical; the understanding and use of principles of design fabrication, processing and production; and the development of skills in the use of hand and machine tools and materials representative of industry in the broadest sense.[104]

Second, it was a fact that satellites were not put into orbit by pure science and mathematics alone. A large number of persons with skilled hands, and with scientific and mathematical minds, were required to make theoretical operation a practical reality. Industrial arts education helped select and motivate the mechanic-technician.

While the current hurrahing for science and mathematics is going on, let us be alert in pointing out that shops are basically laboratories of applied science and mathematics. The potential for teaching and learning that is inherent in our shop facilities has never been fully recognized or utilized. It is true that the conventional way in which we have used these facilities has done little to prove their real potential. For this reason we must be the first to show both the desire and the ability to break away from some of our ideas and actions.[105]

---

[103] S. L. Coover, "Industrial Arts, Past, Present, and Future," *Industrial Arts and Vocational Education*, Vol. XLIII, No. 1, January 1954, p. 7.

[104] Maurice F. Richards, "Sputnik Education and Industrial Arts," *Industrial Arts and Vocational Education*, Vol. XLVII, No. 7, September 1958, p. 214.

[105] Clarence Sparks, "Industrial Education in the Wake of the Satellites," *Industrial Arts and Vocational Education*, Vol. XLVIII, No. 2, February 1959, p. 38.

Industrial arts projects took a turn toward emphasis upon space age values. The test of the contribution seemed to lie in the relative emphasis placed upon the mathematics-science element which had always been present in the curriculum. Projects illustrating scientific principles in the space age were advocated as a part of the modern perspective.[106]

The movement toward restructuring science and mathematics in the curriculum was a definite threat to subjects with less of a foothold. Whether or not industrial arts maintained a place in the space-age curriculum depended largely upon the teacher.[107]

What was obviously needed was more rather than less industrial arts for more students, both boys and girls. Industrial arts teachers had to emphasize (1) the academic standards of the program and (2) the many opportunities for challenging activities in the shop program. Inherent in industrial arts was an untapped opportunity to make the "solids" of education important and valuable to most students.

In a variety of ways industrial arts attempted to meet the challenge of the new era. The term "putter work" induced attention to better educational projects. Teachers studied their programs in challenging ways.[108] Attention was given to *understanding* previous knowledge of objectives, standards, and techniques. Stress was given to written material, homework, and the application of mathematics and science. In turn, industrial and space oriented activities influenced state and local curriculum guides. Reappraisals of the scope of industrial arts led to the view that, "Our program is one which presents a challenge to the most gifted student, provides a liberal education for the average student, yet may be adjusted to fit the needs of the slow learner."[109]

There is evidence to support the contention that industrial arts provides a far better environment for the teaching of general science and mathematics than is presently true of these general courses in the junior high school. Most important, experimental manipulation reinforces knowledge of electronic and mechanical technology. The orientation of industrial arts is more toward the student, the parent, the community, and the general social group than is the orientation of pure science and mathematics; at best, in the junior high school, these subjects have allegiances only to future disciplines.

The space-age of industrial arts provides a fertile field for the testing of hypotheses such as the above.

## Summary

One of the striking aspects of the historical background of industrial arts is its mere continued growth. Despite obstacles that from time to time have threatened its right to inclusion in the

---

[106] It is interesting to note that Woodward's projects in the 1870's were primarily for the purpose of illustrating scientific principles.

[107] Lawrence S. Wright, "Space-Age Industrial Arts," *Industrial Arts and Vocational Education*, Vol. XLVIII, No. 8, October 1959, pp. 223-224.

[108] "A Teachers' Declaration for Space-Age Industrial Arts," *Industrial Arts and Vocational Education*, Vol. L, No. 1, January 1961, pp. 12-14.

[109] *Ibid.*, p. 14.

curriculum, industrial arts has managed to grow. Actually it has seemed to profit from controversial experiences. While there is evidence that might seem to support the opinion that the appeal of the traditional curricular content of industrial arts is sub-educational, it is even more apparent that the field has had as its champions men of superb integrity and high purpose; men who never learned to understand failure—it didn't exist as a dominant element in their lives; they were able to profit even from their less successful experiences.

From 1872 onward, the major values claimed have been educational, intellectual, and general. These values have survived the manual training and manual arts periods and are found to be strong and compelling through the industrial arts period. Throughout all three major periods of industrial arts, its most troublesome aspect has seemed to be its vocational significance. Yet no matter what attitude is assumed or what course of action is taken, vocational significance persists. All attempts to remove this very real attribute have failed. It has been frequently ignored, and in 1917 it was even transferred to trade and industrial education; still it remains. Many students have found vocational values in industrial arts that have carried them into successful careers.

Nevertheless, the traditional and acknowledged general values are unquestionably the major strength of industrial arts. Industrial arts as a vehicle for achieving general values had many dramatic periods in its history, perhaps the most dramatic of all being the Bird House Era. Bird house projects epitomized good relationships of school and community, of student and parent; they enhanced integration of industrial arts with other school subjects, instructor and student rapport, and working relationships among students. The seasonal appeal of the bird house continued more than three decades.

During the depression of the thirties industrial arts made gains in its study of values and showed real profit from self-examination. Changes and adjustments were made because of evidence that signified the need for redirection. Consistency and appropriateness of industrial arts within the general framework of education has been achieved largely because of continued concern for these values, and, sparked by compelling personalities, industrial arts has never been afraid to challenge its own existence. It has grown significantly through these challenges.

Adjustment of industrial arts in terms of requirements of technology and the space age has followed its familiar theme of self-examination. Perhaps the most significant reason for continued successful adjustment of industrial arts has been the primacy of the "boy" as the central theme: the boy as an individual, the boy as a member of a social group, the boy whose interests transcend localism and extend to international and interstellar environments.

## Recall Questions

1. What are some of the dominant influences on industrial arts from World War I through World War II?

2. In what ways did the concepts and images of industrial arts of the 1940's compare with any earlier period?

3. Upon what basis was the push toward state supervision made?

4. What has been the historical relationship between the general educational values of industrial arts and its vocational significance?

5. Justify the persistence of the bird-house project. Why has this project been abandoned in the contemporary period?

## Research Questions

1. Examine the actual growth and development of industrial arts in your state and compare these figures with the total national growth and development of industrial arts. Account for any periods of sudden change of enrollment by comparison with educational, economic, social, or political developments in your state.

2. Prepare a short review of the rationale that justifies the existence of industrial arts in the general curriculum of the schools. Use the most objective evidence you can find, but avoid emotional attitudes or unsupported opinions. Try out your explanation on colleagues and friends; then study their reactions.

## Suggestions for Further Reading

Bawden, William T., *Leaders in Industrial Education.* Milwaukee: The Bruce Publishing Company, 1950.

Bawden, William T., and others, *Industrial Arts in Modern Education.* Peoria, Illinois: The Manual Arts Press, 1934.

Bennett, Charles A., *History of Manual and Industrial Education,* 1870 to 1917. Peoria, Illinois: The Manual Arts Press, 1937.

Dooley, William H., *Principles and Methods of Industrial Education.* Boston: Houghton Mifflin Company, 1919.

Griffith, Ira S., *Teaching Manual and Industrial Arts.* Peoria, Illinois: The Manual Arts Press, 1920.

Leake, Albert H., *Industrial Education: Its Problems, Methods and Dangers.* Boston: Houghton Mifflin Company, 1913.

Person, Harlow S., *Industrial Education.* Boston: Houghton Mifflin Company, 1907.

# Chapter 11

# Influences on Trade and Industrial Education Since 1917

Prior to the passage of the Smith-Hughes Act no general national plan for developing trade and industrial education existed in the United States. Some states conducted programs that reflected purely local interests and needs. Standards of achievement, the nature of the instructional programs, and the content of instruction varied widely but were neither dominated nor encouraged by any one central group, except on a local or state basis. The success of these few programs encouraged the idea of national development to make the benefits of such programs available to more youth throughout the nation. Millions of boys and girls were going to work unprepared to meet the requirements of industrial employment; their industrial education constituted an imperative need of society.

Paralleling the state and local programs were those of private trade schools and factories that had developed near or in the industrial centers. Private schools provided opportunities for the person seeking employment, but the total enrollment was small in comparison with the need for trained workers. Some of the larger industrial organizations had planned and conducted educational programs of their own in order to provide the skills and knowledge required by their corporate interests.

Despite these encouraging developments, a new system of industrial education was urgently needed, a system that would make it more generally available. Many young people could profit from such instruction and could secure employment more nearly suited to their capacities, abilities, and interests.

It was the specific purpose of the Smith-Hughes Act to promote the development of vocational education in cooperation with the states and to "democratize," in a sense, the public school system of the nation by providing practical instruction leading to useful employment.

## World War I

It is not wholly accurate to say that the Smith-Hughes Act was passed because of the possibility of war, but it is apparent that congressional leaders saw a close relationship between the vocational education bill and national preparedness. The provisions of the Act and the requirements for instruction in war-related industrial programs were for the most part in accord. The war programs conducted under the Smith-Hughes Act proved in the first few months that national support of vocational education was appropriate because of its dual aspects—national defense and economic improvement.

While an army for military purposes was being recruited and trained, an army for industrial production was also recruited. It was the latter army that would support the former by providing the material needed at the front.

Although the war created an extraordinary demand for certain kinds of labor, training for these occupations was not limited to wartime purposes; rather it proved to be a valuable preparation for many peacetime occupations. As the war caused many laborers to shift from one occupation to another, vocational training became increasingly important. Educators were not accustomed to going to industry to determine course content, nor had industry been looking to the schools for basic training. However, the coordinating activities of the Federal Board for Vocational Education brought the two elements together. The Board also served as a catalytic agent helping the forces thus united to produce the end results desired.

## War Activities of the Federal Board

The War Department and the United States Shipping Board were quick to recognize that the Federal Board for Vocational Education could stimulate emergency training required by war jobs. Ships were needed, but in order to provide the ships the facilities for building them had to be expanded. Men had to be employed and trained for the new jobs. Agents of the Federal Board conducted a survey of occupations in the shipbuilding field in order to provide instructional material needed for emergency training.

The Federal Board in conference with the War Department worked out a plan of cooperation "for the utilization of the educational facilities of the United States." Although the plan was extensive and provided for a variety of situations, it was mainly concerned with the training of drafted men in various occupations. An order signed on November 3, 1917, to all commanding generals and chiefs of Bureaus read in part as follows:

1. The Secretary of War directs that you be informed as follows: a. The Federal Board of Vocational Education, authorized by act of Congress, February 23,

1917, of which Dr. C. A. Prosser is director, is now organized and is in close cooperation with the vocational schools of the country. This board is prepared to initiate a comprehensive system of preliminary training of men of the second and subsequent drafts prior to their reporting to cantonments.

. . . . . . . . . .

d. It is the desire of the Secretary of War that the Chiefs of Bureaus maintain close cooperation with this board, furnishing such information as to the number of men desired to be trained, necessary courses, etc. For this purpose the chiefs of bureaus will deal directly with Dr. Prosser.[1]

Before the end of November, 48 schools had established classes for the Signal Corps and an intensive study of occupations for the Quartermaster Corps was undertaken by the Board. The Board felt keenly its responsibilities and its opportunity to serve so prominently in the war program.[2] It initiated classes for conscripted men, published ten war emergency courses (the only printed courses of study used in Army Training Camps for such ends), and assisted governmental agencies in an advisory capacity in connection with problems of industrial training.

State Directors of Vocational Education looked to the Federal Board for assistance in promoting exchange of information about methods and procedures of preparing for and actually conducting classes for conscripted men. Draft boards circulated notices of classes to men on draft lists. The Army, by general order, made registration

lists available to vocational school authorities. The Federal Board for Vocational Education urged the states to use its franking privilege, provided that enclosures in franked envelopes contained the name of a properly authorized Board agent.

Getting information to all conscripted men about classes was imperative. The Federal Board recommended that the states use "question and answer" methods to supply the information. Questions such as, Under what conditions may one enter a class? and, What will be the expense?, were answered briefly in communications with conscripted men.

Variety in dealing with actual instructional situations and in providing appropriate tools and equipment appeared to be the rule in the locations where classes were organized. Requirements for instructional facilities were greater than the schools could supply, so other community resources were sought and made available.[3] Municipal garages placed tools, equipment, and machines at the disposal of instructors. City authorities restricted the use of certain streets to provide practice areas in truck driving. Moving and express companies made their trucks and vans available to classes on Saturdays and Sundays. Private garage owners gave their time, and provided facilities in addition, at no expense to the war classes. This was true also of many other commercial firms such as those engaged in oxy-acetylene weld-

[1] *Annual Report of the Federal Board for Vocational Education, 1917.* Washington: Government Printing Office, 1917, p. 14.

[2] Federal Board for Vocational Education, "War Training Work of the Federal Board," *The Vocational Summary,* Vol. I, No. 4, August 1918, p. 2.

[3] Federal Board for Vocational Education, "Promoting War Training Work," *The Vocational Summary,* Vol. I, No. 4, August 1918, p. 14.

ing and commercial telegraphy. In large and small cities and in rural communities the call for industrial instruction was answered in many ways.

States were urged to make the greatest possible use of their Smith-Hughes funds to promote organization of classes in mechanical operations which would be of benefit to the armed forces. The Board made liberal interpretation of the Act for emergency war purposes. Such training was an important investment that would bring returns to post-war industrial America.

### War Bulletins of the Federal Board

The resources of the Federal Board were used extensively to prepare and publish bulletins for the states to use in wartime training. The bulletins became official documents of training, with the approval of the appropriate federal office.

For example, in October, 1917, *Bulletin No. 2 for Use in Training Conscripted Men for Service as Radio and Buzzer Operators in the United States Army* set forth the conditions and preferences of enrollment; length of the course; procedures for obtaining students; nature of the equipment required, and its cost; methods of instruction; certificates of completion; reports and records, and other data. The bulletin also included information on course benefits to the conscripted men and what service the training would render to the nation. The bulletin was widely distributed and had the effect not only of providing basic instructional material but also of insuring to a considerable extent a degree of standardization of programs throughout the nation. Approximately 7,000 men were trained up to August, 1918.

*Bulletin No. 3, Emergency Training in Shipbuilding,* issued in January, 1918, was a guide for evening and part-time classes for shipyard workers. This bulletin had been requested by the United States Shipping Board. It included general information about class procedures, an analysis of shipbuilding and kindred trades, actual job descriptions in the principal occupations, and courses of study. A complete chart of the principal occupations identified the kinds of work done, titles and numbers of men required to do the work, their individual duties, names of the specific jobs to be done, and an analysis of each operation. Large copies of each chart were available from the Federal Board.

*Bulletin No. 4, Mechanical and Technical Training for Conscripted Men,* also issued in January, 1918, was prepared primarily for the Air Division of the U.S. Signal Corps. In addition to information of a general nature, the bulletin included courses of study for cabinet makers and carpenters (wood specialists on airplane work), coppersmiths and sheet-metal workers, engine repair men, ignition repair men, motor car and truck chauffeurs, and welders. The bulletin also contained examination questions for each of the courses.

*Bulletin No. 7, Emergency War Training for Motor-Truck Drivers and Chauffeurs,* published in February, 1918, was based on several months of investigation and study of the Army requirements for these occupations. Therefore both the classroom and shop-work outlines placed emphasis upon the areas which seemed to be critical. Included were 570 examination questions suggested for instructor use.

*Bulletin No. 8, Emergency War Training for Machine-Shop Occupations, Blacksmithing, Sheet-Metal Working, and Pipe Fitting,* published by the Board in February, 1918, differed in its basic orientation from the previous bulletins. Previous bulletins were described by the Board as "Service Bulletins" while Bulletin No. 8 was described as an "Occupational Bulletin." This was evidence of the Board's desire to study and make available information that could have a more general use, rather than being limited to requirements of armed forces. The occupations represented were, however, established areas of work in the Army.

*Bulletin No. 9, Emergency War Training for Electricians, Telephone Repairmen, Linemen, and Cable Splicers; Bulletin No. 10, Emergency War Training for Gas-Engine, Motor-Car, and Motor-Cycle Repairmen; Bulletin No. 11, Emergency War Training for Oxy-Acetylene Welders; and Bulletin No. 12, Emergency War Training for Airplane Mechanics,* issued between February and April, 1918, were all occupational bulletins. Previous formats were followed, with detailed suggestions for conducting classes. Appropriate course outlines and test questions were included in each bulletin.

*Bulletin No. 16, Emergency War Training for Radio Mechanics and Radio Operators,* September, 1918, was the last issued by the Federal Board in its war training series related to industrial education. Although this bulletin was directed toward the war task, it was evidently intended to stimulate similar instruction for civilian occupations.

## Importance of the War Bulletins

In technical content, the ten bulletins when reviewed a half-century later, appear to be thin and elementary. Today they would be almost without value to the average person mechanically and technically inclined. Much of the information they contain is now the common knowledge of any student who has included programs of industrial arts in his junior high school studies. But in 1917-18, general industrial sophistication was not well developed. Radios for the home were not in commercial production, only one out of 22 persons owned an automobile, and many Americans had never even seen an airplane. Therefore elementary information was required. What was most essential in the Board's war emergency work then remains essential in organizing programs of industrial education even today. The principles and processes of occupational analysis, job description, and planning for instruction, which the Board employed in 1917-18, are unmistakably evident in similar publications of the 1960's. These same principles were applied successfully also in World War II.

## War Activities of the Schools

Before 1917, the European war brought clearly to the people of England and France that their vocational education systems were deficient when compared to the system which was used by the Germans.

The Central powers of Europe have taken the lead in practical provision for vocational education, and in the German empire this provision has been well organized under the laws of the several states, fortified by imperial labor laws.[4]

In the United States, the unusual development of trade and industrial education in Germany had been used as a model for emulation when the idea of vocational education was under consideration by the Congress. It was clear that industrial and trade schools could render a valuable service to the nation in time of war, and that they would contribute abundantly to peaceful pursuits following the war. States were urged to follow the leadership of the Federal Board. Note that selfish motivations were not overlooked.

We must keep in mind that the Federal Board for vocational education is in close touch with the National Council of Defense at Washington, and consequently with all departments of the national government which concern war measures. For a local school to jeopardize its chances for national and state aid through failure to follow a program provided by these authorities, or to develop types of work which are out of accord with national needs, will not be the part of wisdom or common sense.[5]

### Military Equivalents

Plans for direct military training in schools, particularly of students between the ages of 16 and 19, met with opposition on the basis that military training, when necessary, was an obligation of citizenship but not of general education. A program of "military equivalents" was suggested as a more appropriate means of utilizing the resources of the "school power."

The military equivalents, in the form of universal training, would be broad enough to anticipate service needs that men at the age of 18 might be called upon to provide. Included in the suggested program was a plan to ascertain the character and extent of the vocational training and experience the boys were currently receiving. Vocational opportunities that would fit boys for service "directly useful to the state" were then to be offered, in the form of school work that would qualify as a partial equivalent for specific military training.

Suggestions that the colleges be closed in order that students might be available for emergency war service met with vigorous opposition from school leaders. There were approximately 20 million persons between the ages of 15 and 24 in the total population; less than 400,000 of these were enrolled in colleges, universities, professional schools, and normal schools. It was argued that the abrupt termination of these educational programs would in the long run not benefit the country and that there were other opportunities for schools to perform patriotic service.

Despite differing points of view it was clear that educational institutions could play a large part in the war effort. Boys who had received industrial and technical instruction in the schools would be a distinct asset either in the Army or in civilian production. Already the call had gone out requesting craftsmen to enter government

---

[4] Anna T. Smith, *Demand for Vocational Education in the Countries at War.* U.S. Department of the Interior, Bureau of Education, Bulletin 1917, No. 36. Washington: Government Printing Office, p. 6.

[5] Arthur D. Dean, *Our Schools in War Time—and After.* Boston: Ginn and Company, 1918, p. 315.

work. The equipment and instructors in vocational schools formed a distinct potential. It had been known by the Congress, while debating the Smith-Hughes Act, that vocational education could "provide for the common defense," and therefore "promote the general welfare."

### Training the Fighting Mechanics [6]

The war found the United States vocationally unprepared. In the early days of the conflict it had been supposed that the general mechanical skills of men brought into the Army would be sufficient to supply the need, but such was not the case. As we have seen, the critical military and industrial shortage of trained workers became the emergency problem for the newly created Federal Board for Vocational Education. Although the Board had the responsibility of building a permanent system of vocational education, it was clear that its emergency task was to train men in skilled occupations useful in actual combat conditions. Both the War Department and the United States Shipping Board requested assistance of the Federal Board in organizing and conducting war classes for various occupations other than actual military training. "Thus for the first time in the history of the United States the schools of the country were called upon by the Federal Government to undertake vocational training." [7] The response of the schools was immediate and enthusiastic. It was evidence of the patriotic responsibility which they felt; they had also an enormous amount of reserve energy to carry on the emergency task.

There was no question about the need for skilled mechanics of all kinds. Transportation required men who could build, equip, maintain, and operate steam and electric railroads; gasoline engines in motorcycles, automobiles, trucks, and tractors. Airplanes required military personnel with special mechanical skills. Methods of communication such as the telephone, telegraph, and wireless required another group of highly skilled men. These demands for mechanical and technical skills became even more pressing after the arrival of the first units of the Army in France.

Committee Organization. Early in February, 1918, the Secretary of War appointed a "Committee on Educational and Special Training." This committee consisted of the following: Colonel Robert I. Rees, General Staff Corps, chairman; Lieutenant Colonel John H. Wigmore, Provost Marshal General's Department; Major William R. Orton, Infantry; Major Grenville Clark, Adjutant General's Department, Secretary. On February 15, the committee appointed Channing R. Dooley as civilian educational director. (Dooley was the director of education for Westinghouse Electric and Manufacturing Co., Pittsburgh.)

An advisory board, appointed to represent educational interests, consisted of the following educators: Professor James R. Angell, University of Chi-

---

[6] Much of the material in this section was either adapted from or suggested by William T. Bawden, "Training the Fighting Mechanic," *Manual Training Magazine*, Vol. XX, No. 1, September 1918, pp. 1-10.

[7] *Annual Report of the Federal Board for Vocational Education.* Washington: Government Printing Office, 1917, p. 10.

cago; Dr. S. P. Capen, U.S. Bureau of Education; J. W. Dietz, president, National Association of Corporation Schools; Hugh Frayne, general organizer, American Federation of Labor; Dr. Charles R. Mann, Massachusetts Institute of Technology; Dean Herman Schneider, University of Cincinnati; and Dr. R. A. Pearson, Assistant Secretary of Agriculture.

The committee rejected armchair methods and lectures in favor of a "learning by doing" program. Theoretical material was to be included in instruction so that the man would come to understand what he was doing, but most important, he would be able to do it. The program was not visualized solely as a means of producing an army of skilled mechanics. The fighting man was the first consideration, and military discipline, military drill, and mastery of combat duties could not be sacrificed. The whole plan would stand or fall upon whether or not the mechanical training added to the general efficiency of servicemen.

**The Plan.** The facilities of existing institutions were to be used. Men would be assigned to the institution in units of 200 to 2,000 and would be known as National Army Training Detachments. They were to be housed and fed at the institutions under conditions of military discipline. Military drill was a part of each day's activity. The nine hour working day consisted of three hours devoted to military drill and six hours to technical and trade training. The program was to consist of short intensive courses with a total time of two months devoted to the program.

The first assignments of men were made on April 1, 1918. A month later 7,500 men were enrolled in 23 institutions; this number increased to 40,000 men in 140 institutions by the first of August. Courses of instruction were provided in about 25 different mechanical trades.

The military organization demanded results; skills must be developed. The reality of performance demonstrations and tests gave definite and tangible form to the program. There was no question whether or not the student fighter had learned; he must produce evidence of learning.

In order to perfect the organization, the nation was divided into ten districts. An inspector or field agent was appointed for each district, as follows:

District 1 Arthur L. Williston, Director, Wentworth Institute, Boston.

District 2 Frank E. Mathewson, Director, Industrial Education Department, Dickinson High School, Jersey City, N.J.

District 3 Stanley A. Zweibel, Director, Vocational Education, Public Schools, Bethlehem, Pennsylvania.

District 4 James A. Pratt, Director of Shops, Williamson Free School of Mechanical Trades, Williamson, Pennsylvania.

District 5 Dean P. B. Woodworth, Lewis Institute, Chicago.

District 6 Robert W. Selvidge, Peabody College for Teachers, Nashville.

District 7 Dean A. A. Potter, Engineering Department, State College of Agriculture and Mechanic Arts, Manhattan, Kansas.

District 8 H. C. Givens, Director, Industrial Education, State Manual Training Normal School, Pittsburg, Kansas.

District 9 Frank H. Shepherd, Oregon Agricultural College, Corvallis, Oregon.

District 10 James A. Addicott, Principal, Polytechnic High School, San Francisco, California.

Another important part of the general plan was preparation of teachers' manuals and the course outlines. The Commissioner of Education detailed to the War Department the specialist in industrial education—William T. Bawden.

## Utilizing the Trade School Resources

The War Department did not commandeer any institutional facilities. Instead, the institutions volunteered their services and were visited by inspectors to determine whether the conditions and facilities were suitable. The program was conducted at no added cost to the institutions, and instruction was limited to areas for which facilities were adequate. With each instruction center the War Department was careful to emphasize the basic goal, which was to give mechanical and technical training to military personnel—not to produce skilled mechanics. Despite the limitations of the two-month courses, the students turned to their task with great enthusiasm and were "working like beavers," as one inspector reported.

## Some Interesting Examples

Bradley Institute. The first detachment arrived at Bradley Institute, Peoria, in April, 1918, for instruction in a number of different trades. The program of instruction in carpentry seemed to pose the major problem because of the lack of definite information concerning requirements of the military; no other such courses were in operation that could be used as a model. Preliminary investigation in the use of hand tools centered upon the construction of equipment for the barracks, chairs, tables, desks, and similar items.

The second detachment was due on June 15, but the Institute did not have dormitory space available. Plans were made for the erection of a 48' x 90' barracks. The first detachment constructed the barracks. The construction was similar to army needs and the men seemed to "turn to" the task with enthusiasm characteristic of interest in "real jobs." An attempt was made to provide assignments in the construction that matched the man's particular abilities. The second detachment built a barracks to house the third, and the third constructed a barracks for the fourth detachment.

Bradley performed notable service in the organization of a special course in lens grinding. Importation of lenses had become almost impossible because of the war, and a critical shortage of skilled lens grinders existed in this country. This shortage made it hard to find an instructor. After a delay while an instructor was obtained and the proper equipment procured, a selected group of men was enrolled in the course. High school graduation and completion of a course in physics were considered as prerequisites. Recognition was given for related technical experience.

Despite the fact that three to five years was considered minimal in learning the trade of lens grinding, Bradley Institute effectively reduced the time. The "short cuts" were principally related to teaching techniques in producing spherical, cylindrical, spherocylindrical, and prismatic lenses, commonly used in spectacles and binoculars. Simple microscopes were also included in the class projects. Lens grinding instruction at Bradley continued for many years after World

War I as a means of preparing men for work in optical industries. The war service activities at Bradley stimulated interest in the vocational program, resulting in administrative changes through which Charles A. Bennett was named Dean of Technology.

**Dunwoody Institute.** Enlisted reserve and conscripted men were trained in both day and evening schools before being called for active service. A large part of the training was for the Quartermaster Corps. Frequently, reserves were called into service but ordered to report to Dunwoody (at Minneapolis) prior to active assignment. Thus they obtained pay and subsistence while in training.

The Baking Department at Dunwoody became in a sense a finishing school for Navy bakers. In other areas Dunwoody acted as a preliminary training school. One of the larger programs of training was for the Signal Corps; in it an estimated 3,500 men were trained as aviation mechanics. These men were on government pay and subsistence while in training. School equipment was supplemented by the Government, and the school was paid an additional amount to cover costs of instruction.

The institution adopted an extremely flexible attitude. Instruction was given in truck driving, radio operation, blacksmithing, carpentry, cooking, coppersmithing, machine shop, motorboat operation and repair, Naval aviation trades, gun and munition work, artillery for officers, and others. The need to provide instructors for all programs including those in the camps made it necessary for Dunwoody to develop its own instructor training sys-

tem. Consequently it drew heavily upon the industrial community for skilled personnel who could be given supplemental teacher training.

Despite the extensive war service, the regular school program at Dunwoody continued with a minimum of interruption.

**University of Wisconsin.** Bench metal work was a common area of instruction for military training detachments. It was also an area in which industrial courses were well established. The shops, equipment, and instructional staff of the University of Wisconsin, Madison, were utilized in part.

Filing was considered the most difficult skill to acquire in bench work.

Students were given drawings and instruction sheets, and under the supervision of an instructor, who made frequent checks of the quality of progress, they proceeded to complete a number of projects. Paperweights, pliers, pencil compasses, tap wrenches, tweezers, combination wrenches, open end wrenches, hand vises, surface blocks, hammers and axes were included.

**Wentworth Institute.** Early in May, 1917, the First Corps Cadets, Massachusetts Volunteer Militia, requested the privilege of recruiting from the student body of Wentworth Institute, Boston. In addition to granting the request the Institute offered to give the cadets practical instruction in courses related to the problems found by Army engineers. Among the recruits were many persons with a variety of mechanical and engineering skills.

Evening classes for the cadets were started on May 5, 1918. Nine courses were offered: (1) timber and woodwork construction, (2) cement and

301

concrete construction, (3) topographical drawing and military surveying, (4) gas and steam engine operating and automobile repair work, (5) electric wiring, (6) applied electricity, (7) machine shop practice, (8) mechanical repair work, (9) forging. Careful attention was given to the students' previous training and experience before assigning them to classes.

A system of trenches was provided by the Reserve Officers' Training Corps at Harvard for the cadets to use, in order that they might have experience in building machine gun shelters, dugouts, and drainage for springs, and in solving other problems common to the engineering corps. In June the War Department accepted the First Corps Cadets as an engineer regiment.

### The War and the National Society for Vocational Education

The eleventh annual convention of the National Society for Vocational Education was held in Philadelphia, February 21-23, 1918, at a time when industrial production was at its height. For nearly a year persons responsible had been exposed to the problems of the war and its effects upon industrial education programs. Seven papers were presented at the convention related to vocational training for war industries.

E. C. Felton, director, Committee on Civilian Service and Labor, Committee on Defense for Pennsylvania, addressed the convention on the topic "War Industries and Their Problems." Felton was of the opinion that the problems that war industries faced were "caused and controlled" by pre-war industrial conditions. He contrasted the situation

of Germany, England, and the United States. Germany—the world's arsenal —was thoroughly prepared for war production with a highly skilled and trained industrial population, but was deprived of many essential materials by England's command of the seas. England, with the world's markets open to her, had available materials and the means of supply, but lacked both the equipment and trained workmen necessary to produce the enormous quantities of materials needed for war. America, with no powerful neighbors, had "given no thought to preparation for such a contingency." America's industry had followed the peaceful unhurried inclination of the American people, which reflected the slow pace in the development of industrial education. Bavaria, with a population about equal to that of New York City, had more trade schools than the entire United States. Changing from a pre-war shipbuilding program of three-quarters of a million tons annually to one of six million tons was a disturbing problem to U.S. industry, but an opportunity for industrial training to show what it could do.

E. E. MacNary, Expert Industrial Training, Division of Construction, U.S. Shipping Board, described the program of "Industrial Training in Shipbuilding." The task was one of taking 150,000 men from different occupations and bringing them in a reasonable time to a degree of competence. In order to accomplish this task a special six-weeks instructor training program was organized at Newport News, Virginia. Shipyard owners sent skilled craftsmen to the instructor training course as a means of upgrading their own instructional program.

302

The instructor training course consisted of (1) analysis and arrangement of trade operations or jobs in good teaching order, (2) methods of effective instruction, and (3) management of instruction under actual production conditions. Charles R. Allen was responsible for laying out the course of instructor training. The training of skilled workers then also became the task of the Industrial Training Department of the Emergency Fleet Corporation, which assisted private industry.

Hugh Frayne, general organizer, American Federation of Labor, and Labor Representative on War Industries Board, Council of National Defense, presented a paper on the topic "War Industries and Their Problems From the Standpoint of Labor." Frayne recognized that war conditions made it imperative for larger numbers of workers to be added to the labor force. He mentioned the ever-present threat of skilled workers being replaced by "poorly trained and specialized inefficient workers," but indicated that labor had faith in the Federal Board for Vocational Education and that if the threat did exist, its extent would not be significant. Frayne made a strong plea for the "promotion of a sound system of vocational education."

Lewis H. Wilson, Director, Division of Agriculture and Industrial Education, New York, indicated that the State of New York was attemping to utilize its existing organization to its maximum capacity. The greatest service had been rendered by the evening schools, where approximately 25,000 students had enrolled in studies directly related to war work. Reports showed a variety of courses in shipbuilding—courses for men employed in Marine Repair Yards, for Hydroplane Boat Builders, in the metal trades, and in buzzer and radio work. In addition thousands of men of draft age were being trained in other military-oriented occupations.

Wesley A. O'Leary, Director, Essex County Vocational Schools, Newark, New Jersey, explained the New Jersey contribution to "Training Equipment Inspectors for the Ordnance Department." Not only were enormous quantities of equipment required for war purposes, but an extremely wide variety of government contracts provided an inspection problem which the Ordnance Department had not previously been required to solve. The particular inspection courses described by O'Leary pertained to leather, textile, and hardware items. These included items such as artillery harness, cavalry outfits, gun cases, pistol holders, haversacks, scabbards, saddle blankets, helmets, cooking utensils, wire cutters, trench tools, buckles, hooks, rings and others common to harness and leather equipment. Prior to the war such equipment was manufactured by Government arsenals which had provided their own inspection.

Courses prepared for inspectors consisted of a unit dealing with the business and accounting side of inspection and a unit concerned with the technical side. The program was approximately two weeks in length.

Major J. E. Bloom, chairman, Military Committee, New Jersey Committee of '76, made "Suggestions for Vocational Training in Connection With the Military Training Camps." Major Bloom, in addition to recounting

303

vocational training activities, had two general suggestions for further training. First, he urged that a general policy be adopted that military units near vocational schools include several months of vocational training in their general program of military training. This was in addition to any other training that had been given. He cited sections of the Selective Service Law which would make this possible. Major Bloom's second suggestion was related to the proposed compulsory military training bill then in Congress. He urged that the bill include vocational training provisions. He also though it wise to make provision for "industrial units for service industries" as a part of the selective service laws.

Thus the National Society, in time of war, presented for the discussion of its members some of the immediate aspects of vocational training. Reviewing the papers leads one to the point of view that industrial educators were proud of their progress and contributions in the war program, but were not satisfied that their potential contribution had been reached. There is also more unmistakable evidence of a strong relationship betwen industrial education and the defense of the nation.

**Lessons of the War**

The twelfth annual conference of the National Society was held in St. Louis, February 20-22, 1919, three months after the end of World War I. A portion of the conference was devoted to an attempt to isolate actual experiences that the war training program had provided, as these would possibly be of value in developing peacetime programs of industrial edu-

cation. From the papers presented at the convention, the following items have been extracted:

1. Peacetime production requirements demand a greater number of considerations than wartime requirements. (Chief differences are cost and quality.)

2. Training time is reduced if implemented by skilled persons who also have been trained as instructors.

3. Training, to be most effective, should be given on actual production jobs under regular conditions.

4. The order in which jobs are given to learners has a great deal to do with the effectiveness of the instruction.

5. In a training department, production should be incidental to training.

6. Foremanship training is essential.

7. Learners profit by association with skilled men while learning.

8. A distinct training department (example refers to shipyards) responsible for the instruction function was found to be most practical. (Instructors assigned to and responsible to production foremen were not satisfactory.)

9. State or Federal Boards should be established to set up standards of training and to prevent exploitation.

10. Only about half the required number of skilled men were available through the draft.

11. Instruction manuals including teaching suggestions and job sheets were effective for instruction and for later use.

12. Adjusting actual operating equipment to introduce one or more "troubles" was found to be an effec-

tive teaching device of a summary nature.

13. About 70,000 men with some vocational training had been sent overseas by the military. Each was able to "do some one thing and do it well." (The quoted words were recommended by C. R. Dooley as a good quality slogan for civilian vocational training.)

14. Short unit courses were found to be satisfactory.

15. The stress of great need and the stimulus of great purpose affect the rate and effectiveness of learning.

16. Men can be trained successfully in evening classes for military occupations.

17. Providing a greater supply of skilled workmen will shorten the period of mobilization for war.

18. Experience with short unit courses suggests that trade and industrial education provides for national defense and for national prosperity.

19. The fact that the military training program was carried on for the most part by twelve states is a challenge to the remaining states to be prepared in the future to render similar service to their country.

20. A nationwide system of evening extension classes for industrial workers is essential as an economic part of a program of national development and security.

The war experience actually provided many more than twenty lessons, but these lessons were clearly defined in the 1919 discussions of the Society.

## Influences and Attitudes

Immediately following the war, attention was turned to reconstruction aspects in which industrial education was thought to figure prominently. Reconstruction—individual, industrial, and social—was more of a process of "getting on" rather than "getting back." Pre-war standards were out of date, and industrial educators were aware of this. In fact there were no true pre-war aspects of vocational-industrial education; it had not existed to any extent before the war! Educators were faced with the problem of creating standards, procedures, and methods; the war had been the laboratory for experimentation. Training for military occupations had to give way to training productive workers to enter a new industrial order. The new skills required of the new order needed to be determined, and then provision made in the states to provide the instruction necessary. Pre-war analyses of vocational opportunities could not be relied upon, and the need for surveys of various types loomed large in the future.

The Federal Board for Vocational Education had gained in status during the war. Its influence was felt immediately; it had accepted the responsibilities imposed upon it. The public image of the Board was good, supported by the ability of industrial education to meet emergency war needs. But the post-war era was in part an unknown quantity. Could industrial education meet the immediate needs of industrial reconstruction and then gradually move into more normal peacetime service? There were no precedents of experience from which to draw ideas, but it seemed likely that industrial development truly depended more upon "development" than upon mere restoration. Promotion and development of industrial education programs had to advance hand in hand with promoting the welfare of workers, which in turn depended in part upon more training and retraining. The funds required to provide instructional programs in industrial education were available. They should be devoted to the needs of employers, boys and girls in school, and returning veterans, and to the needs of the general prosperity of society.

At the time of their discharge from military service, men were told about the opportunities of vocational education. The two cartoons which appear on the following pages are a key to the story.

### From 1917 to 1930

To summarize briefly, World War I exposed an emergency need for skilled workers. The nation was caught "vocationally unprepared" in the area of industrial craftsmanship. In the beginning the trade and industrial education program was directed primarily toward making contributions to the immediate requirements of the war. Concurrently the Federal Board was engaged in making plans for a permanent program of industrial education. "Thus, at a critical time in our national existence a Federal agency came into being, charged with a duty the proper fulfillment of which in war or in peace is vital to national defense and prosperity." [8]

#### Some Points of View

Two very important questions concerning the purpose and direction of the schools developed. (1) First was the problem of production. The tendency for capable students under instruction of capable instructors either to want to, or be expected to, turn out a substantial amount of productive work and thus subordinate the educational ends of the training was apparent. Did the public vocational schools exist primarily to *train producers* or to *make products*? Was it inconsistent to attempt to do both? (2) The second most important question concerned the development of part-time or short-unit courses. Necessity forced the short-unit concept upon the vocational schools. Was the experience sufficiently successful to carry over to the regular school program the concept of intensive courses? Never before had the skilled worker so much opportunity for job promotion through special training. [9]

The manufacturer, as he awakened to his dependency upon educated labor, viewed with much interest the values of part-time education. In fact, the need was so obvious that it could not be thought of as controversial. Action by the school was expected, but the action involved a rather significant shift in emphasis. The lack of interest of students in ordinary school work was frequently cited as the basis for acknowledging their desire "to be getting at some occupation where tangible returns may be had." The attitude of the manufacturer in this regard was reflected by James P. Munroe, vice-chairman of the Federal Board for Vocational Education.

[8] Annual Report of the Federal Board for Vocational Education, 1917, *op. cit.,* p. 7.
[9] The Navy had for a number of years conducted an effective system of trade education through their schools on a short-unit basis. In addition the instruction in the classroom or shop was continued in the actual situation aboard ship or in a naval station.

# The Vocational Summary

**Published Monthly by the Federal Board for Vocational Education**

| VOL. 1 | WASHINGTON, D. C., MARCH, 1919 | No. 11 |

(Reprinted from "The Bayonet," Camp Lee, Virginia.)

# The Vocational Summary

Published Monthly by the Federal Board for Vocational Education

Vol. 2       WASHINGTON, D. C., JUNE, 1919       No. 2

Drawn for "The Vocational Summary," by Sgt. H. E. Homan, 472d Engineers.

The manufacturer is learning rapidly . . . in his new study of industry he will not accept blindly what the schools have been giving him but will demand that the schools be made over to meet the new economic and social situation.[10]

The aroused manufacturer was demanding that the new education be made real, interesting, and businesslike. However, with the manufacturers' interest in a new businesslike type of education, an illusion developed about vocational education that once a person enters a trade he must follow that vocation throughout his life. Such was not the intention of the trade and industrial program in 1918, or at any time thereafter. The focus of attention had been consistently related to beginning levels of occupations. Increasing maturity and experience would assist the person to advance to other levels, and even other occupations, provided his adjustment to the beginning level was complete and backed up by adequate preparation for any particular job.

Early in the new development writers called attention to the objectives of trade education and to the fact that the attainment of these objectives was imperative.[11] A fear frequently expressed concerning teaching of trade and industrial education was that of narrowness. Failure to keep the objectives in clear view might lead to neglect of important instructional responsibilities. Trade skill, trade knowledge, and trade intelligence were the prime objectives. "Doing" situations, gradu-

ated in complexity according to the individual's ability to cope with the tasks, comprised the environment in which trade knowledge and trade intelligence could develop. Achievement of originality, initiative, and problem-solving ability could be attained through jobs, questions, problems, and guided discussions. Rule-of-thumb learning had been warned against by the early theorists in trade and industrial education.

Another view clearly visible at the beginning was related to the "togetherness" of industry and education. When either side attempted to go its own way, the product of instruction was not adequate in relation to the need. Industry fell easily into the trap of narrowness of instruction, to which additional complications were added because the instructor often lacked teaching ability and background. On the other hand pursuing a program of trade training without regard to industry could produce an educated "high-brow" (as industry termed it) who could not meet job requirements. "Education has been self-centered and self-satisfied; industry selfish and narrow; labor snarling and threatening on the leash of social injustice."[12]

## Nature and Size of the Instructional Program

Reports were delayed by confusion concerning terminology and standards, against which the states could measure their progress, and required the joint

[10] James P. Munroe, "The Readjustment of the School From the Viewpoint of a Manufacturer," *Addresses and Proceedings of the Fifty-Sixth Annual Meeting, NEA,* 1918, p. 265.

[11] D. J. McDonald, "Objectives in Trade Education and Suggestions Regarding Their Attainment," *Industrial Arts Magazine,* Vol. VIII, No. 10, October 1919, pp. 379-384.

[12] James McKinney, "The Getting Together of Education and Industry," *Industrial Arts Magazine,* Vol. VIII, No. 12, December 1919, p. 474.

attention of the Federal Board and various state leaders. As may be seen in Chapter 6, statements of general policy were issued frequently by the Board during the early months of its existence. The first report of enrollment in trade and industrial education was made to the Federal Board at the close of the fiscal year 1918. Funds had been allotted to the states late in 1917 and programs were initiated then. However, the most significant work of the first few months appears to be that which was stimulated by the Federal Board in connection with studies and investigations of imperative problems. The studies most closely related to trade and industrial education—not directly connected with the war program—consisted of teacher training for trades and industries, buildings and equipment for schools or departments having classes in trade and industrial subjects, and part-time and general continuation schools.

Six types of trade or industrial schools or classes were authorized for the first year of operation. These were (1) unit trade, (2) general industrial in cities under 25,000, (3) part-time trade extension, (4) part-time trade preparatory, (5) part-time general continuation, and (6) evening industrial. Reports from all of the states indicated a total enrollment for all types of classes for the year ending June 30, 1918, of 117,934.

Immediately after the close of World War I, attention was concentrated on the growth of the regular program, and during the next few years enrollment increased rapidly. A study of the picture in 1923 indicated that of all of the students enrolled in trade and industrial education classes not more than 10 percent were in full-time trade schools, approximately 20 percent were in evening classes, and 70 percent were in part-time schools or classes. Training was offered in 50 occupations by 1923.

Trade and industrial schools are effective in proportion as three principal objectives are realized: (1) An adequate system of selecting persons who will directly profit by the training received; (2) Training under conditions which approximate actual industrial conditions; (3) An adequate system of placing graduates in employment and of following them up during the initial period of work.[13]

It was the Federal Board's consensus that trade schools made good when they were attentive to these objectives and that they experienced disappointment when the objectives had been disregarded—the work then appeared to be "more or less futile."

A review of the number of trade courses offered during the school year ending June 30, 1924, shows the frequency with which programs were offered. The most common course to be offered nationwide in the Day-Unit program was machine shop. This was followed by automechanics, printing, electricity, carpentry, drafting, cabinet making, pattern making, sheet metal, dressmaking, woodworking, millinery, plumbing, and bricklaying. Part-time trade courses for the same year were offered in the following order of frequency: machine shop, automechanics, pattern making, drafting, electricity,

---

[13] Federal Board for Vocational Education, *Yearbook 1923*. Washington: Government Printing Office, January 1924, p. 164.

printing, carpentry, plumbing, brick-laying, cabinet making, sheet metal, dressmaking, woodworking, and millinery. The two programs for 1924 enrolled 409,834 persons.

Noticeable gains were reflected in the areas of teacher training, foreman training, and in providing training for the promotion of leadership within industry. Growth of the teacher training program was particularly significant. Skilled craftsmen were selected from industry as instructors. State and local groups then provided, as required by the Act, a program of professional training to help the craftsmen improve their methods of teaching. Craftsmen-teachers were not required to complete a four-year resident program.

By 1926 the growth of the program was particularly evident in classes that provided for apprenticeship, foreman-ship, plant training, and special services of a specific nature for an industry which had recognized its need for training and had appealed to the trade and industrial education services in any state for assistance. Rising enrollment in evening and part-time courses by 1928 was so pronounced that the Federal Board commented on them as probably the most efficient forms of trade and industrial education.

A study by the Federal Board in 1929 indicated that instruction had been offered in 225 different trade and industrial subjects. The distribution of these courses, which enrolled 563,515 students is shown in the diagram [14] below and on the following page. It can be noted that while the program had continued to expand, a large share of the training was concentrated in basic trades or subjects.

## Number of principal trade courses: 1924

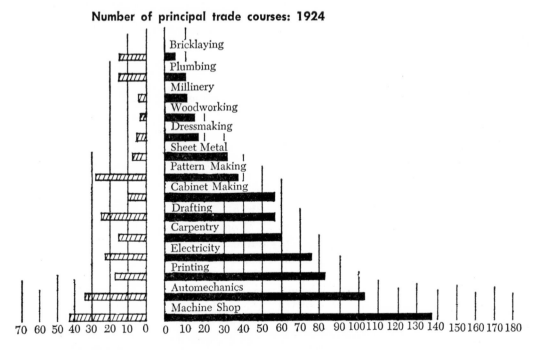

PART-TIME TRADE COURSES          DAY UNIT TRADE COURSES

[14] *Fourteenth Annual Report of the Federal Board for Vocational Education, 1930.* Washington: Government Printing Office, 1930, pp. 37-38.

## Number of principal trade courses: 1929

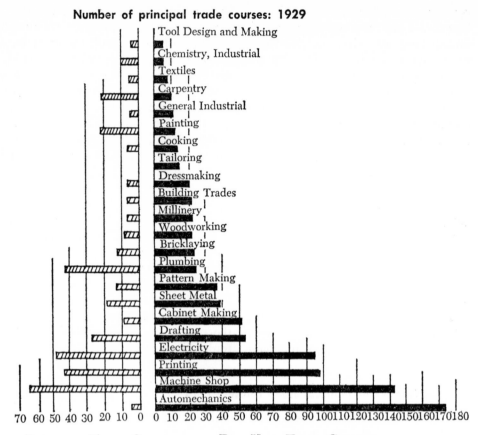

70 60 50 40 30 20 10 0   0 10 20 30 40 50 60 70 80 90 100110120130140150160170180

PART-TIME TRADE COURSES     DAY UNIT TRADE COURSES

### The Depression Years, 1930-1938

The trade and industrial education program reached an enrollment of 618,604 by June 30, 1930. Eight years would pass before this figure would again be reached or exceeded. The decline in the productive industries, due to the economic depression, caused a shrinkage in the number of persons employed. The effects of the economic and social changes were such that trade and industrial education personnel throughout the nation began to focus attention on the problems of the unemployed. Training needs were determined by close cooperation with placement organizations, and an effort was made to discover ways and means of providing training for unemployed workers so that they might find occupations in which there was still an employment demand. Of course many of the unemployed workers were anxious to evaluate their needs for training and were also anxious to improve their occupational abilities.

Enrollment in trade and industrial education dropped to 466,999 by June 30, 1934. Although vocational education could not create jobs, the federal program could adjust in order to serve the need better. Unfortunately changes in the economic scene caused additional demands upon workers and increased their difficulties in finding work. In 1934 the U.S. Office of Education made a special study of the difficulties confronting the worker in the depression and the relationship of these difficulties to a variety of social trends. The major conclusions, while not especially surprising, have had lasting influence because they related the problem of economic depression to vocational education. The conclusions —an apt statement of often neglected principles—were as follows:

1. Most people must work in order to live.
2. In order to work successfully, they must keep up-to-date in their occupational equipment.
3. So rapid and extensive are the changes in occupations and the corresponding changes in the equipment workers need, that the procession of demands on them seems to be continually passing by while they stand still.
4. If workers do not keep up with the procession they meet with lowered wage, reduced employment, and loss of occupation; and the further they lag behind, the sooner they join the unemployable group or become a part of the social scrap heap.
5. The only agency we know, which can help them keep up to date with the occupational equipment in skill and knowledge they need, is some form of vocational training.
6. Only an adequate system of public vocational education will meet the needs of prospective and of employed workers in the various occupations.
7. All the trends in the conditions affecting the matter emphasize the interstate and national character of the problems of vocational education in the States.[15]

From a training point of view it appeared that for various reasons workers could not secure and hold jobs:

Some were not adequately skilled for any production job; the training of others was obsolete and out of date, or too narrow and specialized; in still other cases, too many people were trained for certain types of work.

During periods of depression when jobs are hard to get there has always been a proportionate slump in the enrollment in trade and industrial schools and classes. Theoretically the exact opposite situation should prevail. Periods of part-time employment or actual unemployment might well be regarded by individuals as opportunities to secure additional training, to acquire familiarity with new operations and processes, and in other ways keep up to date vocationally in order to be prepared for the job ahead.[16]

This was an invitation to industrial educators to review carefully the program in their schools and the unemployment situation for the purpose of making whatever adjustments they could. The problem was twofold. On the one hand there were *in-school students* preparing for employment in a world which could not use them adequately. On the other hand there were a large number of *unemployed persons* who had some degree of skill which could be improved with additional study, crowding the market further. It could, of course, be assumed that work was not going out of style and that at some future date economic conditions would improve. The point of view stressed by the Office of Education was that in time of unemployment the trade and industrial program

[15] U.S. Department of the Interior, Office of Education, *Vocational Education and Changing Conditions,* Vocational Education Bulletin 174. Washington: Government Printing Office, 1934, p. 8.

[16] U.S. Department of the Interior, Office of Education, *Digest of Annual Reports of State Boards for Vocational Education.* Washington: Government Printing Office, June 30, 1935, p. 43.

313

should expand with concentrated attention on the true needs of the unemployed.

In the mid-1930's, as business conditions improved, the following situations were noted: Skilled workers were beginning to find employment; a need for training additional skilled workers existed; and persons who were formerly considered efficient workers were seeking additional training, or retraining, in order to adjust to changing conditions of employment and regain high level earnings. The Office of Education reported in 1936 that the two chief tasks then facing trade and industrial education were: (1) to provide preemployment training for youth so that they could be employable when they left a vocational school, and (2) to provide opportunities for employed adults to secure appropriate training in order to maintain their employability. These two tasks were generally regarded as nationwide in urgency, although the conditions under which problems were met and solved differed throughout the nation. Because of the emphasis that had been placed upon training for the unemployed, leaders in trade and industrial education seemed to feel that a "well-planned and efficiently operated program of vocational education" dealt with unemployment to a considerable degree by removing at least one of its causes —low quality skills.

Early in 1936 John W. Studebaker, Commissioner of Education, appointed the special Technical Advisory Committee on Trade and Industrial Education. This had been requested by the American Federation of Labor. The purpose was to study and then make recommendations to the Commissioner concerning plant training. The committee consisted of nine persons, with equal representation from employers, labor, and vocational education. It held its first meeting in Washington, D.C., in the U.S. Office of Education, January 31 and February 1, 1936. In theory the committee was supposed to bring to the Office of Education the same relationship of management and labor that had been characteristic of the Federal Board for Vocational Education. In practice the achievements of the committee tended to be minimal. The presumed fear that the Office of Education would conduct the trade and industrial program without consultation with management and labor was not founded on fact.

The George-Deen Act, which became effective on July 1, 1937, provided for training in various public service occupations that had previously been outside the scope of the Smith-Hughes Act. Considerable attention was therefore given to training in public service occupations such as police work, fire fighting, public sanitation, weights and measures inspection, and other non-clerical occupations. Attention was also given, particularly in the eastern part of the nation, to the formulation of a general program of industrial training which would lead to definite fields of employment hitherto not covered. These new developments did not in any way reduce the training for specific trades.

The reports for the year ending June 30, 1938, revealed a total enrollment in trade and industrial education of 685,804. This represented a new high in the trade areas. Evening trade extension training for journeymen workers had shown definite improvement in terms of numbers of programs. There was some evidence to indicate that this expansion was in a way related to the desire of workers to keep abreast of changes in specific occupational fields. In addition to the increases in this program, and to the increased attention to public service occupations, emphasis had also been placed on occupations which were closely related to the interests of girls and women.

## The Regular Program Through World War II

By the end of the fiscal year 1939 some rather interesting trends could be noted in the development of the trade and industrial education program. The most striking was in the enrollment age of students in trade preparatory classes. At the beginning of the program in 1917, most of those who enrolled had been between 14 and 16 years of age. Gradually an upward shift occurred, so that only a very few students were enrolling before they were 16, and many were 18 and over. The tendency to postpone vocational courses gave rise to the development of many technical-institute type programs in junior colleges or in other post-high school institutions. These programs generally required a longer technical-type training involving a minimum of skills. The needed skills were usually learned on the job in a short time. Such programs competed neither with engineering programs nor with the skilled trades. The training was directed toward a new type of employment for industrial-technical positions in chemistry, textiles, petroleum, electricity, testing, and other fields.

Another significant development, with the beginning of the 1940's, was the increased use of advisory committees in trade and industrial education. Although this had been urged since 1917, suddenly, it seemed, the real values of advisory committees were discovered. When employers and employees had equal representation on the committee, it added strength and direction to the trade and industrial education program. Parallel with the development in the use of advisory committees, and with the general growth of both pre-employment and trade extension programs, came a trend toward issuing certificates to students upon the completion of training. The Trade and Industrial Education Service of the U.S. Office of Education, in cooperation with others, developed a vocational training record card which states could use if they desired to do so; more than a million of these cards were requested by the states.

The passage of the Fair Labor Standards Act (Wage-Hour Law) created problems in the cooperative training program for diversified occupations. Such programs were generally organized in smaller communities where specialized training in a single occupation was not justified. Under the cooperative plan, students were employed half-time in local industries and spent the other half in school, where they received training related to their employment. This plan was somewhat similar to apprenticeship, although the length of time a student was involved with the plan was generally shorter. The U.S. Department of Labor, after careful study, made special wage provisions for these students and thus

315

protected their interests with "no curtailment of opportunities for young people to secure employment." [17]

Beginning in 1917 the largest enrollment in the trade and industrial program had been in the general continuation classes. By 1930 training, which was intended "to enlarge the civic or vocational intelligence" of young workers, amounted to approximately sixty percent of the entire program. Yet ten years later the rate had dropped to ten percent of the total program of trade and industrial education. This decrease in the enrollment in general continuation classes was consistent with the tendency of students to stay in school longer and to enter the labor force at an older age. Other contributing factors were changes in attendance laws and in regulations governing working age. Consequently students who formerly attended the continuation classes now stayed in the regular high school program. As said, by 1940 the continuation program was providing a service to a group of older workers who were in need of a general type of education.

At the beginning of the defense training program, it was feared that enthusiasm of the schools might lead to the abandonment of the regular program. This threat caused the U.S. Office of Education to urge state boards for vocational education to maintain the regular program, and to consider defense-training as superimposed. Federal Acts granting defense training funds in 1940 did have an effect upon the regular program of trade and industrial education and caused a decline in enrollment between the years 1942-45. Despite unusual war conditions, however, occupational opportunities continued to be available and the regular program offered appropriate training.

During the fiscal year ending in 1941, instruction in all-day classes was offered in 101 different areas of trade and industrial education. In addition, the rapid development of instruction for apprentices created the need for training in 95 apprenticeable areas. Altogether 804,515 students were enrolled in the nation's trade and industrial program.

## Trade and Industrial Education During World War II

Despite the declaration of war in December, 1941, the enrollment in trade and industrial education classes increased to a new high of 850,597 for the year ending June 30, 1942. Trends were apparent in the development of new training centers and courses, which provided a broader offering in the regular program. Teacher training activity increased, along with the general use of advisory committees. Pronounced expansions of apprentice training were noted in some sections of the country, particularly in the long-established industries.

By June 30, 1943, the overall enrollment in trade and industrial education classes had dropped by 27 percent. This was natural, considering the war conditions, and was expected. One region indicated that, "Students with one year of training in the day trade schools are at a premium and conse-

---

[17] U.S. Office of Education, *Digest of Annual Reports*, 1940, p. 36.

quently are hard to hold in school." Voluntary attendance in trade extension training decreased, due to the around-the-clock war production program, which limited opportunities for students to attend such classes; and it was reported that some states had actually shifted some of their extension programs to war production training. It was noted also that trade school enrollees tended to be younger than in pre-war years; and that states were providing increased attention to vocational guidance, teacher training, advisory committees, and to cooperation with other Federal and state agencies concerned with training in trade and industrial occupations.

The demand for education of a "technical" nature had been growing constantly, and by 1943 it had grown to such a degree that some positive action was required. Vocational-technical training, although not new, was certainly accentuated by developments related to the war effort. Vocational schools throughout the nation were increasing their programs in the area of vocational-technical training and were offering a large variety of less-than-college-grade courses in response to the demand for new technical workers and for the upgrading of those already employed. During the year a consulting committee on Vocational-Technical Training was appointed by U.S. Commissioner of Education J. W. Studebaker. The 26-member committee (including a 12-member working committee) selected from industry and education, was given three objectives: (1) to study needs for vocational-

technical training; (2) to study present programs and facilities available for such training; and (3) to study additional training services needed.

The regular program of trade and industrial education continued to operate through the war, even though with decreased enrollment. Occupational preparation of students in-school was not neglected and, in fact, was given special attention, as evidenced by the Commissioner's committee, which was intent upon finding evidence that could be used to plan an extension of the program. This foresight was justified by the lack of significant transition problems later when emergency training came to an end.

## The AVA Convention of 1941

The historic scenes of our first war for freedom—Bunker Hill, Lexington, and Concord—must have deeply impressed the early AVA delegates who viewed these sites on Sunday, December 7, 1941. Mingled with the recollections of the past was the reality of the present—the attack at Pearl Harbor. The AVA convention in Boston, December 10-13, 1941, was at once dedicated and thoroughly aware of its responsibility in providing for the defense of the nation. Only a few hours after Congress declared war on the Axis powers, the official representatives of 26,000 AVA members pledged ". . . the united and untiring efforts of our membership and the complete utilization of our vocational schools and training facilities throughout the nation in an all-out TRAINING FOR VICTORY program." [18]

---

[18] L. H. Dennis, "Wartime Problems in Vocational Education Hold Attention at A.V.A. Boston Convention," AVA *Journal and News Bulletin,* Vol. XVII, No. 1, February 1942, p. 34.

The convention picture was revised on the spot. Carefully prepared speeches were discarded or redrafted to involve the important task at hand. The AVA, in a sense, went on a wartime basis. Emphasis centered on the following six points:

1. Speed up training to all-out proportions, so that war production demand for a 24-hour day, 7-day week might receive maximum aid from vocational schools of the nation; retraining of workers displaced in non-defense industries for jobs in war production.

2. Immediate exploration and every possible expansion in the V-Training of qualified women workers for jobs in war industries, especially in sections where there is increasing difficulty in obtaining qualified men for training.

3. That agricultural production must be increased in the "Food for Freedom" campaign with the assistance of every facility available through the agricultural education program; that programs of instruction in repair and maintenance of farm machinery should be made available both to rural youth and adults.

4. Full realization of the fact that the home must play a vital part in the conservation and utilization of material and human resources necessary for military, industrial and civilian defense.

5. Immediate exploration looking to desirable expansion of vocational education in the establishment and assistance in maintenance through federal aid of vocational and trade schools serving large areas.

6. Determination of the place that vocational education will occupy in the period immediately following the war, and what should be done now to prepare for the efficient performance of that duty.[19]

One of the principal convention speakers was Paul V. McNutt, Federal Security Administrator and Director of Defense and Welfare Service. Well informed concerning the service of vocational education, he made a special point of calling attention to the fact that, because of world strife abroad, more than a million and a half defense workers already had been trained under the supervision of vocational educators throughout the country, using school buildings and equipment. He regarded this as a "truly remarkable accomplishment," and noted that since World War I the nation had been quietly developing a basis for war production. This was never its major aim, but the possibility of converting school shops to training schools for war production was not overlooked. Federal aid in support of such programs was a means by which the government realized one of its primary responsibilities to the entire social group, so as to "provide for the common defense."[20]

## Background for War Training

Periodically in 1938 representatives of the Trade and Industrial Education Branch of the U.S. Office of Education met informally with representatives of the War Department for the purpose of discussing the ways and means of providing training for aviation mechanics. Included in these discussions was consideration of the extent to which vocational school facilities might be made available for emergency training. Early in 1939, after an exchange of letters between the Assistant Secretary of War and the

[19] Ibid.

[20] Paul V. McNutt, "Training Our Industrial Army," AVA Journal and News Bulletin, Vol. XVII, No. 1, February 1942, pp. 5-8.

Secretary of the Department of the Interior, an official committee was designated to prepare a plan for the training of mechanics in case an emergency shortage developed. The first task of the committee consisted of making a survey "to learn more accurately the extent to which public and private vocational school facilities might be utilized in case of an emergency."[21] An analysis of nearly 2,000 replies satisfied the committee "that the public vocational schools were definitely in a position to initiate a project of national defense proportions."[22]

President Franklin D. Roosevelt, through the Office of Education, encouraged the states to develop an expanded vocational training program of high quality. Some states were unable to meet their local needs because of the lack of funds and facilities to do so; hence they appealed for assistance. It was decided, after a conference on May 28, that Federal funds were needed to support a national defense training program, and the Office of Education initiated a plan to be used for such training. In rapid succession the following steps were taken:

May 29, 1940. Office of Education proposal for training released.

May 31, 1940. The President in his message to Congress stated that provisions should be made for the expansion of the defense program by the immediate training and retraining of the American people for employment in industry.

June 1, 1940. Commissioner Studebaker mailed copies of the proposal for a training program to all chief State school officers, city superintendents, and presidents and deans of engineering colleges.

June 5, 1940. Dr. [J. C.] Wright and Commissioner Studebaker spent the afternoon at the Bureau of the Budget assisting Mr. Carr, its legal counsel, and Mr. Calhoun, Assistant General Counsel, Federal Security Agency, in the preparation of an authorization for an appropriation of $16,200,000 for initiating the program. It is of historical interest that the term "refresher courses" was first used, in this country, in the language providing for the appropriation.

June 8, 1940. Twenty-five representative school officials assembled in Washington to consider the ways and means of carrying on a national defense training program. The program was unanimously endorsed by this group.

June 19, 1940. The President transmitted his recommendation of the proposed appropriation of $16,200,000 to the Senate Committee on Appropriations as an amendment to a pending appropriations act, H.R. 10104, that had already passed the House.

June 23, 1940. Congress approved an appropriation of $15,000,000 for the program.

June 25, 1940. The Office of Education convened a conference of 42 State leaders in vocational education to map out policies and procedures for beginning the program.

June 27, 1940. The President formally approved the appropriation act known as Public Law No. 668.

July 1, 1940. Hundreds of vocational schools were in operation under the program from coast to coast with enrollment of approximately 75,000 trainees during the month.[23]

In the next five years, ending June 30, 1945, Congress would appropriate $326,900,000 for this work and approximately 7,500,000 would be trained.

[21] Federal Security Agency, U.S. Office of Education, *Vocational Training for War Production Workers*, Final Report, Bulletin 1946, No. 10. Washington: Government Printing Office, 1946, p. 7.

[22] *Ibid.*, p. 9.

[23] *Ibid.*, pp. 18-19.

## The End of the First Year

Although education did tend to mobilize, due to the international crisis, the process was less direct and therefore considerably different from that involving industry and labor.[24] The U.S. Office of Education did not represent a centralized unit capable of immediately placing the resources of education at the disposal of the defense economy. Nevertheless, the nation appeared to look to the Office for leadership and all the elements of education joined in cooperation toward meeting a common goal. Professional associations in education accepted Commissioner George F. Zook's point of view that, "Every educational organization, both technical and general in character, has a solemn obligation to breathe into our national effort in education a deep appreciation of our blessings."[25]

The war efforts of some areas of education were directly represented in products that appeared to have a closer relationship to the material aspects of national defense. But the responsibilities of education were far deeper. F. Theodore Struck described in considerable detail the task of industrial arts as seen in the early stages of the national defense program.[26] Developing understandings, attitudes, and habits of work through representative work experiences common to specialized workers provided a background upon which the skilled worker could develop more fully. In addition Struck could see defense relationships in the safety program of industrial arts and in mental and physical health which contributed to the happy, successful worker.

The pressing need was for an army of trained workers; workers in aircraft, shipbuilding, electricity, machine tools and other areas. The goal for defense vocational education was to meet the need. By the end of the first year 1,565,000 persons were trained. Approximately 800,000 of these enrolled in pre-employment, refresher, and supplementary courses.

For 23 years the nation had been making an investment in defense. "[Years] of cooperation by federal, state, and local forces for vocational training have yielded real preparedness."[27] Vocational education was prepared for the national crisis; also nearly three quarters of a million students were enrolled in industrial arts classes throughout the nation. More than a billion dollars had been invested in buildings and equipment. Equally important was the vast group of experienced administrators and teachers immediately at hand.

"How can you train enough workers to meet the crisis?" a director of vocational education was asked. He replied simply, "We never close."[28] Around-the-clock, 24-hours-a-day vocational

---

[24] George F. Zook, "Organizing Education for National Defense." *AVA Journal and News Bulletin*, Vol. XVI, No. 1, February 1941, pp. 6-7.

[25] *Ibid.*, p. 9.

[26] F. Theodore Struck, "Industrial Arts, Modern Industry and National Defense," *AVA Journal and News Bulletin*, Vol. XVI, No. 1, February 1941, pp. 16-18.

[27] *AVA Journal and News Bulletin*, Special Edition, *Vocational Defense Training*, Vol. XVI, No. 2, July 1941, p. 17.

[28] *Ibid.*, p. 23.

training facilities were meeting the need. In the late afternoon and early evening, classes were filled with defense workers either employed or preparing themselves for employment; these classes were replaced by others past midnight and into the late morning hours—this last group known as the "dawn patrol." During the day the regular students occupied the laboratories and shops, and then the cycle began again.

On June 23, 1941, the American Vocational Association, The American Association of School Administrators, and the National Education Association reported jointly in a letter to the President of the United States:

Dear Mr. President:

On July 1 the schools of the Nation complete the first year of training for defense industries conducted at the request of the Federal Government. The patriotic loyalty of school boards, school administrators, and teachers throughout the country has made possible a unique record, but it is a record which we pledge you to surpass during the coming year.

During the first year of defense training, the schools have performed these services to the Nation in the emergency:

They have trained more than a million and a half persons for defense industries. This, we may add, is more than twice the number which education promised to train with funds allotted by Congress.

They have mobilized more than 10,000 city and rural schools to give defense training.

They have mobilized 142 colleges of engineering (90%) to give short-course training to more than 110,000 engineers.

They have adopted in more than 500 communities the motto, "We never close," in order to use vocational school equipment 24 hours a day.

They have given training to half of all the workers hired by expanding aircraft industries.

They have helped more than 50,000 WPA workers to leave relief rolls and enter defense industries.

They have provided vocational defense training at the low average of 21 cents per man-hour.

They have operated this program at an overhead cost to the Federal Government of approximately 1%.

The school boards of the Nation, Mr. President, have been glad to make available to the Federal Government in this crisis their investment of more than $1,000,000,000 in plant and equipment. The school administrators and teachers have willingly labored long hours overtime to carry defense training forward without slackening their efforts to maintain regular daytime programs.

We also take pride in the fact that education's record in defense training is also a record of the strength of democracy. Defense training programs have been planned and carried forward with the advice and counsel of more than 1,000 State and local advisory committees with equal representation of labor and employers. On these committees approximately 3,500 labor leaders and 3,500 industrial leaders, assisted by more than 5,000 consultants representing NYA, WPA, and local employment services, have given many hours of serious consideration to the development of training in the best interests of the local communities and the Nation as a whole.

We are especially pleased to note that the Congress and the Administration have seen fit to unify the training responsibilities in the official education arm of the United States Government—the United States Office of Education, and to draw upon the immense resources of our state and local systems of education. These systems have been built up over 100 years through the conscientious devotion of citizens and educators, and they now stand ready to serve the Nation in time of need.

As the crisis deepens, the Federal Government may have occasion to call on the forces of education for contributions to defense both greater and wider than the present program. We assure you, Mr. President that the 1,100,000 teachers and school administrators and hundreds of thousands of members of school boards in the United States pledge you to answer any call with the fullest measure of loyal service.[29]

Respectfully yours,

S. D. SHANKLAND
*Executive Secretary*
*American Association of*
*School Administrators*

L. H. DENNIS
*Executive Secretary*
*American Vocational*
*Association*

WILLARD E. GIVENS
*Executive Secretary*
*National Education*
*Association*

## 1941-1942

With the actual declaration of war the educational forces of the nation were called upon for even greater contributions than was the case during national defense training.

The Navy needed 500,000 model airplanes to be used in aircraft recognition training, gunnery sighting practice, and for civilian groups. Commissioner Studebaker, in accepting for the nation's schools the task of making these model planes, stated, "This is one of the largest calls for national service ever made on American schools."[30] Again industrial education was ready for the challenge largely through the thousands of industrial arts departments of the nation. Making models was "old stuff" because the project had been part and parcel of the industrial arts program for a half century and more. The "valuable lessons" which Secretary Knox and Commissioner Studebaker could see in the

performance of the task were inherently a part of industrial arts objectives. So instead of teaching something new the activity merely reinforced learning that was already a part of the program: precision; craftsmanship; following exact specifications; speed of work; community, national, and international relationships; and general expansion of interests beyond the shop. Design related to projects was within the general scope of the nation's industrial education program; the problem was merely one of concentrating effort upon a project conceived and conducted in the national interest.

During the first two years, beginning with the national defense training program, industrial education had provided training for more than 2,500,000 persons. Even though this was an enviable record, the vocational schools were asked to double their output. Production needs had been doubled and trebled, and industry had been ordered on a 24-hour schedule, seven days a week. Industrial educators followed suit and kept their shops open for war production training every day and night throughout the year. Equipment was never idle. This challenge required close evaluation and revision of course content as well as instructional techniques, and adjustment and readjustment of schedules to provide for maximum utilization of equipment. When the national defense training program was started, the "available" equipment was used. However, the need for training required equipment far in excess of that which was available and Congress, through

---

[29] *Ibid.*, pp. 56-57.
[30] "U.S. High School Youth Building 500,000 Model Airplanes for U.S. Navy," *AVA Journal and News Bulletin*, Vol. XVII, No. 1, February 1942, p. 13.

special appropriations, provided millions of dollars of equipment to the schools to use in the war production training program.

The vocational training program had turned from "defense" to "offense." In discussing the problems of vocational training with school administrators, Edwin A. Lee indicated:

Only to the extent that we train these workers can our offensive against the enemy be realized. . . . At the heart of this all-out offensive is a nation of men and women who are trained to work efficiently at the tasks and jobs which need to be done. . . . This has been done in addition to carrying on the regular school program in all communities.[31]

Lee regarded these accomplishments as without parallel in the history of American education and ventured a guess that, "Never again will American schoolmen be superficially critical of vocational education." (Note that within a decade after the end of the war some American schoolmen would tend to forget that vocational education was a basic element in American education.)

One of the key elements of the trade and industrial education program during the war was manifest in the co-operative relationships of labor and industry. Howard A. Campion again stated the case for advisory committees: "The extent to which the existence of functioning advisory committees is regarded as an indispensable condition of a sound training program cannot be overemphasized."[32] The use of advisory committees as a working basis of war training could largely make the difference between success and failure. Advisory committees could function and assist in planning for new courses, locating classes, selecting teachers, organizing course content, selecting equipment, evaluating the program, recruiting trainees, developing instructional projects, and finally, placing the trainee. Campion indicated that some disadvantages might be present, but the advantages far outweighed them.

Because each year during the war millions of young people were entering the labor market for the first time, attention focused again on the importance of appropriate occupational guidance. The industrial arts program of the nation furnished a natural and effective environment in which occupational adjustment could be planned and conducted. "No teacher in any department of the school has a greater responsibility or a greater opportunity to influence and guide our youth than has the industrial arts teacher."[33]

## 1942-1943

July, 1942, marked the end of 25 years of vocational education under the provisions of the Smith-Hughes Act. When the Bill went into effect—July 1, 1917—World War I had necessitated a dedicated, all-out training program. In 1942 a similar condition prevailed, but under much more desirable and effective circumstances from

---

[31] Edwin A. Lee, "Vocational War Training Program Turns From Defense to Offense," *AVA Journal and News Bulletin*, Vol. XVII, No. 2, May 1942, pp. 94-95.

[32] Howard A. Campion, "Labor, Industry, and Vocational Education Cooperate for Victory," *AVA Journal and News Bulletin*, Vol. XVII, No. 2, May 1942, p. 98.

[33] William J. Micheels, "Contributions to Occupational Guidance Through Industrial Arts," *AVA Journal and News Bulletin*, Vol. XVII, No. 2, May 1942, p. 104.

the point of view of actual contributions which trade and industrial education could make. Many years of experience had added a dimension of readiness in trade and industrial education that was visibly effective, even in the darker days of the war. For every trainee who enrolled in the regular program during the first year, fourteen enrolled in 1942. "In all the history of the nations, no other educational or social movement has developed so rapidly and extensively as has vocational education under the Smith-Hughes Act." [34]

Vast as they had become, the expanded training facilities of the armed forces were still not adequate, and again, as in 1917, vocational educators were called upon to provide pre-induction training for draft age out-of-school men and pre-draft age high school and college students. The pre-induction training was voluntary. It consisted of instruction in fundamentals of automechanics, airplane engine mechanics, radio and telegraph operation, general electricity, shop mechanics, principles of aeronautics, and many other subjects. These programs were developed in cooperation with school academic departments. Industrial arts played a particularly significant part. Course outlines were provided to indicate the scope of training. Certificates of completion issued to trainees were valuable in classifying and assigning men to duty. Of interest is a slogan passed on by Army instructors to the teachers participating in the pre-induction training program. "Be

sure that no American soldier is ever killed or injured because YOU failed to do YOUR part to provide him with adequate training." [35]

Vocational and industrial arts students and teachers played an important part in the high school "victory corps," which was organized in answer to a nationwide demand by students for more participation in the war readiness effort. Instruction provided a basis for eventual use in the nation's armed forces.

The 1942 convention of the American Vocational Association became the AVA War Work Training Conference. A major portion of its activities was devoted to the ways and means of increasing efficiency and at the same time accelerating the war production training program. The necessity of specialized skills was never more evident than in the papers and conference discussions of the meeting. Teacher shortages in industrial arts and trade and industrial education had produced serious problems which the AVA faced "without discouragement." While the war problems of industrial education appeared to be oriented in the direction of trade and industrial education, the need for assistance and counsel from leaders of industrial arts was testified to in a resolution at the convention.

Instruction in the Industrial Arts is making a definite contribution to the war. It provides high school boys and girls with opportunity to acquire certain basic hand skills which aid them in the selection of further training and enables boys

[34] Charles A. Prosser, "Then and Now," AVA Journal and News Bulletin, Vol. XVII, No. 3, September 1942, p. 146.

[35] Merwin M. Peake, "The Army Calls Upon Vocational Education for Pre-Induction Training," AVA Journal and News Bulletin, Vol. XVII, No. 3, September 1942, p. 132.

to achieve a more satisfactory Armed Force placement.[36]

**1943-1944**

The May, 1943, issue of the *AVA Journal and News Bulletin* highlighted "Vocational Schools and the War" and included statistical evidence of the schools' contributions. Also, supporting evidence indicated that the regular program was geared in part to the requirements of war. More than 40 percent of the persons enrolled in the regular program of trade and industrial education were receiving instruction in trade areas that were contributing most to war production. To repeat, this was in addition to figures in connection with the war production training program.

Women in the trade and industrial war program accounted for a large part of the total enrollment. They trained for a variety of jobs and were efficient and highly regarded as war workers. Their place and problems in the war effort were constantly under study of the Office of Education. See the case of Augusta H. Clawson, Chapter 12, who was assistant to the special agent for trade and industrial education for girls and women in the Office of Education.[37] The nation had turned to women to help build ships, rivet aircraft parts, run busses, airplanes, and in general share in the step-up of social revolution given impetus by the war.

**Reconversion Training**

Occupational readjustment—reconversion training—commanded atten-tion in 1943, due to the large numbers of service men and women who were seeking employment in civilian activities. Federal legislation was urged to provide financial assistance so that the states could engage in the training.

As early as 1941 the U.S. Office of Education had released war training films related to specific phases of the vocational program. By the spring of 1944 approximately 150 films had been prepared and an additional 250 were either in the process of production or were in the planning stage. The program was experimental in many respects: The areas of the curriculum portrayed were narrow and to the point, the films were designed directly for training courses, and for the most part they represented planned sequences, with each film—although complete in itself—fitting into an integrated series. The films were produced in cooperation with vocational teachers in order that the organization, in terms of difficulty of instruction, would be correct, and the films technically accurate. By early 1944 there were 84 films related to machine shop skills, the largest category. Forty films were related to shipbuilding skills, and 25 were concerned with aircraft manufacturing skills. Paul V. McNutt called the film production program "America's 'Secret' War Training Weapon."

At the same time he was concerned about proper use of surpluses in the postwar world.

If PEACE is a rainbow, one of the largest pots of gold at the end of it will be surplus war materials. Experts place on this stock of war goods a value rang-

---

[36] *AVA Journal and News Bulletin*, Vol. XVIII, No. 2, May 1943, p. 25.

[37] Her diary was later published as *Shipyard Diary of a Woman Welder*. New York: Penguin Books, 1944.

ing between 50 and 75 billion dollars. In this cache is everything imaginable from ships to sealing wax. Machine tools, books, motion pictures, food, jeeps and peeps, radio stations, houses, factories, restaurant equipment—all these and hundreds of thousands of other items will be surplus property.[38]

Educators raised the question, Shall education share in the surplus war materials? This "prize of war," one of the greatest in history, had attracted the attention of many persons. Educators were pressing for top priority in order to insure widest possible use of the surplus in the public interest. Measures they advocated included outright grants of educational materials and supplies for training to the schools, vesting the title to the property in state educational agencies, providing necessary equipment to retrain veterans and war workers, and free distribution to public agencies. (The public had purchased the equipment once. Why should it do so again through school boards?)

By 1944 vocational education, in the midst of a well organized and functioning war production program, had turned its attention vigorously to the problems of reconversion training. "Retooling for Peace" was the central theme for the AVA meeting in Philadelphia, December, 1944. Officially it was a Reconversion Vocational Training Conference. Conference members speculated on the role of vocational education and the size of the problem, and made plans to approach the problem with deliberate, intelligent planning.

The war production training pro-

gram came to a close almost as suddenly as it had begun. The change in the war early in 1945 diminished the need for war training classes. Plans for closing the program were issued by the Commissioner of Education on May 5, 1945.

When the lights went off in Europe they went on in American Vocational Schools. Administrators and teachers practically lived in schools that operated around the clock.

—*AVA Journal,* June 1945

And vice-versa, as the lights went on again in Europe, American vocational schools returned to normal schedules.

### Post-World War II Growth

Industry had leaned heavily upon trade and industrial education during the war. The prospects that this new alliance would be strengthened after the war seemed good. Certainly industry was faced with a multitude of training and retraining problems. In 1943 the Vocational Division of the U.S. Office of Education had suggested that there were twenty problems which would need consideration in terms of the post-war program:

1. Working in harmony with employee and employer organizations through the use of representative advisory committees.
2. Meeting the needs for training and retraining programs demanded by those leaving war production jobs and those mustered out of the military forces.
3. Expanding trade and industrial training opportunities into new fields of employment.
4. Readjustment of women in industrial employment.

---

[38] "Shall Education Share in the 50 Billions of Surplus War Materials?" *AVA Journal and News Bulletin,* Vol. XIX, No. 2, May 1944, p. 5.

5. Greater emphasis upon technical courses. The needs of World War II have indicated *weaknesses* in the technical end of trade courses.

6. Gearing vocational training to employment opportunities.

7. School training for trades and industries vs. apprenticeship.

8. Revising past conceptions of the function of industrial education. There is a growing feeling among the students of industrial problems that our whole conception of *education in general, and of industrial training in particular, needs revision and enlargement.*

9. Meeting increased demand for evening school instruction for employed persons. As soon as employment conditions have been stablized there will be a *great increase in the demand for evening school instruction.*

10. In-service training of teachers.

11. Providing trade and industrial training on post high-school and junior-college levels.

12. Demobilizing VE-ND and reorganizing training in peacetime occupations.

13. The place of specialized training. *Fitting the industrial education programs to the American mass production industrial plan* will call for many modifications, all of which must be in addition to the fine work now being done in a few skilled trades.

14. Preparatory and refresher training for older men now in war-production jobs.

15. Selling vocational education to employers.

16. A study of community needs.

17. Function of the vocational school for training, placement, and follow-up.

18. Training and retraining disabled men and women.

19. The problem of migration of workers.

20. What are the lessons to be learned from the German program of industrial, trade, and technical education?[39]

The 1943 perspective had not included attention to all possibilities that the future undoubtedly would bring; but the view did serve to stimulate thought about the nature of the new day in trade and industrial education. Two years later the Federal Security Agency published another bulletin which suggested the main issues as seen in 1945.

1. The total program should be organized and conducted with the advice and counsel of representative advisory committees.

2. The offerings in the program should be broadened to include a wider range of trades and occupations.

3. All youth who desire training and can profit by it should have an opportunity to secure instruction which will prepare them for specific trades or industrial pursuits.

4. Adequate counseling and guidance should be available to both youth and adults.

5. The program must be adapted to provide training for approximately 60 percent of youth who will become routine workers in industrial and business establishments.

6. Certain phases of trade and industrial training can be given only on the job.

7. The importance of foreman and supervisor training should be recognized in the trade and industrial education program.

8. A full program of trade and industrial education must provide training for apprentices.

9. The trade and industrial education program should extend the in-school training of youth because it is likely that the age of entrance of youth into industry will be advanced.

10. The vocational education and industrial arts programs should be coordinated.

---

[39] Federal Security Agency, U.S. Office of Education, *Vocational Training Problems When the War Ends,* Vocational Division Leaflet No. 12, 1943, pp. 22-27.

11. A job has a definite educational value.

12. The trade and industrial education program should provide an opportunity for everyone to "keep on growing."[40]

As after every major war, education had changed significantly. New occupations had been created during World War II, and their peacetime counterparts would unquestionably continue. Nevertheless, J. C. Wright cautioned industrial educators that although enrollment was extremely sensitive to job opportunities, a lag of six to twelve months might be expected before industrial education could respond to changing economic and social conditions.[41]

### Problems of Expansion

As had been expected, major problems confronting state administrators of trade and industrial education immediately following the end of the war involved (1) selecting and acquiring surplus equipment and supplies and distribution to schools, (2) retraining displaced war workers, (3) providing training for veterans, (4) development of instructional materials, and (5) reorganization of state staffs. Of these five major problems the veteran problem was by far the largest and most demanding.

Day-Trade Programs. Immediately following the war, day-trade programs showed considerable growth—but under somewhat abnormal conditions. Many veterans who had not finished high school were enrolled, conse-

quently, but some states were not able to take care of all of the non-veterans who desired to enroll. A heartening note was that veterans absorbed in the program produced an "unexpectedly satisfactory" response. The seriousness of the veteran had, in general, a stimulating effect upon the younger student. Eventually, after the passage of the George-Barden Act, marked gains were to be noted in the day programs due to the provision for short-unit courses.

By 1947 it was clear that provision for skilled occupations required a higher level technical training than in the past. The vocational-secondary program was functioning as a bridge connecting the student and his preparation for work to his major task of earning a living. A definite trend was noted toward extending the preparatory training to the thirteenth and fourteenth years, in the process achieving a higher level of preparation.

Extension Training. Immediately after the war the major emphasis was on the training of employed workers. In 1947 a 24 percent gain was noted in extension classes, with the major emphasis in the building trades. Thenceforth the enrollment continued to show gains as more occupational areas desired instruction through the schools. The day program and the extension program had as objectives the preparation of persons for entrance upon employment and the better satisfaction of the occupational needs of out-of-school youth and adults. In other words, making people employable and helping

---

[40] Federal Security Agency, U.S. Office of Education, *Vocational Education in the Years Ahead*, Vocational Division Bulletin No. 234, 1945, pp. 282-83.

[41] J. C. Wright, "Reports from All the States Yield Blueprints of Progress," *American Vocational Journal*, Vol. XX, No. 7, September 1945, p. 7.

them to qualify for advancement continued to be major goals.

**Apprenticeship.** The number of apprentices employed after the war grew rapidly and produced two immediate problems. (1) The first was the preparation of sufficient instructional material of a related technical nature. (2) The second consisted of providing appropriate coordination and supervisory services at the state and local levels. The increase in enrollment of apprentices in 1947 over the enrollment in 1946 was 26 percent. Continued increases from year to year heightened the need for instructional material, which the states had only just begun to produce in quantity, and which required nationwide assistance from the U.S. Office of Education.

In some states emphasis on the all-day trade program was actually reduced in order to provide instruction for apprentices. Various laws and regulations facilitated the enrollment of apprentices and magnified the task of providing instructional materials and supervision.

By 1950 many of the states were reporting large percentages of the employed apprentices enrolled in related instruction. Continued cooperation throughout the 1950's by groups concerned with the education of apprentices increased the industrial growth of the nation.

**Public Service Programs.** For decades public service programs had been a part of trade and industrial education. After World War II, however, this phase experienced unusual growth. The training was considered primarily in-service. Thirty-eight states reported programs of public service training in 1946. Then, beginning in 1947, it was confined to the public phases of occupations which were trade and industrial in nature. Persons involved in the program as students were those workers who "sold" a service rather than a skill used in production or processing of goods for consumption. By 1948 the states reported instruction in public service programs as follows: 38 states had programs for the training of firemen; 15 states had programs for custodians, janitors, and building engineers; 22 states were involved in programs for rural electrification; 13 states had programs for peace officer training; and nine states reported training for school bus drivers. These programs have continued to be an essential element of modern trade and industrial training.

**Training Foremen, Supervisors, and Conference Leaders.** The roots of these programs are to be found in World War I experiences. They were used with success again in World War II, and the need for them continued into the post-war years. Conference discussions applied to managerial and supervisory problems had met with unusual success, and the demand for these services required that specially qualified persons be added to state and local staffs to meet the industrial need. Some states—and California is a good example—devoted much time and energy to conducting institutes for the purpose of training leaders who would return to their particular industrial employment and train their own supervisors. During the year 1949 Conference Leadership Training Institutes conducted in southern California enrolled 102 persons. These persons in turn accounted for the training of 1,114 industrial supervisors.

329

Other states—Ohio, for example—approached the problem by providing three weeks or more of summer workshops in cooperation with the state university. The conference leaders trained in this concentrated program returned to train others in local areas.

States employing one or more full time supervisors capable of conducting this work promoted the development of special programs for management personnel which were generously accepted by industry. The unusual development during the post-war years serves as another recognition of the indispensability of a functional relationship with management and labor.

### Standards and Adequacy

Standardization usually suggested a direction opposite to the general tendency of education, and yet orderliness seemed to be appropriate in the early post-war years. Gilbert G. Weaver, not unmindful of the dangers of over-standardization, stressed the fact that properly chosen standards could permit the necessary flexibility in program operation and still move out of what appeared to be an era of overcasualness in trade and industrial education. He suggested the following as reasons for setting up standards:

1. To qualify the understanding of educational objectives.
2. To aid in the uniformity of fundamental educational practices.
3. To aid in the thoroughness with which the work is to be accomplished.
4. To provide efficient guidance of the human product resulting from the total educational process.
5. To assist in the proper selection of facilities for accomplishing the objectives.
6. To permit thorough inspection, evaluation, and comparison of specific accomplishment.
7. To facilitate research in the field of effort by establishment of educational criteria as a basis for scientific study.[42]

Weaver's revolt against loose standards in trade and industrial education is similar to that of others who had dared to challenge hit-or-miss practices. It was possible to reach some professional agreement concerning central issues and to sharpen the ways and means of reaching the goals of industrial education. Quality in trade and industrial education cannot be legislated nor commanded, and a professional approach toward improvement was necessary in order to "prevent or reduce the wide variety of ineffective methods in courses of study."[43]

Improving standards was one thing, but the accomplishments of the program in relation to the need was quite another. "It is wise for industrial educators to examine their efforts with a critical eye from time to time so they can see if what they are accomplishing meets the need of labor, management, youths, and adult workers in an effective way."[44] This was similar to the advice given by the weather expert when he told the apprentice that before mentioning a current dry spell it was always good practice to look out the window to see if it was raining.

Realistic review of the adequacy of

---

[42] Gilbert G. Weaver, "Standards for Vocational-Industrial Education," *American Vocational Journal*, Vol. XXII, No. 4, April 1947, p. 7.

[43] *Ibid.*, p. 8.

[44] Miles H. Anderson, "Is Trade and Industrial Education Adequate?" *American Vocational Journal*, Vol. XXIII, No. 9, December 1948, p. 19.

the program of trade and industrial education was the principal thesis of Miles H. Anderson when he pointed out in 1948 that California's effort in apprentice training, superior though it was, could scarcely be termed a drop in the bucket when related to needs. Anderson viewed the "chief difficulty" of trade and industrial education as a commitment to the skilled trades. But he raised the question of adequacy in a general sense. In the years that followed others would cite time and again the need for expansion of the program to make it (1) more available to youth and adults and (2) to be organized better in relation to employment requirements.

## Era of Technology—After 1950

### Growth and Development

An annual summation of trade and industrial education is prepared by the U.S. Office of Education, based upon the reports sent to Washington by each of the states. This report pertains only to the federally reimbursed program. The descriptive portion is usually quite brief. Despite the many defects that this Digest of Annual Reports of State Boards for Vocational Education has, in terms of presenting a comprehensive review of trade and industrial education, it is still the best source of information available. Studying these digests for the period 1950-62 gives one a broad general view of trends, changes, concerns, and cautions.

In terms of enrollment the program has shown a steady increase, which reflects the increase in the industrial productivity of the nation. Classes were offered in a wider variety of fields as emphasis was concentrated upon specialties made important because of the rapidly developing technology. A definite advance is noted in both the number of girls and women enrolled and in their occupational level upon completion of training.

Accompanying the increases in enrollment were new and extensive developments such as in the new area schools and technical institutes. Also after 1950, substantial progress was made in providing related instruction for apprentices, including attention to the isolated individual. In a number of states, instructional materials laboratories were developed to provide the apprentice with improved aids.

Teacher education figured prominently in the general growth and development trend during the fifties, with changes in the internal program of teacher education and also in services rendered in the form of special institutes for teachers to help upgrade them in new developments. Special programs in the technology of metals, oil production, cosmetology, cleaning and dyeing, electronics, and others were conducted. There were corresponding reports of improvement in supervision and instruction.

Throughout the decade of the 1950's and into the 1960's the generous use of advisory committees and improvement in the working relationships with management and labor were reported. Widespread concern developed for extensive evaluation of many facets of trade and industrial education. Follow-up studies of graduates were broadened. Leadership development became an item of top priority with a number of educators, and the nearly forgotten idea of research in trade and industrial education had a rebirth.

331

Practical Nurse Training. In 1956 the Congress passed Public Law 911 which added Title II to the George-Barden Act and authorized the appropriation of $5,000,000 for the "extension and improvement of practical nurse training." An amount of $2,000,000 was made available for the fiscal year 1957. The response was an immediate increase in student enrollment over the nation in practical nurse training. The appropriation over the years has provided for concentration of effort on curriculum problems, on supervision and improvement of instruction, on follow-up studies of nurse graduates, on selection of students, and on research in the field of practical nursing.

The preparatory program is approximately one year in length and involves approximately 1,750 hours of classroom, laboratory, and clinical instruction. The extension program serves both as an upgrading and as an in-service device. Training has continued to grow under stimulus of federal aid. At the close of the fiscal year 1960 a total enrollment in programs under public supervision and control was reported as 40,250.

Practical nursing emerged from its beginnings as a branch of nursing to a professional status of its own. Licensure laws provided a degree of standardization, and national recognition by professional groups insured continued attention to program improvement. Additional aids came from the Practical Nurse Branch of the U.S. Office of Education and from states employing state supervisors of practical nursing.

## The Crisis

The growth of trade and industrial education was also stimulated by federal appropriations for the training of highly skilled technicians. Automation, technology, emphasis upon science and mathematics, and the rise of the technician as a person in need of special training focused attention upon areas of expansion and growth.

Nevertheless, even during the period of expanding horizons for trade and industrial education came renewed, widespread criticism of vocational education generally. Although criticism hurt, and in some cases was unjustified, it provided an opportunity to review and evaluate results. William T. Bawden sized up the general situation. In 1954, drawing upon his many years as an observer of the field, he noted some conditions that needed special attention.[45] He recalled his attendance at the visitors' galleries of the Senate and House in 1916 and 1917. Federal aid for a nationwide program of vocational education had been proposed. However, opponents predicted that once such aid was started the Government would be saddled with it forever. Bawden raised this question: "Had any appreciable progress been made in the direction of giving the program a momentum of its own, which will carry it forward in the absence of federal aid?"[46] He not only found this difficult to answer, but he held the opinion that little evidence could be found that the question had ever been given serious thought.

---

[45] This grand old man of industrial education passed away at his home in Santa Barbara, California, April 27, 1960.

[46] William T. Bawden, "The Crisis in Vocational Education," *Industrial Arts and Vocational Education*, Vol. XLIII, No. 9, November 1954, p. 296.

Bawden's second question touched upon the relationships between vocational education and the school system. The problem, he said, began in 1917, with the policy of separation.

We learned our lesson once, and we are not going to permit the traditionally minded superintendents and principals to do to vocational education what they did to the manual training movement. We intended to stay away from [the public schools], keep our vocational education separate and independent, and thus avoid any grounds for suspicion that vocational education will ever be dominated by general education.[47]

The fact that separation rather than integration of the program had been the rule made vocational education an ideal target for the critic and accounted in part for any lukewarm and indifferent attitude. Because the problem was so deep-seated Bawden felt that its solution would be rather difficult.

The qualifications of the trade teacher had to be dealt with in the crisis. In 1917 the "contrast" between the industrial arts teacher and the trade teacher was not so obvious or striking as it was in 1954. There was some doubt that either could find employment in 1954 based on the 1917 criteria. The industrial arts teacher had made much progress during the interval, but the trade teacher was suspect.

The real basis of criticism is that during the ensuing 30 years and more so little has been accomplished in the way of raising the standards of qualifications of industrial teachers.[48]

One of the arguments for federal aid had been the unequal abilities of the states to support education. Bawden suggested that possibly those early arguments were no longer valid, or at least not conclusive. "It would be unfortunate if some statistician were to come forward with the report of a study which shows that certain conditions which are vital to the force of the argument are really nonexistent."[49]

There was much opportunity for critics to justify making an appeal for the curtailment of vocational appropriations. Although Bawden did not attempt to answer his questions he did recommend that their existence should be noted and that recognition should be given to the effects that inadequate solutions would have on the future of vocational education.

### A Troublesome Question

As early as 1930 some institutions were granting college credit to trade teachers, based directly upon an evaluation of their trade experience. The case of the craftsman teaching what he had learned as a craftsman was analogous to the case of an academic teacher teaching what he had learned in college. The idea of equivalence of relevant occupational experience and the university program was natural. Some colleges found the idea acceptable and developed policies which would make it possible for the craftsman to pursue a baccalaureate degree that included recognition of his work experience.

Discussion of the policy and its criticisms was common in meetings of the American Vocational Association, and various individuals attempted to deter-

[47] *Ibid.*, p. 296.
[48] *Ibid.*, p. 296.
[49] *Ibid.*, p. 297.

mine answers to the questions which the problem evoked. How much credit should be allowed? What parts of background experience should be eliminated in developing credit values? Was the process of evaluating work experience educationally sound? Reports of continued interest in the practice suggested that it was growing across the country.

In 1955 A. A. Vezzani undertook a study of the nature and extent of the practice of granting college credit for trade experience.[50] Vezzani found that of twenty-eight agencies he studied (in twenty-six states), sixteen allowed college credit for trade experience. Eleven of those responding to the study indicated a definite plan for evaluating trade experience. The practices varied considerably in all details, including the number of credit hours allowed for work experience, which ranged from 16 to 40. Credit granted was in undergraduate terms. The major concern of the institutions granting credit was related to the number of persons involved; the small number appeared to make the work involved unjustifiable.

The problem of evaluating the occupational experience of craftsmen in terms of equivalency of college credit continued to grow during the decade following Vezzani's study. Such granting of credit is a step in the direction of fulfilling future requirements of trade and industrial teachers: possession of a baccalaureate degree.

### Automation Invades the Picture

Automation has brought changes in technical needs. Also, anything that affects the national economy in general and the labor force in particular is certain to have implications for trade and industrial education. When automation began to capture public attention, it created extreme opinions about its relationship to employment, appearing to some as a threat and to others as a boon. Some persons could see large scale unemployment because of automation; others foresaw greater training programs developing in key with newer jobs. The opinion that automation would reduce trade and industrial education's importance in the world of work was commonly held. About the only clear point of view in 1956, amidst the claims and counterclaims, was that it was difficult to be certain about what to believe.

Automation as a control mechanism designed to follow a sequence of predetermined operations was not strictly new. The Monotype caster was a forerunner. In its earlier forms, such as automatic production machinery, automation had only a gradual effect upon industrial education. Over the years appropriate adjustments were made. The only real issue was the rate at which change was developing. This did require special attention, and the call to educators to reappraise their trade and industrial program was urgent. General evaluation would need to be replaced by critical analysis. Again the "tried and true" process of close consultation and cooperation among labor, management, and trade and industrial education appeared to offer the starting point toward solution to problems which might be created.

---

[50] A. A. Vezzani, "Should College Credit Be Granted for Trade Experience?" *Industrial Arts and Vocational Education*, Vol. XLIV, No. 4, April 1955, pp. 117-119.

Present and future problems resulting from the spread of automation will not be solved by any one of these groups working in isolation. What better time than now when industry is standing on the threshold of the automated age? [51]

Automation and its general environment will continue to be a subject for study by trade and industrial educators and representatives of labor and management. To further this study a new element has been added—close correlation with the best national forecasts on the education of technicians, and on population, employment, production manufacturing, and a host of other parameters. Thus the age of technology can, and indeed must, produce solutions for some of the very problems it creates, by providing "instant" information, available simultaneously to every educator who plans for the future.

**The Long View**

At the beginning of each decade it is traditional to look forward to the coming ten years, and 1960 was no exception in contributing its share of predictions about trade and industrial education. Most professional literature that bears upon the topic has a decidedly optimistic outlook, but references to possible roadblocks and the caution to "Look before you leap" appeared.

Change was accepted among industrial educators—not for its own sake, but change based upon evidence of the need. Increased attention to evaluation of every facet of the trade and industrial education program was recommended repeatedly. The worn-out phrase, a "well balanced school program aimed at developing competent workers," was dusted off and attempts were made to breathe live meaning into it. This was essential because of the possibility that some educators might have forgotten the importance of the fact that their dedication was not to skill development alone. Though it was imperative that he have the skill, the competence of the American worker depended upon much more in a technological age.

One observer of the development of vocational education singled out for notice the role that research should play in the decade of the 1960's.

In the field of trade and industrial education, research is needed in almost every aspect of this work and the range of possible research projects is great. Just a few questions illustrate some areas deserving of inquiry: How do persons learn specific manipulative and technical skills? What is the effectiveness of specific instructional aids such as television, filmstrips, instruction sheets, workbooks, and the like? What are optimum teacher qualifications? How much and what types of professional education are really needed by shop teachers, and how much and what kind of practical experience is absolutely required? [52]

Forecasts took on many forms of inquiry that would look a step beyond the factual data of the operating program into the long-range meaning of facts and figures.

Trade and industrial education was intent upon improving its program and

[51] H. Robert Kinker, "Automation and Vocational Education," *Industrial Arts and Vocational Education*, Vol. XLVI, No. 6, June 1957, p. 178.

[52] Lane C. Ash, "What Is Ahead Nationally for Vocational Education," *Industrial Arts and Vocational Education*, Vol. XLIX, No. 7, September 1960, p. 29.

expanding it to serve more of those persons preparing for employment as well as those seeking to move up or to change their employment. A new dimension was added in the form of plans for service to groups of persons previously excluded from the program. The neglected included large numbers of students who had special needs because of handicaps or other conditions beyond their control. The old idea of avoiding these people because of the possible difficulties that might be attached to the relationship gave way to the point of view that these persons could perform some of the work society needed done. Public education had failed to provide a program directed toward their economic stability. It was obvious that many could find employment in occupations related to trade and industrial education. Ralph Wenrich stated that, "We must accept the concept that we have a responsibility for all youth who will work in industry—not just those capable of becoming highly skilled tradesmen and technicians."[53] Wenrich thus invoked a foundation principle, that which places the accent on all youth; it required that "We must . . . study them with as much zeal and enthusiasm as each of us has put into the mastery of a trade or technical occupation or the understanding of some facet of industry."[54]

The long view provided the best evidence that the complexities of the technological age included a significant emphasis upon the emergence of a form of trade and industrial education new from the standpoint of quantity and quality of service to the nation.

It recognized an emergency comparable with that of the war years.

## Summary

Experiences from World War I were exceedingly important in formulating the educational patterns for trade and industrial education. Before the war, planning for the trade and industrial education program had been based largely upon theoretical considerations tempered by limited experience. The war program had the effect of serving as a cruelly urgent "experimental laboratory" for transition. The National Society for the Promotion of Industrial Education made a determined effort to evaluate the World War I experiences and to establish criteria for program operation.

The years between World War I and World War II were a period of growth and adjustment of the program to occupational changes. Value systems developed that highlighted problem characteristics such as the nature of student selection, simulation of industrial conditions, placement of students, and follow-up on their previous success as craftsmen. The interdependence of advisory committees (labor and management) and education became a proved condition for quality programs. The depression provided a critical situation in which new responsibilities were brought into the open. There was no question that trade and industrial education could serve unemployed persons; in fact this was a major social responsibility. One major "holding" point was the passage of the George-

---

[53] Ralph C. Wenrich, *The Youth We Have Neglected.* (Address delivered at the American Vocational Association convention, Atlantic City, N.J., December 10, 1963, Mimeographed.)
[54] *Ibid.*

Deen Act in 1936, at a time when severe cuts in governmental expenditures were the rule.

All through World War II the regular program was conducted along with war training classes, although considerably reduced and overshadowed by the pressure of the war. The rapid adjustment of the nation's trade and industrial shops to war production classes around the clock and seven days a week was a tribute to the foresight of earlier educators who saw a close relationship between trade and industrial education and our national aim "to provide for the common defense."

Conversion from war training to peacetime conditions, with the need for refresher and other courses, was made. Strong attempts to adjust trade and industrial education to economic conditions were an established characteristic of the program. The era of technology after about 1950 again placed emphasis upon a relatively new kind of employee—the technician. Preparations were made to meet the requirement for a large number of technicians and for new programs in the health service field. The responsibilities of the future appeared large and pressing. However, the net result of a national study of vocational education and the Vocational Education Act of 1963 (the Morse-Perkins Bill) set the groundwork for increased service to more of the nation's youth, who must have appropriate training in order to meet the employment requirements of 1960's automated society.

## Recall Questions

1. What particular kinds of trade and industrial programs were developed for training in World War 1?

2. What lessons were learned from World War I which later became recognized parts of the trade and industrial education program?

3. What six types of classes were authorized around which the trade and industrial education program developed?

4. Describe the sequence of events that moved trade and industrial education from its regular program to a wartime basis in 1940.

5. Describe the principal adjustments of trade and industrial education in the post-war era, in terms of attitudes, programs and results obtained.

## Research Questions

1. Gather all possible data about your state's labor force and the distribution of employees in various occupations. Select the occupations that traditionally fall within the trade and industrial category, in terms of work and geographical location.

2. Gather all of the data possible, for your state, about the availability of trade and industrial education. Draw conclusions about the location of training centers in relation to employment centers and the size of the program in relation to employment.

3. On the basis of 1 and 2, prepare some recommendations for any adjustment you think is needed in your state's program.

## Suggestions for Further Reading

Roberts, Roy W., *Vocational and Practical Arts Education, Second Edition*. New York: Harper and Row, 1965.

Lee, Edwin A., *Objectives and Problems of Vocational Education*. New York: McGraw-Hill Book Co., Inc., 1938.

Blauch, Lloyd E., *Federal Cooperation in Agricultural Extension Work, Vocational Education, and Vocational Rehabilitation*. U.S. Department of the Interior, Bulletin 1933, No. 15. Washington: Government Printing Office, 1933.

Hawkins, Layton S., Prosser, Charles A., Wright, John C., *Development of Vocational Education*. Chicago: American Technical Society, 1951.

*Manual Training Magazine* (1899-1922), *Industrial Education Magazine* (1922-1939). Peoria, Illinois: The Manual Arts Press.

*Industrial Arts Magazine* (1914-1930), *Industrial Arts and Vocational Education* (1930-date). Milwaukee, Wisconsin: The Bruce Publishing Company.

# Chapter 12 | Women in Industrial Education

National Society for the Promotion of Industrial Education · Early Schools and Pioneer Women · The Program During the Early Years of the Federal Board · Women and the Labor Force —World War II · Post-War Employment · Summary · Recall Questions · Research Questions · Suggestions for Further Reading

Although some kind of education for girls was available throughout the colonial period, it was meagre and few women were ever able to take advantage of it. Following the Revolutionary War a few inspired people attacked the prevailing complacence in regard to women's education. Their attack resulted in the development of "female seminaries," which "sprang up like mushroom growths" along the Atlantic seaboard and far into frontier areas.

In the early 1800's Emma Willard (1787-1870), Catherine Beecher (1800-1878), and Mary Lyon (1797-1849), the acknowledged pioneers of women's education, proposed some daring innovations in the education of women. One of the best known documents about the reconstruction of women's education is Emma Willard's *A Plan for Improving Female Education*, published in 1819. Emma Willard's Troy Female Seminary opened its doors in September, 1821, to ninety young women from seven states.[1]

There is little, if any, evidence that industrial education for women was ever considered seriously during the early years of the nineteenth century. Later, however, Catherine Beecher shows awareness of the matter, as when she told a Boston Music Hall audience in 1870 that, "Women need as much and even more scientific and practical training for their appropriate duties than men." She was concerned with the plight of unmarried women,

---

[1] A collection of Emma Willard's papers is located in the Library of Russell Sage College, Troy, New York, at the same location where her famous school was established. A statue was erected to her memory on the grounds, and a bronze tablet nearby marks the site of Moulton's Coffee House, where her first classes were conducted on the second floor.

who were dependent upon fathers and brothers, "and yet no openings offer them to earn an independence." Her interests in the lack of education for the "factory girls" contained only a faint suggestion of the need of industrial education for women. Catherine Beecher's Hartford Seminary, which opened in 1828, was devoted largely to general needs in education for women.

Mary Lyon had great interest in the educational problems of the daughters in poor families, the women whom education had passed by. Her plan for a female seminary became a financial possibility after a long and somewhat disappointing fund raising campaign. When her school opened in 1837 (Mount Holyoke, Massachusetts), it was necessary that each of the students perform two hours of domestic work each day in order to reduce the expenses of operation; the rule applied to all, even to Miss Lyon.

Emma Willard, Catherine Beecher, and Mary Lyon were educational reformers whose ideas were thought by many to be visionary and impractical.

They had to fight the inherited social conceptions, which insisted that woman's place was in the home to rear children and care for a family, and the psychological conception that women were inherently inferior intellectually to men.[2]

The Troy, Hartford, and Mount Holyoke seminaries were educational models along a new plan which insisted upon the rights of women to educational equality. There is little to suggest that these pioneers might have become interested in industrial education had they lived a half century later.

Nevertheless, their spirit and enthusiasm were characteristic of those women who stimulated the development of industrial education in the early part of the twentieth century.

## National Society for the Promotion of Industrial Education

From the day of its first meeting the National Society for the Promotion of Industrial Education included vocational preparation of women for the world of work as a normal part of its activity. No special mention was made of this fact; rather, it was just a part of the total consideration. Discussion about its relevance appeared not to be necessary. Jane Addams, Head of Hull House, Chicago, was one of the speakers at the organizational meeting of the Society in November, 1906. Her address did not emphasize the special role of women in industrial education. She confined her discussion to the total task at hand, and the assumption was clearly evident that this was in part a task for women.

But the place of women in the industrial development of the nation was worthy of special study and research, and it was not long after the organization of the Society that a subcommittee on Industrial Education for Women was appointed. Its special purpose was the preparation of a bulletin on the topic. The persons assigned to the subcommittee were Mary Morton Kehey, Chairman, President of Women's Educational and Industrial Union, Boston; Jane Addams, Hull House, Chicago; Sarah Louise Arnold, Dean

---

[2] R. Freeman Butts, *A Cultural History of Education.* New York: McGraw-Hill Book Company, Inc., 1947, p. 506.

of Simmons College, Boston; Emily Green Balch, Professor of Economy and Sociology, Wellesley College; Sophoniaba P. Breckinridge, Chicago University; Susan M. Kingsbury, Professor of History and Economics, Simmons College, Boston; Florence M. Marshall, Director of the Boston Trade School for Girls; and Mary Schenck Woolman, Director of the Manhattan Trade School for Girls.

It was recognized in 1906 that industry presented many occupational opportunities for women and that the position of women in relation to industry had been modified somewhat in recent years. Women had always worked, and across the nation a number of occupational areas were developing which tended to employ women predominantly. "Numerous efforts have been made to fit the woman for some place in the industrial world, but most of these have been desultory, either as evening work, or as part time work, giving a few hours each day."[3] Instruction had been heavily "cultural," rather than practical, and the reference point had been the home more frequently than it had been industry. Nevertheless, some records had been kept by various training centers that indicated the value of the training to the woman worker from the standpoint of enabling her to command a higher salary.

Industrial training schemes for women were considered in Bulletin 4 from four different positions; (1) the girl who is obliged to leave the public school in order that she may contribute to the support of the family, (2) the girl who does not need to start work at 13 or 14 years of age but who knows that she must earn her living by the time she is 16 or 17, (3) the girl who does not feel the pressure of self-support but who can spend any length of time in her educational program, and (4) the girl who is already at work, but who wants to gain greater knowledge so that she can compete more effectively for advancement in her occupation. These considerations provided a framework upon which an educational program could be built for the special needs of girls in each of the above categories.

When one sees the increasing demand for girls in all lines and when one hears the constant complaint of employers that girls are incompetent, unreliable, and disinterested in their work, one is led to feel that it portends nothing but evil for the future of both the industry and the women.[4]

Educators acted on the basis of their belief that industry was entitled to the best possible service that women were capable of giving. The aim of the trade school was to assist the girl to make her contribution to industrial progress and to industrial welfare.

Anna Garlin Spencer, in discussing the social value of industrial education for girls, cited five prevalent fallacies in relation to women and girls. First, the number of girls and women concerned was too small. Second, industrial education was unnecessary because industrial employment was merely an interlude between home life

---

[3] Florence M. Marshall, *Industrial Training for Women,* National Society for the Promotion of Industrial Education, Bulletin No. 4, October 1907, p. 41.

[4] National Society for the Promotion of Industrial Education, Bulletin No. 6, *Proceedings of First Annual Meeting,* Chicago, Part II, May 1908, p. 33.

HISTORY OF INDUSTRIAL EDUCATION IN THE U.S.

before she entered the industrial field and her home life afterward. Third, that the trend to employ women in industrial pursuits was somewhat new. Fourth, that the problem of industrial education for girls was just as simple as it was for boys. Fifth, the difficulties and complexities of industrial education for girls were so great as to be impossible of solution.[5] But this was only an identification of fallacies. It accomplished little toward the solution of the problem. Anna Spencer thought that the girl's first need of self-support and her later need, or desire, for employment after her children had grown up made it advantageous for industry to consider with care the opportunity to provide industrial education for women.

Henry S. Pritchett, President of the Society, talked about its aims in Chicago in January, 1908, and referred frequently to "our men and our women," "the boys and the girls," or "any boy or any girl," implying that it was unquestionably the purpose of the Society to give attention to the needs of people who work or who are preparing for work, men or women.

The second annual convention of the Society provided two major addresses related to industrial education and women. One, by Anna C. Hedges, Superintendent of the Hebrew Technical School for Girls, was concerned with woman's work in industrial education. The other, by Florence M. Marshall, provided a special review of

trade school education for girls. Miss Marshall made some interesting assumptions that she thought important in organizing trade education for girls. These were as follows:

1. Nearly half of the girls leave school to go to work between the ages of 14 and 16.
2. The occupations which these girls enter are unskilled, temporary, often detrimental physically, and lead to nothing in the future.
3. Skilled occupations in which there is opportunity for advancement will not admit girls who come directly from the schools without technical training, but are suffering because of a lack of skilled workers.
4. Girls who are leaving school to go to work are in the main from families who cannot afford to give their children a prolonged education but who could and would gladly keep them in school a few years more if this resulted in increased earning capacity.
5. Industries such as custom dressmaking and similar lines of sewing, millinery, glove, shoe and clothing manufacture, straw hatmaking, and salesmanship are dependent for their growth upon women employees and offer a grade of work that can be well done only by hand and mind trained to be intelligent.
6. Women employed in these industries are having, because of the nature of their work, a chance for development and an opportunity for a kind of social contact which will make them more intelligent and capable homemakers, if in time they are called upon to perform such duties.[6]

Miss Marshall's assumptions were more nearly representative of actual conditions than of hypothetical con-

---

[5] Anna Garlin Spencer, "The Social Value of Industrial Education for Girls," National Society for the Promotion of Industrial Education, Bulletin No. 6, *Proceedings of the First Annual Meeting*, Chicago, Part II, May 1908, pp. 38-45.

[6] Florence M. Marshall, "How to Conduct A Trade School for Girls," National Society for the Promotion of Industrial Education, Bulletin No. 9, *Proceedings of the Second Annual Meeting*, Atlanta, Georgia, June 1909, pp. 93-94.

ditions. Educational programs should be organized around the needs of girls who were potential enrollees in the school and in consideration of the needs of the industry that would offer them employment. Cherished notions about girls, and the facts about them, were two entirely different things. Instead of all girls being comfortably settled in homes of their own Miss Marshall indicated that in some of the large cities 77 out of 100 girls 16 to 20 years of age were working for pay outside the home, and that thousands of little girls 14 and 15 years of age were entering temporary juvenile occupations. In her opinion this was a condition, not a theory, that demanded practical treatment in the field of industrial education.

Mrs. Raymond Robins, National Women's Trade Union League, Chicago, informed the Society at its Milwaukee meeting in 1909 that there were six million wage-earning women in the United States. More than 250,000 of the young women working in Illinois had a statistical average wage of $270 per year. She made a plea for training that would equip better the young women who were in the industrial world or were preparing to enter.

In 1910 the Society issued a list of trade and industrial schools in the United States. Of the schools in the list 19 indicated that they had programs for women; nine of these were in New York; five in Massachusetts; and one each in California, Louisiana, Georgia, Virginia, and Wisconsin.

In connection with industrial educa-

tion for women, the major problems that occupied the attention of the Society concerned understanding the need as indicated by the industries, and then translating this need into an actual program of instruction that would lead to employment. The aim was to make it possible for the woman to be successful in her work and receive an adequate compensation for her service. Once the nature of the jobs to be filled was thoroughly understood, the school needed to explore ways and means of providing the most meaningful instruction.

In 1911 the Society issued its Bulletin No. 13, Part I of which was devoted entirely to the topic, "Trade Education for Girls." One of the reports, by Susan M. Kingsbury, consisted of a detailed study of the needle trades. A second report focused attention on the needs of department stores. Altogether there seemed to be evidence to indicate that the schools were beginning to meet the needs of the trades. The following quotation was indicative of reports from students and employers:

Our graduates are satisfying the trades. The call comes for "more girls like Fannie," or it is reported "Trade School girls can do what I tell them without much explanation."

Many employers pay at once the wage we recommend the girl is competent to earn. They have found we do not overrate ability.

The average girl having completed the course is paid $4 to $6—maximum to a few $11, and girls out at trade some time are earning as high as $7 to $12, maximum to a few $20-$30, and some are being made forewomen.[7]

[7] Helen R. Hildreth, "How the Manhattan Trade School for Girls Meets Trade Demands," *Trade Education for Girls,* National Society for the Promotion of Industrial Education, Bulletin No. 13, Part I, 1911, p. 25.

At one point in the promotional program of the National Society, Prosser appealed to the General Federation of Women's Clubs for aid in the vocational movement. In a short pamphlet he explained what vocational education was and why it was important, and then he suggested that women's clubs could (1) cooperate with other agencies that were working on the problem, (2) study the Page Bill and then write to their members in Congress, (3) start a movement of concern for vocational education in their own state and attempt to get state legislation for vocational education, (4) start work of a promotional nature in their own communities, (5) assign committees to study the problem of the wage-earner who leaves school at age 14, (6) assist industrial organizations to present the problem to the public schools, and (7) read some of the many publications which were suggested in the pamphlet.[8]

Prosser's appeal did bring assistance from women's clubs, and in the followings years evidence could be found frequently that they had taken the crusade for vocational education as an item of responsibility. Their work was particularly noticeable in the fight to influence Congress favorably in connection with the Page Bill.

During the next annual convention of the Society attention was drawn to teacher training for women. High standards were set for occupational efficiency and for an additional amount of pedagogical training. The women in industrial education helped mold the standards for teacher training and selection, standards that were to be incorporated into the federal legislation in the years to come.

Year after year the record of the Society contained pages and pages of the rationale concerning appropriate industrial education for women. Laura Drake Gill, President of the College for Women, Sewanee, Tennessee, was much impressed with the value of industrial education on the social bearing of women, even arguing for such training as a compulsory matter in the school. Ida M. Tarbell, Associate Editor, *American Magazine*, described for the Society in 1913 a complete education for women, which emphasized their need for education in relation to the home and to industry. Her concluding statements were:

There is nothing in this scheme of training all girls in the domestic industries which need interfere with training for special shop, factory, or office work. Such training would do much to develop the faculties which are required in all industries—the hand sense—the attention and appreciation of material things—the correlation of hand and brain—all things in which the average girl is deficient now. She would be better able to take the training for some special industry because of the domestic training, and when she left that industry to marry, as she is almost certain to do, she will not go to her difficult business as an unskilled laborer. She, her family, and we, society, would be spared the economic, the moral, and the social consequences of her lack of knowledge and skill.[9]

---

[8] C. A. Prosser, *What Can the Members of the General Federation of Women's Clubs Do to Aid the Movement for Vocational Education.* [Not dated, but probably 1912.]

[9] Ida M. Tarbell, "What Industrial Training Should We Give the Average Girl?" National Society for the Promotion of Industrial Education, *Proceedings of the Seventh Annual Meet-*

## Value of the Society's Role

The meetings of the Society provided a sounding board for discussion of the various facets of industrial education for women. Slowly but surely these discussions produced some fundamental principles of trade and industrial education for women. Investigation into the nature of these principles was carried out by special studies initiated by some of the pioneer women and later reported in detail in the proceedings of the Society. Representatives of management and labor were involved in planning the structure of industrial education for women, and they frequently assumed the leadership role in these undertakings. The product of the industrial education class was fashioned to fit industrial needs, and the investment of time and energy produced results in women employees who were readily adaptable to the industrial environment.

During the period 1906-17, the Society and its activities continued to be the focal point for all of the significant developments in industrial education for women; there were no secondary centers for growth of the movement. The work of the Society in relation to the program for women was widely publicized, and the Society drew into its membership all of the women with active interest in industrial education. This was an entirely new movement, directed toward filling an urgent social need. The planning of the movement from stage to stage was promoted by the National Society for the Promotion of Industrial Education.

## Early Schools and Pioneer Women

The trend toward a national program of industrial education included programs for women as an integral part of the total movement because, among other reasons, a number of such schools were already in operation. These schools provided a valuable source of information for the National Society as its plans unfolded. Because information about industrial education efforts was so important in planning, it was necessary to know of the actual status of all trade and industrial schools in operation. A study of such schools in 1910 reveals much about the availability of trade and industrial instruction for women.[10]

Some of the schools that offered instruction for girls and women were private, some public; some charged tuition, and others were entirely free; but all intended to provide some instruction that would improve the vocational opportunities of women. In order to identify some of the schools and to suggest the general development of trade and industrial education for women, the list of schools is divided into two parts, those that developed prior to 1900, and those established between 1900 and 1910.

### Schools Prior to 1900

1859, Cooper Union for the Advancement of Science and Art, New York City. Women could enroll in courses for which they had the appropriate educational background, but three courses—stenography, typewriting, and telegraphy—were exclusively for them.

---

ing, October 1913, p. 135. [Note: Ida Tarbell is perhaps better known for her *History of the Standard Oil Company* (1904), one of several books of the period exposing corruption in business and politics.]

[10] Edward H. Reisner, *A Descriptive List of Industrial Schools in the United States*, Bulletin No. 11, National Society for the Promotion of Industrial Education, August 1910.

1868, The Hampton Normal and Agricultural Institute, Hampton, Virginia. The school was established to provide educational facilities for Negroes and Indians, to "prepare them for productive citizenship." The program for girls was largely in the area of domestic science and arts.

1868, The Schofield Normal and Industrial School, Aiken, South Carolina. The program provided for ten years of schooling, the last four of which were devoted to specialized industrial work. It is presumed that Negro girls were enrolled principally in the sewing program.

1869, The Miller School of Albemarle County, Virginia. The school was founded according to the terms of the will of Samuel Miller. (Instruction did not begin until 1878.) Instruction was provided for children 12 to 16 years of age whose parents had been unable to educate them. Between 1878 and 1910, the total number of girls enrolled was 316. The school program was general but combined with "agriculture and the useful arts."

1879, The United States Indian School, Carlisle, Pennsylvania. The school was supported financially by the U.S. Department of the Interior. The program for girls included nursing, cooking, laundering, and housekeeping.

1880, The Tuskegee Normal and Industrial Institute, Tuskegee, Alabama, was established by an act of the Alabama Legislature to provide "young colored men and women the opportunity of learning a vocation, and at the same time of gaining a sound moral and literary training." The famous director of the school was Booker T. Washington. Instruction for girls was

provided in dressmaking, soapmaking, domestic training, mattress making, basketry, and broom making.

1887, The Hebrew Technical School for Girls, New York City. The school prepared students for work in the trades and in commercial occupations and also "for the management of the home."

1893, The Hebrew Education Society, Philadelphia, Pennsylvania, was established to offer instruction to pupils 14 years of age and over in several trade areas. Presumably the instruction areas offered for girls included garment cutting, millinery, and dressmaking.

1894, The Manassas Industrial School, Manassas, Virginia, was established to give elementary education and trade knowledge to colored youth. Admission requirements included the ability to do fourth grade work. Such trade work as was available for girls was limited to sewing and to domestic science.

1894, The California School of Mechanical Arts, San Francisco. This school was established by an endowment of James Lick, an early California pioneer. A grammar school diploma was required for admission. Elementary and advanced courses were provided for girls in the areas of household art and science, dressmaking, domestic science, and millinery.

1895, The Fessenden Academy and Industrial School, Fessenden, Florida, was established for the benefit of the colored race. The program for girls was limited to sewing, cooking and general household-related subjects. Students between the ages of 9 and 21 could be admitted, provided they could show a certificate of good character.

1896, Lewis Institute, Chicago, Illinois, was established as a polytechnic institute for both boys and girls. Vocational and liberal instruction was provided; the special program for girls was limited to domestic economy.

1896, The Christiansburg Industrial Institute, Cambria, Virginia. The school was established to give industrial training to Negro youth and was modeled after the Tuskegee Normal and Industrial Institute. Negro youth who had attained the age of 14 and could give evidence of good character and health were admitted. Cooking, sewing, millinery, and laundry work were offered for girls.

1896, The Montgomery Industrial School for Girls, Montgomery, Alabama, was established "to uplift the women and to elevate the home life of the colored race." General elementary education was included in the program of instruction along with domestic science, sewing, housework, simple nursing, and basketry.

1897, The Vorhees Industrial School, Denmark, South Carolina. The school was established by Elizabeth Evelyn Wright, a graduate of Tuskegee in 1894. An age requirement of 14 years was imposed, but no literary requirement was enforced. Instruction for girls was offered in sewing, laundering, millinery, basketry, nursing, broom making, cooking, and housekeeping.

1897, Manual Training and Industrial School for Colored Youth, Bordentown, New Jersey. Alternate days were spent in academic and industrial work. Children who could read and write were admitted. Programs for girls included cooking, dressmaking, basketry, and needle work.

In addition to the schools listed above there were others that identified the enrollees as "students" or as "pupils," without specific indications of special attention for girls and women. It may be presumed that a number of these schools did offer special instruction for girls and that in part the instruction was vocationally oriented.

## Schools Organized Between 1900 and 1910

1902, Manhattan Trade School for Girls, New York City. The aim of the school was to prepare for self-supporting work in the trades for girls who were forced to labor at the earliest time allowed by law for entrance into a skilled trade. A variety of occupational instruction was offered in dressmaking, millinery, and related areas. Girls were required to have completed the 5A grade and the age of entrance was 14 to 17 years.

1902, The Okolona Industrial College, Okolona, Mississippi. The school was organized for colored youth and included a "practical literary education" and trade instruction. The programs of nursing, sewing, millinery, typewriting, and housekeeping were presumably for women.

1904, The Colored Industrial and Normal School, Salisbury, Maryland. Instruction was directed toward making colored children proficient in the common school subjects and to provide in addition special attention to industrial training. The school admitted children at six years of age. Instruction in sewing and cooking were included in the program for girls.

1905, The New York Trade School for Girls, Syracuse, New York. The school's particular aim was to provide

347

trade instruction for girls who were compelled to go to work upon leaving the elementary schools. Instruction was offered in dressmaking, cooking, plain sewing, and millinery. An extensive program for employed girls was also available in the afternoon, evening, and Saturday classes.

1905, The Long Island City Evening High and Trade School, Long Island City, New York. The particular aim of the school was to provide instruction for employed workers which would improve their proficiency. Employed women could find advanced work in dressmaking, millinery, and domestic science.

1906, The Secondary Industrial School of Columbus, Georgia. This school was established to prepare boys and girls "for intelligent and efficient service and for good earning power in business life or the more important industries." Consequently a wide variety of general courses was offered in addition to courses related to mechanics, textiles, business, home economics, and domestic science.

1907, The High School of Practical Arts for Girls, Boston, Massachusetts. The school provided emphasis upon occupations that employed large numbers of women. A grammar school diploma was required for admission. Courses in household science and arts, sewing, dressmaking, and millinery were offered in the industrial department in addition to a substantial general program required of all students.

1908, The New York Evening High School for Women, New York City. The work in this school was devoted exclusively to occupational preparation, from general trade work to highly specialized programs. Students were required to have completed six years of elementary school for admission. The course selection procedures included a plan of vocational guidance.

1908, The Technical High School, Cleveland, Ohio. Emphasis in this high school program was directed toward industrial employment. Instruction in domestic science and applied art was based upon a comprehensive program of general studies. It was intended that such instruction would make it possible for graduates "to assume positions of industrial leadership in which skill and technical knowledge are prerequisite."

1908, The Evening Industrial School, Boston, Massachusetts. This school was originally established in 1848 and reorganized in 1908 in order to make it more effective in its vocational objectives. Students were admitted on the basis of an examination in the subject matter of the elementary school, and were required to have reached the age of 15 years. Girls could receive instruction in dressmaking, sewing, millinery, embroidery, and cooking.

1909, The Five Points Italian Trade School, New York City. "The aim of the school is to give elementary trade instruction that will decrease the years of apprenticeship and in certain trades such as Power Sewing Machine Work, eliminate apprenticeship altogether." Admission required the ability to read and write. Students must have reached the age of 14 years as a minimum.

1909, The New Bedford Industrial School, New Bedford, Massachusetts. The school provided instruction for girls over 14 years of age in domestic arts. Applicants were required to have the ability to read, write, and speak the English language.

348

1909, The Lawrence Industrial School, Lawrence, Massachusetts. The school did not propose to provide a student ready to enter into a highly skilled trade but rather to provide a background which would open avenues to industrial employment. Any girl in Massachusetts 14 years of age or over who had completed the first six years of the public school could enter the domestic science program.

1909, The 63rd Street Evening Trade School of the Children's Aid Society, New York City. The aim of the school was to give "elementary or introductory trade instruction" in the following areas to students over 14 years of age who could read and write: restaurant cooking, home cooking, dressmaking, millinery, housekeeping, carpentry, janitor work, plain sewing, basket making, chair caning, and grade work.

1909, The Albany Vocational School, Albany, New York. "The aim of the school is to give boys and girls 14 years of age a training that will prepare them to enter advantageously some branch of industrial work." A student of 12 years might be admitted provided that she had completed the first six years of schooling. The four-year program was comprehensive, with roughly half of the instruction in general subjects.

1909, The Hudson Industrial School, Hudson, New York. The program was designed to interest students of the grammar grades in vocational pursuits, and the hours of study were equally divided between "bookwork and shopwork."

1909, Saunders' School of Trades, Yonkers, New York, (previously known as the Yonkers Trade School.) The school was endowed with $500,000 from the estate of Ervin S. Saunders, but otherwise supported by state funds. The purpose of the school was to prepare pupils directly for work in the trades. Possession of a grammar school diploma or evidence of ability to undertake the work of the school were the only requirements. About half of the school day was devoted to instruction in English, mathematics, history, and citizenship. Instruction for girls was evidently limited to sewing and cooking.

1909, The Girls' Trade School, Boston, Massachusetts, proposed a program of instruction "to fit girls to become skilled workwomen." Admission required girls to be able to read and write English and to have some knowledge of hand sewing. The minimum age for admission was 14 years. Courses were offered in dressmaking, millinery, clothing machine operating, and straw machine operating. Supplementary work in related subjects was also provided.

1909, The Milwaukee School of Trades for Girls, Milwaukee, Wisconsin, was established with the definite aim of teaching trades to girls. Admission requirements included an age level of 14 years and ability to read and write English and to perform fundamental operations of arithmetic. Dressmaking and millinery, cooking and housekeeping, art and design, industrial history, workshop mathematics, English and physical culture were included in the program of instruction.

1910, The School of Domestic Science, Rochester, New York, provided training for girls "for home or for vocations." Pupils were required to have completed the sixth grade and be 14 years old "or nearly so." Instruction

349

was offered in dressmaking, millinery, and cooking.

### Significance of the Early Schools

Establishment of schools to provide instruction of an industrial nature for girls and women is clearly a reflection of the needs of the time. Interest in a national movement for the benefit of industrial education developed rapidly as a result of the progress noted in the early schools.

Organization, content, and direction of the early schools followed no single plan, and the schools were representative of purely local conditions. Obviously one school would profit from the experiences of another and would in turn influence other schools as they developed industrial programs. It is evident that most of the schools recognized the need for pre-employment instruction and also for instruction for employed women. The age of admission of 14 years was almost universal. Value was placed upon completion of the elementary school and upon skill in the fundamental operations. Many of the schools of high school grade planned industrial instruction as a part of the total school program, though not at the expense of the common learning. These trends, easily identifiable in the programs of the early schools, were carried as principles into the Smith-Hughes Act.

Significant also is the wide range of interests represented in the formation of industrial education programs for girls and women. Public and private school groups, religious and fraternal groups, and civic groups all partici-

pated in the organization and development of schools. No small part of the movement toward schools that would provide industrial instruction for girls and women came from the influence of wealthy persons who provided substantial financial support. On the other extreme even the schools that started largely with an "idea and determination" seemed somehow to find a sufficient number of willing contributors to keep their programs in operation.

### Pioneer Women in Industrial Education [11]

*Elizabeth M. Fish (1875-1939).* Miss Elizabeth M. Fish, native of Minnesota, was graduated from the University of Minnesota in 1897 and continued graduate work in later years at the University of Chicago and the University of Munich. From 1903 to 1914 she taught school in several cities in Minnesota and in Spokane, Washington. In 1914 she was invited to Minneapolis to organize and become the principal of the newly established Girls' Vocational High School.

The high school was organized to provide training for girls who intended to seek employment at an early age in the industrial occupations in Minneapolis and nearby communities. Courses were offered in a variety of women's trades. The quality of instruction and the achievement of graduates brought national recognition to the school. Graduates of the cosmetology program made excellent records in state examinations, and graduates of the practical nurse program were sought eagerly by employers because

[11] Adapted from, Helen Livingstone and Blanch Nechanicky, *The Women Pioneers in Trade and Industrial Education in the United States.* American Vocational Association, May 1952.

of the quality of their classroom instruction and their clinical training in the sponsoring hospital.

Miss Fish was unique in her organization and management of the school. Her administrative practices were democratic in nature. She did not impose or direct, but provided leadership conducive to the development of good working relationships among colleagues. Faculty meetings were laboratory clinics in which the group assessed their needs and proposed action to solve problems in a cordial atmosphere devoid of stress.

Graduates of the school were not given trade diplomas until they had been successful in employment in the occupation for which they were trained. When trial employment showed that a student's preparation was inadequate, the student returned to school to make up deficiencies.

**Helen Rebecca Hildreth (1864-1921).** After high school graduation Helen Rebecca Hildreth prepared for teaching by attending the state normal school at Winona, Minnesota. After several years of teaching in the West she returned to her native New York and completed a baccalaureate degree at Columbia University.

Miss Hildreth's first experience in trade education came with her appointment as Executive Secretary of the Manhattan Trade School where she served until 1910. For a year she held the position of principal of the State Trade School for Girls in New Britain, Connecticut. She then served as Director of the Education Department of the Women's Educational and Industrial Union, where she was involved in teacher training and in the supervision of girls' vocational schools in Massachusetts.

In 1913 Miss Hildreth was appointed director of the Worcester Trade School for Girls. But her fame as an industrial educator of girls transcended the confines of the Worcester school. She was soon involved in a country-wide demand for her services, and she traveled widely in response to such requests.

Students drew inspiration for their work from Miss Hildreth, and she was unusually successful in motivating them to become better workers, to develop pride in what they did, and to share in the dignity of work.

Miss Hildreth's demonstrated administrative ability gave her properly the rank of one of the "foremost executives of trade schools in this country."

**Helen Livingstone (1882?-1958).** Helen Livingstone, native of New York, was graduated from the Northfield School for Girls (Massachusetts) in 1900. She taught for two years in Connecticut and then entered Pratt Institute, Brooklyn, New York, in the teacher training class, graduating in 1904.

From 1904 to 1907 she taught industrial arts to boys and girls in the elementary grades in Pittsburgh, Pennsylvania. During the period 1907-12 she taught trade dressmaking and food service in the industrial education department of the high school. Beginning in 1917 she served for seven years as a city supervisor in Pittsburgh and as a part-time teacher in the City Teachers College. She received her bachelor's degree from the University of Pittsburgh in 1916.

351

In 1919 Miss Livingstone began a 10-year career in Detroit in connection with vocational programs for girls at the Cass Technical High School. In addition, for two years she served as Director of the Continuation School for Girls.

In 1929 she returned to New York to reorganize an old technical school for girls and to serve as its principal until 1932. During her spare time she offered extension courses in methods of teaching for women trade teachers, and in 1936 she was appointed to the regular teacher training staff of the Industrial Education Bureau, State Education Department, University of the State of New York, and assigned to the New York City office.

Her work in teacher education and her publications related to vocational education, together with her vast background of actual teaching and administrative work in vocational education, gave her a reputation as an authority on industrial education for women and girls. Miss Livingstone retired in 1947.

**Florence M. Marshall (1870-1947).** Miss Marshall received her bachelor's degree from Boston University in 1899 and a professional diploma from Teachers College, Columbia University in 1901. In 1903 she founded the Boston Trade School, the first trade school for girls in this country. She owned the school and served as its director until 1908.

Miss Marshall was a staff member of the Douglas Commission, appointed by Governor Douglas of Massachusetts in 1905 to study that state's need for trade education.[12] She also served on numerous other commissions and committees in this country and abroad. In 1914 she was appointed by President Wilson as a member of the Commission on National Aid to Vocational Education. In 1911 Miss Marshall was appointed principal of the Manhattan Trade School for Girls.

The Manhattan Trade School for Girls changed frequently in organization and character during Miss Marshall's administration, as it was gradually transformed from a one-year trade school to a thoroughly accredited high school, but high standards of occupational competency were always required. Deportment, good manners, and fundamentals of good citizenship were given equal attention, for Miss Marshall thought these essential to a good trade worker.

Close relationships were established with industry and with former students. Classrooms simulated industrial environment, and the school was on the frontier of new programs in industrial education. Beauty culture as a trade training course offered by the public schools had its start there.

The Manhattan Trade School for Girls set many standards, and its program was emulated by other schools. Miss Marshall believed in the work she was doing and was an active and tireless promoter of industrial education and truly one of its pioneers.

**Cleo Murtland (1873-1965).** Miss Cleo Murtland received her bachelor's degree from Teachers College, Columbia University in 1917 and her master's degree in 1921. She was a teacher in the Manhattan Trade School for Girls,

---

[12] One of the results of the findings of the Commission was that the Boston Trade School was taken over by the City to become the first public trade school in the country.

1907-11, and principal of the David Hale Fanning Trade School for Girls, Worcester, Massachusetts, 1911-13.

In 1913 Miss Murtland became the Assistant Secretary of the National Society for the Promotion of Industrial Education, and for three years her work was closely related to industrial development, particularly the development which was significant in promoting the vocational education movement in the United States.

For two years Miss Murtland served as principal of the Philadelphia Trade School for Girls, and then in 1919 she began her long and distinguished career as an associate professor of vocational education at the University of Michigan. She was the author of several books, contributor of numerous magazine articles, and participant in a number of special studies and surveys related to vocational education.

Throughout her professional life she contributed generously to the improvement and expansion of industrial education for women. Her advice and service were sought frequently in connection with the major developments in industrial education. She retired in 1943.

*Mary Schenck Woolman (1860-1940).*[13] Mary Schenck's early life followed a pattern characteristic of the well-to-do New Jersey family: cultural atmosphere, a library of fine books, private schools, and an invigorating family environment. Her early schooling in Philadelphia (private Quaker school) included household studies along with the language and history which were her specialities. She also attended classes at the University of Pennsylvania, but that university did not offer degrees to women.

She was married in 1882 to John Woolman, a well known New Jersey lawyer. Ill health of her husband and mother reduced financial resources, and with other increasing responsibilities forced the sale of the New Jersey home. The family moved to New York City in 1891, where Mrs. Woolman was employed in correcting manuscripts for publication. Her critical reviews attracted the attention of the president of Teachers College and in 1892 she became a member of the science department staff.

Mrs. Woolman entered upon this work with enthusiasm and determination. She spread the idea of sewing as a day-school subject and served as an active member, and later an officer, of the New York Association of Sewing Schools. She changed sewing instruction from practice for its own sake to constructive work on useful articles of clothing. Her methods were advanced for the time, but at length her domestic arts course at Teachers College moved toward a scientific basis which attracted attention, and Mrs. Woolman was much in demand as a teacher and lecturer.

In 1902 Mrs. Woolman was released half-time from her Teachers College assignment to participate in the development of the Manhattan Trade School for Girls. For eight years she was the director of that school which in 1910 became a part of the public school system of New York City. Students did not enroll in a narrow oc-

---

[13] See also *Journal of Home Economics,* November 1940, for a comprehensive review by Anna M. Cooley of the life and contributions of Mary Schenck Woolman.

cupational program but one which involved art, English, design, textiles, mathematics, and other subjects thought to contribute to the development of citizenship.[14]

Mary Schenck Woolman's later activities were numerous. She was at one time or another the director of the Women's Educational and Industrial Union, Boston; head of the home economics department, Simmons College; and textile specialist for the General Federation of Women's Clubs. Coincident with these employments she lectured and worked with professional associations. Creative and imaginative, she seemed as well to have unlimited energy and strength, all of which made her contributions to trade education for girls a valuable social service.

### Significance of the Work of the Pioneer Women

Many other women are no doubt entitled to recognition for having shared in the pioneer efforts in industrial education for women. It can be said, however, that in the historical record these six are prominent, and their achievements are representative of the development of industrial education for women.

Common elements are strikingly evident in the work of these pioneers of industrial education for women. Each was well educated, much better in fact than was customarily the case of women in the early 1900's. Each appeared to have a sense of deep social concern for the plight of the working woman. All were aware of the lack of appropriate instruction for women who worked or planned to work. They were aware also of the necessity for instruction to be directly related to the needs of industry. Not one of the six pioneers thought of industrial education for women in a narrow sense. Their programs tended to be comprehensive but directed toward both occupational and personal needs. Each had the rare ability to work effectively with others, and each believed in the dignity of work.

## The Program During the Early Years of the Federal Board

With the formation of the Federal Board for Vocational Education the active role in the development of industrial education for women was transferred from the National Society for the Promotion of Industrial Education to the Federal Board. The Society did not cease to function in relation to the development of industrial education for women; the spotlight was merely focused on the activities of the Federal Board because this was the source that would generate new programs under the Smith-Hughes Act.

### The Girls Go to War

During the early part of World War I women were encouraged to enter industrial employment, but were not urged to enter the emergency training programs provided by the Federal Board. The thought here was that women would release men from a number of occupations and thus the men would be available for war work. The point of view was short-lived, however, because of the growing attitude

---

[14] Mary S. Woolman, *The Making of a Trade School*. Boston: Whitcomb and Barrows, 1910.

that women could be employed in any industry, although many positions in these industries were at the time unsuitable for women. The whole problem boiled down to what kinds of occupations the women were willing to undertake.[15]

More than one and a half million women were reported to be at work in war-related industries in the early part of 1918. Large industrial plants opened positions for women, and many of the plants started their own programs of instruction; the public schools offered supplementary courses. Success stories of women in war work were the rule. Stories about failures were hard to find. Much had been said about the Smith-Hughes Act as a means of providing democracy in education. Democracy had meant also "equal opportunity," and the facts about women, industry, and education for war work seemed to prove that discrimination in regard to women at work was beginning to become a thing of the past.[16]

**Post-War Expansion**

The total problem of the growth of industrial education following the war included some significant changes in relation to employment of women. Attention to "employment management" by industry enlarged the occupational areas open to women.[17] Compulsory education laws and the part-time continuation education classes that were established throughout the United States were factors in the expansion of opportunity for women. Concepts of the employment of women were changing rapidly. The use of power driven machines in industry facilitated development of new opportunities.

Enlarging the scope of women's work is a matter of breaking down prejudices and seeking an outlook toward better opportunities for them and a broader vision of what technical education may accomplish.[18]

The experience in some of the trade schools indicated that the trained worker was able to command a good wage almost regardless of her age. The Manhattan Trade School for Girls had requests for over 3,000 positions which it could not fill and the indications were that the girls who were out of work were those without training for a particular line of work. The trade school experience also indicated the necessity of vocational guidance and the need for proper information about trade positions.[19]

Interest in vocational education for girls developed also in foreign lands after the war. This was a direct result of the participation of women in the war work of their countries. News about the development of industrial education for women in the United States had been widely circulated, and

---

[15] "Women and War Work," *The Vocational Summary,* Vol. 1, No. 3, July 1918, p. 22.

[16] Anna L. Burdick, "Training of Girls and Women for Emergency War Work," *The Vocational Summary,* Vol. 1, No. 4, August 1918, pp. 8-10.

[17] "The Federal Vocational Education Act and Employment Management as Factors in Developing Industrial Training for Women," *The Vocational Summary,* Vol. 1, No. 6, October 1918, p. 24.

[18] *Third Annual Report of the Federal Board for Vocational Education,* Vol. I, 1919, p. 66.

[19] Anna L. Burdick, "The Manhattan Trade School for Girls," *The Vocational Summary,* Vol. 2, No. 6, October 1919, p. 111.

it was not long before visitors from other lands were traveling in the United States. The Mayor of Rome, Italy, sent Countess Maria A. Loschi to visit schools and report on the training of girls and women in wage-earning occupations. Miss S. Chang of the Shin Chow Girls' High School, Shanghai, was sent by the Chinese Ministry of Education, "to inspect schools and classes for vocational education for girls and women." Mlle. Marg Bourat, representing the French Minister of Labor, visited many of the schools for girls in the United States.[20] The Federal Board arranged the itineraries for these visitors and provided opportunities for discussion of the general problem of vocational education with American women. The American Academy of Political Science in New York invited Mlle. Bourat to present a paper to that group related to her observations about vocational education. Such exchanges of information created additional emphasis upon the role of woman in industrial education.

The immediate post-war expansion was a period of discovery of new relationships between women at work and the vocational education program. The theoretical view that employees could attend classes after their work hours and thereby improve their opportunity for higher pay and advancement actually worked out in practice. As a specific example, the garment industry in California (75 percent of the employees were women) encouraged establishment of classes in power machine stitching in the evening program of vocational education.[21] In addition to perfecting skills at the machines, the women were taught a technical knowledge of the machines. The net result of the instruction was satisfactory from the standpoint of increased wages and for promotion to the first steps of supervision and administration.

## Some Trends

The necessities of the war produced evidence that women could perform a greater variety of industrial work than had previously been recognized.

Some industries had jobs suitable for women but had not provided a suitable working environment.

Consideration was given to the idea that different types of industrial education were necessary to accommodate the different objectives women had in relation to the world of work.

The public had tended largely to accept the idea of women in the industrial scene, and without prejudice or discrimination. Public and private schools expanded their curricula, and new opportunities were offered to women in industrial education.

## Growth of the Program for Women

Prior to the twentieth century, women had not been employed in industry in sufficient numbers to demand any particular consideration from the point of view of vocational training. The public attitude had in fact been one of prejudice against industrial training for women. Women had usually stayed in industry only briefly,

---

[20] Anna L. Burdick, "Foreign Interest in Training Girls for Wage-Earning Occupations," *The Vocational Summary*, Vol. 1, No. 10, February 1919, p. 14.

[21] "Women Workers are Trained for Promotion," *The Vocational Summary*, Vol. 2, No. 2, June 1919, p. 34.

and there had been few occupations open to them that required specialized training or skill. But by 1919 there were 11,000,000 wage-earning women in the United States.

There was no central source that received reports on the enrollment of women in industrial education prior to the beginning of the national program. After 1917 state boards for vocational education reported their enrollments for all students involved in vocational education under the Smith-Hughes and subsequent acts. Such figures of enrollment would not account for private, corporation, or other schools that had no reason to report their activities.

The purpose of the trade and industrial education program for girls and women was expressed in three parts:

1. To prepare the girl to enter the field of wage earning;
2. To enable the girl or woman already employed to improve or to change to a more congenial or profitable occupation; and
3. To insure progression or advancement in the type of work in which she is already engaged.[22]

These purposes were directed toward improved products, increased output, higher wages, and better standards of living.

Some states had not taken seriously any obligation to stimulate programs of industrial education for women, and the Federal Board urged them to move toward more programs for women. Lack of such programs was a definite

handicap to the woman worker. In this connection the Board reached three general conclusions about employment of women, which were brought to the attention of industrial education leaders.

1. That lack of vocational training works an immeasurable hardship on the young wage earner by holding her productive efficiency below the normal standard of wage.
2. That inexperience, lack of confidence, and ignorance of industrial organization and requirements seriously embarrass and handicap the mature woman who returns to employment or who enters an industrial organization for the first time.
3. That the adult woman worker continuing in employment, partly through lack of opportunity for training and partly because of the prevailing attitude that greater responsibilities and their rewards are closed to her, seldom advances from the lower or intermediate states of employment to positions of responsibility which increased maturity and experience justify.[23]

Not only was it necessary to arouse the school authorities to action but the women themselves needed to promote the need for industrial education among the communities and employers.

In 1923, after six years of promotion under the Smith-Hughes Act, the Board could report significant gains both in the enrollment of girls and women and in the expansion of the program to new areas of instruction.[24] Trade courses for girls in all-day trade schools were operating in 25 centers

---

[22] *Fourth Annual Report of the Federal Board for Vocational Education.* Washington: Government Printing Office, 1920, p. 40.

[23] *Ibid.,* p. 41.

[24] Federal Board for Vocational Education, *Yearbook, 1923.* Washington: Government Printing Office, 1924, pp. 173-174, 274-287.

throughout the country. Many courses that had previously been open only to boys were now admitting girls. Women were enrolling in evening trade extension classes, and the growth in part-time cooperative courses was encouraging.

The increase in enrollment for women in trade and industrial education from 1920 to 1930 exceeded 225 percent. A comparison of the growth for the decade is shown below.[25]

|  | Enrollment 1920 | Enrollment 1930 |
| --- | --- | --- |
| Evening Classes | 1,424 | 9,902 |
| Trade Extension | 5,445 | 9,834 |
| General Continuation | 40,298 | 166,788 |
| All-Day | 3,780 | 9,575 |

Although these changes imply a significant change in program growth, the actual number of women enrolled in trade and industrial education classes was far below occupational needs.

## Women and the Labor Force— World War II

In the fall of 1941, just prior to Pearl Harbor, Eunice S. Harrison reviewed the progress of women's work in trade and industrial education.[26] Her analysis of the general situation was much like the view one would have from a high elevation, where down below could be seen the entire scene in all its detail. Nationwide, the public school trade and industrial education program had established courses for the full-time student. Evening courses designed to supplement the skill and

trade knowledge of employed women were being conducted with attention to expanding the program to cover a wide variety of need. Even in the new national defense education program a large number of women had enrolled for instruction that would lead to industrial jobs.

One of the striking elements in the panorama of women's trade instruction in 1941 was the variety of trade areas involved (46 separate occupations as Mrs. Harrison reports) and in the obvious attempts to keep instruction up to date with the change in women's occupations. The learning environment reflected as closely as possible the working environment. Increased attention to the occupational needs for nursing, dental assisting, medical secretaries, and similar laboratory type occupations had produced a small group of very successful programs over the United States.

What was happening in related instruction for women's occupations was an indication that basic scientific knowledge underlying the materials and processes for each trade was rapidly becoming an integral part of the instruction. It was believed "that fundamental facts in bacteriology, biology, chemistry, physics, physiology, anatomy, and dermatology can be painlessly taught if practically demonstrated." [27]

### First War Training Efforts

The first major production and training efforts of the national defense

---

[25] Adapted from, *Fourteenth Annual Report of the Federal Board for Vocational Education, 1930.* Washington: Government Printing Office, 1930, p. 83.

[26] Eunice S. Harrison, "Women's Trades March Onward," *AVA Journal and News Bulletin,* Vol. XVI, No. 3, September 1941, pp. 88-90.

[27] *Ibid.,* p. 90.

program were initiated while the nation was still in the period of economic depression. Employment of women while men were still out of work was of national concern; consequently, few women were involved in the training programs during the early months of national defense training.

But employment requirements for the future appeared to be extensive, and involvement of large numbers of women was unavoidable. Manpower shortages after January, 1942, were critical, and by October there were 74,675 women enrolled in war production training classes. The average monthly enrollment of women during 1943 was 48,383.

The numbers were consistently largest in a few states. California, first to pioneer in the extensive use of women, trained the largest number, 221,609, which was 15 percent of all women trained. New York ranked next with 130,446, then Pennsylvania with 117,533. New York trained the largest number in preemployment courses and California, the largest number in supplementary courses.[28]

At first women were trained for the lighter types of work, and standards for age and physical condition were required. Later nearly all restrictions were removed, and women were trained across the board for any occupation in war production. The early practice of segregated vocational education classes for women gave way to no distinction in training classes, "since it was soon apparent that no distinction would be made on the job."[29]

Elaborate publicity schemes of vocational educators and the employment services attracted new groups of women to training classes. Unusual performance of women in war production work was cited. Speakers reached thousands of women through their club activities, and appeals were based upon the "patriotism aspect rather than upon monetary gains."

Women did not lack mechanical aptitude, although many were not familiar with mechanical terminology. Training was adjusted to the ability of the learner. "The greater number of trainees were enrolled in classes for aviation services, machine shop work, shipbuilding, radio services, and welding."[30] The total number of women trained during the entire war production training program was 1,501,453, which was 20 percent of all vocational training offered.

Many women were inexperienced in work outside the homes, and they needed assistance in many ways. Women counselors helped trainees select clothing and reach other decisions about their training and work. "When the trainees knew what to expect on the job and when they became skilled in doing their work they proved acceptable and proficient war production workers."[31]

### Instruction and Supervision of Women

It is significant that war experience proved that training for women need not be essentially different than for

---

[28] W. Daniel Musser, *Vocational Training for War Production Workers, Final Report*, Bulletin 1946, No. 10. Washington: Federal Security Agency, U.S. Office of Education, 1946, p. 75.

[29] *Ibid.*, p. 75.

[30] *Ibid.*, p. 76.

[31] *Ibid.*, p. 77.

men, even though working in industry was largely a new experience for most of the women. Women teachers soon were added to the instructor ranks, and in some cases all of the students in their classes would be men. The "chilly reception" accorded women students by some instructors who had never previously had women in their classes wore off when women proved to be able and intelligent workers. Some men claimed that women were among the most successful workers. There were, however, a few instructors who refused to instruct women on the grounds that, "Women were a distracting influence, and could never learn to do any work." [32]

Stories about women in classes, although mostly not true, would arise from instructional situations, and men would have capital fun based on the inexperience of women with industrial tools and processes. Take the case of the woman who told her roommate, "I learned to read a micrometer today and I can read to one thousandth of an inch." "That's nice," her roommate replied, "How many thousandths are there in an inch?" "I don't know," the woman answered, "but there must be millions of them." This was a part of the environment that added fun and zest to the seriousness of the business at hand.

The states varied considerably in the ways in which they attempted to meet all of the problems of women and war work. A countless number of conferences were held throughout the nation on problems of training, supervision, counseling, and general management as related to women at work. One of the striking examples of this work was the report from the state of Tennessee of the conferences conducted with women representatives of industry concerning the general topic of "More Efficient Use of Women in Industry." The simplified analysis presented the key issues met in conference discussion. Cartoons were used to drive home particular points. Important items affecting the work of the woman worker were isolated, and a number of solutions were suggested. This was a thoroughly sound review by the people most concerned with the many problems war work presented to the woman worker. The report was a source of information that in effect set standard procedures, or perhaps more accurately identified areas of consensus, so that the best possible solutions to particular difficulties were identified for any person confronted with similiar problems.

In addition to the thoroughly professional report that presented practical solutions to real situations, a poem in the lighter vein was reproduced from the *Press Piper*, Kingsport Press, Kingsport, Tennessee:

> There's lipstick on the drinking
>   fountain,
> There's talcum on the bench,
> There's cold cream on the surface plate,
> Hand lotion on the wrench.
> And "Evening in Paris" in the air,
> That once held lube oil smell,
> I just picked up a bobby pin,
> Believe me, war is hell!

W. J. McAuliffe suggested that the writer of the poem was writing for the eyes of "Friend Wife," otherwise it would read as follows:

---

[32] *Ibid.*, p. 114.

A cutie bent over the drinking fountain,
Is a quite attractive sight,
And a pretty gal on the next bench
As company, suits me all right.
The smell of perfume as she leans close
To see how I handle a tool,
Don't make my job any tougher,
But admit it? I ain't no fool!
She don't borry my chawin' tobaccy
Nor ask for the loan of my dough,
And besides the dame ain't wacky,
What she's here for she seems to know.
Oh, what this war's done to the old
shop,
May make some dumbbells mad,
But, brother, I really ain't kicking
a-tall,
This war stuff ain't so bad! [33]

This story like countless others reflected the changes in industry with the employment of large numbers of women workers. Told in fun and jest, the poem has an unmistakable thread of recognition of and tribute to the fine work characteristic of the women in war production.[34]

Louise Moore in discussing some of the early apprehensions concerning women trainees indicated that management was reluctant to engage women in production work because they feared a low level of mechanical aptitude, a high accident rate, and the possibility that they would constitute a disturbing element in the factory. Vocational school authorities visual-ized difficulties in the differing rates at which women would progress in instruction. Such fears were largely groundless. "No training opened to women has subsequently been closed to them because they proved incapable of doing the job. Some women have been available for work in every field, no matter how hard, hot, or dirty." [35]

## The Augusta Clawson Story

For a short time during World War II, Augusta H. Clawson was a welder in an Oregon shipyard. Among the thousands of women who did similar work during the war, her story is unique.

Early in 1943 the War Production Training Branch of the Vocational Division, U.S. Office of Education, became aware that a large number of women who were trained for work in shipyards were quitting soon after beginning their employment. Why? At this point Augusta Clawson enters the story. As she put it, "In April 1943 I made a strange bargain and because of it I have four ships at sea." [36]

In 1943 Augusta Clawson was serving as Special Agent Training Women for War Production, Vocational Division, U.S. Office of Education. Since

[33] Tennessee State Board for Vocational Education, *More Efficient Use of Women in Industry.* Nashville, Tennessee, 1944, p. iv.

[34] Extraordinary performance and patriotic attitude of women was more of a rule than an exception. In one instance, while the author was involved with vocational training in the Navy, a woman and her daughter applied for work. Their husbands were both in the service and they requested the "hardest work we can get." They were totally unconcerned about the pay. Both women were trained as fork-lift operators and they became quite adept in the work at the U.S. Naval Supply Depot at San Pedro, California.

[35] Louise Moore, *Training Women War Production Workers: The Work of the Public Vocational Schools,* VE-ND Misc. 3674, Federal Security Agency, Office of Education, August 1943, pp. 4-5.

[36] Augusta H. Clawson, *Shipyard Diary of a Woman Welder.* New York: Penguin Books, 1944, p. vii.

Miss Clawson's office had responsibilities concerning training of women welders, it was reasonable that the office should direct some effort toward learning if the shipyard training was in any way at fault in relation to the short period of employment. First hand experience with the problem was necessary if the problem was to be solved. Her "strange bargain" was her agreement to go through a welding training program in a shipyard and then go to work as a welder—in other words to have a critical look at the problem where it existed and in the environment where it occurred. So, early in April, 1943, Miss Augusta H. Clawson, Special Agent of the Office of Education, left Washington, D.C. and reappeared in an Oregon shipyard as Miss Gus Clawson from New Jersey. Only a handful of people knew of her true identity and purpose.

*Welding Trainee.* The routine procedures of the U.S. Employment Service and the Union Hiring Hall were completed, and Gus was assigned to a shipyard school. Counseling was provided by both the employment service and the hiring hall; still there were a number of routine problems which she had to solve for herself concerning the clothing needed as a trainee and other things about the job in general.

At school she started immediately to weld and to adjust to the new environment of heavy clothes, confined quarters, dirt, grime, and heat. There were movies about welding, lectures about health and safety, and there were people and trainee talk. Mothers with sons in the service, mothers with small children and nursery school problems, and a grandmother were among Gus's trainee companions.

There were the ones they called "Colorado," and "Missouri," and "Shorty," and the two instructors, and the two pretty cousins who had to take a day off to get their hair done, and the couple who put half their pay into war bonds. There were also hospitality and friendliness and sore muscles. Soon Gus mastered the new environment and learned how to "discipline unruly bubbles" of molten iron. With assistance from her instructor she progressed from horizontal, to vertical, to overhead welding. ("Overhead is fun and not hard.") And she passed her welding tests. So after eight days of training Gus Clawson reported to the shipyard as a welder operator.

*Gus the Welder.* After the first day on the real job Gus summed up her experience by saying, "It's incredible! It's inhuman! It's horrible! And it's marvelous! I don't believe the blitz could be noisier." During the following days she worked on command—a tack here, a brace there—up the ladder, down the ladder, into tiny spaces, and in the sunshine and in the rain. Teamwork and understanding developed with experience as did satisfaction when difficult welds met inspection. Because shipfitting was not as continuous as production, Gus learned that idle workers were not necessarily loafing. The shipfitter depends upon the burner, a welder waits for the shipfitter, but all "must be on the spot when needed." Her pride was without measure when her attendance badge, which had read "New Hire," was replaced by one reading "Welder."

After seven days of shipyard welding Gus realized that she had no fear or dread of the work but was apprehensive concerning overhead welding in which her training was not as thorough at it could have been. And the noise didn't seem to matter anymore.

When the new girls began to brag about having had special attention because they were all taken to the school for a lecture about the shipyard, Gus could only glow in silent satisfaction —the orientation course had been started because of her report on the confusion of the first day.

An accident caused by a broken welding lead line brought the price of carelessness to everyone's attention. Ten men had been on the brink of death in the blaze because "workers were careless." A drive on safety was instigated—air hoses, electrician's tape, and more lighting appeared, but the work went on as if nothing had happened. Gus became thoroughly convinced that the quality and quantity of training had to be increased—there was too much at stake, including human life.

Augusta Clawson continued her role as a welder until May 27 (nearly two months, with a few days out to report her experiences to a meeting of the State Directors of Vocational Education who were meeting in Cincinnati) and then left the yard to resume her work as Special Agent of the Office of Education. There was more than just a little reluctance to leave; she had made many friends and the work had become exciting despite its harshness. But she had attained the goal she desired, and her "strange bargain" had been completed. She could speak with authority about women welders in the shipyards because she could speak from experience—and speak she did, to educators everywhere in the interests of improving training for women.

**Aphorisms of Gus.** Throughout her report on experiences as a welder Miss Clawson made observations that seem to summarize her thoughts and provide other insight into her fabulous experience. The following is a sample:

There is nothing in training to prepare you for the excruciating noise you get down in the ship. (p. 59)

I wonder, too, whether in our training we couldn't be taught to weld from unusual angles and positions. (p. 60)

More and more I marvel at training that in eight days can give enough to make us worth anything on the job. And we are worth something. We're building ships. (pp. 70-71)

It isn't only your muscles that must harden. It's your nerve too. (p. 73)

There was a grand feeling of all working together. (p. 75)

I have come to the firm conviction that what wears one out is not work—it's apprehension. (p. 89)

I think we college graduates flatter ourselves when we think our academic degrees somehow set us apart from other people. (p. 95)

I am impressed by the poor work habits of many. (p. 111)

One can't (despair) of real democracy when one finds what I found in this cross-section of the average American. (p. 157)

There is much more of the Augusta Clawson story than can be told here. She made a deep impression upon the industrial educators she met and talked with, and they carried her ideas into practice. Her story is a part of the total background of the development of industrial education for women.

NOTE: In a letter to the author, dated October 27, 1966, Miss Clawson said, "Believe it or not, I still hear from a few of my shipyard pals after all these years."

363

## Statistical Data

Welding was only one of many occupations in which women provided a full measure of devotion during the war. With few exceptions they worked in all of the occupations required by the demands of the war, and each of these occupations had its training programs. The following tabulation shows the distribution of training of women during the period of July 1, 1940 through June 30, 1945.[37]

|  | Enrollment in Preemployment Courses | Enrollment in Supplementary Courses |
|---|---|---|
| All Courses | 554,722 | 946,731 |
| Automotive | 1,935 | 5,606 |
| Aviation | 194,065 | 435,188 |
| Electrical | 6,873 | 6,760 |
| Forging | 238 | 125 |
| Foundry | 1,081 | 2,211 |
| Machine Shop | 148,028 | 73,370 |
| Radio | 21,984 | 31,859 |
| Sheet Metal | 13,311 | 1,778 |
| Shipbuilding | 68,118 | 185,661 |
| Welding | 24,520 | 15,927 |
| Others | 74,569 | 188,246 |

## Implications of the War Training of Women

Experience gained during the war training program for women did much to dispel the last remaining prejudices about the kinds of work women could do. It appeared that women could succeed in virtually any line of work. In their achievement and production they were in no way inferior to men. Employers developed new attitudes about the employment of women. Salary and responsibility ceased to be factors of major significance; emphasis was placed on quality of work done and not on the sex of the employee.

The women who joined the labor force in unprecedented numbers during the 1950's and 1960's were not faced with the previous uncertainties about their abilities, and they usually found working conditions satisfactory. The ease of their transition into industrial work made it difficult for them to believe that not many years earlier it would have been virtually impossible to have gotten a job in their present field. The women who continued in industrial employment after the war could put their experience to use in satisfying peacetime production requirements. Many returned to vocational schools to acquire additional skill and knowledge for new jobs.

## Post-War Employment

Employment conditions for women improved immeasurably following the war. Although much of the employment had to be redirected from war activities to other occupations, appropriate training programs were available, or were developed, in the vocational schools of the nation. The attention given to selection of training, the vocational advisement practices, and the generous use of advisory committees strengthened the training programs.[38]

The depression emphasis upon industrial training in the area of household employment gave way to a wider view of employment opportunities.[39]

---

[37] W. Daniel Musser, *op. cit.*, Adapted from tabulated data shown on pages 168 and 170.

[38] Celia D. Shelton, "Training Girls for Occupations," *AVA Journal and News Bulletin,* Vol. XII, No. 2, May 1937, pp. 110-112.

[39] United States Department of the Interior, Office of Education, *Vocational Training for Household Employment*, Misc. 1613, 1935.

The technological age had changed the attitude of parents about the "worldly ambitions of their daughters." "Now the majority of them believe it essential to prepare their daughters to meet the demands for a specialized occupation." [40]

It was evident that in the 1950's most women worked outside their homes at some time during their lives. In 1900 only about 20 percent of women over 14 were in the labor force; by 1949 this percentage had increased to about 32. "For the first time in our history married workers outnumbered single women workers." [41] Furthermore, the number of working women with children under 18 years of age represented about 20 percent of all women with children under 18 years of age. The economic aspects of the increase in women workers were significant. Although it was apparent that many of the women worked in order to improve the standard of living of the family, the total family income had increased substantially. "In terms of wage and salary income in 1939, wives whose husbands were in the $1,000 to $1,500 bracket, for example, were twice as likely to be in the labor market as wives whose husbands were in the $2,000 to $3,000 bracket." [42] Kaplan believed that many low-income families were held intact only because of income obtained by women

who had gone to work. It was clear that women had become a fixed part of the American labor force.

## Federal Attention to Industrial Education for Women

This part of the historical background really goes back much further than post-World War II developments, and in order to indicate specifically the attention of the Office of Education to this area of training, and to maintain continuity, we must pick up the threads at the beginning late in 1917.

About a year after the passage of the Smith-Hughes Act the Federal Board provided a staff position for a person whose time would be devoted entirely to the interests of women in industrial education. As has been pointed out previously, interest in industrial education for women was built into the structure of vocational education from the beginning of the National Society for the Promotion of Industrial Education, in 1906. For more than a decade, therefore, promotion of industrial education for women had been an integral part of the program. Staffing the position was merely a step in the total plan of the Federal Board. Prosser investigated the availability of women for this position and found that Anna L. Burdick had the background and experience required. [43]

---

[40] Eva Wingert, "Vocational Education for Girls," *American Vocational Journal*, Vol. 23, No. 5, May 1948, p. 23.

[41] David L. Kaplan, "Women in Industry," *American Vocational Journal*, Vol. 25, No. 5, May 1950, p. 3.

[42] *Ibid.*, p. 4.

[43] The principal sources of information for this section, unless otherwise indicated, are two mimeographed booklets: (1) Helen Livingstone and Blanche Nechanicky, *The Women Pioneers in Trade and Industrial Education in the United States*, American Vocational Association, May 1952; and (2) Cleo Murtland, *Women-in-Industry of the American Vocational Association*, April 1960.

*Anna Lalor Burdick* (1869-1944), a native of Iowa, graduated from the State University of Iowa in 1889. She was a high school teacher, principal, and one of the first women to hold the position of city superintendent of schools. During the period 1913-1917 she was Director of Vocational Guidance in Des Moines, Iowa; reportedly the first person in a public school system to have that title and responsibility.

Her career from 1889 to 1917 was marked by an intense interest and concern for young people. During her professional career in Iowa she was an active participant in social and civic clubs. In part this experience was closely related to providing educational opportunity for work, and to enlisting support of industrialists and parents in these endeavors. In 1917 she was invited to join the staff of the Federal Board for Vocational Education as Special Agent in Charge of Industrial Education for Girls and Women.

During her 22 years with the Federal Board and the U.S. Office of Education, she stimulated nationwide interest in the needs of women in industrial education. She traveled to every state in the nation many times. Her enthusiasm was catching and she commanded the attention and respect of her colleagues. Her work was imaginative and creative, yet her practical ideas produced action among those with whom she worked.

Her sphere of influence and activity extended into the international scene by virtue of travel to Europe and Central and South America, and by her participation on official committees and commissions having concern for inter-national education problems. Mrs. Burdick was a well known public speaker, and her professional publications on a variety of themes were continuous throughout her career. Her achievements, which were acknowledged in many ways and at many times, were given especially fitting tribute in 1939 when Rutgers University conferred on her the degree of Doctor of Letters.

She devoted a lifetime of effort to establishing increasingly effective programs of vocational preparation for women and to relating this preparation to social and economic progress. On the day of her retirement she reported that she had completed exactly 50 years to the day in public education.

*Miss Louise Moore* was appointed to the position vacated by Mrs. Burdick in 1939 and remained there until her retirement in 1955. Miss Moore had been a teacher for a number of years when she entered industry in the Nellie Don Dress Factory in Kansas City. She was employed by the Dutchess Manufacturing Company, Poughkeepsie, New York, at the time she was called to the position in the U.S. Office of Education. An admirer of Mrs. Burdick, she carried out her work in the "Burdick spirit," promoting, encouraging, and developing vocational education for women.

*Mary S. Resh* came to the U.S. Office of Education as a Program Specialist, Trade and Industrial Education, to give special attention to the industrial education programs for women. Mrs. Resh had been the Principal of the Anna Lalor Burdick Vocational School for Girls in Washington, D.C., just prior to her appointment to the Office of Education. Like her predecessors,

Mrs. Resh entered upon a vigorous campaign to stimulate nationwide interest in developing an expanded program of trade and industrial education for women. She became actively engaged in the Women-in-Industry section of the American Vocational Association and served as editor of the Newsletter that was sent to members of the section.

She was prominently involved in the National Leadership Development Conferences of the Trade and Industrial Education Branch, Office of Education, and in other national conferences as a representative of women's interest in the industrial world. Mrs. Resh resigned her position in the Office of Education in 1962 to continue similar work in the Office of Manpower, Automation and Training, U.S. Department of Labor.

The work of Mrs. Burdick, Miss Moore, and Mrs. Resh represents a significant part of the total development of industrial education for women. Their influence in connection with actual development of programs at the local level and upon the attitude and interest of state leaders has unquestionably been responsible for much of the growth of the program. Furthermore, the fact that the U.S. Office of Education had a person especially in charge of such work influenced some states to appoint women to similar positions.

### The Nature of the Program in 1960

The necessity for wider and wiser utilization of womanpower as a national resource became a compelling issue in the late 1950's. Consequently the industrial education of women who were employed in industry, and the preparation of those who would be so employed, commanded the attention of industrial educators in the various states. It was anticipated that girls and women would participate in the world of work to a greater extent than ever before. The importance of highly developed skills for women in some occupations and the need for instruction in diversified training programs were common items of discussion in trade and industrial education meetings. In order to provide some background information about the nature and extent of programs throughout the nation, the Office of Education, under the direction of Mary Resh, compiled a listing of programs that were established and operating during the school year 1958-59.[44]

The following tabulations were derived from the directory of training programs for women, prepared by Mrs. Resh.

|  | Number of States and Territories Offering Program |
|---|---|
| Practical Nursing | 50 |
| Cosmetology | 39 |
| Commercial Foods | 34 |
| Power Machine Operation | 25 |
| Dressmaking | 21 |
| Advertising & Commercial Art | 19 |
| Tailoring | 15 |
| Dental Assisting | 14 |
| Drafting | 11 |
| Needle Trades | 9 |
| Baking | 8 |
| Laundry, Dry Cleaning & Pressing | 8 |
| Cafeteria & Restaurant Management | 7 |

[44] Mary S. Resh, *Trade and Industrial Education for Girls and Women*, U.S. Department of Health, Education, and Welfare, Office of Education, OE-84002. Washington: Government Printing Office, 1960.

|  | Number of States and Territories Offering Program |
|---|---|
| Medical Assistant Training | 7 |
| Nursery Assistant Training | 7 |
| Photography | 7 |
| Tea Room & Waitress Training | 6 |
| Nurse's Aide Training | 6 |
| Dress Design | 6 |
| Household & Domestic Service | 5 |
| Industrial Supervisory Training | 5 |
| Laboratory Technician Training | 5 |
| Printing | 5 |
| Patternmaking & Drafting | 4 |
| Millinery | 4 |
| Maid Training | 4 |
| Executive & Institutional Housekeeping | 4 |
| Dietary Technician Training | 4 |
| Interior Decorating | 3 |
| Upholstery | 2 |
| Sanitary Food Handling | 2 |
| Catering | 1 |
| Dental Technician Training | 1 |
| Embroidery Mending | 1 |
| Enameling | 1 |
| Fashion Illustration | 1 |
| Floral Design | 1 |
| Glovemaking | 1 |
| Institutional Service | 1 |
| Jewelry Making | 1 |
| Knitting | 1 |
| Looping | 1 |
| Masseuse Training | 1 |
| Needle Work | 1 |
| Rug Hooking | 1 |
| Sign & Showcard Making | 1 |
| Silk Screen Painting | 1 |
| Stagecraft | 1 |
| Stenciling | 1 |
| Woodworking & Carving | 1 |
| X-Ray Technician Training | 1 |

The preceding list does not account for all of the women enrolled in trade and industrial education programs, because women were accepted without a special note being made of it in any of the trade and industrial education programs. Although the list does show a fairly wide variety of occupations, it is evident that the bulk of industrial education effort for women was concentrated in a few occupations.

The following list shows the number of programs offered in 1958-59 for women in each of the states and territories. It should be noted that in some states the number of programs listed is not representative of different kinds of programs (Practical Nursing listed in 20 schools in one state, for example). However, the list does show the relative effort of the various states in industrial education for women.

|  | Number of Programs |
|---|---|
| Alabama | 25 |
| Alaska | 1 |
| Arizona | 8 |
| Arkansas | 13 |
| California | 128 |
| Colorado | 14 |
| Connecticut | 24 |
| Delaware | 6 |
| District of Columbia | 19 |
| Florida | 92 |
| Georgia | 32 |
| Hawaii | 11 |
| Idaho | 25 |
| Illinois | 36 |
| Indiana | 4 |
| Iowa | 10 |
| Kansas | 7 |
| Kentucky | 32 |
| Louisiana | 21 |
| Maine | 4 |
| Maryland | 17 |
| Massachusetts | 25 |
| Michigan | 17 |
| Minnesota | 29 |
| Mississippi | 11 |
| Missouri | 27 |
| Montana | 2 |
| Nebraska | 7 |
| Nevada | 4 |
| New Hampshire | 50 |
| New Jersey | 39 |
| New Mexico | 5 |
| New York | 145 |
| North Carolina | 37 |
| North Dakota | 1 |
| Ohio | 37 |
| Oklahoma | 53 |
| Oregon | 8 |
| Pennsylvania | 71 |
| Puerto Rico | 36 |

| | Number of Programs |
|---|---|
| Rhode Island | 1 |
| South Carolina | 29 |
| South Dakota | 3 |
| Tennessee | 55 |
| Texas | 68 |
| Utah | 9 |
| Vermont | 4 |
| Virgin Islands | 1 |
| Virginia | 52 |
| Washington | 35 |
| West Virginia | 4 |
| Wisconsin | 14 |
| Wyoming | 10 |

The problem of the availability of industrial education is not alone a problem of the women's occupations. Despite evidence which one sees in the data about the lack of availability in breadth of occupational programs and their lack of comprehensiveness, it is still true that the nation has moved a long way toward meeting the needs of women for occupational preparation. A realistic readjustment of the program is a task for the future.

## A Dozen Questions[45]

An Act of Congress, approved June 5, 1920, established the Women's Bureau in the U.S. Department of Labor.

It shall be the duty of said bureau to formulate standards and policies which shall promote the welfare of wage-earning women, improve their working conditions, increase their efficiency, and advance their opportunities for profitable employment.[46]

During the first forty years of operation the Bureau issued 275 bulletins, 20 special bulletins, 32 leaflets, 8 pamphlets, and 29 miscellaneous unnumbered publications in relation to its congressional charge. The Bureau

has had an obvious interest in and concern for industrial training for women. The size and nature of the problem of employment was portrayed by the Bureau in its publication *A Dozen Questions,* issued in 1961. From the facts as seen by the Women's Bureau one may gain some insight into the industrial training problem facing the states and local communities of the nation.

1. *How many women workers are there in the United States?* Actually there were nearly 24 million women in the nation's labor force. This number was more than four million larger than the peak of employment of women during World War II.

2. *Of all women, what percent work?* About 37 percent of all women of working age were in the labor force. The percentage varied considerably for different age groups and with marital status.

3. *Of all workers, what percent are women?* Women comprised one-third of the labor force. There was a gradual rise in the percentage up through World War II when the percentage dropped off to about 28 percent and then rose again.

4. *What is the average age of women workers?* The median age in 1960 was slightly more than forty years, although nearly forty percent were 45 or older.

5. *Are many women workers married?* Over half of all women workers were living with their husbands.

6. *Are there many working mothers?* Five million women workers had children between the ages of six and 17,

---

[45] Material for this section was prepared from data gleaned from a publication of the Women's Bureau, U.S. Department of Labor, *A Dozen Questions,* 1961.
[46] 66th Congress, *Public Law 259,* June 5, 1920.

and three million had children under the age of six.

7. *How many women are heads of families?* The family head is a woman in 4½ million families (1 family in 10). Half of the women family heads were in the labor force.

8. *How many women work at part-time jobs, or for only part of the year?* About 29 million women worked at some time during the year 1959. Of these, about 14 million either worked at a part-time job or a full-time job for only part of the year.

9. *What occupational fields employ the most women?* Of over 22 million employed women workers in April, 1961, more than 6¾ million were in clerical jobs. Between 2¼ and 3⅓ million women were employed in each of the following broad occupational groups: factory and other operatives; service workers, such as waitresses, beauticians, and practical nurses; professional and technical workers; and private-household workers.

10. *What are the most important specific occupations for women?* Nearly half of the women workers were employed in the following nine specific occupations in April, 1961: stenographers, typists, secretaries; operatives in nondurable-goods manufacturing; sales workers in retail trade; teachers (except college); waitresses, cooks, and similar workers (other than in private households); operatives in durable-goods manufacturing; medical and other professional health workers; farm laborers (unpaid family); proprietors in retail trade.

11. *How many working women belong to labor unions?* About 3.3 million. This was about one-sixth of the total union members and about one-seventh of the number of women workers.

12. *How does education affect the kind of jobs women hold?* Women college graduates were employed primarily in professional or technical work; high school graduates, in clerical work; and those with an eighth-grade education or less, in factory, private-household or service jobs.

The increase in the number of women in the employment structure had been so large and so rapid after World War II that most Americans were scarcely aware of the dynamic and dramatic changes that were occurring.[47] Realignment of industrial jobs had facilitated solutions to the problem of how women could be employed in "tomorrow's world." John P. Walsh noted that in the restructuring of industrial groups in space, missile, aircraft, electronics, and other areas, the problems connected with employment of women had been recognized, and firms which could use women extensively for industrial tasks were making progress in changeovers to provide adequately for their employment.[48] He noted particularly that training was an important factor in the successful adjustment of women to industrial work. Many other significant comparisons could be made of the numerous changes related to the employment of women in industry—for example, the change in completion of higher edu-

[47] U.S. Department of Labor, Women's Bureau, *Today's Woman in Tomorrow's World.* Washington: Government Printing Office, 1960, p. 5.
[48] *Ibid.,* pp. 44-45.

cation. Women were granted 156,000 degrees in 1960; nine times the number granted in 1920.

### Review of Women in Training, 1962

The total number of women enrolled in public school industrial education at any one time would consist of the enrollment in industrial arts, trade and industrial education, practical nursing and other health occupations, and technical education. In addition to the public school program women are enrolled in industrial education in private, parochial, government-operated, labor unemployment, corporation, correspondence, and armed forces schools. Hence obtaining an accurate enrollment figure is extremely difficult. About the best index readily available consists of the *Digest of Annual Reports of State Boards for Vocational Education*. These reports are issued annually and consist of a compilation of records sent to the U.S. Office of Education by each of the states.

The industrial education-related data consist of reports for trade and industrial education, technical education, and practical nursing and other health occupations. The chart below, with data obtained from the Digest for 1961-62, shows relationships for the United States as a whole.

Enrollment figures have little meaning unless compared with other data. For example, considering the total U.S. population, there are more women than men; women comprise about one-third of the total labor force; educational requirements in general are rising in all occupations; and it appears that a woman's chance of being hired is enhanced materially when she has completed specialized training before seeking employment. (Opportunities for upgrading in employment are also improved if the worker participates in in-service schooling.)

One tentative conclusion that can be reached from the above data and general rationale is that there are not enough women enrolled in industrial-related educational programs. Also, it follows that the breadth of occupational training for women needs to be expanded both in terms of the kinds of occupations concerned and of the general availability of instruction throughout the various states.

The chart on the following page shows the distribution of enrollment for women as a percentage of the total trade and industrial education enrollment for 1961-62. The range is from 0.2 percent (North Dakota) to 36.4 percent (New Hampshire); the national average is 11 percent.

| | *Total Enrollment* | *Enrollment of Women* | *Percentage* |
|---|---|---|---|
| Trade and Industrial Education | 1,005,383 | 110,867 | 10.9 |
| Practical Nursing and Other Health Occupations | 48,985 | 47,877 | 98.0 |
| Technical Education | 148,920 | 6,820 | 3.9 |
| Total-National | 1,203,288 | 165,564 | 13.9 |

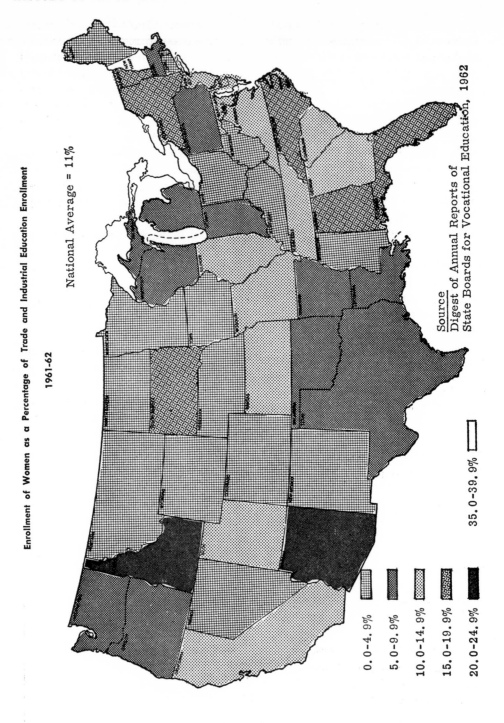

Enrollment of Women as a Percentage of Trade and Industrial Education Enrollment

1961-62

National Average = 11%

Source
Digest of Annual Reports of
State Boards for Vocational Education, 1962

0.0-4.9%
5.0-9.9%
10.0-14.9%
15.0-19.9%
20.0-24.9%
35.0-39.9%

It would be unwise to jump immediately to final conclusions on the basis of the data presented in the chart. The data account only for the number of women reported by the states as enrolled in trade and industrial education. Obviously all states are somewhat better off in regard to industrial education for women, since the enrollment from all other sources is not accounted for.

What the chart does show is that there are extreme differences among the states. (Theoretically, a girl seeking instruction in trade and industrial education is much better off in some states than in others.) The chart also suggests that one of the major problems of each of the states is providing industrial education for women.

## Summary

Industrial education for women which led to employment could be found in a number of special schools prior to 1900. It was narrow in scope, but so were women's occupational opportunities. However, the value of special training for work, in terms of wages and advancement, was readily apparent. The schools established after 1900 were patterned largely after earlier models. In many of the early schools attention was given to the 3 R's and to related general work, and a distinct tendency toward comprehensiveness in the education of girls and women is found in the work of those schools. One of the major drawbacks was the lack of definite attention to the problem as a national issue.

The National Society for the Promotion of Industrial Education acted in part as the unifying force for women's industrial education, and the passage of the Smith-Hughes Act provided the basis for a nationwide organization of effort in the public schools. Once under way, and supported and stimulated by federal funds, the program grew slowly. Discrimination and narrow views about women at work were largely overcome during World War I, but many early public school programs were strongly oriented toward the so-called "women's trades"—the occupations that traditionally employed large numbers of women.

Statistical data about the enrollment of women show that the number enrolled has always been small in comparison with occupational needs. Nevertheless, the growth of the program in the public schools has been encouraging. Industry's experience with women employees in World War II, in which many previous myths were found to be without foundation, provided the final emancipation of women at work. Women could do any work they wanted to do; they learned rapidly and their latent mechanical skills were easily developed.

One source of strength in the development of trade and industrial education programs for women has been the special attention given this area by the U.S. Office of Education. Since 1917 a woman has held a position in the Office of Education, concerned specifically with trade and industrial education for women. Congressional appropriations in the late 1950's for practical nursing and other health occupations improved and expanded these occupational opportunities throughout the nation.

373

By the 1960's it was generally acknowledged that the employment of women in a wide variety of occupations was a fixed element, and predictions for future needs and changes of occupations assumed that a large percentage of nation's women would work.

---

## Recall Questions

1. What was the role of the National Society for the Promotion of Industrial Education in the development of industrial education for women?
2. What occupational areas were most frequently mentioned in the programs of the early schools?
3. Identify some of the specific attitudes about women at work that developed in World War II.
4. Recall some of the factual data about women in the labor force in the 1960's.
5. What traits of those who pioneered industrial education for women seemed to have lasting value in promoting the growth and development of such education?

## Research Questions

1. Gather all of the data available for your state concerning industrial education opportunities for women. Show the distribution of availability of instruction for various areas, and reach conclusions concerning any changes you think are necessary to make instruction more uniformly available to girls and women.
2. Gather all of the data available for your state about trends and current employment of women. How extensive is employment in terms of different occupational areas? Prepare a tabulation of employment by occupations. How many different occupations employ 90 percent of the women at work? Show other relationships and trends.

## Suggestions for Further Reading

*American Vocational Journal*
Publications of the Women's Bureau, U.S. Department of Labor.
Publications of the U.S. Office of Education.

# Chapter 13

# Organized Labor and Industrial Education

Labor's Early National Concern for Industrial Education · Labor's Point of View, 1917-1938 · Labor and Industrial Education, 1939-1950 · Post-War and the Space Age—Labor and Industrial Education After 1950 · Summary · Recall Questions · Research Questions · Suggestions for Further Reading

The attitude of labor has always been an important factor in the progress of industrial education. Throughout the nineteenth century labor demonstrated its interest in education by promoting free schools, free textbooks, and the general extension of educational facilities. It is clear that labor was in support of industrial education under public rather than private control. In 1829 the organized working men and women in New York adopted resolutions concerning the regeneration of national education "which shall secure equality to every child which is born to the Republic, an enlightened, practical and systematic course of instruction, including the knowledge of at least one trade or useful occupation . . . at public expense." [1] Two years later the working men of Boston passed similar resolutions demanding a liberal system of education, with particular reference to employment in mechanical occupations. In the beginning labor simply wanted a better break in the fundamentals of education, but later it began to seek consideration of its specific technical needs.

## Labor's Early National Concern for Industrial Education

Some of the well established labor unions—Typographers, Pressmen, Bricklayers, and Electrical Workers—organized vocational schools of their

---

[1] Original source quoted in National Society for the Promotion of Industrial Education, *The Social Significance of Industrial Education*, Bulletin No. 13, Part IV, January 1911, pp. 170-171.

own. Because of their success the development of interest in industrial education on a broader base was natural. As early as 1903 committees on education functioned as a regular part of the annual meetings of the American Federation of Labor. The committees fostered every legitimate enterprise of the movement toward industrial education, regarding such education as "necessary and inevitable" for the progress of the workers in industry. They opposed "sham" in any form in the plans of industrial education. The welfare of labor depended in a large measure upon the sound development of industrial education.

The 1907 convention of the American Federation of Labor in Norfolk, Virginia, recognized by special resolution the formation of the National Society for the Promotion of Industrial Education. The Society had been apprehensive about the attitude of labor toward it because many of the national unions were suspicious of the so-called "trade" schools, particularly those which appeared to offer short cuts to a trade. But the AFL was emphatic in its support of the National Society, saying in the resolution: ". . . We do endorse any policy, or any society or association having for its object the raising of the standard of industrial education and the teaching of the higher techniques of our various industries."[2]

Special committees of the American Federation of Labor were appointed to make studies of industrial education in 1908 and 1909. Their reports indicated that a general demand for industrial education was expressed by business organizations, boards of trade, labor organizations, and by a significant number of educators and other persons who held public office. They also reported that they had found "sufficient proof that the right kind of education for a boy or girl who expects to enter upon a vocational career is second only in importance to their having an education at all."[3]

The 1910 committee report requested:

. . . the officers of all organizations affiliated with the American Federation of Labor to supply us with all information they may have relative to industrial education as soon as possible. And this for the purpose of getting an up-to-date report with up-to-date methods of how industrial education should be taught, conducted and promoted.[4]

John Golden, President of the United Textile Workers of America, came forward with a strong note of support in 1909.[5] Having served on the Douglas Commission in Massachusetts four years earlier, and having thus been party to a significant study of industrial education, Golden could speak with more authority than most labor leaders. He shared the contemporary

---

[2] Samuel Gompers, *The Attitude of the American Federation of Labor Toward Industrial Education.* An address before the Eighth Annual Convention of the National Society for the Promotion of Industrial Education, Richmond, Virginia, December 10, 1914, p. 9.

[3] American Federation of Labor, *Industrial Education.* Washington: American Federation of Labor, 1910, p. 9.

[4] *Ibid.,* p. 15.

[5] John Golden, "The Position of Labor Unions Regarding Industrial Education," *The Annals of the American Academy of Political and Social Science,* Vol. XXXIII, No. 1, January 1909, pp. 185-187.

opposition to substandard trade schools operated purely for profit, schools that turned out a "half-baked" journeyman in a few months. Such schools were dubbed as "scab-hatcheries."

On the other hand, Golden could find no basis for opposition to the schools and the program proposed by the National Society for the Promotion of Industrial Education. "In such a movement I feel safe in saying organized labor is with you heart and soul." [6]

The facts were simple. Labor regarded a skilled trade as the most valuable asset a workman could possess. Any movement that threatened this asset was in opposition to labor's views; movements that enhanced this asset had labor's wholehearted support.

Specialization in industry had all but wrecked the old apprenticeship system; at the turn of the century children of the "great wage-working class" generally came from poor families and entered the labor market at an early age, most often unprepared to do so. That the problem needed attention was quite evident to AFL study groups.

The one trouble in America to-day is that too many of our youths who have graduated from the grammar or high school are misfits industrially. If we are to secure industrial supremacy, or even maintain our present standards in the industrial world, we must in some way in our educational system acquire an equivalent to our old apprenticeship system.[7]

As noted, organized labor was solidly opposed to the injustices of nar-row training and exploitation which produced "half-trained mechanics." Labor was solidly for education that emphasized the human element because the mere *production* of future workers *in the image of automatic machines* was untenable. The committees could see a close relationship between the future welfare of America and industrial training of workers, provided that some means could be devised to insure the protection of the workers in the process.

Concern was expressed frequently about the dangers to high standards of efficiency among American workmen if the problems of the beginners in the occupational world were ignored. Educated hands and brains were required if the boys and girls of the nation were to have an opportunity "to earn a living in a self-selected vocation and acquire an intelligent understanding of the duties of good citizenship." [8] Not only is it possible in these reports to see definite trends toward labor's concept of a total program of industrial education which was broad in scope, but one also gets a faint hint of the importance of the newly discovered vocational guidance movement.

Education committee reports of the AFL during the formative years of the industrial education movement ultimately had an impact on the actual wording of the Smith-Hughes Act. Labor particularly favored the establishment of industrial education in the public school system in order to make it available to all youths 14 to 16 years

---

[6] *Ibid.*, p. 187.

[7] AFL, Industrial Education, *op. cit.*, p. 9.

[8] *Ibid.*, p. 13.

of age. The committees recognized continuously that the program was a "public necessity" and therefore should be conducted at "public expense." The necessity for competent trained teachers was stressed repeatedly. Suggestions for the curriculum specified instruction in English, mathematics, physics, chemistry, elementary mechanics, drawing, history of the trade, economics, and philosophy of collective bargaining. It was definitely labor's view that students should be prepared to pursue advanced study in their respective fields. Advisory boards, "including representatives of the industries, employers, and organized labor," were recommended in order that the schools would maintain close relationships with the actual occupational conditions.

One of the comprehensive reports of the Committee on Industrial Education of the American Federation of Labor, compiled and edited by Charles H. Winslow, was presented to the United States Senate on August 17, 1912, by Senator Carroll S. Page of Vermont, and was ordered to be printed.[9] The report stated plainly that labor needed a new approach to the problem of industrial education: Twenty-five years of manual training had not provided satisfactory replacements for the depleted ranks of skilled labor. Since the state had provided schools to teach trades to the mentally, morally, and physically deficient, the report strongly urged the state not to deny the same chance to the normal boy or girl. A similar question was raised in connection with the disproportionate attention that the state gave the ten percent who entered the professions, while ignoring the other ninety percent who, by and large, went into manual occupations.

When the AFL met in Rochester in the late fall of 1912, one of their resolutions was directed toward total and complete support of vocational education. The president, the legislative committee, and the education committee had studied the direction of education in the United States and expressed concern for the large school dropout at the end of the sixth grade.

In the committee members' view, the Page bill moved in the direction of America's greatest educational need. The resolution of November 19, 1912, read in part as follows:

The Vocational Education bill, known as Senate 3, introduced by Senator Page of Vermont (a similar bill having been introduced in the House of Representatives by Congressman Wilson) is one of the several introduced in Congress to advance the cause of vocational education throughout the states by a liberal Federal grant for agriculture, the trades and industries, as well as home economics. The Page bill creates a plan for Federal grants to secondary public schools, thus giving direction to a complete scheme of education in which all of the children of the nation should receive a just and equitable share of attention.[10]

Labor was intent upon securing the passage of this legislation. It provided for high standards and wide latitude within the states for adaptation to

---

[9] *Industrial Education,* 62nd Congress, 2nd Session, Senate Document No. 936, August 17, 1912.

[10] Resolution passed by the American Federation of Labor in annual convention in the city of Rochester, Tuesday, November 19, 1912, favoring the Page Bill, (Senate No. 3). (Mimeographed.)

specific needs in a particular community.

The revolution in the making, with respect to the curriculum in the public schools, did not go unnoticed by national media. The efforts of organized labor and the National Society for the Promotion of Industrial Education were recognized, and frequently with general approval, by national magazines. *The Saturday Evening Post* of March 4, 1911, is a good example.

Manual training was the first step in the right direction; and even before that was generally adopted there were a few wise teachers who had learned how to spread what is called "general culture" by an appeal to the hands of their pupils.

Manual training was one thing and actual preparation for a specific work in life was quite another. Sometimes, particularly when manual training is taught by a charming young woman who specializes in hammered brass, it is a most snobbish performance.

Not much longer will Johnny Jones and his sister be turned out of the grammar grades in millions, with their heads stuffed with a smattering of general information, and left to face without further aid the bitter competition of present-day life. Education must put on its overalls and give them at least an opportunity to get ready for their waiting jobs.[11]

From the beginning of the work to promote the interest in industrial education, the National Association of Manufacturers had provided parallel support. The Association formed a committee on industrial education which kept all members informed on the progress of the industrial education movement. Up to the middle of 1913, the NAM had published five bulletins about industrial education. The fifth bulletin, No. 34 in the series, is important because it lists four points that reinforce labor's position. These points, which were adopted by the NAM at its eighteenth annual convention in Detroit, May, 1913,[12] were essentially as follows:

1. Fifty percent of the children who leave school at the end of the sixth grade, "undirected, unskilled, uninformed," would be saved educationally by vocational education.

2. Teachers in the new program must have "extended experience in actual employment in the occupations taught" in order to provide up-to-date practical instruction.

3. State and local boards of control should have adequate representation of labor and management: Failure has marked every great attempt at Vocational Education not so directed.

4. Emphasis should be placed on the continuation school; trade schools should draw their students from the successful graduates of continuation schools.

The influence of this forthright stand by NAM came at a time when the Page Bill, then under consideration in Congress, needed support.

Because labor's position was so clearly a central element in the promotion of industrial education, it was often misunderstood. Samuel Gompers pointed out that a large portion of his life had been devoted "to combating

---

[11] Henry M. Hyde, "Making Over the Public Schools—Education With Its Overalls On," *The Saturday Evening Post*, March 4, 1911, p. 56.

[12] National Association of Manufacturers, *Industrial Education*, Bulletin No. 34, Detroit, Michigan, May 21, 1913.

wrong-headed notions about the attitude of organized labor with reference to every sort of social and economic question." [13] So the key question during the early years of the twentieth century concerning the growing interest in industrial education was, "Where does labor stand?"

"I can assure you," said Gompers in his address to the National Society for the Promotion of Industrial Education in 1914, "that no disposition will be found anywhere among workingmen to oppose this effort to make our schools more democratic in serving the real bread-and-butter needs of the community." [14] For more than a century prior to 1917 labor had sought to have its educational needs satisfied. It was only natural that labor leaders should be concerned about any educational proposal that would produce an excess of potential workers which exceeded the real demand. A fair and proper apportionment of the supply of labor power must be maintained in relation to the demand for labor. In this connection industrial surveys and accumulation of facts regarding employment in a community were essential elements for planning industrial education.

Labor followed the developments of the national legislation continuously up to the passage of the Smith-Hughes Act. In fact, Arthur E. Holder, the AFL legislative representative, was involved in the meetings and discussions concerning vocational education during the years prior to the passage of the Act. When the Federal Board for Vocational Education was appointed,

Holder was named labor's representative on the Board.

## Labor's Point of View, 1917-1938

Labor's interest in education extended far beyond considerations of industrial education. In every annual convention, the American Federation of Labor stated and restated its point of view concerning many aspects of education. That labor supported public education there can be no doubt; that labor expected quality in public education is likewise beyond question. As previously said, labor was concerned with the education of *all* children, and the education committees of the AFL were as apt to defend free textbooks, teacher tenure, English, foreign language, and education for retarded children as they were to defend measures related to industrial education. So-called "inquisitions by school authorities" into the personal, religious, political, and economic views of teachers were sharply protested as "intolerable in a free country."

Upon the passage of the Smith-Hughes Act all affiliated bodies of the AFL were urged to help carry out the provisions of the bill directly and to lend support to states as they developed their systems of vocational education. The affiliated groups were urged also to prevent any attempt "to pervert industrial education to the purposes of exploitation." Increasing facilities in public normal schools desiring to train teachers for trade and industrial education was recommended

[13] Samuel Gompers, *op. cit.*, p. 3.
[14] *Ibid.*, p. 7.

strongly, as was the necessity to improve teaching related to the "privileges and obligations of citizenship."

## Adjustment to the Smith-Hughes Act

In 1918 the AFL reviewed the distinctive features of the Smith-Hughes Act for the benefit of its membership and expressed satisfaction that all of the 48 states had accepted the provisions of the Act within six months after the Federal Board had been appointed.

As noted, the necessity of vocational education in the public schools was a product of modern industry. Two developments stood out clearly: first, the decrease in the use of the apprenticeship system, and second, the tendency to train workers as specialists. In a sense both elements were penalties of the new system, but they could not be ignored because of their potential disadvantage both to labor and to the employer. After making extensive studies labor reached what might be called a unanimous conclusion that through the Smith-Hughes Act both developments could be controlled. The federal law was intended to be elastic and flexible and could therefore "fit" a variety of situations encountered in the states.

For the full-time student the industrial program was regarded by labor as pre-apprentice training. Arthur E. Holder illustrated the point as follows:

When a boy has spent two years in such a school he should receive some equivalent credit on his apprenticeship so that his apprenticeship would be shortened by whatever arrangement has been agreed upon in the locality of the school after full

consideration by accredited representatives of the community.[15]

The provisions for trade-extension classes provided better means for employed workers to extend their skill and technical knowledge and thus reduce the evils of the specialist or special operator classifications which were common in American industry. Taken as a whole, the Smith-Hughes Act appeared to provide more "opportunity for all," and this was precisely the intent of labor in its efforts to secure a broader base for the superior craftsman. Workers were encouraged to take advantage of the programs of vocational education.

It was necessary that labor should be reassured in connection with the purposes of the schools and classes created in response to the Smith-Hughes Act. Arthur E. Holder attempted to explain the concept as follows:

It is not expected or intended that the output of such schools will ever disturb the labor conditions. It is not intended that the business of the school is simply to make goods or commodities. The real, genuine business of the school is to give practical instruction, and to give instruction that will be completely and properly digested by the scholars.[16]

Another element about which labor needed assurance was the intention of the Act with regard to the person who had completed his training. The leaders in the vocational education movement never thought of the product of the school as a competent all-round mechanic or as a limited specialist. Such an outcome would have defeated

[15] Arthur E. Holder, "Labor and the Smith-Hughes Vocational Education Act," *The Vocational Summary*, Vol. 1, No. 3, July 1918, pp. 6-7.
[16] *Ibid.*, p. 7.

the purposes of the law: All that was intended was that the student have adequate preparatory training. It was expected that the employed worker would become an all-round artisan by attendance at evening classes.

Stimulation by the AFL encouraged state and local labor unions to be concerned about education in general and about industrial education in particular. The report of the committee on education of the New York State Federation of Labor, at its annual convention in 1918, is an example of the intensity with which labor turned its attention to education. Among other things the committee recommended compulsory education, free textbooks, school lunches, physical education, teacher education for trade and industrial teachers, establishment of a minimum state salary, vocational guidance, and restricted class size. The committee also desired representation on boards of education and advisory committees. With respect to the ages of the students eligible for various classes the committee indicated:

That prevocational training shall be limited to children of 12 years and over, and vocational training to children of 14 years and over, but under no circumstances should this training take time that should be devoted to the fundamentals of the three R's.[17]

The committee again pointed out that the industrial and vocational courses should include teaching related to "the privileges and obligations of intelligent citizenship" and further recommended an industrial history that would include an accurate account of the organization of workers. When the courses under the Smith-Hughes Act were organized, labor emphasized the point of view that the instruction should be conducted in a way that would be most profitable to all concerned.

## Mutual Assistance

Labor's assistance with industrial education programs was encouraged to the point that we find labor and industrial education each involved in attempting to lead the other. Of course, relationships between the school and industry were desirable, but both groups had to learn how to make these relationships effective. An analysis of the general situation in 1921 focused attention upon the necessity of "vital contacts."

1. In the first place, *the existing social and industrial order has brought about a condition which leaves the average youth wholly isolated from the world in which men do their work, and gives him no opportunity to observe the doing of such tasks as would give an incentive for achievement.*
2. *Vital contacts are needed in order that certain influential personalities of industry may be a power in re-enforcing the good influences of the school.*
3. *There is need for very vital contacts in order that the school may more effectively train for the demands of industry; and especially that for the pupil going from school to industry that a minimum of specialized additional training may be necessary in order to make him competent in a specialized task.*[18]

Implicit in Morgan's suggestions is

---

[17] "Report of the Committee on Education," *The Vocational Summary,* Vol. 1, No. 7, November 1918, p. 10.

[18] DeWitt S. Morgan, "The Need of More Vital Contacts Between the School and Industry," *Industrial Arts Magazine,* Vol. 10, No. 2, February 1921, pp. 46-47.

the principle that neither the school nor the industry can be entirely successful in doing the training job independently, but that both working in harmony can provide the best possible program of training for industry.

Matthew Woll, member of the committee on education, AFL, informed the vocational educators that the labor movement did not conceive of education as a process of simply teaching what to think, but rather as the process of teaching how to think. Similarly, labor did not regard vocational education as a process of teaching the worker merely what to do, but how to find out what to do. "We want all of education to contribute to establish a habit of mind that is creative which will find expression in every relation in life." [19] It was labor's hope, according to Woll, that through vocational education the whole work process could become educational in character. To achieve this required the cooperation of management, labor, and education.

Though our schools may develop the highest type of creative energy, if industries are so backward that there is no opportunity for creative ability to function, we can do little to stop the resulting industrial and social waste. Vocational education that stops with the training of workers is far from complete or effective. It must be so developed as to mesh into the wider educational plan that ought to comprehend the whole industry.[20]

At the 1924 convention in El Paso, it was recommended that the permanent committee on education, AFL, take as a project for the next year the topic of the Best Method of Promoting Trade Education.

As the thirties began, labor was strong in its advocacy of the use of vocational training, and retraining, as a means to cope with problems of unemployment in the depression years. The great army of the unemployed stood as a menace to the security of governmental institutions, and labor's continued endorsement of vocational education was with the expressed hope that in some measure vocational education could make a contribution toward relieving the problems of unemployment.

The re-orientation of vocational education was a frequent topic, so there could be no doubt but that effort was to be expended to cope with problems of national stress, such as the depression, and to adjust better to technological progress and science on the move. Matthew Woll told the American Vocational Association, at their meeting in December, 1931, in New York City:

As vocational education must fit boys and girls for industrial life and for citizenship in a democratic society, there should be tripartite control, thus permitting the experience of industrialists, labor and executives to enrich and direct its course.[21]

On the same program, National Association of Manufacturers President John E. Edgerton indicated his continued support of the national program of industrial education. He urged that it become more available to the employed population and that it be

[19] Matthew Woll, "Vocational Training and American Labor," *Vocational Education Magazine*, Vol. II, No. 2, October 1923, p. 23.

[20] *Ibid.*

[21] Matthew Woll, "Vocational Education and Our Changing Civilization," *American Vocational Association, Bulletin No. 9*, February 1932, p. 8.

strengthened in a variety of ways. Prophetically, Edgerton said that restless science would produce new employment situations, of which vocational education must be aware. "Furthermore, we must reconcile ourselves to the fact that science cannot be suppressed or curbed," he said. "It is not only the most dependable, but the most restless agent of material progress. It is a dynamic force which is constantly disturbing static states." [22] Science had in the past created periods of readjustment and frequently brought to light the need for labor to sharpen its skills and knowledges to cope with the new industrial developments. "Vocational education, therefore, is at least the partial answer to the question raised by the unrestrainable operations of science." [23]

Labor vigorously supported teacher training programs for "those who would teach our working people," and openly encouraged capable members to become instructors. Efforts in advancing concepts of special training for trade instructors were based upon a belief that competent instructors needed to study "the art of imparting trade knowledge."

The thread of cooperative attitudes among labor, management, and education is evident at any point in the history of industrial education. This relationship became one of the foundation principles of successful industrial programs, honored and respected by all concerned. At the annual meetings of the American Vocational Associa-

tion, labor and management occupied prominent positions. Furthermore, committees of the AVA were at work continuously on mutual problems.

### Resisting the Depression Squeeze

During the depression, particularly in the early thirties, when government economy measures were producing consolidation of activities and other changes, labor was alert to the long term effect of these reorganization plans. The Executive Council of AFL, meeting in Washington, D.C., in October, 1933, considered what was happening to the nation's schools. The Council accepted the idea of state and local responsibility for education—in fact insisted upon it—but they were convinced that the social obligations for education were not being met adequately. They feared particularly that proposed economies might deny an education to boys and girls in one state, and that, should they migrate to another state, they might therefore become a social burden. "We can not simply sit by and watch the passing of the free public school. . . ." [24]

The Council held the opinion that prevailing educational philosophy accorded a "distinct and highly important place" to vocational education. This was recognition that ours was a culture both of the humanities and of industrial life and living. Vocational education was of "peculiar and most intimate concern" to labor, but this did not deny the necessity that it be correlated with other educational work.

---

[22] John E. Edgerton, "Education and Industry," *American Vocational Association, Bulletin No. 8,* 1932, p. 6.

[23] *Ibid.,* p. 7.

[24] American Federation of Labor, *Report of the Executive Council,* Fifty-third Annual Convention, Washington, D.C., October 2, 1933, p. 119.

In the spring of 1933 because of the nation's economic depression, it seemed possible that the government would not only abolish the Federal Board for Vocational Education but would also reduce by 25 percent the federal money for vocational education and grants for Agricultural and Mechanical Colleges. The AFL was alarmed to the fighting point by these proposals and set out to defeat them.

Later, when President Roosevelt ordered retention of appropriations, the AFL continued its review of the total national picture of education to the end that further improvements might become realities. The prospects were gloomy: The school year might be shortened in three-fourths of the states; in nearly half of the states current expenditures for education might be reduced; teachers' salaries might be reduced; an increase in the number of unemployed teachers and in the number of pupils per teacher could be expected. These were sufficient reasons for immediate action. The immediate problem was serious, but narrow planning would make the problem extremely critical in the near future.[25]

The AFL Executive Council invited —actually demanded—governmental cooperation in matters relating to vocational education.

". . . It is to be expected that the Secretary of the Interior will confer and advise with the American Federation of Labor . . . before any departure from the existing plan is decided upon."[26] The action of labor during the difficult times of the depression is further recognition of the constructive part it has played in furthering the interests of vocational education.

## Discord

At both the local and state levels the story was not always one of mutual trust. It is a fact that making a theory work is much more difficult than making the theory, and so, when people with diverse interests—students, job seekers, school personnel, labor representatives, educational leaders, and management—were mixed together, the pot would occasionally boil.

Therefore to imply that the relationships between trade and industrial education and labor were always smooth during the first twenty years of the Smith-Hughes Act would be entirely incorrect. There were many evidences of dissatisfaction. Some of these erupted in boiling furore about the time that President Roosevelt signed the George-Deen Act on June 8, 1936. Labor opposed an increase in the appropriations for vocational education— as represented by the George-Deen Act—because of fears that the program was too narrow, merely requiring the trainees to acquire a specific skill for a specific job, and that vocational education would become an adjunct to the employment and management divisions of big corporations.

Subsequently, the President, aware of the many criticisms, invited a group of disinterested persons to review the existing program of federal aid for vocational education and the relationship of this program to education in general and to social and economic conditions. Although the committee studied the

---

[25] *Ibid.*, p. 120.
[26] *Ibid.*, p. 121.

total program of vocational education, labor's relationship had been primarily concerned with the trade and industrial area. In order to determine the reasons for dissatisfaction with trade and industrial education, the committee sent questionnaires to state federations of labor, central labor unions, building trades councils, and local unions to ask for their comments.

By 1936, labor's enthusiasm for trade and industrial education had soured to the point that its attitude seemed to be that of protecting itself from the abuses of vocational education. To indicate the factors which brought about the change, the committee summarized the attitude of labor from the questionnaires as follows:

Failure to encourage or allow labor participation in the development of the program.

Disregard of the apprentice method of training and, hence, creation of substandard craftsmen.

Failure to balance trade training programs to personnel needs of the industry, thus creating an artificial surplus.

Disregard of proper labor standards as to wages in placing trade school students and graduates.

Unconcern as to whether such placements displaced adult workers.

Domination of many vocational training systems by "chiseling" employers.

Complaisance on the part of educators toward the use of Federal funds to train new sources of labor for migratory industries.

Training workers under so-called vocational education plans for mere routine processes.

Permitting student employees to work on a production basis without wages.

Encouraging boys to go into trade courses to the detriment of their general education.

Lack of cooperation with union apprentice training programs.

Failure to supply trade extension courses for union journeymen already employed and seeking to keep abreast of technical changes in a trade.

Susceptibility of vocational educators to employer propaganda, such as the cry of labor shortage, without regard to the real facts as to shortage or whether the school can actually do anything about it, or whether another depression will hit us before the "shortage" could be met.

Failure to give trade school students any instruction on subjects which would prepare them for a proper understanding of industrial life.

Inculcation of anti-union propaganda and fostering of employer-dominated philosophies that tend toward company unionism, such as seen in movements such as the Future Craftsmen of America.[27]

## Labor Prepares a Guide

Concurrently with the publication of the Russell report, the AFL issued a *Guide for Vocational Education* which was distributed to labor and education groups throughout the United States.[28] The report contained three parts. *Part one* reviewed material about "The Future Labor Army." Labor presented the general rationale for vocational education, stressing its importance to the boy and girl, to the economy, and to the welfare of the nation. Questionable practices related to selecting students for vocational classes in high schools were stated succinctly. There was not the slightest room for disagreement by vocational

---

[27] John Dale Russell and Associates, *Vocational Education*, Staff Study No. 8, Prepared for the Advisory Committee on Education. Washington: Government Printing Office, 1938, pp. 258-259.

[28] *Guide for Vocational Education*. Washington: American Federation of Labor, 1938.

educators; the suggestions followed accepted points of view.

If organized labor will insist upon vocational training that meets the standards that labor had in mind when it first demanded and got vocational training, and if the unions in every State and local community will help to keep that vocational training up to standard, all of labor can march forward toward the promise of America.[29]

*Part two* of the report was concerned with "Keeping Skill in Line with Industrial Change." The rationale related to this point followed representative ideas equally acceptable to vocational education and labor.

The AFL was critical of proposals which had been discussed for several years to organize a student group to be known as "Future Craftsmen of America." The proposed organization probably appeared as a threat to the apprenticeship system, but even more threatening was the possibility of compromising quality by producing large numbers of low-skilled workers. Of course, vocational educators had no intention of upsetting the balance of skill level and industrial change, but plans for the student organization had not been developed in a manner which would secure the support of labor. Insight into the labor point of view may be gained from the following quotation in the report.

We must remember that it is a highly skilled task to create and maintain a working program of vocational education that effectively meets labor's practical needs. It demands the best educational methods we know. It takes unusual understanding of business and industry as well as unusual insight into labor's problems and into the labor movement. The people who plan and who teach the vocational education courses must rate high in all of these respects. Organized labor can only help to choose these experts wisely—making sure that they know their job and that they know labor—and can only help to keep vocational education in line with workers' needs at every step in the program if the union members study the problem. We cannot learn how to direct vocational education by inspiration any more than one can learn a highly skilled trade in any other way than by setting himself to learn it.[30]

The responsibility was placed clearly upon labor to have all of the facts so that it could provide effective assistance.

*Part three* of the report consisted of "General Exploratory Questions for the Local Committee on Education," which would help local groups to get together on the "knotty" problems of planning and administration of vocational education in a local school.

It is significant that this report, issued at a time of severe stress in vocational education, presented a rational point of view, which, if followed, would presumably have reduced conflict. The AFL pointed out to its membership the kinds of questions they should ask to get the information necessary in helping build the kinds of vocational education that were thought to be desirable. The report was not vindictive in any way. The accusing finger was pointed as much at labor as at vocational education. It was quite definite that labor regarded the success of the vocational education program as a joint responsibility. Labor's

---

[29] *Ibid.*, p. 4.
[30] *Ibid.*, p. 11.

support of trade and industrial education was not in any sense a blind one.

## Labor and Industrial Education, 1939-1950

By 1939 the depression and its wide-scale unemployment had lessened. After the Congressional elections of 1938, the influence of the New Deal was somewhat reduced, and its effects on labor and industrial education could be listed on both the negative and positive sides of the ledger. The Congress of Industrial Organizations had been created. A European war was imminent. Ideas of neutrality quickly gave way to the necessity for the United States to look to its own military defense. Thus the year 1939 is a convenient separation point between two eras in industrial education —one a time of unemployment, the next a period of increasing jobs related to World War II. The year 1950 is likewise something of a turning point since by then World War II was over and a certain amount of post-war readjustment had taken place, yet the impact of science and outer space was only beginning to be felt.

### Labor Looks Ahead in Vocational Education

The American Federation of Labor took the point of view that the major problem of vocational education was poor coordination with general education. This, labor felt, was the stumbling block that prevented achievement of the objectives set forth in the first days of the vocational education movement.

The danger was ever present that vocational education might degenerate into scholastic ineffectiveness. It was the opinion of labor that general educators needed to take the initiative in the matter. Lack of coordination appeared to develop from the fact that vocational education was largely under federal control while general education was responsible largely to local jurisdiction. Labor had opposed federal control from the time when the Smith-Hughes Act was passed, although labor readily admitted that "labor standards" did need federal control.

There was increasing evidence that labor and industrial education treasured quality and effectiveness in vocational education. The growth of enrollment in vocational education to approximately two million students by 1939 was pleasing to labor. George L. Googe explained the periods of discord as follows:

Indeed it is because labor, more than any other group in society, recognizes the power of the vocational education instrumentality and consequently the social loss if it is vitiated, and its power for evil if misdirected, that the American Federation of Labor has at times been vocational education's severe critic.[31]

Evidently labor's critical evaluation of vocational education was directed toward making possible continued "mutual helpfulness," but then that had also become an accepted principle of vocational education.

In the period 1939-1950 labor's interests were broadly established in the field of vocational education; conse-

---

[31] George L. Googe, "Labor Looks Ahead in Vocational Education," *AVA Journal and News Bulletin*, Vol. XIV, No. 1, February 1939, p. 12.

quently, representatives of labor were giving attention to particular facets of the program. Teacher education was one of the elements that received such attention. Labor had long accepted the principle that teacher training was imperative and had urged higher and higher standards in teacher training and selection. "Vocational education should no longer content itself with an under-standardized faculty. Neither the mere academic student nor the mere tradesmen can adequately do the job." [32]

### Stress on Working Relationships

Working relationships among industry, labor, and industrial education have continuously been strong elements in the progress of industrial education, and many factors have combined to bring this about. The frequent stress upon working relationships does not imply lagging interest on the part of the groups concerned; rather it implies an emphasis upon cooperation as an essential aspect of sound industrial education. The literature abounds with examples of cooperative relationships. These examples, which are found in the reports of industry, labor, and industrial education, indicate the pride of all of these groups in their contributions.

An interesting example is the experience of the Structural Clay Products Institute which had organized its own apprenticeship programs. During the depression, however, many of the apprentices left these programs and the Institute wanted to devise a system of

building up enrollment in brick-masonry classes. They sought advice of L. H. Dennis, Secretary of the American Vocational Association, and learned that classes could be organized as a part of the national vocational education program in the public schools.[33] This procedure would enable the Institute to meet its objectives and at the same time be relieved of the necessity of being totally responsible for all of the details of organizing and conducting the training programs. Evidently they were delighted with the prospects and indicated that the Washington staff of the Institute was "sold on vocational education."

After reclarification of motives, meanings, and established procedures of vocational education, the Institute, together with representatives of the U.S. Office of Education and the Federal Committee on Apprentice Training, studied ways of improving the training program as it had existed at the time of the depression. Then, with the help of these groups, the Institute presented the problem to selected schools, with the result that programs for the training of brick masons were started in Indianapolis; Newark; St. Louis; Waterloo, Iowa; and Lincoln, Nebraska. The outcome of this cooperative action was immediately satisfactory, so the Institute expanded the program.

Another example of working relationships among labor, federal government, and industrial educators developed in connection with the Fair Labor Standards Act of 1938. The Act provided

[32] Henry Ohl, "Labor Views Vocational Education," AVA Journal and News Bulletin, Vol. XIV, No. 1, February 1939, p. 43.

[33] Douglas Whitlock, "Industry, Labor and Vocational Schools Cooperate in Training Bricklayers," AVA Journal and News Bulletin, Vol. XIII, No. 3, September 1938, p. 154.

for minimum wage arrangements. Although certain groups of employees were exempt, vocational students were not. Working out the complex plan for these students required the cooperative action of the U.S. Office of Education, the Wage and Hour Division and the Division of Labor Standards of the U.S. Department of Labor, and representatives of state departments of education.[34] Instructions were detailed to guide school administrators in meeting the requirements imposed by the Act. Thus through the cooperation of several groups the interests of industry, education, labor, and the student were preserved and served better.

The policies and practices of American industry certainly had implications for industrial education; therefore, continuous review of these policies and practices was essential in improving working relationships. With this in mind, John R. Ludington concluded:

> . . . that as a nation we are entering an era of industrial development marked by the need for deliberate and continuous planning. The cooperative use of intelligence must become the guide for future progress in opposition to traditional forces and the perpetuation of institutional idea systems and patterns.[35]

Other events have shown the necessity of strengthening working relationships in order to achieve general social goals. The CIO resolutions of 1949 relating to federal aid to education, labor extension service programs, and education of children were strong statements of belief and dedication to certain principles related to each.[36] In addition, embodied in the resolutions are the bases for cooperative working relationships in order that the practical reality of the resolutions be achieved.

## Cooperation in Apprenticeship

Apprenticeship has been the perennial educational medium of labor. It has suffered the ravages of time, has been submerged, suppressed, and neglected, but it has never disappeared completely. For many trades the apprentice programs are sound, and the fact that such training has persisted under adverse conditions is some indication of its merits as a means of providing skilled craftsmen. Beginning in the 1930's a determined effort was made to rescue and strengthen the apprenticeship system of the nation.

A national apprenticeship program was not established until 1937, when the Fitzgerald Act was passed. However, the need for the Act grew from earlier attitudes and related activities. Some states had apprenticeship laws (Wisconsin started the movement in 1911), but the lack of national coordination would occasionally create problems in relation to the employment of youth. Frank Cushman's, *Report of a Conference on Apprentice Education in the Building Trades*, 1923, pointed

---

[34] Oscar W. Ross, "Vocational Training Under the Fair Labor Standards Act," *AVA Journal and News Bulletin*, Vol. XV, No. 3, September 1940, p. 152.

[35] John R. Ludington, *A Study of Certain Policies and Practices of Organized American Industry With Implications for Education*. (Unpublished Doctoral Dissertation, The Ohio State University.) Abstracts of Doctoral Dissertations, No. 33, The Ohio State University Press, 1940, pp. 138-139.

[36] Congress of Industrial Organizations, *CIO Resolutions on Education*, 11th Constitutional Convention, Cleveland, Ohio, October 31-November 4, 1949.

up the need for national review and standards. Early in 1934 the NRA appointed an Advisory Committee on Apprenticeship. The results of these meetings led to an Executive Order (6750C) authorizing the Secretary of Labor to create a Federal Committee on Apprenticeship. In the fall of 1934 regional conferences were held to develop working relationships between the states and the Federal Apprenticeship Committee. The entire operation was, however, conducted on an insecure footing until the passage of the Fitzgerald Act.

The Fitzgerald Act of 1937 provided incentive from the national level. By 1940 eleven states had enacted apprenticeship laws, and in 13 others apprenticeship councils had been formed. At least half of the states, therefore, had some organized means of carrying on apprenticeship programs. Recommendations adopted by the International Labor Organization during the summer of 1939 were given wide publicity in the United States jointly by labor and the U.S. Office of Education. These recommendations included provision for: (1) written agreements showing the terms of the apprentice relationship, (2) learning schedule in the various aspects of the trade, (3) a scale of wages with periodic increases, (4) attendance in classes for related instruction, (5) continuous employment, and (6) approval by joint committees of employers and employees.[37]

Wilson Frankland, writing from the point of view of labor, was aware of the difficulty in trying to list all factors representing labor's interest in apprenticeship. He did, however, identify four as particularly important and representative of cooperative relationships.

First, cooperation between employers, journeymen trade organizations (where apprentices are affiliated with such groups), manufacturers of equipment, and public school authorities. Second, adequate provision for housing, shop equipment, and laboratories needed (physical equipment). Third, courses of study laid out to meet modern conditions. Fourth, skilled trade and properly qualified shop and subject related teachers.[38]

Involvement of labor in apprenticeship programs can stimulate interest in retraining programs for journeymen. Frankland cited specific examples of the formulation of such courses at the Washburne Trade School, Chicago.

### Push Toward Committee Representation

Historically, labor's demand that industrial education have advisory committees with labor representation has been continuous and persistent. There has been no conflict at the conceptual level on this point because the idea was fundamental in the Smith-Hughes Act. Labor's complaint was that the committees did not work. There was nothing wrong with the policy; it was the practice that did not measure up to labor's expectations.

In 1941 a resolution was adopted by the AFL calling for affiliated state and central bodies to name committees on vocational training. Each committee was asked to: (1) gather and analyze information on vocational education in

---

[37] Clara M. Beyer, "Labor's Interest in Apprenticeship and Vocational Education," *AVA Journal and News Bulletin*, Vol. XV, No. 1, February 1940, pp. 30-31.
[38] Wilson Frankland, "The Point of View of Labor," *AVA Journal and News Bulletin*, Vol. XV, No. 2, May 1940, p. 99.

its community; (2) examine training programs, particularly of the emergency nature of government agencies; (3) keep before civic and socially minded organizations the social and economic aims of labor; (4) assist in organizing vocational teachers into the American Federation of Teachers. Each unit of AFL was requested to send reports of its findings to the national Committee on Education.

Discussions on the national level between labor and representatives of vocational education in the U.S. Office of Education resulted in an agreement in 1942 that programs of vocational education should be established on the basis of actual need and only on the advice and counsel of a representative advisory committee. All units of labor were requested to lend all possible assistance in developing such advisory committees. "In this way such programs become joint enterprises, based upon the knowledge and experience of all groups interested or concerned in the training." [39]

Then, in 1943, the reports of the AFL indicated that labor was not contributing much to the membership of the advisory committees. Requests by vocational education for labor representation on these committees were sometimes not even acknowledged, or if acknowledged the member often did not attend the meetings. This situation caused the AFL to stress in its reports that this was a responsibility of labor, and labor's representatives should attend to their obligations. [40]

## CIO Activities in Industrial Education

Prior to merging with the AFL in 1955, the Congress of Industrial Organizations did not follow the same general procedures as the AFL regarding the pattern of educational activities. Industrial education activities were obviously important to CIO but were manifested primarily in training programs of an in-plant nature. Resolutions in support of legislation for vocational education are not uncommon in the proceedings of CIO meetings. However, a full-scale continuous program of educational activity was not a part of its national organization.

## Labor, Management, and Education Speak

A grave question immediately following World War II concerned the changes needed in industrial education to conform better to post-war conditions. In 1946 an opinion survey undertaken by H. H. London and Ivan Hostetler reported data concerning fifty issues from 900 representatives of labor, management, and education. [41] All groups agreed on the greater need for industrial training in the post-war years. The schools were urged to provide basic industrial education as a foundation for further development of specialists. (Note how this reverts to early opinion, when labor championed general public training.) "A large percentage of all groups would confine preemployment training to job families

---

[39] *Labor and Education.* American Federation of Labor, Reports of the Executive Council to the annual conventions, 1939-1954, p. 10.

[40] *Ibid.,* p. 23.

[41] H. H. London and Ivan Hostetler, "Labor Management and Education Speak," *American Vocational Journal,* Vol. 21, No. 7, September 1946, pp. 25, 32.

392

rather than to specific jobs."[42] Vocational guidance was thought essential. Ninety percent of the labor leaders favored industrial education programs in junior colleges. Expansion of technical institutes and technical high schools was urged.

While a large percentage of all groups would confine industrial education in the full-time general high school to industrial arts, a majority of all except management would not. This would suggest that the majority favor day trade classes as well as industrial arts in the general high school.[43]

Other significant opinions were reported, and, while differences were observed, the report showed unmistakably that the three primary groups —labor, management, and education— were of one voice concerning the necessity to improve in all aspects of industrial education. Furthermore, one concludes from the report of the survey that the groups were anxious to continue their cooperative endeavors.

S. Lewis Land determined from other studies that there were eight investigative factors of importance to management and labor that might be used as guides to measure the adequacy and success of vocational training programs.[44] The points he suggested investigating are paraphrased as follows:

1. Extent to which training reduces the time of adapting new workers to production.

2. Evidence that trade extension classes contribute to effective utilization of manpower.

3. Need for conservation of time of supervisory personnel.

4. Relationship of training and effective use of production machines.

5. Evidence that training programs lessen material losses.

6. Relationship of shop accidents and training.

7. Effect of training on labor turnover.

8. Effect of training on absenteeism.

Land also reviewed the methods used by local directors of vocational education in establishing sound working relationships with labor and management. These were reported as: "(1) advisory committees; (2) first hand contacts with plant managers, superintendents, and foremen; (3) first hand contacts with labor unions; and (4) effective public relations in keeping the public thoroughly informed of the program conducted by the schools."[45] Lewis Land spoke for vocational education. It is quite obvious that management, labor, and education have maintained lines of communication concerning their common interests in industrial education; it is equally obvious that when these lines break down, one party does not hesitate to bring the matter to the attention of those who might help correct it.

## A Critical Review of Industrial Education

Through the years spokesmen for all facets of labor stood ready to be critical of practices in trade and

---

[42] *Ibid.*, p. 25.
[43] *Ibid.*, p. 32.
[44] S. Lewis Land, "Establishing and Maintaining Relationships With Management, Labor, and the Public," *Industrial Arts and Vocational Education*, Vol. 38, No. 8, October 1949, p. 305.
[45] *Ibid.*, p. 305.

industrial education when these practices seemed to be in conflict with labor's view; at the same time labor would speak with pride of the achievements of trade and industrial education. Labor had played an important part in the national development of trade and industrial education; hence it had a right to re-evaluate the work from time to time with praise or criticism according to its own criteria. Now and then labor interpreted its role as one which made suggestions of tasks to be completed, at times demanding that the work be done.

It was not surprising therefore to find the Executive Council of the AFL recommending that the Vocational Division of the U.S. Office of Education make a major evaluative study of vocational education. The proposed study was to cover the entire field, including related academic subjects, counseling and guidance. Note that a strong old theme was repeated: "All trade unionists believe the academic work to be of equally as great importance as the vocational work for the pupil." [46] Of course, labor wanted to determine the extent to which the trade and industrial program tended to produce low-paid "specialty" workers, poorly equipped for advancement —which had always been one of labor's chief suspicions about the national program. Labor continued to maintain that the vocational education program should provide a "well rounded education" for a complete life rather than make of students "mere tools" for industry.

Yet in nearly every convention the AFL tended to reaffirm its faith in the principles of vocational education. Some practices they could never support. At times they were bitter in opposition to a part of the program; but that labor's faith in the educational goal was not shaken may be seen by the point of view expressed at the 1949 convention.

Vocational training, formal and informal, must help establish standards for work proficiency as well as help provide to equip the worker for his work. Education must be continuous. Adult education is as essential in our complex society as is elementary education or any other level of education. [47]

Both immediate and long range interests of labor were involved in the development of vocational education. These interests, it had been discovered, could not be served except upon the basis of an improved functional relationship between labor, education, and the general community.

The national study requested by labor, undertaken in cooperation with the U.S. Office of Education and the U.S. Department of Labor, had progressed to the extent that the AFL Executive Committee could report to its national convention some specific problems which had been found:

1. Lack of effective labor representation on Boards of Education and other administrative units.
2. Lack of labor representation on policy-making boards at the state and local level.
3. Lack of definite programs which labor should propose for consideration.

---

[46] American Federation of Labor, *Labor and Education in 1948*, p. 20.
[47] American Federation of Labor, *Report of the Executive Council*, Sixty-eighth Convention, St. Paul, Minnesota, October 3, 1949, p. 103.

4. Lack of understanding of the basic importance of learning on the job.

5. Lack of coordination between vocational education and general education, between on-the-job training and apprenticeship training, and with a lack of information and understanding on the part of each of what the other program seeks to accomplish.

6. Lack of appreciation by the general public of the social and economic objectives of labor's approach to the problem.

7. Traditional, formal school organization regulations prevent a more fluid vocational program from being adopted more readily to meet local needs.[48]

## Post-War and the Space Age— Labor and Industrial Education After 1950

Labor's role in education cannot be described at any time as limited in purpose. Although emphasis is concentrated here in the area of industrial education, labor's attention was by no stretch of the imagination so limited. Any area of education could expect to receive a comment of appreciation or admonition, depending upon labor's regard for the achievements in the area.

Naturally, at times labor called attention to its part in certain achievements, as for example, the extensive development of vocational education during World War II, when this pronouncement was made: "The American Federation of Labor looks with pride on this record and rejoices in the large part it played in establishing the vast system of vocational training in the United States."[49]

Labor had participated in a sufficient number of studies to be aware of the fact that post-war technology was producing an emphasis upon the technical side of education, and it readily agreed that this trend should be followed and developed. The rapid occupational changes would have a bearing upon vocational guidance services, requiring the schools to follow employment trends closely. "It is unfair both to the students in vocational schools and to the labor movement to direct large numbers of children into trades and vocations in which there are no opportunities to secure employment."[50]

So, as the nation moved into the second half of the twentieth century, we find labor watchful of progress, or the lack of it, on many fronts.

### Inspection Reports

The studies requested of the U.S. Office of Education were producing guide lines for future action in industrial education, while sustaining both hopes and fears that had arisen out of previous subjective evaluations. William Green, President of the AFL, reported that effective results in vocational education were obtained where "purposeful joint advisory committees of management and unions" were at work.[51] Green was referring to the four pilot projects being carried on in Alabama, California, Michigan, and New Jersey. At the 1951 AFL convention, the subcommittee on vocational education was able to report that:

---

[48] American Federation of Labor, *Labor and Education in 1950*, p. 16.

[49] American Federation of Labor, *Labor and Education, 1939-1954*, p. 27.

[50] *Ibid.*, p. 20.

[51] "A. F. of L. President William Green Endorses the Nation's Program of Vocational Education," (Reprinted from the August, 1951, issue of *The American Federationist*.) *American Vocational Journal*, Vol. 26, No. 8, November 1951, p. 23.

The study in Alabama showed particularly the need for a more active participation on the part of the trade union leaders in the state's vocational training program. The Alabama study showed also the need for more constructive cooperation between the Vocational Training program and the Apprenticeship Training program.

The California study revealed entirely different conditions. Here, an active labor movement, well experienced in working with public and private agencies, was taking a leading part in bringing a real value to the program. Here, however, also, the study shows that local labor leaders must work more actively in close cooperation with the authorities sponsoring the project.[52]

Why was labor so intent upon its inspection of industrial education and its advisory groups? Obviously the area of industrial education was closely related to labor's interests, but it is possible that a larger and more significant issue was related to a point of view often expressed by labor: "Differences in education constitute the widest and most formidable chasms between groups of citizens." This was the view of William Green in 1951.

**The Dumping Ground and a Plan of Action**

Periodically the AFL committee on education would call attention to what it defined as a "caste system" in the national educational structure. In support of this criticism the committee would cite situations such as pupils with low IQ's being told to take vocational work while those with high IQ's were advised not to do so, vocational schools and academic schools with different scholastic standings, prospective vocational teachers with college degrees and minimum work experience having preference over skilled craftsmen without college degrees. The committee was alarmed at these developments because of the effect they could have on instruction and upon a "sound social conception of the community."

Vocational education, let us frankly admit, is widely regarded as suitable for the "educationally and socially inferior pupil," only. In too many communities the vocational school is the institution to which are sent pupils of low I.Q., and pupils who are social behavior problems.[53]

Such a situation justifiably was regarded by the AFL as harmful to the community, to the pupils enrolled in vocational work, and, most of all, to those who did not take vocational work because this attitude prevailed. "We are concerned about the effect that these unreasonable, unsound attitudes have on the child whose parents work in practical jobs—jobs their schools look upon as suited for the inferior person."[54]

Reasoning followed lines that demanded action. The problem was discussed at the 1952 convention in New York City.

At this time, when more and more the real experts and authorities in American education, and indeed in education throughout the world, recognize the absolute necessity of developing manual skills and the necessity of adapting school programs to have them meet the needs of a changing social order, and to have them secure and maintain the interest of

---

[52] American Federation of Labor, *Labor and Education in 1951*, pp. 11-12.
[53] American Federation of Labor, *Labor and Education in 1953*, p. 15.
[54] *Ibid.*, pp. 15-16.

396

the pupil who is in school because he has to be there, it is imperative that the entire vocational program conducted jointly by the Federal Government, the states, and local communities, be critically reevaluated.[55]

Samuel Gompers had been identified prominently in the events leading up to the passage of the Smith-Hughes Act, and labor was proud of that fact. But in the early 1950's, labor stated that the program had "grown but not developed."

Just talking about the problem will do nothing to help us understand the issues involved and try to meet them. Neither will the repeated enunciation of statements of policy, as we have done from year to year, accomplish our purpose.[56]

In reality, however, some progress had been made. The Committee on Education had been working for some time with representatives of the Vocational Division of the U.S. Office of Education. Nevertheless, in 1952 the AFL advocated that at least four steps be taken immediately.

1. That we ask the Division of Vocational Education in the Office of Education to call a conference to which representatives of Labor, industry, the schools, and experts in academic training in the field of vocational education be invited so that a frank and full discussion of the present status of the law as it is actually administered may be held.

2. That we recommend to state federations and to central bodies that steps be taken by them to have schools require practical working experience of not less than three years of any person employed to teach a vocational subject.

3. That we advise our state federations

and city central bodies to arrange in co-operation with other civic bodies for a city-wide or state-wide conference to evaluate the present status of mental and achievement tests and the role they play in shaping general school policy, as well as the adjustment of the individual child.

4. That steps be taken to present to community civic bodies the importance of recognizing the social contribution made by all workers whether manual or non-manual, and the need for developing a respect for all who contribute to the social good through their work.[57]

One result was that states were encouraged to step up their activities along the lines of the recommendations, but it would be nearly a decade before a substantial review of all facets of the nation's program of vocational education would actually take place, and even later before the results of the review could be evaluated.

## Cooperative Working Relationships— the Perennial Issue

The continuous written record of labor and industrial education periodically produces a review of the "working relationships" issue. It shows up with amazing regularity each year; its appearance is as dependable as the sunrise. Consequently, the story has a repetitious nature that could be boring, were it not for two important facts: First, the "brickbats" and "bouquets" were not always aimed at vocational education. Labor can be as critical of its own performance as of vocational education. Similarly, commendations for a job well done are accorded both to vocational educators

---

[55] American Federation of Labor, *Report of the Proceedings of the Seventy-first Convention of the American Federation of Labor,* New York, N.Y., September 15-23, 1952, p. 211.

[56] *Ibid.,* p. 211.

[57] *Ibid.,* p. 211.

and to labor. Second, the issue of co-operative working relationships is, in fact, important. Labor believes this, and no effort has been spared to keep the idea prominently in view of all concerned.

So, despite the fact that the story of labor and industrial education is loaded with references to the cooperative working relationships issue, it seems justifiable to add more examples from the 1950's.

At the 1953 convention of the AFL in St. Louis, James Brownlow of the Metal Trades Department introduced a resolution related to vocational education:

WHEREAS, The American Federation of Labor played a major role in the establishment of a Federal-State vocational education program, and

WHEREAS, The maintenance and development of such a program must involve

1. A thorough understanding on the part of all interested parties of the legal basis within which the program must operate.

2. A respect for and appreciation of the standards of training which are an integral part of the philosophy and practices of the American Federation of Labor.

3. A complete knowledge of the social and educational aim of the program, as well as of its essential characteristics, as well as its operational practice.

4. A well-planned practical program of cooperation with the American labor movement is essential to the effective development of the program, therefore, be it

RESOLVED, That the Officers of the State Federations and of the City Central Bodies and of all affiliated national and international unions be informed fully of the aims, purposes, and administration of the Federal-State vocational education program as set forth in the charts and explanatory matter hereto attached and as further interpreted by the committee on vocational education of the American Federation of Labor, and be it further

RESOLVED, That we urge responsible officers of our trade union movement to inform the subcommittee on vocational education of the A. F. of L. of any problems that have arisen in the conduct of the program.[58]

The resolution was adopted unanimously.

In the 1954 report the committee cited the joint project of the AFL and the Vocational Division of the U.S. Office of Education in which all affiliated bodies of the AFL were sent a report of the aims, purposes, and administration of the Federal-State vocational program. This project improved the attitude between the two groups, which promoted better working relationships.

Labor again pressed for the appointment (actually re-establishment) of the Advisory Committee on Vocational Education and the Advisory Committee on Trade and Industrial Education. This was not done immediately, because of the view of the Commissioner of Education that the appointment of such committees was not timely. Labor indicated that it would again bring this matter to the attention of the Commissioner, which it did in 1955, but the appointments were not made.

The AFL committee cited many successful and pleasing evidences of cooperative activity with public education and urged labor to unite with an open mind in developing state and local relationships.

---

[58] American Federation of Labor, *Proceedings, Seventy-second Convention,* St. Louis, Missouri, September 21, 1953, p. 454.

Again we comment on the need for all who are concerned with education to become alert to the problem of developing a more wholesome appreciation and attitude toward vocational education and the development of manual skills which are so vital to our continued national progress.

Every effort must be made to avoid vocational classes as a dumping ground for pupils who may be judged as intellectually inferior. The strength of our nation is steadily becoming more dependent upon the skill and training of its work force.

Vocational education programs, properly administered, will play an increasingly important part in developing the strength of our country.[59]

### Formation of the Labor-Management Relations Committee, AVA

An agenda item before the Executive Committee of AVA at its Chicago meeting, November 19-27, 1953, was as follows: "Consideration of ways by which the AVA can contribute to better public relations with labor, management and vocational education at the national, state and local levels."[60] Consideration of labor-management relations was not particularly a new venture with AVA, but the item has importance as the beginning of a new emphasis. The minutes contain only a brief note about the agenda item. "This item was discussed in some detail. It was decided that our relations with labor, management and other groups should be given much consid-

eration and should be included in our program of work."[61]

An *ad hoc* committee was appointed to study the problem. The first meeting of the committee was held February 8-9, 1954. A report of this meeting, made to the Executive Committee March 30, 1954, contained a resolution that cited the need for sustained committee action, and a recommendation that the committee be formalized by the Executive Committee. On March 31, 1954, the Executive Committee agreed unanimously to the formation of a Labor-Management Relations Committee.[62]

The committee was authorized "to make a comprehensive study of the objectives, organization and implementation of Advisory Committees, functioning at the state and local levels within the several states and territories, in order to determine the relationship that exists between vocational education and labor-management groups."[63] The following persons were appointed members of the Labor-Management Relations Committee: Lawrence Borosage, Chairman (Michigan); Thos. H. Quigley, (Georgia); Samuel L. Fick, (California); Cecil E. Stanley, (Nebraska); Robert M. Reese (Ohio); Howard K. Hogan, (U.S. Office of Education); Frank P. Johnson, (New York); and M. D. Mobley, (Executive Secretary, American Vocational Association).

---

[59] American Federation of Labor and Congress of Industrial Organizations, *Labor and Education in 1955*, p. 39.

[60] American Vocational Association, *Minutes of the Executive Committee*, November 19, 1953. (Hereafter cited as AVA *Minutes*.)

[61] *Ibid.*

[62] AVA *Minutes*, March 31, 1954.

[63] *Ibid.*

At the annual convention in December, 1954, the Executive Committee gave further attention to the matter particularly with reference to inviting the major labor and management groups to appoint representatives to the Labor-Management Relations Committee.[64]

Activities of the Labor-Management Relations Committee were cited briefly in the minutes of the Executive Committee in the spring of 1955, saying that, "Contacts made during the past year were invaluable and that much progress had been made."[65]

Although the Executive Committee agenda for the meeting of December 1-9, 1955, made provision for a report and discussion of progress of the Labor-Management Relations Committee, a report was not made and the official minutes do not contain any reference to the Labor-Management Committee's action. At this point it appears that the Committee was slowly passing into oblivion. However, on December 4, 1956, a motion was made by AVA Vice President Samuel L. Fick to reactivate the Committee. "It was agreed that in these crucial times, we should maintain the gains we have made with labor and management."[66]

Early in March, 1957, Borosage outlined the progress of the Committee since its inception, indicating the contacts made and citing some imperative objectives for the Committee. Borosage asked to be relieved as chairman, but requested that he be allowed to continue to serve as a member. The size of the task and the press of other business made it impossible for him to devote the required time to the chairman's task.

At the spring 1957 meeting of the Executive Committee it was decided that Samuel L. Fick should be named chairman of the Labor-Management Relations Committee.[67] Fick announced the dates of the next meeting of the Committee as May 8-9, 1957. The meeting, held in Washington, D.C., was productive of ideas, and the report of the meeting was accepted by the Executive Committee which acted favorably upon a recommendation that another meeting be held in the fall to explore manpower needs.[68]

In April, 1958, Fick reported to the Executive Committee that the meeting with representatives of the National Association of Manufacturers, AFL-CIO, and the U.S. Chamber of Commerce had been successful. He also reported that representatives of the U.S. Office of Education and the U.S. Department of Labor would be invited to participate in the next meeting of the Labor-Management Relations Committee. The Executive Committee approved this action.[69] In August it was pointed out that, "It is tremendously important for members of this committee to be selected from states that have good relationships with both management and labor."[70]

[64] AVA *Minutes,* December 4, 1954.
[65] AVA *Minutes,* April 15, 1955.
[66] AVA *Minutes,* December 4, 1956.
[67] AVA *Minutes,* March 27-30, 1957.
[68] AVA *Minutes,* August 1-9, 1957.
[69] AVA *Minutes,* April 9-12, 1958.
[70] AVA *Minutes,* August 7-15, 1958.

From time to time during the next two years, the Committee met and general progress was reported. At the meeting in Washington, D.C., March 9-10, 1960, the discussion was related to advisory committees, coordination, improving instruction, and defining the term "technician." Following this meeting the Executive Committee of AVA encouraged continued activity of the Labor-Management Relations Committee and approved travel funds for the Committee for the spring of 1961.[71]

The Labor-Management Relations Committee had recommended that it hold two meetings each year, one in the spring and one during the annual AVA convention. The record indicates enthusiasm for the work of the Committee, but documentation of concrete achievement is lacking. This may have been the reason why, on May 10, 1962, the Committee prepared a statement of *policy*, defined its *responsibilities*, and suggested procedures to be used in continuing its work.

I. STATEMENT OF POLICY. The functions of the LABOR MANAGEMENT RELATIONS COMMITTEE of the AMERICAN VOCATIONAL ASSOCIATION, INC., are to:

Relate national labor, employer and management groups to the American Vocational Association looking toward the ultimate and continuous concern of these groups in understanding the principles and policies enunciated from time to time by the Association.

Enlist the support of labor and management for the principles and policies of vocational education nationally and within the states.

Make recommendations to the Executive Committee of AVA regarding the Association's relations to labor and management groups.

Carry out such other labor and management group relation responsibilities as the Executive Committee of A.V.A. may assign.

II. RESPONSIBILITIES

1. Assess the status of relationships of vocational education with labor and management.

2. Identify specific problems of concern to vocational education as they relate to labor and management groups.

3. Involve all groups concerned (labor, management, vocational education, government agencies) in the study of problems related to vocational education.

4. Seek ways and means to resolve these problems identified with 2 and 3 above.

5. Give leadership to movements and projects that will improve relationships between vocational education and labor and/or management groups.

6. Provide a means for improving communication between vocational education and labor and/or management groups.

7. Recommend preparation, production and distribution of appropriate publications that will facilitate the work of this committee.

8. Serve in a consultative capacity to organizations and agencies in matters falling within the jurisdiction of this committee.

9. Prepare an annual budget.

III. PROCEDURES

1. Meet annually during A.V.A. conventions and special meetings at the call of the chairman.

2. Keep appropriate minutes and distribute copies as follows: Executive Committee of A.V.A.; All members (appointed and ex-officio) of the committee; State Supervisors of Trade and Industrial Education; Executive Committee of the following affiliated and associated organizations of A.V.A., N.C.L.A., A.T.E.A., N.A.I.T.E.

---

[71] AVA *Minutes,* November 30-December 9, 1960.

3. Report annually to the Executive Committee of A.V.A. those activities not included in the minutes referred to above.

4. Keep the A.V. Journal advised of important activities that should be reported to the general membership.

5. Prepare and distribute in advance the agenda for each meeting of the committee.

6. Encourage and request certain "face to face" meetings when appropriate to carry on the work of the committee.

7. Review publications and speeches and be continually sensitive to matters affecting relationships with vocational education.

8. Act on assignments from the Executive Committee of A.V.A.

9. Survey needs and problems and bring to the attention of the committee for consideration.

10. Select action which first places responsibility on the Labor Management Relations Committee and only refer problems for consideration by others when advisable.

11. Follow up the results of action to completion.[72]

The importance of the Labor-Management Relations Committee of AVA, from a historical point of view, lies in the fact that its formation is further evidence of the dependence of vocational education upon its relationships with labor and management. This dependency was apparent in 1906, when the National Society for the Promotion of Industrial Education was founded, and it has been acknowledged and implemented many times by the professional association of vocational education. This element of consistency adds emphasis to the centrality of labor and management in the progress of industrial education.

## Training Agreement—IBEW and Vocational Education

In the spring of 1962 a proposed training agreement between the International Brotherhood of Electrical Workers and Vocational Education was announced. The agreement provided for a cooperative plan of relationships to further and improve training in the electrical area.

The agreement represented the joint efforts of Fred Irwin, Assistant to the President of IBEW, and John P. Walsh, Director, Trade and Industrial Education Branch, U.S. Office of Education. The idea grew out of a session entitled, "Working with Labor and Management," a part of the National Leadership Development Conference at Cornell University in 1957. Subsequent meetings, including the 1961 national conference of state supervisors of trade and industrial education in Kansas City, brought the plan to completion.

The agreement identifies the responsibilities of IBEW and those of vocational education. In effect each group pledged to go out of its way to be of assistance to the other, and at the same time each group would respect the particular responsibilities of the other. The agreement was indeed a major step forward. IBEW had pledged cooperation throughout its complex organization from the national headquarters to the smallest local unit. Similarly the trade and industrial educators from the national to the state and local level gave the idea a cordial reception.

The agreement should serve to unite leaders in industry and education at the

---

[72] Minutes of the Labor Management Relations Committee, AVA, May 10, 1962.

national, state, and local levels. Vocational educators everywhere should hail this as a forward looking step in the relationships with one of the outstanding industries of the nation.[73]

## The Changing Needs of Vocational Education

Appointment of the Panel of Consultants on Vocational Education in 1961 gave labor the national study it had sought for so long a time. Labor was properly represented on the Panel, as were other groups that labor thought indispensable to a proper study of vocational education.

On September 15, 1962, the AFL-CIO Committee on Education presented its views to the Panel in a paper entitled, *The Changing Needs of Vocational Education*.[74] Peter T. Schoemann, Chairman of the AFL-CIO Education Committee and a member of the Panel (also President, United Association of Journeymen and Apprentices of the Plumbing and Pipe Fitting Industry), had long been identified with vocational education and was a highly able representative of labor's views.

The AFL-CIO statement contained a review of labor's positive stand on vocational education over the years. It also contained a summary of the contemporary socio-technological situation, a factual analysis of the national vocational education program, a review of the educational needs of youth and employed workers, and a number of recommendations related to specific details of the vocational education program.

The Committee identified some of the major problems that vocational education needed to solve in the next decade as:

How to train youth for entering employment in a rapidly changing economy;

How to teach new skills to workers whose jobs are lost because of technological changes;

How to prepare inexperienced and untrained young workers who have not completed school;

How to improve teacher training;

How to keep abreast of ever-changing technical progress.[75]

One of the significant points, expressed immediately following the listing of problems, indicated labor's mature view of vocational education. "Today training is never finished. To remain employed a worker must train all his working life to keep up and to anticipate the technological changes in his occupation."[76]

The Committee's statement—a short, simple, straightforward, imaginative, broad, and forward-looking document—was firm but not critical, professed faith in vocational education, and pledged labor's cooperation to expand and improve the program. It would be difficult for any educator to contest the issue.

## The Secretary of Labor Speaks

"There is no future in this country for the unskilled worker," W. Willard Wirtz, Secretary, U.S. Department of

---

[73] American Vocational Association, "IBEW and Vocational Education," *American Vocational Journal*, Vol. 37, No. 3, March 1962, p. 6.

[74] AFL-CIO Committee on Education, *The Changing Needs of Vocational Education*, September 15, 1962. (Mimeographed.)

[75] *Ibid.*, pp. 3-4.

[76] *Ibid.*

Labor, reported to the General Subcommittee on Education, on March 26, 1963.[77] Automation and technological change reportedly had the effect of creating as well as destroying jobs. The new jobs, however, required some skill; those they replaced were not as demanding.

There was a place in the old work force for the boy or girl who left high school, either dropping out or with diploma in hand, and entered the work force with no skill training. He or she could, and did, take an unskilled job and worked up from there. Now such jobs are vanishing. And so today there are over 700,000 16-to-21 year olds out of school and out of work. Every American youngster *has* to be given today, as a part of his education, some know-how about making a living—which means, for a great many of them, vocational education.[78]

Secretary Wirtz stressed the necessity of immediate reforms so that education and training would in fact be responsive to the needs of the economy. This was a "Wake up America!" point of view. The challenge was to all phases of education, to labor, to government, and also to the public at large.

The attack upon hard-core unemployment in the United States (through the Manpower Development and Training Act) stressed needs such as adult basic education in order to overcome functional illiteracy. Some applicants for assistance had so little education that they could not absorb the training for any of the occupations in need of workers. Experimental programs for the chronically unemployed had been established—teaching "the

3 R's along with specific occupational skills."

The contemporary task involved meeting the needs, whatever they were and wherever they existed. However, the major issue confronting all education and training was one of preventing the perpetuation of the problem. Although the total responsibility was a task for many persons, the Secretary could see the central issue as a need "for *more* vocational education—and earlier."

### Labor and Industrial Education at State Level

The topic of labor and industrial education has been considered largely from a national viewpoint and therefore the activities of national labor organizations have been cited. The work of state and local labor groups cannot be ignored, but at the same time their unique contributions are too numerous to be documented in this general treatment of labor and industrial education.

State labor groups have, of course, contributed much to the development of good relationships between labor and industrial education. Examples can be chosen from any state. The persistent stand of the Wisconsin State Federation of Labor during the crisis of the 1930's is one. An apparently organized effort by many forces to cripple the vocational schools of the nation alerted the Wisconsin group into positive action. Its efforts were unquestionably a major factor in preventing both a reduction in federal expenditures and less emphasis upon industrial education.

---

[77] W. Willard Wirtz, *Labor and Vocational Education*, March 26, 1963. (Mimeographed.)
[78] *Ibid.*, p. 2.

The story of the state action therefore could be told from fifty sources. One other case, however, may illustrate the contemporary relationship which is so valuable in the development of industrial education.

In January, 1964, the California Labor Federation, AFL-CIO, was invited to testify before a subcommittee of the State Assembly Interim Committee on Education concerning the basic purposes and broader function of the public school system in America.

The Federation explained to the subcommittee the general background, not unlike that presented earlier in this chapter. Much had been said about a crisis in education, which the Federation rejected. Its argument was that it was more appropriate to consider "change and challenge," than crisis.

If a crisis does in fact exist today, it is a crisis that existed prior to the Soviet scientific advances, and one that stems basically from the failure of a wealthy nation to give education the priority access it must have to the public treasury of a free society.[79]

Labor has considered that if an educational crisis does exist, it is located in "our thinking and in the assertion of our values."

The labor movement today, it should be clarified, is concerned not only with the inadequate amount of total resources society is making available for education, but also with the vast inequalities that exist in the manner these inadequate resources are being made available as between income groups and social classes within our society.[80]

The Federation discussed the problem of the dropouts and agreed that many such persons could be guided into vocational education. This would be meaningful only if the vocational curriculum were geared to the realities of the labor market. If the practice in a particular school permitted the use of the vocational classes as a depository for the "misfits," then it was unlikely that such a program could provide appropriately for dropouts.

Stress was placed on the necessity of a master plan for public schools which would elevate the position and status of vocational education in the thinking of students and educators. The phrase "dignity of labor," old though it was, was given renewed meaning.

In school programming, curriculum development, training and compensation of school teachers—across the board—vocational education in its broadest context must be raised to a level of recognition commensurate with academic and scientific training.[81]

To the Federation, evidence indicated that some schools were "floundering" in their vocational education programs. But part of the blame fell on the public, industry, and labor-management groups for not assuming their responsibilities in meaningful projection of future technologies and basic skill needs.

Thus 1.4 million men and women of the organized state labor group are speaking for their schools in general and of their particular needs—a group

[79] California Labor Federation, AFL-CIO, *Statement Before the Subcommittee on Research, Structure and Function, Assembly Interim Committee on Education,* Monterey, California, January 9-10, 1964, p. 5. (Mimeographed.)

[80] *Ibid.,* p. 7.

[81] *Ibid.,* p. 17.

405

that can criticize and share part of the criticism, or glorify and deserve a share of the glory. "The labor movement is part and parcel of the same moving force of freedom in our society that gave birth to the public school system." [82]

## Summary

Organized labor's relationship to industrial education can be represented in a very brief statement: For more than a half century it has been one of wholehearted support and encouragement.

Much like the responsible parent and a child, with periods of stress and severe discipline, but always with interest in family welfare finally prevailing, labor and industrial education have managed to work out their problems to the gain of both groups. The long road from the beginning of the century has been rough—at places nearly impassable—but the road has never reached a dead end nor an impenetrable barrier, and probably never will. One reason that good relations will prevail is that both labor and industrial education are dedicated to the same fundamental principles. They differ frequently upon the implementation of the principles, which is to be expected in any healthy relationship. Differences, therefore, often become a strength rather than a weakness.

Over the years labor and industrial education have set consistently higher standards in all phases of their relationship. At times labor has had to run interference for industrial education, as in the periods of legislation or threats to annihilate the program. When labor "throws its weight around," government and the public are prone to listen, but labor's influence on behalf of industrial education has generally been within the bounds of reasonableness.

The mutual dependency of labor and industrial education must never end; otherwise the goals of each group will be far ahead of actual performance. One of the great problems of labor and industrial education continues to be the acceptance of industrial education on a par with other educational endeavors; this must be accomplished without predatory destruction of other educational areas. Labor has maintained this goal firmly since the beginning of the modern public vocational education movement.

---

[82] *Ibid.*, p. 1.

---

## Recall Questions

1. What has been labor's attitude in general about the quality of industrial education? The extent of the program?

2. Cooperative working relationships have been presented as a perennial issue. What are some of the historical events that bear out this point of view?

3. Identify the references to labor and education that show labor's broad view about vocational training.

## Research Questions

1. Study the reports of your state labor organization and identify the specific action, resolutions, or points of view in relation to industrial education since 1950.

Interview members of various advisory committees and summarize their points of view about the quality and quantity of industrial education in your local area. With what major issues are these persons concerned?

## Suggestions for Further Reading

American Federation of Labor, *Labor and Education,* 1881-1954.

American Federation of Labor and Congress of Industrial Organizations, *Labor and Education,* Yearly publications since 1955.

American Federation of Labor, *Proceedings of Annual Conventions,* 1881-1954.

American Federation of Labor, *Annual Reports of the Executive Committee,* 1881-1954.

American Federation of Labor and Congress of Industrial Organizations, *Proceedings of Annual Conventions,* and *Annual Reports,* since 1955.

# Chapter 14

# Educating the Technician

The Technician and Technical Occupations · National Defense Education Act · Conferences · Emphasis upon the Technically Talented · Occupational Criteria and Curriculum Patterns · American Technical Education Association · Industrial Arts and Technician Education · A Round-Up of Conclusions · Summary · Recall Questions · Research Questions · Suggestions for Further Reading

Although the occupation of technician is of comparatively recent origin, the concept of things technical is rooted in the remote past. Time seems to change the nature of the "technical" so that continuously the older technical knowledge tends to become common or general. Technical, when applied to education, has a strong scientific emphasis and implies a knowledge over and beyond manipulative skill. At an earlier historical period in industrial education, reference was made to the "mysteries" of an occupation. One who understood the mysteries (science and mathematics) of an occupation was considered infinitely better prepared than one who did not.

Woodward's manual training of the 1870's rested solidly upon the desire to reinforce learning by reference to models, constructed by students, to represent scientific principles. Thus modern industrial arts evolved as a union of the practical and the technical (scientific), to the end that the knowledge acquired would become functional in the lives of students.

The trade school of the 1880's survived and grew in almost direct relationship to the technical nature of its program. Besides instruction in ordinary trade skills, the schools began to teach related technical knowledge; the resulting education was a marketable commodity in competitive society.

Technical knowledge alters man's relationship to his environment. Industrial education is engaged in providing a means of satisfactory adjustment to the changed environment on a broad

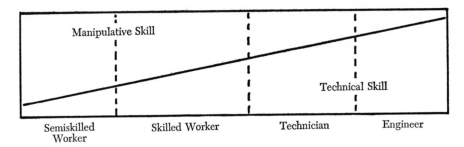

basis from general to highly complex relationships. The greater the impact of technology upon society, the greater the need for industrial education in all of its forms.[1]

## The Technician and Technical Occupations

One of the troublesome issues in the area of technical education is the difficulty of precisely defining many terms. Such education includes preparation for a variety of occupations, covering a wide range of physical and mental effort, yet having a great deal of similarity. Therefore clearcut distinctions are difficult to make.

A simple diagram is frequently used to show relationships between manipulative skill and technical skill for various types of workers and to suggest the approximate location of the technician in the hierarchy of occupations.[2]

The relationships indicated above show the position of the technician in relation to the emphasis upon manipulative skill and technical skill, and in relationship to other kinds of workers. Quantitative values cannot be interpreted from the diagram. Technician occupations in research and development, service, industrial, or manufacturing environments would vary greatly in the relative emphasis placed upon manipulative and technical skill.

Emerson describes the situation further by reference to four variations within the technician complex.[3]

A. **Narrow-scope limited-level technical occupation.** Such occupations are not considered a "technician" occupation due to the relatively simple technical skills required and the short learning period.

B. **Technical specialist occupation.** This occupation is narrow in scope but requires a high level of ability. The training required is generally shorter than that for technician occupations.

---

[1] Of necessity this chapter can review the historical development of only a small part of technical education. In the main the chapter will be limited to the period since World War II. Although the larger topic of "educating the technician" would include reference to engineering, agriculture, business, and other areas, it is the purpose of this chapter to focus upon the education of the technician from the standpoint of the vocational-industrial program found in high schools and in institutions beyond the high school, but not including the four-year program of colleges and universities. An additional severe limitation is that the fine work of private schools, and of governmental and private industry, must be ignored.

[2] Adapted from Lynn A. Emerson, *Education for a Changing World of Work*, Appendix I, "Technical Training in the United States." U.S. Department of Health, Education, and Welfare, Office of Education. Washington: Government Printing Office, 1963, p. 1A.

[3] *Ibid.*, p. 5.

C. *Industrial-type technician occupation.* The scope of such occupations is broad and requires a high level of ability. Training period may be as long as that required for an engineering technician but with an emphasis upon applied technology. "Occupations of this type may include technical maintenance jobs of broad scope, technical production jobs, and the like."

D. *Engineering-type technician occupation.* These occupations are broad in scope, requiring a high level of ability and at least two years of post-high school education with an emphasis upon mathematics, science, and applied technology. "Persons in these occupations have sufficient background to be able to work effectively as aides to engineers and scientists."

The range of tasks performed by technicians includes a wide variety of specific responsibilities such as making drawings or charts, analyzing and interpreting plans, supplying details for an overall design, testing, inspecting, supervising, diagnosing, marketing, reporting, operating, servicing, and many others.

## Paths to Technician Jobs

Educational experience leading to employment as a technician is provided through a number of formal programs, beyond the high school. Emphasis upon the need for technicians has not only tended to cause existing educational institutions to stress such training but has also created a number of new institutions of the "Area School" type which include in their instructional program preparation for technician occupations. Emerson

has visualized some of the more common pathways in the chart which appears on the following page.[4]

Reaching the goal of employment as a technician can be achieved by many paths. All of these paths were open to high school graduates, and the supply of technicians was provided—though never adequately from the standpoint of numbers—by those completing the educational journey beyond high school.

In a direct relationship to technological demand, after World War II the nation became acutely aware of the necessity for a stepped-up program to educate an abundant supply of technicians. The need was nationwide, and the Congress initiated action in the form of special legislation to promote and develop technical education.

### National Defense Education Act

Prior to World War II, programs of a "technical institute type" were developed in many states as a part of the trade and industrial education program. The programs were "vocational in nature and technical in content" and were applied to specific occupational areas: Petroleum Technology, for example. Changing industrial conditions produced the need for this type of instruction. Experience of World War II emphasized further the development of vocational-technical programs—this was one of the lessons of the war. During the post-war years considerable attention was devoted to technical education, in direct proportion to the explosion of scientific knowl-

[4] *Ibid.*, p. 38.

410

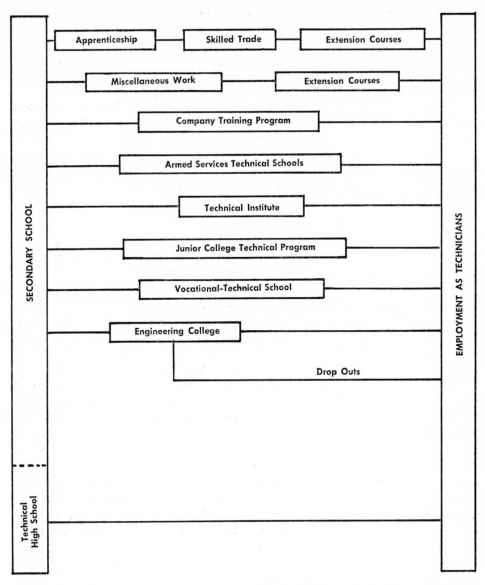

edge and the beginnings of the space age.

### Title VIII, Public Law 85-864

On September 2, 1958, an Act of Congress was passed "to strengthen the national defense and to encourage and assist in the expansion and improvement of educational programs to meet critical national needs; and for other purposes." Title VIII of the Act was devoted to *Area Vocational Education Programs.* The Congress, well aware of the past achievements of vocational education, sought to provide: (1) an extension of vocational education to residents of areas inadequately served, and (2) for national defense requirements of personnel equipped to render skilled assistance in fields particularly affected by scientific and technological developments. The Act further proposed assistance to state boards of vocational education to provide "vocational and related technical training and retraining for youths, adults, and older persons, including

411

related instruction for apprentices, designed to fit them for useful employment as technicians or skilled workers in scientific or technical fields."

The provisions of Title VIII, NDEA, amended and became Title III of the George-Barden Act. An authorization for appropriation of $15,000,000 a year for three years was made.

## Area Vocational Education

As indicated in Chapter 7 the Office of Education responded to the emphasis upon technical education by establishing a new branch of the Office, Area Vocational Education; Walter M. Arnold was appointed director.[5] This move made it possible to focus attention upon the development of technical education.

The Area Vocational Education program had been established as a new title of the George-Barden Act; therefore organization for the new programs followed the established patterns of other areas of vocational education, i.e., state plans, state boards for vocational education, and other characteristic elements of federal-state cooperation.

Because of the special nature of the new program, it was necessary to emphasize and realign certain basic criteria. These were identified as follows:

1. An employment market must exist for the persons trained.
2. Course content must be determined upon the basis of an analysis of the occupation or family of occupations.
3. Students must have appropriate general education backgrounds. (Or the appropriate general and scientific educa-

tion must be included as a part of their total curriculum.)
4. The length and technical content of the program must "fit those enrolled for employment."
5. "Classrooms, shop and laboratory facilities, including instructional equipment and supplies for effective instruction" must be available.
6. Instructors and supervisors must have "professional and technical preparation and experience."
7. An appropriate student selection program must be maintained.[6]

Emphasis was also placed upon the "area" concept—the programs were not to be limited to a particular school district. Large geographical areas would improve recruitment of students, thus making it possible to establish comprehensive programs. It was known that the states would vary in the ways the area concept was interpreted, and they were cautioned not to consider this problem lightly. Designating each school district as an area vocational education program would "defeat the purposes and intent of the area idea."

Defining the task of the technician and adjusting the point of view in regard to the special training required became persistent problems. The point of view of the Area Branch in 1959 was stated as follows:

The main requirement of highly skilled technicians in recognized occupations is technical knowledge and how to apply it. Such occupations demand the practical application of technology in specific fields and require specialized and technical skills developed through intensive training. They require more than just the understanding of scientific principles.

---

[5] On August 1, 1961, Arnold was named Assistant Commissioner for Vocational Education.

[6] Adapted from, U.S. Department of Health, Education, and Welfare, Office of Education, *Area Vocational Education Programs*, Misc. 3561, Revised September 1959.

Basic science and mathematics are foundations for the applied technology, and on these foundations the special applications are developed.[7]

Instruction in basic science and mathematics alone was not sufficient— "The heart of the technician operation is the application of technology to a real job situation."[8]

Objectives and program standards for area vocational education were discussed in detail in various publications and kept prominently before the vocational educators of the nation. Failure to appreciate the significance of the Act could mean failure of the schools to make appropriate educational contributions to their communities.[9]

## Conferences

Success of the area vocational education program depended in a large measure upon the extent to which the states developed an understanding of the unique nature of the program. In order to facilitate this degree of understanding, the Area Branch arranged for a number of meetings in which persons from the various states could share ideas and suggest solutions for problems encountered in operating the program.[10]

### Kansas City, 1960

Sixty-six state representatives having responsibility for technical education programs met with members of the Office of Education in a three-day conference, June 20-22, 1960, in Kansas City. In purpose the conference intended to look at the record of achievement for the past two years and to plan ahead.

At the outset the purpose of the Area Vocational program was stated as follows:

The purpose of title VIII is to alleviate the technical manpower shortage by assisting the States in providing, through area vocational education programs, training of less than college grade for youth, adults, and older persons, which are designed to fit them for useful employment as highly skilled technicians in recognized occupations requiring scientific knowledge in fields necessary for the national defense as determined by the State board for such state.[11]

The following trends and changes— here abstracted from the report—were observed.

1. The area concept was gaining acceptance.
2. The challenge of and responsibility for training highly skilled technical workers under Title VIII was being universally accepted.
3. The states and local communities were providing new buildings and facilities.
4. Industry and labor had shown interest in the program and were providing encouragement and support.
5. Students of high-level ability were attracted to the program.
6. A trend toward preparatory technician training had developed at the post high school level.

---

[7] *Ibid.,* p. 9.

[8] *Ibid.,* p. 10.

[9] Walter M. Arnold, "Area Vocational Education Programs," *School Life,* January 1960, pp. 16-21.

[10] See section in Chapter 7, "Area Vocational Education Branch," for a discussion of conferences during the period 1956-1959.

[11] U.S. Department of Health, Education, and Welfare, Office of Education, *1960 National Conference of State Supervisors of Title VIII Programs,* OE-80011, September 1960, p. 3.

413

7. Employed workers were requesting highly technical short-unit extension classes.

8. During the developmental stages of the program the services and facilities of public agencies were being used.

9. Expansion of the program and elimination of duplication of facilities could be traced to "the larger administrative unit" characteristic of area programs.

10. Some states had passed legislation to implement the program.

11. The evidence indicated that an emphasis was placed on upgrading the quality of the program.

12. Standards were being developed through cooperative means.

13. Guidance personnel were being oriented to the need for highly qualified students.

14. Preparatory training was offered in eight technologies: electronic, mechanical, electrical, chemical, aeronautical, production, civil, and instrumentation.

15. States were preparing curriculums in other areas of technology.

16. The range of course offerings was much wider in extension classes than in pre-employment classes.

The conference touched upon areas of critical need and placed stress upon the pursuit of quality in the many facets of technical education. The conference was important not so much because of the new ideas developed as because of the emphasis upon a new level of alertness and sensitivity in relation to the program of technical education.

### Multi-State Conferences During 1961

The Kansas City conference provided a means whereby key persons responsible for the development of technical education could discuss their common problems. The program was new and it was essential that state leaders have an opportunity to share ideas, review the growth of the program, and plan cooperatively for further development of technician training.

In recognition of the value of such conferences Walter M. Arnold, Director of the Area Vocational Education Branch, proposed in October, 1960, that multi-state conferences be held during 1961, and scheduled meetings in Baltimore, Maryland; Atlanta, Georgia; Springfield, Massachusetts; Pittsburgh, Pennsylvania; Oklahoma City, Oklahoma; Pocatello, Idaho; and Minneapolis, Minnesota during the period February 27 to May 10, 1961.[12] A planning committee was selected by the Office of Education, and the committee met during the AVA convention in Los Angeles in December, 1960, to recommend the areas of emphasis for the 1961 conferences.

The conferences were developed around six areas of emphasis: (1) a progress report of Title VIII programs with a focus upon statistical, financial, and general information, and upon other related concerns such as schools, surveys, working relationships, publications, and training needs; (2) the needs and requirements of equipment for technical education; (3) criteria for developing quality; (4) extension training in technical education; (5) teacher education; and (6) problems of supervision.[13]

---

[12] U.S. Office of Education, Division of Vocational Education, *Circular Letter 3543*, dated October 31, 1960.

[13] Frequently throughout these chapters reference has been made to the central position of the Division of Vocational Education (later the Division of Vocational and Technical Education) as a motivator in program development. That the Division has been effective in its leadership

## Seven Regional Conferences Held During 1962

During the period February to May 1962 the Area Vocational Education Branch of the Office of Education conducted conferences in Philadelphia, Pennsylvania; Orlando, Florida; Norwalk, Connecticut; Carbondale, Illinois; Milwaukee, Wisconsin; Phoenix, Arizona; and Portland, Oregon. More than 400 persons attended the conferences whose theme was "Improving the Organization and Operation of Technical Education Programs."

The Office of Education reported on the status and trends in the area of technical education. Discussion topics centered around (1) the need for technical teachers, supervisors, administrators, and (2) teacher education and problems of curriculum design. The conferences were capped by visits to schools and industrial plants.[14]

The report indicates that previously accepted principles were reaffirmed and that interest in technical education continued to grow throughout the nation. One highlight of the report was stated as follows:

Completion of a good technical curriculum should prepare the graduate to be employable and immediately productive in one of several entry jobs in a technological field; able to progress to positions of increasing responsibility; and able to increase his technical skills by means of advanced technical study.[15]

One notes in the point of view the persistent theme of vocational education—employability and quality of product.

### Other Conferences and Outcomes

Similar conferences were held in other years and were devoted to exchange of information and to discussion of particular trends and relationships. Placement studies, in 1962, indicated that 82.9 percent of the graduates were placed in positions either directly or closely related to the training.[16] The Office of Education held the opinion that "the report of graduates reveals that the efforts of educators in the field of technical education have been successful in providing programs that are of a rigorous nature and high in quality."[17]

It was indicated earlier that technical education programs had previously been established in the two-year curriculums of junior colleges or technical institutions; but these programs had, by and large, not increased in proportion to the need for highly skilled technicians. By 1962, however, it appeared that Title VIII had awakened the interest of the public in general and of educators in particular to this "neglected area of education." This

role accounts in a large measure for successful developments in the states. The conferences on technical education stimulated by the Area Education Branch are merely additional evidence of the desirability of strong leadership at the Federal level in order to promote quality of program performance in the States.

[14] U.S. Office of Education, Division of Vocational and Technical Education, *Improving the Organization and Operation of Technical Education Programs,* Spring 1962. (Mimeographed.)
[15] *Ibid.*
[16] U.S. Office of Education, Area Vocational Education Branch, *Placement of Graduates from Technical Education Preparatory Programs, Fiscal Year, 1961,* Misc. No. 3612, August 1962. (Mimeographed.)
[17] *Ibid.,* p. iii.

|  | *Preparatory Program* | *Extension Program* | *Total* |
|---|---|---|---|
| 1958-59 | 19,243 | 29,321 | 48,564 |
| 1959-60 | 32,937 | 68,342 | 101,279 |
| 1960-61 | 39,224 | 83,728 | 122,952 |
| 1961-62 | 53,071 | 95,849 | 148,920 |
| 1962-63 | 75,888 | 108,707 | 184,595 |

was thought to be one of the significant outcomes of the legislation.[18] Significant also was the rapid expansion in extension programs, indicating a definite movement toward retraining employed technical workers and providing an opportunity to keep pace with occupational changes.

## Emphasis upon the Technically Talented

The National Defense Education Act, with its emphasis upon training highly skilled technicians necessary to the national defense, was a boon to vocational education. A means was provided which enabled vocational education to expand program ideas established prior to World War II. It reestablished the idea that, "It [vocational education] performs a prime function by providing a means for early identification of the technically talented student and a way to foster his abilities."[19] Industrial educators in every state moved rapidly to meet the challenge of technology by establishing new courses in technical education.

## Summary of Federally Aided Programs

Growth of the program in terms of enrollment was rapid during the first five years. (See chart at top of the page.)

The gain in enrollment during the second year represented an increase of 109 percent; (part of this increase resulted from including the enrollment figures for technical students previously reported in other tabulations.) The gain during the next three years averaged 22 percent each year. Approximately fifty percent of the enrollment was in the field of electronics, and nearly 22 percent in a variety of mechanical occupations. Ninety-four percent of the enrollees during the year 1962-63 were men. Four states, California, Florida, Texas, and Washington, accounted for 52 percent of the total enrollment that year.

More impressive than the statistics concerning the growth of enrollment was the action reported in nearly all of the states to improve their ability to educate the technicians. Some states more than doubled the number of schools. "The skilled hands and trained minds of a nation's citizens comprise

---

[18] A mimeographed paper, "Title VIII—Area Vocational Education Programs," dated January 1962, evidently prepared by the Area Vocational Education office, cites this impact as important; presumably this was representative of a nationwide trend.

[19] U.S. Department of Health, Education, and Welfare, Office of Education, *Vocational and Technical Education, A Review of Activities in Federally Aided Programs, Fiscal Year 1963*, OE-80008-63. Washington: Government Prining Office, 1964, p. 6.

a major part of her wealth and basic source of her strength." [20]

## Occupational Criteria and Curriculum Patterns

The history of technical education provides few clear-cut definitions that can be used to plan and conduct future programs. This confusion has been detected by a number of persons aware of the many variables involved, such as the wide range of job classifications and the educational programs required. But workers called technicians do exist, and the number of such persons in the labor force continues to increase.

When the NDEA made funds available to promote and develop technical training, the Act did not provide guidelines to reduce the complexity of the general situation. Hundreds of additional teachers and educators throughout the nation became involved in technical education, which only compounded the complex issues. The conferences of the 1960's, conducted by the Office of Education, were directed in part toward finding some common bases for administration, supervision, and operation of technical education programs. In addition the Office of Education issued in 1962 a general guide for the benefit of persons concerned with these programs. The publication of *Occupational Criteria and Preparatory Curriculum Patterns in Technical Education Programs* was prepared by Maurice W. Roney who at that time was a program specialist in the Area Education Branch of the Division of Vocational Education.

Roney called attention to the fact that *the central concern of technical education is with a body of knowledge rather than with specific jobs.* The term "technician" then referred to scope of training and work capability rather than to employment classifications. Two basic assumptions were made:

1. The technical occupations, whether or not they are closely related to engineering functions, require broad technical competence based on a knowledge of engineering and scientific principles.
2. A significant part of this knowledge can best be provided by formal systematic training in organized programs of instruction. [21]

### Occupational Criteria

As a prelude to developing criteria to identify occupations that require technical education, Roney proposed five points related to technical abilities which were essential as a reference base. These were stated as follows:

1. Facility with mathematics; ability to use algebra and trigonometry as tools in the development of ideas that make use of scientific and engineering principles; an understanding of, though not necessarily facility with, higher mathematics through analytical geometry, calculus, and differential equations, according to the requirements of the technology.
2. Proficiency in the application of physical science principles, including the basic concepts and laws of physics and chemistry that are pertinent to the individual's field of technology.
3. An understanding of the materials and processes commonly used in the technology.

---

[20] *Ibid.*, p. 14.

[21] U.S. Department of Health, Education, and Welfare, Office of Education, *Occupational Criteria and Preparatory Curriculum Patterns in Technical Education Programs*, OE-80015. Washington: Government Printing Office, 1962, p. 3.

4. An extensive knowledge of a field of specialization with an understanding of the engineering and scientific activities that distinguish the technology of the field. The degree of competency and the depth of understanding should be sufficient to enable the individual to do such work as detail design using established design procedures.

5. Communication skills that include the ability to interpret, analyze, and transmit facts and ideas graphically, orally, and in writing.[22]

These general abilities were "essentially universal" in that nearly any conception of technician education would find them appropriate. It is true that the five abilities do not recognize the necessity of many personal characteristics, but the impersonal approach was an aid to objectivity in developing criteria for identifying occupations that require technical education.

Roney identified 12 criteria, in terms of activities of an individual in a technician occupation, that could be used to identify appropriate occupations. An individual whose activities could be described by the criteria was thought to be involved in an occupation that required technical education. No occupation would require all 12 of the criteria, and Roney assigned no value to the order or weight each should have. The criteria were as follows:

1. Applies knowledge of science and mathematics extensively in rendering direct technical assistance to scientists or engineers engaged in scientific research and experimentation.

2. Designs, develops, or plans modifications of new products and processes under the supervision of engineering personnel in applied engineering research, design, and development.

3. Plans and inspects the installation of complex equipment and control systems.

4. Advises regarding the maintenance and repair of complex equipment with extensive control systems.

5. Plans production as a member of the management unit responsible for efficient use of manpower, materials and machines in mass production.

6. Advises, plans, and estimates costs as a field representative of a manufacturer or distributor of technical equipment and/or products.

7. Is responsible for performance or environmental tests of mechanical, hydraulic, pneumatic, electrical or electronic components or systems and the preparation of appropriate technical reports covering the tests.

8. Prepares or interprets engineering drawings and sketches.

9. Selects, compiles, and uses technical information from references such as engineering standards, handbooks, and technical digests of research findings.

10. Analyzes and interprets information obtained from precision measuring and recording instruments and makes evaluations upon which technical decisions are based.

11. Analyzes and diagnoses technical problems that involve independent decisions.

12. Deals with a variety of technical problems involving many factors and variables which require an understanding of several technical fields.[23]

In applying the *criteria* to the *educational program*, Roney called attention to their interdependence: "Neither can be correctly interpreted without a clear understanding of the other."

**Educational Implications**

For applying the "five imperatives of technical education" and the criteria,

[22] *Ibid.*, p. 5.
[23] *Ibid.*, pp. 6-8.

there were certain suggested balances to be maintained among the components of the program. "The educational program must be specialized without overspecialization; theoretical but not impractical; and scientific without sacrificing the learning values that come from the realistic application of scientific principles." [24]

Roney analyzed a number of two-year programs of technical education and found that the curriculums averaged 71 semester credit hours for completion. Technical courses made up 59 percent of the credit-hour requirements; however, because of the laboratory work involved, these courses required 69 percent of the student's time. [25]

### Significance of the Roney Study

The bulletin, *Occupational Criteria and Preparatory Curriculum Patterns in Technical Education Programs,* was intended to influence the development of technician education and consequently was directed toward the interests of a large number of people concerned with it. The bulletin was widely distributed and presumably readily accepted as a guide by those most directly concerned with technical education—at least by those persons conducting programs influenced by the NDEA.

It is too early to review the actual impact of the bulletin or to observe its effect upon the technical curriculum. It is significant that the Office of Education, early in the period of rapid growth of attention to educating the technician, detected basic stumbling blocks and made a determined effort to provide a base of reference for technical educators.

### American Technical Education Association

The American Technical Education Association is an organization whose purpose is to bring together in professional association persons interested in technical education. The first meeting was held December 30-31, 1927, at the Brooklyn Chamber of Commerce, and was devoted largely to organizational details. The Association was formally organized in December, 1928, at a meeting held in Detroit. Albert L. Colston, Brooklyn Technical High School, was the first president.

During the first years the annual meetings were held in cooperation with the National Education Association. Some other meetings were held independently. At the Brooklyn meeting in December, 1944, the group decided to seek affiliation with the American Vocational Association. This move was prompted by the attention given to technical education by a publication of the U.S. Office of Education (1944) entitled *Vocational-Technical Education for Industrial Organizations.* Accordingly, ATEA President A. D. Althouse, Vocational Education Department, Detroit, Michigan, conferred with the AVA executive committee at its meeting in Philadelphia in December, 1944, and approval of affiliation was given. The Buffalo meeting of ATEA in February, 1946, was held as a sectional meeting of the AVA.

---

[24] *Ibid.,* pp. 10-11.

[25] *Ibid.,* pp. 12-17, 25. (Sample curriculums.)

The 1946 yearbook committee restated the definitions of technical education and trade education in an effort to delineate properly the area of technical education and to show common relationships and concerns. "The two curriculums differ principally in emphasis upon the shopwork in contrast with the laboratory, mathematics, drawing, and technology related to an occupation." [26]

At the same meeting the constitution was approved. Article II states the purpose of ATEA.

The purpose of the American Technical Education Association is to promote technical education for the interested and qualified American youth; to recommend standards for technical education; and to provide an opportunity for an exchange of ideas among persons in the technical education field.[27]

The ATEA pressed forward year after year with studies to keep up with the programs of technical education. Presentations of trends, status, future requirements, technological impact, improvements, needs related to secondary and higher schools, relationships to industry and education, and similar topics were made at the annual meetings. Little by little the ATEA increased its membership, expanded the scope of its interest in technical education (in the early years the concern was devoted largely to the technical high school), and moved directly into a review of standards and the promotion of excellence in technical education. From the beginning ATEA has had an attentive ear close to industrial change in an attempt to match the expectations of industry with the capabilities of technical education graduates.

## Industrial Arts and Technician Education

One of the significant historical trends to be found in a study of industrial arts, and its predecessors—manual arts and manual training—is its close resemblance to new developments in education and industry. Prior to 1890 the attachment of manual training to faculty psychology was indeed strong. During the early years of the twentieth century the virtues of manual arts were closely identified with pragmatism. John Dewey was an ardent proponent of manual arts, and the subject matter area found fertile ground in the elementary schools of the nation. Good elementary schools had strong programs of manual arts. Later, when junior high schools were invented, manual arts (industrial arts) found an identity with the purposes of junior high school education. This was reason to stress the functions of industrial arts as an interpreter of industry for students in the high school sequence.

Throughout its long historical period industrial arts has maintained steadfastly an attachment to the educative process as an intellectual discipline. In recent years this attachment has been seen clearly as a part of the general education of youth. Despite its critics, industrial arts has over the years been persistent in its claim to fundamental values on the one hand, and to the major forces of the social and eco-

---

[26] American Technical Education Association, *Yearbook December 1956*, p. 5.
[27] *Ibid.*, p. 8.

nomic environment on the other. In a way industrial arts has stood on solid ground on one foot, and with the other has used each newly emerged facet of education and technology as a temporary stepping stone. This was natural and consistent with the general rationale for industrial arts in education. Since industrial arts has interpreted its role in terms of each new area of emphasis in social life, it is reasonable to expect evidence of relationships to contemporary technology.[28]

## Emphasis on Science and Mathematics

In Chapter 10 the impact of the space age upon industrial arts was discussed briefly. It is from this same era —the period after about 1955—that we derive some of the relationships of industrial arts to the education of technicians. The relationships are difficult to trace, but the impact of technology on industrial arts has made many industrial arts educators aware that science and mathematics must be emphasized. Consequently industrial arts programs were revised to provide opportunity for students to apply scientific principles through "creative experimentation" in the fabrication of projects.[29] Automation with its scientific emphasis captured the attention

of instructors. Suggestions appeared for instructors to use in the general orientation of students of technology.[30] Industrial arts educators rediscovered the occupational implications of industrial arts and sought ways and means of making full use of its potential to answer industry's cry for technologists.[31]

The Industrial Arts Conference in 1961 (the Mississippi Valley Conference) was conducted around a theme of science, mathematics, and technology. Delegates reviewed industrial arts content in terms of science, mathematics, experimentation, and technology. Emphasis was upon change in content due to requirements of the technological age.

In the process of preparing individuals for the technological culture of the present and future, ideas of an articulated curriculum in industrial arts from elementary grades through technical and professional schools were brought into review.[32] The emphasis was definitely upon the occupational significance of industrial arts. Norman Stanger analyzed the objectives and outcomes of industrial arts and vocational trade and industrial education.[33] The analysis was presented in chart form showing the continuum of industrial education by grade levels as it

---

[28] This is a brief summary of material which has been developed more fully in other chapters, notably Chapters 10 and 11. The review seems necessary at this point in order to explain some of the direction and concern of industrial arts in technician education.

[29] "Integrating Science and Industrial Arts," *Industrial Arts and Vocational Education,* Vol. 49, No. 5, May 1960, p. 62.

[30] O. S. Harrison, "Automation and Industrial Arts," *Industrial Arts and Vocational Education,* Vol. 50, No. 9, September 1961, pp. 20-21.

[31] William Plutte, "The New Industrial Arts Frontier: Technical Education," *Industrial Arts and Vocational Education,* Vol. 51, No. 1, January 1962, pp. 8-10.

[32] Jerry Streichler, "How Can We Put Industrial Education in Step With Technology," *Industrial Arts and Vocational Education,* Vol. 52, No. 9, November 1963, pp. 16-18.

[33] Norman R. Stanger, "The Total Program of Industrial Education," *Industrial Arts and Vocational Education,* Vol. 52, No. 9, November 1963, pp. 18-19.

related to four basic elements (1) general information and growing up, (2) guidance and human relations, (3) industry—its processes and significance, and (4) job skills and knowledge. His intent was to show a "commonsensical pattern of articulation and coordination of the total program of industrial education." Joseph W. Duffy in a proposal to revamp industrial arts to reflect technological needs suggested that it was possible to revise industrial arts significantly without "scuttling our present program."[34]

Marshall Schmitt in a review of trends in industrial arts pointed out that:

The establishment of new courses in the industrial arts curriculum is an indication of change in the program. Course titles, such as heat treatment of metals, industrial processes, pre-engineering laboratory, applied shop, industrial materials, industrial arts science, group manufacturing, industrial technology, and strength of materials, are examples of this new change in the industrial arts public secondary school program.

Insofar as course titles are predictive of the content of the course, it appears that industrial arts is emphasizing the application of science in solving technical problems.[35]

Certainly technology and social change were elements to be reckoned with, but how? This problem was reviewed for industrial arts educators by J. Herbert Hollomon, Assistant Secretary of Commerce, at the annual convention of the American Industrial Arts Association in Tulsa on April 13, 1965. Hollomon pointed out that our world was changing—increasingly urban, international, and heavily dependent upon science and technology. Society therefore had new and different needs—renewal of cities, transportation, recreation, solving pollution problems—and that new skills would be required. He predicted, however, that:

Future education will be based largely upon information, and it will be the manipulation of information which will be the basis of industrial arts in the future—not the manipulation of materials or energy.[36]

## So What!

A clear view of the implications of industrial arts for technician education is clouded by many variables. But like the wind, which we can feel but can't see, the consensus seems to favor the point of view that implications do exist which relate to industrial arts and technician education. Despite difficulties of program implementation, the educational climate of industrial arts is favorable for assuming a portion of the responsibility for technician education.

Providing an appropriate program of industrial arts requires clear and realistic understanding of objectives. Statements of purpose unique to industrial arts were stressed by the American Council of Industrial Arts Supervisors.

*To develop in each student an insight and understanding of industry and its place in our society.* Since industry is a constructive, dynamic force in the world

---

[34] Joseph W. Duffy, "Let's Revamp Industrial Arts Programs to Reflect Technological Needs," *Industrial Arts and Vocational Education*, Vol. 52, No. 9, November 1963, pp. 20-21, 55-56.

[35] Marshall J. Schmitt, "Trends and Development in Industrial Arts," *Industrial Arts and Vocational Education*, Vol. 52, No. 1, January 1963, p. 17.

[36] J. Herbert Hollomon, "Technology and Social Change," *The Journal of Industrial Arts Education*, Vol. 24, No. 5, May-June 1965, p. 20.

today, it is the responsibility of the school to provide opportunities for each student to understand this force better. Industrial arts provides significant learning experiences relating to industry in which students acquire skill in performance and knowledge of principles and theory through study and application.

*To discover and develop student talents in industrial-technical fields.* Students have a diversity of talents. The school's responsibility is to assist students in discovering and developing these talents. It is the responsibility of industrial arts education to identify special talents in industrial-technical fields.

*To develop problem-solving abilities related to the materials, processes, and products of industry.* The problem-solving approach in industrial arts involves creative thinking, and gives the student opportunity to apply principles of planning and design, construction techniques, industrial processes, scientific principles, and mathematical computations to the solution of problems.

*To develop in each student skill in the safe use of tools and machines.* Industrial arts provides planning, construction and production activities which enable students to acquire industrial-technical skills. These activities offer opportunities to develop tool and machine skills commensurate with the mental and physical maturity of the student.[37]

This statement of basic objectives is one of the evidences of thoughtful movement toward appropriate action in technician education. Two opinions characteristic of the mood of industrial arts further illustrate the trend:

Since industrial arts is a derived discipline growing out of the dynamic needs of our culture, its one constant characteristic should be its adaptability. Change is the characteristic of the day and it is manual and mechanical change which gave birth to industrial arts. It is technological change which demands that we must modify in order to impart the character of a true discipline to our field. We must conceive of industrial arts as a way of thinking—as a way of life—wherein the techniques of the industrial arts is as illuminating as the content. Just as the light of the techniques of the liberal arts tends to brighten our lives, so should the light of the techniques of the industrial arts brighten the vision of the world.[38]

The second point of view, derived also from considerations of the implications of automation, suggests a practical approach for industrial arts educators as they "tune-up" to technology.

It is our responsibility, as industrial arts teacher educators, to attempt to keep abreast of all new technological developments, through increased research and industrial contacts, and reduce the traditional technological lag between industry and school in an era of rapid technological progress.[39]

Two points, conspicuous in the contemporary literature are significant. First, stress upon the general objectives of industrial arts has not decreased under the pressure of technological change—this is the foot on the solid foundation. Second, industrial arts is searching with determination for its appropriate role in the complexity of technology—this is the foot that rests upon the contemporary concerns of society.

---

[37] American Council of Industrial Arts Supervisors, *Industrial Arts Education: Purposes, Program, Facilities, Instruction.* Washington: American Industrial Arts Association, 1963, pp. 4-5.
[38] H. O. Schorling, "Automation: Educational Implications and Commitments," *The California Council on Industrial Arts Teacher Education Journal,* Vol. 1, No. 5, Spring 1965, p. 8.
[39] James E. Ryan, "Some Implications of Automation on Industrial Arts Education," *The California Council on Industrial Arts Teacher Education Journal,* Vol. 1, No. 5, Spring 1965, p. 20.

## A Round-Up of Conclusions [40]

A newcomer to the field of technician education would be confronted with a mass of ideas, points of view, trends, relationships, and predictions that seemingly have no relationship and that lead to a confused educational situation. This is merely an indication of the complexity of the total problem and suggests that the educaional specialist must pay more than usual attention to the nature of this rapidly changing field. Fortunately study of technician education has been sufficient to provide us with some reasonably sound points of view.

Technology has influenced occupations at every level, and the trend is toward increasing the amounts of technology in these occupations. Technical occupations are found throughout industry "from narrow-scope limited-level jobs to those filled by highly skilled technicians and technical specialists." The technical type of job is not limited to the field of industry; many such occupations are appearing in other fields.

As industry disperses into labor market areas, geographical areas not previously considered industrial are finding increasing need to provide technician education. Women are entering the field of technical employment in increasing numbers. The great need for technicians appears to be growing, with no indication that the field will be saturated in the near future. The supply of new technical workers will need to come from pre-employment programs organized in educational institutions.

The curriculum in post-secondary institutions will have a base of applied science, mathematics, drawing, general technology, and an appropriate program of general education. Review of the curriculums offered indicates little standardization of content. The tendency of such curriculums is, however, directed toward clusters of closely related occupations rather than the needs of a single occupation.

The evening and part-time programs for technicians rank equally in importance with the pre-employment programs. In addition to extension programs, the need for correspondence courses in technical subjects is growing. Not all people who have the need for special technical instruction live close to an educational institution that offers it.

Despite increasing enrollment in technical courses the production of technicians falls far short of the need. Estimates of actual need show wide variation, but programs of technician education can be increased vastly without endangering employment conditions. The position of the United States in world technological development depends greatly upon the attention given to technician education. Expanded programs of research in technical education are needed.

### Summary

The historical background of technician education includes a variety of

---

[40] Lynn A. Emerson, *op. cit.* I have chosen to approach a review of significant conclusions about technician education by close reference to a study by Lynn A. Emerson prepared for the Panel of Consultants on Vocational Education. The material appearing in this section is paraphrased from Emerson's conclusions and recommendations as found on pp. 158-162.

424

developments throughout the nineteenth century and early years of the twentieth. The education of the technician has been important for a long time and many private schools, industry schools, and governmental units have made significant contributions. However, the greatest developments in technician education have occurred since World War II when this phase of education seemed more directly connected to the economic progress of the nation. Its proper concern became a necessity in our national life.

Definitions of technical education and descriptions of the work of the technicians are exceedingly complex because of the number of variables involved and because of the wide range of occupations to which the term "technical" may be applied. Despite such difficulties some generalities concerning definition have emerged. The pathways for education of the technician are numerous; consequently many different types of educational institutions are involved.

Critical need for technicians after World War II became a matter of national concern and the Congress made provisions for technical education in the National Defense Education Act of 1958. At the national level attention was focused on technician education in the Area Vocational Education Branch of the Division of Vocational and Technical Education, U.S. Office of Education. The Area Branch conducted a number of conferences throughout the United States in order to stimulate the development of technical education and to provide standards for program operation. Interest in technical education developed rapidly.

Reports from schools indicated growth in enrollment, increase in the number of different types of programs, and satisfactory results from the standpoint of placement and earnings of graduates. Title VIII of NDEA had brought this "neglected area of education" into national view, and placed an emphasis upon technically talented persons.

Functional occupational criteria and curriculum patterns emerged with increased clarity when attention was drawn to considerations of technical education as a body of knowledge rather than as a particular job. Occupations for which technical education was required were identified on the basis of five general abilities to be developed. Twelve criteria were suggested which would identify the activities of an individual in a technical occupation.

The American Technical Education Association is the national professional organization with concerns centralized in the area of technician education. In 1944 it became affiliated with the American Vocational Association. Annual meetings of the AVA are devoted to the pursuit of quality in technical education.

Industrial arts education is a strong basic element in technical education with a primary opportunity to introduce the technical world to students. It can take principles of the technological age, related largely to science and mathematics, and develop within the student a deep understanding of these principles. Trends in recent years show that industrial arts has tended to become increasingly aware of the opportunity to provide instruction in applied science and mathematics, and

425

many new courses have developed as evidence of this trend. Recent statements of objectives of industrial arts have placed emphasis on its fundamental mission in educating the technician.

Despite the complexities of definition and the vast range of occupations affected by technology, general conclusions show extreme need for an expanded program of technician education.

---

### Recall Questions

1. What are the specific problems involved in defining technician education?
2. Discuss the pathways to technician jobs.
3. Describe the activities of the Area Vocational Education Branch of the Office of Education.
4. What criteria were suggested as a means of determining that an occupation required technical education?
5. What is the function of the ATEA?
6. Discuss the role of industrial arts in technician education.

### Research Questions

1. Select one foreign industrial nation and prepare a paper about its development of technician education.
2. Using the reports from the U.S. Office of Education prepare an analysis of the growth and development of technical education in your state since 1958. How does this growth compare with other states, and with the nation as a whole? Describe the nature of this growth, from data obtained within your state, in terms of enrollment, scope of program, and other factors.

### Suggestions for Further Reading

Emerson, Lynn A., "Technical Training in the United States, Appendix I," *Education for a Changing World of Work*, OE-80022. Washington: Government Printing Office, 1963.

Henninger, G. Ross, *The Technical Institute in America*. New York: McGraw-Hill Book Company, Inc., 1959.

Venables, P. F. R., *Technical Education*. London: G. Bell and Sons Ltd., 1955.

# Chapter 15

# Panel of Consultants on Vocational Education

Selecting the Panel · The Panel and Its Work · The Vocational Education Act of 1963 · The Panel and the Act of '63 · Summary · Recall Questions · Research Questions · Suggestions for Further Reading

### Prelude—Budget Hearings

Each year a committee of the Congress of the United States conducts hearings on appropriations for all government agencies. These are held to determine if adjustments of appropriations for any activity of the federal government are necessary, and the committee's conclusions are embodied in a recommended budget. The hearings in 1960 were thus a part of the normal routine of the Congress, but included in the recommendations for the fiscal year 1961 was a cut of $2 million in the authorization for vocational education.

During the normal course of events, the committee took up the matter of the appropriations for education, and the recommended cut in vocational funds came into full view. This recommendation did not have the approval of either the United States Commis-

sioner of Education or the Secretary of Health, Education, and Welfare. During the discussion of vocational education, Commissioner Lawrence G. Derthick referred to the National Defense Education Act as the "third great milestone in education." Congressman John Fogerty (Rhode Island) immediately inquired about the other two milestones. These were identified by Commissioner Derthick as the Northwest Ordinances of 1785 and 1787 and, not forgetting the Morrill Act of 1862, the Vocational Education Act of 1917 (the Smith-Hughes Act) with its amendments. Congressman Fogerty replied that to cut funds for an Act referred to as the "third milestone" in education did not seem appropriate.

The probe into the deep recesses of the appropriations for vocational education brought forth the idea (evidently suggested by Arthur S. Flemming, Secretary of Health, Education, and Welfare) that the national vocational education program needed redirection. Vocational education programs had been experiencing continuous readjustment because of social, economic, and technological change. New courses were being added in response to new occupations and to the growing importance of science and mathematics as related to the processes of technology. Further evidence of change was the development of area vocational schools and other special training programs for displaced and unemployed persons. At length, on the basis of testimony before the committee, the cut was adjudged ill timed and inconsistent with the needs of the nation, and the committee restored the $2 million to the budget.

## Presidential Candidates React to Vocational Education

In the presidential election year 1960, following an established custom, the American Vocational Association sought the presidential candidates' views on the matter of vocational education. Of particular concern were reactions of the candidates to cuts or increases in vocational education appropriations. Letters were sent to Senator John F. Kennedy (Massachusetts) and to Vice President Richard M. Nixon.

On August 17, 1960, Senator Kennedy replied to the inquiry from the American Vocational Association as follows:

The continuation of federal funds for vocational education at the full amounts authorized by existing law is vital to the security and economic health of our nation. This is why I co-authored the area vocational education measure that became a law in 1958.

Vocational education plays an important part in the program of the Democratic Party for acceleration of our nation's growth. Growing needs mean expansion of vocational education. As the skill of our workers increases, their contribution to the economy increases.

I wholly subscribe to the pledge contained in the 1960 Democratic Platform to "further federal support for all phases of vocational education."

I am aware of the efforts of the present administration to make drastic cuts in appropriations for such education or to repeal existing laws dealing with the subject. I am proud of the record of the Democratic Congress in continuing this effort.[1]

On October 7, 1960, Vice President Nixon replied to the letter from the American Vocational Association pledging his "wholehearted support," recognizing the importance of vocational education, and giving an unqualified answer of "yes" to the questions about continuing and increasing funds for vocational education. Vice President Nixon indicated that:

The nation's growing economy demands that we use the talents of every worker to the fullest degree. Vocational education plays a vital role in ensuring that each individual may make the greatest contribution to our economy.

He called attention to a position paper, published in September, in which he had given his views about national support of education, and he quoted a section from that paper in reference

---

[1] *American Vocational Journal,* Vol 35, No. 7, October 1960, p. 22.

specifically to vocational education. He concluded his letter as follows:

I concur that today millions of Americans who have received vocational training are making a great contribution to the nation's welfare and economy. They must continue to make that contribution.[2]

The views of prominent Americans in and out of the government were studied by the delegates to the American Vocational Association convention at Los Angeles in December, 1960. Matching these views with insights into the extraordinary changes in technological development produced in the delegates a conviction that they must become dedicated to an even greater effort in the area of vocational education.

### President Kennedy Requests a Study

John F. Kennedy was inaugurated as President on January 20, 1961. With a new administration in power, the American Vocational Association began an intensive study of the needs of vocational education. The Program Development Committee of the Association met in Washington, D.C., February 8-11, 1961, to discuss what the attitude and program of the AVA should be in regard to legislation. On February 10, 1961, the Committee met with Secretary of Health, Education, and Welfare Abraham Ribicoff and Assistant Secretary Wilbur Cohen about a number of items related to vocational education. During the discussion, the AVA Committee indicated that there was a growing feeling that a task force should be appointed to

make a comprehensive study of vocational education. Secretary Ribicoff told the Committee that the President, in his message to Congress on education (February 20, 1961), would call for such a study. The Secretary then asked the AVA Committee to assist him in suggesting the names of prominent persons who might make a contribution to the study. In the weeks that followed, the AVA worked closely with the Secretary's office in this matter.

In his message to Congress on American Education, President Kennedy said:

The National Vocational Education Acts, first enacted by the Congress in 1917 and subsequently amended, have provided a program of training for industry, agriculture, and other occupational areas. The basic purpose of our vocational education effort is sound and sufficiently broad to provide a basis for meeting future needs. However, the technological changes which have occurred in all occupations call for a review and re-evaluation of these acts, with a view toward their modernization.

To that end, I am requesting the Secretary of Health, Education, and Welfare to convene an advisory body drawn from the education profession, labor, industry, and agriculture, as well as the lay public, together with representatives from the Departments of Agriculture and Labor, to be charged with the responsibility of reviewing and evaluating the current National Vocational Education Acts, and making recommendations for improving and redirecting the program.[3]

This announcement assured a major study of vocational education. The message was greeted with enthusiasm by vocational educators throughout the

---

[2] *American Vocational Journal*, Vol. 35, No. 8, November 1960, p. 6.

[3] *American Education*, Message of the President of the United States, 87th Congress, First Session, House of Representatives Document No. 92, February 20, 1961, p. 5.

nation. However, they were naturally concerned that the persons chosen to be members of the advisory body be well informed and able. Provincialism and lack of perspective about vocational education could create new problems rather than solve existing ones and prepare for the future.

## Selecting the Panel

It was nearly seven and a half months from the time of the President's request for a Panel of Consultants on Vocational Education until the White House announced the appointment of the Panel. In part this long period reflected the seriousness accorded the selection by the Secretary of Health, Education, and Welfare, but in part the interval also reflected turmoil and confusion.

There was no question about the desirability of making a study of vocational education, but there were sharp differences of opinion about who should do the studying. Almost immediately after the President's request for a Panel, members of Congress, government officials, and professional organizations were flooded with recommendations concerning appointments. This was expected and, in fact, was entirely in line with Secretary Ribicoff's request of the Program Development Committee of AVA prior to the President's message to Congress.

It was obvious that any appointment to the Panel should be above "political favors" and that the persons appointed should have definite qualifications which entitle them to consideration. As far as possible, the Panel was supposed to be representative of a cross-section

of American life. This precluded the possibility of loading the Panel with persons whose total occupational experience had been in the field of vocational education. On the other hand, knowledge of vocational education was an imperative element in the list of characteristics desirable in the persons to be selected. Furthermore, members of the Panel should be generally favorable toward the vocational education movement and federal participation in it. The Panel's task, simply stated, was to review the past program, evaluate the existing program, and make recommendations for improvement and redirection. This was a practical, down-to-earth task and not an invitation to debate theoretical issues.

Despite the complications just mentioned, the field of candidates was gradually narrowed, and Secretary Ribicoff sent invitations to those approved by President Kennedy. On October 5, 1961, a press release from the Office of the White House Press Secretary read as follows:

The President today announced the appointment of a panel of consultants to the Secretary of Health, Education, and Welfare to review and evaluate the National Vocational Education Act and make recommendations for improving and re-directing the program.

This panel, which will consist of 25 members drawn from labor, industry, agriculture, education, Government, and the general public, was named by Secretary Ribicoff at the request of the President. It is expected that its recommendations will be placed before the Congress in January 1963.

The Chairman of the panel will be Benjamin C. Willis, Superintendent of Schools, Chicago, Illinois. The other members are:

CHARLES W. ENGLEHARD, JR.
*Chairman of the Board*
*Englehard Industries*
*Newark, New Jersey*

DAEL WOLFLE
*Executive Officer, American Association*
*for the Advancement of Science*
*Washington, D.C.*

FRANCIS A. GREGORY
*Assistant Superintendent and Director*
*of Vocational Education*
*District of Columbia Schools,*
*Washington, D.C.*

THEODORE SCHULTZ
*Chairman, Department of Economics,*
*University of Chicago,*
*Chicago, Illinois*

FREDERICK T. CORLETO
*Corleto Buick Agency, Inc.*
*South Philadelphia, Pennsylvania*

PETER T. SCHOEMANN
*President, United Association of*
*Journeymen and Apprentices of the*
*Plumbing and Pipefitting Industry,*
*Washington, D.C.*

CHARLES O'DELL
*Assistant Director of Retired Workers'*
*Department of the International Union*
*of the United Auto Workers,*
*Detroit, Michigan*

WILLIAM B. LOGAN
*Director of Distributive Education and*
*Professor of Education*
*Ohio State University,*
*Columbus, Ohio*

CHARLES F. CARROLL
*Superintendent of Public Instruction,*
*State Department of Public Instruction*
*Raleigh, North Carolina*

THOMAS H. QUIGLEY
*Professor and Head, Department of*
*Trade and Industrial Education,*
*Engineering Extension Division,*
*Georgia Institute of Technology*
*Atlanta, Georgia*

EDWARD B. EVANS
*President, Prairie View Agricultural*
*and Mechanical College*
*Prairie View, Texas*

HENRY A. GONZALES
*State Supervisor of Trade and*
*Industrial Education*
*Sante Fe, New Mexico*

ERNEST H. DEAN
*Speaker of the House of*
*Representatives of the State of Utah*
*Salt Lake City, Utah*

PAUL SHEATS
*Director of Extension and Adult*
*Education*
*University of California*
*Los Angeles, California*

MARGARET C. ELLS
*American International College*
*Springfield, Massachusetts*

JERRY R. HOLLEMAN
*Assistant Secretary of Labor*
*Washington, D.C.*

FLOYD D. JOHNSON
*Teacher of Vocational Agriculture*
*York, South Carolina*

MRS. MARY CAPERTON BINGHAM
*Louisville, Kentucky*

J. B. PERKY
*Director of Vocational Education*
*State Department of Education*
*Stillwater, Oklahoma*

JAMES PATTON
*President, National Farmers Union*
*Denver, Colorado*

MRS. HELEN RADKE
*Member of Port Angeles Public School*
*Board (and Member of State Board of*
*Education)*
*Port Angeles, Washington*

MARK ELLINGSON
*President, Rochester Institute of*
*Technology*
*Rochester, New York*

E. T. YORK
*Director of Federal Extension Service,*
*Department of Agriculture*
*Washington, D.C.*

HYMAN H. BOOKBINDER
*Special Assistant to the Secretary of*
*Commerce*
*Washington, D.C.*

431

Theodore Schultz did not serve, and later Helen LeBaron, Home Economics Education, Iowa State College, Ames, Iowa, was appointed to the Panel. J. Chester Swanson, Professor of School Administration, University of California, Berkeley, was selected as the director of the study and was in charge of the Panel staff in Washington, D.C.

## The Panel and Its Work

### The First Meeting

The Panel held its first meeting in Washington, D.C., November 9-11, 1961. Sterling M. McMurrin, U.S. Commissioner of Education, opened the meeting and reviewed the charge to the Panel which President Kennedy had established nearly nine months earlier.

Wilbur Cohen, Assistant Secretary for Legislation, Department of Health, Education, and Welfare, read a message of greetings from President Kennedy. The President reminded the Panel of the industrial, economic, and labor force conditions, and focused attention upon the changes anticipated in the next decade. The President's message concluded with the following statement:

It is timely, in view of these rapidly changing conditions, to convene an advisory body to take a close look at vocational education. It will study the manpower requirements of the Nation and attempt to determine the amount and type of vocational education needed to provide the trained manpower necessary for the future welfare of our country. The advisory body will assess the effectiveness of current vocational education programs in serving groups that do not now have the opportunity to enroll for such training. It will then study the various Federal acts and recommend revisions to put vocational education in a position to render the greatest service possible during the years ahead.[4]

Mr. Cohen assured the Panel that its recommendations would receive the careful attention of the Department of Health, Education, and Welfare. Congressman Fogerty also attended the opening meeting and spoke briefly of his interest in the work of the Panel and in the development of vocational education.

Thus the Panel started its work on a note of praise and optimism. Commissioner McMurrin, Seymour Wolfbein of the Department of Labor, J. Chester Swanson, and Walter M. Arnold, Assistant Commissioner for Vocational Education, and members of his staff, made presentations to the Panel. During the three-day meeting, the Panel raised many questions, suggested issues which were thought to be of importance to the general problem, and moved toward defining the plan by which the Panel could meet its responsibilities.

Because they represent the widespread interests of the Panel and the variety of situations or conditions members considered important in preparing their report, the questions and issues raised during the first meeting are here reported in full.

1. An identification of "hard policy" issues with which the Panel should concern itself.
   a. What should be included in Federal Vocational Education acts?
   b. What is the national interest in vocational education?

---

[4] Statement presented to the Panel, November 9, 1961. (Mimeographed.)

c. How do the mobility and urbanization of population relate to vocational education?

2. The most neglected youth in America today are the non-college bound and the high school dropouts. What can vocational education do to help these people? Basic to any consideration of the task of training and rehabilitating the large group of school dropouts is the need for remedial reading instruction.

3. An effort should be made to challenge the potential of all youth. The present Federal laws should be studied as to their age restrictions for workers, etc., to determine how these laws relate to preparation for employment.

4. The world of work should be examined; information should be gathered from studies already made; the labor market should be analyzed to compare existing vocational education programs to our national manpower needs; the structure of education should be analyzed in relation to present legislation, and how needs are being met.

5. One objective should be to develop a flexible system of vocational education and these points should be considered:

a. What are the rewards to society of an ideal program of vocational education?

b. How can a program be developed which will make it possible for individuals to change their jobs when their present skills become obsolete?

c. New and different institutions should be considered in an effort to meet new needs of our society.

6. The national interest in vocational education should be determined and the roles of education, industry, and various levels of government in this activity should be defined.

7. Specialized education rapidly becomes obsolete in our highly technical world. Many skills may be good only for a few years. We must take account of these facts.

8. Many people in rural areas of America are unemployed or underemployed. Their needs should be considered.

9. Great technical changes have occurred in America in the last few years.

Some radically new concept in the field of vocational education may be necessary to serve these changes.

10. There is a need for special attention to the education of women, to prepare them for the dual role of employment and maintaining a home.

11. It is necessary to improve the image of vocational education.

12. The philosophical basis of our present vocational legislation should be re-examined. For example, much of our present program was based on the assumption that one of the fundamentals of our economy is the small farm-owner operation. This seems to be no longer the case.

13. A careful examination of the relationships of other laws to vocational education (i.e., Child Labor Law) should be made.

14. The role of the Federal government should be examined to determine whether it should provide substantial financial support or seed money support for vocational education.

15. Some of the terms in vocational education should be re-examined, possibly eliminating such terms as sub-professional, semi-skilled, and other terms that indicate partial achievement on the part of whole individuals.

16. Priority groups to be served by vocational education will need to be determined: 14 to 18 year-olds, 18 to 20 year-olds, adults, etc.

17. Should someone in our social structure (probably the public schools) maintain contact with all students until the students have become gainfully employed?

18. What changes have occurred in the economic nature of America since 1917 when the Smith-Hughes Act was approved? What social and economic trends will likely prevail for the next decade?

19. Are there any aspects of the present vocational education program which contribute to any difficulties that minority groups may experience in acquiring the skills needed for job opportunities? Are there any special programs, within the general vocational education program,

which can be developed and promoted to maximize attention to the special problems faced by minority youth? [5]

## Analysis of the First Meeting

There was nothing really new in the Panel's 19 questions and issues. Some of these matters had been discussed in the literature of vocational education for years. What was important was the avowed intention of the Panel to attempt *to do something* about these well known problems in vocational education. The fact that the 19 points were well known, accounts for the agreement of the Panel that their action should encompass these areas. Any doubt or disagreements which may have occurred during the meeting did not filter into the official record.

The Panel's first meeting resulted in some rather interesting conclusions. For example, the Panel recognized that:

- The major portion of the youth of the nation were neglected from the standpoint of occupational preparation.
- Minority groups had special problems and could get lost unless definite and deliberate care was taken to keep their interests in view.
- The key word for the future was *flexibility*.
- Vocational education and the labor market were inseparable.
- Social and economic trends were closely related to the programs of vocational education.
- Vocational education was a national problem and mobility and urbanization were critical issues.

Much of what the Panel said was an updated version of comments which had been made frequently throughout the history of vocational education.

This provides evidence that such education is based on principles which are largely unchanged by time.

## Position Papers and Meetings With Special Groups

The first meeting of the Panel pointed up the value of having various groups present their conceptions of new directions for vocational education. To this end, the Panel invited a number of individuals to present special reports at future meetings and also invited organized groups to present "position papers" stating their views concerning their particular area of vocational education.

Position reports were presented by home economics educators, distributive education supervisors and teacher educators, trade and industrial educators, The National University Extension Association, The Association of State Colleges and Universities, AFL-CIO Education Committee, and others. Letters were sent to the Panel which oulined views of individuals, and the Panel solicited studies and publications from the states, which provided supplementary information. Special studies of administration, agriculture, sociology and economics of vocational education, financing vocational education, technical education, and the manpower requirements through the 1960's were requested by the Panel.

On one occasion, July 23, 1962, delegates to a manpower conference in Washington, D.C., were invited by J. Chester Swanson, staff director of the Panel, to an evening meeting to review some of the tentative conclusions of the study. Swanson presented to the group

---

[5] *Report of Conference, November 9-11, 1961*, pp. 3-5. (Mimeographed.)

the five basic assumptions that guided the work of the staff:

1. Vocational-technical education is a program of training with the objective of making youth and adults effective workers. It is a unique facet of education which develops in individuals qualities and values that are basic to our social and economic well-being. The changing needs of our economy and the mobile nature of our population make such training programs of primary national importance rather than of state and local interest only.

2. This Panel is considering all such training which qualifies one to enter employment without a baccalaureate degree. The major areas for consideration are: (a) the traditional secondary level in-school vocational courses; (b) the post-high school vocational or technical level in-school courses (as given in grades 13 and 14, the junior college, the community college, the technical institute, or a college with such non-degree programs); (c) courses for out-of-school youth and adults (pre-employment, retraining, or job upgrading).

3. The charge to this Panel involves a consideration of the present activities of vocational-technical education and the relation of these activities to the Smith-Hughes Act, the George-Barden Act, the training activities of the Area Redevelopment Act, and the possibilities of training under the Manpower Act of 1962.

4. Good vocational-technical training programs require students who have achieved adequate basic education skills. The Panel therefore recognizes the importance of maintaining quality programs in elementary schools and providing academic instruction coordinate with occupational skill training in secondary schools.

5. Consideration should be given to the types of service that vocational education can render our society and a search made for the most effective means for using vocational education to perform these services effectively.[6]

The basic assumptions scarcely left room for argument, and the manpower conference delegates expressed no opposition. They did, however, discuss the assumptions in some detail and expressed great interest in the progressive outlook the Panel had established in relation to the future role of vocational education.

These meetings and the position papers magnified the effectiveness of the Panel in its approach toward a consensus in relation to the major issues before it.

## Other Meetings of the Panel

The Panel visited programs of vocational education in Chicago, Philadelphia, and Baltimore. Regional conferences in a number of areas were conducted by members of the staff. Although the visits and regional conferences were productive of many views, it was apparent that great interest had developed over the nation in connection with two problems: (1) What vocational education could do to reduce unemployment, and (2) how vocational education could work toward the elimination of the school dropout problem.

Both of these problems were much in the news, and it was natural to look toward a national study for some positive action in regard to these matters. The Panel therefore was conscious of the prominence of these issues as it continued its deliberations.

At a meeting on March 9-10, 1962, Chairman Willis appointed working subcommittees to develop guidelines that could be used in preparing the Panel's final report. Among other

---

[6] Panel of Consultants on Vocational Education, *Staff Report, July 1962.* (Mimeographed.)

things, the reports of the subcommittees specified 13 areas for concentrated effort or specific study by the Washington staff. These areas were defined in the following manner:

1. Scholarships for impoverished youth who cannot now take advantage of opportunities under other Federal programs.

2. Specific information about the labor market, not only in agriculture, but in all vocational areas. We should determine manpower needs in each of these areas and determine how vocational education might assist in meeting needs for training.

3. Geographical information about the labor market.

4. The kind and level of training that will meet manpower needs, and the manner in which programs of adult education may help to meet these needs.

5. Specific information on how an adequate program of vocational training will affect the problem of unemployment.

6. Information regarding proper administration of vocational programs and allocation of funds to States.

7. The staff should consider rather intensive efforts in acquainting the public with problems and opportunities in vocational education, directing these efforts toward conditioning Congress to an acceptance of the needs of vocational education.

8. Rural America is not too different from the rest of the country—those areas have dropouts, unemployed and underemployed. The changing picture of agriculture is serious. We need information on special needs of rural areas.

9. A review of the lack of instructional materials in vocational education is indicated.

10. What about equipment in vocational education shops? To what extent is teacher education in vocational education current?

11. The staff should take a look at accrediting agencies with respect to people who are to teach in the programs under discussion. What are these agencies saying with respect to qualifications of people who are to teach vocational education subjects?

12. Guidance and counseling will play an important role in vocational education. This role should be considered and defined.

13. A portion of the final report of this Panel should deal with youth groups in vocational education—FFA, FHA, DECA, etc.[7]

Little by little the Panel was closing in on the specific elements that would comprise its final report. In producing the evidence that led to answers to the problems and questions, the staff utilized resources of various government agencies and the wealth of material that had been provided previously by individuals and groups throughout the nation.

By the time the Panel met again, May 3-5, 1962, its subcommittees and Washington staff had assembled and organized some of the desired information, and the report was beginning to take its first shape. The larger issues were coming into full view, making it possible to attend to subordinate issues; still the report would undergo many revisions during the next six months before it was to have unanimous acceptance by the Panel.

At the request of the Panel, M. D. Mobley, Executive Secretary of the AVA, presented the views of that group concerning the general problems of vocational education. These views were most valuable since they not only presented the position of a leading organization but also indirectly reflected Mobley's own insights gained during many years as a distinguished

---

[7] Panel of Consultants on Vocational Education, *Conference Summary, March 7-10, 1962.* (Mimeographed.)

observer of the national program. Full cooperation and support by AVA had been pledged previously, and Mobley emphasized that the AVA had confidence in the Panel and the staff. He then reviewed a number of specific items which he felt were *strong features of vocational education.*

1. It operates as a part of the public school education program of the nation.
2. It takes into consideration the needs for training at all levels except in those occupational fields requiring a baccalaureate degree.
3. It provides education and training for both entrance into and progress in an occupational field.
4. It has built up a healthy federal-state-local relationship which provides training programs to contribute to the social and economic welfare of each of these levels of our government and nation.
5. It has developed teacher education as an integral part of each phase of the program.
6. It has developed minimum standards for the several vocational education programs.
7. It has established advisory committees to help determine vocational training needs and content of courses.
8. It has employed the use of surveys and studies to determine the types of programs needed in a given community.
9. It has developed a philosophy of education which takes into consideration a program of education for those who are not academically talented.
10. It has been able to adjust its program to meet education and training needs in times of national emergency.[8]

Mobley also presented the Panel with a list of *features of the program which needed strengthening.*

1. Periodic evaluations should be made of each program to keep it up-to-date.
2. School administrators of programs must become better informed regarding the philosophy of vocational education and the "tried and tested" techniques in administering programs.
3. Teachers must be better paid in order for schools to compete with industry in the employment of competent personnel.
4. Much of the school equipment must be updated—*this is a must.*
5. The social stigma on vocational education must be removed and respect for those who work in fields trained by vocational educators must be improved.
6. Vocational education and industrial arts should be defined so that the public will understand the objectives of each.
7. The scope of vocational education must be broadened to take care of education and training needs in occupational fields requiring only limited skills and knowledge as well as occupations requiring a high degree of skill and technical knowledge.
8. Teacher education must be expanded and improved.
9. Research in the field of vocational education must be expanded.
10. Vocational programs must be extended to more sparsely populated areas such as conceived through area vocational schools and programs.
11. Teachers must be required to keep up-to-date in their occupational fields.[9]

An objective of the Panel was to define as accurately as possible the status of vocational education in the nation. In its search for all available evidence, the list of factors needing strengthening was as valuable as the list of strengths.

Each meeting brought the Panel closer to the main issues to be faced,

---

[8] Presentation by M. D. Mobley, Executive Secretary, American Vocational Association, to the Panel of Consultants on Vocational Education, Washington, D.C., May 3, 1962, pp. 14-15. (Mimeographed.)
[9] *Ibid.*

and the meetings changed from "hearings" to "work groups." The meeting of July 14-17, 1962, was devoted largely to subcommittee work. The vast amount of information received by the Panel had been reviewed, evaluated, and distributed to its proper place in the outline of the report. During August two subgroups met with the staff in connection with special problems.

When the Panel returned to Washington in September, the first draft of a portion of the report was ready for review. At meetings in October and November, the remainder of the text of the report was reviewed and directions were given to the staff concerning the preparation of the report for publication. By this time, the Panel had agreed that the title of the report should be *Education for a Changing World of Work.*

### The Final Meeting, November 25-27, 1962

In the fall the Washington staff prepared a Summary Report containing charts and diagrams illustrating the problems to be solved by vocational education. Succinct statements of the Panel's major conclusions were included in the summary report.

On the morning of November 27, 1962, President Kennedy received the Panel at the White House. Chairman Willis presented a copy of the Summary Report to the President and expressed the appreciation of all the members for the privilege of serving. The President thanked the members for their service and spoke briefly of the values of vocational education to the nation; he was particularly concerned about high school dropouts and other young people who needed to develop skills in order to compete effectively in the economic life of the nation. A note of humor was introduced into the proceedings when the President remarked that every time he asked Dr. Willis to serve on a panel, it cost the government money; Dr. Willis replied that the Panel was only requesting $400 million, to which the President replied, "That isn't much money."

Following the White House reception, the Panel held a press conference. Copies of the Summary Report were distributed to the press, and Chairman Willis answered questions concerning the report. There were no negative overtones to the conference. The press appeared to accept the report without even the suggestion of a critical note. They wanted to know the facts and seemed generally of the opinion that the report represented an appropriate direction for the nation. The resulting press reviews were pleasing to vocational educators.

The Panel completed its task on November 27, 1962, discharging its obligations in connection with the report.[10] All that remained was to prepare a draft of the final report for publication, a task that was completed late in December.

### Publications of the Panel of Consultants

The total report of the Panel was published in five separate documents:

---

[10] Members of the Panel did meet again at the American Vocational Association meeting in Milwaukee in December, 1962, where they were honored by the Association.

the summary report, the comprehensive report, and three appendices. The reports were printed by the Government Printing Office and were listed as publications of the U.S. Department of Health, Education, and Welfare, Office of Education:

*Education for a Changing World of Work*

Summary Report, OE-80020
The Report of the Panel, OE-80021

Appendix I, OE-80022
Technical Training in the United States

Appendix II, OE-80025
Manpower in Farming and Related Occupations

Appendix III, OE-80026
The Economic and Social Background of Vocational Education in the United States

A Sociological Analysis of Vocational Education in the United States

The Case for Education for Home and Family Living

The Contributions to the National Economy of the Use of Resources Within and by the Family

### Harmony

It is significant that the Panel completed its work with strong support and approval of all of the groups with interests in the study. No minority reports were necessary. When misunderstandings arose, the Panel or the staff met the challenge and worked with the dissident group until an acceptable understanding had been reached. In many instances, sections of the Panel report were presented to special groups; their review and recommendations were requested. Every effort was made to prepare a report that would be acceptable to all concerned with vocational education. This was not ap-

peasement; it was a straightforward approach finding the proper direction for vocational education in the future. When differences developed among Panel members, the problem was discussed until the issues were resolved. Few public documents have had such wholehearted approval.

### The Vocational Education Act of 1963

During the late fall of 1962, when the structure of the Administration's bill on education was developed, it was apparent that legislation for vocational education would be presented as part of a larger bill. Vocational educators were wary of this approach because controversy over any other section of the bill might endanger its vocational provisions.

On January 29, 1963, Senate Bill 580, House Bill 3000, *A Bill to Strengthen and Improve Educational Quality and Educational Opportunities in the Nation*, was introduced in the respective Houses and referred to appropriate committees. Title V of each bill contained the provisions for vocational education.

The fundamental recommendations of the Panel of Consultants were integrated into the provisions of these bills; increases in federal funds were authorized, although in amounts far short of the Panel's proposals. Furthermore, Title V of the bill replaced the George-Barden Act in its entirety and eliminated earmarked funds. Removal of earmarked funds was contrary to a resolution of the American Vocational Association, House of Delegates (Milwaukee, December, 1962), which called for their retention. AVA informed its

439

members that it would take appropriate steps to secure changes in the bill, and it was confident that the members of Congress would cooperate wholeheartedly in developing a bill that would meet the approval of a vast majority of vocational educators.

Prior to the end of December, 1962, a group of vocational educators was at work on provisions for a substitute bill that would overcome the objections to the omnibus bill. The Program Development Committee of AVA met in Washington January 31-February 4, 1963, to review and agree upon the final recommendations. The Program Development Committee worked closely with Representative Carl D. Perkins (Kentucky) and Representative Phillip M. Landrum (Georgia), who had requested recommendations from AVA for a substitute bill. It was intended that the new measure would retain the Smith-Hughes and George-Barden Acts intact, thus making provision for earmarked funds, and that it would provide a bill constructed along the lines of the recommendations of the Panel of Consultants. These recommendations were incorporated into the bill introduced by Congressman Perkins in the House of Representatives (HR 4955) on March 18, 1963. The bill was referred to the Committee on Education and Labor.

### "The Forgotten Youth"

In the meantime, the Senate Republican Policy Committee had undertaken an independent study of the problem and on March 4, 1963, issued a statement bearing the title of *The Forgotten Youth, Vocational Education in the United States.* The Administration had stated that ignorance and illiteracy, unskilled workers and school dropouts, and "other failures in our educational system have bred failures in our social and economic system," producing juvenile delinquency, unemployment, and chronic dependency. The Senate Republican Policy Committee took the opposite stand, stating that it was "failures in our social and economic system" that bred failures in our educational system. However, the Committee did claim that there was a systematic refusal of the educational system in general to acknowledge that vast changes were taking place in the social and economic mores of the American people. The Committee further charged that the Administration placed emphasis on "glamour" aspects of education leading to college entrance and, in effect, endorsed "trends already observed in American education to classify all other educational courses as being just a shade lower in dignity than the academic course."

A partial solution to the problems of unemployed youth as well as those of the employer looking for skilled or semiskilled help does exist within our educational system—the VOCATIONAL or TECHNICAL school—but it has been neglected and ignored. In some cases it almost seems that our school administrators have taken the attitude that if they don't look maybe these schools will go away.[11]

The Republican Policy Committee did not offer vocational education as an

---

[11] *The Forgotten Youth.* Prepared by the staff of the Senate Republican Policy Committee, Senator Bourke B. Hickenlooper, Chairman. Issued by the Committee, Washington, D.C., March 4, 1963, p. 7.

absolute solution to the social and economic problems, but it did recommend that vocational education should be pushed vigorously, administered better, and financed more fully. Its report called attention to the point of view of the experts (the Panel of Consultants on Vocational Education), who agreed that a deep-seated need for vocational and technical education existed and would increase. It noted that the Panel had set a price tag of $400 million as a reasonable figure, yet the Administration suggested *$73 million*. Finally, the Committee cited obstacles to the creation of a truly effective vocational education program; the greatest of these barriers was the attitude of the Administration, school boards, school officials, and the public. "Their apathy and even hostility mitigate against a sound program and must be changed before effective steps can be taken."

The statement of the Senate Republican Policy Committee contained nothing new but it was a strong emphasis of the party's policy in the matter of vocational education; it was also a convenient means for a strong attack on the Administration. The importance of the statement is that it verified again the bipartisan support that vocational education always has had in the Congress, it showed unquestionably that the members were aroused to the importance of vocational education, and it recognized that other groups must be similarly aroused. Both major political parties supported vocational education, but they fought bitterly over

the details of how Congress should act to provide the most effective program. A challenging finger was pointed toward the education profession to use the legislation wisely. The Policy Committee report was widely distributed among all the members of the Congress and it became available at a time when the legislative problems of the omnibus bill seemed to spell doom for the vocational provisions of the bill. Whatever impact the report may have had was cut short by the Administration's message to Congress on June 19, 1963, requesting an expanded program of vocational education.

It is very doubtful that the report had any effect on the administration; the administration policy-makers gave it only cursory attention. It is difficult to explain why the report was so thoroughly ignored. One probable reason for the lack of attention given to the report was that it was never formally accepted by the Policy Committee. Thus, it was impossible to tell what kind of support the report had behind it.[12]

### Action in the House of Representatives

Hearings before the General Subcommittee on Education of the Committee on Education and Labor began on March 25, 1963, and concluded on April 30, 1963. Testimony and documents submitted in relation to vocational education came from a large number of individuals and groups. Fifteen witnesses (ten representing AVA) appeared before the House Subcommittee, in support of vocational legislation. The witnesses were carefully selected to be representative of

---

[12] Douglas E. Kliever, *Vocational Education Act of 1963: A Case Study in Legislation.* (Senior Thesis, Princeton University, Woodrow Wilson School of Public and International Affairs and the Department of Politics, April 17, 1964.) Washington: American Vocational Association, 1964, pp. 20-21.

many sections of the country and also of various phases of vocational education. Their prepared statements and direct testimony were in support of the Perkins bill. Government witnesses had no choice but to support the Administration bill. The 700-page report of the hearings contained the evidence that would prevail in the restructuring of HR 4955 by the House committees.

Later, while the subcommittee was considering the bill in executive session, two serious problems arose. The first concerned agriculture and home economics. An amendment was proposed that would have eliminated funds entirely for these programs. The proposed amendment was rejected by "a very close vote." The second problem concerned home economics. An amendment was proposed to make it mandatory that 50 percent of the funds allocated to home economics be used for job-oriented training in occupations related to home economics. This amendment was also voted down. These amendments would have caused serious problems in the nation's operating program of vocational education had they gone into the final law.

On June 18, 1963, the bill was reported back to the House with amendments and was accompanied by House of Representatives Report No. 393, which included an analysis of the bill and several supplementary statements.

The bill was debated on August 6, 1963. Carl Elliott (Alabama), member of the Committee on Rules, called for House Resolution 469 to be read. The resolution outlined the procedures for consideration of the vocational education bill, HR 4955. Mr. Elliott indicated that he would support the bill because increased efforts in education would approach hard-core unemployment and also provide for the training of highly-skilled persons. "There is no need for further evidence that vocational education is a key to our national economic security and our citizens' personal self-fulfillment," he said.[13] Continuing his introduction to the bill he pointed out that, "It is economic as well as common sense that says we must invest now in vocational education, and invest heavily."[14]

Congressman Elliott reviewed briefly the provisions of the bill, showing that it followed closely the report of the Panel of Consultants on Vocational Education. It was the Congressman's opinion that the bill was "a landmark in education. I think it may well be the most important piece of legislation this session of Congress will consider."[15] He concluded his remarks by urging the House to vote against the so-called "Powell Amendment." This was a civil rights amendment which had been attached to other legislation. Some members of the House had asked that such an amendment be added to the vocational education bill in order to insure that benefits of the program would be available to all citizens without discrimination because of race or color. However, Elliott and others felt that the amendment would kill the bill. "This bill should not be made a vehicle of racial agitation," Elliott said.[16]

---

[13] *Congressional Record*, Vol. 109, No. 120 (August 6, 1963), p. 13462.
[14] *Ibid.*
[15] *Ibid.*, p. 13464.
[16] *Ibid.*

At this point Clarence J. Brown (Ohio), also a member of the Rules Committee, spoke glowingly in support of the vocational bill despite the fact that he had "not been enamored of most of the Federal aid to education measures or bills that have been introduced in this House."[17] Mr. Brown said that the amount of money was not large, particularly when compared to other appropriations, such as the $2,087 million for one year for a moon shot, a venture surrounded by doubt. He noted that the expenditure for vocational education was in fact an investment, and said, "I am wondering how we fix values in our minds."

Howard W. Smith (Virginia), Chairman of the Rules Committee, expressed his opposition to federal aid to education but cited vocational education as worthy. "This is a thing that is very much desired, and is very much needed."[18] Smith did have reservations about some sections of the bill and was definitely against the "Powell Amendment."

After other points of view had been expressed concerning civil rights and the appropriateness or inappropriateness of such an amendment to the vocational bill, the House resolved itself into the Committee of the Whole House on the State of the Union to consider HR 4955—Vocational Education.

The bill came from the Committee on Education and Labor with bipartisan support. In the debate that followed, it appeared that nearly unanimous support had developed.

The bill was hailed as a *significant advance*, as *a milestone in vocational education*, as *the answer to a great crisis*, as *representative of imagination and vision*, and finally as *good sound legislation*. There was no opposition to the bill, although members of the House did disagree about some of its provisions.

Representative Silvio O. Conte (Massachusetts) told the members of the House that he was a graduate of a vocational high school. "I, for one, will never forget or play down my vocational training . . . I think the practical experience and knowledge I gained at that time were essential to my future."[19]

When the discussion had been completed, the Clerk read the bill and Alphonzo Bell (California) offered an amendment which inserted at various sections in the bill phrases which included the words "nondiscrimination" or "racially nondiscriminatory." Bell indicated his support of vocational education, but stated his belief that many members of the House could not support the bill without the amendment. There were differences of opinion about the amendment. Some of the members were for the amendment on the basis that similar amendments had been attached to other legislation and that it was appropriate to do so with with HR 4955.

Others saw a larger issue.

Augustus F. Hawkins (a Negro Congressman from Los Angeles) spoke against the amendment, indicating that it was not a proper introduction

[17] *Ibid.*
[18] *Ibid.*, p. 13465.
[19] *Ibid.*, p. 13481.

of civil rights. "It can only prostitute that which to me is sacred," he said, and he further stated that the amendment was technically incorrect, that it would not threaten any state in defiance of the Constitution, and that it would endanger the operation of the vocational program if it should pass. "I come from and I represent a district which is between the noise of downtown Los Angeles and the stockyards, and the poor Negro boys and girls in my district need this training. For that reason I oppose the amendment." [20]

At no time during the debate were protests directed against vocational education, but rather they were against the proposed amendment which was alleged to open a back door to the racial issue. Some opponents of the amendment called it a "phony" measure. There were those who went even further, charging that those who favored the amendment had "phony" ideas about civil rights. Such accusations created a minor revolution in the House. It was reported that if the amendment failed to pass, a motion to recommit the bill to committee would be offered.[21] The time allocated to debate on the amendment expired and the question of the amendment was put to a vote. Yeas were 146, nays 194, so the amendment was rejected. There still remained the question of whether the bill could pass without the amendment.

William T. Cahill (New Jersey) then offered an amendment to strike out the words "under public supervision and control," and insert the words "in pub-

lic or other nonprofit educational institutions." [22] As it turned out, the debate on this amendment was entirely between Cahill and Frank Thompson Jr., also of New Jersey. The question was whether the state could, if it desired to do so, support worthy programs in nonprofit educational institutions. The Congressmen differed on the issue, and it was not clear whether the amendment would actually accomplish its purpose. The amendment lost by a vote of 44 for and 123 against.

M. G. Snyder (Kentucky) then introduced a motion to recommit the bill to committee with instructions that the Bell amendment be added to the bill. This motion lost by a vote of 181 for and 217 against.

When the final vote on the bill was taken, the yeas were 377, the nays 21 (35 did not vote) and the bill was passed.

### Action in the Senate

Hearings on S. 580, the omnibus bill, were conducted during the period June 10-14, 1963, by the Subcommittee on Education of the Senate Committee on Labor and Public Welfare. Before the bill was returned to the Senate, the Congress received a message from President Kennedy (June 19, 1963) with the following recommendations:

That the pending vocational education amendments, which would greatly update and expand this program of teaching job skills to those in school, be strengthened by the appropriation of additional funds, with some of the added money earmarked for those areas with a high incidence of school dropouts and youth unemployment,

---

[20] *Ibid.*, p. 13499.
[21] The amendment had been proposed previously in committee and was not supported.
[22] *Ibid.*, p. 13504.

444

and by the addition of a new program of demonstration youth training projects to be conducted in these areas;

That the vocational education program be further amended to provide a work-study program for youth of high school age, with Federal funds helping their school or other local public agency employ them part time in order to enable and encourage them to complete their training.[23]

On July 18, 1963, the recommendations of the Presidential message were introduced as an amendment to Title V-A of S. 580. On August 7, 1963, HR 4955 was received in the Senate and referred to the Committee on Labor and Public Welfare. In an executive session on September 10 and 11, 1963, the Education Subcommittee considered HR 4955 and S. 580 in the light of the Presidential message and recommended revision of the text of HR 4955 to provide for an expanded program of vocational education, an extension of NDEA, and other items. On September 25, 1963, the Committee on Labor and Public Welfare made further adjustments in the report of the Education Subcommittee and ordered HR 4955 reported favorably to the Senate as amended.

On October 7, 1963, the Senate took up the matter of vocational education. Senator Wayne Morse (Oregon) opened debate on the bill. He noted that Senator Jacob K. Javits (New York) and Senator Winston L. Prouty (Vermont) had amendments to introduce and suggested time limits of 30 minutes to each side of the house in debate on amendments and one hour to each side of the house in debate on the bill. Senator Thomas Kuchel (California) inquired if there were other amendments, and Senator Morse indicated that the Senator from Arizona (Goldwater) might have an amendment, but that he had not had final notice of it.

Senator Morse then discussed the education legislation which was before the 88th Congress and said of HR 4955 that it represented the best judgment of the majority of the Committee. He pointedly cited many facts about the educational needs and said he felt the rationale which promoted the passage of the Smith-Hughes Act in 1917 was applicable to the present bill. He paid special tribute to Senator Lister Hill (Alabama), the Panel of Consultants, and the Secretary of Health, Education, and Welfare and his assistants, and then reviewed the essential features of the bill, indicating that, "The findings of the panel which were published in its report are the basis of the bill before the Senate." [24]

Senator Morse compared the Senate and House versions of the bill and explained why the differences existed. In connection with increased authorization for financing in the Senate bill, the Committee had carried out the request of the President. In concluding his introduction to the bill Morse said,

I urge my colleagues to help American girls and boys of all ages to obtain, [in] all the areas covered by the bill, educational objectives suited to their individual talents and abilities. In my judgment, this can be done at this time through support of this first installment of educational legislation in the 88th Congress, without amendment.[25]

[23] *Congressional Record*, Vol. 109, No. 159 (October 7, 1963), p. 17839.
[24] *Ibid.*, p. 17838.
[25] *Ibid.*, p. 17842.

445

Senator Abraham Ribicoff (Connecticut), formerly Secretary of Health, Education, and Welfare, spoke highly of the Panel and its work. He commented:

It would be a tragedy for the country if this legislation is not enacted. Its underlying purpose is to improve our vocational education system so that all people, whatever their age or level of academic achievement, may have an opportunity to acquire the education and training necessary to make them employable.[26]

Senator Frank Carlson (Kansas) rose in support of the bill. "It is my own opinion that we have failed to stress nationally the importance of the vocational phase of our educational program." [27] Senator Carlson continued with emphasis upon the need for more time and money, the need to evaluate the esteem in which vocational education was held, and the need to take a lesson from some of the foreign countries who had learned of the necessity of vocational education in their total education program.

The possibility of amendments either on October 7 or 8 was brought into the discussion by several of the Senators, and finally a "Unanimous Consent Agreement" was suggested to regulate the procedures in connection with the bill. In the discussion that followed, the Senators pledged approval of vocational education and mentioned experiences in their own states as specific evidence of the need and importance of vocational education.

Senator Joseph S. Clark (Pennsylvania) indicated the necessity of arousing people to the seriousness of the crisis which the vocational education bill would help eliminate:

. . . in many ways we are engaged in a race between education and catastrophe; at present catastrophe is winning, because there is no sense of urgency in the White House, in the Senate, in the House, or, I regret to say, among the American people. We come out with fine words; we receive wonderful messages; we make splendid speeches; and we hear excellent testimony. But—to use an analogy which I have used before on the floor of the Senate—then, like Ferdinand the bull, we sit down under a tree, smell the beautiful flowers, and let the rest of the world go by.[28]

The views of Senator Clark were not unlike those of other members of the Senate as they presented explanations of numerous other details of the bill and each in his turn expressed satisfaction that federal aid to vocational education was a move in the right direction. Senator Ralph Yarborough (Texas), co-sponsor of the National Defense Education Act of 1958, cited many achievements of vocational education and presented information to the Senate in the form of evidence that federal funds for vocational education had produced much in return and actually had achieved the objectives for which the money was appropriated. "Vocational education is a field in which Congress wisely has been active for many years." [29]

At this point in the debate, Senator Barry Goldwater (Arizona) offered an amendment to reduce the funds and strike out the work-study program.

[26] *Ibid.*, p. 17843.
[27] *Ibid.*, p. 17844.
[28] *Ibid.*, p. 17850.
[29] *Ibid.*, p. 17863.

I wish to make it abundantly clear that I do not oppose vocational training. I believe the program, ever since its inception in 1917, has been one of the better programs engaged in by the Federal Government. It has been operated in an orderly fashion. It has not involved the expenditure of overly large sums by the Federal Government; and I believe that, on the whole, the States have done an exceedingly good job in managing the programs.

My whole objection to the bill as it now stands is that it would be much too costly; it would cost too much money. No need has actually been shown for this great increase—which is 15 times greater, I may say, than what the President originally asked for, early this year, in his first message to Congress on this subject. In short, there is no demonstrable need for this costly addition.[30]

In the discussion that followed, Senator Goldwater made his position quite clear and submitted additional evidence in support of his position, but he lacked the support of the Senate as a whole. Evidently a large number of the Senators had accepted the rationale of the Panel of Consultants and were of the opinion that the $400 million, which the Panel had recommended, was not out of line with the need. It was obvious, however, that the national program which had been conducted on an appropriation of about $57 million could not move overnight into an expansion that could use $400 million. This was one of the key points in Senator Goldwater's proposed amendment.

Senator Morse rose in objection to the amendment and presented extensive evidence in support of additional funds. Senator Kenneth B. Keating (New York) also objected to the amendment, and provided a succinct review of the general rationale for vocational education.

The United States is today in a 20th-century, space-age world. It is no longer enough for our youngsters to learn the three R's. Unless they learn a trade or profession, they may find themselves filling unemployment forms instead of filling a worthwhile job.[31]

At length, the Presiding Officer of the Senate raised the question on the amendment suggested by Senator Goldwater. The roll call vote was recorded as yeas 23, nays 52, not voting 25. "So Mr. Goldwater's amendment to the committee amendment in the nature of a substitute was rejected."[32]

The next day, October 8, the Senate continued the debate on HR 4955 as amended by the Committee on Labor and Public Welfare. Senator Birch Bayh (Junior Senator from Indiana) offered an amendment that further increased the amounts recommended by the Committee. Senator Bayh had only one reservation in his wholehearted support of HR 4955—"It is only half a loaf." Not enough money, he felt, was provided to cope with the great economic problem of the age—providing skills needed by industry. Although the Senator regarded the bill as a step forward, he thought the amount of money proposed by the Committee was like delegating "one beaver to dam the roaring Colorado." His amendment would implement the minimum recommendations of the President's Panel of Consultants on Vocational Education.

[30] *Ibid.*, p. 17867.
[31] *Ibid.*, p. 17871.
[32] *Ibid.*, p. 17872.

He urged adoption of his amendment for three basic reasons:

First. History has shown that for each Federal dollar expended for vocational education, State and local governments have provided more than $4.

Second. The demand for skilled and highly trained workmen has never been greater.

Third. Although the amendment would considerably increase the long-range allocation of resources for vocational education, the increase would be comparatively gradual. The step-by-step, 4-year increase would enable the development of adequate programing and planning to insure the efficient assimilation of all additional funds.[33]

Senator Bayh developed his arguments in detail, carefully providing supporting evidence for each. He ran out of time and Senator Morse granted him additional time. During his final argument he said:

Mr. President, in the past we have tended to downgrade technical education. It has played what could be called the role of Cinderella to its more glamorous stepsisters in the field of education. It is time that we stopped thinking that vocational education is for the deadheads, that it is the solution for the culturally deprived, or that it is a convenient dumping ground for those problem youngsters whom the regular teachers cannot handle.

This has never been the case, but now, more than ever before, we must look upon vocational education as a part of a balanced, overall program designed to meet the manifold complications of our industrial society. We must look upon vocational education as one means of meeting the need for specialization, as one way of preparing our youth for the more diversified labor market of tomorrow. In short, vocational training is one means of preparing our young people for useful roles in modern society.

Mr. President, I should like to make one final plea for my amendment, a plea for more resources in vocational education. In this era, when a diploma does not guarantee a job, let us fully implement this program designed to see that each student is "job trained." "Job trained" with the skills needed today and tomorrow.[34]

The Senate was moved by what must have been a stirring address. Senator Daniel K. Inouye (Hawaii) voiced his approval and offered to give his support to the amendment.

When the time had expired Senator Morse congratulated Bayh on his speech, saying: "If I were to make a maiden speech this year, I do not know of a better subject than a plea for more support for the youth of America."[35]

Senator Morse also indicated that the amendment by Senator Goldwater and the amendment by Senator Bayh would move the nation further toward an improved program of vocational education in the years ahead, because the senators had shown two sides of the picture. Then Senator Morse explained his position as a "political realist" and gave the reasons why he could not support Senator Bayh's amendment.

My answer is this: not only do we have a problem in the Senate and the House; but we also have the greater problem of explaining this situation to the American people, who still do not understand the facts. We cannot go too far ahead of them. However, the fact that we are proposing this amount this year does not mean, I say to the Senator from Indiana, that next year—if public opinion demands it—we

---

[33] *Congressional Record,* Vol. 109, No. 160 (October 8, 1963), p. 17982.

[34] *Ibid.,* p. 17984.

[35] *Ibid.,* p. 17984.

cannot amend the existing legislation so as to provide for increased amounts.[36]

He concluded with the view that the committee amendment to HR 4955 was the wisest course to follow with the new vocational education program.

Senator Hubert H. Humphrey (Minnesota) complimented Senator Bayh on his maiden address to the Senate and on his forthright stand on vocational education.

The Senator from Indiana ought to rejoice in the fact that by his good judgment he has selected this subject as the project to which he wishes to dedicate his energies, and, indeed, to give his life to during his career in the Senate and as a matter of public service.

I believe the history books of our Nation will have a special chapter for men and women who at an early time saw the importance of improvement in educational facilities, instruction, educational curriculum, and educational programs. The Senator is correct. No Nation ever spent itself into bankruptcy by educating its people.[37]

Other Senators extended their congratulations to Senator Bayh and in each case assurances were given him that his dynamic view of the need for additional financing was a step in the right direction. However, it became obvious that although the facts did demonstrate the need, providing money in the full amount recommended by the Panel should await another day. On the basis of these assurances, Senator Bayh withdrew his amendment.

During the continuing debate on HR 4955, other members of the Senate spoke in approval of the bill. One amendment was tabled and another

was withdrawn. When the final vote on the bill was called for, the result was yeas 80, nays 4, not voting 16. The bill was passed.

## Conference Committee

The situation on October 8 concerning vocational education consisted of one version of HR 4955 which had passed the House and a second version which had passed the Senate. Both Houses were in agreement that a vocational education bill was needed, but they were miles apart concerning the text of the bill. A Committee of Conference, consisting of representatives from both Houses, was appointed to prepare a bill to be submitted to both bodies. The Senate appointed Senators Wayne Morse, Lister Hill, Pat McNamara, Ralph W. Yarborough, Joseph Clark, Jennings Randolph, Winston L. Prouty, Barry Goldwater, and Jacob K. Javits as their conferees on October 8, the day they asked for a conference. It was not until October 29 that the House agreed to a conference and appointed Representatives Adam C. Powell, Carl D. Perkins, John Brademas, Peter Frelinghuysen, Jr., Charles E. Goodell, Dave Martin (Nebraska), Albert H. Quie, Alphonzo Bell, and Mrs. Edith Green as conferees.

The conference committee was slow in reaching agreement on all of the issues, most of which were large. For example, the House had recommended funds in a step-by-step range of $45 million to $180 million; the Senate recommendation was a range of $108

---

[36] *Ibid.*, p. 17985.
[37] *Ibid.*, p. 17986.

million to $243 million. But this was only one of the issues involved. The conference was conducted in closed session, and the information that filtered out to the public was at times encouraging and at other times discouraging.

The tragic death of President Kennedy, on November 22, 1963, came in the midst of the conference proceedings. Vocational education had lost one of its strong supporters. Just a year earlier President Kennedy had received the Panel of Consultants at the White House. The informal reception in the rose garden just outside his office brought to each person a vivid experience of the President's warmth and dynamic personality. The group was impressed with his sincerity and his remarkable understanding of the program of vocational education. He had asked that the national study be made, had followed the project into its legislative phase, and had further stressed its importance by special messages to Congress.

Formal recognition to President Kennedy's faith in vocational education was given at the American Vocational Association meeting in Atlantic City a few weeks later, and the continuing sense of personal loss among the vocational educators of the nation was strong.

On Friday, December 6, 1963, as the delegates to the annual convention of the American Vocational Association were assembling in Atlantic City, the outlook concerning the bill was not good. The report was that the conferees were "chasms apart." The major stumbling block appeared to be the formula for allocating vocational education grants to the states. The House bill would not give financial advantage to the states with small per capita incomes.

The unfavorable report about the position of the conference committee cast a shadow over preliminary meetings of the AVA convention. Saturday and Sunday were indeed dark days. When the convention opened officially on Monday, December 9, no one could tell what the outcome might be, and many feared the worst.

Over the weekend in Washington the picture changed completely. "Part of the sudden spirit of compromise was attributed to President Johnson who reportedly telephoned key members of the conference committee to urge that no effort be spared to hammer out an agreement now that passage was 'so near'." [38]

House of Representatives Report No. 1025 (December 10, 1963), contained the conference report. The preamble to the report stated:

The committee of conference on the disagreeing votes of the two Houses on the Amendment of the Senate to the bill (HR 4955) to strengthen and improve the quality of vocational education opportunities in the Nation, having met, after full and free conference, have agreed to recommend and do recommend to their respective Houses as follows: [39]

At this point the text of the bill, which represented the agreement of

[38] "Hill Deadlock Broken Over School Bills," *The Washington Post*, December 10, 1963, p. A-11.
[39] House of Representatives, Report No. 1025, 88th Congress, 1st Session, *Amendments to the Vocational Education Program, National Defense Education Act of 1958, and Public Laws 815 and 174, 81st Congress*, December 10, 1963.

450

the conference committee, was included in the report. Outwardly, prospects for the bill seemed good. The deadlock between the Houses was apparently resolved, and there was time for both Houses to consider the compromise bill and place it on the President's desk before the first session of the 88th Congress ended.

Beneath the surface, however, all was not so tranquil. Some members of the Committee of Conference, particularly Congressman Frelinghuysen, were far from satisfied and held that that bill should have continued study. More strife lay ahead.

### House of Representatives, December 12, 1963

Congressman Powell called up the conference report on HR 4955 and asked that the clerk read the report and the statement of the managers on the part of the House. Powell then reviewed the background of the conference report and indicated that:

From every avenue in American life, our attention has been called to the importance of strengthening the quality of vocational education if we are to maintain America's position as a leader in the world of work.[40]

At this point in the discussion on the floor of the House of Representatives one gets a glimpse into the activities of the conference committee. Congressman Frelinghuysen wanted to recommit the bill to the conference committee because of some of the new provisions which had been added at the insistence of the senators. Two

items—which Frelinghuysen said were unrelated to the bill—were (1) an extension of the impacted areas legislation, and (2) extension of the National Defense legislation. Two other items which he thought were "novel, expensive, and quite possibly unwise Federal vocational programs" consisted of (1) federal residential schools, and (2) federally financed work-study programs. He urged that the House not "yield to the blackmail of the other body" in these respects.

Evidently the conference committee had almost broken up over these matters. Congressman John H. Dent (Pennsylvania) paid tribute to Congressman Phil M. Landrum (Georgia) for having eased the situation "and kept us talking instead of walking."[41]

Sentiment to recommit the bill was strong among the House members of the conference committee. Others opposed this, arguing that recommitment would kill the bill. However, Congressman Albert Quie (Minnesota), supporting Frelinghuysen, called that "the silliest argument I have heard all day."[42] He continued by saying, "The impacted-aid lobby, the NDEA lobby and the vocational education lobby would descend on this Congress and make certain that we report out a bill."[43] Under these conditions the bill could not possibly get lost in legislative maneuvers. Quie then offered a motion to recommit the bill to committee. The vote was yeas 180, nays, 192, not voting 69, so the motion lost. At this point, the conference report was

---

[40] *Congressional Record*, Vol. 109, No. 204 (December 12, 1963), p. 23105.
[41] *Ibid.*, p. 23111.
[42] *Ibid.*, p. 23117.
[43] *Ibid.*, p. 23111.

put to a vote with the result of yeas 300, nays 65, not voting 69. So the conference report was agreed to, and the House passed the vocational education bill.

### The Senate, December 13, 1963

Senator Wayne Morse submitted to the Senate the report of the Committee of Conference and asked for unanimous consent. He claimed that the conference compromise was sound and deserved the support of the Senate.

The discussions that followed consisted largely of support for the conference report and praise to the members of the Senate who had been engaged in working on the bill. There was a faint boast that the Senate had lost very little in the conference with the House. A vote on the bill was called for. The yeas were 82, nays 4, not voting 14. So the report was agreed to and the Senate passed the vocational education bill.

### The White House, December 18, 1963

In the Cabinet Room of the White House, surrounded by leaders of Congress and special guests, President Lyndon B. Johnson signed into law the Vocational Education Act of 1963 (Public Law 88-210), on December 18, 1963.

The President expressed his personal satisfaction with the legislation and in addition said:

Modern demands upon labor and industry require new skills and an upgrading of old skills, require more education and greater knowledge. It has been said

that we need over 100,000 technicians a year just to meet our needs in the engineering field alone but all of our present programs combined, we are told, turn out a maximum not of 100,000 a year but only 20,000 technicians a year. We believe that this new law will help close this gap. Under this law high school students will be encouraged to stay in school. If they need financial assistance, they may receive it under a work and study program.

. . .

For the first time Federal funds are going to be available to construct new vocational schools. Demonstration and research projects authorized under this law will vastly improve the quality of our vocational training. Where there is severe unemployment and high numbers of school dropouts, special experimental programs of residential vocational education schools are authorized.

. . .

Finally, the extension of the program of aid to schools and districts affected by Federal activities will permit a continuation of Federal assistance where we have a special responsibility. I believe that this measure, together with a Manpower Development and Training Act, places us in a position to make a major attack on one of the most important obstacles to economic growth and productivity. It is a reaffirmation of our conviction that education is the cornerstone of our freedom.[44]

## The Panel and the Act of '63

A strong parallel exists between the relation of the Panel of Consultants on Vocational Education to the Vocational Education Act of 1963, and the relation of the Commission on National Aid to Vocational Education to the Vocational Education Act of 1917. In both instances, the problems of vocational education loomed sufficiently

[44] *Selected Education Acts of 1963*, Prepared for the Subcommittee on Education of the Committee on Labor and Public Welfare, United States Senate, Washington: Government Printing Office, 1963, p. 89.

large in the public eye to attract presidential interest. Both the Commission and the Panel were created at the request of a President. Members of the two groups were chosen carefully to represent the essential segments of society most concerned with the problem. The two groups followed similar practices in determining the needs for vocational education. Each group reported its findings to the Congress. The two reports became the basis upon which the bills of 1917 and 1963 were constructed. The *Congressional Record* for 1917 cited the Commission report as a document of authority; the *Congressional Record* of 1963 contained the essence, and much of the actual text, of the report of the Panel and pointed to the work of the Panel as the authority in matters of vocational education.

It is apparent that each Congress had regarded the passage of its Vocational Education Act as a contribution that would benefit the masses of the people. In many respects, the Panel and its report are reflections of the Commission and its report, displaced in time by 46 years and adjusted to the requirements of contemporary society. In the years ahead, the one single document which will have the greatest impact upon the program of vocational education will be the report of the Panel of Consultants on Vocational Education.

## Summary

For nearly a decade prior to the election of John F. Kennedy as President of the United States, the White House had been urged to reduce the funds devoted to vocational education.

On a number of occasions the preparation of the national budget presented new threats of financial problems for vocational education. Each threat was countered by presenting evidence of the value of vocational education and the need for continued financial support at the federal level.

Vocational education did have major issues to resolve, but reduction in expenditure of federal funds was scarcely an appropriate aid toward meeting the required vocational education adjustments. The action by President Kennedy in requesting the appointment of the Panel of Consultants brought the program of vocational education into national view. It had been 46 years since President Woodrow Wilson had performed a similar service in the appointment of the Commission on National Aid to Vocational Education.

The diversity among the members of the Panel aided in the study of vocational education. The Panel consisted of persons from 19 states. Included were teachers, chief state school officers, university professors, state supervisors of vocational education, and representatives of industry, business, labor, state and federal governments, agriculture, racial minorities, boards of education, and professional associations. Geographically, too, the representation was broad; the Far West, the Mountain States, the Plains States, Eastern States, the South all had their spokesmen. Likewise the members displayed a wide range of educational achievement and educational interests.

This diversity entered into the Panel discussions, producing the specific ideas, the generalizations, the patterns, the procedures, and the recommendations which finally became the report

453

of the Panel, *Education for a Changing World of Work.*

This report was the source of authority used in preparing the various versions of the legislative bills. Members of Congress supported their personal views in debate by reference to the report. The final structure of the Vocational Education Act of 1963 was in accord with the major recommendations of the Panel. Congress did reach some decisions that had not been specifically identified by the Panel, but even these could be inferred from the report.

The drama of congressional action shows clearly that the members of Congress considered vocational education essential to the well-being of the people, and through the people, to the well-being of the nation. They fought bitterly over certain issues, but when the question was Yes or No in relation to vocational education the vote was an overwhelming Yes.

The Panel, its report, the bills, and the final passage of the Vocational Education Act of 1963 (Morse-Perkins Act) combined to usher in a new age of industrial education.

---

## Recall Questions

1. What was President Kennedy's specific charge to the Panel?
2. What were the strengths and weaknesses of vocational education as viewed by the American Vocational Association?
3. What was the origin of *The Forgotten Youth*? What was the significance of this publication?
4. Why was the omnibus bill a threat to legislation for vocational education?
5. What amendments were proposed in the House and the Senate concerning the vocational bill?

## Research Questions

1. Review all of the testimony in the *Congressional Record* pertinent to the Vocational Education Act of 1963 and prepare a list of the principal issues on which Congress justified the need for this legislation.
2. Study the reports of hearings held in connection with the Vocational Education Act of 1963. Upon what bases did witnesses urge legislation?

## Suggestions for Further Reading

U.S. Department of Health, Education, and Welfare, Office of Education, *Education for a Changing World of Work,* OE-80021. Washington: Government Printing Office, 1963.

*Congressional Record,* 88th Congress, First Session
    Vol. 109, No. 120, Tuesday, August 6, 1963, pp. 13462-13507.
    Vol. 109, No. 159, Monday, October 7, 1963, pp. 17799, 17837-51, 17853, 17862-72.
    Vol. 109, No. 160, Tuesday, October 8, 1963, pp. 17977, 17981-98, 18000, 18023-45.
    Vol. 109, No. 205, Friday, December 13, 1963, pp. 23277, 23298-23312.

# Chapter 16

# Industrial Education in Other Nations

International Vocational Training Information and Research Center, CIRF · Analysis of Contemporary Developments · Latin America (The Charter of Punta del Este) · United States Personnel in Other Nations · Summary · Recall Questions · Research Questions · Suggestions for Further Reading

**D**uring America's colonial period and for a large part of the 19th century, the number of craftsmen supplied through domestic apprenticeship was never sufficient to satisfy the country's ever-increasing requirements. We always depended upon craftsmen from Europe to supply our skill needs, almost completely in the beginning, and to some degree even into the twentieth century. This dependence was reduced and eventually ended by America's growing strength on the one hand, and on the other by a series of immigration laws which shut off the supply of craftsmen from abroad.

But even while we were becoming physically independent of European craftsmen, their reputation lingered on. German and Scandinavian craftsmanship was considered representative of the best; also when we were establishing our own programs of industrial education we looked to these countries for models and for principles.

One example may serve to illustrate how the ideas of European industrial educators entered into American thinking. Dr. George Kerschensteiner's manual training work in Munich after 1896 was especially well-known among leading American educators. His essay "The Education of German Youth for Citizenship" in 1900 won a prize from the Royal Academy of Useful Knowledge.[1] He also won the right to put

---

[1] Charles A. Bennett, *History of Manual and Industrial Education, 1870-1917.* Peoria, Illinois: The Manual Arts Press, 1937, pp. 197-199.

his ideas into educational practice. Interest in Kerschensteiner's educational philosophy had developed in the United States from the reports of Paul H. Hanus, who visited him in 1904; from the reports of Charles A. Bennett, who interviewed him in Munich some years later; and from Frank A. Manny's reviews of Kerschensteiner's publications.

In 1910, at the invitation of the National Society for the Promotion of Industrial Education, Kerschensteiner spent two months in America.[2] He lectured before the Society and before the Commercial Club of Chicago. He visited Cincinnati, St. Louis, New York, and Philadelphia, and talked with Thomas A. Edison. Upon his return home he recorded his impressions of the public school system in the United States in a series of five articles. When the House of Representatives was studying the Smith-Hughes bill, Kerschensteiner's views were cited as relevant evidence for supporting it.

But American knowledge about foreign industrial education was not limited to developments in Germany. American educators visited many European countries and reported their observations.[3]

During the first half of the twentieth century the program of industrial education developed in accord with need in certain countries, and not at all in others. The march of technology did not produce more than the normal gains required by increased employment in industry. Apprenticeship continued to play a significant role in most of the industrialized nations. Despite the importance of these developments their historical significance seems to be of less note (to the purposes of this history) than the dynamic developments which have been forced by modern technology.

### Technology of Modern Times

The technological revolution following World War II has had an impact upon all nations. Their economic stability has depended in large measure upon their possession of skills and upon their use of these skills for their own benefit. In consequence industrial education has developed rapidly in previously industrialized countries, and industrially impoverished nations have appealed to the better developed nations for assistance. These appeals have been recognized in a variety of ways; the United Nations Educational, Scientific, and Cultural Organization (UNESCO) and the International Labor Organization (ILO) have played leading roles in aiding the new developing nations.

In America, efforts of private foundations and branches of the United States Government have placed emphasis upon lending assistance to countries weak in basic industrial education. Hundreds of American industrial educators have accepted the challenge of living in other countries to help de-

---

[2] Emil O. Toews, *The Life and Professional Works of George Michael Kerschensteiner (1854-1932)*. Unpublished doctoral dissertation, University of California, Los Angeles, 1955, pp. 154-162.

[3] Bennett, *op. cit.* Bennett's book contains a review of industrial education in Russia, Scandinavia, France, Germany, and England. He was one of many observers of the European programs.

velop the field. Similarly, thousands of students from other nations have come to America to study industrial education. Schools in all fifty states have organized special programs for foreign students or have sent task forces from their faculties to other nations. These cooperative relationships produced the need for an appropriately organized means of exchange of information on an international basis and for the promotion of research.

## International Vocational Training Information and Research Center, CIRF

The International Vocational Training Information and Research Center, CIRF, was established in January, 1961, as a joint undertaking of the International Labor Organization and the Council of Europe.[4] Cooperating with ILO and the Council of Europe in CIRF are three other groups: OECD, the Organization for Economic Co-operation and Development; EEC, the European Economic Community (Common Market); and ECSC, the European Coal and Steel Community. CIRF constitutes a section within the International Labor Organization and operates on an extra-budgetary account to which the participating organizations contribute. The Center publishes reports and manuals, abstracts of articles on vocational education, and a magazine, *Training for Progress*.

The principal functions of the Center are to:

1. *Collect information* about developments in the fields of vocational and technical education, and the training of workers, supervisors, technicians, and associated staff;

2. *Carry out international research* on vocational training requirements, organization, and methods and means, and to co-ordinate national research undertaken in specialized fields; and

3. *Provide information* on vocational training and technical education activities in the various countries of the world.[5]

The program of CIRF is ambitious and much needed: its goals of registering research projects throughout the world and publishing abstracts of such research are exciting to research workers in industrial education because the task of discovering what is going on in the field is thereby greatly simplified. In 1962 CIRF indicated that its abstracts were based upon scanning systematically more than 1,000 periodicals, in 18 languages, published in 50 countries. The official languages of CIRF are French and English; the abstracts, as well as all other documents, are published in both languages. CIRF explains that its abstracts are intended for those industrial educators who want to "dig deep" into that field of education. The publications provide an international equivalent of our national professional journals.

---

[4] The letters CIRF are derived from the Center's French name, *Centre International d'Information et de Recherche sur la Formation Professionnelle.*

[5] Sven Grabe, *Memo on the Activities of the International Vocational Training Information and Research Center.* Prepared for the Research and Publications Committee, American Vocational Association, November 6, 1962. (Mimeographed.)

## The Research Program

The Center places priority on studies and research related to the need for skilled workers in the rapidly changing repair and maintenance operations. Parallel with these studies are investigations of the organization and control of vocational education, including emphasis upon many components such as finance, teachers, and buildings. The intensified research program of the Center is based upon the assumption that technological change and automation are affecting the foundations upon which national systems of training were developed. The skilled worker is regarded as the key factor in technological progress, since worldwide shortages of such craftsmen tend to retard the speed of technology.

The major research efforts of CIRF, completed through 1964, are as follows: [6]

### A. National organisation of training.

A study of the organisational structure and legislative basis of vocational training activities of the various countries of Europe.

### B. Training of teaching and instructing staff.

A study of the status and arrangements for basic and further training of vocational teachers and manual skills instructors in public and private schools and training centres.

### C. Technological change.

A study of the influence of technological change on the job descriptions, training syllabi and examination requirements in selected industrial occupations.

### D. Trade tests and examinations.

A study of the general principles and rules applied in the examination of trade skills and knowledge acquired in an industrial, agricultural and artisan trades training.

### E. Cost of training.

A study of accountancy methods used to determine the cost of training, including regulations for public contributions aiming at a reimbursement of such expenditure.

### F. Repercussions of technical change on the recruitment and training of personnel in steel furnaces.

A study of the work force in older and new blast furnaces in operation in six European steel plants, undertaken at the request of the European Coal and Steel Community. Study completed in 1963.

### G. Repercussions of technical change on the recruitment and training of personnel in steel furnaces.

Continuation of project F.

### H. Trends in European apprenticeship related to accelerated technical development.

A study of recent (last ten years) changes in apprenticeship regulations, syllabi and examination requirements made necessary by technical change. Undertaken on contract with the U.S. Department of Labor, Office of Manpower, Automation and Training.

### I. Training of maintenance workers.

A study of how chemical and food processing plants in some European countries are catering for their rapidly growing need of highly skilled maintenance staff caused by increasingly complex equipment. Undertaken on contract with the U.S. Department of Labor, Office of Manpower, Automation and Training.

### J. Training of skilled workers.

A comparative pilot study of the results

---

[6] CIRF Information Brochure, dated March, 1964.

458

obtained in apprenticeship training in four industrial towns (Bristol, United Kingdom; Dordrecht, Netherlands; Karlsruhe, Germany; and Mechelen [Malines], Belgium), as demonstrated by employer preferences and further training action. Undertaken under contract with the Organisation for Economic Co-operation and Development. Completed.

The Center indicates that its services are available to outside organizations on a cost reimbursement basis but that its comprehensive program is devoted to projects that are related to the improvement of vocational training practices at the "worker, supervisor and technician levels in industry and in other fields of economic activity."

## Analysis of Contemporary Developments

The following review of industrial education in its contemporary aspects in other nations is gleaned largely from CIRF *Abstracts*. Data provided in the *Abstracts* is classified into 15 training-related categories. The term *training* is frequently used in the *Abstracts*, but it implies more than rapid skill development. Eight of these categories —the next eight headings in this chapter—have been selected for review here, and in each category only those references to education of an industrial nature have been included. The identifying feature in the review is the category and not the nation; particular nations are cited only to illustrate the kind of work being done in each category.

[7] CIRF *Abstract* No. 01561, March 1963.
[8] CIRF *Abstract* No. 00884, August 1962.
[9] CIRF *Abstract* No. 00111, November 1961.
[10] *Ibid.*

### Vocational Training Systems in General

Manpower is the most abundant resource of developing nations, but to be useful it needs skill training. Because facilities for training are generally lacking in these nations, the demand for skilled workers can not be satisfied. The aim of European nations has been and is to establish permanent vocational training systems.

The aim of vocational training should be to provide broad basic training on which basic specialized training and retraining can be given. In modern technological societies, skill requirements change rapidly and continuous adaptation and upgrading of skills are needed.[7]

Recognition that availability of skilled manpower was a significant factor of economic growth was widespread throughout the nations. "Skilled manpower for continents in a hurry" could be satisfied in an emergency situation by the easily adaptable "American Area Vocational School."[8] But long-term measures were imperative. Cooperation of technical institutions, education in general, and industry was held to be vital to the international scene. Sven Grabe, head of CIRF, summarized one aspect of the international development by saying, ". . . there will be a closer connection between general education and vocational training; these two will together absorb 80 to 90 per cent of all European youth."[9] Prerequisite to all improvements, in the international view, was the necessity for expanded research in "vocational education sciences."[10]

In 1961 the European Coal and Steel Community was actively at work on the problem of improving a common policy within the Community. Specific studies were evolved, dealing with critical problems which must be solved to reap the advantages of a common policy.

Norway, Sweden, Denmark, and Finland studied the changes in vocational training needed to promote a free exchange of labor among the Nordic countries.[11] In both Norway and Sweden the primary program of adult training had focused upon combating unemployment and underemployment. Emphasis upon training in Finland had been concentrated upon "unemployed youth lacking vocational qualifications," while in Denmark vocational training had been based mainly on apprenticeship to fill the needs of industry. Norway's ten year plan for seamen's training begun in 1961, represented a drastic reform in the training of common seamen, ship machinists, radio operators, cooks, stewards, and navigators. Modifications in the vocational training act provided for attention to improvements in instruction and for general upgrading of vocational education.

The pros and cons of a central administration of the education system in Sweden in 1962 created the necessity for attention to the welfare of vocaional education.

Vocational training has developed outside the educational system. It has been,

and will always be, dependent upon initiative on the part of workers and employers, and groups representing commerce, the artisan trades, and small industries.[12]

On the other hand the centralized authority held the possibility of "making vocational training equivalent in the eyes of the public to the theoretical streams in the general school system."[13] The new central school agency finally prevailed, becoming effective October 1, 1964.

Denmark's entry into the common market focused attention upon greater manpower training. As indicated, the quality of apprentice training in Denmark was on a par with that of other common market countries. However, reforms were needed to bring all training under one ministry, and recognition of the influence and contribution of employers' and workers' organizations was imperative. "Not to take action now in vocational training matters would mean a loss in competitive ability."[14]

Full agreement was reached in regard to bringing all training under the Ministry of Education in Denmark, and due regard was given to problems of reaching more appropriate cooperative arrangements.[15] Writing from the point of view of a workers' representative, Henry Grunbaum expressed satisfaction with the law that provided for the training of unskilled and semi-skilled workers, but he had the following suggestion for further consideration.

---

[11] CIRF *Abstract* No. 01576, March 1963.
[12] CIRF *Abstract* No. 01581, March 1963.
[13] *Ibid.*
[14] CIRF *Abstract* No. 00089, October 1961.
[15] CIRF *Abstract* No. 00278, January 1962.

In the more distant future it might be well to modify present skill training into a basic training for all young school leavers, followed by specialised training, taking into account the individual's interests and abilities and the actual requirements of the economy.[16]

Arne Lund, writing from the point of view of an employers' representative, regarded the change as desirable and stressed the need for full cooperation of all groups concerned with training. He also stressed the need to expand further the facilities for training.[17]

Erik Dreyer, citing the view of an official responsible for training, described the development of schools and programs in response to the new laws and organization. Some requests for programs had been refused because of narrowness in scope and the consequent doubt about educational value. Dreyer indicated also that attention to teacher training was so imperative that, as soon as the general development of the program was well under way, it would become a priority consideration.[18]

Switzerland passed a new law related to vocational training on September 20, 1963. It upgraded and strengthened previous plans, providing further regulations. Provisions related to apprenticeship made basic vocational training compulsory. Compulsory "related instruction" also formed a part of the new law, and vocational teachers were required to be properly trained. The law contained other provisions identifying responsibilities of various groups for the operation of vocational training.

In the early 1960's, the United Kingdom and the Federal Republic of Germany placed concentrated attention upon their respective systems of vocational training. Emphasis was given to new laws, new relationships, expansion and availability of vocational education, examinations for both teachers and trainees, cooperation with industry, relation of vocational training to economic need, and implementation of program objectives.

Similarly other nations gave attention to their particular needs in vocational training. New laws supporting vocational education were passed in France, Morocco, Senegal, Poland, Spain, India, Pakistan, and New Zealand among other nations. The CIRF *Abstracts* identify more than fifty specific developments in other countries beween 1961 and 1963 that show concern for vocational training systems in general.

### Economic, Technical, and Social Aspects

The practical aspects of adult education for the developing countries were identified as inseparable from economic development, and successful programs were judged to be those that would fit into the economic and social change, not get ahead of it. Furthermore, because education and training were usually lengthy processes, attention to these factors early in the consideration of economic and social

---

[16] CIRF *Abstract* No. 01165, November 1962.
[17] CIRF *Abstract* No. 01164, November 1962.
[18] CIRF *Abstract* No. 01163, November 1962.

461

development was recommended. Nor was the need overlooked to "concentrate on the training of instructors." [19] Emphasis was also placed on having a centralized influence upon the development of industrial education so that the whole program could be considered, not just one aspect of it.

In the European Economic Community measures were developed for the free circulation of workers between countries.

Each member country should organise accelerated training courses for their workers to help them acquire the qualifications necessary to take employment in the sectors in which the lack of manpower exists.[20]

Many of the nations studied the changes in the labor force and the vocational characteristics of their change, in order to establish adequate methods of training. The USSR is a good example of a nation that has used research data as a basis for establishing a network of vocational-technical schools.

France has moved rapidly in the direction of considering vocational training along with manpower needs in problems of economic expansion. In the process France has discovered that *the numerical expansion in the evolution of technical education gave rise to the need for adaptability in employees.*

Adaptability became more important than manual skill outside a few remaining traditional trades. This has brought with it a change of attitude towards specialization in technical and vocational training.[21]

In 1963 the Federal Republic of Germany adopted a vocational training bill in an effort to stimulate upgrading of vocational skills. Financial assistance was available to youths under 25 years of age. Although there were a number of restrictions in regard to the bill, and some negative viewpoints, the idea had the support of many organized youth groups. Those who supported the bill could see the social and economic advantages inherent in it. "The encouragement of vocational training is a prime public duty." [22] Objections to the bill were principally on the grounds that it was created as a social welfare measure and therefore did not have uniform basis for granting aid to all persons.

In Switzerland industry and technology were dynamic influences in the social order that required more skilled craftsmen and technicians. However, the vocational training system tended to be static, preserving traditional practices. It seemed obvious that some effort should be directed toward understanding the nature, scope, and depth of industry and technology, and their occupational needs. It was equally obvious that significant educational adjustments were needed in vocational education. "The future of the country depends on a good performance record in vocational education." [23] Education of the rising generation should be more clearly related to the occupational needs of the national economy. Meas-

[19] CIRF *Abstract* No. 01562, March 1963.
[20] CIRF *Abstract* No. 00085, October 1961.
[21] CIRF *Abstract* No. 00168, November 1961.
[22] CIRF *Abstract* No. 01847, October 1963.
[23] CIRF *Abstract* No. 00444, March 1963.

ures to improve the situation were recommended in the form of vocational guidance, study of long-range economic trends and their effect upon employment, and encouragement to gifted young people to enter occupations requiring a high degree of skill.

Educational reforms, particularly in the system of vocational education, were of practical concern in Sweden, Norway, Denmark, Finland, Nigeria, Poland, Italy, Madagascar, and in nearly every other country, because such reforms were related to the economic and social progress.

## Relationships Between Education and Training

The problem of whether the basic school should consist of broad preparatory trade training or more direct skill training has been of concern in many nations. In Sweden the labor unions pointed out that certain differences existed in regard to whether or not vocational training should be extended to the basic school. They cited the opinion—and claimed research would bear it out—that the basic school should be the same for all persons up to the age of 16, or approximately the 9th year of schooling. The lack of stability of vocational interests was thought to be the major issue.

Tuition in all streams and districts must be so broad that children are not predestined for a narrow work sector. Training for particular occupations should take place only after the basic school.[24]

As might be expected, one of the stumbling blocks in the planning for

vocational education had been related to the responsibility of the local school to supply manpower to local industries. Employers could agree that the basic schooling was important and that the program in the 9th school year might provide a broad basic vocational training, but they were insistent upon a degree of flexibility in school laws that would permit their adaptation to local needs.

In England, A. D. C. Peterson, writing about "Education for the Seventies" as applied to the United Kingdom, pointed out that the expansion of human knowledge and its application to human life should be matched by a corresponding revolutionary trend in education. But here we find the familiar refrain that this had not been the case largely because of the continued dominance of pure science over applied science. He pointed out that the educational system was prejudiced against "using for educational purposes any area of study which has direct utilitarian applications," and that behind this situation was the fact that the teachers were trained to foster that point of view.

The schools are prepared to teach the social organization of the mediaeval manor but not that of the 20th century factory; they refuse to teach new subjects on the grounds that they are still in the experimental stage, that there are not yet any orthodox textbooks or examination criteria.[25]

In the Federal Republic of Germany the controversy concerning the ninth year of compulsory schooling centered around the tendency to increase the

[24] CIRF *Abstract* No. 00119, November 1961.
[25] CIRF *Abstract* No. 04636, November 1963.

extent of general education at the expense of vocational training. Admitting the values of general education in the employment structure, Paul Lumpp held the opinion that "the 9th year of compulsory schooling must therefore be used for vocational or prevocational training in order to satisfy the ever stiffer requirements of some of the technical trades."[26] General trade union policy had demanded a "second road to education" which would lead those students trained in vocational centers to the open door of the university.

The second road should, by its educational content of social, economic and technical experience, give the same chances as the general school, which through its emphasis on languages, literature and history, mathematics and natural sciences has given us a mistaken, too narrow concept of what education means.[27]

M. N. Skatkin, writing about the relation between instruction and practical work in the USSR, stressed the necessity of an appropriate combination of the two. Like an echo of our early leaders, in a list of principles concerning the problem, he noted that many of the goals and purposes of instruction could be realized in practical work and, for that matter, should be integrated into the framework of practical study. He did not accept it as the core of education, however.

Though practical work is essential it cannot be the center of education, since instruction has to impart much experience drawn from history to supplement personal experience which is an inadequate foundation for vocational life. Crea-

tiveness on a progressive scale is all important. Young people must not work only to orders, which generates mental passivity; they must learn to think independently and to solve technical problems through personal initiative. In this way technical progress will be accelerated.[28]

Similar discussions are reported during 1961-63 in Belgium, Eastern Germany, France, Austria, Canada, and other countries. Hard and fast lines of organization backed up by long tradition were causing adequate development of vocational training in relation to the needs of developing industries. Despite such gains, lack of balance was everywhere indicated as a problem, and the need for expanded vocational education services was compelling. It is notable, however, that in one way or another many leaders were fighting for an adjustment of the general and the practical.

## Organization

During the early 1960's, nations gave attention to a general plan of organization for vocational and technical education. Through agreements by professional groups, labor unions, and a variety of city, district, and national government representatives, the general organization and administration of vocational education was streamlined. The most frequent reason for attention to rapid organization was the pressure of economic need, exhibited largely by shortages of skilled manpower.

In Poland resolutions were adopted that focused attention upon the num-

[26] CIRF *Abstract* No. 05482, December 1963.
[27] CIRF *Abstract* No. 00112, November 1961.
[28] CIRF *Abstract* No. 00637, May 1962.

ber of apprentices in relation to total employees in any particular establishment. A fixed number was not specified by the resolution; instead it required appropriate groups (The Praesidiums of National Councils) to establish minimum ratios.[29] The Warsaw Pedagogical Institute extended the scope of its activities to include vocational and adult education.

The Institute's work in the field of research on the structure and organization of the school system includes research into the problem of the vocational training and further training of teachers.[30]

A committee of the Trade Union's Central Board drew up schemes and courses to promote adult education in part-time schools, to facilitate training and further training of workers.[31]

Sweden moved toward establishment of an optimum number of students per instructor in order to provide closer supervision and to improve the quality of learning.

The basic figure of 16 trainees is valid throughout the vocational [workshop] school system. A change in the number of trainees would necessitate adaptation in regard to the organisation and the equipment of the workshops. Perhaps the solution lies in the use of a senior instructor with assistant instructors. The introduction of such a system has been opposed by the teachers' organisations, as it would constitute different qualifications. These objections could be overcome by reorganising the teaching career and starting at assistant-teacher level. The assistant teach-

ers should be first-class craftsmen and have had a certain amount of training as teachers. In any case, it is necessary to avoid the mistakes of the military system.[32]

In Norway the reorganization of school administration gave much attention to the special requirements of vocational education. The Vocational Training Division had four sections: (1) the office for vocational training in the artisan trades and industry, (2) the office for technical schools, (3) the office for commercial vocational training, and (4) the office for domestic work and feminine crafts. The training of teachers and instructors was assigned to the office for teacher training within the general education division.[33]

France strengthened its organization for vocational guidance,[34] modifying its structure in the Ministry of Education to provide a more direct centralized authority for vocational activities, and focusing attention upon further education for rural populations.[35]

In addition, revision in the structure of the "Electricité de France" technical school at Gurcy-le-Châtel provided a model for electrical schools. Attention was given to vocational, physical, and "human" education. This boarding school of 360 boys, 16 to 18 years of age, provided training periods varying from 1 to 2½ years.

In the sphere of international technical co-operation, the Gurcy school has become a study centre for foreign nationals

[29] CIRF *Abstract* No. 00950, August 1962.
[30] CIRF *Abstract* No. 00309, February 1962.
[31] CIRF *Abstract* No. 04846, November 1963.
[32] CIRF *Abstract* No. 01428, February 1963.
[33] CIRF *Abstract* No. 00361, February 1962.
[34] CIRF *Abstract* No. 00413, February 1962.
[35] CIRF *Abstract* No. 00080, October 1961.

who, on their return to their home country, will be responsible for organising centres for training workers and supervisors in the electrical and electromechanical industries, and for establishing the corresponding pedagogical material. Study visits of about 3 months are arranged for foreign engineers and technicians from Africa, Latin America and the Middle East to familiarise them with the various teaching methods they will subsequently apply in their own country.[36]

Similarly, in the Federal Republic of Germany organizational reviews include evening classes, artisan trades, related instruction, and identification of goals to be achieved in the future.[37]

Extensive revisions in the USSR were reported on a variety of topics: production training in Novosibirsk schools, the role of labor statistics in planning the national economy and training measures, technical progress and vocational training, syllabi and establishment of schools, structure of general education schools providing vocational training, production training in general, liaison between schools and plants, and others.[38] Clearly the USSR undertook a search for new ways to improve the organization for vocational education based upon a critical review of past experience.

## Vocational Guidance, Selection, and Pre-Vocational Training

In 1963, vocational guidance was emphasized as a necessity for the child, adolescent, or young adult in a general resolution by representatives of Austria, Belgium, France, Federal Republic of Germany, Italy, Luxembourg, the Netherlands, and Switzerland. Such services were recommended for youths between the ages of 10 and 25. The school was held to be the institution in the best position to provide the assistance required.

The international consensus was summarized in the following manner:

Guidance services should supply adolescents with occupational information and documentation describing the different occupations and directing them into different lines which will give them the appropriate training. Individual guidance enables the adolescent to choose his future occupation in full knowledge of the different factors involved and practical consequences of his choice.[39]

In addition, the international view suggested that vocational guidance services should be free and that financial support should be provided for non-profit organizations to support their guidance services. It was recommended also that knowledge of the adolescent be obtained not only by psychological testing, but that school marks, health and physical data, and family and social background also be considered. Pleas were made for higher standards among counselors and for the establishment of an "ethical code by competent authorities."

In the USSR, helping the student to choose a trade or occupation at the secondary school level was recommended as a task for a new type of school

---

[36] CIRF *Abstract* No. 01488, February 1963.

[37] CIRF *Abstract* Nos. 00415, 05242, 00963, 00952, 01515, August 1962 to March 1963.

[38] CIRF *Abstract* Nos. 01136, 01589, 00123, 01790, 01754, 01006, 00982, 01212, 01406, 00731, 00211, November 1961 to June 1963.

[39] CIRF *Abstract* No. 01841, September 1963.

combining general and vocational education.[40] Although students were in theory free to choose any trade they wished, in practice the needs of the national economy, and the needs in certain economic areas, placed some priority upon occupational selection.

Inquiries in the Federal Republic of Germany in the fall of 1963 sought to determine how the choice of trade was made by vocational school pupils. The study concluded:

. . . that most of the pupils concerned had made their choice with the help of their parents; the role of the vocational guidance services seems less important than official statistics would give one to believe. The enquiry also revealed that girls often choose a trade which is not typically feminine.[41]

Experiments were also under way with a preparatory basic training year for young persons interested in deciding upon a career. Students who had left school were given practical instruction in a variety of occupational choices. Although the results of the experiment were not made available, it is apparent that the Federal Republic of Germany was engaged in trying out a number of new ideas, including science expositions, in an attempt to determine the nature of deep-seated vocational interests.

In Eastern Germany attention was given to providing a systematic vocational program that would lead to vocational choice in conformity with the need of the economy.[42] In Brazil care-

fully prepared training courses for school teachers and vocational guidance counselors were inaugurated.[43] In Switzerland increased efforts among business establishments, schools and parents were directed toward improving the vocational guidance system.[44]

Similarly in other nations guidance was reported as an imperative contemporary matter in the general improvement of vocational education.

Selection procedures, closely related to vocational guidance, were given attention in several nations. Poland experimented in the use of selection committees to assure a better distribution of students among the various types of schools.[45] The United Kingdom explored the problem of school leavers and the transition from school to work and recommended that:

The youth employment officer should have at least 2 interviews with each school leaver.

Employers should be obliged to report to the Ministry of labor the engagement of anyone under 18, giving details on pay, type of employment, training, and day-release.

The practice of appointing careers masters and mistresses should be encouraged.

The establishment of a national apprenticeship authority through which all young workers can receive training is recommended.

Part-time further education is recommended for all who are under 18 years of age.[46]

Such studies were not unlike those made in the United States; in fact the

---

[40] CIRF *Abstract* No. 00925, August 1962.
[41] CIRF *Abstract* No. 05521, December 1963.
[42] CIRF *Abstract* No. 05384, December 1963.
[43] CIRF *Abstract* No. 01843, September 1963.
[44] CIRF *Abstract* No. 01177, November 1962.
[45] CIRF *Abstract* No. 01772, May 1963.
[46] CIRF *Abstract* No. 01342, January 1963.

reason for studying selection procedures appears to have many identical elements the world over—improvement in the process of matching youth with jobs.

Concern for pre-vocational education in Switzerland, France, Eastern Germany, Italy, Denmark, and the developing countries was evident in a number of reports of reforms and new practices.[47] Such experimentation included reviews of effectiveness of the programs and an analysis of staffing for all branches of vocational education, with special attention given both to apprenticeship and the needs of rural youth.

**Instructors and Teachers**

Preparation of instructors at teacher training institutes in the USSR has been subjected in the 1960's to almost constant review and evaluation. No one system of instructor training appears to be dominant, but all systems have undergone experimentation with the result that in the future basic principles may emerge as standards. Physics teachers are used to teach "work and production" in the electro-technical and electronics fields.[48] This necessitates a highly integrated theory-practice system in order that the desired experiences may be achieved.

The teaching staff of the technical secondary schools is recruited chiefly among engineers. The latter are also required to act as teachers at general education schools for production training. Engineers who are to teach must undergo thorough and methodical pedagogical training.[49]

Follow-up of young instructors in technical schools (technikum) is carried out on a regular basis. Through exchanges of correspondence the instructors continue to receive assistance; their difficulties are studied carefully and answers to particular problems are prompt. The instructor's criticism of their teacher training leads to reforms for future groups of teachers.[50]

I. G. Sandomirskij, USSR, writing about the "instructor's rights and duties," provides some interesting data that may be compared with points of view in the United States. The CIRF *Abstract* is presented in full, as follows:

1. *Preparatory to giving practical training, the instructor must:*
- have drawn up an annual work plan and made a list of tasks that pupils will have to accomplish, bringing together practical training and production work;
- have prepared a schedule of rotation between the various jobs;
- have checked the condition of tools and equipment of the work benches provided for the pupils;
- have made sure that the safety and hygiene conditions of the work are in conformity with the regulations.

2. *During the practical training, the instructor must:*
- give directions to pupils at each of the three stages of the practical training lesson: initiation of the work, actual training processes, analysis of progress achieved and mistakes made;

[47] CIRF *Abstract* Nos. 01647, 04931, 07236, 00442, 00346, 07270, 04426, February 1962 to May 1964.
[48] CIRF *Abstract* No. 00125, November 1961.
[49] CIRF *Abstract* No. 01535, March 1963.
[50] CIRF *Abstract* No. 01699, April 1963.

- make sure that the work carried out by the pupils conforms with technical requirements and that output norms correspond with the time allowed;
- systematically check the level of skill and knowledge acquired by the pupils and take in good time any measures needed to prevent them from acquiring poor working techniques;
- make the maximum use of the pupils' theoretical knowledge;
- get them used to using tools economically and economising in materials and electric current.

3. *The instructor has educational duties to perform in the course of practical training. They are:*

- to develop a spirit of initiative in his pupils, accustom them to checking on their own progress and to using worktime to the full, and to instil in them an interest in and liking for the trade taught;
- to make them respect work discipline and get them used to doing their work conscientiously.

4. *In evaluating his pupils' efficiency, the instructor must check it in 3 ways:*

- regular control of pupils' progress at every lesson;
- observation of their work, examination of objects manufactured by them, oral questioning;
- periodic checks at the end of term (6 months);
- to assess the extent of the pupils' knowledge; the instructor must take into account tests (semestrial) as well as pupils' efficiency, evaluated during the regular progress control at each lesson;
- testing in the form of qualifying examinations at the end of the course.

5. *The instructor's rights.* An instructor may:

- mention daily, before the whole group, the names of the best pupils and give them prizes;
- criticise, before the whole group, any pupils who have not complied with the work discipline, or who have not been sufficiently conscientious in carrying out their tasks; inflict disciplinary sanctions for repeated or premeditated offences;
- combine teaching of theory with practical training, provided he has the appropriate qualifications and has been trained for this purpose;
- sit on the board of adjudicators when pupils are to be promoted.[51]

Prospective teachers have extensive experience in demonstration teaching and also the benefit of review and analysis of their demonstration by competent observers. It is interesting to note that, "The teacher who gave the lesson criticises it, recognising and pointing out its possible defects." [52]

Contemporary needs in the USSR make it imperative that teachers become qualified to teach two or more subjects—for example, biology, chemistry, and basic agriculture, or physics, electro-technics, and the study of machines.[53] Although specialization for teachers is important, and the practice of a teacher learning three trades during his practical training period is becoming common, the problem is by no means resolved, and the Ministry of Education may in the future develop specific criteria to be followed.[54] Modern experimental teaching schools have been established, and the general improvement of pedagogical training is an imperative task.

---

[51] CIRF *Abstract* No. 05419, December 1963.
[52] CIRF *Abstract* No. 05327, December 1963.
[53] CIRF *Abstract* No. 01021, October 1962.
[54] CIRF *Abstract* No. 01620, March 1963.

In the Federal Republic of Germany the aims of vocational school education are clearly defined. Vocational training cannot be separated from the general, and consequently the vocational teacher must be carefully selected and examined during the process of his training.[55]

Pilot studies have been made on the status and the role in society of the vocational school teacher showing that his social status is in a no-man's land in many respects. He is looked down upon because he has not completed a full course of academic studies, and skilled workmen believe him incapable of meeting the demands of economic competition. It is planned that these pilot studies be expanded to a broader sample and subjected to international comparisons.[56]

Today vocational schools are not only expected to impart limited theoretical knowledge in special trades but also to give general education to young people. The effectiveness of teaching depends upon the quality of the teacher. He must be very well acquainted with didactic and teaching methods as applied in vocational schools. Competency in this field cannot be acquired in too brief a period of studies. The vocational school teacher must have also mastered his technical subject well. . . . [He] must have the mental capacity and general education of university students.

Education of teachers needs the atmosphere of a university and must have a special centre in the form of a university institute which has a constant exchange of ideas with all other university activities. Isolation would be detrimental to the education of teachers. In the proposed institute teaching and research should go hand in hand. Didactic and teaching methods of vocational schools require research. Teacher training must also include the study of arts and political subjects. Since, in the future, the vocational school will have the function of selecting the able trainees for further training and studies, additional training for special courses (mathematics, German, etc.) should be taken into consideration.[57]

As said, all nations appear to be sensitive to the needs of teacher education, and a variety of plans and suggestions have been made. The Swiss Vocational Schools Association has proposed accelerated courses in methodology. The Association is opposed to the practice of having one kind of vocational teacher for general knowledge and another for trade knowledge. It suggests three 20-week terms of scientific training and one term of pedagogical training, believes no single type of training will fit all vocational teachers, requests that teaching certificates be given after the examination for teaching for full-time teachers, desires an independent teacher training institution, is satisfied with the contemporary system of training part-time teachers, claims that further training of all teachers is indispensable, and urges expansion of teacher training without delay.[58] Reports from Luxembourg, Poland, Australia, Yugoslavia, Eastern Germany, Sweden, and the United Kingdom cite a variety of needs, make proposals, suggest standards and procedures, and in general demand an upgrading on every front in teaching and teacher education.

---

[55] CIRF *Abstract* No. 01827, September 1963.

[56] CIRF *Abstract* No. 00961, August 1962.

[57] CIRF *Abstract* No. 00774, June 1962.

[58] CIRF *Abstract* No. 01812, September 1963.

## Teaching Methods, Examinations, Research Methods

Teaching methods are a popular subject for discussion the world over. No attempt is made here to document fully all of the observations, suggestions, and results of experiences available from the countries that have expressed views on the subject. Nevertheless, a tremendous amount of data is already available and it continues to build up at an astounding rate. This may occur because instructors everywhere recognize that the methodological phase of industrial education is important. With all of the discussion, however, they apparently hold no hope of resolving the problem of methodology in the near future. A listing of some of the topics, selected at random, may suffice to indicate the nature of the thinking about teaching methods in other nations:

1. The role of lesson plans in adult education.
2. How to teach the mineralogical composition of rocks to future road-building technicians.
3. The role of the instructor in organizing groups for creative technical work.
4. Organizing correspondence courses in industrial training.
5. Teaching new techniques in the metal trades.
6. Principles of syllabus development.
7. Instruction sheet on the teacher's approach to a class.
8. Job files instead of notebooks for practical vocational training.
9. Social and human aspects of training in technical education.
10. Trade journals as teaching aids.
11. Systematic reporting as a method of teaching in industrial arts.
12. Giving a lecture by telephone to a student body.
13. What to do when trainees fail in related instruction classes.
14. How to organize workshop visits from apprentices.
15. "Discussion-Lessons" in a technical secondary school.
16. Teaching methods for mathematics in vocational training.
17. Methodology of practical instruction in the electrical trade.
18. Use of the case method of instruction.
19. Using experimental methods of teaching.
20. Teaching of work science in technical schools.

A much longer list of topics could be made. The use of films and other audio-visual material was described in many settings. Teaching machines, programmed instruction, and automated devices of many classifications have captured the attention of instructors throughout the world. The area of teaching methods is wide open for continued study and research.

Examinations go hand in hand with teaching methods as an item of instructor concern. Student qualifications, achievement, rate of progress, and a host of other elements need to have evaluative treatment; nearly everyone has an idea, and many ideas are projected as having unusual merit. Concern for examination ran the gamut from theoretical approaches to exceedingly simple, practical, easy-to-use methods of reaching evaluative positions.

Although research in industrial education in other nations occupies a high status position among educators, comparatively little research appears to be underway. On the other hand the activity of CIRF seems to have produced some rather substantial projects in other nations, and CIRF itself is gearing up to engage in comprehensive research on a broad scale.

A listing of a few of the reports of research will indicate in part the kinds of studies other nations are including in their program.

1. Development of a structure for vocational training research. (Poland)
2. The psychological factors in vocational education and aspects of new occupations. (USSR)
3. A study of methods used by pupils in independent study (correspondence courses). (USSR)
4. Learning curves and the impact of different teaching methods. (Sweden)
5. Training for perceptual skills. (United Kingdom)
6. Extension of experimental work in teaching. (USSR)
7. Organization of methodological research in technical secondary schools. (USSR)
8. Effectiveness of training provided for future technician mechanics. (Poland)
9. Reasons why building trades trainees abandon their courses. (Poland)
10. A teaching experiment of alternated school and plant training. (Federal Republic of Germany)

In nations having a background of industrial training over a long period of time, one finds rather extensive progress in the study of teaching methods, in concern for examinations, and in research development. In the nations where industrial training has been formalized only recently, there is some evidence of concern for these three areas and a desire to develop rapidly.

### Training Facilities, Equipment, Teaching Aids[59]

*Training Facilities.* One of the significant contributions in industrial education for the developing countries is a publication entitled *Model of a Skilled Workers' School.* The book, written by Jurgen A. Wissing and published in 1944, contains plans for the metal trades. Prepared as a guide for experts in developing countries, the material was based on experience gained in Asia, Africa, and Latin America. The guide is complete from the standpoint of shop arrangements, tools, equipment lists, curriculum, staffing, and materials.

A new training course, Service-Station School, announced in June, 1964, was attached to a vocational school at Braunschweig, Federal Republic of Germany. The school proposes to correct defects in the training of pump attendants. It represents a new service to an industry in need of assistance. The program includes minor repairing in addition to complete automobile servicing.

On March 7, 1963, the Institute for

---

[59] The resource material for this section consisted of the CIRF *Abstracts* (Section 14) for the years 1961-64. No attempt has been made to document the specific facts by reference to a particular abstract. All quoted material is, however, related to data found in Section 14.

Industrial Reconstruction announced the opening of new training facilities at Naples, Italy. Instruction was provided in fitting, welding, carpentry, milling, and turning. In addition, drafting, chemistry, and physics laboratories were provided. A gymnasium and theatre provided recreational facilities. The training facility complex was set in an attractive environment of lawns and trees; similar centers have been planned for Genoa, Trieste, Taranto, Terni, and Milan. "The purpose of all of them is to train young people from both the human and technical point of view. This contribution to vocational training will be of special importance in South Italy in creating suitable conditions for economic and social development."

In 1962 a Polish mining school developed a special gallery, constructed above ground, for training young miners and apprentices under 17 who are not allowed to go underground. This training facility provides a realistic environment for introductory training. "In the training galleries the theoretical part of this subject [gasses] can be supplemented by actual testing for the presence of gasses introduced for this purpose."

A research center, founded in 1962 in the Netherlands as a non-profit organization, "aims at gathering, elaborating, increasing, and spreading knowledge about data processing." Courses, lectures, syllabi, and a variety of teaching aids are provided. The center's program is flexible to allow short and long-term conferences for managers and professional directors, and a range of symposia for employees.

The Production Engineering Research Association (United Kingdom) reported successful experiences with a new training facility in the form of a mobile demonstration unit using instructional films and a choice of 17 sessions. The mobile unit, operating since 1954, provided 6,860 sessions to 1962, for 130,000 works (factory) personnel.

Training centers in the Federal Republic of Germany have expanded facilities in the form of special advanced programs for employed workers and have experimented with special training centers under the sponsorship of chambers of commerce. A strong case was presented in February, 1962, in relation to the need for the establishment of a documentation center for vocational training in West Germany.

"The tasks of a documentation Centre would be to make available to all interested parties comprehensive information about the development of vocational training to be used within undertakings in schools, courses, etc., and to supply the basic material for scientific work, teaching, etc. This is an important and urgent need."

*Equipment.* A variety of equipment for specialized training has been reported in other nations as a means of improving instruction. In Poland new equipment was devised to improve teaching standards in schools training drivers of motor vehicles. In the United Kingdom a portable foundry was developed for classroom demonstration of foundry processes. It is especially adaptable to industrial situations in engineering, in technical schools, and in the science departments of secondary schools. Auxiliary equipment for machine shop operators was introduced in the Netherlands in

March, 1962. "Auxiliary apparatuses do not replace normal machine tools, but they make it possible to learn to operate them with speed and understanding. Trainees show great interest and participate in working with the apparatuses. Learning is intensified. Results are better than with the current methods of instruction."

*Teaching Aids.* Reports of training aids describe numerous devices, many with unique features, that have been found to be successful.

Review of the CIRF *Abstracts* reveals examples such as teaching machines and programmed teaching in Norway, and peg boards for transistor circuits in East Germany. A technical college crew in the USSR has created special types of teaching machines— "During the academic year 1963-64 a large number of teachers will be given the opportunity to become familiar with the machines."

In Switzerland an illustrated horological dictionary in four languages (French, German, English, and Spanish) was published in 1962, for horologists, traders, factory employees, retailers, instructors, and laymen. The first edition contained about 4,500 items.

The Moscow Technical-Scientific Public Library (USSR) prepared bibliographical lists of new techniques for workers who desired to upgrade their knowledge about their occupational area. These aids were prepared because of the inherent difficulty people have in keeping up to date with current literature. Expansion of the service was anticipated.

Use of professional literature in practical vocational training was urged in East Germany. "Vocational instruc-tors must understand the importance of making extensive use of professional literature and other printed material. In particular, the use of professional literature is an important means of educating the trainees for independent work."

### European Summary

The European view of industrial education, as reflected from the analysis of CIRF *Abstracts,* consists of a review of contemporary developments related to eight major categories:

1. Vocational training systems in general.
2. Economic, technical, and social aspects.
3. Relationship between education and training.
4. Organization.
5. Vocational guidance, selection, and pre-vocational training.
6. Instructors and teachers.
7. Teaching methods, examinations, research methods.
8. Training facilities, equipment, teaching aids.

It seemed best not to attempt to sketch the historical development of industrial education in each country. See early chapters for some related influences.

The nations with well established programs of industrial education are devoting much effort to improvements throughout—in national laws, in administration and supervision, in buildings, in financing, in teacher education, in instructional materials, in student selection, and in still other areas. A distinct tendency to secure some consensus in methodology, in content, and in organization is observed. This is

474

particularly true in the countries sustaining the common market because of the advantages similar efforts have in the free exchange of labor. The movement toward quality and excellence in the many facets of industrial education is evident in all of the established programs.

The developing nations have had the benefit of aid from established programs throughout the world. At no previous time has so much attention been devoted to industrial education, throughout the world, nor has the relationship of a nation's economic stability to its industrial education ever been so pronounced as it is now.

### Latin America
### The Charter of Punta del Este

The educational goals of twenty Latin-American countries are set forth in the Charter of Punta del Este, 1961, which identified also the crucial role of education in the achievement of the objectives of the Alliance for Progress.[60]

From 1955 to 1965, the population of Latin America increased at approximately 2.6 percent annually and is expected to reach a total of about 200 million persons by 1970. In 1960 about 41.1 percent of the population was under 15 years of age.

More than fifty percent of the population was engaged in agriculture in 1950; but the migration of rural masses to the industries of the cities has increased at a rapid rate.

The bottleneck resulting from the defective agrarian structure accounts in good part for the paralysis of Latin American development, because it leaves millions of human beings outside the consumer circuit, with little purchasing power or opportunity to change.[61]

The Charter of Punta del Este places importance upon the study of population and economic and social factors as a means of developing long-term objectives for educational progress. Cultural imbalance, changes in occupational patterns, social barriers, and health and nutrition are important factors requiring consideration in preparing for future educational programs.

A study made in 1960 found that the school dropout rate was high; retention of learning was low; 44 percent of the teachers were uncertificated; teachers' salaries were low ("barely sufficient to cover their most basic needs"); teacher training programs had serious shortcomings. And yet the situation had been even worse; progress was being made.

**Industrial Education.** Of the nearly 4 million students enrolled in secondary schools in Latin America in 1960, 9 percent were enrolled in industrial schools, 15 percent in commercial schools, 1 percent in agricultural schools, and 2 percent in home economics courses; but 73 percent were enrolled in normal schools and general secondary schools. "Obviously, a sound policy of vocational training and technical education is of paramount importance for economic and

---

[60] See: Organization of American States, Inter-American Economic and Social Council, special meeting at the ministerial level, Punta del Este, Uruguay, 1961, Alliance for Progress: Official Documents. Washington, D. C., Pan American Union, 1961, Resolution A. 1.

[61] *Third Inter-American Meeting of Ministers of Education*, Bogota, Colombia, August 4-10, 1963. Washington: Pan American Union, 1964, p. 10.

social development . . ."[62] The shortage of industrial technicians accounted largely for the low industrial productivity and for the poor quality of manufactured products. The problem, however, was not simple; attempts to solve it had to take into account a variety of factors, all in the developmental stage and in short supply: organization, teachers, supervisory personnel, vocational guidance, textbooks, buildings, laboratories, and money. These elements could be obtained only with general social development.

## Goals for Vocational and Technical Education

One of the results of the Third Inter-American Meeting of the Ministers of Education was a statement of goals for education. The goals for vocational and technical education were described as follows:

1. Technical education and vocational training in various fields should be included as a basic element in the general economic and social development plans of the countries.
2. Vocational training and the training of middle-level technicians should be an integral part of the educational system of a country. Coordination between these two and other branches of intermediate education is essential.
3. An essential requirement for admission to vocational training courses should be successful completion of primary education and, for middle-level technicians, completion of the common basic post-primary cycle.
4. The two sexes should be given equal access to technical education and vocational training.
5. The second cycle of intermediate education should preferably be used for technical training in various specific fields,

[such as] industry, commerce, and agriculture. Students who complete these courses of study, like those in other branches of education, should have the possibility of going on to higher education.
6. The objective with regard to occupational level should be clearly determined, for the training of both technicians and skilled workers.
7. [In addition to solid technical knowledge] technical and industrial schools in Latin America should provide the individual with a general culture equivalent to that provided by the other branches of intermediate education; they should [also] prepare him to direct work, administer resources, and, in certain cases, teach his staff.
8. Trade schools, also, should give students a general cultural background and help them to develop the skills, abilities, and work habits that will fit them to become efficient workers.
9. In order to overcome the present shortage of skilled manpower and to ensure adequate training in industrial techniques, in addition to systematic vocational training, preferential attention should also be given to other types, such as on-the-job training for young people, and basic, complementary, or highly specialized training for adult workers.
10. It is suggested that the agencies in charge of technical education cooperate with and give technical assistance to employers, labor organizations, and other institutions that intend to carry out training programs for workers.
11. Because of the close relationship between technical education and work, employers and labor organizations should be encouraged to give advice on orientation and development of plans. Among other advantages, this will ensure that financial support is forthcoming from the various sectors of production.
12. Efforts must be made to foster the collaboration of private business firms: apart from the undeniable financial advantages the schools will be most efficient

[62] *Ibid.*, p. 28.

476

if they adapt their methods, equipment, and specialities to the requirements of industry, which in turn would benefit by receiving workers and technicians trained in the skills it needs.

13. Industrial and commercial firms situated near trade schools can help them, first by providing machines, tools, and workshop or laboratory equipment that is badly needed by most of them, but no longer of use to the firms, and second by giving students the opportunity to do practice work in their plants and offices.

14. It is especially recommended that governments of countries having developed systems of technical education create "study centers" to promote educational research and training of teachers for trade schools, technological and scientific research, and to foster the preparation and specialized training of technicians and skilled workers. These activities should be carried out independently in specialized institutes, but they should be coordinated.

15. Each school should have scholastic and vocational guidance services to counsel students in regard to existing educational opportunities, employment possibilities, and the special branch for which they are best suited.

16. It is suggested that courses should be organized to train "bachilleres" (academic secondary school graduates) who have not been able to follow university studies, in technical work . . . that does not call for a high degree of special training, such as that of foremen, and jobs in production control, sales, and procurement, as chemical assistants, in industrial public relations, and so on, or in very definite specialities.[63]

These goals are cited out of the context of the total purposes and expectations of the Ministers of Education, who included specifications for the related necessities, such as administra-tion, teacher education, and buildings.

*Immediate Action Projects.* Once the goals to be achieved had been outlined, attention was turned to specific tasks that needed immediate attention. Complete implementation of these tasks would in some instances require several years. Nevertheless the Ministers proposed projects to be studied by "experts," who were to design the means of solving particular problems.

Many of the 25 projects which were defined cut across, or have implications for, industrial education, but one of the projects was defined specifically for the field. This project was titled "Middle-Level Technical Education, Project No. 11." Its provisions were:

a. That middle-level education be strengthened and diversified through the provision of suitable equipment for workshops and laboratories and the training of teachers who will use such equipment.

b. That special attention be given to technical and agricultural schools so that they may produce sufficient skilled middle-level personnel to give impetus to agrarian reforms and industrial development.[64]

A study of technical education in Latin America by Ernesto F. Babino attempts to deal with the specific problems of each nation because the extreme variation and great differences among the countries makes generalizations of little value.[65]

## Significance of Activities in Latin America

The countries of Latin America fall broadly in the category of developing

---

[63] *Ibid.*, pp. 73-74.

[64] *Ibid.*, p. 93.

[65] Ernesto F. Babino, *Estudio Comparado de la Education Technica en America Latina.* Washington: Pan American Union, 1963.

nations. The needs of each are general and the total development of these nations involves many considerations outside the realm of industrial education, but such education clearly is an imperative aspect of national development. In fact economic progress depends upon the development of industrial education to such a great extent that failure at this point would doom the entire proposal.

There is a parallel between the stated goals of the Ministers of Education in Latin America and the goals of industrial education in the United States. Obviously the Ministers were influenced strongly by U.S. developments; however, the goals were accepted as being appropriate for Latin America. Of course, principles of industrial education in the United States would apply in Latin America. But tremendous differences in resources for implementing the principles occur. In view of these differences, the situation can be understood only by one who takes full account of the social and economic structure of each nation and its goals.

## United States Personnel in Other Nations

Since the end of World War II, hundreds of industrial educators from the United States have worked in many developing nations. Actual assistance has taken many forms from purely advisory to on-the-spot instruction in specific courses or occupational areas, especially for countries committed to industrial and technical development.

1. One area of assistance was concerned with the general industrial ori-

entation of youth in school. Reaching this objective required the adaptation of industrial arts instruction to the general school program. In many instances introducing industrial arts instruction was a part of the total educational development rather than a revision of existing patterns. Generalizations concerning the actual trends of development of industrial arts in other nations would be difficult to make and most likely misleading because of the numerous special or unique educational situations represented by these nations. However, the general goals were associated with the development of "mechanical" or "industrial" intelligence among students.

2. A second major area of assistance was related to systems of industrial instruction leading directly to employment in the new industries of developing countries.

In both cases success depended first upon strengthening the general program of education in order to have a base upon which industrial, trade, and technical education programs could be built.

Industrial educators were recruited from the total resources of the United States by many organizations having concern for international problems. UNESCO, ILO (International Labor Organization), private foundations, the United States Department of State, the United States Office of Education, the Agency for International Development, religious organizations, and many other groups including the World Bank sought the services of men in the programs of their special interests. Because of the variety of methods of recruitment, it is virtually impossible to cite specific facts and figures con-

478

cerning the numbers of persons involved, their length of service, and the nature and location of their work. The situation becomes even more complex because some of the agencies contracted with educational institutions to send teams to other nations. Thus contributions tended to "pile up."

There is no one central source of information to provide data related to this vast program. Even within a single agency, such as the Agency for International Development, it is not possible to ferret out specific data concerning industrial educators and their contributions. The agencies have been concerned with other areas of assistance so that the data about industrial education is lost within the complexity of the total endeavors. Some exceptions did occur, however. Information is available on agencies with special projects of an industrial character.

Generally the story of the activities of industrial educators can be told only by reference to isolated experiences of persons who have chosen to write or speak about their work in other nations. Without more encompassing records no sound evaluation of the work can be made; in fact it might be too early to make an accurate determination of long-term gains for any of the nations concerned, even if better records were available.

## Summary

The roots of industrial education in the United States are found in the educational histories of other nations. American pioneers in industrial education studied them carefully. The program that evolved in the United States is somewhat eclectic; no one national system was used as a pattern. Many practices and philosophies have been combined and thoroughly adapted to meet the needs of American industry and technology, so the contemporary program of industrial education in the United States has a character that is distinct from that of programs in other nations.

Current programs of industrial education in other nations are exceedingly important to the United States because they increasingly represent vitally needed attempts to solve complex industrial problems on an international basis, and because of the opportunity for industrial educators in the United States to participate in the programs of the developing countries.

A bright spot marks the work of the International Vocational Training Information and Research Center, CIRF, located at Geneva, Switzerland. The Center, established in 1961 as a part of the International Labor Organization, ILO, has embarked upon a comprehensive program of documentation and research which can produce instructional standards for industrial education. The Center is sensitive to the many factors that determine the nature of industrial education: economic and social change, automation and technology, labor needs and requirements, and similar basics. From the documentation provided by CIRF, it is possible to develop a tenable point of view about the status and trends of the international program.

CIRF provides documentation for 15 different categories of vocational education. Eight of these categories were selected for review, and only the references related to industrial education were used. These categories are:

479

- Vocational training systems in general.
- Economic, technical, and social aspects.
- Relationships between education and training.
- Organization.
- Vocational guidance, selection, prevocational training.
- Instructors and teachers.
- Teaching methods, examinations, research methods.
- Training facilities, equipment, teaching aids.

The awakening of Latin America to the need for industrial education furnishes a fascinating prospect for future gains. Goals have been established by the Ministers of Education, and action programs are under way.

The prospect is strong that industrial educators in the United States may participate to a greater extent in these projects. Many industrial educators from the United States have served abroad in various capacities, particularly in the new developing nations. A thorough, documented appraisal of the nature, extent, and current status of their contributions unfortunately does not exist. It seems certain, however, that the work of these educators is vital to the future development of industrial education in the United States, since this development can hardly be effective without knowledge and understanding of the international scene.

### Recall Questions

1. Identify the German educator who influenced industrial education during its formative years in the United States.
2. Describe the program and purposes of CIRF.
3. Summarize the key points in each of the eight categories described for the international program of industrial education.
4. What organization is the prime mover for the potential development of industrial education in Latin America? What are its goals?

### Research Questions

1. Using issues of the CIRF magazine, *Training for Progress*, summarize what has been written on the following themes:

- Technical change.
- Glimpses of the future.
- Changing policies.
- Planning ahead.
- Group training.
- Research.

2. Using the CIRF *Abstracts*, develop a paper about industrial education for any nation of your choice. Refer to all 15 categories for which information is available.

### Suggestions for Further Reading

Although isolated references to industrial education may be found in educational journals of the United States, the most significant and up-to-date documentation for other nations may be found in the *Abstracts* and other publications of the International Vocational Training Information and Research Center, CIRF, Geneva, Switzerland. Research-oriented industrial educators should possess the publications of CIRF. Write to:

International Vocational Training
   Information and Research Center
   c/o International Labor Office

917 15th St. NW
Washington, D.C. 20005

# Chapter 17

# Summary and a Look Ahead

Social Emphasis · Emergence of the Industrial Education Enterprise · Dependency upon Professional Association · Significance
of Federal Leadership · Teacher Education: The Cornerstone
· Milestones · A View from the Crystal Ball

A study of the history of industrial education provides a fascinating insight into fundamental values of education and points toward the fulfillment of democracy's desire to educate all of its people. Industrial education has been close to the mainstream of American life and has reflected the needs of the great mass of the American people. During our early national period attention was focused upon making the common learnings freely available to all of the people. Later, extension of educational opportunities beyond the grammar school became an obsession, but required nearly a century to achieve. Parallel to educational progress in general we find the evidences of industrial education development.

Our changing orientation from an agrarian to an industrial economy brought into focus the desirability of industrial education. With the spread of formal education came the desire of the masses for educational consideration of their occupational needs. In the early years of the nineteenth century, agricultural societies flourished throughout the nation. Deliberate attempts were made to share information for the benefit of all and thereby increase the productive capacity of the farms. In time the need for such information exceeded the ability of the societies to provide it. Soon there was talk about agricultural schools, and in 1862 the Congress, in passing the Morrill Land Grant Act, sought to provide in part for this need by establishing Agricultural and Mechanical Colleges in each of the states. Similarly the mechanics had developed institutes, which they supported vigorously, in an attempt to provide a means of meeting the requirements of an advancing industrial economy. In time these efforts, noble as they were, failed to make adequate provision, and the industrialists turned to the Congress for legislation to support industrial education in the secondary schools. It was not until 1917 that their efforts bore fruit in the form of the Smith-Hughes Act.

Labor had worked continuously throughout the nineteenth century for more and better education in the common school, and later turned its support toward its particular needs in the secondary school. It supported the National Society for the Promotion of Industrial Education and for a decade encouraged Congress in the legislation which ultimately resulted in 1917 to promote and develop industrial education in the secondary school.

Three basic threads, visible throughout our history, have had direct bearing upon the development of industrial education in the public schools: the growing importance of education in general, the change in the basic economy of the nation, and the activities of labor.

### Duality of Industrial Education

Throughout this treatment of the history of industrial education, the generic term "industrial education" has been thought of as having two parts. Part one consists of Manual Training, Manual Arts, and Industrial Arts. Part two consists of Trade and Industrial Education, and Technical Education. In effect the two parts become a continuum providing industrial education experiences from the elementary school through two years of post-high school educational experience. This might appear to oversimplify the study of industrial education, and to a certain extent it does. But the historical record has a habit of clouding the issue at times, making clear cut delineations of the two parts impossible. To make the

situation even more difficult both parts were derived from the same roots; at certain historical periods we are concerned with identical twins and at others with members of the same family group.

### Nature of the Summary

I have chosen in the summary to emphasize impressions, to develop certain trends, and to call attention to issues that have fundamental significance in the historical period of industrial education. I make no attempt to follow the main text chapter by chapter, but instead I follow the general development of the text, choosing my major areas of emphasis to reflect a personal bent—the net result of 25 years of the study of industrial education. But, let's get on with the story, starting with early evidences.

### Social Emphasis

Articles of pottery and bronze were made in abundance by Greek craftsmen and, with the advent of colonial expansion and the Aegean trade, were transported to distant shores. Increase in manufacturing provided employment for larger numbers of craftsmen. A high point in craftsmanship was reached during the period of Pericles (460-429 B.C.). Increased earnings made it possible for craft clubs to develop and for some of the craftsmen to enjoy a rather high social position. The wealth of Greece depended in a large part upon the development and recognition of craftsmanship. Economic gains by workers raised standards of living.

The relationship between social development and craftsmanship was apparently well known at least a millennium earlier than the "Golden Age of Greece," but a long time would pass before man became important as man, even though the product of his skill was important to economic development. The elements of industrial education, exemplified characteristically by the father-son-family relationship, were found in the slave or near-slave existence of the masses of the people. But artistry in copper, iron, stone, pottery, and building construction continued to show up over a vast geographical area. Rome, Ephesus, and even the caravanserai, along the ancient trade routes of present day Turkey, displayed remarkable advancement of craftsmanship which was somehow taught and passed on to the next generation.

Though there were many interesting and significant relationships between industrial education and social development in the Middle Ages and the Renaissance, the big gain did not develop until the beginning of modern industry with its factories and mass production. Industrialization began in England around 1750, and during the next century and a half, it spread around the world. Booming industrial cities developed which destroyed rural industry of the home, and men began to work together in large numbers rather than as individuals or small family groups. But again one notes the close relationship of social well-being and the ability to produce the goods and services needed by a new industrial economy.

Spinning replaced hand weaving, steam power replaced the sail and the horse; steel production, coal mining, transportation, and communication were revolutionized under the impact of industrialism. The effect upon the people was astonishing. A quiet rural agricultural life gave way to crowded cities with slums, unsanitary living and working conditions, long hours of employment, child labor, exploitation of women, malnutrition, and disease. The situation got worse before it began to change for better social conditions. Education for the masses of the workers was almost non-existent.

Little by little attempts were made to correct the extensive social injustices. Jean Jacques Rousseau challenged the evils of society and urged a return to nature in order that man regain his liberty and happiness. Utopian schemes were suggested, tried, and discarded. Leadership in factory reform came from Robert Owen, a mill owner in Scotland, who provided adequate wages, good working conditions, houses for workers, and schools for their children. He was instrumental in promoting governmental reforms in Parliament. Later when his reform interests were broadened he tried a social experiment in New Harmony, Indiana. These efforts of 1825 and a few years thereafter failed because the effort was directed at only a part of the problem of workers as a whole.

During our colonial period industrial education was manifest largely in the apprenticeship system. It was well regulated by colonial laws and provided the age-old values of apprenticeship—food, clothing, shelter, religious training, common schooling, trade instruction, and related technical instruction. Apprenticeship was a social device which honored the basic rights of man. But these social values fell before the onslaught of industrialism

483

in the United States. The social plight of industrial workers in America was somewhat akin to that in England. The American people were faced also with the necessity of social reform.

Concurrently with the social conditions of advancing industry, America moved toward the development of free public schools. The idea of universal public education became accepted and did in part provide the basic ingredient of the goal of an "educated" labor force. But it did little to provide actual instruction of an industrial education nature.

[Note: An interesting parallel to the need for education in the early years of the nineteenth century occurred in the 1960's as an outgrowth of the Manpower Development and Training Act. Attack upon the hard core unemployment problems forced organization of classes in reading, writing, and arithmetic for unemployed adults—illiteracy has never been a very good starting point for making people employable.]

Few people complained about the lack of industrial education in the public schools during the first half of the nineteenth century. The needs, such as they were, became the responsibilities of a variety of societies, assemblies, associations, and institutes, sponsored by the initiative of workers themselves. They satisfied their industrial education need by special classes and lectures. The General Society of Mechanics and Tradesmen, established in New York in 1785, is an example of the emergence of these efforts; it is of particular interest because it is still active. A similar institution—also still active—was the San Francisco Mechanics Institute, established in 1855, only five years after California was admitted to the Union.

There was little industry in California at that time, but a handful of industrialists looked toward the future and began the arduous task of providing by their own means the industrial education needed by the growing state.

Many such institutions developed in the United States, and although they gave attention to industrial education they also made provision for the well-being of their members. Only a few of these institutions survived, and those that remained changed their educational bent in accord with the general development of public education in the United States. Corporation schools also provided instruction in relation to the corporate needs; this was still another part of the total development of industrial education.

Concern for the social plight of ethnic groups has long been a characteristic of industrial education. The historical record abounds with evidence of attention to the needs of Negroes, Italians, Spanish Americans, American Indians, and other groups. At one time special schools and youth organizations were provided for various ethnic groups, and industrial education was a part of their instructional program. Hampton Institute, one of the earliest trade schools, was established with the intent of assisting Negro youth to find its rightful place in society. But society changes, and with the change great concern developed for man, as man, without regard to race, creed, or color.

It is interesting to note that the vocational education acts were developed in their basic structure without ethnic classification. Their provisions applied to Negro schools on the same basis as to other schools. Consequently, social adjustment (civil rights) in the 1960's proceeded without any major changes in industrial education. Such education was already intended for people of all ethnic groups.

The intent here is to point out in summary form that industrial education is a social process and that its social roots extend back to very early historical periods. Industrial education performs a social function in interpreting the industrial environment, in assisting students to take full advantage of knowledge of the impact and influence of technology, and in providing experience in basic industrial skills of value in the cultural mores of contemporary society. Industrial education also provides an essential social service by (1) providing direct instruction leading to employment, and (2) providing instruction for employed (and unemployed) workers so that they can keep up with the technology of their area and thereby become mobile with the increasing technical requirements of industry. Industrial education deals directly with the ability of persons to become independent economic units, the social consequences of which are far reaching and obvious.

## Emergence of the Industrial Education Enterprise

Following the Civil War and the Reconstruction period, a variety of forces developed which created the environment for industrial education. Westward migration was accelerated and thousands of persons moved into areas which had previously been uninhabited by white men. By 1890 the Census Bureau said it could no longer distinguish a frontier and declared officially that

such areas no longer existed. Railroads pushed into these lands and a semblance of industry sprang up. Industrialism grew rapidly in the populated areas and exerted an influence felt far and wide.

The impact of industrial and social changes made it clear that education must be expanded and brought within reach of all persons—the progress of democracy was at stake. By 1870 there were approximately 500 free public high schools in the nation. This number increased to over 6,000 by the end of the century. Similarly, about two percent of the students of high school age were in school in 1870, but by 1900 this figure had increased to about nine percent. New conceptions of educational need were in order. Older ideas, which had served society so long and so well were no longer tenable. Committees and commissions pondered the problem and prepared reports, and general controversy developed over the direction and content of education. Into this controversy, strongly supported on the one hand and violently opposed on the other, industrial education made its debut.

Educational developments abroad had a strong effect upon American educators. A new kind of education, compounded of the ideas of Johann Pestalozzi and Friedrich Froebel, was introduced into the schools of Finland in 1886 by Uno Cygnaeus. This new manual work, involving wood, metal, and basket-weaving, became a compulsory phase of education in Finland, and in 1872 a sloyd school to train teachers was established. The program of Cygnaeus did not have the trade orientation advocated by Rousseau, nor did it have as its basic

485

purpose the sense-perception of Pestalozzi; the manual activities were a form of educational expression calculated to release the creative abilities of children. The idea spread to other countries of Europe and eventually took root in the educational growth of America.

Three men made significant contributions to the development of a manual activities type of education in the United States. John D. Runkle, who was inspired by the Russian exhibit at the Centennial Exposition in 1876; Calvin M. Woodward, who developed preliminary ideas between 1872 and 1878, and who, with the assistance of business men and industrial leaders in St. Louis, founded the Manual Training School in 1880; and Gustav Larsson, who came to Boston from Sweden in 1886 to start a sloyd school, were the early motivators. The educational climate was good. The programs prospered, but a strong current of opposition appeared from educators who denied the existence of educational and intellectual values in these manual activities. But manual training and sloyd were introduced into the public educational system. The critics actually assisted in the process because they caused the manual training leaders to look sharply at their educational program.

One prominent educational leader who came to the aid of the program was John Dewey. He wrote in the May, 1913, issue of *Vocational Education* that the question of industrial education had great consequences for the future of democracy—its right treatment would make public education "truly democratic," and its wrong treatment would accentuate "undemocratic tendencies." When the vocational significance of industrial education came into full view, labor vigorously supported its development and promoted its interest.

What was industrial education like around the turn of the century? Was it educational? Intellectual? Vocational? Apparently it was all of these and more. The writers of the period didn't always take the trouble to explain, but then, such was the nature of the industrial education movement. Some industrial educators were staunch supporters of educational and intellectual values. They ignored tendencies to use the manual training experiences as preparation for employment. Other educators faced the problem more realistically and little by little stimulated the idea that some positive steps should be taken to provide for occupational preparation in industrial education, rather than to leave the matter to chance. This idea was aided by a study of industrial education in Massachusetts in 1905.

An Act of the Massachusetts legislature in 1905 authorized Governor William L. Douglas to appoint a commission to study the nature of industrial education and the need for it, and to make recommendations concerning the responsibility for providing such education. The commission consulted with a large group of people in the United States and abroad and published its report in June, 1906. This document marked a turning point. (In fact it is frequently referred to as a history-making document.) Massachusetts became the first state to adopt a system of free industrial education. Other states followed and the vocational side of industrial education began to receive attention. But some industrial educators were still not satis-fied—they wanted the movement to be national in scope.

Accordingly a group of industrial educators met in June, 1906, in New York City, to take some positive action, and out of this meeting came the Na-tional Society for the Promotion of In-dustrial Education. The Society in a careful review and study of the many facets of industrial education, and with the wholehearted support of labor, in eleven years secured the passage of the Smith-Hughes Act, giving national rec-ognition to the movement. The pro-ceedings of the annual meetings of the Society, and its many special publica-tions, comprise the primary literature of vocational-industrial education. Principles determined during this pe-riod have withstood the test of time.

This is the way things stood in 1917. First, we had a program of industrial arts which had emerged from manual arts and manual training. Its efforts were primarily educational but it was multi-purpose in nature. The program was growing and becoming more so-phisticated as time moved on. It was swept into the curriculum in a minor wave of enthusiasm for things of prac-tical significance, and it appeared to have developed along the lines of the educational temperament of the time. In a way the movement could be thought of as reactionary in order to contrast a break with the so-called tra-ditional curriculum. Second, the ground work had been prepared for a full-scale program of trade education. It was created by industrial arts educa-tors in order to focus attention upon the much needed vocational aspects of industrial education. Prior to the pas-sage of the Smith-Hughes Act a few states made significant moves toward a vocational emphasis upon industrial education, but the Act brought all of the states into the plan. It has been de-termined by the Commission on Na-tional Aid to Vocational Education that the vocational problem was a national problem and needed such stimulation as could come from national legisla-tion.

So, as we moved toward the 1920's, industrial education faced many prob-lems of organization and operation, and some of these problems would become the concern of professional as-sociations.

## Dependency upon Professional Association

The first professional teachers' or-ganizations were developed in the United States in the period 1830-1850. Rhode Island was the first to organize a state association in 1845. There were, of course, a number of other organiza-tions composed largely of public-spirited citizens who were interested in the general development of educa-tion, but professional advancement came from teachers who organized to consider the problems of the profes-sion. The National Education Associa-tion traces its beginnings to the year 1857. Some of the professional associa-tions published journals as a means of taking educational ideas and ideals to all members. The progress of public education depended in part upon professional organizations. It is not sur-prising therefore that industrial edu-cators would seek to develop ways and means to meet in professional groups. There were common professional needs and only through group consideration

487

could these needs have adequate attention.

As the manual training movement advanced, it was common to find local groups of manual training and drawing teachers forming associations. Frequently these became statewide in nature due to the fact that many schools had only one manual training teacher. Activities were varied and some of these associations produced deep-seated concern for purely professional activities. Nearly all, however, capitalized upon socialization among group members as a means of reaching their principal objectives.

During the formative years of industrial education, the annual meetings of the National Education Association became the professional proving ground. The proceedings of NEA of the 1880's and 90's contain most of the record of professional activity in industrial education. A department of industrial education was organized by NEA in 1875. For many years thereafter a surprising amount of the total professional discussion of education was related to industrial education.

The art motif of manual arts brought teachers into the Eastern Arts Association and the Western Arts Association. For many years the majority of the members of these two associations were composed of manual arts teachers. The professional purposes were highly oriented toward industrial concerns. Manual training needed the influence of art, and association of manual arts teachers in the arts associations was urged by some leaders in the field of manual arts. The wedding of art and manual arts was never really accomplished. There were obvious differences of concentrated interest, and

as the association grew larger and tended to departmentalize, the two groups drifted apart. But there was some common ground, and the arts associations did provide significant professional challenge toward understanding the nature of art in manual arts.

When the National Society for the Promotion of Industrial Education was formed, it became the center around which the vocational aspects of industrial education developed. The society grew strong in membership and influence (its counterparts were reflected in many new state associations), and manual arts educators were involved as an integral part of the society. In fact one can get the impression that NSPIE provided more of a professional home for manual arts educators than did the arts associations. It is significant, however, to note that the professional attention of manual arts educators was divided.

Although the National Society professed nationwide interests, it was made up largely of persons who resided along the Atlantic coast. The desire for professional expression was strong among the vocational educators of the Middle West, and in 1914 an organization known as the Vocational Education Association of the Middle West was formed. Now two groups competed for the allegiance of largely the same group of educators. With the passage of the Smith-Hughes Act, the NSPIE changed its name to the National Society for Vocational Education. Almost concurrently with these developments the NEA department changed its name to the Department of Vocational Education, and there was no indication by organizational name of the existence of a professional group of industrial arts educators. Actually they did participate in these organizations and looked to them as a professional base. When the two vocational associations joined in 1925 to form the American Vocational Association, a vice presidency was established for industrial arts in AVA, giving it an equal status with the other areas of emphasis.

It was not until just prior to World War II that any attempt was made to form a national organization of industrial arts educators. These efforts were continued after the war, but it was not until January 1, 1961, that a full-time executive secretary was appointed for the American Industrial Arts Association. AIAA is a department of NEA. Since 1961 the professionalization of industrial arts has moved forward at a rapid pace.

One of the professional associations whose work has had a significant impact upon the development of industrial education is the Mississippi Valley Conference. It has operated as a closed group with limited membership, and its real significance is not well known among industrial educators generally. However, from the time it was only an idea, back in 1908, until at least the beginning of World War II, it served a professional need. There was no way for manual arts teacher educators to discuss professional issues. Bennett and Selvidge sought to fill this need by getting the men in industrial arts teacher education in the Mississippi Valley together for occasional meetings. In the beginning they struggled with fundamental issues and pooled their professional experience to find new approaches to critical problems.

This was professional activity at its best and it paid off. The meetings were highly constructive, challenged depth of thinking, and must have provided excellent motivation during the early years. Much of the progress in teacher education for manual arts came from the influence of the men of the Mississippi Valley. Although the meetings are still held each year and may have a significant stimulating effect upon its members, their relative importance is now somewhat diminished because there are other avenues by which the issues of industrial arts are subjected to professional inspection.

The work of professional associations is essential to progressive development of industrial education. Appraisal of patterns of industrial education can have an important bearing upon progress and can be productive of new ideas, directions, and innovations. The value of professional association may be illustrated by a remark made by Bennett when he returned home from a poor professional meeting. He said that there wasn't enough difference of opinion to have a good discussion.

## Significance of Federal Leadership

The place of national leadership, particularly by an element of the Federal government, is all too frequently misunderstood. When money is involved the cry of "federal control" is heard. Any development that appears to have possibilities of federal intervention in a local or state program of industrial education is regarded under some circumstances as a hope and under others as a threat. Without arguing the issue of "federal control," let us see from historical perspective what influences actually evolved from leadership at the federal level.

The industrial education movement in the United States came to the attention of the federal Office of Education. William T. Harris fought the idea of industrial education prior to his appointment as Commissioner in 1889, and his attitude did not change during his tenure which lasted until June 30, 1906, although he did make objective reference in his reports to the growth of the program.

In June, 1906, things changed. First, the report of the Douglas Commission had been made available. Second, the National Society for the Promotion of Industrial Education was formed. And third, Elmer E. Brown became the United States Commissioner of Education. Brown's attitude was exactly opposite to that of Harris. He encouraged the movement throughout his period in office, which lasted until June, 1911. Brown's successor was Philander P. Claxton who served from 1911 to 1921. Claxton was as vigorous as Brown had been in his support of industrial education. Furthermore he frequently engaged the services of specialists to provide him with specific information. His enthusiasm was marked by the success of his efforts to establish in his staff the position of specialist in industrial education. To this position Claxton invited William T. Bawden in 1914.

There were only a handful of people on the staff of the Commissioner of Education in 1914, and the appointment of a specialist in industrial education is significant. Bawden played his role to perfection. He was honored and respected by industrial educators

throughout the nation, and he used his office to promote standards, to inspire quality, and to encourage innovations. He was Mr. Industrial Education, and a comfortable feeling must have existed among industrial educators with Bawden in this position. He represented the best of industrial education and he held a high position of trust in the federal government. If Bawden ever had enemies, they didn't cite, in public documents, objections to him personally or suggest any negative aspects of the influence of his office.

The Vocational Education Act of 1917 provided for a Federal Board to administer the provisions of the Act. Although Claxton served on the Board, he declined to administer the Act through his office; rather he advocated an independent Board responsible directly to Congress and the President. The evidence does not suggest that Claxton had any fears of federal control, but the nature of the vocational movement—involving management, labor, industry, and agriculture—was in many respects beyond the scope of his office.

So the Federal Board for Vocational Education went to work to provide the instructional material needed, and to call conferences of state leaders to develop criteria—in general to round out the identity of the vocational phase of industrial education, which was entirely new in the public schools. The activities of the Board were much like those of Bawden in the earlier years, but operated on a vast scale. Bawden continued to represent industrial education, including the vocational aspects, in the Office of Education. One needs only to see a compilation of all of the publications of the Federal

Board to gain a view of the impact the Board had upon the development of trade education.

Federal leadership then, during the period 1917-1933, came from an independent federal board, and from a specialist assigned to the Office of Education. Economy moves during the depression forced the functions of the Federal Board into the Office of Education, but as a staff separate from the activities of the specialist in industrial education.

Adjustment to this change came quickly and again the industrial educators of the nation looked to the U.S. Office of Education for continued leadership. Unfortunately the growth of industrial arts in the nation was not reflected in staff appointments in the Office of Education, and it was not until the 1960's that additional assistance was provided. However, except for a few short periods, industrial arts has had representation in the Office of Education continuously since 1914. The leadership has been significant, but seriously handicapped by the lack of staff.

On the vocational side of industrial education the Office of Education did exert an influence and did provide motivation and inspiration for the states in the development of their programs. Through the professional meetings of AVA, industrial educators have frequently called upon the Office of Education to provide leadership. The list of such activities includes requests for conferences for development of instructional material, supervision, research, administrative reform, teacher education, *ad infinitum*.

When this leadership role appeared to be endangered by reorganization in the Office of Education, the American Vocational Association protested vigorously. As late as February, 1966, the AVA, by the direction of its House of Delegates, became involved in a national survey to show the need for this leadership.

## Teacher Education: The Cornerstone

The historical record of industrial education shows clearly the centrality of teacher education in the development of industrial education. The conclusion that improvements in industrial education must start with the teacher —and hence with teacher education —seems to be beyond debate. The quality of the product of industrial education—the students—is a direct measure of the quality of the teaching. This in turn places the burden directly upon the teacher education institutions.

Bennett was aware of this fundamental responsibility when he taught the first formal course in teacher education for manual training teachers in 1891. Bennett and Selvidge were aware of teacher education as a central issue when they discussed the formation of a study group in 1908 (the Mississippi Valley Conference). Leadership from NSPIE also focused early attention upon teacher education.

These concerns, of course, did not originate with manual and trade training. A long historical background of teacher education preceded the emergence of industrial education. In 1685 Robert Cavalier Sieur de la Salle established a normal school in France. In the years that followed, concern for the training of teachers was felt by

491

others, including Pestalozzi, and the net effect in the United States was increased interest in teacher education by the early nineteenth century. Except for the teacher training in the Lancastrian schools, 1818, the first private normal school for teachers was established by Samuel R. Hall in 1823 in Concord, Vermont. Hall's celebrated book, *Lectures in Schoolkeeping*, 1829, was the first professional book written in English and published in America, intended primarily for teachers. The book was instantly successful and was widely distributed throughout the nation. The first state normal school, established in Albany, New York, in 1844, under the direction of David P. Page, was followed by similar institutions in other states.

So, when industrial education entered the scene, teacher education had been established in America. The success of these teacher education ventures did not impress the early leaders in industrial education, and their inclination was to establish separate programs. It was a long hard task to develop some degree of uniformity about content and standards. Early surveys showed extreme diversity. Identifying areas of central importance in teacher education was one of the tasks of the Mississippi Valley Conferences. Bawden exerted leadership in marshalling the forces of industrial education to the end that the tempo of activity toward improvement in teacher education was increased.

One of the most significant elements in the history of industrial teacher education is the dogged determination exhibited by industrial arts teacher educators as they surveyed, studied, reviewed, and then recommended criteria toward increasing the quality of teacher education. Publication of the AVA bulletins on improving instruction was undertaken by industrial arts educators in 1927 and continued for many years. The bulletins did have a direct effect upon teacher education. They were reprinted and widely distributed. After all, when standards of attainment in industrial arts are sharpened, the implication for teacher education is obvious—the old, old story of the centrality of the teacher. It was 1950, however, when the major emphasis came from the newly created American Council on Industrial Arts Teacher Education, that depth reviews were introduced. The Council is intent upon providing continuing evaluative efforts and it would appear, at long last, that industrial arts has secured the necessary organizational structure to provide professional attention to teacher education.

Trade and technical teacher education was born in the same era as the vocational movement. Convictions were strong during the period 1906-1917 concerning the program of teacher education as an essential element. The whole procedure was carefully worked out before 1917, and during the early years the Federal Board exerted strong leadership toward development of programs of teacher education in each of the states. The Bulletins of the NSPIE prior to 1917 pinpointed teacher education as a fundamental element in the program, and the Act of 1917 reflected these goals as basic requirements.

Although the rationale for teacher education had been carefully worked out, definite plans to implement such programs were not available. This task of selecting craftsmen and preparing them to become teachers was new in most of the states. There was strong reaction against turning the teacher education problem over to the normal schools, which were not generally in tune with industrial education and furthermore showed very little interest in it.

The Federal Board managed to move toward achieving "a complete corps of specially trained teachers" by means of bulletins and meetings directly related to teacher education. Little by little the states showed progress toward giving teacher education a position of importance, but there were many varieties of the program. Although the Federal Board had a definite responsibility to urge progress in teacher education, this task was shared by AVA. Committees of the Association studied various elements of teacher education, reported their findings, and made recommendations. This twofold attack on the problems of teacher education—AVA and the Federal Board (USOE)—could only appeal to the professional responsibility of the people in the field; no force or authority could be exerted. Under these influences, however, trade and industrial educators were prone to set higher and higher goals for themselves. Even so, progress toward quality in teacher education was not uniform among the states.

One can only conclude that industrial education over the years has placed value on teacher education. It has made continuous effort to secure the best possible program, conducted under the best possible conditions, and a persistent enthusiasm among teacher educators is apparent.

## Milestones

The historical record repeats itself many times, emphasizing developments, trends, and achievements, with the effect that certain facets of history stand out in bold relief. These underlying basic themes, as they reappear from time to time, lead one to conclusions that they constitute milestones. In addition single events so definitely mark turning points that they also appear as significant.

**Industrial Education and National Security.** At the beginning of World Wars I and II, industrial arts mobilized immediately to contribute directly to the national defense needs. This took the form of an emphasis upon industrial arts rather than a change in the basic program. Articles requested by the Red Cross were made, and models for instructional purposes were constructed in response to requests from the armed services. Industrial arts students realistically backed up war requirements. Instructional emphasis in industrial arts was adjusted so that new needs were reflected; radio in 1917, airplanes in 1940, are examples of this adjustment of emphasis.

Trade and technical education provided a direct service in both wars by preparing people to enter war industry jobs. The schools never closed, and the war contributions were made at little expense to the regular program of vocational education. The fact that the shops and laboratories of industrial education are "in reserve" but ready for immediate use is exceedingly important. The cherished words, "to provide for the common defense," find practical expression in the area of industrial education.

493

*Industrial Education and the General Goals of Education.* Few people realize the extent to which industrial education can contribute to the general goals of education. The industrial education environment provides reality for abstract concepts and real-life experiences. It is strange, however, when every industrial educator knows well the potential of industrial education in relation to the general goals of education, that he has not capitalized more fully upon this potential. The bird-house era is a good example of an almost complete relationship of the student and his teacher, his family, his community, his general geographical environment, and the other disciplines of the school community.

Opportunities for achieving the general goals of education are far more obvious in the industrial arts area than in the trade and technical area, but by no means are these opportunities absent from the latter. The early leaders of industrial education were well aware of the potential of industrial education for educational goals generally.

This is not to say that industrial education can be all things to all people, but it is to say that the potential of industrial education in relation to the general goals of education has not been tapped, and that the future possibilities are almost unlimited.

*Dynamism and Industrial Education.* The forces of society bear heavily upon the program of industrial education, and it is in the nature of industrial education to reflect these forces accurately. Industrial education has been conditioned to change, particularly change of a social and economic nature. The actual program of modern

industrial arts bears little resemblance to the manual training of the early years. The content and procedures have been adjusted continuously. Fundamental principles remain the same, but a change in social and economic environment demands that these principles be interpreted, and as far as possible implemented, according to this environment.

Similarly the vocational aspects of industrial education have adjusted according to social and technological requirements. The purpose of modern trade and technical education—to prepare people for jobs—was the same in 1917. But the contemporary program bears little resemblance to its earlier counterpart.

It is the nature of industrial education that it continually react to the dynamic nature of contemporary society. What appears to be a confusion of concepts is in reality a determined effort by leading industrial educators to see that the field is properly influenced by a variety of forces. The historical record cites in much detail the impact of the social and economic forces.

*Improving the Standard of Living.* An incident in the early history of the trade school movement cites the case of a graduate who reported to his instructor that prior to enrolling in the course his pay was twenty-five cents an hour, but upon completing the program his pay had increased to fifty cents per hour, and this on the basis of his new knowledge. What is the impact upon the standard of living when a person's economic return is doubled?

It was hypothesized early in the vocational movement that appropriate instruction would indeed enable a person to compete more effectively for available job opportunities. The record bears out the hypothesis. It is even more significant that this occurs under the aegis of a free system of public education. Trade and technical education can and does hit hard at the point of improving a person's economic position.

In theory no person was to be denied the opportunity of preparing himself to enter the labor force as a producer of the goods and services that society requires. In practice this has been carried out only insofar as appropriate instruction has been available. Furthermore some public educational institutions have not taken full advantage of the opportunity to provide appropriate training for the world of work. However, some gains, such as the area school development, have recently been made.

It is a milestone of industrial education that it has made provision for occupational education of people during periods of economic recession and technological advances. The traditional scope of the program has included instruction of a pre-employment nature for persons who have not yet entered the labor force, and industrial education for those who are employed, as well as those who have lost their jobs or who otherwise need retraining.

The Panel of Consultants on Vocational Education recognized the need to expand the scope of industrial education still further, and the Vocational Education Act of 1963 provided implementation of the idea. This direct attempt to reach more of the people in need of vocational education is a direct attempt to maintain the goal of improving the standard of living as an essential element of industrial education.

**Women and the Work Force.** One of the significant achievements of industrial education has been its recognition of the employment needs of women. Both private and public schools existed around the turn of the century to provide instruction in "women's occupations." The idea became a part of the first vocational education act, and such opportunities were extended.

The whole concept of women at work changed during World War II. Long-standing prejudices evaporated and about one-third of the labor force after the war consisted of women. Provision for women has grown in the vocational phase of industrial education. A significant part of this growth in recent years has been in the health occupations. Since women were involved in the beginnings of the vocational education movement, their increased participation may not be precisely a milestone in the historical scene, but it is definitely worth noting.

**Industrial Education in Other Nations.** The activities of industrial educators overseas became a significant milestone after World War II. The developing nations had immediate need for consultation with industrial educators from the United States. A large number of industrial arts and trade and technical teachers joined other persons to help in the readjustment of education in various nations around the world. As significant as the migration of industrial educators to other countries is the provision made for students of other nations to study in the United States with industrial educators.

The International Vocational Training Information and Research Center, located at Geneva, Switzerland, adds emphasis to this milestone of industrial education. The Center has secured the cooperation of industrial educators in the industrial nations of the world and provides a worldwide clearing house for industrial education information. The substance of industrial education is recognized as essential to economic development, and the nations of the world have subscribed to this point of view with enthusiasm.

**The Panel of Consultants on Vocational Education.** When President Kennedy asked for a national study of vocational education, he opened a new era in industrial education. It had been 47 years since President Wilson had made a similar request. The report of the Panel was recast into the legislation of the Vocational Education Act of 1963. The Panel report bears the same relationship to the Morse-Perkins Act as did the report of the National Commission to the Smith-Hughes Act in 1917.

The real impact of the Panel report can scarcely be identified in 1966. However, the increased funds for program development and for research will unquestionably have a strong influence upon the progress of industrial education. The nature of this impact must, however, be detailed at a later historical period.

**The Compact for Education.** Since the Constitution made no provisions for an educational system, colonial responsibility for education carried over as a state responsibility at the beginning of our national period in 1789. But the federal government could not ignore education completely, and in 1867 it established a federal office of education with responsibility for providing statistics and other educational data of value to the states. Although the *concern* of the federal government for education has changed much over the years, as reflected by its increasingly substantial grants to the states, education has remained a *function* of state government.

By the mid-1960's development of educational policy within the states had become a complex venture, and into the chaos came the voice of James B. Conant appealing for a degree of order. His appeal was contained in the form of a bold suggestion that the fifty states enter into a compact to create an interstate commission for planning educational policy on a nationwide basis. Conant did not think of the commission as a primary *source of action*, but rather as a new mechanism to *stimulate action*, state by state. His idea was to provide a new study of the educational problem, a study that would place no restraints on the states but that would instead provide the resource material needed by a state for wise action.

Governor Terry Sanford (North Carolina) initiated action by writing to other governors, pointing out that the process of improving education needed the involvement of governors and other state leadership. Meetings were held in May, 1965, and during the rest of that summer, followed by a general meeting in Kansas City on September 29-30, 1965. On February 18, 1966, ten states had ratified the charter, and the compact became a reality. By September, 37 states had joined the compact.

The Commission identified what it could accomplish as follows:

1. A *partnership* between the educational and political forces for *advancement* of education.
2. A stimulus for *State* action in education.
3. A means of *interchange of information* and ideas and successful programs across state lines and regions for the benefit of states.
4. A *forum* for discussion and recommendation of various policy *alternatives* for state consideration and decision.
5. A way to collect, correlate, analyze and interpret data for use *by the states*.
6. A way to assemble the best minds and the most experienced opinions into working parties to *explore new ways* for the states to attack the problems and *carry out research* on all aspects of education.
7. A way to encourage the states to *fulfill* their *role* as the *senior partner* in American education.
8. A place for individual states to call on for *specialized* help in evaluating programs and *getting new ideas*.[1]

One of the studies initiated during 1966 involved the formation of a *Task Force on Vocational Education*. Leon Minear, Superintendent of Public Instruction (Oregon), a member of the steering committee of the Commission, was appointed chairman of the Task Force. The first meeting was held in Portland, Oregon, November 29-30, 1966. The following were identified as members:

DR. WALTER M. ARNOLD
*Asst. Comm., Vocational and Technical Education, Dept. of Health, Education, and Welfare, Office of Education, Washington, D.C. 20202*

DR. MELVIN L. BARLOW
*Director, Division of Vocational Education, University of California, 131 Moore Hall, Los Angeles, California 90024*

DR. MELVIN BARNES
*Superintendent, Portland Public Schools, 631 NE Clackamas, Portland, Oregon*

MR. LOWELL BURKETT
*Executive Director, American Vocational Association, 1025 15th Street, NW, Washington, D.C. 20005*

DR. JOHN COSTER
*Director, Center for Occupational Education, North Carolina State University, Raleigh, North Carolina*

DR. ALBERT L. DEMOND
*President's Commission on Manpower, San Francisco, California*

MR. STEVEN FARBER
*Longworth House Office Building, Room 1026, Washington, D.C.*

DR. MARVIN FELDMAN
*The Ford Foundation, 477 Madison Avenue, New York, New York*

DR. N. H. FRANK
*Professor of Physics, Massachusetts Institute of Technology, Cambridge, Massachusetts*

DR. ALLEN LEE
*Director, Research and Development Program for Vocational and Technical Education, University of California, 2510 Channing Way, Berkeley, California*

DR. JOHN LEFSON
*Superintendent of Schools, Atlanta, Georgia*

DR. WILLIAM LOOMIS
*Director, Vocational Education, Oregon State Department of Education, Salem, Oregon*

[1] *The Compact for Education*, Education Commission of the States. Cincinnati, Ohio, December 1965, p. 15.

Dr. Leon P. Minear
*Superintendent of Public Instruction, State Department of Education, Salem, Oregon*

Mr. Joe Murphy
*State Director of Vocational Education, State Department of Education, Hartford, Connecticut*

Dr. Arthur Pearl
*Associate Professor, University of Oregon, Eugene, Oregon*

Mr. Stan Swan
*Portland Office of Congresswoman Edith Green, 313 Pioneer Post Office, Portland, Oregon*

Dr. J. Chester Swanson
*University of California, Berkeley, California*

Dr. Robert E. Taylor
*Director, Center for Vocational and Technical Education, 980 Kinnear Road, Columbus, Ohio 43212*

Dr. Grant Venn
*Associate Commissioner of Education, U.S. Office of Education, Washington, D.C. 20202*

An evaluation of the activities of the Task Force cannot be made because of the recency of its organization. However, its potential impact upon the development of trade and technical education in the various states would seem to be substantial.

**Advisory Council on Vocational Education.** The Panel of Consultants on Vocational Education, appointed by President Kennedy in 1961, indicated succinctly that frequent reviews of the national program of vocational education were imperative. The long period of time between the report of the National Commission in 1914 and the report of the Panel of Consultants in 1963 had been marked by numerous changes in the social and economic mores of the American people. Such

changes had not been reviewed to determine implications for vocational education.

Congress adopted the recommendations of the Panel of Consultants and included them in the Vocational Education Act of 1963. The first paragraph of Section 12 of the Act reads as follows:

The Secretary [of Health, Education, and Welfare] shall, during 1966, appoint an Advisory Council on Vocational Education for the purpose of reviewing the administration of the vocational education programs for which funds are appropriated pursuant to this Act and other vocational education Acts and making recommendations for improvement of such administration, and reviewing the status of and making recommendations with respect to such vocational education programs and the Acts under which funds are so appropriated.

The Act further provided that the Council submit its report to the Secretary no later than January 1, 1968; in turn the Secretary was required to transmit the report to the President and the Congress.

No action was taken on this matter until late in 1966. On November 22, President Johnson identified the Advisory Council as consisting of the following persons:

Martin W. Essex (Chairman)
*Superintendent of Public Instruction, State Department of Education, Columbus, Ohio*

Rupert N. Evans
*Dean, College of Education, University of Illinois, Urbana, Illinois*

James T. Harris
*Vice President, African-American Institute, 866 United Nations Plaza, New York, New York 10017*

Malcolm G. Hunt
*State Director of Vocational Education, Santa Fe, New Mexico*

JOHN W. LETSON
*Superintendent of Schools, Atlanta, Georgia*

GARTH L. MANGUM
*Director, Manpower Policy Evaluation Project, W. E. Upjohn Institute for Employee Research, Washington, D.C.*

LELA O'TOOLE
*Dean, Division of Home Economics, Oklahoma State University, Stillwater, Oklahoma*

CHARLES W. PATRICK
*President, San Diego Junior Colleges, San Diego, California*

OTTO PRAGAN
*Department of Education, AFL-CIO, Washington, D.C.*

LEONARD H. ROSENBERG
*President, The Chesapeake Life Insurance Co., Baltimore, Maryland*

C. VANNOY STEWART
*Associate Professor of Agriculture and Head Teacher Trainer, Sam Houston State College, Huntsville, Texas*

The first meeting of the Council was held on December 19, 1966, and the second on January 29-30, 1967. The report of the Council—the first evaluation under the Vocational Education Act of 1963—will be a significant milestone in the history of vocational education in the United States.

## A View from the Crystal Ball

History takes the heterogeneous events of the past—a mass of confusion, at first glance—and attempts to learn about how the pieces of the puzzle fit together. What influences have produced what trends? Who? what? when? where? why? and so what? are questions asked continuously. Sometimes the answers form a pattern but frequently their significance is not

apparent. Nevertheless strong impressions are formed, and some of these impressions seem to reveal the fundamental values which industrial education may well continue to seek in the future.

Has industrial education created the basis of social progress or has it merely reacted to a social situation? In a way it has done both. The entire history of industrial education is one of continuous change serving as both the ounce of prevention and as the pound of cure. Take the contemporary situation of chronic unemployment. Here the pound of cure fits in to change what is regarded as an unwanted social situation. At the same time the ounce of prevention is at work in providing the background of skills, knowledges, and appreciations to enable persons to enter upon the work of society. Solving the immediate problem for some persons and at the same time preventing the problem from occuring in the experience of others has been a persistent goal of industrial education.

The nineteenth century literature of industrial education frequently brings out, in one way or another, the need for "mechanical intelligence." A person wise in the ways of applying a knowledge based upon the operational requirements of society has always been in demand. Woodward was in search of improving mechanical intelligence when he had his engineering students make models to demonstrate scientific principles. Runkle found in the applied concepts of industrial education a means of developing mechanical intelligence. His students were excellent theoreticians—they just had five thumbs on each hand. The beginnings of manual training represented a start

499

toward development of mechanical intelligence. This need is present in contemporary society but with many modifications as dictated by contemporary needs. Generalities alone did not put vehicles into outer space.

The personalities of industrial education, as they pass in historical review, bring one to think about the "stature" of these persons. They had visions of great achievements, and they were able to provide concentration upon specific elements of industrial education without losing their broad general perspective. Their personal magnetism captured the minds and hearts of those they worked with and their leadership stands out prominently. They never developed a working pattern for industrial education that would stand for all time (in fact the first evidence of success always brought forth evaluative attitudes.) They were never satisfied; success was merely a step toward further gains. Each in his own way added emphasis and strength to the industrial education movement. Bawden, Bennett, Prosser, Allen, Merrill, Woodward, Page, Richards, Gompers, Dean, Pritchett, Florence Marshall, Holder, and many others are names that stand out in the significant achievements of industrial education. One of the unfortunate aspects of the history of industrial education is the lack of adequate biographies.

At this point, as we look back upon the leadership of the past, we wonder if the contemporary scene matches up with the men and women of stature in industrial education. Where are the great leaders among us today?

Industrial education faces the future with a greater leadership potential than it has ever had in the past. We have among us not the small handful of prominent people, but scores of creative, imaginative people producing innovations in industrial education. They are hard to see because there are so many of them. Also our concepts of leadership are changing. Instead of a few great men with all around competency and depth of perception, there are many. We require much of our leaders today and we insist upon competencies far greater than were achieved in the earlier period. The industrial arts and trade teacher, the teacher educator, and the administrator of 1917 couldn't get a job in today's industrial education program.

Such comparisons are somewhat unfair. There is no doubt that the leaders of the past matched up with the social and economic conditions of their age. They produced the theory and adapted it to the needs of the time. So it is true today. The displacement by time and circumstance of continuing needs requires that industrial educators provide an appropriate industry-education posture. The industrial education program must work in the educational process of today and reflect the need of the time, and we have hundreds of people who are masters of the art of making the program work. The hard work of keeping the program in operation has not been conducive to the production of philosophers, sociologists, historians, economists, or psychologists in industrial education, but this need too must be satisfied.

At every turn in the historical scene we see that change has been an inherent quality of industrial education. There are no flat or dead spots during

500

which change did not occur. Change has tended to reflect industrial education in terms of social, economic, and educational needs. If the past is any predictor of the future, the concept of change appears to be appropriately integrated into the industrial education system so that we will be able to adapt to the environment of the future. Despite the emotion surrounding automation there is little evidence that work is going out of style. That it is changing there can be no doubt. That the rate of change is perceptibly greater than ever is quite clear. But this is not an overwhelming problem in industrial education, a field that is accustomed to change. Obviously industrial educators must sharpen their perceptions to change, but this is now one of the major issues confronting industrial education.

There are two major evidences of change immediately at hand. The first is in industrial arts. Industrial arts has traditionally been a part of the total educational program and it has had to fit into educational planning. Some of the hard, fast lines marking off subject matter areas are likely to fade somewhat, and industrial arts teachers will join other subject matter specialists to become *teachers* of students—the process of subject matter integration—but the resulting program of team teaching must have a strong industrial-technological emphasis. Industrial arts teacher education institutions, which for so long were solely intent upon producing industrial arts teachers, are now expanding their programs along lines that provide an industrial curriculum leading to employment in other than teaching. This change appears to be be completely in order and in tune with the increase of students in college programs.

The second major change is in the vocational aspects of industrial education—the trade and technical program. In purpose this program will still provide instruction for persons who are entering the labor force for the first time and for persons who need to upgrade and update their skills and knowledge as employed workers. However, the scope of the program has changed to bring into view a much larger group of students, and therefore the number and kinds of courses to meet their occupational needs will increase. Greater concern for unemployment and retraining has developed; this fact must find expression in programs for adults. The assumption that most people will devote more and more time, during their working lives, to keeping occupationally competent seems to be founded upon reasonable grounds. This tends to broaden the scope of trade and technical education programs.

The challenge of the future in both areas of industrial education means that all industrial educators have greater responsibility to look to their personal program of self-development. The educational possibilities are unlimited, but they are dependent upon the ways and means whereby education in general interprets its role as the guardian of occupational competency for all.

## Projections

From historical perspective a variety of trends and directions become apparent. Some of these pathways are so clearly marked and generally supported by objective evidence that little room exists for doubt about the validity of the trend and direction. Other pathways are blazed only by an occasional marker, and the trail is faint, thus making historical travel difficult. But, "the past is prologue," and of much service to any prophet.

Therefore, despite the limited nature of historical evidence, the urge to look into the uncertain future, where history has not yet trod, is irresistible. Today is anxious about tomorrow. We hope that understanding today's experiences will aid us in avoiding errors tomorrow because, as the philosopher George Santayana once said, "Those who cannot remember the past are condemned to repeat it." Projections into the future can represent a reasonable description of coming events, a guess as to what could happen, or at least a hope of what the future ought to be. Viewed in the crystal ball are three major points:

### 1. *Industrial Education—One Program or Two?*

The viewpoint expressed in earlier chapters concerning the term "industrial education" is that it represents a combination of two programs—industrial arts education and trade and technical education. Implied in the use of the inclusive term is a continuum of experiences starting with early student interests in the industrial world and culminating in preparation for employment. This interpretation has been widely held since the beginning of the vocational education movement.

Industrial arts objectives, covering a wide range of student goals, have been traditionally centered around educational and intellectual purposes. Trade and technical education has sighted its objectives along a central purpose of occupational preparation. The transition area between the two programs has been the cause of some concern in the 1960's because of increased attention to education's commitment for occupational preparation.

It is to be expected that industrial arts will continue to move more prominently into the technological era— history shows that manual training, manual arts, and industrial arts programs have always been associated with contemporary issues. In fact, this is one of the strengths of the movement.

More specifically, the future (in relation to point one) would appear to have these characteristics:

- The transition area (grey area, as it is sometimes called) will be reviewed to the extent that industrial arts will sharpen its identity and responsibility in the area of occupational training.
- An emphasis will be placed on vocational guidance throughout the industrial arts program.
- Trade and technical education will increase its sensitivity to general values in education in order to establish a basis for further student gains in skill and technical knowledge.
- Although the two programs are "elements in the same series," they will continue to exist as units with identifiable parts. The two programs will not combine, as in a chemical combination, with the resulting product having no resemblance to the separate elements. The relationship will continue to be that of a mechanical mixture. Any other relationship will

502

defeat foundation principles of these two autonomous areas of education.

## 2. *Toward Realizing the Potential of Industrial Education*

The "educational mind" of America does not really understand industrial education and its potential. Few industrial educators have been able to demonstrate the real values of industrial education. They do not lack ability to do so; it just hasn't been done. Central in the future is *exploration in depth of the potential of industrial education.*

The stakes are high; therefore if industrial education does not become involved in depth and in a much wider range of endeavor it is most certain that some other agency will. Already in the 1960's we have seen private industry and other branches of government take on a responsibility for education for which they have no previous tradition or history. A major part of this responsibility should have fallen to industrial education.

It seems no rash prediction to say that in the future industrial education:

- Will at least partly solve the dropout problem.
- Will provide instruction leading to a wider range of occupational interests.
- Will inspire the slow or reluctant learner.
- Will provide all of the requirements necessary to improving competency of the unemployed.
- Will open new worlds of conquest for talented students.

The list is actually endless. The environment of industrial education is conducive to the solution of numerous social and occupational problems. Its only limitation is the imagination and drive of industrial educators themselves. In other words, permission for industrial education to hold its rightful place in the future depends upon the "educational mind" and the interpretation it makes of the range of its responsibility.

## 3. *Future Leadership in Industrial Education*

Observers of the contemporary educational scene imagine they see significant changes in the future—a "revolution" in education unlike any previous major departures. They say that new approaches to the education of youth and adults will tend to break down the barriers of the subject matter areas as these unfold in the educational experiences of students. Revolution or not, leadership in the new structure of education can, and must, come from industrial educators.

Before we revolutionize anything, remember that education has a commitment to all of the children of all of the people, and yet some of the children can't perform satisfactorily in relation to the general demands of society. Some of the children tend to react against the acquisition of knowledge, no matter how we change our methods. Many of them cannot get jobs either as youths or as adults. So the commitment as an ideal goal, valuable though it is, has not yet produced the desired achievements.

The secret to be found in the future involves a more imaginative, creative, and intelligent use of ideas presently recognized (and those to come in the future) so that the resources of education apply more effectively to all in-school and out-of-school youth and adults. Team teaching, TV, and a variety of automated devices are finding new uses. Experimentation is progressing at a rapid pace. Research specifically provided for in the Vocational Education Act of 1963 was intended to produce a wealth of information which could be used to direct the movement toward the future more effectively.

The pace of educational activity induces new requirements in industrial education at every wave of its advance. The extent to which industrial education maximizes its contribution to the education of the future is dependent upon a number of specific competencies, but—again it must be said—most important of all is the *leadership* industrial education produces.

Over the years the concepts of leadership have changed. We have had our "great men" in industrial education, and still do. They are essential to continued development. But we must —and will, far more than in early years —recognize and produce leadership in great abundance at every level and on every facet of industrial education. Strong leadership must and will continue at the national level, in the federal government and in national professional associations. We seem headed toward the same kind of continuing leadership development in state departments of education, colleges, and in professional associations. By and large, leadership at state and national levels has been good and can reasonably be expected to become even more extensive and sophisticated in the future.

A target in leadership for the future, which has been only loosely developed, is leadership at the school and classroom levels. Leadership at these points is likely to improve because national interest in such improvement is strong. All of the improvements, goals, expectations, and achievements must ultimately occur in an environment where teachers and students work together. A thousand leaders of national stature—in their remote position—cannot replace one creative, imaginative, and dedicated teacher, if he has strong local support, as well as national. *All other leadership is essentially devoted to providing the environment so that teacher leadership can develop under the most desirable of conditions.*

Achievement of these major points in the future includes using national resources to upgrade and update a number of standards and procedural elements. When this occurs, industrial education will have been accorded its rightful position of prestige among the subject matter areas of education.

# INDEX

NOTE—This index is not intended to give all references to each proper name or piece of legislation, for example, Charles A. Bennett or Smith-Hughes Act, but rather to list highlights.

## A

Addams, Jane, 53, 340
Addicott, James A., 299
Advisory Council on Vocational Education, 498, 499
Agricultural and mechanical colleges, 27, 32
Allen, Charles R., 209, 229, 303
Allen, David, 89
Althouse, A. D., 419
American Association of School Administrators, 321, 322
American Council for Industrial Arts Teacher Education, 84
American Council of Industrial Arts Supervisors, 84, 422, 423
American Federation of Labor (See *Organized labor*)
American Federation of Teachers, 392
American Home Economics Association, 78
American Industrial Arts Association (AIAA), 83-85, 287, 422, 489
American Lyceum of Science and Arts, 26
American Technical Education Association (ATEA), 419, 420
American Technical Society, 214
American Vocational Association (AVA)
   bulletins, 181
   contribution to Vocational Education Act of 1963, 429, 436-441
   formation of, 77-81
   labor-management committee, 324
   report to President, 321, 322
   research activities, 160-163
   war work training conference (1942), 324

*American Vocational Journal,* 75
Anderson, Miles H., 331
Angell, James R., 298
*A Plan for Improving Female Education,* 339
Apprenticeship
   after World War II, 329
   ancient and medieval, 17-20
   decay of, 33
   Federal Committee on, 391
   in Colonial America, 25, 26
   trends in Europe today, 459, 464
Armstrong, Gen. Samuel Chapman, 42
Aristotle, 17
Arnold, Sarah Louise, 341
Arnold, Walter M., 157, 164, 412, 432
Artisans and artists, 17, 19
Assembly of Athens, 16
Associations, professional, 67-91, 487, 488
Athens, 16, 17
Auchtmuty, Richard Tylden, 42
Automation, 334, 335

## B

Bacon, L. C., 93
Bailey, C. H., 93
Balch, Emily Green, 341
Baldwin Locomotive Works, training program, 44
Ball, Frank J., 258
Barlow, Melvin L., 497
Barlow, R. R., 89
Barnes, Melvin, 497
Bauder, C. F., 181

Bawden, William T.
  as Specialist in Industrial Education, 135,
    180, 241, 245, 300
  death of, 111
  in Mississippi Valley Conferences, 93, 95,
    97, 102-106
  role seen in retrospect, 490
Bayh, Sen. Birch, 447-449
Beecher, Catherine, 339
Belfield, H. H., 46
Bell, Rep. Alphonzo, 443
Bennett, Charles A.
  death of, 111
  general references, 208, 241, 244, 245, 301,
    456
  honored by The Ship, 87
  in Mississippi Valley Conferences, 92, 93,
    99, 101, 489
Bingham, Mrs. Mary Caperton, 431
Bingham, Lt. Col. W. V., 215
Bird House Era, 257-265
Bishop, Fred, 86
Bloom, Maj. J. E., 303
Bogan, William J., 75, 101, 241
Bookbinder, Hyman H., 431
Borosage, Lawrence, 142, 399
Boston Asylum and Farm School, 26
Boston Manual Training Club, 89
Bourat, Mlle. Marg, 356
Bowler, Earl M., 142, 157
Bowman, C. A., 106, 181
Boy Scouts of America, 260
Brademas, Rep. John, 449
Bradley Institute, 174, 300
Breckinridge, Sophoniaba P., 341
Briggs, Howard L., 251
Brown, Rep. Clarence J., 443
Brown, Elmer Ellsworth, 56, 135, 490
Brownlow, James, 398
Bruch, L. H., 93
Buchanan, J. R., 31, 40
Bulletins, NSPIE, 53
Bureau of Education, Industrial Education
  Circulars, 98
Burdick, Anna Lalor, 365-367
Burgess, L. G., 89
Burgess, T. C., 93
Burgher class, 20
Burkett, Lowell, 498
Butler, Nicholas Murray, 52
Butterfield, Ernest W., 70
Buxton, George F., 93, 241

**C**

Cahill, Rep. William T., 444
Campion, Howard A., 323
Capen, S. P., 299
Carlson, Sen. Frank, 446
Carnegie Foundation, 54
Carnegie Institute of Technology, 215
Carris, Lewis H., 115
Carroll, Charles F., 431
Cary, C. P., 120
Caswell, William E., 284
Centennial Exposition (1876), 38
Chang, Miss S., 356
Charter of Punta del Este (1961), 475

Charts
  Division of Vocational and Technical Edu-
    cation, 165, 168
  Educational Requirements of Industrial
    Arts Teachers, 193
  Employment as Technicians, 411
  Enrollment of women as a percentage of
    trade and industrial education (1961-
    1962), 372
  Number of principal trade courses: (1924
    and 1929), 311, 312
  Percentage distribution of women in trade
    and industrial education, 371
  Preservice Preparation of I. A. Teachers,
    204
  Professional Associations, 74
  "The Boy," 269
  (Also see *Tables*)
Chumpacker, Sanger, 262
CIRF *Abstracts*, 459-474
Clark College, 54
Clark, Maj. Grenville, 298
Clark, Sen. Joseph S., 446
Clawson, Augusta H., 325, 361-363
Claxton, Philander P., 97, 115, 135, 243, 490
Cohen, Wilbur, 429
Colston, Albert L., 419
Committee on Education (House of Repre-
  sentatives), 61
Commodus, 17
Common school, 30, 31
Compact for Education, 496-498
Compulsory school attendance, 30
Conant, James B., 496
Congress of Industrial Organizations (See
  *Organized labor*)
Conte, Rep. Silvio O., 443
Cooper Union, 52
Cooper, Walter H., 142
Cooper, William John, 256
Corleto, Frederick T., 431
Corporation schools, 44, 45
Coster, John, 497
Cotter, Carl T., 87
Council for Vocational Education, 78
Crawshaw, Fred D., 93
Criticisms of manual training and industrial
  arts
  19th century, 37, 39-41
  by Commissioner Harris, 134
  by Executive Council of AFL, 393-395
  by Virgil Volla, "4 F's," 283, 284
Curriculum
  balance, 39
  combination of subjects, 97
  four-year college training recommended, 95
  graduate programs, 108
  space age, 289
Cushman, Frank, 142, 390
Cutten, George, 287
Cygnaeus, Uno, 25, 485

**D**

Davis, Rep. Charles R., 55
Dawson, Kenneth E., 84
Dean, Arthur D., 46, 85, 87, 246

r